Introduction to Law Enforcement and Criminal Justice

Second Edition

Introduction to Law Enforcement and Criminal Justice

Second Edition

Henry M. Wrobleski
> Normandale Community College
> Bloomington, Minnesota

Kären M. Hess
> Normandale Community College
> Bloomington, Minnesota

Criminal Justice Series

West Publishing Company

St. Paul • New York • Los Angeles • San Francisco

Cover Design: Henning & Associates
Text Design: Henning & Associates
Copyeditor: Lucy Paschke
Composition: Metro Graphic Arts, Inc.
Photo Credits:

Section 1. J.D. Stinchcomb. **Chapter 1.** *Opener:* Minnesota Historical Society; *pp. 9, 15, 18:* J.D. Stinchcomb. **Chapter 2.** *Opener:* AP/Wide World Photos; *p. 55:* UPI/Bettmann Newsphotos. **Chapter 3.** *Opener:* Jeffrey Blankfort/Jeroboam, Inc.; *p. 75:* UPI/Bettmann Newsphotos. **Chapter 4.** *Opener:* UPI/Bettmann Newsphotos. **Chapter 5.** *Opener:* West Publishing; *p. 127:* AP/Wide World Photos. **Section 2.** J.D. Stinchcomb. **Chapter 6.** *Opener:* AP/Wide World Photos; *p. 143:* Courtesy of the Federal Bureau of Investigation; *p. 149:* Courtesy of U.S. Secret Service. **Chapter 7.** *Opener:* UPI/Bettmann Newsphotos; *p. 187:* Captain Bob Mack/Minneapolis Police Reserve Underwater Recovery Unit; *p. 189:* West Publishing; **Section 3.** J.D. Stinchcomb. **Chapter 8.** *Opener:* AP/Wide World Photos; *p. 219:* West Publishing. **Chapter 9.** *Opener:* Bob Eckert/EKM-Nepenthe; *p. 238:* UPI/Bettmann Newsphotos. **Chapter 10.** *Opener:* J.D. Stinchcomb; *pp. 265, 266:* West Publishing. **Chapter 11.** *Opener:* Bob Eckert/EKM-Nepenthe; *p. 302:* UPI/Bettmann Newsphotos. **Chapter 12.** *Opener:* AP/Wide World Photos; *p. 314:* J.D. Stinchcomb; *p. 320:* Henry Wrobleski. **Section 4.** Courtesy of the San Diego Police Department. **Chapter 13.** *Opener:* AP/Wide World Photos; *p. 339:* AP/Wide World Photos. **Chapter 14.** *Opener:* Bob Eckert/EKM-Nepenthe; *p. 392:* J.D. Stinchcomb. **Section 5.** John Maher/EKM-Nepenthe. **Chapter 15.** *Opener:* John Maher/EKM-Nepenthe. **Chapter 16.** *Opener:* AP/Wide World Photos. **Chapter 17.** *Opener:* UPI/Bettmann Newsphotos. **Section 6.** Courtesy of the Federal Bureau of Investigation. **Chapter 18.** *Opener:* UPI/Bettmann Newsphotos. *p. 507:* Bob Eckert/EKM-Nepenthe. **Chapter 19.** *Opener:* John Maher/EKM-Nepenthe; *p. 531:* AP/Wide World Photos. **Chapter 20.** *Opener:* UPI/Bettmann Newsphotos.

A student workbook has been developed to assist students in mastering the concepts presented in this text. The workbook reinforces concepts by presenting them in a concise format with self-testing exercises. An examination copy is available to instructors by contacting West Publishing Company at the address below. Students can purchase the workbook from the local bookstore under the title *Student Workbook to Accompany Introduction to Law Enforcement and Criminal Justice, Second Edition,* prepared by Henry M. Wrobleski and Kären M. Hess.

COPYRIGHT © 1986 By WEST PUBLISHING COMPANY
50 West Kellogg Boulevard
P.O. Box 64526
St. Paul, MN 55164-1003

Library of Congress Cataloging-in-Publication Data

Wrobleski, Henry M., 1922-
   Introduction to law enforcement and criminal justice.

   (Criminal justice series)
   Includes index.
   1. Law enforcement—United States. 2. Police—United States. 3. Crime and criminals—United States. 4. Criminal justice, Administration of—United States.
I. Hess, Karen M., 1939- . II. Title.
HV8138.W76 1986   364'.973   85-22639
ISBN 0-314-93527-4

To Our Families

Contents
In Brief

Contents

Figures

Tables

Preface

The future of our lawful, democratic society depends in large part upon those of you currently in the field of law enforcement and those of you preparing to enter this field. The law enforcement officer is responsible for assisting those in distress, providing services to persons who request them, preserving peace and order in the community, preventing unlawful acts, and apprehending those who violate the law. These complex responsibilities must be met under constantly changing conditions and in a manner which assures the rights of the individual. Increased technology, industrialization, urbanization, and mobility have brought new problems to law enforcement requiring the law enforcement officer to be knowledgeable in a wide varity of areas.

Introduction to Law Enforcement and Criminal Justice provides basic information which should serve as an overview of the entire field as well as a solid foundation for future course work. The content in each chapter could easily be expanded into an entire book or course, but the basic concepts in each area have been included. You will be introduced to the history of law enforcement and crime as it exists in the United States, including juvenile delinquency and organized crime. After familiarizing yourself with this general background of law enforcement, you will learn about the agencies engaged in law enforcement activities, the general organization of most police departments, and the goals most seek to accomplish. Next you will study the complex role of the police officer in depth—the functions performed in fulfilling extremely difficult responsibilities, including traffic, patrol, investigation, and community service. Then you will be introduced to the police officer's role in the criminal justice system, from the investigation and search through the arrest and the court trial including the nature of civil rights and civil liberties and our courts and corrections systems. Finally, you will learn about the requirements for becoming a law enforcement officer, what occurs during the recruitment, probation, and training periods; what opportunities in law enforcement are available to members of minority groups and women; the image of the law enforcement officer; and, finally, critical issues facing those involved in law enforcement.

Important court cases and decision are presented throughout the book rather than being isolated in a single chapter. Likewise, modern advancements in law enforcement are integrated into chapters rather than presented as a separate subject. The content of the book is based on the result of ten years of classroom research among law enforcement officers and preservice students as to what subject matter is most important and useful to the future police officer. The book itself has been classroom tested and reviewed by several experts in the field.

The authors recognize the importance of women in law enforcement. The fact that the authors have occasionally chosen to use the masculine pronoun when a pronoun is called for should in no way be construed as implying bias.

How to Use This Book

Introduction to Law Enforcement and Criminal Justice is more than a textbook; it is a learning experience requiring your active participation to obtain best results. You will get the most out of the book if you first familiarize yourself with the total scope of law enforcement: read and think about the Table of Contents and what is included. Then follow these steps as you read each chapter:

1. Read the objectives at the beginning of each chapter:

Do You Know . . .

■ What the basic instrument of government is?

Think about your current knowledge on each question.
What preconceptions do you hold?

2. Read the chapter (underlining or taking notes if that is your preferred study style).
   a. Pay special attention to all information that is shaded:

> *The United States Constitution is the basic instrument of government and the supreme law of the United States.*

The key concepts of each chapter are highlighted in this manner.
   b. Look up unfamiliar words in the glossary at the back of the book.

3. When you have finished reading the chapter, reread the list of objectives given at the beginning of the chapter to make certain you are able to give a response to each question. If you find yourself stumped, find the appropriate material in the chapter and review it.

4. Next, complete the Application, if appropriate, at the end of the chapter. The application exercises provide an opportunity to use the concepts in actual or hypothetical cases. After you have made your responses, compare them with the sample answers provided.

5. Finally, read the Discussion Questions, think about possible responses, and be prepared to contribute to a class discussion.

Good reading and learning!

Acknowledgments

We would like to thank the following individuals and organizations for their contributions to *Introduction to Law Enforcement and Criminal Justice.*

Thank you to Larry Gaines, Eastern Kentucky University; Professor George Green, Mankato State University; Robert Ingram, Florida International University; Glen Morgan, Lincolnland Community College; Professor Frank Post, Fullerton College; Jack Spurlin, Missouri Southern State College; and Larry Tuttle; Palm Beach Junior College for their helpful reviews of the manuscript and their suggestions for changes. A special thank you to Professor Post for his valuable additions, particularly in the areas of law enforcement agencies and the police career.

For their valuable suggestions for the second edition of *Introduction to Law Enforcement and Criminal Justice,* thank you to Robert Ives, Rockford Police Department; Sergeant James Walsh, Mount San Jacinto College; Paul H. Johnson, Murry State University; Roger Brown, Golden Valley Lutheran College; Dr. Jack Taylor, Oscar Rose Junior College; Lt. David A. Wilson, Turmbull Police Department; Professor Joseph Polanski, Sinclair Community College; Dr. David G. Epstein, Burnswick Junior College; Professor Kenneth Bowser, Westfield State College; Myron Utech, University of Wisconsin at Eau Claire; and Dr. Steven Brown, East Tennessee State University.

Thank you to the administration and staff of Normandale Community College for their assistance and support during the classroom testing of the manuscript, to the students in Law Enforcement 050 for providing ideas and suggestions, and to Pamela Reierson, media specialist, for her invaluable assistance in locating sources and information.

Thank you to the Department of Justice; the Federal Bureau of Investigation; the Federal Drug Enforcement Administration; the International Association of Chiefs of Police; the Minnesota Attorney General's Office, Civil Service Department, County Attorney's Association, Governor's Commission on Crime Prevention and Control, and State Highway Department; the National Council of

Christians and Jews; the National Safety Council; and police departments of Philadelphia, San Diego, and St. Louis Park; and the publishers for permission to include their materials in our text.

Thank you also to Susan Tubb and to Solveig Tyler-Robinson, our editors, for their patience, their attention to detail, and their encouragement and support. It is largely through their efforts that this second edition has a new look.

Finally, thank you to our families and collegues for their support and assistance during the development of *Introduction to Law Enforcement and Criminal Justice*. A special thank you to Adina Wrobleski for her careful, thorough review of the entire manuscript.

Introduction to Law Enforcement and Criminal Justice

Second Edition

Background

The chapters in Section One present the rich heritage of law enforcement, and how our laws and our system of enforcing them evolved from ancient to modern times (Chapter 1).

Rules for conduct within society and laws regarding violations of these rules have been clearly specified in our criminal statutes, which not only define crimes but prescribe punishments. The crimes range from violent crimes such as murder and rape to costly white-collar crime, to the illegal use, possession, and sale of narcotics and dangerous drugs (Chapter 2). The multiple causes of crime and factors causing people to become criminals or juvenile delinquents underscore the complexity of the crime problem (Chapter 3). Dealing with victims of crime is also an important function of the law enforcement officer, including understanding how such victimization might affect individuals (Chapter 4). In addition, although not a crime in itself, organized crime, with its corrupting and strong-arm tactics, poses a direct threat to our national security and a difficult challenge to individuals in law enforcement (Chapter 5).

It is within this context that the modern law enforcement officer functions. An awareness of the heritage of law enforcement, the types of crimes occurring in the United States, who commits them and why, and how victims are affected—all these understandings contribute to effective performance of law enforcement responsibilities.

The Rondo Street Police Station, St. Paul, Minnesota, in 1900. Note the four staff officers on the right and how their uniforms differ from the patrol.

A Brief History

*The Evolution of Modern Law
and Law Enforcement*

Do You Know . . .

- What a law is?

- When and why law enforcement began?

- The origins of features of our law enforcement system such as:
    The offices of sheriff, constable, and justice of the peace?
    General alarms and citizen's arrests?
    Jury by peers, grand jury, and due process?
    Separation between enforcing laws and judging offenders?
    Division of offenses into felonies and misdemeanors?
    Local responsibility for law enforcement?
    Paid law enforcement officers?
    Women in law enforcement?

- The significance of the tithing system, the Frankpledge system, Leges Henrici, the Magna Carta, the Parish Constable system, and the Watch and Ward system?

- How law enforcement has traditionally responded to increased crime?

- What significant contributions to law enforcement were made by Sir Robert Peel?

- Where and when the first police department was established in England and what it was called?

- What systems of law enforcement were brought from England and adopted in the United States in colonial New England and the South?

- When and where the first modern American police force began and what it was modeled after?

- When and how state and federal law enforcement agencies originated in the United States?

- What effect the spoils system had on law enforcement in the 1900s?

- What the Pendelton Act accomplished?

- What organizational systems of law enforcement have been tried in the United States and which have been most successful?

History is a vast early warning system.
—Norman Cousins

Introduction

A brief look into the history of laws and law enforcement will give you answers to many of the preceding questions. The heritage of law enforcement is a source of pride as well as a guide to avoiding mistakes in the future.

Specific dates and events are not as important as acquiring a sense of the sequence or chronology of how our present-day laws and system of law enforcement came into existence. As you read, watch for information related to the preceding questions. You may want to take notes or to underline in your book.

Law

We all have an idea of what a law is; we all have to live by laws or face the consequences. We may not know how laws originated, what they cover, or how they are enforced.

Law is a body of rules for human conduct which are enforced by imposing penalties for their violation. Technically, laws are made and passed by the legislative branches of our federal, state, county, and city governments. They are based on customs, traditions, mores, and current need.

Law refers to all the rules of conduct established and enforced by the custom, authority, or legislation of a group, community, or country.

Notice that law implies both prescription (rule) and enforcement by authority. It might seem that the term *law enforcement* is redundant since law refers to both the rules and their enforcement. But, in the United States, those who enforce the laws are *not* the same as those who make them. This has not always been true.

Primitive and Ancient Law

Even the cavemen had certain rules they were expected to follow or face death or banishment from the tribe. The customs depicted in early cave-dwelling drawings may well represent the beginning of law and law enforcement.

The prehistoric social order consisted of small family groups living together as tribes or clans. Group living gave rise to certain customs that everyone was expected to observe. The chief of the tribe had executive, legislative, and judicial powers and often appointed members of the tribe to perform special tasks such as serving as his bodyguard or enforcing his edicts. Crimes committed against individuals were handled by the victim or the victim's family. The philosophy of justice was retaliatory, that is, punish the offender. A person who stole the game from his neighbor's traps could expect to pay for the crime by being thrown into a pot of boiling oil or a cage of wild beasts. Other common punishments for serious offenses were flaying, impalement, burning at the stake, stoning, branding, mutilation, and crucifixion.

> *A system of law and law enforcement began earlier than 2000 B.C. as a means of controlling human conduct and enforcing society's rules.*

The earliest record of ancient man's need to organize and standardize rules and methods of enforcement to control human behavior dates back to approximately 2300 B.C. when the Sumerian rulers Lipitshtar and Eshumma set forth standards on what did and did not constitute an offense against society. A hundred years later, the Babylonian King Hammurabi established rules for his kingdom that designated not only offenses but punishments as well. In fact, Hammurabi established the oldest known building code. Although the penalties prescribed were often barbaric by today's standards, the relationship between the crime and the punishment are of interest.

The Code of Hammurabi consisted of 300 legal provisions concerning such matters as false accusations, witchcraft, military service, land and business regulations, family laws, tariffs, wages, loans, and debts. The main principle of the code was that "the strong shall not injure the weak." The code also established a social order based on individual rights. With Hammurabi we find the origin of the legal principle of *lex talions*— an eye for an eye.

The first accounts of a developing court system came from Egypt in approximately 1500 B.C. The sophisticated court system was presided over by judges appointed by the Pharaoh. About 1000 B.C. in Egypt, public officers performed police functions. Their weapon and symbol of authority was a staff topped by a metal knob engraved with the king's name. The baton carried by the modern police officer may have its origin in that staff.

Figure 1–1.   **The Oldest Known Building Code.**

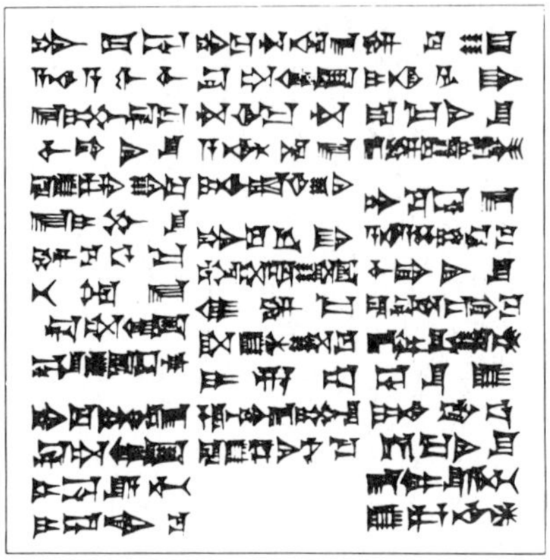

From the Code of Hammurabi (2200 B.C.)

If a builder builds a house for a man and does not make its construction firm and the house collapses and causes the death of the owner of the house—that builder shall be put to death. If it causes the death of a son of the owner—they shall put to death a son of that builder. If it causes the death of a slave of the owner—he shall give to the owner a slave of equal value. If it destroys property he shall restore whatever it destroyed and because he did not make the house firm he shall rebuild the house which collapsed at his own expense. If a builder builds a house and does not make its construction meet the requirements and a wall falls in—that builder shall strengthen the wall at his own expense.

Source: Masonry Institute, 55 New Montgomery Street, San Francisco, Cal. 94105.

The Greeks had an impressive form of law enforcement called the *epohri*. Each year at Sparta a body of five epohrs was elected and given almost unlimited powers. They were the highest executive power in the land, being investigator, judge, jury, and executioner. These five men also presided over the Senate and Assembly, assuring that their rules and decrees were followed. One problem with this system, however, was that it promoted corrupt enforcement.

From the Greek philosopher Plato, who lived from 427 to 347 B.C., came the idea that punishment should serve a purpose rather than just being retaliation. Note the similarity between this concept and the relationship between the crimes and punishments set forth by Hammurabi in 2200 B.C. This relationship is the basis of equity and the basis of law in America, as will be discussed later.

Like the Greeks, the Romans had a highly developed system for the administration of justice. The Twelve Tables were the first written laws of the Roman Empire. Drawn up by ten of the wisest men in Rome in 451 and 450 B.C., the Twelve Tables were fastened to the speakers' stand in the Roman Forum. The tablets dealt with legal procedures, property ownership, building codes, marriage customs, and punishment for crimes.

About the time of Christ, the Roman Emperor Augustus chose members from his military to form the Praetorian Guard to protect the palace and the Urban Cohort to patrol the city. Augustus also established the Vigiles of Rome. Initially assigned as fire fighters, they were eventually also given law enforcement responsibilities; consequently, they are sometimes referred to as the first integrated police-fire service. As the first civilian police force, the Vigiles sometimes kept the peace very ruthlessly. It is from these Vigiles that we derive the word *vigilante*.

In the Roman Empire during the first century A.D., public officials (called *lictors*) acted as bodyguards for magistrates (judges). When the magistrate ordered, the lictor would bring criminals before him and carry out the magistrate's prescribed punishments, even the death penalty. Their symbol of public authority was a *fasces,* a bundle of rods tied by a red thong around an axe, which represented their absolute authority of life and limb. Within the city of Rome itself, however, the fasces had no axe because there was a right to appeal a capital sentence (Hall, 1974, p. 119).

Figure 1–2.   **Fasces.**

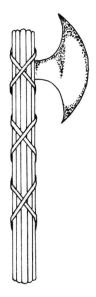

Drawing by Ione Bell.

Another important contribution from the Roman Empire was the Justinian Code. Justinian I, ruler of the Eastern Roman Empire from 527 to 565 A.D., collected all the existing Roman laws. They became known as the Corpus Juris Civilis, meaning body of law. The Corpus Juris Civilis consisted of all Roman laws and legal principles, illustrated by cases, as well as explanations of new laws under proposal.

English Law and Law Enforcement

The early beginnings of just laws and social control were destroyed during the Dark Ages as the Roman Empire disintegrated. Hordes of Germanic invaders swept into the old Roman territory of Britain, bringing with them their own laws and customs. These German invaders intermarried with conquered English, the result being the hardy Anglo-Saxon.

The Anglo-Saxons grouped their farms around small, self-governing villages that policed themselves. When criminals were caught, the punishment was often severe, as in ancient times. Sometimes, however, the tribe would let an offender prove his innocence through battle. And sometimes they allowed testimony by other tribespeople willing to swear that the accused was innocent. In addition, the practice of allowing a criminal to pay a fine for committing a crime or to work off the debt was beginning to come into vogue.

As time went on, the informal grouping of families became more structured. Alfred the Great (849-899 A.D.) first set down the guideline that all freemen should belong to an association that binds them with a certain group of people. The idea was that if one person in the group committed a crime and was convicted, all people in the group were responsible for the person's fine. Consequently, all members of the group were very careful to see that no one in the group broke the law. Every male, unless excused by the king, was enrolled for police purposes in a group of ten families known as a **tithing.** To maintain order in the tithing, they had a leader or chief tithingman who was the mayor, council, and judge all in one. Society was so basic at this time that they needed to enforce only two laws: laws against murder and theft.

The tithing system established the principle of collective responsibility for maintaining local law and order.

Any victim or person who discovered a crime would put out the "Hue and Cry" (Lunt, 1938), for example, "Stop, thief." Anyone who heard the cry would stop whatever he was doing and help capture the suspect. This may be the forerunner of both the general alarm and the citizen's arrest.

The Hue and Cry may be the origin of the general alarm and the citizen's arrest.

When capture was made, the suspect was brought before the chief tithingman, who determined innocence or guilt plus punishment. Theft was often punished by civil restitution or working off the loss by bondage or servitude—the basis for civil law, restitution for financial loss (Lunt, 1938).

If a criminal sought refuge in a neighboring village, that village was expected to return the criminal for punishment. This cooperation among villagers eventually resulted in the formation of hundreds, which were groups of ten tithings. The top official of the hundred was called a reeve. The hundreds also elected a constable to lead them in pursuit of any lawbreakers. The constable was the first English police officer and, as such, had charge of the weapons and horses of the whole community.

Finally the hundreds were consolidated into shires, or counties. The head of the shire was called, quite logically, the shire-reeve, which is the forerunner of our county sheriff. The shire-reeve acted as both police officer and judge for his territory, traveling from hundred to hundred. The shire-reeve had the power of *posse commitatus,* meaning he could gather all the men of a shire together when he needed assistance in pursuing a lawbreaker. This is the forerunner of our posse.

In 1066, William the Conqueror, a Norman, invaded and conquered England. As king of a conquered nation, William was too concerned about national security to allow the tithings to keep their own system of home rule. He established fifty-five military districts each headed by a Norman shire-reeve who answered directly to the crown. William also decided that shire-reeves should not try cases, but should serve only as police officers. He selected his own judges who traveled around and tried cases. These were the forerunners of our circuit judges. Even more important, however, is that this separated the law enforcement and judicial roles.

Under William the Conqueror, the shire-reeves were limited to law enforcement and separate judges were appointed to try cases.

Constables on duty during Anglo-Saxon times.

William established a highly centralized bureaucracy that also unified the country's law enforcement. He introduced the curfew, requiring that all fires be extinguished or covered during the night; and he developed a doomsday book, a tax roll listing the landowners and the extent of their land. The doomsday book was also a legal code with penalties for infractions—an idea formulated by King Alfred the Great 150 years earlier.

In addition, the Normans modified the tithing system into the Frankpledge system, which refers to the guarantee for peace maintenance that the king demanded from all free Englishmen.

The Frankpledge system required loyalty to the king's law and mutual local responsibility in maintaining the peace.

William's son, Henry I, who ruled England from 1100 to 1135, also made significant contributions to law enforcement. In fact, he came to be known as Henry the Lawgiver after he issued the **Leges Henrici** which established certain offenses such as arson, robbery, murder, counterfeiting, and crimes of violence as being against the king's peace. The Leges Henrici set the precedent that for certain crimes a person should be punished by the state rather than by the victim or his group. It also divided crimes into felonies and misdemeanors.

The Leges Henrici made law enforcement a public matter and separated offenses into felonies and misdemeanors.

Henry I's reign ended in 1135 and was followed by many years of turmoil that lasted until Henry II became king in 1154. Henry II's greatest contribution to law enforcement was the jury system. Called an inquisition, people were required to give information to a panel of judges who then determined the guilt or innocence of the accused.

For the next hundred years the kings appointed enforcement officers to meet the king's needs but had no real control over their power. However, when John became king in 1199, he abused his power by demanding more military service from the feudal class, selling royal positions to the highest bidder, and increasing taxes without obtaining consent from the barons—actions all contrary to feudal custom. In addition, John's courts decided cases according to his wishes, not according to law.

In 1213, a group of barons and church leaders met near London to call for a halt to the king's injustices. They drew up a list of rights they wanted King John to grant them. After the king refused to grant these rights on two separate occasions, the barons raised an army and forced him to meet their demands. On June 15, 1215, King John signed the Magna Carta.

Among the provisions of the **Magna Carta** were the right to fair taxation; the right of **habeas corpus,** which promised not to hold a person for any length of time without a hearing; and the right to a trial by jury. It also separated state and local government. This document served as a model for our Bill of Rights.

The original charter was concerned mostly with guaranteeing feudal laws and benefited only the feudal nobility. It granted freedom and privileges to the church, and a few clauses relieved the economic pressure on the middle class. The common freeman and peasant were scarcely mentioned. Nonetheless, this document was the beginning of democracy in England because for the first time the king was subject to the law and his power was checked.

In 1285 King Edward I set up a curfew and night watch program which allowed for the gates of Westminster, then capital of England, to be locked. This would keep the city's occupants in and unwanted persons out. Bailiffs were hired as night watchmen to enforce the curfew and guard the gates. Edward I also mandated that groups of one hundred merchants be responsible for keeping peace in their districts, thus making law enforcement a local responsibility. This system of law enforcement, called the **Watch and Ward**, provided citizens protection twenty-four hours a day. The term ''Watch and Ward'' originated from the name of the shifts, with the day shift called ''ward'' and the night shift ''watch.''

With an ever-increasing population and a trend toward urbanization, society in England became increasingly complex. Law enforcement became truly a collective responsibility. If a man's next-door-neighbor broke the law, the man was responsible for bringing the lawbreaker before the shire-reeve. This prompted the development of a system under which the hundred would decide yearly who would be responsible for maintaining law and order. Responsibility rotated among community members. It was inevitable that some people, not wanting to serve their turn, would seek other members of the hundred to serve in their place for pay. This was the beginning of the system of paid deputies appointed to be responsible for law and order. The paid deputy system was then formalized so that those whose turn it was to pay for protecting the hundred met and appointed the law enforcers. The abuse of citizen duty to serve as watchmen was pervasive, however, and led to the dregs of society, such as petty thieves and town drunks, serving as the watchmen.

During the fourteenth century the office of Justice of the Peace was established to replace the shire-reeve. The Justice of the Peace was assisted by the constables and by three or four men knowledgeable of the country's laws. At first the Justice of the Peace was involved in both judicial matters and law enforcement, but later his powers became strictly judicial. He was responsible for settling matters of wages, prices, conditions of labor, and pre-trial preliminary hearings to determine if there was enough evidence to keep a man in jail to await trial. The Justice of the Peace eventually became the real power of local government (Lunt, 1938).

> *During the fourteenth century, the shire-reeve was replaced by the Justice of the Peace.*

With the passing of feudal times and rise in the power of the church, the unit of local government in rural areas progressed from the hundred to the parish, that is, the area in which people lived who worshipped in a particular parish church. Once each year the parish appointed a person to be **parish constable** and to act as their law officer. This system of maintaining law and order in rural Britain lasted from the Middle Ages until the eighteenth century.

> *During the Middle Ages, the Parish Constable system was used for rural law enforcement; the Watch and Ward system was used for urban law enforcement.*

Developments in urban England required a different system of law enforcement. With urbanization came commerce, industry, and a variety of buildings usually made of wood since England was primarily forest land. For purposes of fire prevention, the town guild appointed men known as the Watch and Ward who patrolled at night on fire watch. They assumed the coincidental responsibility of preventing people from breaking into houses and shops.

Although the Watch and Ward system was primitive and not too effective, it was adequate until the Industrial Revolution (1750) began. About the same time famine struck the rural areas, and large numbers of people moved from the country into the towns seeking work in weaving and knitting mills and in factories. Many, however, failed to find work, and England experienced much unemployment, poverty, and crime.

In addition, political extremists often aroused mobs and incited them to march upon Parliament. These mobs were usually unruly, destructive, and indifferent to the safety of local residents and their property. The government had no civil police force to deal with mob violence, so they ordered a magistrate to read the "riot act," which permitted the magistrate to call the military to quell the riot.

The use of a military force to repress civil disobedience did not work very well. Soldiers hesitated to fire on their own townspeople, and the townspeople, who actually paid the soldiers' wages, resented being fired on by soldiers they had hired to protect them. Consequently, when the riot act was read and the military were called into action, citizen unrest usually mounted.

In addition to unemployment, poverty, and resentment against use of military force, the invention of gin and whiskey in the seventeenth century and the subsequent increase in the liquor trade also caused a great rise in violent crimes and theft.

> *The government responded to the increase in crime by improving street lighting, hiring more watchmen, and greatly increasing the severity of punishment for all kinds of crimes.*

In 1736 a law was passed requiring every gin and whiskey seller and manufacturer to purchase exorbitantly priced licenses. This law did not stop the flow of gin and whiskey, but instead greatly increased the corruption of the constables. Since the constables were often employed in the liquor trade, it was impossible for them to honestly enforce the regulations governing taverns and inns. Additionally, the London watchmen who were responsible for regulating the morals of the townspeople were highly susceptible to bribes and payoffs.

Around 1750 Henry Fielding, an English magistrate and novelist (author of *Tom Jones*), was instrumental in establishing the **Bow Street Runners,** the first detective unit in London and an indicator of the increasing problems faced by law enforcement officials.

The Bow Street Runners, first called ''Thief-takers,'' were specially chosen men with reliable characters who were paid a weekly wage so they would not be tempted by bribes. Known for their incorruptibility, physical strength, and tenacity, they soon became the terror of all street gangs. Because of their skill and reputation, other agencies from throughout England often hired them. The most famous runner was Townsend, who was hired to guard the royal family and became a close friend of the king.

When these runners proved successful, other units were organized. Foot patrols of armed men guarded the city's streets during the day and a horse patrol combatted highway robbery on the main roads up to twenty-five miles from Bow Street.

Although the Bow Street Runners and patrols greatly improved control in the Bow Street area of London, other parts of London were overwhelmed by the impact of the Industrial Revolution. Machines were taking the place of many jobs, causing unemployment and poverty. The cities were developing into huge slums and the crime rate soared. Children were often trained to be thieves, and for the first time in England's history, juvenile delinquency became a problem. Citizens began to carry weapons, and the courts used long-term prison sentences, resulting in overcrowding in the jails and prisons. Punishments were also severe, with over 160 crimes punishable by death. Despite the rampant crime, however, most Londoners resisted an organized police force, seeing it as restricting their liberty.

They had fought long and hard to overcome the historical abuse of military power by the English kings and resisted any return to centralized military power.

Then, in 1819 and 1820, two incidents occurred that helped people change their minds. The first incident was an attack by armed soldiers on a meeting of unemployed workers that left eleven people dead and hundreds injured. This incident, known as the Peterloo Massacre, was a vivid example of the result of using soldiers to maintain peace. In contrast, in the second incident the Bow Street Runners were able to break up a conspiracy to murder a number of government officials. When the conspirators were executed, people were well aware that actions by a group of professional peace keepers could prevent a major insurrection.

In addition to rampant crime, Parliament was also justifiably concerned about poverty, unemployment, and general conditions. Five Parliamentary commissions of inquiry met in London between 1780 and 1820 to determine what should be done about the public order. It was not until Sir Robert (Bobbie) Peel was appointed Home Secretary that the first really constructive proposal was brought before Parliament.

Peelian Reform

Sir Robert Peel, often referred to as the "father of modern policing," proposed a return to the Anglo-Saxon principle of individual community responsibility for preserving law and order. He proposed that London have a body of civilians appointed and paid by the community to serve as police officers.* Parliament agreed and passed the Metropolitan Police Act of 1829, creating the Metropolitan Police of London.

Many of the fundamental principles of Peelian Reform are as applicable today as they were in 1829:

- Police must be stable, efficient, and organized militarily.
- Police must be under governmental control.
- The distribution of crime news is essential.
- The deployment of police strength by both time and area is essential.
- No quality is more indispensable to a policeman than a perfect command of temper; a quiet, determined manner has more effect than violent action.
- Good appearance commands respect.
- The securing and training of proper persons is at the root of efficiency.
- Public security demands that every police officer be given a number.
- Police headquarters should be centrally located and easily accessible.

*The name *police,* introduced into England from France, is derived from the Greek word *polis* meaning "city." Originally, in continental Europe, the term included all activities of a state which had not been segregated into special administrative branches. By the middle of the eighteenth century, the scope of police activity had narrowed to two main classifications: security police, charged with preserving the individual from dangers threatening his person or property, and welfare police, charged with fostering the public welfare by promoting interests beneficial to society.

■ Policemen should be hired on a probationary basis.

■ Police records are necessary to the correct distribution of police strength.

In addition, one of Peel's first steps was to introduce reform that abolished the death penalty for over 100 offenses.

Although most of these principles make sense to us in the twentieth century, they were not readily accepted in nineteenth-century England. During the first few years of Peelian Reform, strong opposition was encountered. In addition to this opposition, Peel was faced with the problem of finding a building for the newly created London Police. He chose an abandoned building that had been built many years before for the Scottish nobility to use when they visited London. This building housed the London Metropolitan Police, and it became known the world over as Scotland Yard, as immortalized by A. Conan Doyle in his Sherlock Holmes mysteries.

Peel eventually became a national hero, and his reforms led to increased status and prestige for all who entered a career in law enforcement. His principles also became the basis of police reform in many large cities in America.

> *Peel's principles for reform called for: local responsibility for law and order; appointed, paid civilians to assume this responsibility; and standards for these individuals' conduct and organization. His proposals resulted in the organization of the Metropolitan Police of London.*

London Metropolitan Police (1829)

The London Metropolitan Police was uniformed for easy identification—top hats, three-quarter-length royal blue coats and white trousers—and were armed only with a truncheon. They were obviously not soldiers as they had no guns. They were (and still are) called ''Bobbies'' after Sir ''Bobbie'' Peel.

Unfortunately, the London Metroplitan Police were not popular. Soon after the force went on street duty in 1829, a London mob assembled, prepared to march on Parliament. A police sergeant and two constables asked the mob leaders to send their people home. The police, trained to be courteous but firm, did their job properly; however, the mob did not disperse. Instead they attacked the sergeant and constables, killing the sergeant and critically injuring the constables. A jury of London citizens, after hearing evidence clearly indicative of a cold, brutal murder, returned a verdict of justifiable homicide. In time, however, the effect of the policemen discharging their duties with professional integrity created a respect for the law which still exists today in England.

City and Borough Police Forces (1835)

With the coming of broad public use of the steam engine and railways and the building of better roads, many criminals moved from London to provincial cities such as Birmingham, Liverpool, and Manchester. Soon the citizens of these cities demanded some police organization similar to that of London. In 1835 Parliament

An English Bobby: A new breed of British constable.

enacted permissive legislation allowing (but not requiring) every city or borough (unincorporated township) over 20,000 people to form a police force. The act called for the town council, a body of elected representatives who administered the city's affairs, to appoint from its members a watch committee to (1) appoint a chief of police, (2) appoint the officers of the force, and (3) administer the force.

County Police Act (1839)

The counties had no collective system of local government larger than the individual parish, yet they, too, felt the need for an organized police force. This prompted Parliament to pass the County Police Act (1839) giving magistrates the responsibility to fix the strength of the force and to appoint and dismiss the chief constable. Unlike his borough counterpart, the parish magistrate, once appointed, had absolute rights of appointment over his subordinates. The new force was paid for by citizens' taxes.

The County Police Act produced an uneven response. Only fifteen of the fifty-two counties had adopted it by the end of 1840. Reluctance to implement the legislation came from several sources, the most important being financial interests. The decision rested with the magistrates, the principle landowners in each county, and they had a vested interest in keeping taxes down.

Women Enter Law Enforcement

In 1883 the London Metropolitan Police appointed two women to supervise women convicts. Their numbers and functions later expanded. In 1905 a woman was attached to the London Metropolitan Police force to conduct inquiries in cases involving women and children. Each year an increasing number of police matrons were hired.

Around 1914 considerable public concern arose in favor of the employment of women police as part of the organization for the prevention and detection of crime. The Penal Reform League passed a resolution urging the appointment of women police constables with powers equal to those of men constables in all county boroughs and the metropolitan boroughs of the County of London (Chapman and Johnston, 1962).

Soon after, the Criminal Law Amendment Committee and the National Vigilance Association sent delegates to interview the Secretary of State on the subject. Delegates were then appointed by the Women's Industrial Council to serve on the Parks Committee of the London Council.

Early in World War I, two separate movements for women police began. The Women Police Volunteers was formed and later came to be called the Women Police Service. In 1920 the group split into the Women's Auxiliary Service and the Women Patrols of the National Union of Women Workers of Great Britian and Ireland. The present official women police are largely a direct continuation of the Women Patrols (Chapman and Johnston, 1962).

In 1883 the London Metropolitan Police appointed two women to supervise women convicts. Their numbers and functions later expanded.

Early Law Enforcement in the United States

The early colonial American settlements relied heavily on self-policing to assure the peace. Communal pressure rather than formal policing was the backbone of law enforcement. The colonists were of similar background, most held similar religious beliefs, and there was actually little worth stealing. However, the seeds of vice and crime were there, as noted by political scientist David Perry (1973, p. 24):

> These colonists were far from the cream of European society; in many cases they represented the legal and religious castoffs.* Their migration served the dual purpose of removing socially undesirable persons from the Mother country and providing manpower for the outposts of imperial expansion. The governors of the new colonies were responsible for keeping such people in line.

Many features of British law enforcement were present in early American colonial settlements. In New England, where people depended on commerce and industry, the night watchman or constable served as protector of public order. In

---

*Persons found guilty of criminal or religious offenses who were banished from Europe and exported to the New World.

the South, where agriculture played a dominate role, the office of **sheriff** was established as the means of area law enforcement. Most of the watchmen and sheriffs were volunteers, but many were paid to serve in the place of others who were supposed to patrol as a civic duty.

New England adopted the night watchman or constable as the chief means of law enforcement; the South adopted the office of sheriff.

Many different types of law enforcement were tried in many different parts of the country. Almost all used some kind of night watch system, with little or no protection during the day. As might be expected, the fastest growing municipalities were the first to organize legal forces.

Creation of the Boston Police

In 1631 the Boston court ordered a six man force to be established to guard the city from sunset to sunup. This was the first night watch in colonial America. In 1636 a town watch was created. This watch consisted of a group of citizens appointed by the town council and stayed in effect for over two hundred years. During this time the services performed by the watch changed significantly. At first the primary function was to ring a bell in case of fire. In 1702 the police were to patrol the streets in silence; in 1735 they were required to call out the time of day and state of the weather.

In 1801 Boston became the first city in the United States to acquire a permanent night watch. These men were paid fifty cents a night. In 1807 the first police precincts were formed, and in 1838 a day force was created to supplement the night force.

Creation of the New York Police

The New York police began in 1652 with the creation of the Rattle Watch, a group of citizens armed with a rattle to call for help. The first police force was formed in 1658. It consisted of eight night watchmen. In 1693 the first precinct station was established, called the Watch House.

The system of watchmen was very ineffective. Often the person on watch was a person sentenced to be a watchman as a form of punishment for a misdemeanor. In addition, citizens could avoid the watch duty by hiring someone to take their place. Although this practice eventually led to a paid police force, it did have its problems. Wealthy citizens came to rely on hiring others, and the men they hired were then hesitant to invoke their authority against the well-to-do. According to Richardson (1970, p. 10), by the mid-1700s New York City's night watch was described as a:

> . . . parcel of idle, drinking, vigilant snorers, who never quell'd any nocturnal tumult in their lives; . . . but would, perhaps, be as ready to join in a burglary as any thief in Christendom.

Due to a continuing increase in crime during the daytime, New York City hired an assortment of watchmen, fire marshals, and bell ringers to patrol during the day and night. In 1844 a paid day watch was established, consisting of sixteen officers appointed by the mayor. At this time the night watch consisted of 1,100 watchmen and was completely separate from the day force. As might be expected, friction existed between the day and night forces, and it became an impossible arrangement, totally incapable of combatting the growing lawlessness in the city.

The practice of hiring substitutes for watch duty eventually led to a paid police force.

Legislators from New York City visited the London Metropolitan Police Department and were so highly impressed that, in 1844, New York City followed the pattern set in England fifteen years earlier by Sir Robert Peel and established a round-the-clock, paid police force.

In 1844 New York City established the first modern American city police force, modeled after London's Metropolitan Police Department.

Soon other police forces similar to that in New York developed, including forces in Chicago, Cincinnati, New Orleans, Philadelphia, Boston, Baltimore, and San Francisco.

In 1856 New York adopted a full uniform for each ward.

In spite of patterning themselves after the London Metropolitan Police, New York police officers vigorously protested against wearing uniforms. It wasn't until twelve years later that the New York police adopted a full police uniform and became the first uniformed law enforcement agency in the country. Likewise, although Henry Fielding established the Bow Street Runners (the first detective unit) in 1750, it was over a hundred years later before American police agencies recognized a need for detective units. In 1866 Detroit established the first detective bureau, followed by New York in 1882, and Cincinnati in 1886.

Evolution of the City Police

When city police were first established, their only contact with their departments was face-to-face meetings or messengers. However, during the 1850s telegraph networks linked police headquarters directly with their districts, making unnecessary the daily meetings between the captains and the commissioners. Several decades later a modified telegraph system linked the patrolman directly to his station. A fire alarm system, first introduced in Boston, was adopted for police use. Call boxes placed on city street corners became a common sight. These boxes were equipped with a simple lever which signalled the station that the officer was at his post. A bell system was then added that allowed the patrolman to use a few simple signals to call an ambulance, a "slow wagon" for routine duties, or a "fast wagon" for emergencies. The introduction of a special "Gamewell" telephone into the call box in 1880 made this a truly two-way communication system, greatly improving the contact between the patrolmen and their station house.

The Civil War brought new problems of social control. Municipal forces tried to meet these problems by organizing new divisions and specializing the force. As centers of population became increasingly urbanized and fringe areas became incorporated suburbs of the hub city, a trend developed to add forces to the police organization rather than to centralize or consolidate them. Consequently, newly developed fringe cities had their own forces which, rather than improving efficiency, fostered complex, uncoordinated relationships, compartmentalization, and inefficiency.

Establishment of State Law Enforcement Agencies

In 1835, when Texas was still a republic, the Texas provisional government established the Texas Rangers. The Texas Rangers were actually a military unit established into three companies which were responsible for border patrol. The apprehension of Mexican cattle rustlers was a primary task (Folley, 1973, p. 64).

In 1874 the Texas Rangers were commissioned as police officers in the state of Texas. At that time there were 450 Rangers, and their duties included tracking down murderers, robbers, smugglers, and mine bandits.

Massachusetts was the next state to establish a state law enforcement agency by appointing a small force of state officers in 1865 to control vice within the state. The state also granted them general police powers; therefore, Massachusetts is usually credited with establishing the first law enforcement agency with general police authority throughout the state.

The Texas Rangers were the first agency similar to our present-day state police.

Establishment of Federal Law Enforcement Agencies

Several federal law enforcement agencies were created by Congress to meet demands created by the changing conditions of the nation.

The oldest federal agency is the U.S. Marshals Office, created in 1789. Thirteen U.S. Marshals were assigned to President George Washington's attorney general. As the nation began to grow westward, the U.S. Marshals were the main law enforcement in the territories. When the Civil War ended (1865) and most of the territories had become states, the U.S. Marshals became the bailiffs of the U.S. District Courts, where violations of federal crimes are tried.

The Justice Department established other federal law enforcement agencies such as the Immigration and Naturalization Service (1891), of which the Border Patrol is a well-known division.

The Treasury Department established federal law enforcement agencies which are still well known today. The Secret Service was created in 1865 to control the flood of counterfeit currency bankrupting the war effort. After President McKinley was assassinated in 1901, the Secret Service was authorized to protect the president and his family.

Another well-known federal agency established within the Treasury Department was the Internal Revenue Service (1862) and its famous Intelligence Division agents whose income tax evasion cases brought long prison sentences to such infamous criminals as Al Capone, Vito Genovese, and many others.

Among the earliest federal law enforcement agencies were: United States Marshals, Immigration and Naturalization Service, the Secret Service, and the Internal Revenue Service.

The Problem of Corruption

Just as earlier in other countries, corruption became a problem in United States law enforcement. One primary factor underlying this corruption was the prevelant **spoils system** which placed rewards in the hands of victors. This system led politicians to staff many of the nation's police forces with incompetent people as rewards for support, "fixing" arrests or assuring that arrests were not made, and securing immunity from supervision for certain establishments or people.

The spoils system encouraged politicians to reward their "friends" by giving them key positions in police departments.

As noted by Walker (1983, p. 7):

> The quality of American police service in the 19th century could hardly have been worse. The police were completely unprofessional and police work was dominated by corruption and inefficiency. The source of these problems was *politics*. Local government was viewed primarily as a source of opportunity—for jobs, for profit, for social mobility, for corruption . . . Selection standards for police personnel were nonexistent. Officers obtained their jobs through political contacts . . . In 1880 most big cities paid their police $900 a year; a factory worker could expect to earn only about $450 a year.

Reform movements began early but moved slowly against the solidly entrenched political "untouchables." Cities sought to break political control by a variety of organizational techniques, including the election of policemen and chiefs, administering forces through bipartisan lay boards, asking states to assume local policing, and instituting mayor-council or council-city manager municipal government—which has proved to be the most effective thus far.

The election of the municipal **chief of police** was common with the establishment of local departments. Remembering the corrupt officials who served as long as they pleased the king, the people elected police officials to serve short terms so they would not have time to become too powerful or corrupt. But this system had its drawbacks. Not only were the officials not in office long enough to become corrupt, they were not in office long enough to gain proficiency in their job. In fact, officials would just get to know their own officers and have enough experience to run the police department when their terms would expire. Additionally, since terms were so short, officials kept their civilian jobs and generally devoted most of their time to them, giving only spare time to running the police force. This system lacked professionalism; the position of police chief became a popularity contest. Therefore, it was decided that a permanent police chief, qualified with experience and ability, was the best way to have effective law enforcement. Today the elected police chief system remains in only a few cities.

In the mid-1800s administrative police boards or commissions were established. They were made up of judges, mayors, and private citizens who served as the head of the police department with the police chief following their orders. The rationale was that the chief of police should be a professional and keep his job continuously, but that civilian control was necessary to maintain responsibility to community needs. This system lasted many years, but it had serious weaknesses. The board members often proved more of a hindrance than a help, and the system fostered political corruption.

As a reaction against local boards, and in an attempt to control corrupt police agencies, state control of local agencies was developed in some areas of the country. It was believed that if the state controlled local agencies, citizens would be assured of adequate and uniform law enforcement. While some cities still operate within this framework, most cities and states found this was not the answer to the problem because the laws were not equally enforced. In some areas the laws were under-enforced and in other areas, over-enforced. The system also lacked responsiveness to local demands and needs. Therefore, control was again given to the local government in most instances.

The next system to be tried was the commission government charter. Commissioners were elected and charged with various branches of city government. This system, also on the decline, was as inadequate as the administrative police board.

The most efficient and prevalent current local system is the mayor-council or council-city manager government. The former is very efficient when the mayor is a full-time, capable administrator. The latter assures more continuity in the business administration and executive control of the overall operations because a professional, nonpolitical administrator is managing the affairs of the community. Either way the chief of police is selected on the basis of merit.

> Cities sought to break political control by a variety of organizational techniques, including the election of policemen and chiefs, administering forces through bipartisan lay boards, asking states to assume local policing, and instituting mayor-council or council-city manager municipal government—which has proved to be the most effective thus far.

In 1883, a major step toward reducing corruption within the police department occurred when Congress passed the Pendelton Act. Prior to this act, most government positions were filled by political appointment. Frequently the people appointed were incapable of performing their tasks well. One government worker who was going to be replaced by President Garfield shot and killed the president. This incident caused a public outcry and resulted in passage of the Pendelton Act. The act established a Civil Service Commission to enforce its provisions. The new laws called for an examination open to all citizens and for new workers to be hired on the basis of who had the highest grades. The act also made it unlawful to fire or demote workers for political reasons and relieved government workers from any obligation to give political service or payments.

> The Pendelton Act created the civil service system for government employees and made it unlawful to fire or demote a worker for political reasons.

Developments in the Early 1900s

In the early 1900s state and federal law enforcement agencies continued to emerge, and national attention began to focus on the police as a profession.

Development of State Law Enforcement Agencies

Most state police agenices established prior to the twentieth century were created as a response to a limited need such as the control of vice. Such was not the case in Pennsylvania.

The first modern state police agency was the Pennsylvania Constabulary, which originated in 1905 to meet several needs. As noted by Folley (1973, p. 66), the **Pennsylvania Constabulary** (1) provided the governor an executive arm to assist him in accomplishing his responsibilities, (2) provided a means to quell riots occurring during labor disputes in the coal regions, and (3) improved law enforcement services in the rural portions of the state where county officials were generally ineffective. Governor Pennypacker's rationale for the first need to be met by such a state agency is vividly described by Katherine Mayo (1917, pp. 5-6):

> In the year 1903, when I assumed the office of chief executive of the state, I found myself thereby invested with supreme executive authority. I found that no power existed to interfere with me in my duty to enforce the laws of the state, and that by the same token, no conditions could release me from my duty so to do. I then looked about me to see what instruments I possessed wherewith to accomplish this bounden obligation—what instruments on whose loyalty and obedience I could truly rely. I perceived three such instruments—my private secretary, a very small man; my woman stenographer; and the janitor. . . . So I made the state police.

Humorous as it may sound, there was a large element of truth in the governor's thinking. Further, the labor riots were real and had to be faced. Perhaps most important, however, was the emphasis on rural law enforcement and the establishment of a uniformed mounted force offering protection in even the most remote areas of Pennsylvania. Although they were organized originally for the purpose of and functioned as strikebreakers, the Pennsylvania state police served as a model for other states and heralded the advent of modern state policing.

The first modern state police agency was the Pennsylvania Constabulary, which originated in 1905 to meet several needs.

Development of Federal Law Enforcement Agencies

The world-famous Federal Bureau of Investigation (FBI) was not created by Congress until 1908. Six attorney agents were hired, but they were not allowed to use guns. In 1924 J. Edgar Hoover was appointed director, and he completely reorganized the Bureau. Shortly thereafter it reached national stature. The FBI has jurisdiction in three general areas encompassing some 180 different criminal matters: (1) crimes involving national security, (2) interstate crimes, and (3) crimes on the high seas. The importance of the FBI as well as other federal and state agencies will be discussed in detail in Chapter 6.

The most important federal law enforcement agency created in the twentieth century is the Federal Bureau of Investigation, better known as the FBI.

The Wickersham Commission and Police Professionalism. In 1929 President Herbert Hoover appointed the national Commission on Law Observance and Enforcement to study the American criminal justice system. The

Commission, named after its chairman, George Wickersham, devoted two of its fourteen reports to the police. Report 11, *Lawlessness in Law Enforcement,* delineated the problem of police brutality. The report concluded that "The third degree—the inflicting of pain, physical or mental, to extract confessions or statements—is extensively practiced." Report 14, *The Police,* concentrated on police adminstration and called for expert leadership, centralized administrative control, and higher personnel standards, in short, police professionalism.

The Evolution of Modern Law Enforcement

Largely because of civil service and a grassroots-inspired groundswell of general reform, most police forces have shaken the influence of corrupt politics. In contrast to conditions at the turn of the century, appointment to the forces and police adminstration generally is vastly improved. Police recruitment, discipline, and promotion have been removed from politics in most cities.

Communications involving police service have also greatly improved. The radio and patrol car transformed the relationship between the police and the public and offered increased protection for everyone. The continuous expansion of the telephone in the 1960s and 1970s made it easier for people to call the police. Police dispatchers were added to tie radio systems directly into telephone networks. The use of fingerprint systems and the increased employment of policewomen as well as many other advances occurred at an accelerated pace.

However, despite the advanced technology which greatly improved the police officer's ability to respond to requests for aid and increased his mobility, the basic strategy of police has not altered.

> *Crime waves in metropolitan areas prompt cities to improve their street lighting, increase the number of police officers on the streets, and demand more severe punishment for the convicted criminals.*

In the last three decades, the human factor has assumed greater importance as police agencies cope with the tensions and dislocations of population growth, increasing urbanization, developing technology, the civil rights movement, changing social norms, and a breakdown of traditional values. These factors have enormously complicated law enforcement, making more critical the need for truly professional police officers.

Today's local police officers must be law enforcement generalists with a working knowledge of federal, state, county, and municipal law, traffic law, criminal law, juvenile law, narcotics, liquor control, and countless other areas. But this only accounts for approximately 10 percent of what a modern police officer does. Today's police officers spend 90 percent of their time providing a variety of services while protecting life, property, and personal liberty. They must be aware of human factors and understand the psychological and sociological implications of their work for their community. They must deal with all citizens, rich and poor, young and old, in ways which will maintain the community's support and confidence. This is no small responsibility.

Summary

Our current laws and the means by which they are enforced have their origins in the distant past, perhaps as far back as the cave dwellers. Laws and law enforcement began several thousand years B.C. as a means of controlling human conduct and enforcing society's rules. Many features of our present system of law enforcement have been borrowed from the Greeks, Romans, and particularly the English.

The English tithing system established the principle of collective responsibility for maintaining local law and order. This system was modified by the Normans into the Frankpledge system which required loyalty to the king's law and mutual local responsibility in maintaining the peace. During the Middle Ages, the Parish Constable system was used for law enforcement; the Watch and Ward system was used for urban law enforcement. The government responded to increases in crime by improving street lighting, hiring more watchmen, and greatly increasing the severity of punishment for all kinds of crimes.

In 1829 the Metropolitan Police Act created the first true police force, the Metropolitan Police of London. Sir Robert Peel was the driving force behind this act.

The early American settlers brought with them several features of English law and law enforcement including those found in Leges Henrici, which made law enforcement a public matter, and in the Magna Carta, which provided for due process of law. Law enforcement in colonial America was frequently patterned after England's Watch and Ward system and later after the London Metropolitan Police and the principles for reform set forth by Sir Robert Peel.

Although law enforcement was generally considered a local responsibility, the early beginning of state law enforcement agencies occurred with the establishment of the Texas Rangers, and the early beginning of federal law enforcement agencies with the establishment of U.S. Marshals. After the turn of the century other state agencies, notably the Pennsylvania Constabulary, and other federal agencies, notably the Federal Bureau of Investigation, were established.

The spoils system encouraged politicians to reward their friends by giving them key positions in police departments. Cities fought to break political control by a variety of organizational techniques, including the election of policemen and chiefs, adminstering forces through bipartisan lay boards, asking states to assume local policing, and instituting mayor-council or council-city manager municipal government—which has proved to be the most effective thus far. In addition, in 1883 the Pendelton Act created the civil service system for government employees and made it unlawful to fire or demote a worker for political reasons.

Discussion Questions

1. What common problems have existed throughout the centuries for people in law enforcement?

2. How have these common problems been approached at different points in history?

3. What demands are made on the modern police officer which were not present twenty or thirty years ago?

4. What is the difference between someone seeking vengeance on his own for a wrong against him and a court imposing a fine or prison sentence on a wrongdoer?

5. Why was there no law enforcement during the daytime for many centuries?

6. Why did it take so long to develop a police force in England? In the United States?

7. Should police officers be appointed or elected?

References

Chapman, S.G., and Johnston, Colonel T.E. St. *The police heritage in England and America.* East Lansing, Mich.: Michigan State University, 1962.

Eldefonso, E.; Coffey, A.; and Grace, R.C. *Principles of law enforcement.* 4th ed. New York: John Wiley & Sons, 1983.

Ferguson, R.W., and Stokke, A.H. *Concepts of criminal law.* Boston: Holbrook Press, 1976.

Fitzgerald, P. *Chronicles of the Bow Street office.* 1888. Reprint. Montclair, N.J.: Patterson Smith Publishing Corp., 1972.

Folley, V.L. *American law enforcement.* Boston: Holbrook Press, 1973.

Hall, J. *Dictionary of subjects and symbols in art.* New York: Harper and Row, 1974.

Kadish, S.H., ed. *Encyclopedia of crime and justice. Vol. 3.* New York: The Free Press, 1983.

Levin, J.P.; Musheno, M.C.; and Palumbo, D.J. *Criminal justice: A public policy approach.* New York: Harcourt Brace Jovanovich, 1980.

Lunt, W.E. *History of England.* New York: Harper and Brothers, 1938.

McKay, J.P.; Hill, B.D.; and Buckler, J. *A history of western society.* 2d ed. Boston: Houghton Mifflin Company, 1983.

Mayo, K.M. *Justice to all: The story of the Pennsylvania state police.* New York: G.P. Putnam's Sons, 1917.

Owings, C. *Women police.* Montclair, N.J.: Patterson Smith Publishing Corp., 1969.

Perry, D.C. *Police in the metropolis.* Columbus, Ohio: Charles E. Merrill, 1973.

Quinney, R. *Criminology.* Boston: Little, Brown & Company, 1975.

Richardson, J.F. *The New York police.* New York: Oxford University Press, 1970.

Rubinstein, J. *City police.* New York: Farrar, Straus & Giroux, 1973.

Saunders, C. *Upgrading the American police*. Washington, D.C.: The Brookings Institution, 1970.

Walker, S. *The police in America: An introduction*. New York: McGraw-Hill, 1983.

Wickersham Commission. *Wickersham Commission reports*. Montclair, N.J.: Patterson Smith Publishing Corp. 1968.

Officers prepare to handle a violent confrontation with a suspect. It is estimated that two violent crimes are committed in the United States every minute.

Crime in the United States

Laws and Crimes

Do You Know . . .

- How to define and differentiate: law, moral law, common law, criminal law, civil law, tort, equity, statute, crime, misdemeanor, and felony?

- What law takes precedence if two laws conflict?

- How crimes and punishments are determined in the United States?

- What the characteristics of a crime are?

- How to define the crimes of murder, assault, rape, robbery, burglary, larceny/theft, motor vehicle theft, and arson?

- What is meant by white-collar crime and what specific types of crimes are included in this general classification?

- How to define narcotics and dangerous drugs? What the three general classifications of dangerous drugs are?

- What restrictions are placed on the possession, sale, and use of narcotics and dangerous drugs?

- What relationship exists between drinking alcohol and fatal motor vehicle accidents?

There is no man so good, who, were he to submit all his thoughts and actions to the laws would not deserve hanging ten times in his life.

—*Montaigne*

Introduction

To assure to each United States citizen the right to "life, liberty, and the pursuit of happiness," society has established laws which all are expected to obey. It is up to individuals in law enforcement to assure that the laws *are* obeyed. To do so effectively, it is important to know what constitutes crime in the United States, what actions are illegal, and under what circumstances. The seriousness of crime in the United States is well illustrated by the FBI's "Crime Clock" in Figure 2–1.

Figure 2–1.   *Crime Clock.*

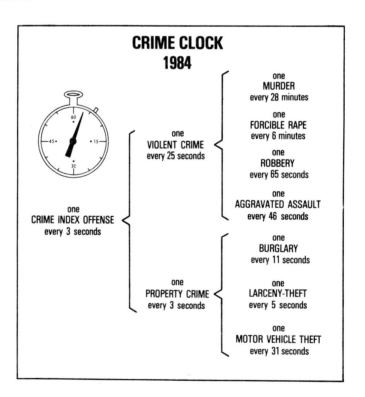

Source: Uniform Crime Reports, 1984.

Law Enforcement and the Law

Folley (1980, p. 12) notes that: "To fully appreciate the significance and complexities of law and to place the police role in proper perspective, familiarity with several types of law is important."

Law

Recall that this book began with a discussion of what law is: Law is a body of rules for human conduct which are enforced by imposing penalties for their violation. Laws define man's social obligations and determine the relations of individuals to society and to each other. The purpose of law is to regulate the actions of individuals to conform to the way of life that the people's elected representatives or the community consider essential.

Social or Moral Law

Often obedience to law is obtained through social pressure—ridicule, contempt, scorn, or ostracism. Such methods are called moral or social sanctions, and the laws they enforce are called moral or social laws.

> *Moral or social laws are laws made by society and enforced solely by social pressure.*

Moral or social laws include laws of etiquette, "honor," and morality. When moral laws break down and social sanctions fail to obtain conformity, other laws may be enacted and enforced.

Precedents: Common Law and Case Law

The beginnings of law are found in social habit or custom. Custom is simply precedent—doing what has been done before. In early times custom, religion, morals, and the law were intermingled. Some early customs have, over the centuries, become law.

Some customs were enforced physically rather than morally, the violator being expelled from the community, sacrificed to the gods, or hanged. Other violations of custom which were not felt to be harmful to the whole community were punished by the injured group or the injured individual with the aid of his family (self-help, vengeance, feud). As long as such acts of vengeance, although regarded as right by the victim, might lead to retaliation, the sanction behind the rules of custom were still purely moral. But when the community began to protect those who had taken *rightful* vengeance, these persons became agents of the community. This kind of self-help met early society's needs when the right to take vengeance or redress was clear. It did not provide a way to settle controversies. Therefore courts were established to interpret customs and settle controversies.

Custom was replaced by judicial precedent. Legally, however, precedents or decisions are not law, but only evidence of the law. Even if the precedent or decision is written, the law in them is "unwritten."

In England, **common law** was the term applied to the laws and customs of the realm applied by the royal courts. It was defined as the customary law of England set by the judges as disputes rose. This was in contrast to local custom, equity, or ecclesiastical (church) law. When Parliament supplemented and modified the existing legal principles, the term *common law* was used to describe the law in force before, and independent of, any acts of the legislature.

> *Common law refers to the precedents set by the judges in the royal courts in England.*

The common law brought to the United States by the early settlers and established in the various colonies forms the basis of modern American law. The common law of the states has one exception, Louisiana, which established and kept the system of French civil law.

In a nontechnical sense, common law describes the precedent generally followed in the absence of a specific law. In the United States this has come to be known as **case law.**

> *Case law refers to the settling of judicial precedents; no specific law exists, but a similar case serves as a model to be followed.*

According to Oran's *Dictionary of the Law:* "Case law summarizes how statutes and constitutional problems have been interpreted by judges in cases coming before them." When cases which are not covered by the law come before the courts, the judges' rulings on previous similar cases will, for all practical purposes, be treated as law.

Statutory Law

In an advanced society, legislation becomes an increasingly important agency of legal development. The United States, as well as many other countries, has largely succeeded in replacing common law (unwritten law) with **statutory law** (legislated and written law). However, much of our law still rests upon judicial precedent; that is, common law and case law.

> *Statutory law is law passed by the legislature. It may be passed at the federal or state level, and at either level it includes constitutional and ordinary law.*

Federal constitutional law is based on the United States Constitution, its amendments, and interpretations of the Constitution by the federal courts. As discussed in Chapters 13 and 14, law enforcement officers must comply with constitutional law which places numerous restrictions on their actions. Ordinary federal law consists of acts of Congress, treaties with foreign states, executive orders and regulations, and interpretation of the preceding by federal courts.

State constitutional law is based on the individual state's constitution, its amendments, and interpretations of them by the state's courts. State ordinary law consists of acts of the state legislatures, decisions of the federal courts in interpreting or developing the common law, executive orders and regulations, and municipal ordinances.

In addition, in most states, each county and city is given the right to make and pass laws for its local jurisdiction, providing the law does not conflict or pre-empt the state's laws. The basis of the local ordinances (laws) are primarily enacted to protect the individual community.

Order of Authority of Law

If two laws conflict, a set order of authority has been established.

The order of authority of law is: the federal Constitution, treaties with foreign powers, acts of Congress, the state constitutions, state statutes, and finally, common law or case law.

Equity

Before leaving the general discussion of laws and looking at criminal and civil laws, one other concept is important; that is, the concept of **equity.**

Equity means to resort to general principles of fairness and justice whenever existing law is inadequate.

Neither the Roman praetors nor the English chancellors made rigid rules like legislators; instead they found law in the decisions of single cases as judges do. They did not, however, regard themselves bound by precedents. The new rules were not regarded as law at first, but rather as arbitrary assertions of governmental power. However, both in Rome and in England, equity, following its own precedents, soon developed a new body of judicial custom recognized as law. In England and in the United States today, equity is recognized as judge-made law, that is, a legal ruling by a judge based on fairness. In the United States, equity describes a system of rules and doctrines supplementing common and statutory law and superseding laws which are inadequate for fair settlement of a case. In other words, equity requires that the ''spirit of the law'' take precedence over the ''letter of the law.''

As noted by Ferguson and Stokke (1976, p. 64): ''The rule of thumb in construing penal statutes is that criminal statutes are not to be strictly construed, but rather should be interpreted so as to promote fairness and justice. When construing penal statutes, one must take into consideration the 'spirit of the law, not the letter of the law.' '' This imperative to justice is echoed by Germann, Day, and Gallati (1972, p. 16): ''In order that justice might prevail, the strict letter of the law is not always satisfactory; often equity must be considered, and legal justice corrected or supplemented by reference to the spirit of the law rather than to the letter of the law.''

Criminal Law

Criminal law defines crimes and fixes punishment for them. Criminal law includes rules and procedures for investigating crimes and prosecuting criminals; regulations governing the constitution of courts, the conduct of trials; and the administration of penal institutions.

American criminal law has a number of unique features. In establishing criminal law, the federal government and each state government are sovereign within the limits of their authority as defined by the Constitution. Therefore, criminal law varies from state to state. Although there are many differences, most of them have a tradition derived from English common law. There is no federal common law jurisdiction in criminal cases, however (*U.S. v. Hudson*).

> *Criminal law defines crimes and fixes punishments for them.*

The statutes that define what acts constitute social harm are called substantive criminal law, for example, a statute defining homicide. A substantive criminal law not only defines the offense, but also states the punishment. The omission of the punishment invalidates the criminal law.

In most countries crimes and punishments are expressed in statutes. Punishments include removal from public office, fines, exile, imprisonment, and death. Unless the act of which a defendant is accused is expressly defined by statute as a crime, no indictment or conviction for the commission of the act is legal. This provision is important in establishing the difference between government by law and arbitrary dictatorial government.

Criminal law in the Unites States generally defines seven classes of crimes. It includes offenses against (1) international law, (2) the dispensation of justice and the legitimate exercise of governmental authority, (3) the public peace, (4) property, (5) trade, (6) public decency, and (7) persons.

And, like English law, American criminal law also classifies crimes with respect to their gravity as treason, felonies, and misdemeanors. **Felony** refers to serious crimes, generally those punishable by death or by imprisonment for more than one year in a state prison or penitentiary. The court may inflict a lesser punishment. **Misdemeanor** is a term applied to any minor offense, generally punishable by a fine or a short imprisonment, usually not to exceed one year, in a jail or workhouse.

No crime is a felony unless made so by statute, or unless it is a felony under common law. Formerly a felony was a crime punishable by forfeiture of the criminal's lands, or goods, or both. In addition, other punishment might be added, according to the degree of guilt. In England for a long time most felonies were punishable by death.

> *Felony refers to serious crimes, generally those punishable by death or by imprisonment for more than one year in a state prison or penitentiary. The court may inflict a lesser punishment.*

The criminal codes of the states vary in their classification of offenses that are considered misdemeanors. Examples of crimes usually defined as misdemeanors include libel, assault and battery, malicious mischief, and petty theft.

Misdemeanor is a term applied to any minor offense, generally punishable by a fine or a short term, usually not to exceed one year, in a jail or workhouse.

In some states the distinction between felonies and misdemeanors is practically discarded, the punishment for each particular crime being prescribed by statute.

The same situation existed under common law. Although under common law a crime was generally classified as treason, felony, or misdemeanor, many offenses could not be defined exactly, so the rule was adopted that any immoral act harmful to the community was, in itself, a crime, punishable by the courts. Crimes were classified as *mala in se* (bad in itself), based to a large degree on religious doctrine, or as *mala prohibita* (bad because it is forbidden). A *mala in se* crime is one which is so offensive that it is obviously criminal, for example, murder or rape. A *mala prohibita* crime is one which violates a specific regulatory statute, certain traffic violations, for example. These would not usually be considered crimes if no law prohibited them.

Civil Law and Torts

Civil law refers to all noncriminal restrictions placed upon individuals. Although laws vary from state to state, generally such actions as trespassing, desertion of family, slander, failure to make good on a contract, or similar actions against an individual would be covered under civil law.

 Civil law refers to all noncriminal restrictions placed upon individuals. It seeks not punishment, but restitution.

As Prosser notes (1955, p. 7):

A **tort** is not the same thing as a crime, although the two sometimes have many features in common. The distinction between them lies in the interests affected and the remedy afforded by the law. A crime is an offense against the public at large, for which the state, as the representative of the public, will bring proceedings in the form of criminal prosecution. . . . A criminal prosecution is not concerned in any way with compensation of the injured individual against whom the crime is committed. . . . The civil action for a tort, on the other hand, is commenced and maintained by the injured person himself, and its purpose is to compensate him for the damage he has suffered, at the expense of the wrongdoer.

 A tort is a civil wrong for which the court will seek a remedy in the form of damages to be paid. People's court

Sutherland and Cressey (1978, p. 8) clarify the distinction between a tort and a crime:

> The conventional view is that a crime is an offense against the state, while, in contrast, a tort in violation of civil law is an offense against an individual. A particular act may be considered as an offense against an individual and also against the state, and is either a tort or a crime or both, according to the way it is handled. A person who has committed an act of assault, for example, may be ordered by the civil court to pay the victim a sum of $500 for the damages to his interests, and may also be ordered by the criminal court to pay a fine of $500 to the state. The payment of the first $500 is not punishment, but payment of the second $500 is punishment.

It is important that law enforcement officers recognize when a matter is covered by criminal law and when it is covered by civil law (noncriminal matters). Sometimes police officers are asked to describe a citizen's rights in a noncriminal matter and what legal options are open.

we do not give legal advice !!!

A Close-Up on Crime

Haskell and Yablonsky (1983, p. *ix*) suggest that "crime exists in all societies. Wherever there are laws or moral prescriptions for behavior, there is always a segment of society that will violate these norms."

The Bureau of Justice Statistics (1983, p. 2) defines **crime** as follows: "We define crime as all behaviors and acts for which a society provides formally sanctioned punishment." Crimes are made so by law. State and federal statutes define each crime, the elements involved, and the penalty attached to each.

Crime is defined as any behavior for which society sanctions a punishment.

Sutherland and Cressey (1978, pp. 12-14) have summarized seven inter-related and overlapping characteristics of crime delineated by Jerome Hall:

1. A crime has certain external consequences called a harm. Crime has a harmful impact on social interests; mere intention without resulting in such a harm is not a crime.
2. The harm must be specifically outlawed in advance.
3. Conduct must occur, either intentional or reckless action or inaction, to bring about the harmful consequences. *overt conduct*
4. **Criminal intent** must be present. Criminal intent must not be confused with motivation. The motive might be "good," but if the intention is to perform an act specifically outlawed, it is still a crime. For example, if a person steals from the rich to give to the poor, his motives are "good," but his intention is still wrong.

5. The criminal intent and conduct must be related. For example, a salesman who enters a home on business and then decides to steal something cannot be charged with breaking and entering.

Act must cause the harm

6. A causal relation must exist between the outlawed harm and the intentional act. For example, if a person shoots someone and the victim suffocates while in the hospital recovering from the wound, the causal relation is not clear-cut.

7. The punishment must be legally prescribed the action must be punishable by law.

Crimes can be categorized in many different ways. You have already seen one such classification—a criminal act can be either a misdemeanor or a felony. Another common classification is to differentiate between violent crimes and property crimes. Violent crimes include homicide, rape, assault, and robbery—actions that involve the use of force or the threat of force against a person. In contrast, property crimes do not involve such force. They include larceny, burglary, and motor vehicle theft.

The three classifications of crime discussed in this chapter are: (1) Part I and Part II Index Crimes, (2) white-collar crimes, and (3) crimes related to narcotics and dangerous drugs.

Part I Index Crimes

Crimes reported to local police departments or to the FBI are listed in an *Index of Uniform Crime Reports* (UCR), issued yearly by the FBI. How much crime is unreported, however, is not known.

As noted by Nettler (1978, p. 55): "The most popular measure of crime is official statistics of offenses 'known to the police.' . . . Crimes known to the police are themselves a result of social processing. . . . Complaints to the police are subject to errors that result from mistakes and from lies." In addition, "Official statistics on crime are imperfect not only because of what is and is not included but also because of imperfections in those who do the counting" (Nettler 1978, p. 63).

This point is reiterated by the Brantinghams (1984, p. 56): "Criminal justice statistics do not enumerate all crimes. They enumerate only those crimes made known to the criminal justice system. A substantial number of crimes are never reported to the police or any other agent of criminal justice. The true number of crimes, called the dark figure of criminality is unknown." In spite of these difficulties, police departments do make frequent use of the information from the Uniform Crime Reports.

The Uniform Crime Reports divide crimes into Part I and Part II crimes, with Part I crimes being those which are most serious in terms of either their use of violence or the value of the property involved.

The eight Part I crimes are (1) murder, (2) aggravated assault causing serious bodily harm, (3) forcible rape, (4) robbery, (5) burglary, (6) larceny/theft, (7) motor vehicle theft, and (8) arson.

Murder (Homicide)

Murder is defined in the Uniform Crime Reporting Program as the willful killing of another person. Deaths caused by negligence, suicide, accident, justifiable homicide, attempts to murder, or assaults to murder are *not* included.

 Murder (homicide) is the willful killing of a human by another human.

The generally recognized levels of homicide are: (1) first-degree murder, (2) second-degree murder, (3) manslaughter (or non-negligent manslaughter), and (4) negligent homicide. The first three categories, considered to be willful acts, are classified as felonies. Negligent homicide, however, is usually considered a misdemeanor.

First-degree murder is willful, deliberate, and *premeditated* (planned) taking of another person's life. A homicide which occurs during the commission or attempted commission of arson, robbery, rape, or burglary is also usually classified as first-degree murder, even though it was not willful, deliberate, or premeditated. The question of premeditation is always left up to the jury.

Second-degree murder is one which is *not* premeditated but the intent to kill is present. The charge of murder in the second degree or manslaughter often results from killings which do not involve weapons.

Manslaughter is differentiated from murder in that the element of malice is absent, that is, the death was accidental; there was no original intent, hatred, ill-will, or disregard for the lives of others. In many states manslaughter is classified as either voluntary or involuntary. *Involuntary* manslaughter involves killing someone while doing some lawful act negligently or while negligently failing to perform some legal duty. Many deaths resulting from automobile accidents are classified as involuntary manslaughter. If there is no malice or intent to harm, and if the the activity which led to the death is not a felony and would not usually cause bodily harm, most state statutes define it as involuntary manslaughter. In contrast, *voluntary* manslaughter is intentionally killing someone without previous malice, but in the sudden heat of passion due to adequate provocation. For example, a man who kills another man whom he found in bed with his wife would probably be found guilty of voluntary manslaughter. If a store owner kills a robber in his store, his act and many other instances of self-defense are often defined as voluntary manslaughter.

Negligent homicide refers to an accidental death which results from the reckless operation of a motor vehicle, boat, plane, or firearm.

According to the UCR, 19,000 to 21,000 homicides are committed per year. The Bureau of Justice Statistics cites these facts regarding homicide:

- Homicide is the least frequent violent crime.
- Ninety-five percent of the victims were slain in single victim situations.
- At least 55 percent of the murderers were relatives or acquaintances of the victim.
- Twenty-four percent of all murders occurred or were suspected to have occurred as the result of some felonious activity.

Assault

Assault is the unlawful attack by one person upon another for the purpose of inflicting severe bodily injury. Aggravated assault is usually accompanied by the use of a weapon or other means likely to produce serious bodily harm or death. Attempts are included since it is not necessary that an injury result when a gun, knife, or other weapon is used which could and probably would result in serious personal injury if the crime were successfully completed.

> *Assault is attacking a person. It may be aggravated or simple.*

Whether an assault is aggravated or simple is determined by the prosecuting attorney and is based on the intent of the attacker. Some states include the term *battery* in their statutes; others omit the term and allow the term *assault* to refer to both the blow and threats of attack. Assaults are frequently committed in conjunction with rape, burglary, and robbery.

Aggravated assault is an unlawful attack upon a person for the purpose of inflicting severe bodily injury or death. Assault can safely be classified as *aggravated* if a gun, knife, or other weapon is used and serious personal injury is inflicted. In most states aggravated assault is a felony and carries severe penalties because it would have been murder if the victim died. The intent of the act ''appears'' to be murder and not simply injury.

Simple assault, the most frequent type of assault, has no intent of serious injury. It may or may not be accompanied by a threat. Hands, fists, or feet are the most frequently used weapons. Most simple assaults result from emotional conflicts and are classified as misdemeanors. The mere pointing of a gun at a person or threatening a person with bodily harm may constitute simple assault in certain situations.

The UCR estimates that between 640,000 and 660,000 aggravated assaults occur annually. The Bureau of Justice Statistics cites these facts about assault:

- Assault is the most common type of violent crime.
- Simple assault occurs more frequently than aggravated assault.

Rape

Rape, as defined in the Index Program, is the carnal knowledge of a female through the use of force or the threat of force. Assaults to commit forcible rape are also included in the definition; however, statutory rape (without force) is not.

> *Rape is having sexual intercourse with a female through the use or threat of force. Rape may be aggravated or simple.*

Aggravated rape involves using force, threats of immediate use of force, or taking advantage of an unconscious or helpless woman or a woman incapable of consent because of mental illness or a defect reasonably known to the attacker.

Simple rape involves misleading a victim about the nature of the act being performed; for example, having intercourse under the guise of a medical examination or treatment or knowingly destroying the victim's will to resist by use of a drug or intoxicant.

According to the UCR, between 78,000 and 79,000 forcible rapes occur annually. Rape is a violent crime against the person, yet it is probably one of the most under-reported crimes because the victim fears her assailant or is extremely embarrassed. According to the Bureau of Justice Statistics:

- Most rapes involved a lone offender and a lone victim.
- About 36 percent of the rapes were committed in the victim's home.
- Fifty-eight percent of the rapes occurred at night between 6 P.M. and 6 A.M.

It should be noted that some states have deleted the word *female* from their rape statutes and substituted the word *person*. This, in effect, includes males as potential victims of rape. This not only has social significance, but it also indicates a problem with the figures included in the Uniform Crime Reports.

Robbery

Robbery is stealing or taking anything of value from the care, custody, or control of a person in his presence, by force or by threat of force. Assault to commit robbery and attempts are included in the definition. This violent crime frequently results in injury to the victim.

> *Robbery is stealing anything of value ~~from the control, care, or custody of a person~~ by force or threat of force.*

In 50 percent of the cases, robbery is accompanied by an assault upon the victim. Sometimes labeled as the most brutal and vicious of all crimes, robberies occur in all parts of the country; its victims are people of all ages, incomes, and backgrounds. Robbers may shoot, assault, or torture their victims to find where their valuables are located. Many victims who have refused to cooperate, and even some who have, have been ruthlessly killed. Further, robbery calls are the third ranking cause of police fatalities.

The favorite weapon of most robbers is the handgun. Other weapons used include knives, acids, baseball bats, and explosives. Armed robbers frequently attack drug stores (often for narcotics), supermarkets, liquor stores, jewelry stores, gas stations, banks, residential homes, cab drivers, and pedestrians.

The classic image of a robber is a masked man pointing a gun at a lone pedestrian on a city street or in a small grocery store at night. Frequently the victims are old people who are robbed of a small amount of money and are knocked to the ground, sometimes suffering permanent injuries or even death.

Robbery produces millions of dollars for criminals and is the most frequently reported crime. Approximately 10 percent of all willful homicides are the result of robbery attempts. But statistics do not reflect the human loss and tragedy often involved in robbery.

Not all robberies are aggravated, however. Some states have a category of simple robbery where no force or threat is used. A usual element of the crime of robbery is force and fear, not stealth. If a thief jostles a victim in a crowd to divert atttention and picks his pocket, the crime is robbery. A normal pickpocket operation or purse-snatching is larceny, not robbery, unless there is resistance or bodily contact.

Nationally about 50 percent of the robberies committed are street robberies. Large cities commonly have twenty to thirty robberies reported in a twenty-four-hour period on Fridays and Saturdays.

According to the UCR, between 500,000 and 550,000 robberies are committed annually. The Bureau of Justice Statistics states that:

- Robbery is a violent crime that typically involves more than one offender (in about half of all cases).
- Slightly less than half of all robberies involved the use of a weapon.
- Less than 2 percent of the robberies reported to the police were bank robberies.

Burglary

The Uniform Crime Reporting Program defines **burglary** as the unlawful entry into a structure to commit a felony or theft. The use of force to gain entry is not required to classify the crime as a burglary. Burglary has three sub-classifications: forcible entry, unlawful entry where no force is used, and attempted forcible entry.

Burglary is unlawful entrance into a building to commit theft or other felony.

Many dictionaries have as their first (most common) definition of burglary, "the act of breaking into a house at night to commit theft or other felony." This definition reflects what burglary was historically (under common law)—breaking and entering a dwelling of another in the night. Modern-day statutes reflect numerous changes in that definition, broadening its scope considerably.

Some states, for example, have eliminated the word *breaking* and require only a trespass. Burglaries can occur by forcible or attempted forcible entry, unlawful entry, or without force as when a burglar opens an unlocked door or window, or remains in a building without the consent of the person in charge with the intention of committing a crime. Department stores often have been the victims of burglars who hide in the store at closing time and wait until everyone else has left, take what they want, and then break out of the store to escape.

State statutes usually define *building* as a dwelling or other structure suitable for human shelter or connected to such a structure. Warehouses, barns, garages, and some types of shelters have also been defined by the courts as buildings. For example, California defines burglary as the entry of a structure for the specific purpose of committing theft or some other felony. A structure is anything having continuous walls, a floor and roof, windows and doors included.

State statutes also vary as to whether the crime must occur at night to be a burglary. Some states say it may occur at any time of the day or night. If entry occurs during the night, breaking may not be an essential element of the crime.

Punishments are usually most severe if the burglar has an explosive or tool in his possession, if the building entered is a dwelling and the burglar has a dangerous weapon when entering, or if he assaults someone while committing the burglary.

Some states have a modified charge of "breaking and entering" which is a lesser charge than burglary. The intricacies in defining burglary are interesting. For instance, if a salesperson pockets a diamond ring while making a sales call in a home, it is not burglary. However, if a person poses as a salesperson to get into a home and then steals a diamond ring, it is burglary in most states.

The UCR estimates between 3 and 3½ million burglaries are committed annually. According to the Bureau of Justice Statistics:

- Forty-two percent of all household burglaries occurred without forced entry. 3y at night
- In the burglary of more than 3 million American households, the offenders entered through an unlocked window or door or used a key (for example, a key hidden under a doormat).
- About 34% of the no-force household burglaries were known to have occurred between 6 A.M. and 6 P.M.
- Residential property was targeted in 67 percent of reported burglaries; non-residential property accounted for the remaining 33 percent.
- Three-quarters of the non-residential burglaries for which the time of occurrence was known took place at night.

Larceny/Theft

Larceny/theft is the unlawful taking or stealing of property or articles without the use of force, violence, or fraud. It includes shoplifting, pocket-picking, purse-snatching, thefts from motor vehicles, thefts of motor vehicle parts and accessories, and bicycle thefts. The category does not include embezzlement, "con" games, forgery, and passing worthless checks, to be discussed shortly under Part II crimes. It also does not include motor vehicle theft which is a separate Crime Index offense.

motor vehical items most stolen

> *Larceny/theft is unlawfully taking and removing another's personal property with the intent of permanently depriving the owner of the property.*

Larceny/theft may be classified as either a misdemeanor or a felony. It differs from robbery in that it does not involve threats of force, force, or violence. The severity of punishment usually depends on the value and type of property taken, whether it was taken from a building or a person, and the specific circumstances of the case.

Most theft statutes indicate situations where the value of the article is immaterial in determining whether the offense is a felony or misdemeanor. These situations include stealing from the person of another or a grave or a corpse, stealing public records or public funds, looting, and stealing articles representing trade secrets.

Some states categorize larceny into degrees. Grand and petty larceny are common identifications for value of property taken and punishment. First-, second-, and third-degree larceny also indicate a certain minimum value of the property taken and various degrees of punishment.

The most common type of theft is the theft of items from motor vehicles and motor vehicle parts and accessories. The files of police departments throughout the country are filled with reports of losses such as CB radios, stereo tape decks, clothing, and photographic equipment taken from motor vehicles.

Other common forms of larceny are thefts from buildings such as underground garages where maintenance equipment such as lawnmowers, snowblowers, lawn hoses, and fertilizers are the target. Bicycles are also a common target for thieves. Because they are easily removed and lack serial number markings, bicycle theft has become big business for many criminals. Police departments find that in some cities dealers specialize in the sale of stolen bicycles.

Thefts from coin-operated vending machines, pocket-picking, purse-snatching, and shoplifting are other common forms of larceny/theft. Shoplifting accounts for an estimated 2 billion dollars lost each year. Shoplifters range in age from five to eighty-five. The great majority are amateurs, but there are professional shoplifters (called ''boosters'') as well as itinerant schools for professionals. The vast majority of shoplifters apprehended are not prosecuted because merchants do not want to alienate good customers or spend the time involved in prosecution, so the customers pay for the shoplifting losses in higher prices.

The UCR estimates approximately 7 million larceny/thefts annually in the United States. According to the Bureau of Justice Statistics:

- Pocket-picking and purse-snatching most frequently occur inside non-residential buildings or on street locations.

■ Unlike most other crimes, pocket-picking and purse-snatching affect the elderly as much as other age groups.

■ Most personal larcenies with contact occur during the daytime, but most household larcenies occur at night.

Motor Vehicle Theft

In Uniform Crime reporting, motor vehicle theft is defined as the unlawful taking or stealing of a motor vehicle, including attempts. This definition excludes taking a vehicle for temporary use by those persons having lawful access to the vehicle. Motor vehicle theft includes automobiles, trucks, buses, motorcycles, motorized boats, and aircraft.

> *Motor vehicle theft is the unlawful taking or stealing of a motor vehicle without the authority or permission of the owner.*

Motor vehicle theft rates show this crime to be primarily a large city problem; the highest rates appear in the most heavily populated sections of the country.

It is difficult to obtain a conviction for auto theft unless witnesses see the person drive the vehicle away and make positive identification later. It is also difficult to prove if the suspect intended to permanently deprive the rightful owner of its use. Therefore, another category of auto theft has been created called "Unlawful Use of a Motor Vehicle" which applies to suspects who merely have possession of a vehicle reported stolen.

Auto thefts represent the greatest monetary property loss—greater than the combined total of all other offenses. The police are not only charged with the recovery of stolen vehicles, but with the apprehension of the guilty parties.

Of the many motives for auto theft, joy-riding* leads the list. Young people steal a car, take it for ride, and then abandon it. Autos are also stolen for revenge, for transportation, for commercial use, and for use in committing other crimes such as kidnapping, burglary, and bank robbery. Autos are stolen and stripped for such parts as transmissions, engines, and seats. Sale of stolen auto parts is one of the fastest growing businesses today because of the high cost of replacement parts and the unavailability of parts for foreign-made cars. Automobiles are also stolen, modified, and given altered serial numbers, fraudulent titles, and sold to an unsuspecting public.

With the increased number of foreign students attending our universities, a relatively new scheme has caused millions of dollars of losses to Amercian banks. The fraudulent car scheme has accelerated to a new high under the guise of car loans from banks. Foreign students buy new cars, obtain loans on them, and then ship them to foreign countries which require no proof of ownership. In addition,

---

*Joy-riding is often a separate charge where intent to permanently deprive is not in evidence.

many vehicles reported as stolen are actually driven into lakes and rivers or buried by their owners to defraud insurance companies.

The UCR estimates over 2 million motor vehicle thefts are reported annually. The Bureau of Justice Statistics reports that:

- Motor vehicle theft is relatively well reported to the police because reporting is required for insurance claims, and vehicles are more likely than other stolen property to be recovered.
- About three-fifths of all motor vehicle thefts occurred at night.

Arson

Arson is intentionally damaging or destroying or attempting to damage or destroy property by means of fire or explosion. It is a felony in all fifty states. It was not until 1978 that Congress made arson a Class I (Part I) crime. During the subcommittee hearings, *Arson for Profit: Its Impact on States and Localities,* Senator John Glenn noted that: "We have an arson epidemic that has now spread to the suburbs and the rural areas. Arson has increased over 400% in the past ten years (1967-1977). An estimated 1,000 people, including 45 firefighters die each year in arson fires, 10,000 people are injured annually. Annual damage estimates are as high as $15 billion. Insurance losses exceed $3 billion. . . . New York's arson task force estimates that New York loses about 300-400 buildings a month by fire, the majority of which are arson."

> Arson is intentionally damaging or destroying or attempting to damage or destroy by means of fire or explosion the property of another without the consent of the owner or one's own property, with or without the intent to defraud.

One of the most serious problems often encountered in arson investigations is the joint jurisdiction of firefighters and law enforcement officers. All too frequently this results in duplication of effort and inefficiency.

The Uniform Crime Reports carry only trend and clearance tables for arson, stating that sufficient data is not available to estimate totals for this offense. The Bureau of Justice Statistics states the following regarding arson:

- Single-family residences were the most frequent targets of arson.
- Fifteen percent of all structures where arson occurred were not in use.

Comparative Statistics for the Part I Index Offenses

Table 2–1 summarizes the number of offenses reported in seven of the Part I Index crimes from 1974 through 1983.

Table 2–1.   *Index of Crime, United States, 1974–1984.*

	Population[1]	Crime Index total[2]	Modified Crime Index total[3]	Violent crime[4]	Property crime[4]	Murder and non-negligent manslaughter	Forcible rape	Robbery	Aggravated assault	Burglary	Larceny-theft	Motor vehicle theft	Arson[3]
Number of offenses:[5]													
1975	213,124,000	11,292,400		1,039,710	10,252,700	20,510	56,090	470,500	492,620	3,265,300	5,977,700	1,009,600	
1976	214,659,000	11,349,700		1,004,210	10,345,500	18,780	57,080	427,810	500,530	3,108,700	6,270,800	966,000	
1977	216,332,000	10,984,500		1,029,580	9,955,000	19,120	63,500	412,610	534,350	3,071,500	5,905,700	977,700	
1978	218,059,000	11,209,000		1,085,550	10,123,400	19,560	67,610	426,930	571,460	3,128,300	5,991,000	1,004,100	
1979	220,099,000	12,249,500		1,208,030	11,041,500	21,460	76,390	480,700	629,480	3,327,700	6,601,000	1,112,800	
1980	225,349,264	13,408,300		1,344,520	12,063,700	23,040	82,990	565,840	672,650	3,795,200	7,136,900	1,131,700	
1981	229,146,000	13,423,800		1,361,820	12,061,900	22,520	82,500	592,910	663,900	3,779,700	7,194,400	1,087,800	
1982	231,534,000	12,974,400		1,322,390	11,652,000	21,010	78,770	553,130	669,480	3,447,100	7,142,500	1,062,400	
1983	233,981,000	12,108,600		1,258,090	10,850,500	19,310	78,920	506,570	653,290	3,129,900	6,712,800	1,007,900	
1984	236,158,000	11,881,800		1,273,280	10,608,500	18,690	84,230	485,010	685,350	2,984,400	6,591,900	1,032,200	
Percent change; number of offenses:													
1984/1983		−1.9		+1.2	−2.2	−3.2	+6.7	−4.3	+4.9	−4.6	−1.8	+2.4	
1984/1980		−11.4		−5.3	−12.1	−18.9	+1.5	−14.3	+1.9	−21.4	−7.6	−8.8	
1984/1975		+5.2		+22.5	+3.5	−8.9	+50.2	+3.1	+39.1	−8.6	+10.3	+2.2	
Rate per 100,000 inhabitants:													
1975		5,298.5		487.8	4,810.7	9.6	26.3	220.8	231.1	1,532.1	2,804.8	473.7	
1976		5,287.3		467.8	4,819.5	8.8	26.6	199.3	233.2	1,448.2	2,921.3	450.0	
1977		5,077.6		475.9	4,601.7	8.8	29.4	190.7	247.0	1,419.8	2,729.9	451.9	
1978		5,140.3		497.8	4,642.5	9.0	31.0	195.8	262.1	1,434.6	2,747.4	460.5	
1979		5,565.5		548.9	5,016.6	9.7	34.7	218.4	286.0	1,511.9	2,999.1	505.6	
1980		5,950.0		596.6	5,353.3	10.2	36.8	251.1	298.5	1,684.1	3,167.0	502.2	
1981		5,858.2		594.3	5,263.9	9.8	36.0	258.7	289.7	1,649.5	3,139.7	474.7	
1982		5,603.6		571.1	5,032.5	9.1	34.0	238.9	289.2	1,488.8	3,084.8	458.8	
1983		5,175.0		537.7	4,637.4	8.3	33.7	216.5	279.2	1,337.7	2,868.9	430.8	
1984		5,031.3		539.2	4,492.1	7.9	35.7	205.4	290.2	1,263.7	2,791.3	437.1	
Percent change; rate per 100,000 inhabitants:													
1984/1983		−2.8		+.3	−3.1	−4.8	+5.9	−5.1	+3.9	−5.5	−2.7	+1.5	
1984/1980		−15.4		−9.6	−16.1	−22.5	−3.0	−18.2	−2.8	−25.0	−11.9	−13.0	
1984/1975		−5.0		+10.5	−6.6	−17.7	+35.7	−7.0	+25.6	−17.5	−.5	−7.7	

[1]Populations are Bureau of the Census provisional estimates as of July 1, except April 1, 1980, preliminary census counts, and are subject to change.

[2]Because of rounding, the offenses may not add to totals.

[3]Although arson data are included in the trend and clearance tables, sufficient data are not available to estimate totals for this offense.

[4]Violent crimes are offenses of murder, forcible rape, robbery, and aggravated assault. Property crimes are offenses of burglary, larceny-theft, and motor vehicle theft. Data are not included for the property crime of arson.

[5]Annual totals for years prior to 1984 have been adjusted and may not be consistent with those in prior editions of this publication. See "Offense Estimation", pages 3 and 4 for details.

All rates were calculated on the offenses before rounding.

Source: Uniform Crime Reports, 1984.

Part II Index Crimes

The Part II offenses consist of several other crimes that can be either misdemeanors or felonies. They are as follows:

- Other assaults (intimidation, coercion, hazing, etc.)
- Forgery and counterfeiting
- Fraud (confidence games, etc.)
- Embezzlement
- Stolen property: buying, receiving, possessing.
- Vandalism
- Weapons: carrying, possessing, etc.
- Prostitution and commercialized vice
- Sex offenses (except forcible rape, prostitution, and commercialized vice)
- Drug abuse violations
- Gambling
- Offenses against the family and children (child abuse, neglect, nonsupport)
- Driving under the influence
- Liquor laws (liquor law violations, bootlegging, etc.)
- Drunkenness
- Disorderly conduct
- Vagrancy
- Curfew and loitering (juveniles)
- Runaway (juveniles)
- All other offenses (abortion, bigamy, contempt of court, the list goes on and on)

White-Collar Crime

White-collar crime is an occupational or business-related crime. The Part I offense of larceny/theft and several of the Part II offenses can also be classified as white-collar crimes. These crimes often involve billions of dollars and pose an extremely difficult challenge to law enforcement officers.

 White-collar crime is occupational or business-related crime.

In a large southern city recently, a grand jury brought indictments on thirty-two counts against a vice-president of a bank for embezzling funds. Outstanding community leader, father of several children—a respectable individual in the community was suddenly disgraced. At the same time in a western city, a grand jury brought indictments on twelve counts against a warehouse employee who had taken merchandise from his employer's warehouse, loaded it on a friend's truck, sold it, and divided the profits. The warehouse employee, a family man who attended church regularly, was shunned by his friends and fired by his employer.

Although most people in business are honest, corruption does exist. Security abuses, tax frauds, embezzlements, bribes, and kickbacks frequently occur, often the result of a "look the other way" attitude of co-workers and employers. Not only do employees and employers frequently ignore dishonesty within their businesses, they frequently engage in such practices themselves, rationalizing their actions as acquiring something they really were entitled to. For example, the employee who makes long-distance calls on his employer's phone or who pads his expense account may tell himself that since he is underpaid, this is simply one way of getting what he has coming to him.

When stealing from the boss (company, firm, business), most employees do not consider what they are doing as theft but merely a fringe benefit of the job. Going across the street and taking the same thing from another firm would be considered dishonest—but not when taken from one's own employer.

The Chamber of Commerce of the United States (1974) has identified nine categories of white-collar crime: (1) securities theft and fraud, (2) insurance fraud, (3) credit card and check fraud, (4) consumer fraud, illegal competition, and deceptive practices, (5) bankruptcy fraud, (6) computer-related fraud, (7) embezzlement and pilferage, (8) bribes, kickbacks, and payoffs, and (9) receiving stolen property.

Eldefonso, et al. (1974, p. 2) note that the existence of white-collar crime has an extremely demoralizing effect upon those who lack material possessions. Such individuals, while not having the opportunity to engage in white-collar crime, may follow the example of illegal means to obtain material gain.

Criminals involved in fraudulent schemes of all types are usually extremely mobile, moving from city to city and state to state, ruining individuals and small businesses.

> *White-collar crime includes: (1) securities theft and fraud, (2) insurance fraud, (3) credit card and check fraud, (4) consumer fraud, illegal competition, and deceptive practices, (5) bankruptcy fraud, (6) computer-related fraud, (7) embezzlement and pilferage, (8) bribes, kickbacks, and payoffs, and (9) receiving stolen property.*

Securities Theft and Fraud

Securities theft and fraud may be perpetrated by clerks acting independently, by individuals who rob messengers and steal from the mails, or by well-organized rings, one of which was reported as stealing approximately five million dollars worth of stock monthly.* The total value of all outstanding lost, stolen, or missing

---

*The statistics in this section are from *White Collar Crime: Everyone's Problem, Everyone's Loss.* Chamber of Commerce of the United States, 1974.

securities has been placed at $50 billion. Most security thefts involve cooperation of dishonest employees (''inside'' people) and may involve counterfeit and bogus securities as well.

Insurance Fraud

Insurance fraud losses are approximately $1.5 billion yearly, leading to higher premiums for consumers. Since insurance is important to businesses and individuals, false claims for life, health, and accident benefits affect almost everyone.

Especially prevalent are fraudulent auto accident claims seeking compensation for treatments for personal injury, time lost from work, and automobile repairs.

Many white-collar crime experts exclude insurance fraud since it is not typically done in the course of a white-collar occupation.

Credit Card and Check Fraud

The approximately 26 billion checks and 300 million credit cards in circulation each year present limitless opportunity for crime. Unauthorized use of credit cards (found, stolen, or counterfeited) results in an estimated loss of $100 million annually.

Check fraud, including checks passed with insufficient funds or with no account, forged checks, counterfeit checks, stolen travelers' checks, money orders, and payroll checks, costs an estimated $1 billion annually.

As with insurance fraud, many white-collar crime experts exclude credit card and check fraud since they are not typically done in the course of a white-collar occupation.

Consumer Fraud, Illegal Competition, and Deceptive Practices

Thousands of different schemes have been reported to defraud the public, including offers for ''free'' articles, advice, vacations, mailing or unordered merchandise, phony contests, recommendations for unneeded repairs, ''going-out-of-business'' sales, unqualified correspondence schools, and price-fixing. Hundreds of other schemes undoubtedly exist but have not been reported because although the victims may realize the swindle, they do not want to admit having been ''taken in.''

Bankruptcy Fraud

Bankruptcy fraud, also called planned bankruptcy, scam, or bust-out, accounts for estimated annual losses of $80 million. This white-collar crime involves purchasing merchandise on credit from many different suppliers, selling the merchandise for cash which is ''hidden,'' and then claiming bankruptcy, not paying the creditors. A small business which has extended a large amount of credit to a company that declares bankruptcy (legitimately or not) may be forced out of business. Such an owner may then decide to use the same tactic himself, rationalizing the fraud as a justified effort to save his debt-ridden business.

Computer-Related Crime

Computer-related crime is a relatively new, yet highly profitable, type of white-collar crime. As noted in the *Washington Post,* December 6, 1976:

> The federal government is becoming increasingly concerned with the growing misuse of computers to steal, defraud, embezzle, sabotage and blackmail people in private and public agencies. According to a study by the General Accounting Office, 69 computer crimes defrauded federal agencies of $2 million over the last two years. In addition, more than 400 crimes-by-computer cases have been documented over the last eight years with victims losing $200 million.

The Bureau of Justice Statistics (1983, p. 3) states that: ''. . . the dramatic growth in high technology has brought with it sensational accounts of computerized 'heists' by sophisticated felons seated safely behind computer terminals.'' Computer fraud may involve the input data, the output data, the program itself, or computer time.

Input data may be altered; for example, fictitious suppliers may be entered, figures may be changed, or data may be removed. Some universities have experienced difficulties with student grades being illegally changed on computer cards.

Output data may be obtained by unauthorized persons through such means as wiretapping, electromagnetic pickup, or theft of data sheets.

The computer program itself might be tampered with to add costs to purchased items or to establish a double set of records.

Computer time may be used for personal use, an example of pilferage to be discussed shortly. Some employees have even used their employer's hardware and company time to set up their own computer services for personal profit.

According to Siegel (1983, pp. 332–333):

> A number of common techniques are used by computer criminals. In fact, computer theft has become so common that experts have created their own jargon to describe theft styles and methods:
>
> - *The trojan horse.*   One computer is used to reprogram another for illicit purposes. In a recent incident, two high-school-age computer users reprogrammed the computer at DePaul University, preventing that institution from using its own processing facilities. The youths were convicted of a misdemeanor.
> - *The salami slice.*   An employee sets up a dummy account in the company's computerized records. A small amount—even a few pennies—is

subtracted from customers' accounts and added to the account of the thief. Even if they detect the loss, the customers don't complain, since a few cents is an insignificant amount to them. The pennies picked up here and there eventually amount to thousands of dollars in losses.

- *Super-zapping.* Most computer programs used in business have built-in antitheft safeguards. However, employees can use a repair or maintenance program to supersede the antitheft program. Some tinkering with the program is required, but the "super-zapper" is soon able to order the system to issue checks to his or her private account.
- *The logic bomb.* A program is secretly attached to the company's computer system. The new program monitors the company's work and waits for a sign of error to appear, some illogic that was designed for the computer to follow. Illogic causes the "logic bomb" to kick into action and exploit the weakness. The way the thief exploits the situation depends on his or her original intent—theft of money, theft of defense secrets, sabotage, and so on.
- *Impersonation.* An unauthorized person uses the identity of an authorized computer user in order to use the computer in his or her stead.
- *Data leakage.* A person illegally obtains data from a computer system by leaking it out in small amounts.

Embezzlement and Pilferage

Many businessmen consider embezzlement and pilferage to be their most serious problem. Both are, in effect, theft. To embezzle is to steal or use for oneself money or property entrusted to the person. To pilfer is basically the same, but on a much smaller scale. The pilferer usually takes such things as office supplies, spare parts, and materials rather than money, but the result is the same. Cumulatively, the losses from pilferage may be much greater than what some other dishonest employee might embezzle. Equally dishonest is unauthorized use of company equipment, personnel, and time.

Bribes, Kickbacks, and Payoffs

Bribes, kickbacks, and payoffs are pervasive in the business world and are frequently used to obtain new clients, to keep old clients, to influence decisions, or to obtain favors. They can involve anyone from the custodian to the company president, and they can occur in any aspect of a company's operation.

Receiving Stolen Property

Although classified as a white-collar crime, receiving stolen property frequently occurs in conjunction with crimes such as robbery and burglary. The individual who buys and sells stolen property is of vital importance to the success of most burglars, robbers, and hijackers. Criminals depend upon a "fence" (a professional receiver and seller of stolen property) to convert what they have stolen to cash.

Other Types of White-Collar Crime

Police officers may also be called upon to investigate such white-collar crimes as crimes by businesses, as well as violent white-collar crimes such as selling dangerous products or intentional violation of safety codes. Investigating such crimes is difficult because usually individuals in top management are suspects and, consequently, uncooperative.

Illegal Possession, Sale, or Distribution of Narcotics and Dangerous Drugs*

> *Narcotics are drugs that produce sleep, lethargy, or relief of pain, including heroin, cocaine, and marijuana. Dangerous drugs are addicting, mind-altering drugs such as depressants, stimulants, and hallucinogens.*

It is a crime in most states to use or sell **narcotics** and dangerous drugs without a prescription. Additionally, the abuse of these substances is often closely connected to other types of crime. Homicide, rape, burglary, armed robbery, and shoplifting have been connected with the use of narcotics and dangerous drugs and with the drug abuser's need for money to support his habit.

The misuse and abuse of drugs and their illegal sale and disposition have become a national problem not limited to slum areas or to the use of hard narcotics. Consequently, new amendments by Congress, laws by state legislatures, and ordinances by local political subdivisions provide stronger regulation of the manufacture, distribution, delivery, and possession of many narcotics, depressants, stimulants, and hallucinogens.

> *In most states narcotics and dangerous drugs may not be used or sold without a prescription. Federal law prohibits sale or distribution not covered by prescription, but it does not prohibit possession for personal use.*

Calculations based upon the excess of legitimate production over estimated medical need and illegal production, coupled with direct evidence of misuse and abuse, suggest a level of total abuse of an estimated 5 percent of the United States population or nearly 10 million people.

Narcotics produce sleep and relieve pain

Prohibited narcotics include heroin, cocaine, and marijauna.

Heroin is the most commonly abused narcotic. It is synthesized from morphine and is up to ten times more potent in its effects. Heroin is physically addictive and expensive. It causes an easing of fears, followed by euphoria, and finally stupor.

---

*The following information on narcotics and dangerous drugs is adapted from *Fact Sheet,* Drug Enforcement Administration, U.S. Department of Justice (no date).

Heroin is considered a major factor in contributing to crime because of its street cost and its continuous necessity to be used; therefore, law enforcement narcotics divisions frequently concentrate their efforts on apprehending the suppliers and pushers of heroin.

Cocaine was once widely used as a local anesthetic in surgery. It is a white or colorless crystalline powder that is inhaled or injected, producing euphoria, excitation, anxiety, a sense of increased muscular strength, talkativeness, and a reduction in feelings of fatigue. The pupils frequently become dilated, and the heart rate and blood pressure usually increase.

Marijuana is probably the most socially acceptable of the illegal drugs; legislation lessening penalties for its use has frequently been proposed. Although it has been known for nearly 5,000 years, it is one of the least understood of all natural drugs, yet one of the most versatile: derived from the cannabis plant which still grows wild in many parts of the United States, marijuana is frequently used in the form of cigarettes. When smoked, marjuana enters the bloodstream quickly, causing rapid onset of symptoms. The effects of the drug on the user's mood and thinking vary widely, depending on the amount and strength of the marijuana as well as the social setting and the effects anticipated. The drug usually takes effect in about fifteen minutes and lasts from two to four hours.

''Social'' doses of one or two cigarettes may cause an increased sense of well being; initial restlessness and hilarity followed by a dreamy, carefree state of relaxation; alteration of sensory perceptions including expansion of space and time; and/or a more vivid sense of touch, sight, smell, taste, and sound; a feeling of hunger, especially craving for sweets; and subtle changes in thought formation and expression.

Dangerous Drugs

Depressants (Barbiturates). Depressants or **barbiturates** are sedatives taken orally as a small tablet or capsule to induce sleep or to relieve tension. Housewives are the most common abusers of barbiturates.

Small amounts of barbiturates make the user relaxed, sociable, and good-humored. Heavy doses cause sluggishness, depression, deep sleep, or coma. A barbiturate addict usually takes ten to twenty pills a day and often shows symptoms of drunkenness: speech becomes slurred and indistinct, physical coordination is impaired, and mental and emotional instability occurs. Many barbiturate addicts are quarrelsome and have a ''short fuse.'' Overdoses are common and frequently cause intentional or accidental death.

Stimulants (Amphetamines). **Amphetamines** are stimulants taken orally as a tablet or capsules, or intravenously, to reduce appetite and/or relieve mental depression. They are often taken by truck drivers, salespeople, college students, and businesspeople who want to stay awake for long periods and by people who want to lost weight.

Normal doses produce wakefulness, increased alertness and initiative, and hyperactivity. Large doses produce exaggerated feelings of confidence, power, and well-being.

Habitual users may take amphetamines for three or four days, eat nothing, and drive themselves until they black out from exhaustion. Heavy users may exhibit restlessness, nervousness, hand tremors, pupil dilation, dryness of mouth, and excessive perspiration. They may be talkative and experience delusions and/or hallucinations. Although small doses may produce cheerfulness and unusual increase in activity, heavy and prolonged use may produce symptoms resembling paranoid schizophrenia. Handling this deviant behavior has always been a source of concern and danger for law enforcement officers.

Hallucinogens. **Hallucinogens** may produce distortion, intensify sensory perception, and lessen the ability to discriminate between fact and fantasy. The unpredictable mental effects include illusions, panic, psychotic or antisocial behavior, and impulses toward violence and self-destruction. Probably the best known hallucinogen is LSD, which gets its name from the colorless, odorless substance lysergic acid diethylamide from which it is made.

Although hallucinogens are usually taken orally as a tablet or capsule, their physical characterstsic allow them to be disguised as various commonly used powders or liquids. LSD has been found on chewing gum, hard candy, crackers, vitamin pills, aspirin, blotting paper, and postage stamps.

Other hallucinogens include DMT (dimethyltryptamine), a powerful drug similar to LSD; mescaline, a chemical derived from the peyote cactus; and psilocybin, a natural ingredient in a species of Mexican mushroom.

> *The three general classifications of dangerous drugs are depressants (barbiturates), stimulants (amphetamines), and hallucinogens.*

Deliriants

Deliriants are volatile chemicals that include airplane glue, gasoline, lighter fluid, paint thinner, Freon, carbon tetrachloride, and other volatile commerical products. Although technically neither narcotics nor dangerous drugs, deliriants may be a prime cause of psychological dependency among young people.

Deliriants may be sniffed or inhaled either directly from a container or from a paper or plastic bag or cloth. Redness or irritation commonly occurs around the nostrils and lips. Other reactions vary according to the deliriant used and the amount inhaled. However, deliriants generally produce a ''high'' similar to that produced by alcohol.

Common Factors

In spite of numerous differences produced by use of various kinds of narcotics and dangerous drugs, certain common factors occur, the most important of which are

(1) they are mind-altering, (2) they may become addicting—either physically or psychologically, and (3) overdosage may result in convulsions and death.

Societal Effects

Although the drug abuser may claim that it is his right to ingest, smoke, sniff, or inject whatever he wants into his own body, the results of such actions do have serious implications for society as the user is no longer in control of what he thinks, says, or does, and often poses a threat to other members of society.

The occasional user of marijuana may argue that no harm is being done to anyone, but researchers point out that a person predisposed to the abuse of one drug may be likely to abuse other, stronger drugs (*Fact Sheet*). Also users of one drug may be exposed to a variety of other drug users and sellers and, through this association, may be encouraged to experiment with more potent drugs. More importantly, however, is the expense involved in supporting a drug habit. Frequently this expense causes the addict to turn to crime to obtain money with which to purchase the needed drugs.

Alcohol

Although drinking alcohol is not illegal, laws have been established that regulate the age at which it becomes legal to drink as well as the amount that a person can drink and then operate a vehicle. The problem of the drunk driver is well known to police officers. Drunk drivers are a menace to themselves and to others. "Drinking

A sobriety test is administered to a DWI suspect.

is a factor in at least half of all fatal motor vehicle accidents.'' (*Accident Facts,* 1984, p. 53). According to *Accident Facts*: ''Since 1980 numerous activities have been directed at combating the drinking driver problem. States are passing stricter anti-drinking and driving laws and are increasing the enforcement of existing laws. On the Federal level, a bill has been enacted to encourage the states to adopt uniform 21 year old drinking age laws. Twenty-three states now have 21 year old drinking age laws. Since 1980, twenty states have raised the legal drinking age, 10 of which raised the drinking age to 21.''

> *Drinking is a factor in at least half of all fatal motor vehicle accidents.*

In addition, according to the Bureau of Justice Statistics (1983, p. 39), alcohol abuse is common among criminals, with more than a third of all prison inmates indicating they drank heavily. Approximately 10 percent of the offenders indicated they were ''very drunk'' at the time of the offense.

Summary

Just as our current methods of enforcing the laws have slowly evolved, so have the laws themselves. In the beginning most laws were set by a ruler or were moral or social laws, enforced by social pressure. This was followed by common law—law based on precedent. In the United States common law became known as case law. Statutory law has replaced most common and case law. Statutory law consists of laws passed by federal and state legislatures regarding both constitutional and nonconstitutional (ordinary) matters.

As the legal system developed, a distinction arose between an action which was considered a crime and one which was not considered a crime even though it did violate a law (tort). This division was reflected in the establishment of two separate bodies of law: criminal law and civil law. Criminal law defines what action constitutes a specific crime and establishes punishments for each. Civil law, on the other hand, sets forth laws which citizens are expected to obey, but if they do not they are not considered criminals. Civil law seeks to establish restitution for a wrong against an individual.

Laws, by their very definition, imply both the rule and its enforcement. To ensure enforcement, police have been given power and authority from local, state, and federal sources; but they are also restricted in their use of this power by the Constitution, the Fourteenth Amendment, and the courts. They have the power to enforce the laws so long as they do not violate the civil rights and liberties of any individual.

The law enforcement officer functions in a society where the citizens enjoy great freedom. Sometimes, however, this freedom is viewed by citizens as license to do as they please, to ignore the laws of society. State and federal statutes have defined actions which are not to be tolerated—crimes—and have set specified penalties for each. Although state statutes vary in their definitions of and penalties for crimes, certain generalizations can be made. Generally, a crime is an intentional action which is prohibited by law and for which punishment is legally prescribed, which directly causes an actual harm.

The crimes most frequently reported to police, the most serious crimes in the nation, are called Part I Index Crimes. They include murder, assault, rape, robbery, burglary, larceny/theft, motor vehicle theft, and arson.

White-collar crime—occupational or business-related crime—includes fraud involving securities, insurance, credit cards, checks, bankruptcy, and computers, as well as illegal competition, deceptive practices, embezzlement and pilferage, bribes, kickbacks, payoffs, and receiving stolen property. White-collar crime involves billions of dollars annually.

A third category, drug-related crime, includes illegal possession, sale, or distribution of narcotics and dangerous drugs. (Narcotics are drugs that produce sleep, lethargy, or relief of pain, including heroin, cocaine, and marijuana; dangerous drugs are addicting, mind-altering drugs including depressants, stimulants, and hallucinogens.) In most states narcotics and dangerous drugs may not be used or sold without a prescription. Federal law also prohibits sale or distribution not covered by prescription, but it does not prohibit possession for personal use. Finally, although drinking alcoholic beverages in not in itself a crime, drinking is a factor in at least half of the fatal motor vehicle accidents, and, consequently, is of great concern to law enforcement officers.

Discussion Questions

1. If a person's reckless driving of a car injures another person who dies two weeks later as a result of the injuries, could the reckless driver be charged for a crime, sued for a tort, or both? How would the type of charge affect the possible consequences faced by the reckless driver?

2. Why is motor vehicle theft in a different category than larceny/theft?

3. Why are some crimes divided into categories or degrees?

4. Where does alcohol fall in the categories of drugs and crimes?

5. How does our city rank in the United States as far as occurrence of Index Crimes? Drug abuse?

6. Which drugs pose the greatest problem for law enforcement?

References

Barlow, H.D. *Introduction to criminology.* Boston: Little, Brown and Company, 1978.

Brandstatter, A.F., and Hyman, A.A. *Fundamentals of law enforcement.* Beverly Hills: Glencoe Press, 1971.

Brantingham, P., and Brantingham, P. *Patterns in crime.* New York: Macmillan Publishing Company, 1984.

Chamber of Commerce of the United States. *White collar crime: Everyone's problem, everyone's loss*. Washington, D.C.: U.S. Government Printing Office, 1974.

Clark, R. *Crime in America*. New York: Simon and Schuster, 1970.

Driscoll, J.P. *Criminology—instructor's guide*. Philadelphia: Lippincott, 1978.

Eldefonso, E.; Coffey, A.; and Grace, R.C. *Principles of law enforcement*. New York: John Wiley & Sons, 1974, 1983.

Ferguson, R.W., and Stokke, A.H. *Concepts of criminal law*. Boston: Holbrook Press, 1976.

Folley, V.L. *American law enforcement*. Boston: Holbrook Press, 1980.

Germann, A.C.; Day, F.D.; and Gallati, R.B. *Introduction to law enforcement and criminal justice*. Springfield, Ill.: Charles C. Thomas, 1972, 1978.

Haskell, M.R., and Yablonsky, L. *Crime and criminality*. Boston: Houghton Mifflin Co., 1983.

Hood, R., and Sparks, R. *Key issues in criminology*. New York: McGraw-Hill, 1970.

National Safety Council. *Accident facts*. 1984.

Nettler, G. *Explaining crime*. 2d ed. New York: McGraw-Hill, 1978.

Oran, D. *Dictionary of the law*. St. Paul, Minn.: West Publishing Company, 1983.

Pepinsky, H.E. *Crime control strategies: An introduction to the study of crime*. New York: Oxford University Press, 1980.

President's Commission on Law Enforcement and Administration of Justice. *The challenge of crime in a free society*. Washington, D.C.: U.S. Government Printing Office, February 1967.

Prosser, W.L. *Handbook of the law of torts*. 2d ed. St. Paul, Minn.: West Publishing Company, 1955.

Rainwater, L. *Inequality and justice*. Chicago: Adline Publishing Company, 1974.

Reid, S.T. *Crime and criminology*. New York: Holt, Rinehart and Winston, 1982.

Sheley, J.F. *America's crime problem: An introduction to criminology*. Belmont, Cal.: Wadsworth Publishing Co. 1985.

Siegel, L.J. *Criminology*. St. Paul, Minn.: West Publishing Company, 1983.

Sutherland, E.H. *The professional thief*. Chicago: University of Chicago Press, 1937.

Sutherland, E.H., and Cressey, D.R. *Criminology*. 10th ed. Philadelphia: Lippincott, 1978.

Sutherland, E.H., and Cressey, D.R. *Principles of criminology*. 5th ed. Philadelphia: Lippincott, 1955.

Sykes, G.M. *The future of crime*. Washington, D.C.: U.S. Government Printing Office, 1980.

Tittle, C. *Sanction and social deviance*. New York: Praeger Publishers, 1980.

U.S Congress. Senate. Committee on Governmental Affairs. *Arson for profit: Its impact on states and localities*. 95th Cong., December 14, 1977.

U.S. Department of Justice. Bureau of Justice Statistics. *Report to the nation on crime and justice*. Washington, D.C.: U.S. Government Printing Office, 1983.

U.S. Department of Justice. Drug Enforcement Administration. *Fact sheet*. Washington, D.C.: (no date).

U.S. Department of Justice. *Crime and alcohol.* Washington, D.C.: U.S. Government Printing Office, 1982.

U.S. Department of Justice. *Dictionary of criminal justice data terminology.* Washington, D.C.: U.S. Government Printing Office, 1981.

U.S. Department of Justice. Uniform Crime Reports. *Crime in the United States.* Washington, D.C.: July 28, 1985.

Vetter, H.J., and Silverman, I.J. *The nature of crime.* Philadelphia: W.B. Saunders Company, 1978.

Walker, S. *Sense and nonsense about crime: A policy guide.* Monterey, Cal.: Brooks/Cole Publishing Co., 1985.

Criminal behavior frequently begins during a person's youth. Juvenile delinquency is a severe problem in the United States, where youths are responsible for a disproportionate part of the nation's crime.

Criminals and Juvenile Delinquents
Who Are the Offenders?

Do You Know . . .

- What the major causes of criminal behavior are?

- How most criminal behavior comes about?

- How to define juvenile delinquency?

- How severe the problem of juvenile delinquency is in the United States?

- What status offenses are and what is included in this category?

- What some major causes of juvenile delinquency seem to be?

- How parents, school, and society can help prevent children from becoming delinquents?

- What dangers are inherent in labeling people?

The most conservative estimates suggest that 36 to 40 million persons—16–18% of the total U.S. population—have arrest records for nontraffic offenses.
— Report to the Nation on Crime and Justice.

Introduction

Just as since ancient times, society makes laws to protect its members, and there are those individuals who do not abide by the laws. Sometimes breaking the law is not considered criminal; for example, a person who breaks a traffic law by speeding would not be considered by most as a criminal. Other offenses, however, are serious enough that the person committing them is called a criminal or, if under legal age, a juvenile delinquent.

Sutherland and Cressey (1978, pp. 20–21) indicate that sociological criminologists take three different positions on who is a criminal. The first group is legally oriented, confident that statutes clearly describe criminal behavior and, consequently, anyone who violates a statutue is a criminal, whether apprehended or not. A second group takes the opposite position, arguing that laws are irrelevant, that "persons of little power are criminals according to the law in action, but more powerful people are not." The third group takes a position in between, contending that statutory definitions are used as reference points by both ordinary citizens and criminal justice personnel. They note that most people, for example, know it is against the law to rob, even if they do not know the legal definition of robbery and often confuse it with burglary. This group of criminologists feels you can speak of "unapprehended criminals" and "criminals at large," even if no one has been arrested or even detected.

Multiple Causes of Criminal Behavior

Rainwater (1974. p. 7) has identified five different perspectives on the causation of crime:

> For the social pathologist, the problem is the defective character of individuals in society. . . . For the sociologist who focuses on social disorganization, the problem is in ineffectiveness of rules for organizing constructive social processes. For the value conflict theorist, the problem can be understood only as a result either of conflicts among groups in society or of conflicting interests held by a single individual. For the deviance theorist, the problem lies in the instigations to rule violation created by the unequal distribution of opportunities for self-realization in society. For the labeling

theorist, the problem is very much in the eye of the beholder, and in the process by which society separates its members into the moral and the immoral, the conforming and the deviant.

Each perspective offers some insight into the complexity of the causations of crime, and each illustrates that there is no single factor responsible for the existence of crime, a fact long accepted by criminologists.

> *No definitive answer exists as to why people commit crimes. Of the several theories set forth, several suggest a combination of sociological, psychological, and biological factors.*

According to the Bureau of Justice Statistics (1983, p. 30):

Historically, the causes of criminal behavior have included explanations ranging from the influnces of evil spirits to the abnormal shape of the skull. Contemporary theories for the causes of crime still abound, but can be grouped into three general explanations:

- The sociogenic—focuses on the environment's effect on the individual and places responsibility for crime on society. It identifies as the causes of crime such factors as poverty, ignorance, high unemployment, inadequate housing, and poor health. To these general environmental factors, it adds the impact of unstable homes, viewing their consequent discord, absence of affection and consistent discipline, and improper moral instruction as especially contributory to juvenile delinquency and youth crime. However, recent research has shown that these factors do not account for long-term fluctuations in crime. Moreover, these factors cannot explain why under certain circumstances, one individual commits a crime and another does not.

- The psychogenic—focuses on psychological factors and understands crime to be the result of an individual's propensity and inducement toward crime. Propensity toward crime is determined by the individual's ability to conceptualize right and wrong, to manage impulse and postpone present gratifications, and to anticipate and take into account consequences that lie in the future as well as the individual's fondness of risk and willingness to inflict injury on others. Inducement relates to situational factors such as access and opportunity that may provide the individual with the necessary incentives to commit a crime. Under this explanation, while many environmental factors contribute to an individual's propensity to commit crime, the individual is responsible for his behavior. Further, inducement toward committing crime may be inherent in our technological age which, among other things, allows increased access through greater mobility.

- The biogenic—focuses on biological functions and processes and relates human behavior, specifically criminal behavior, to such biological variables as brain tumors and other disorders of the limbic system, endocrine abnormalities, neurological dysfunction produced by prenatal and postnatal experience of infants, and chromosomal abnormalities (the XYY chromosomal pattern).

Further support for the multiplicity of causes for crime is presented by Hood and Sparks (1970) who note that numerous comparisons of groups of criminals with groups of noncriminals have failed to produce any single characteristic or "factor" which absolutely distinguishes the two groups. Further, since the concepts of crime, delinquency, deviant behavior, and the like apply to such a wide range of different kinds of behavior, having in common only the fact that they have been declared contrary to legal rules in various times and places, no single causal explanation can possibly cover this wide range of behaviors.

Many Americans have come to accept the existence of crime as a part of life, a price paid by a democratic society for its high standard of living where those who "have not" seek to get their fair share in any way possible.

Crime has always been a local problem and responsibility, yet it is a social problem which concerns the entire country. Its causative factors and effects have been studied by scientists and researchers for over a century. Its increase in the last quarter-century has so alarmed the country and cities that in the sixties and seventies politicians often dictated a "law and order" platform.

Many of the causative factors of crime are well beyond the control of the law enforcement officer. Included among these are the population, its density and size, that is, how many people live in a square mile; economics; the legal policies of prosecutors; the educational system of the community; the recreational areas and facilities available; and the religious characteristics of some communities. With a breakdown in discipline in many schools with open, permissive policies and a breakdown in the family value system, crime has become one of America's gravest social problems.

The high level of unemployment, especially among the young, increases the problem. With teen-age unemployment in some large cities running forty percent, attitudes and values may change considerably. The free enterprise system may appear to have little to offer a young person who cannot gain access to the system because no jobs are available. For some the logical alternative is to engage in crime. When frustration, emotional conflict, and desperation overcome individuals because of social and economic conditions, they frequently resort to a crime against property or persons. The result is that those individuals who have been able to cope with the stresses of the free enterprise system and are law-abiding find themselves victimized by those who have turned to crime.

Criminologist Edwin H. Sutherland (1937) has postulated a theory concerning the genesis of criminal behavior called *differential association*. He explains the beginning of criminal behavior in the group-based learning experiences of the individual based on the following assumptions (Vetter and Silverman, 1978, p. 325):

- Criminal behavior is learned.
- Criminal behavior is learned in interaction with other persons in a process of communication.

- The principal part of the learning of criminal behavior occurs within intimate personal groups.
- When criminal behavior is learned, the learning includes: (a) techniques of committing the crime . . . and (b) the specific direction of motives, drives, rationalizations, and attitudes.
- The specific direction of motives and drives is learned from definitions of the legal codes as favorable or unfavorable.
- A person becomes delinquent because of an excess of definitions favorable to violation of the law over definitions unfavorable to violation of the law.
- Differential associations may vary in frequency, duration, priority, and intensity.
- The process of learning criminal behavior by association with criminal and anticriminal patterns involves all the mechanisms that are involved in any other kind of learning.
- While criminal behavior is an expression of general needs and values, it is not explained by those general needs and values since noncriminal behavior is an expression of the same needs and values.

Most criminal behavior is learned.

Everyone at one time or another is exposed to criminal behavior; some learn and acquire criminal actions; some do not. Why? Again, no simple reason can be given. Often a large part of the answer is found in what happens to individuals in their early years. Some children cause no problems for parents, school, and the community; others are incorrigible, creating a serious problem not only for their parents, teachers, and neighbors, but for law enforcement officers.

Criminals—Who Commits Crime?

The Bureau of Justice Statistics (1983, pp. 31–34) answers the question "Who is the 'typical' offender?" with the following facts:

- Most crimes are committed by men, especially by men under age 20.
- Offenders described in arrest, jail, and prison data are disproportionately young, black, unmarried males. Violent offenders are typically low-income youth with a high likelihood of unemployment.
- Serious crime arrests are highest in young age groups; participation in crime declines with age.
- Property crimes are more typical of youths than of older offenders.
- Violent juvenile offenders and adult felons have very similar characteristics.
- Gang membership is a major difference between youth and adult criminals.

Table 3–1.   *Who is the "Typical" Offender?*

What are the characteristics of offenders?

	U.S. population 1980	1981				
		Index crime arrestees		Convicted jail inmates	State prison inmates	Federal prison inmates
		Violent	Property			
	226,545,805	464,826	1,828,928	91,411	340,639	28,133
Sex						
Male	49%	90%	79%	94%	96%	94%
Female	51	10	21	6	4	6
Race						
White	86	53	67	58	52	63
Black	12	46	31	40	47	35
Other	2	1	2	2	1	2
Ethnic origin						
Hispanic	6	12	10	10	9	16
Non-Hispanic	94	88	90	90	91	84
Age						
Under 15	23	5	14	*	0	0
15–19	9	25	36	14	7	0
20–29	18	42	31	53	56	34
30-39	14	17	11	19	25	40
40–49	10	7	4	9	8	17
50–59	10	3	2	4	3	7
60 +	16	1	2	1	1	2

*Less than 0.5%.

For what mix of offenses are persons arrested, jailed, and imprisoned?

Arrestees
include many later released
—most arrests are for less
serious offenses

Jail inmates
include those awaiting
trial or sentencing and
those serving short
sentences for less
serious crimes

Prison inmates
are those sentenced
to more than one
year—generally
for serious crimes

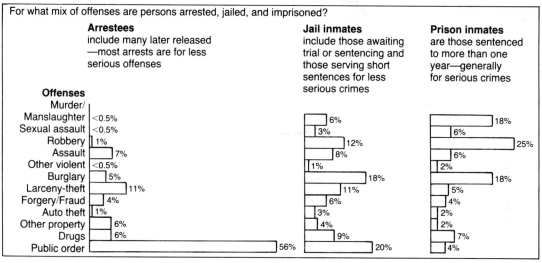

Offenses	Arrestees	Jail inmates	Prison inmates
Murder/Manslaughter	<0.5%	6%	18%
Sexual assault	<0.5%	3%	6%
Robbery	1%	12%	25%
Assault	7%	8%	6%
Other violent	<0.5%	1%	2%
Burglary	5%	18%	18%
Larceny-theft	11%	11%	5%
Forgery/Fraud	4%	6%	4%
Auto theft	1%	3%	2%
Other property	6%	4%	2%
Drugs	6%	9%	7%
Public order	56%	20%	4%

Source: Bureau of Justice Statistics, *Report To The Nation On Crime and Justice,* 1983.

- Relatively few offenders are career criminals.
- Career criminals, though few in number, account for most crime.
- Chronic violent offenders start out and remain violent.
- Prior criminal behavior is one of the best predictors of future criminality.
- Relatively few offenders are female.
- A relatively large proportion of offenders come from minority groups.
- Many offenders have backgrounds that include a turbulent home life, lack of family ties, and poor education. Most offenders were not married; yet most inmates had dependent children.
- Prior to arrest many inmates had little or no legal income.
- Drug and alcohol abuse is common among offenders. Two out of five prison inmates reported they were under the influences of drugs or were very drunk around the time of the offense.

Juvenile Delinquency

States vary as to the age of a juvenile, but most state statutes specify an individual under the age of sixteen or eighteen. **Juvenile delinquency** is behavior by a person not of legal age that violates a local, state, or federal law.

Kratcoski and Walker (1978, p. 261) note that: "delinquency encompasses a wide range of youthful behavior. It applies to juveniles who have committed rape or murder and those who have run away from home to escape intolerable or even threatening situations. Juvenile delinquency, in various jurisdictions, also includes having a fist fight; fishing without a license; taking a ride in a car without the owner's knowledge; buying beer, wine or liquor; drag racing; having sexual relations with a person of the opposite sex; skipping school; gambling for money in card games; or staying out after a certain hour at night."

> *Juvenile delinquency is behavior by a person not of legal age that violates a local, state, or federal law.* criminal law

Juvenile delinquency presents a serious problem with an enormous number of youngsters involved. Self-report studies indicate that approximately 90 percent of all young people have committed at least one act for which they could be brought to juvenile court (*The Challenge of Crime in a Free Society,* 1967, p. 55). However, many of these offenses are minor (for example, fighting, truancy, and running away from home), and state statutes often define juvenile delinquency so broadly that virtually all youngsters could be classified as delinquent.

Even though many offenses are minor, and even though many juvenile offenders are never arrested or referred to juvenile court, alarming numbers are. The Children's Bureau estimates that one in every nine youths and one in every six male youths will be referred to juvenile court for a delinquent act (excluding traffic offenses) before his eighteenth birthday (*The Challenge of Crime,* p. 56).

Arrest statistics point out the severity of the problem, although such statistics may be somewhat exaggerated as juveniles are often more easily caught than adults, and they often act in groups when committing the crimes, thereby producing a greater number of arrests than crimes committed.

Table 3–2 from the Uniform Crime Reports indicates the type and extent of crimes in which youth are involved:

The seriousness of the problem is evident in the amount of relatively serious property crimes: burglary, larceny, and motor vehicle thefts. In addition, although juveniles account for more than their share of arrests for several serious crimes, such arrests are only a small part of all juvenile arrests. Juveniles are most often arrested for petty larceny, fighting, disorderly conduct, liquor-related offenses, and noncriminal conduct such as curfew violations, truancy, incorrigibility, or running away from home.

Table 3–2.   Total Arrests of Persons under 15, 18, 21 and 25 Years of Age, 1983.

[9,879 agencies; 1984 estimated population 179,871,000]

Offense charged	Total all ages	Number of persons arrested				Percent of total all ages			
		Under 15	Under 18	Under 21	Under 25	Under 15	Under 18	Under 21	Under 25
TOTAL	8,921,708	524,760	1,537,688	2,868,066	4,507,344	5.9	17.2	32.1	50.5
Murder and nonnegligent manslaughter	13,676	138	1,004	2,918	5,649	1.0	7.3	21.3	41.3
Forcible rape	28,336	1,481	4,397	8,214	13,264	5.2	15.5	29.0	46.8
Robbery	108,614	7,206	27,795	50,603	72,682	6.6	25.6	46.6	66.9
Aggravated assault	231,620	9,966	31,148	60,808	103,643	4.3	13.4	26.3	44.7
Burglary	334,399	49,704	127,708	195,201	248,346	14.9	38.2	58.4	74.3
Larceny-theft	1,009,743	156,595	338,785	488,668	627,122	15.5	33.6	48.4	62.1
Motor vehicle theft	93,285	8,504	33,838	52,204	67,177	9.1	36.3	56.0	72.0
Arson	14,675	4,091	6,244	7,728	9,388	27.9	42.5	52.7	64.0
Violent crime[1]	382,246	18,791	64,344	122,543	195,238	4.9	16.8	32.1	51.1
Property crime[2]	1,452,102	218,894	506,575	743,801	952,033	15.1	34.9	51.2	65.6
Crime Index total[3]	1,834,348	237,685	570,919	866,344	1,147,271	13.0	31.1	47.2	62.5
Other assaults	408,389	26,014	66,880	117,588	196,109	6.4	16.4	28.8	48.0
Forgery and counterfeiting	63,359	1,206	6,179	15,982	29,522	1.9	9.8	25.2	46.6
Fraud	203,175	7,850	16,997	35,194	72,013	3.9	8.4	17.3	35.4
Embezzlement	6,290	65	455	1,414	2,643	1.0	7.2	22.5	42.0
Stolen property; buying, receiving, possessing	95,527	6,665	22,989	42,014	59,462	7.0	24.1	44.0	62.2
Vandalism	189,524	46,016	87,135	115,304	141,026	24.3	46.0	60.8	74.4
Weapons; carrying, possessing, etc.	137,909	5,769	20,657	41,540	67,418	4.2	15.0	30.1	48.9
Prostitution and commercialized vice	88,337	261	2,375	15,856	44,410	.3	2.7	17.9	50.3
Sex offenses (except forcible rape and prostitution)	75,709	6,401	13,409	20,693	31,553	8.5	17.7	27.3	41.7
Drug abuse violations	562,255	11,407	67,211	169,709	308,175	2.0	12.0	30.2	54.8
Gambling	27,377	104	671	2,372	5,810	.4	2.5	8.7	21.2
Offenses against family and children	32,877	690	1,577	4,820	10,204	2.1	4.8	14.7	31.0
Driving under the influence	1,346,586	457	18,563	157,078	432,939	(4)	1.4	11.7	32.2
Liquor laws	383,234	8,476	101,904	247,084	297,755	2.2	26.6	64.5	77.7
Drunkenness	886,434	2,704	23,582	108,760	261,504	.3	2.7	12.3	29.5
Disorderly conduct	514,403	22,111	73,552	161,474	272,385	4.3	14.3	31.4	53.0
Vagrancy	22,640	582	2,044	5,674	9,352	2.6	9.0	25.1	41.3
All other offenses (except traffic)	1,845,398	70,453	256,575	552,982	928,602	3.8	13.9	30.0	50.3
Suspicion	16,419	927	2,496	4,666	7,673	5.6	15.2	28.4	46.7
Curfew and loitering law violations	67,243	18,905	67,243	67,243	67,243	28.1	100.0	100.0	100.0
Runaways	114,275	50,012	114,275	114,275	114,275	43.8	100.0	100.0	100.0

[1] Violent crimes are offenses of murder, forcible rape, robbery, and aggravated assault.
[2] Property crimes are offenses of burglary, larceny-theft, motor vehicle theft, and arson.
[3] Includes arson.
[4] Less than one-tenth of 1 percent.

Source: Uniform Crime Reports, Crime in the United States, 1984.

Youth is responsible for a substantial and disproportionate part of the national crime problem.

A special category of offenses has been established for juveniles, designating certain actions as illegal for any person under the state's defined juvenile age of sixteen or eighteen. These are status offenses.

Status offenses are violations of the law applying only to those under legal age. They include absenting from home, truancy, drinking alcoholic beverages, smoking, violating curfew, and incorrigibility.

Factors Related to Juvenile Delinquency

Delinquents often come from backgrounds of social and economic deprivation, that is, their families have lower than average incomes and social status. Equally or perhaps even more important, however, is the area in which the youth lives. One study showed that lower-class youths will seldom be classified as delinquents if they live in upper-class neighborhoods, and numerous other studies have established the relationship between certain deprived areas, especially the slums of large cities, and delinquency *(The Challenge of Crime,* p. 189).

As with most crime, arrest rates for delinquents are highest in the cities, particularly the larger cities, next highest in the suburbs, and lowest in rural areas. The delinquency rate is high among children from broken homes as well as among children who have several brothers and/or sisters. Delinquents often do poorly in school, are below their normal grade level, and have dropped classes or have dropped out of school completely when they are old enough to do so.

According to a press clipping, a fourteen-year-old boy was brought into court on charges of robbing and assaulting a sixty-five-year-old woman with a knife. Sitting in the closed session court room was a woman to whom the judge pointed and asked the boy if he knew. The youngster antagonistically stated, "No." The judge then informed the boy that she was his mother whom he had not seen since she had left him at the age of four months on the steps of the city general hospital because "she did not like the child or child's father." The boy subsequently lived in ten orphanages and foster homes. Following his sentence to a state training school, the boy bitterly stated to the judge, "The world has done me wrong, and it will have to pay me back. If it doesn't give me what I have coming I'll take it."

This is not a unique situation. The question is how to deal with such attitudes. Constructive prevention and correction of such attitudes and behaviors is desperately needed. However, to attempt to prevent or correct juvenile antisocial behavior without an understanding of the underlying causes is futile. What accounts for the juvenile brutalities that too frequently capture the headlines, the gang beatings of people, the torturing to death of elderly people "for fun," the deadly juvenile gang wars, the vandalism in schools and churches? Society must give reasonable answers to such questions rather that blaming all delinquency on crime comics, movies, sparing the rod, or mollycoddling young offenders.

The societal focus on the causes of delinquent behavior in children is justifiable because juvenile delinquents commit a disturbing proportion of serious offenses and because many of them grow up to be habitual offenders. Consequently, the prevention and correction of juvenile delinquent behavior offers one potential means of reducing our nation's high adult crime rate.

Historical Assumptions

Historically simplistic answers have been sought for complex, baffling problems. For example, for centuries the western world operated on the belief that everyone knew the difference between right and wrong, and that if anyone did wrong and broke the law, it was because he willfully chose to do so. This belief underlies our system of criminal law and its reliance on punishment.

Closely related to this concept was the idea that delinquents and criminals differed from the rest of the population in being "born bad." Over the last two decades people have blamed all the misbehavior of the age on one factor or another: feeblemindedness, poverty, slums, gangs, drinking, broken homes, lack of playgrounds, failure to punish children, nutrition, divorce, depression, inflation, and on and on. Today crime and horror comics, pornography, violence on television and in the movies, and parental permissiveness are bearing the brunt of the blame for juvenile delinquency. It has even been said that there are no delinquent children, only delinquent parents.

Rarely does a simple explanation exist for a serious or chronic misbehavior by a particular child except in the infrequent cases of brain damage, disease, or accident. Children grow into chronic behavior given certain combinations of situations and their own unique personalities.

> *Children are directly influenced by their own basic individuality, their home, their school, and their community (society).*

Basic Individuality

Babies start life as self-centered, dependent beings who, although they have absolutely no control over themselves or their environment, have an urge for self-preservation, aggressive drives, emotions such as love, anger, and fear, and basic needs which must be met. If their wants are denied, they cry, scream, and sometimes show aggression that might be murderous if they were not so helpless. If permitted to continue in this self-centered world of infancy and given free rein to their impulsive actions to satisfy their wants, any child could grow up to be a thief, killer, or rapist.

In the growing-up process it is normal for a child to be dirty, to fight, to grab, to steal, to tear things apart, to talk back, to disobey, and to lie. As noted by Ilg and Ames (1955, p. 137):

> Finding a 6-year-old who lies or steals, who has moments of nearly ungovernable rage and who thinks the world ought to revolve around him is not much of a surprise to a psychologist, however hard it may be, temporarily, on

parents, relatives, and the neighborhood. But finding the same behavior in a 14- or 15-year-old can be frightening. The whole question of why growth went wrong is a tremendously complicated one. . . .

To teach its youth self-discipline and conformity to societal expectations, most societies depend largely on authority expressed through various pressures. It depends on the pressures of physical realities such as the hazards imposed by fire, knives, and stairways, which children must learn to respect if they do not want to get hurt. It depends on the pressures of the competing needs of brothers and sisters, neighbors, and peers. It depends upon the rules and sanctions imposed by parents, schools, custom, laws, police, and the courts.

From infancy on, every child needs the continuous but reasonable discipline of adults. However, intense authority, strict regimentation, or harsh and frequent whippings may build resentment, hate, and a sense of guilt. Dr. Haim G. Ginott (1965, p. 72) warns: "Parents who are in the midst of a declared or undeclared war with their children . . . should recognize the fact that this war cannot be won. . . . Even if we win a battle and succeed in enforcing our will, they may retaliate by becoming spiritless and neurotic, or rebellious and delinquent."

In addition to reasonable discipline, children must have their basic emotional needs satisfied. Haskell and Yablonsky (1970) cite four basic needs which must be met. First and most important is the need for emotional security, the assurance that one belongs, is loved, and wanted. Infants get this from their parents. As they grow older this sense of security is nurtured by belonging to the family, the neighborhood, the gang, the club, the union, etc. Few people seek or tolerate isolation or ostracism.

A second basic need is for a sense of adequacy or worthiness, the feeling of being competent in at least one activity for which the child gets recognition and praise and gains the crucial sense of being useful. A third need is for new experiences, for adventure and excitement. And a fourth need is an increasing desire for independence as the child advances toward manhood or womanhood.

It is largely through satisfying these basic emotional needs for security, self-worth, excitement, and independence that parents, the school, and the community persuade youth to give up immediate satisfaction of their desires, to exercise self-control, to conform to society's standards, and to avoid delinquent behavior. With some children this is easier than with others. Ilg and Ames (1955, pp. 317–19) have identified three general groups of children: (1) those made of basically sturdy "stuff," who are stable and able to rise above the most adverse circumstances; (2) those who are susceptible to their surroundings and need good upbringing and positive influences to become good citizens; and (3) those who have an inadequacy in their basic individuality. It is from the third group which the majority of delinquents come.

The parents, the school, and society must teach youth self-discipline and adherence to societal expectations, and must, at the same time, provide for meeting the child's basic needs.

Ilg and Ames contend that these children are not "born criminals," but that the task of growing up to accept and follow society's rules is hard for them, sometimes impossible. Some are lacking in intelligence. Some never develop emotionally. Some lack inhibition and restraint or the ability to foresee the end result of their actions. They caution: "Here as elsewhere the best that parents and society can do for our children may not be too good. And here as elsewhere it is not all up to the parents or to society. Even though there is much that they can do, we must always remember that at least a part of the answer—sometimes most of it—lies in the organism itself."

Parental Influence

The mechanisms at work in good parent-child relationships can be seen all around us. Although there is no one way to be a good parent, certain principles recur in the literature on child development. The child's need to belong, to be loved and approved is just as insistent as the need for food. In effect, parents might offer their children this love and approval in exchange for giving up infantile habits and sources of pleasure. Gradually children accept the frustrations, nonaggressions, and the endless "don'ts" and "nos" of their early years. Soon they develop their own control mechanism, their conscience, to govern their behavior according to the beliefs, values, and attitudes they have adopted from those they love and admire.

We can also see the failure of these mechanisms, where instead of love, approval, consistent discipline, and respect for their individuality, children experience from their parents excessively harsh discipline, constant criticism, indifference, or unpredictable swings between harshness and laxness. Such children with no incentive to control their aggressions, are likely to be cruel, quarrelsome, destructive, defiant, selfish, jealous, and to show little feelings of remorse or guilt. If brutality in their early years clamped down on their every effort to let out some of their hostility, the hostility may, in time, explode in torturing a dog or cat, in hurting other children, in setting fire to the school building, in theft, murder, and other heinous crimes. Such is the background of some of the children whose atrocious behavior makes the headlines.

Influence of the School

Children spend a great deal of time in school; consequently, its influence is often profound. According to some, the school is the most important influence on a child's development. Dr. William Glasser (1969, pp. 2–5) states: "If school failure does not exist, other handicaps (poverty, color, broken home, poor relationship with parents) can be more easily overcome." Dr. Glasser places highest emphasis on success: "I do not accept the rationalization of failure commonly accepted today, that these young people are products of a social situation that precludes success. Blaming their failure upon their homes, their communities, their culture, their background, their race, or their poverty is a dead end for two reasons: (1) it removes personal responsibility for failure, and (2) it does not recognize that school success

Big City theory
→ Reality theory

is potentially open to all young people. . . ." According to Dr. Glasser, the most critical years are ages five to ten, but failure at any stage in a student's education can greatly diminish chances for success in life:

> Very few children come to school failures, none come labeled failures; it is school and school alone which pins the label of failure on children. . . . If, however, the child experienced failure in school during these five years (ages five to ten), by the age of ten his confidence will be shattered, his motivation will be destroyed, and he will have begun to identify with failure. Convinced that he is unable to fulfill his needs through the logical use of his brain, he will return to behavior directed by his emotions. . . . He will abandon the pathways of love and self-worth and grope blindly toward what seem to him to be the only paths left open, those of delinquency and withdrawal (pp. 26–27).

Influence of Society

The social aspects of an individual's environment, his neighborhood, associates, customs, beliefs, attitudes, also shape the individual's personality. Just as some place emphasis on the parents' influence and others emphasize the school's influence, many such as Ramsey Clark (1970, p. 17) stress societal influences: "Crime reflects more than the character of the pitiful few who commit it. It reflects the character of the entire society. . . . What they are and what they experienced came largely from society—for its influence on them and on their forebearers."

Among most primitive people the basic emotional needs of children were met automatically by the group or tribe as well as by the parents. The tribe or village was small and everyone knew everyone else. All shared the same activities in work, education, and recreation; all shared the same beliefs and superstitions. The adaptations demanded of children were comparatively few and simple, with practically no choice of beliefs or behavior patterns to create conflicts within the child. Consequently, although the group's behavioral standards were often primitive, nonconformity to those standards (delinquency) was almost unknown. As society progressed, however, this was no longer true:

> Our youth now love luxury—they have bad manners and contempt for authority. They show disrespect for their elders and love idle chatter in place of exercise. . . . Children are now tyrants—not the servants of their households. They no longer rise when elders enter the room. They contradict their parents, chatter before company, gobble up their food, and tyrannize their teachers. (Socrates, Fifth Century B.C.)

Upon first reading, the above statement might seem to apply to today's youth as well. It is obvious that the problem of juvenile behavior has been of concern for centuries.

Records going back to colonial times indicate that a considerable amount of juvenile delinquency has always existed in this country. Nevertheless, the lifestyle of earlier days was less conducive to delinquent behavior. Before the automobile, life centered in the home, the church, and the school, in relatively stable neighbor-hoods. A child might grow to adulthood without going ten miles from his birthplace. The family was likely to be a clan of many members. Children whose parents were missing, brutal, indifferent, or failed to meet the children's emotional needs, might get satisfaction and guidance from a grandmother, an aunt, the woman next door, the minister, the priest, or the teacher. The self-contained neigh-borhood and the self-contained classrooms, like the tribe, gave children support and imposed powerful controls on their behavior.

As for the other basic needs, the typical youngster was from early years a useful hand on the farm, in the family shop, or in the home, obtaining a sense of competence, usefulness, and growing independence while learning a vocation. Youths fit into life by living and sharing. Untamed country surrounding even the big cities provided excitement and new experiences. The rebels and the violent could always escape to the frontier and not influence less rebellious and violent youth.

Today, however, industrialization, mechanization, mobility, urbanization, and teeming populations have transformed the conditions of life and multiplied the problems of adjustment for children. The clan family with its helpful grandparents and maiden aunts has disappeared. The automobile has obliterated the self-contained neighborhood and, by enabling youth on the farms as well as in the cities to seek recreation in the anonymity of distance, has practically ended the neighbor-hood's control over youths' behavior. At the same time the car invites delinquency over a larger geographical area and vastly increases its dangers. In addition, boys and girls seldom grow into a vocation in the family business, and modern technol-ogy has almost eliminated daily chores like carrying out the trash, beating the rugs, picking vegetables, and even mowing the lawn. In too many homes, today's young-sters feel unneeded, superfluous, almost a kind of toy.

Simultaneously mechanical inventions take children farther from nature, its satisfactions, and its lessons. The house is too small for recreation; the streets are dangerous. Today's youth often have no permissible readily available outlet for their energies. It is understandable that our streets are clogged with souped-up cars, children breaking school windows and street lights, experimenting with liquor, narcotics, and drugs.

Seriously and chronically delinquent children are produced in rural areas and in well-to-do neighborhoods, but the majority come from slums which magnify all the modern social conditions, making it difficult for today's children to grow up as well-adjusted adults.

In blighted neighborhoods, with run-down, overcrowded housing, few churches, poor schools, and no playgrounds, with constantly changing populations and without neighborhood consciousness, pride or leadership, where vice flourishes and derelicts, crooks, and gangs seek refuge, children from emotionally impoverished homes have a far greater chance of becoming serious delinquents than if they lived in a more favorable neighborhood. Slums contribute dis-proportionately to the load of the juvenile courts and are a prime factor in precipitat-ing delinquent behavior in children whose family relationships have predisposed them towards it.

Officers participate in a reach out program for juveniles.

When gangs dominate the social life of adolescents in blighted areas, they may even enlist some emotionally well-adjusted youngsters in delinquency. In today's society of interdependent, fragmented families, few homes can satisfy all the economic, vocational, social, and recreational needs of its children. The family and child depend upon the community as never before. If the needs of children for constructive citizenship are to be satisfied in this age of machines and technology, the home, the schools, the community, and individuals in law enforcement will have to shoulder a large part of the job. If they do not, the danger of high juvenile crime rates and the formation of juvenile gangs is great.

The Hazards of Labeling

We have talked about crimes, criminals, and juvenile delinquents. Such labels are helpful in discussion and in academic situations, but they should be avoided as much as possible when actually dealing with individuals. The following observations by D.F. Duncan (1969, pp. 41–45), although referring specifically to delinquency, apply equally to all other types of labels which we often thoughtlessly apply to individuals.

The delinquent label accomplishes four major changes in the life of the child to whom it is attached. First, as a self-fulfilling prophecy, it encourages the child to identify himself as a delinquent and bad. He organizes his behavior, attitudes, and ambitions accordingly.

Secondly, the label acts to strip the youth's community of the positive means of control it normally employs to hold the behavior of its youth in line with its values. By rejecting the child who has acquired a delinquent label, society withdraws its recognition and affirmation.

Third, the label serves effectively to cut off legitimate opportunities for success and recognition. The most significant people in a child's life—his peers, family, neighbors and authority figures react to the child labeled delinquent with mistrust, suspicion and caution.

The fourth and most critical result of the delinquent label is that it opens the door to illegitimate opportunities to the child. If a youth accepts its delinquent label and seeks out friends who have also been labeled, his behavior will tend to conform to the standards of those friends from whom he is forced to seek recognition and approval.

> *Labels are dangerous because they may become "self-fulfilling," they may impair society's control mechanism, cut off legitimate opportunities for success and recognition, and cause the person so labeled to seek out others who have been similarly labeled.*

Although individuals may engage in criminal acts, they should still be regarded as persons, not criminals per se. In addition, people's behavior can change. As noted by Driscoll (1978, pp. 76–77), although studies of the careers of adult criminals demonstrate the importance of delinquency as a harbinger of criminality, they also show that the great majority of delinquents never reach criminal maturity and do not move into adult criminality. Conversely, some adult criminals have no history of delinquency because such a history would preclude their appointment to positions of trust; that is particularly true of those who commit white-collar crimes. Driscoll notes that an older embezzler may never attain "criminal maturity" because he does not incorporate criminal attitudes into his personality and does not have the self-concept of a criminal. He sees himself as a normal person caught in a unique circumstance that permits no alternative except the violation of a financial trust.

Summary

Criminal behavior results from an individual's basic personality and environment. No definitive answer exists as to why people commit crimes. Of the several theories set forth, several suggest a combination of sociological, psychological, and biological factors. It should be recognized, however, that most criminal behavior is learned. Such learning often starts at an early age, resulting in juvenile delinquency, that is, behavior by a person not of legal age that violates a local, state, or federal law. Youth is responsible for a substantial and disproportionate part of the national crime problem. Any discussion of juvenile delinquency must take into consideration status offenses, violations of the law applying only to those under legal age. They include absenting from home, truancy, drinking alcoholic beverages, smoking, violating curfew, and incorrigibility.

The same social and economic conditions operate in the youth's development as operate in the development of adult criminal behavior. Children are directly influenced by their own basic individuality, their home, their school, and their community. All must share in teaching youth self-discipline and adherence to societal expectation, and all must assist in meeting the child's basic needs.

In spite of the necessity of labels such as criminal and juvenile delinquent, the dangers of such labels should be recognized. Although crime does exist, by law, criminal behavior is engaged in by individuals who, in spite of their actions, are entitled by law to their civil rights and civil liberties.

Application

Many notorious criminals have committed serious crimes and are either presently serving long prison terms or have been executed. Research the background of one such individual and determine whether there were any indicators in the person's youth that might suggest a future career in serious crime.

Discussion Questions

1. What helps kids in trouble?
2. What problems can arise in the legal definition of a juvenile delinquent and serious crimes such as murder?
3. Where does our attitude that most juveniles are violent individuals come from?
4. Is there one single causative factor for crime today?
5. How can the personal biases of those in the criminal justice system be avoided in handling criminals in the community?
6. What are some high risk factors that contribute to a criminal career?
7. How long does one remain a criminal— until the crime has been "paid for" or for a lifetime?

References

Clark, R. *Crime in America.* New York: Simon and Schuster, 1970.

Department of Health and Human Services. *Television and behavior.* Washington, D.C.: Government Printing Office, 1982.

Driscoll, J.P. *Criminology—instructor's guide.* Philadelphia: Lippincott, 1978.

Duncan, D.F. "Stigma and delinquency." *Cornell journal of social relations* 4 (1969): 41–45.

Eldefonso, E., and Hartinger, W. *Control, treatment, and rehabilitation of juvenile offenders.* Beverly Hills: Glencoe Press, 1976.

Finckenauer, J.O. *Juvenile delinquency and corrections: The gap between theory and practice.* Orlando, Fla.: Academic Press, 1984.

Ginott, H.G. *Between parent and child.* New York: MacMillan, 1965.

Glasser, W. *Schools without failure.* New York: Harper and Row, 1969.

Haskell, M.R., and Yablonsky, L. *Crime and delinquency.* Chicago: Rand McNally and Company, 1970.

Hood, R., and Sparks, R. *Key issues in criminology.* New York: McGraw-Hill, 1970.

Ilg, F.L., and Ames, L.B. *Child behavior.* Gesell Institute. New York: Dell Publishing, 1955

Jensen, G.F., and Rojek, D.G. *Delinquency: A sociological view.* Lexington, Mass.: D.C. Heath and Company, 1980.

Kratcoski, P.C., and Walker, D.B. *Criminal justice in America: Process and issues.* Glenview, Ill.: Scott Foresman and Company, 1978.

Murrell, M.A., and Lester, D. *Introduction to juvenile delinquency.* New York: MacMillan, 1981.

Nettler, G. *Explaining crime.* 2d ed. New York: McGraw-Hill, 1978.

President's Commission on Law Enforcement and Administration of Justice. *The challenge of crime in a free society.* Washington, D.C.: U.S. Government Printing Office, February 1967.

Rainwater, L. *Inequality and justice.* Chicago: Adline Publishing Company, 1974.

Sutherland, E.H. *The professional thief.* Chicago: University of Chicago Press, 1937.

Sutherland, E.H., and Cressey, D.R. *Criminology.* 10th ed. Philadelphia: Lippincott, 1978.

U.S. Department of Justice. Bureau of Justice Statistics. *Report to the nation on crime and justice.* Washington, D.C.: U.S. Government Printing Office, 1983.

U.S. Department of Justice. Law Enforcement Assistance Administration. *Children in custody.* Advance report on the juvenile detention and correctional facility census of 1972–1973. Washington, D.C.: National Criminal Justice Information and Statistics Service, May 1975.

U.S. Department of Justice. Uniform Crime Reports. *Crime in the United States, 1977.* Washington, D.C.: U.S. Government Printing Office, September 9, 1984.

Vetter, H.J., and Silverman, I.J. *The nature of crime.* Philadelphia: W.B. Saunders Company, 1978.

A police evidence technician investigates the scene of a burglary. Burglaries are frequently accompanied by vandalism.

Victimization

The Victims of Crime

Do You Know . . .

- What percentage of households in the United States are touched by crime each year?

- What households are at greatest risk of violent crime?

- What groups of people are most likely and least likely to become victims of crime?

- If a person is more likely to be victimized by a stranger or by a relative or acquaintance?

- How victims of violent crime protect themselves?

- How crime affects its victims?

- How crime rates compare with the rates of other serious life events?

- What percentage of all crimes against people and their households are not reported to police?

- How many states have compensation programs to help victims of violent crimes and what these programs typically offer?

Answers to the preceding questions are contained in *Report to the Nation on Crime and Justice*, chapter 2, prepared by the Bureau of Justice Statistics of the U.S. Department of Justice. Unless otherwise noted, all information, statistics, figures, and tables are adapted from this reference. The report uses crime statistics from several different sources, including the National Crime Survey (conducted since 1973), the Uniform Crime Reports (analyzed for eleven years from 1971-81), and homicide statistics from coroners' reports to the National Center for Health Statistics (NCHS).

Something insidious has happened in America: crime has made victims of us all. Awareness of its danger affects the way we think, where we live, where we go, what we buy, how we raise our children, and the quality of our lives as we age. The specter of violent crime and the knowledge that, without warning, any person can be attacked or crippled, robbed, or killed, lurks at the fringes of consciousness.

—Statement of the Chairman, President's Task Force on Victims of Crime

Introduction

It is common knowledge that law enforcement officers must know how to deal with criminals. Even more important, however, is the officers' ability to deal with those who are victims of crime. This is critical, not only because personal concern and establishment of rapport will enhance communications, and consequently, result in the officers' ability to obtain more information related to the crime, but also because this will enhance the image of the police officer as a professional.

Victimization Rates

Although some crimes have increased in frequency and others have decreased in frequency, the percentage of households victimized yearly by at least one crime has stayed virtually the same from 1975 to 1981. In 1981 almost a third (30 percent) of all households were victimized by violence or theft. Each of these households was victimized by at least one burglary, larceny, or motor vehicle theft, or one or more of its members were victims of a rape, robbery, or assault.

✳ *In 1981 almost a third (30 percent) of all households were victimized by violence or theft.*

Nearly 25 million households were victimized by at least one crime of violence or theft, and 6 percent of all households had members who were victims of at least one violent crime of rape, robbery, or aggravated or simple assault.

According to the Uniform Crime Reports 41 million victimizations occurred in 1981, with property crimes outnumbering violent crimes nine to one, as summarized in Table 4–1.

Also, as might be expected, the great majority of commercial burglaries and robberies occurred at night. The most frequently burglarized or robbed businesses were stores, gas stations, convenience stores, and banks. Banks accounted for only 1.3 percent, but received more publicity and investigative resources than most other burglaries or robberies.

Figure 4–1.   **Victimization Rates between 1973 and 1981.**

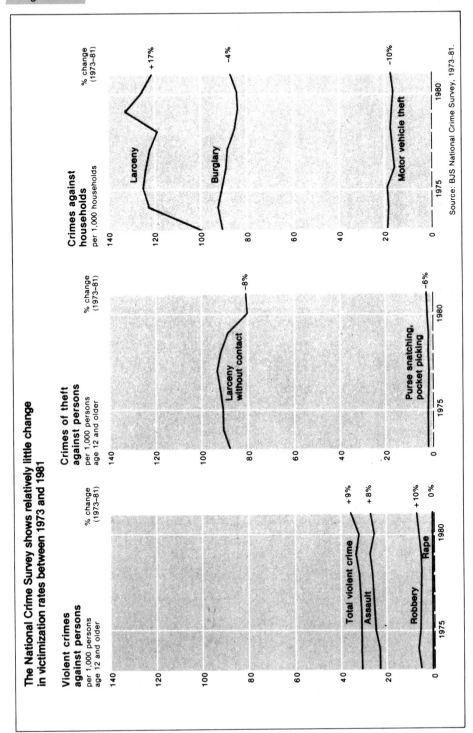

Table 4–1.   *Summary of Victimization in 1981 and Comparison of Property versus Violent Crimes.*

41 million victimizations occurred in 1981

Personal crimes

Crimes of violence
Rape	178,000
Robbery	1,381,000
Aggravated assault	1,796,000
Simple assault	3,228,000

Crimes of theft
Larceny with contact	605,000
Larceny without contact	15,258,000

Household crimes
Burglary	7,394,000
Larceny	10,176,000
Motor vehicle theft	1,439,000

Total	41,455,000

Source: BJS National Crime Survey, 1981.

13 million UCR Index Crimes were reported to police in 1981

Violent crimes	1,321,900
Murder	22,520
Forcible rape	81,540
Robbery	574,130
Aggravated assault	643,720

Property crimes	11,968,400
Burglary	3,739,800
Larceny-theft	7,154,500
Motor vehicle theft	1,074,000

Total	13,290,300

Note: Offenses may not add to totals due to rounding.

Source: FBI Uniform Crime Reports, 1981

Property crimes outnumbered violent crimes by 9 to 1

Property crimes

5,223 per 100,000
U.S. population

Property crimes

Larceny-theft	53.8%
Burglary	28.1%
Motor vehicle theft	8.1%

Violent crimes

Aggravated assault	4.8%
Robbery	4.3%
Forcible rape	0.6%
Murder	0.2%
	100.0%*

Violent crimes

577 per 100,000
U.S. population

*Percents do not add to 100% because of rounding

Source: FBI Uniform Crime Reports, 1981.

Household Risk Factors

Certain types of households are more likely to be victims of crime than others. Included in the high risk category are Hispanics, renters, households headed by younger persons, households containing six or more people, and households in urban areas.

National Crime Survey data for 1980 indicates that only 24 percent of all violent crimes occurred in and around the victim's home, but that 30 percent of all rapes occurred there.

> ◄ Hispanics are more often victims of household crimes that non-Hispanics.
>
> ◄ Renters have higher household crime rates than home owners.
>
> ◄ Household crime more often affects households headed by younger people.
>
> ◄ Household crime rates are highest for households with six or more people.
>
> ◄ Households in cities have higher crime rates than suburban or rural households.

Individual Risk Factors

Just as certain types of households are at greater risk of being victimized, certain individuals are also at greater risk than others, as summarized in Table 4–2.

As noted by the Bureau of Justice Statistics:

- ▪ Victims of crime are more often men than women.
- ▪ Younger people are much more likely than the elderly to be victims of crime. (But the elderly have a greater fear of crime and may restrict their lives in ways that reduce their chances of being victimized.)
- ▪ Blacks are more likely to be victims of violent crime than whites or members of other racial groups.
- ▪ The divorced and the never married are more likely than the married or the widowed to be victims of crime.
- ▪ Violent crime rates are higher for lower income people.
- ▪ Theft rates are highest for people with low incomes (less than $3,000 per year) and those with high incomes (more than $25,000 per year).
- ▪ Students and the unemployed are more likely than housewives, retirees, or the employed to be victims of crime.
- ▪ Rural residents are less often crime victims than are people living in cities.

> *Young, black, unemployed males living in the city have the highest victimization rates; elderly white females living in rural areas have the lowest victimization rates.*

Table 4–2.   *Factors Associated with Risk of Victimization.*

	Personal crimes of . . .			Personal crimes of . . .			Personal crimes of . . .	
	violence*	theft*		violence*	theft*		violence*	theft*
Total (U.S.)	35	85	**Income**			**Race, sex, and age summary**		
			Less than $3,000	67	106	White males		
Sex			$3,000-$7,499	45	66	12-15	69	139
Male	46	91	$7,500-$9,999	43	71	16-19	95	144
Female	25	80	$10,000-$14,999	40	82	20-24	91	145
			$15,000-$24,999	31	84	25-34	52	104
Age			$25,000 or more	28	104	35-49	28	76
12-15	59	128				50-64	14	50
16-19	68	132	**Education**			65 and over	8	26
20-24	68	133	0-4 years	14	26	White females		
25-34	44	101	5-7 years	19	28	12-15	40	133
35-49	23	78	8 years	13	29	16-19	37	133
50-64	13	51	9-11 years	25	46	20-24	44	124
65 and over	8	22	High school			25-34	35	95
			grad.	20	63	35-49	16	80
Race and origin			1-3 yrs. college	36	94	50-64	10	55
White	33	85	College graduate	27	105	65 and over	6	18
Black	50	85				Black males		
Other	38	81	**Employment status**			12-15	95	92
Hispanic	39	86	Retired	10	27	16-19	112	111
Non-Hispanic	35	85	Keeping house	15	41	20-24	86	164
			Unable to work	24	26	25-34	57	124
Marital status by sex			Employed	37	97	35-49	35	85
Males			In school	56	121	50-64	28	40
Never married	80	137	Unemployed	76	118	65 and over	28	38
Divorced/						Black females		
separated	68	133	**Residence**			12-15	69	90
Married	26	63	Central city	52	101	16-19	49	81
Widowed	15	40	1,000,000 or			20-24	61	88
Females			more	64	113	25-34	40	103
Never married	42	120	500,000-999,999	54	106	35-49	36	80
Divorced/			250,000-499,999	45	91	50-64	27	37
separated	65	112	50,000-249,999	42	93	65 and over	12	28
Married	13	64	Suburban	33	94			
Widowed	11	34	Rural	24	60			

*Personal crimes of violence include rape, robbery, and assault. Personal crimes of theft include larceny without contact, purse snatching, and pocket picking.

	Rates per 1,000 persons		
	Robbery	Assault	Rape
Sex			
Male	10	36	*
Female	5	18	2**
Age			
12-15	12	46	1
16-19	12	53	2
20-24	12	54	2
25-34	8	35	1
35-49	5	17	*
50-64	5	8	*
65 and over	4	4	*
Race and origin			
White	6	26	1
Black	17	31	2
Other	10	27	*
Hispanic	12	25	*
Non-Hispanic	7	27	1
Marital status			
Divorced/separated	15	48	3
Never married	13	47	2
Married	4	16	*
Widowed	5	6	*
Income			
Less than $3,000	16	47	4
$3,000-$7,499	12	31	2
$7,500-$9,999	9	32	1
$10,000-$14,999	8	31	1
$15,000-$24,999	6	25	1
$25,000 or more	5	23	*
Employment status			
Retired	6	4	*
Keeping house	4	11	1
Unable to work	6	18	*
Employed	7	29	1
In school	11	44	*
Unemployed	13	60	3
Residence			
Central city	15	35	1
Suburban	6	26	1
Rural	3	21	1

	Rates per 1,000 persons		
	Burglary	House-hold larceny	Motor vehicle theft
Age of household head			
12-19	218	184	29
20-34	115	156	25
35-49	95	138	20
50-64	68	104	12
65 and over	54	63	7
Race or origin of household head			
White	83	119	16
Black	134	142	24
Other	68	118	13
Hispanic	104	148	29
Non-Hispanic	87	120	17
Income			
Less than $3,000	132	118	12
$3,000-$7,499	99	120	12
$7,500-$9,999	89	121	14
$10,000-$14,999	87	123	20
$15,000-$24,999	80	128	19
$25,000 or more	83	123	18
Number of persons in household			
1	84	77	15
2-3	86	115	17
4-5	93	165	19
6 or more	109	196	21
Form of tenure			
Home owned or being bought	73	110	13
Home rented	115	141	25
Place of residence			
Central city	120	149	26
1,000,000 or more	115	116	38
5,000-999,999	126	166	27
250,000-499,999	129	159	24
50,000-249,999	114	163	15
Outside central city (suburban)	80	119	17
Nonmetropolitan (rural)	68	98	8

* Too few cases in the survey sample to obtain statistically reliable data.
** This rate based on women only; the rate based on the total population is 1.

Source: BJS National Crime Survey, 1981.

Homicide Rates

Both the Uniform Crime Reports and statistics from the Public Health Department indicate that the homicide rate has been rising since 1961. Reasons for the rise in the homicide rate include the fact that babies born during the "baby boom" reached age sixteen in the early 1960s. Since violent victimization is more prevalent among people under age thirty, it might be expected that the homicide rate would increase as a large proportion of the population reached the victimization-prone ages.

The Relationship Between Victim and Offender

When people worry about crime, they are most often worried about being attacked by strangers. This fear is frequently justifiable: With the exception of murder and rape, most violent crimes are committed by strangers. Males, blacks, and young people face the greatest risk of violent crime by strangers, and are victimized by violent strangers at an annual rate almost triple that of women. Blacks are more than twice as likely as whites to be robbed by strangers.

> *Most violent crimes except murder and rape are committed by strangers.*

The risk of robbery is less for older people, but this may be because many older people are no longer physically able to move about outside their homes and many others may fear crime and, consequently, remain at home most of the time. It may be that older people who are active and mobile may be at as much risk as the general population.

Figure 4–2.   *Race of Victims and Offenders.*

Victims and offenders are of the same race in 3 out of 4 violent crimes.

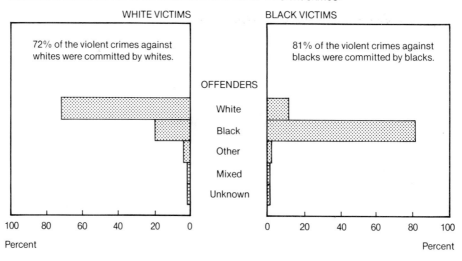

Table 4–3. **Involvement of Weapons in Crime.**

Except for homicide, most violent crimes do not involve the use of weapons

Weapon use	Homicide	Rape	Robbery	Assault**
Firearm	62%	7%	18%	9%
Knife	19	15	21	9
Other	13	1*	9	14
Type unknown	0	2*	2	1
None used	6	77	54	68
Total	100%	100%	100%	100%

Note: Because some victimizations involve more than one type of weapon, detail may add to more than 100%.
*Estimate is based on 10 or fewer samples and is therefore statistically unreliable.
**Includes simple assaults, which by definition do not involve the use of a weapon.

Source: National Crime Survey, 1981.
Uniform Crime Report, 1981.

Women are more vulnerable than men to assaults by acquaintances and relatives, with two-thirds of all assaults on divorced and separated women being committed by acquaintances and relatives. Spouses or former spouses committed only 5 percent of the assaults by single offenders. In almost three-fourths of spouse versus spouse assaults, the victim was divorced or seprated at the time of the incident.

More than half of all homicides are committed by someone known to the victim. Acquaintances commit more than 39 percent of all homicides; relatives commit 17 percent of all homicides.

It is of interest to note that victims and offenders are usually of the same race, as summarized in Figure 4–2.

Use of Weapons in Victimization

Except for homicide, most violent crimes do not involve the use of weapons (see Table 4–3). When a weapon is used, the likelihood that a victim will lose property in a robbery attempt is greater. The likelihood of losing property is:

- Eighty percent if the robber wields a gun.
- Sixty percent if the robber wields a knife.
- Fifty-four percent if the robber is unarmed or threatens the victim with a stick, bottle, club, or other such weapon.

However, according to statistics, the likelihood of being injured by a stranger is less if the stranger is armed. The likelihood of injury to a robbery victim is:

- Fifty-three percent if the robber displays a stick, bottle, or other such weapon.

Table 4-4.	Use of Weapons in Assaults on Law Enforcement Officers.

Means of assault	% of all assaults	% resulting in personal injury
Firearm	6%	18%
Knife	3	34
Other weapon	8	41
Hands, fists, feet, etc.	83	36
Total	100%	

Source: FBI Uniform Crime Reports, 1981.

■ Thirty-four percent if the robber is unarmed.

■ Twenty-five percent if the robber is armed with a knife.

■ Seventeen percent if the robber is armed with a gun.

One logical explanation for this is that victims will be less likely to resist a robber armed with a gun or knife.

Likewise, police officers assaulted by gun bearing offenders sustained the lowest percentage of injuries (see Table 4-4). This is not to imply that a gun wielding offender is not a threat to citizens and law enforcement officers. Of the 91 law enforcement officers killed in the line of duty in 1981, three-quarters (69 officers) were killed by handguns, 12 by rifles and 5 by shotguns. Only five died from other than firearm wounds: one was stabbed, two were struck by vehicles, one was killed by a blunt instrument, and one was drowned.

And, as noted previously, more than half of all homicides are committed with handguns (see Figure 4-3).

How Victims Protect Themselves

Victims rarely respond by wielding a weapon. However, rape victims are more likely to use force, try a verbal response, or attract attention, and are less likely than others to do nothing to protect themselves. In contrast, robbery victims are least likely to try to talk themselves out of being victimized and the most likely to do nothing, as summarized in Table 4-5.

Of all responses reported by victims to the National Crime Survey, physical force, trying to attract attention, and doing nothing to protect oneself or property resulted in the highest proportions of seriously injured victims (16 percent, 14 percent, and 12 percent, respectively). In contrast, those who tried to talk themselves out of the situation or took nonviolent evasive actions were less likely to incur serious injury (both six percent).

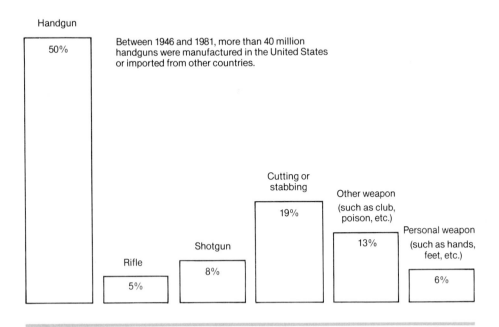

Figure 4–3.   **Weapons Used to Commit Homicide.**

Half of all homicides are committed with handguns.

Handgun

50%

Between 1946 and 1981, more than 40 million handguns were manufactured in the United States or imported from other countries.

Cutting or stabbing

19%

Other weapon

(such as club, poison, etc.)

13%

Personal weapon

(such as hands, feet, etc.)

6%

Shotgun

8%

Rifle

5%

Victims of violent crime can protect themselves by returning physical force, by verbal response, by attracting attention, by nonviolent evasion, or by brandishing a weapon.

Crime's Effect on Its Victims

National Crime Survey and UCR data suggest that losses from personal and household crime exceeded $10 billion in 1980 and that 2 million injuries or deaths resulted from violent crime.

Violent crime can affect its victim physically, economically, and emotionally.

The economic impact of crime must also take into consideration time lost from work, medical costs, and the introduction of security measures to prevent future victimization.

Simon, Witte, et al. (1982) estimate the total income for the "underground economy" to be between $170 and $300 billion in 1980. They suggest that the social cost of underground activity included lost tax revenues, treatment programs

Table 4–5.   **How Victims of Violent Crime Protect Themselves.**

Victim response*	Percent of victims who used response by type of crime*		
	Rape	Robbery	Assault
Weapons use Used or brandished gun or knife	1%	2%	2%
Physical force Used or tried physical force	33	23	23
Verbal response Threatened, argued, reasoned, etc. with offender	17	8	13
Attracting attention Tried to get help, attract attention, scare offender away	15	7	6
Nonviolent evasion Resisted without force, used evasive action	10	11	19
Other	5	4	7
No self-protective actions	19	45	30
Total	100% (873)	100% (5.868)	100% (24.876)

*Victim self-protective responses are listed in the table in order of assertiveness. If victims indicated that they took more than one type of action, only the most assertive action was used in the analysis.

Source: BJS National Crime Survey, 1973-79.

for drug abusers, higher insurance premiums, and increased law enforcement efforts. In fact, the entire cost of the criminal justice system is an indirect cost of crime.

The economic impact of crime usually hits the poor the hardest. The Bureau of Justice Statistics found that in 1980 the relative impact per incident was five times greater on families with yearly incomes of less than $6,000 than for those with incomes of $25,000 or more, but that the gap has been narrowing in recent years.

Crime Rates Compared with Other Life Events

It is human nature to worry about the misfortunes that might come one's way and to try to protect against such misfortunes. The rates of some violent crimes are higher than those of some other serious life events (see Table 4–6).

> *The chance of being a victim of a violent crime, with or without injury, is greater than that of being hurt in a traffic accident, being affected by divorce, death from cancer, or injury or death from fire. However, a person is much more likely to die from natural causes than as a result of a criminal victimization.*

Table 4–6.   *Comparison of Crime Rates with Other Serious Life Event Rates.*

How do crime rates compare with the rates of other life events?

Events	Rate per 1,000 adults per year*	Events	Rate per 1,000 adults per year*
Accidental injury, all circumstances	290	Heart disease death	4
Accidental injury at home	105	Cancer death	2
Personal theft	82	Rape (women only)	2
Accidental injury at work	68	Accidental death, all circumstances	0.5
Violent victimization	33		
Assault (aggravated and simple)	25	Motor vehicle accident death	0.3
Injury in motor vehicle accident	23	Pneumonia/influenza death	0.3
Divorce	23	Suicide	0.2
Death, all causes	11	Injury from fire	0.1
Serious (aggravated) assault	9	Homicide/legal intervention death	0.1
Death of spouse	9	Death from fire	0.03
Robbery	7		

These rates are an approximate assessment of your chances of becoming a victim of these events. More precise estimates can be derived by taking account of such factors as age, sex, race, place of residence, and lifestyle. Findings are based on 1979-81 data, but there is little variation in rates from year to year.

*These rates have been standardized to exclude children (those under age 15 to 17, depending on the series). Fire injury/death data are based on the total population, because no age-specific data are available in this series.

Sources: Current estimates from the National Health Interview Survey, United States, 1981, Vital and Health Statistics Series 10, no. 141, October 1982; *Advance report of final divorce statistics,* 1979, Monthly Vital Statistics Report, vol. 30, no. 2, supplement. May 29, 1981; *Advance report on final mortality statistics,* Monthly Vital Statistics Report, vol. 31, no. 6, supplement, September 30, 1982, National Center to Health Statistics, U.S. Public Health Service, Washington, D.C. *Preliminary estimates of the population of the United States, by age, sex, and race. 1970 to 1981,* Series P-25, no. 917, U.S. Bureau of the Census, Washington, D.C., 1982. "Fire loss in the United States during 1981," Michael J. Karter, Jr., *Fire Journal,* vol. 76, no. 5, National Fire Protection Association, Qunicy, Mass., September 1982.

Fear of Victimization

Public opinion polls have found that people do fear crime in general, but they generally feel their own neighborhoods are relatively safe. If someone in the neighborhood is victimized, however, the entire neighborhood may feel much more vulnerable.

Interestingly, the people who express the greatest fear of being victimized are females and the elderly, and, as previously stated, they are at lower risk than other segments of the population. Whether they are at lower risk because they take measures to reduce their chances of being victimized is not known. If the elderly, for example, restrict their activities because they are afraid of becoming victims of crime, this fear is, in itself, a sort of victimization.

Reporting of Crimes to the Authorities

Chapter 3 made reference to the "dark figures" of crime—the vast amount of crime that goes unreported. Two-thirds of all crimes are not reported to the police. The statistics must be interpreted with caution, however. It is certain, nonetheless, that a great deal of crime is not reported to the police. Reporting rates have been found to vary by type of crime and by age and sex of the victim, but not by the victim's race. In 1981 reporting rates were higher for violent crimes than for personal crimes (47 percent versus 27 percent), for female than for male victims of violent crimes (52 percent versus 44 percent), and for older than for younger victims. Reporting rates were also higher for motor vehicle theft than for burglary and for household larceny. Homeowners and high income groups were more likely to report household crimes than renters and low income groups.

• *Two-thirds of all crimes are not reported to the police.*

Reasons for not reporting violent crimes to the police were varied, with the most common being private/personal matter (see Table 4–7).

Table 4–7.   ***Reasons Given for Not Reporting Violent Crimes to the Police.***

Many violent crimes were unreported because they were "private matters," and many crimes of theft were "not important enough to report"

Percent of victimizations not reported to the police, by reason for not reporting

	Private/ personal matter	Nothing could be done/lack of proof	Not important enough	Reported to some- one else	Police wouldn't want to be bothered	Too inconvenient	Fear of reprisal	All other reasons	Not given
Crimes of violence									
Rape	35%	18%	4%	8%	*%	2%	16%	42%	2%
Robbery	15	21	15	9	9	6	7	39	5
Aggravated assault	31	10	22	11	7	3	5	22	4
Simple assault	32	8	30	14	7	2	3	14	3
Crimes of theft									
Burglary	9	23	23	7	10	2	1	44	2
Larceny	8	23	39	3	10	2	1	32	2
Motor vehicle theft	12	18	16	8	8	3	*	52	1

Note: Percents add to more than 100% for each type of crime because some people gave more than one reason for not reporting.
*0 or less than 0.5%.

Source: BJS National Crime Survey, 1981.

Victim Compensation Programs

As noted in the *Encyclopedia of Crime and Justice* (1983, p. 1606): "The use of public monies to aid persons victimized by crime has roots in antiquity. The policy goes back at least to the ancient Babylonian Code of Hammurabi which decreed communal responsibility when it proved impossible to establish individual blame for a crime. . . . Such compensatory approaches were also characteristic of Anglo-Saxon law, but they gave way in the thirteenth and fourteenth centuries to a system of state-operated criminal prosecution."

The encyclopedia goes on to say that during the nineteenth century several reformers advocated reviving the system of compensating crime victims, but it was not until the 1960s that the movement gained momentum. This momentum was initiated in large measure by an article in the London *Observer* written by Margery Fry, proposing that victims should no longer have to rely on civil lawsuits to recover losses sustained because of violent crimes. According to the encyclopedia: "Fry cited a 1951 court award of £11,500 to a man blinded in an assault. The amount was to be paid at the rate of five shillings a week, which meant that it would take 442 years for the victim to recover the full amount. Fry wrote: 'The logical way of providing for criminally inflicted injuries would be to tax every adult citizen . . . to cover a risk to which each is exposed.' "

In 1965 California initiated the first state-wide victim compensation program, and since then more than half of the states have started similar programs. These programs supplement existing programs that assist victims, such as rape crisis centers and prosecutors' victim assistance programs.

In some programs, if a victim dies, the family is reimbursed for out-of-pocket medical and funeral expenses. Most states deny awards to a victim who provoked the crime, was involved in an illegal activity when the crime occurred, or was related to the offender. Some states require that the victim be a state resident, not a visitor to the state.

> Thirty-seven states and the District of Columbia have victim compensation programs. Most programs provide for recovery of medical expenses and some lost earnings.

In 1980 victim compensation awards totaled $34 million. Fourteen states pay for their victim compensation programs through penalty assessments against convicted offenders; another fourteen states use legislative appropriations; and the remaining states use a combination of these two sources. See Table 4–8 for a list of states having victim compensation programs, as well as the range of awards and how victims can qualify.

Table 4–8.   *Summary of Current Victim Compensation Programs in the United States.*

37 States and the District of Columbia have compensation programs to help victims of violent crime

State	Financial award	To qualify, victim must—		
		show financial need	report to police within:	file claim within:
Alaska	$0-40,000	No	5 days	24 months
California	$100-23,000	Yes	*	12 months
Colorado	$25- 1,500	No	3 days	6 months
Connecticut	$100-10,000	No	5 days	24 months
Delaware	$25-10,000	No	*	12 months
D.C.	$0-25,000	Yes	7 days	6 months
Florida	$0-10,000	Yes	3 days	12 months
Hawaii	$0-10,000	No	*	18 months
Illinois	$0-15,000	No	3 days	12 months
Indiana	$100-10,000	No	2 days	3 months
Iowa	$0- 2,000	No	1 day	6 months
Kansas	$100-10,000	Yes	3 days	12 months
Kentucky	$100-15,000	Yes	2 days	12 months
Louisiana	$250-10,000	No	3 days	12 months
Maryland	$100-45,000	Yes	2 days	6 months
Massachusetts	$100-10,000	No	2 days	12 months
Michigan	$100-15,000	Yes	2 days	1 month
Minnesota	$100-25,000	No	5 days	12 months
Missouri	$200-10,000	No	2 days	12 months
Montana	$0-25,000	No	3 days	12 months
Nebraska	$0-10,000	No	3 days	24 months
Nevada	$100- 5,000	Yes	5 days	12 months
New Jersey	$100-25,000	No	90 days	24 months
New Mexico	$0-12,500	No	30 days	12 months
New York	$0-20,000†	Yes	7 days	12 months
North Dakota	$100-25,000	No	3 days	12 months
Ohio	$0-25,000	No	3 days	12 months
Oklahoma	$0-10,000	No	3 days	12 months
Oregon	$250-23,000	No	3 days	6 months
Pennsylvania	$100-25,000	No	3 days	12 months
Rhode Island	$0-25,000	No	10 days	24 months
South Carolina	$300-10,000	No	2 days	6 months
Tennessee	$100-10,000	No	2 days	12 months
Texas	$0-50,000	Yes	3 days	6 months
Virginia	$100-10,000	Yes	2 days	6 months
Washington	$200-15,000†	No	3 days	12 months
West Virginia	$0-20,000	No	3 days	24 months
Wisconsin	$0-12,000	No	5 days	24 months

*Must report but no time limit specified.
†Plus unlimited medical expenses.
Source: State Legislatures, November/December 1981; with additions from the National Organization of Victim Assistance.

Summary

In 1981 almost a third (30 percent) of all households were victimized by violence or theft. Households at greatest risk are those rented by Hispanics in central cities, headed by younger people, and having more than six people living in the same household.

Individuals having the highest victimization risk are young, black, unemployed males living in the city; those having the lowest victimization risk are elderly white females living in rural areas.

Most violent crimes except murder and rape are committed by strangers. Victims of violent crime have protected themselves by returning physical force, by verbal response, by attracting attention, by nonviolent evasion, or by brandishing a weapon.

Violent crime can affect its victim physically, economically and emotionally. The chance of being a victim of a violent crime, with or without injury, is greater than that of being hurt in a traffic accident or being affected by divorce, or death from fire. However, a person is much more likely to die from natural causes than as a result of a criminal victimization.

When people are victimized, they often do not report it to police. In fact, two-thirds of all crimes are not reported to police. If a person is seriously injured, a victim compensation program may be available. Thirty-seven states and the District of Columbia have such programs. Most provide for recovery of medical expenses and some for lost earnings.

Application

In 1977 a National Survey of Crime Severity (NSCS) was conducted. This survey described 204 illegal events, ranging from playing hooky from school to planting a bomb that killed twenty people in a public building. This nation-wide survey is the largest measure ever made of how the public ranks the seriousness of specific crimes.

The results of this survey follow. As you read through the results, see if you agree with or if you would change some of the ratings. Also see if you can see any generalizations that can be made about how the public views the seriousness of various types of crimes.

1. Would you change any of the ratings? If so, which ones?
2. Can you make any generalizations based on the findings?

Table 4–9.   How Do People Rank the Severity of Crime?

Severity score and offense

72.1—Planting a bomb in a public building. The bomb explodes and 20 people are killed.

52.8—A man forcibly rapes a woman. As a result of physical injuries, she dies.

43.2—Robbing a victim at gunpoint. The victim struggles and is shot to death.

39.2—A man stabs his wife. As a result, she dies.

35.7—Intentionally injuring a victim. As a result, the victim dies.

33.8—Running a narcotics ring.

27.9—A woman stabs her husband. As a result, he dies.

26.3—An armed person skyjacks an airplane and demands to be flown to another country.

25.9—A man forcibly rapes a woman. No other physical injury occurs.

24.9—Intentionally setting fire to a building causing $100,000 worth of damage.

22.9—A parent beats his young child with his fists. The child requires hospitalization.

21.2—Kidnaping a victim.

20.7—Selling heroin to others for resale.

19.5—Smuggling heroin into the country.

19.5—Killing a victim by recklessly driving an automobile.

17.9—Robbing a victim of $10 at gunpoint. The victim is wounded and requires hospitalization.

16.9—A man drags a woman into an alley, tears her clothes, but flees before she is physically harmed or sexually attacked.

16.4—Attempting to kill a victim with a gun. The gun misfires and the victim escapes unharmed.

15.9—A teenager boy beats his mother with his fists. The mother requires hospitalization.

15.5—Breaking into a bank at night and stealing $100,000.

14.1—A doctor cheats on claims he makes to a Federal health insurance plan for patient services.

13.9—A legislator takes a bribe from a company to vote for a law favoring the company.

13.0—A factory knowingly gets rid of its waste in a way that pollutes the water supply of a city.

12.2—Paying a witness to give false testimony in a criminal trial.

12.0—A police officer takes a bribe not to interfere with an illegal gambling operation.

12.0—Intentionally injuring a victim. The victim is treated by a doctor and hospitalized.

11.8—A man beats a stranger with his fists. He requires hospitalization.

11.4—Knowlingly lying under oath during a trial.

11.2—A company pays a bribe to a legislator to vote for a law favoring the company.

10.9—Stealing property worth $10,000 from outside a building.

10.5—Smuggling marijuana into the country for resale.

10.4—Intentionally hitting a victim with a lead pipe. The victim requires hospitalization.

10.3—Illegally selling barbiturates, such as prescription sleeping pills, to others for resale.

10.3—Operating a store that knowingly sells stolen property.

10.0—A government official intentionally hinders the investigation of a criminal offense.

9.7—Breaking into a school and stealing equipment worth $1,000.

9.7—Walking into a public museum and stealing a painting worth $1,000.

9.6—Breaking into a home and stealing $1,000.

9.6—A police officer knowlingly makes a false arrest.

9.5—A public official takes $1,000 of public money for his own use.

9.4—Robbing a victim of $10 at gunpoint. No physical harm occurs.

9.3—Threatening to seriously injure a victim.

9.2—Several large companies illegally fix the retail prices of their products.

8.6—Performing an illegal abortion.

8.5—Selling marijuana to others for resale.

8.5—Intentionally injuring a victim. The victim is treated by a doctor but is not hospitalized.

8.2—Knowing that a shipment of cooking oil is bad, a store owner decides to sell it anyway. Only one bottle is sold and the purchaser is treated by a doctor but not hospitalized.

7.9—A teenage boy beats his father with his fists. The father requires hospitalization.

7.7—Knowing that a shipment of cooking oil is bad, a store owner decides to sell it anyway.

7.5—A person, armed with a lead pipe, robs a victim of $10. No physical harm occurs.

Answers

1. Answers will vary considerably.

2. It appears that people agree that violent crime is more serious than property crime. Other things you may have noticed include the fact that people seem to take into account the ability of the victim to protect him/ herself, the extent of injury and loss, the type of business or organization from which property is stolen, and the relationship of the offender to the

7.4—Illegally getting monthly welfare checks.

7.3—Threatening a victim with a weapon unless the victim gives money. The victim gives $10 and is not harmed.

7.3—Breaking into a department store and stealing merchandise worth $1,000.

7.2—Signing someone else's name to a check and cashing it.

6.9—Stealing property worth $1,000 from outside a building.

6.5—Using heroin.

6.5—An employer refuses to hire a qualified person because of that person's race.

6.4—Getting customers for a prostitute.

6.3—A person, free on bail for committing a serious crime, purposefully fails to appear in court on the day of his trial.

6.2—An employee embezzles $1,000 from his employer.

5.4—Possessing some heroin for personal use.

5.4—A real estate agent refuses to sell a house to a person because of that person's race.

5.4—Threatening to harm a victim unless the victim gives money. The victim gives $10 and is not harmed.

5.3—Loaning money at an illegally high interest rate.

5.1—A man runs his hands over the body of a female victim, then runs away.

5.1—A person, using force, robs a victim of $10. No physical harm occurs.

4.9—Snatching a handbag containing $10 from a victim on the street.

4.8—A man exposes himself in public.

4.6—Carrying a gun illegally.

4.5—Cheating on Federal income tax return.

4.4—Picking a victim's pocket of $100.

4.2—Attempting to break into a home but running away when a police car approaches.

3.8—Turning in a false fire alarm.

3.7—A labor union official illegally threatens to organize a strike if an employer hires nonunion workers.

3.6—Knowingly passing a bad check.

3.6—Stealing property worth $100 from outside a building.

3.5—Running a place that permits gambling to occur illegally.

3.2—An employer illegally threatens to fire employees if they join a labor union.

2.4—Knowingly carrying an illegal knife.

2.2—Stealing $10 worth of merchandise from the counter of a department store.

2.1—A person is found firing a rifle for which he knows he has no permit.

2.1—A woman engages in prostitution.

1.9—Making an obscene phone call.

1.9—A store owner knowingly puts "large" eggs into containers marked "extra large."

1.8—A youngster under 16 years old is drunk in public.

1.8—Knowingly being a customer in a place where gambling occurs illegally.

1.7—Stealing property worth $10 from outside a building.

1.6—Being a customer in a house of prostitution.

1.6—A male, over 16 years of age, has sexual relations with a willing female under 16.

1.5—Taking barbiturates, such as sleeping pills, without a legal prescription.

1.5—Intentionally shoving or pushing a victim. No medical treatment is required.

1.4—Smoking marijuana.

1.3—Two persons willingly engage in a homosexual act.

1.1—Disturbing the neighborhood with loud, noisy behavior.

1.1—Taking bets on the numbers.

1.1—A group continues to hang around a corner after being told to break up by a police officer.

0.9—A youngster under 16 years old runs away from home.

0.8—Being drunk in public.

0.7—A youngster under 16 years old breaks a curfew law by being out on the street after the hour permitted by law.

0.6—Trespassing in the backyard of a private home.

0.3—A person is a vagrant. That is, he has no home and no visible means of support.

0.2—A youngster under 16 years old plays hooky from school.

Source: The seriousness of crime: Results of a national survey. Center for Studies in Criminology and Criminal Law, University of Pennsylvania, Philadelphia. The entire questionnaire will be published verbatim in a forthcoming technical report of the Bureau of Justice Statistics. (The entries here have been slightly edited.)

victim. You may also have noticed that white-collar crimes such as fraud, cheating on income taxes, and accepting bribes are viewed as seriously as (or more seriously than) many of the conventional property and violent crimes. In addition, within particular categories of crime, deciding severity was affected by whether an injury occurred and the extent of property loss.

Discussion Questions

1. Does our state have victim compensation laws? If so, how do they compare to those provided in the other states?
2. Have you ever been victimized? Has a member of your family? A friend or neighbor? What were the effects?
3. Why is it so difficult for a victim of a crime to accept its consequences?
4. Thirty-seven states and the District of Columbia have victim compensation programs. What one common concern do they all share?
5. How can prosecutors assist victims in their experiences with the criminal justice system?

References

Chambliss, W., and Seidman, R. *Law, order and power.* 2d ed. Reading, Mass.: Addison-Wesley Publishing Co., 1982.

Encyclopedia of crime and justice. New York: The Free Press, 1983.

Finn, P., and Lee, B. *Serving two masters: The issue of victim assistance.* Cambridge, Mass.: Abt Associates, 1981.

President's Task Force on Victims of Crime. *Final report.* Washington, D.C.: U.S. Government Printing Office, 1982.

Reiss, A.J., Jr., and Biderman, A.D. *Data sources on white-collar lawbreaking.* National Institute of Justice, U.S. Department of Justice. Washington, D.C.: U.S. Government Printing Office, 1980.

Simon, C.P., et al. *Beating the system: The underground economy.* Boston: Auburn House Publishing Company, 1982.

U.S. Department of Justice. Attorney General's Task Force on Violent Crime. *Final report.* Washington, D.C.: U.S. Government Printing Office, 1981.

U.S. Department of Justice. Bureau of Justice Statistics. *Report to the nation on crime and justice.* Washington, D.C.: U.S. Government Printing Office, 1983.

Wright, J.D.; Rossi, P.H.; and Daly, K. *Under the gun: Weapons, crime and violence in America.* New York: Aldine Publishing Co., 1983.

Organized crime is deeply involved in gambling, drugs, prostitution, pornography, loansharking, and infiltration of legitimate businesses.

Organized Crime in the United States

A National Threat

Do You Know . . .

- How organized crime is usually defined?

- What names organized crime is known by?

- What two characteristics of organized crime set it apart from other crimes committed by a group of individuals?

- How the Mafia originated?

- What the typical structure of organized crime is?

- What types of crime are most frequently engaged in by members of organized crime?

- What is organized crime's largest source of revenue?

- What specific threats organized crime poses to the United States?

- What special problems organized crime presents to law enforcement?

- What major federal legislation has been enacted to deal with organized crime?

> *Organized crime will put a man in the White House some day, and he won't know it until they hand him the bill.*
>
> —*Ralph Salerno*

Introduction

According to the *Report of the Task Force on Organized Crime* (1976, p. 7):

> Organized crime exists in both urban and rural areas. . . . Organized crime income is presently invested in a variety of businesses, including liquor establishments, nightclubs, health spas, travel agencies, massage parlors, motels, real estate agencies, nursing homes, and pornographic book stores and films. There are no "safe" enterprises, for organized crime may choose to infiltrate and take over wherever there is potential profit. Tactics adopted by organized crime include homicide, arson, and intimidation.

Organized Crime Defined

Definitions of **organized crime** vary, from lengthy, detailed statements to simple eleven-word definitions. California's definition of organized crime is one of the more detailed (*Organized Crime*, 1976, p. 214):

> Organized crime consists of two or more persons who, with continuity of purpose, engage in one or more of the following activities:
>
> 1. The supplying of illegal goods and services, i.e., vice, loan-sharking, etc. . . .
> 2. Predatory crime, i.e., theft, assault, etc. . . .

Several distinct types of criminal activity fall within this definition of organized crime. The types may be grouped into five general categories:

1. Racketeering.
2. Vice Operations (narcotics, prostitution, loansharking, gambling).
3. Theft/fence rings (fraud, bunco schemes, fraudulent document passers, burglary rings, car thieves, truck hijackers).
4. Gangs (youth gangs, outlaw motorcycle gangs, prison gangs).
5. Terrorists.

A New York Conference on Combatting Organized Crime (Office of the New York Counsel to the Governor, 1966) defined organized crime as follows:

Organized crime is the product of a self-perpetutating, criminal conspiracy to wring exhorbitant profits from our society by any means—fair and foul, legal and illegal. Despite personnel changes, the conspiratorial entity continues. It is a malignant parasite which fattens on human weakness. It survives on fear and corruption. By one or another means, it obtains a high degree of immunity from the law. It is totalitarian in its organization. A way of life, it imposes rigid discipline on underlings who do the dirty work while the top men of organized crime are generally insulated from the criminal act and the consequent danger of prosecution.

Rhodes (1984, p. 46) cites a 1967 Task Force Report that describes organized crime as a "society":

Organized crime is a society that seeks to operate outside the control of the American people and their governments. It involves thousands of criminals, working within structures as complex as those of any large corporation, subject to laws more rigidly enforced than those of legitimate governments. Its actions are not impulsive, but rather the result of intricate conspiracies, carried on over many years and aimed at gaining control over whole fields of activity in order to amass huge profits.

And, as noted by Rhodes (1984, p. 47), by 1971 the National Advisory Commission recognized the wide variety of types of organized crime in its definition.

Organized crimes is a type of conspiratorial crime, sometimes involving the hierarchial coordination of a number of persons in the planning of illegal acts, or in the pursuit of a legitimate objective by unlawful means. Organized crime involves continuous commitment by key members, although some individuals with specialized skills may participate only briefly in the ongoing conspiracies.

The Task Force on Organized Crime (*Organized Crime*, p. 7) notes:

In nonlegal terms, organized crime has been called everything from non-existent to a vast conspiracy. As one observer of the organized crime scene noted, "For most purposes the term 'organized crime' has no precise legal configuration, although some specific attributes of syndicated criminal operations can be accurately defined."

Another problem encountered in discussing the problem of organized crime and possible solutions to it is the fact that organized crime itself is not illegal. According to Cressey (1969, p. 229):

It is not against the law for an individual or group of individuals rationally to plan, establish, develop, and administer an organization designed for the perpetration of crime. Neither is it against the law for a person to participate in such an organization. What is against the law is bet-taking, usury, smuggling and selling narcotics and untaxed liquor, extortion, murder, and conspiracy to commit these and other specific crimes. Because "organized crime'' is merely a social category, rather than a legal category, police and other governmental agencies cannot even routinely compile information on it as they do for other categories of crime.

> *Organized crime is a type of conspiratorial crime, sometimes involving the hierarchial coordination of a number of persons in the planning and execution of illegal acts, or in the pursuit of a legitimate objective by unlawful means. Organized crime involves continuous commitment by key members, although some individuals with specialized skills may participate only briefly in the ongoing conspiracies.*

Distinctive Characteristics of Organized Crime

All crime is a threat to our country, but organized crime poses a unique threat. Two features of organized crime, corruption and enforcement powers, set it apart from other types of crime and make it especially threatening, not only to police officers, but to our entire democratic process.

> *Organized crime is distinct from other forms of crime in that it is characterized by corruption and enforcement powers.*

Figure 5–1.   *The Classic Pattern of Organized Crime.*

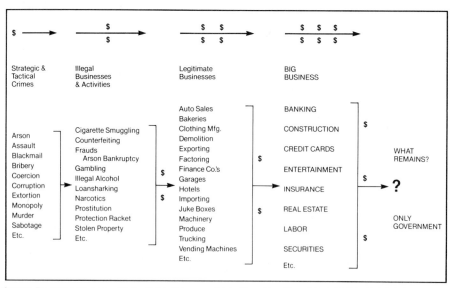

Source: *The Crime Confederation* by Ralph Salerno and John Tompkins. Copyright © 1969 by Ralph Salerno and John S. Tompkins. Used by permission of Doubleday & Company, Inc.

Corruption

The President's Commission on Law Enforcement and Administration *(Challenge of Crime,* 1967, p. 241) drew the following conclusions about organized crime in the United States.

> In many ways organized crime is the most sinister kind of crime in America. The men who control it have become rich and powerful by encouraging the needy to gamble, by luring the troubled to destroy themselves with drugs, by extorting profits from honest and hardworking businessmen, by collecting usury from those in financial plight, by maiming or murdering those who oppose them, by bribing those sworn to destroy them. Organized crime is not merely a few preying on a few. In a very real sense, it is dedicated to subverting not only American institutions, but the very decency and integrity that are the most cherished attributes of a free society. As the leaders of Cosa Nostra and their racketeering allies pursue their conspiracy unmolested, in open and continuous defiance of the law, they preach a sermon that all too many Americans heed: The government is for sale; lawlessness is the road to wealth; honesty is a pitfall and morality a trap for suckers.

Corruption poses an extremely serious threat to police professionalism, discipline, and efficiency, and the greatest source of that corruption is organized crime. (The types of corruption associated with organized crime are illustrated in Table 5–1.)

Enforcement Powers

A second unique characteristic of organized crime is the use of enforcement activities. Perhaps the gravest threat of organized crime is this assumption of enforcement powers. In our society, only legitimate government has the power to coerce its citizens through due process and the criminal justice system. When another group, such as organized crime, usurps that coercive power, it nullifies our legitimate government.

Organized crime usually has one or more fixed positions for "enforcers" who maintain organizational integrity by arranging for the maiming and killing of recalcitrant members and those who oppose them.

Unfortunately, organized crime's violent tactics seem to have caught the public's fancy, as evidenced by the tremendous success of books and movies about the Mafia. The public interest in gangsters' activities implies an element of voyeurism in participating vicariously in something illegal, yet exotic and tacitly approved. Because of the popularity of books and movies concerning organized crime, many Americans are much more aware of its existence than was formerly true, but few realize the true threat it poses to our society.

A History of Organized Crime

Organized crime in America is almost synonymous with the Mafia or Cosa Nostra. Therefore, we begin our mini-history of organized crime with the origins of the Mafia.

> *Organized crime has many names including the mob, the syndicate, the rackets, the Mafia, and Cosa Nostra.*

Mafia is an Italian word which refers to the lawless, violent bands of criminals who engaged in cattle-stealing, kidnapping, and extortion in Sicily in the nineteenth and early twentieth centuries. Members of the Mafia were bound by a

Table 5–1.   *A Typology of Organized Crime Payoffs.*

Participants	How Obligations Are Incurred	How the Debts Are Paid
Elected Officials (Federal)	Support in political campaigns. Trips, vacations on company expense accounts, cash through foundations, and cash bribes through lobbyists, etc.	Political appointments Contracts Personal favors Paroles, pardons
Appointed Staff	Campaign workers Liaison with revenue sources Cash payoffs	Hired as staff worker Retains contact with revenue sources Conducts business for elected official
The Elected Official	State Campaign contributions Trips on private accounts Cash through lobbyists Tips on investments, i.e., public franchises and licenses Local Campaign contributions Promise to self interest groups—gamblers, etc. Money to citizens' committees during preelection campaign Cash payoffs through lobbyists	Contracts Allocations of franchises Granting licenses such as liquor Contracts for local service— garbage, ambulance, towing, etc. Abstain from enforcing certain type of laws
The Judge	All Levels Campaign contributions Cash payoffs	Favorable decisions Probation, parole and select court assignment
The Lawyer	Client contacts and referrals Campaign workers Liaison with business and criminal clientele Cash payoffs (fees)	Appointments to positions to keep contacts with proper clients Consultants on contracts, crime commissions, etc.
The Police	All Levels Political patronage Campaign contributions to elected offices Budget manipulation Cash payoffs	Select enforcement methods Preferential treatment in the degree of enforcement Lack of enforcement

Source: Denny F. Pace, Jimmie C. Styles, *Organized Crime: Concepts and Control* © 1975, p. 31. Reprinted by permission of Prentice-Hall, Inc., Englewood Cliffs, New Jersey.

rigid ethical code, the **omerta**, which required any member who suffered an in-justice to take personal vengeance without contacting the law. The Mafia was not a centralized organization; it had no official hierarchy, but rather it consisted of many small groups, each autonomous in its own district.

The Mafia used terrorist methods against the peasant electorate to obtain political office in many communities, giving them influence with the police force and legal access to weapons.

Late in the nineteenth century the Italian government's efforts to suppress the Mafia caused many of its leaders to leave the country. Many came to the United States and maintained their organizations here. They found ample opportunity for their traditional occupation. New immigrants, bewildered by America's language and customs and gathered together in "Little Italys" in New York, Chicago, New Orleans, and other cities, were easy prey for the Mafia who had brought all their talents and philosophy with them. Word of their success quickly reached Sicily, and many more Mafia members came to America.

Prosperous Italian farmers and merchants who understood the Mafia's capabilities were among the first targets of the brotherhood. A truck farmer, for example, might receive a notice to leave a hundred dollars in a shed "or else." The note would be written in the unmistakable Mafia dialect and signed with the Black Hand. If the farmer did not do as instructed, he would find a black hand stenciled on his fence, shed, or house—the final warning. The truck farmer would pay; he would not go to the police, for he knew that even in Italy the police were helpless against the Mafia. In America the police could not possibly know their power, and they were not especially friendly to the new immigrants. The Italian immigrants believed they must pay or be killed. The police were, for the most part, completely unaware of the situation.

Toward the end of the nineteenth century, however, the situation changed. The first American policeman to openly oppose the Mafia was Chief David Hennessey of New Orleans. A group of mafiosi (Mafia members) headed by Antonio and Carlo Matranga controlled the New Orleans docks, the center of the country's rapidly growing fruit trade from Latin America. No freighter could un-load until the importer paid them a fee. No longshoreman would work without orders from a Mafia boss. Since dock racketeering was common all along the seaboard, the importers did not complain.

Then, in 1890, a series of brutal murders shook the city (Gage, 1972, p. 73): "One Italian had his throat cut and was dumped into a canal. Another, almost decapitated, was found with what was left of his head stuffed into his own roaring fireplace. Shotguns, bombs and daggers—the traditional Mafia methods—were accounting for several murders a week."

Chief Hennessey, an honest, intelligent, imaginative policeman, personally conducted a thorough investigation and came up against the system created by the New Orleans Mafia. Suddenly he lost all support. His own police officers, many Italian, would not assist, nor would members of the Italian colony, even though most of them were being extorted by the Mafia.

Hennessey persisted despite numerous warnings and offers of bribes. He continued to piece together the network through which the Matranga family ruled the New Orleans docks. He discovered that the brutal murders resulted from a feud between the Matrangas and the Provenzano brothers who had tried to move in on their territory. Hennessey was able to build a case and was ready to present it to the grand jury. However:

> The brotherhood decided that he had moved in too close and knew too much. A few days before he was to testify, as he was walking home from police headquarters one evening, a salvo of shotgun blasts cut him down. He was terribly wounded, but he managed as he staggered and fell, to pull his service revolver from its holster. Heaving himself up in a last gesture of defiance, he emptied his gun. A detective who happened to be nearby and heard the shooting dashed up and found the chief sitting on the stoop of a house, gun still clutched in his fingers. . . . A few hours later, after a number of violent struggles in the hospital against the paralysis that prevented him from speaking, he was dead (Gage, 1972, p. 74).

Public pressure forced the police to seek out and prosecute those responsible for Chief Hennessey's death. Several Mafia members were captured and brought to trial. However, the Mafia hired the best legal talent available and also bribed and intimidated the jury. The result was that the jury could not decide on the guilt of three of the men, and they found all the rest innocent.

Citizens of New Orleans called a protest meeting which began peacefully, but which erupted into a roaring, bloodthirsty mob of several thousand citizens who marched on the jail, battered down the gates, and dragged the Mafia members out into the street. (The Mafia members had been taken back to the Parish Prison following the trial to complete various legal formalities.) The violent mob hung two Mafia members from a city lamp post and riddled them with bullets. They lined up nine other mafiosi in front of the prison wall and shot them.

Counteractions against the Mafia did not destroy them; they simply made them more secretive, more prone to use terrorist tactics.

A few years later, another wave of Mafia immigration began as the result of Mussolini's decision to make Sicily the political and intellectual center of his Mediterranean Fascist empire. To do this, he realized he must break the brotherhood's rule of the island. He selected Colonel Cesare Mori, a professional policeman who hated the Mafia, to do the job. He gave him extraordinary powers and over a thousand hand-picked policemen. Mori instituted a ruthless campaign of arrests and prosecutions which resulted in another wave of Mafia immigrants to the United States. In Sicily, many of the Mafia members simply stopped operations for a while, waiting for the time when they could again function. Although Mori believed he had crushed the Mafia, he was mistaken.

The new Mafia immigrants joined friends and relatives already established in the United States. Sondern reports that: "By 1925 the Mafia in the United States was reaching new and undreamed of heights of wealth and power as a result of Prohibition and the organizing genius of Al Capone in Chicago and Charlie 'Lucky' Luciano in New York" (Gage, 1972, p. 79).

The Mafia probably originated with the lawless, violent criminal bands who dominated nineteenth-century Sicily. They came to the United States in 1880 and continued their terrorism and extortion. By 1925 they were a wealthy, powerful, highly organized operation.

During Prohibition, the Italian, German, Irish, and Jewish groups competed with each other in racket operations. The Italian groups were successful in switching their enterprises from prostitution and bootlegging to gambling, extortion, and other illegal activities. They consolidated their power through murder and violence.

According to Cressey (1969, p. 9):

Near the end of Prohibition, the basic framework of the current structure of American organized crime . . . was established as the final product of a series of "gangland wars" in which an alliance of Italians and Sicilians first conquered other groups and then fought each other. During these conflicts the Italian-Sicilian alliance was called the "Mafia," among other things. . . . The Italian-Sicilian apparatus set up as a result of a 1930-1931 war between Italian and Sicilian criminals continues to dominate organized crime in America, and it is still called "The Mafia" in many quarters.

Organized criminal activities in the United States are characterized by secrecy, gang wars, violence, and occasional prison sentences. From the early days of the Matrangas and the Provenzano brothers in New Orleans to the present time, constant gang wars and assassinations to control the illicit activities in this country have occurred. There was open warfare in Chicago in 1929 when Al Capone and Bugs Moran fought constantly for control of the underworld traffic in liquor. Finally Capone's gunmen invaded Moran's headquarters, herded seven men into a garage, lined them up against a wall, and killed them in the infamous St. Valentine's Day Massacre.

In 1936 Charles "Lucky" Luciano was sentenced to fifty years in prison on prostitution charges and was subsequently deported to Italy. In 1947 Benjamin "Bugsy" Segal was murdered in his Beverly Hills home. In 1957 Albert Anastasia was gunned down in a barber shop as he was getting a haircut; his assassins were never apprehended. In 1971 Joseph Colombo Sr. was gunned down in a New York Italian Day Rally; he survived but was totally disabled. He ultimately died from the injuries in 1978. In 1972 Joey Gallo was shot to death in Umberto's Clam House in New York's Little Italy, perhaps in retaliation for the assassination attempt on Joseph Colombo Sr.

In addition to violence, leaders of the various organized crime families obtain and maintain their positions of power through a code of conduct similar to, and just as effective as, the Mafia's code. The code requires underlings not to seek police protection, but to be "standup guys," going to prison for the boss if necessary. The code gives the leaders complete power over everyone in the organization. Loyalty, honor, respect, and absolute obedience are ingrained in family members through ritualistic initiations and customs, through monetary rewards, and, when necessary, through violence.

Although no one is to inform to the outside world, if such an event occurs, the organization has its own elaborate system of internal informants. Therefore, the code not only protects leadership, it makes it very difficult for law enforcement to cultivate and maintain informants within the organization. Despite prescribed mechanisms for peaceful settlement of disputes between family members, the boss may order the execution of any family member for any reason.

One of the best known Mafia members, Joseph Valachi, a narcotic traffiker and organized crime baron, was the first man to violate the oath of silence. Valachi was the first to say that the members of the Mafia actually called their organization the Cosa Nostra, which means "our thing." In 1963 Valachi testified before the McClellan Committee in Washington, for the first time exposing the innermost secrets of the Cosa Nostra, naming those responsible for gangland killings, and describing the structure of the organization.

A member of the Mafia for thirty years, Valachi spent a week on the witness stand outlining for national television his life story from his first burglary in 1921 to 1962 when he killed a man in an Atlanta prison yard. Valachi described routine business deals and matter-of-fact murders. He identified hundreds of Cosa Nostra members and described the organization in great detail. It was the first time law enforcement officials in the United States had corroboration that organized crime had a structure.

The Structure of Organized Crime

The President's Commission on Law Enforcement and the Administration of Justice (*Challenge of Crime*, 1967, pp. 192-193) described the basic structure of organized crime:

> Today the core of organized crime in the United States consists of 24 groups operating as criminal cartels in large cities across the Nation. Their membership is exclusively Italian, they are in frequent communication with each other, and their smooth functioning is insured by a national body of overseers. . . .
>
> These 24 groups work with and control other racket groups, whose leaders are of various ethnic derivations. In addition, the thousands of employees who perform the street-level functions of organized crime's gambling, usury, and other illegal activities represent a cross-section of the Nation's population groups.
>
> The scope and effect of their criminal operations and penetration of legitimate businesses vary from area to area. The wealthiest and most influential core groups operate in New York, New Jersey, Illinois, Florida, Louisiana, Nevada, Michigan and Rhode Island.

Each group is known as a family, with membership varying from as many as seven hundred men to as few as twenty (*Challenge of Crime*, p. 193): "Each family can participate in the full range of activities in which organized crime generally is known to engage. Family organization is rationally designed with an integrated set of positions geared to maximize profits. Like any large corporation, the organization functions regardless of personnel changes, and no individual—not even the leader—is indispensable. If he dies or goes to jail, business goes on.

The hierarchial structure of the families resembles that of the Mafia groups that have operated for almost a century on the island of Sicily. *Theft of the Nation* (Cressey, 1969) describes in detail the national structure as well as the intricate structure of the family itself.

The **Commission,** also called the "High Commission," the "Grand Council," the "Administration," the "Roundtable," and the "Inner Circle," is a combination board of business directors, legislators, supreme court justices, and arbitrators, but its primary function is judicial.

The ultimate authority on organizational disagreements, the Commission is made up of nine to twelve bosses of the most powerful families in the country. Some families do not have members on the Commission, but they usually have a specified Commission member to look after their interests. Commissioners are not equal in power and authority; informal understandings give one member authority over another.

> *The Commission is the highest ruling body of Cosa Nostra.*

Within the family itself, an intricate structure has been established.

Each family is headed by one man, a boss, who maintains order and maximizes profits. He is subject only to the national advisory group, the Commission; his authority in all family matters is absolute.

Each boss has an *underboss*, a vice-president or deputy-director, who collects information, relays messages, passes instructions down to his own underlings, and acts for the boss in his absence.

The boss also has a *consigliere* (counselor or advisor) who is on the same level as the underboss, but who operates in a staff capacity. He is often an elder member of the family, partially retired from a criminal career, who gives advice to family members including the boss and underboss; therefore, he has great influence and power.

Below the underboss are the *caporegime* (lieutenants), lower-echelon personnel. Some caporegime serve as buffers between the top members of the family and the law. To maintain their insulation from the police, the boss will usually insist that all commands, information, complaints, and money flow through a trusted go-between. A caporegima does not make decisions or assume any of the boss's authority.

Other caporegime are chiefs of operating units which vary with the size and activities of particular families. The caporegima often has one or two associates who work closely with him, carrying orders, information, and money to the men in his unit. The caporegima is similar to a plant supervisor or sales manager.

The lowest level members of the family are the *soldiers* or "button men" who report to the caporegima. Soldiers may operate illicit enterprises such as loan-sharking operations, dice games, bookmaking operations, smuggling operations, or vending machine businesses on a commission basis. Or they may "own" the business and pay a percentage to the organization for the right to operate. Frequently soldiers form partnerships with one another or with caporegime. Some soldiers and most upper-echelon family members are involved in more than one enterprise.

The soldiers oversee a large number of employees, not family members and not necessarily Italian. Employees do most of the actual work, but they have no buffers or insulation from the law. They take bets, answer phones, sell drugs, make book, and work in legitimate businesses. For example, in a major lottery business which operated in black neighborhoods in Chicago, the workers were blacks, the bankers for the lottery were Japanese-Americans, but the game, including the banking operation, was licensed for a fee by a family member.

> *An organized crime family consists of a boss, an underboss, a consigliere, caporegime, and soldiers.*

The Chain of Command

The hierarchy or chain of command within a family is illustrated in Figure 5–2. Notice that the soldiers are responsible for corruption of police and public officials as well as for exercising control (enforcing). Notice also the illegal activities as well as the legitimate businesses in which organized crime is involved. It should also be noted, however, that not all who study organized crime agree with this description of organized crime as a clear organizational hierarchy.

Figure 5–2. *An Organized Crime Family.*

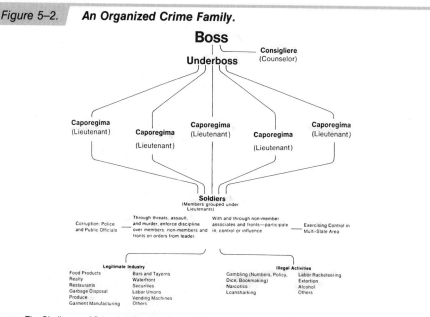

Source: The Challenge of Crime in a Free Society. 1967, p. 194, President's Commission on Law Enforcement and Administration of Justice.

The Nature and Extent of Organized Crime Activities in the United States

The diversified yet interrelated nature of organized crime activities is evident in the Task Force Report (Organized Crime, pp. 10-12):

> Gambling has long been a traditional arena for organized crime, and is one area law enforcement officials fear that there may be attempts by organized crime elements to take over any gambling operations that may be legalized in the future. As for other activities, the drug business (notably cocaine trafficking) is growing; pornography also is showing astronomical distribution profits. Loansharking is found to be tied into several other activities, including gambling, and arson and fraud are tied into insurance irregularities.
>
> There are also large, organized hijacking rings, armed robbery groups, and increasing vehicle losses, including heavy equipment. Untaxed cigarettes are another major problem. Credit card and stock frauds, sale of stolen and counterfeit securities, and the manufacture and distribution of counterfeit money are among prevalent white-collar crimes.
>
> There apparently is a link between organized crime and street crime where drug operations, fencing, gambling, and certain burglaries are concerned.
>
> Drug addicts pose a major problem in terms of burglaries. Some law enforcement people believe that most established crime figures began their careers in street crime operations. They also point to ties between organized crime and thefts of credit cards, airline tickets, securities, and money. They believe that channels controlled by organized crime are used to launder stolen money and to distribute stolen credit cards.
>
> The relationship between corruption and street crime also is important, with elements creating a subculture in which certain people believe they are above the law. In some communities their impact is so strong that they in fact become the law, maintaining a well-insulated position and buying official protection.
>
> Legitimate businesses are not only infiltrated or manipulated, but also are taken over by organized crime. For example, the liquor industry is a primary arena for organized crime operations—one often ignored in crime reports and one that benefits from weaknesses in law enforcement. Alcoholic beverage outlets are the underworld's retail market for all its goods and activities, and tax fraud is a frequent occurrence in connection with liquor operations.
>
> Another vulnerable area is the vending machine industry—whether the machines are operated for services, entertainment, or other purposes. Because they involve large cash flows, these machines are a growing operational area for organized crime.
>
> Organized crime figures are believed to have influence over the banking industries, grand juries, and some members of the legal profession.

Organized crime is heavily involved in gambling, drugs, prostitution, pornography, loan-sharking, and infiltration of legitimate businesses.

Gambling

Illegal gambling (placing bets with bookmakers) is a billion-dollar business in the United States. It occurs throughout the country with organized crime maintaining control by violence and by providing services including protection, sharing of financial risks(layoffs), legal assistance, and financial aid.

Figure 5–3.   The Web of Organized Crime.

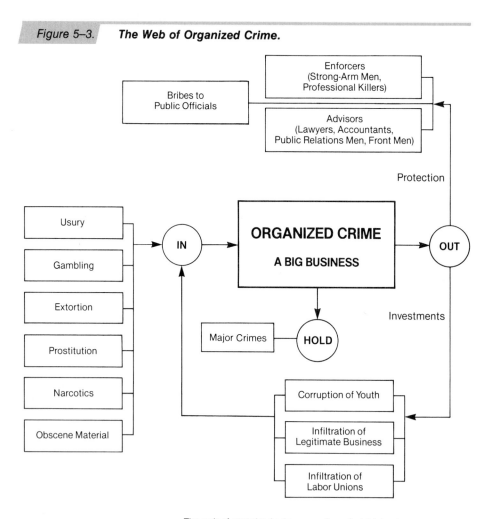

The web of organized crime, a portion of which is shown above, reaches into every part of the nation and affects all levels of society.

Source: Courtesy of the Federal Bureau of Investigation.

Wagers on football are most popular. Organized crime often either controls gambling operations or takes a cut of someone else's operation. The "street people" (bookies) are part of the organized crime network, but they are not part of organized crime itself, and they know little about it.

Organized crime is also involved in legal gambling, such as the casinos in Las Vegas, race tracks throughout the country, and even legal charity games. Only lotteries seem to have escaped the infiltration of organized crime.

Without participation of "law-abiding" citizens, organized crime would lose billions of dollars and much of its power. Unfortunately, countless millions of citizens contribute to the wealth and power of organized crime by making illegal bets. The benefits to the bettor are numerous, even when legitimate games are available. Illegal games offer greater variety, better odds, regular service, and a fast, guaranteed payoff. The bettor can phone in bets, charge them, preserve anonymity, and avoid having to pay taxes on winnings. These advantages offset the risks of getting caught or becoming indebted to organized crime.

Sports betting, supported by millions of American citizens, is organized crime's largest source of revenue.

Betting on Sports.   Most bets are made on football, baseball, and basketball, both professional and college. Although the majority of bets are made between acquaintances, the vast majority of money wagered is bet through bookmakers. The bookie handles larger bets which cannot comfortably be made between friends. He acts as a broker for those who want to bet large amounts of money on a given team.

Many bookmakers subscribe to a national handicapping service which provides detailed information about the teams playing and a list of point spreads. The bookmaker begins his day on a telephone, with a call to the biggest book in town, getting the opening odds or point spreads on the day's games. In exchange, for this service, he bets approximately $1,000 a month with the "big man" who himself has obtained the line from a syndicate in a distant city and who places at least $5,000 a month with the syndicate in exchange for its expertly calculated line.

The bookmaker often makes his calls from public phone booths as federal authorities frequently check telephone bills to see who is being called and where they are located.

When the bettors call in, the bookie writes down the wagers on a single sheet of paper which he can stuff under a floor board or into a slit in a door if raided. Some bookies use combustible paper treated chemically to vanish in a puff of smoke when touched with a cigarette or match, leaving no ashes. Other bookies use water-soluable paper which disintegrates when dropped into a toilet or sink, leaving no evidence.

The Numbers Game.   Betting on numbers is legal in a few states, but operating a numbers game is not legal. The most popular form of the numbers game consists of a player choosing any three-digit number from 0 to 999. The player has one in a thousand chances to win. The winning number is determined by betting totals or payoff odds on selected races at horse racing tracks. The two most common systems are the Brooklyn System and the New York System.

Figure 5–4.   **Illegal Numbers Game Structure.**

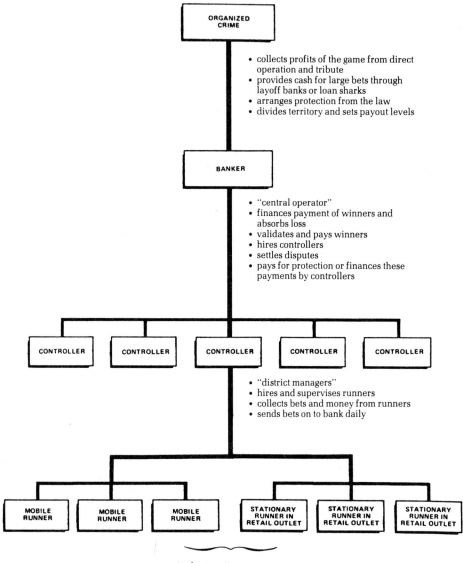

Source: Legal Gambling in New York, p. 47. Reprinted by permission of the Fund for the City of New York, 342 Madison Avenue, N.Y.

The Brooklyn number is the last three digits of the track's total parimutuel handle for the day. The New York number is more complicated, combining the payoff odds for win, place, and show horses in the first seven races. Because the first digit is calculated after the third race, the second digit after the fifth race, and the last digit after the seventh race, the New York number is often referred to as playing 3-5-7.

Numbers are played in offices, factories, and residential areas. The numbers organization has three layers. At the bottom are many runners and collectors who report to a smaller number of controllers, the agent or associates of a relative handful of bankers at the top. The runner, controller, and banker are somewhat comparable to salesman, district manager, and president in a legitimate business. Figure 5–4 illustrates the structure of the illegal numbers game.

Illegal numbers game operators require several services, including access to large amounts of money in case they are heavily hit and protection from the law. Organized crime's capital and contacts put it in a position to provide the money and the protection. Since the numbers game is the most visible of organized crime's activities, it is peculiarly susceptible to police interference and requires an extensive network of contacts with public officials at many levels. Therefore, it provides an entry point to the law enforcement structure. Corruption related to the numbers game is pervasive, affecting arrests, investigations, prosecutions, and sentencing.

Drugs

Organized crime's involvement in drugs concentrates on heroin and cocaine, a trade made to order because of its large demand, substantial profit, and need for an efficient organization with a good deal of capital as well as street-level protection.

The sale of narcotics is usually organized like a legitimate import business. Organized crime purchases large quantities of drugs from Europe, Asia, or Mexico and then distributes it in smaller lots to middle-level wholesalers who cut it further and sell it to dealers on the street.

Organized crime figures usually do not become directly involved beyond the middle level, thus protecting themselves from the authorities. They are primarily financiers, putting up capital for large-scale purchases. Frequently even import and distribution is taken over by others.

Organized crime may also be involved in the illegal production or distribution of prescription drugs. In the early 1970s the New Jersey State Commission on Investigation found evidence that organized crime and some newer black groups were financing illegal laboratories to produce "speed" in Newark, Atlantic City, Philadelphia, Detroit, and Canada.

Prostitution

Prostitution, one of organized crime's rackets since the turn of the twentieth century, reached its peak during the Depression, but since that time has declined.

The Organized Crime Task Force of the President's Commission on Law Enforcement *(Organized Crime,* 1976) quoted from the 1952 Second Interim Report of the United States Senate's Kefauver Committee which investigated organized crime:

> Before the First World War, the major profits or organized criminals were obtained from prostitution. The passage of the Mann White Slave Act, the changing sexual mores, and public opinion combined to make commercialized prostitution a less profitable and more hazardous enterprise. . . . Prostitution is difficult to organize and discipline is hard to maintain.

One form of prostitution—streetwalking—was probably too conspicuous and hard to regulate for organized crime. Not only do streetwalkers get arrested frequently, they also may be involved in prostitution-related crimes (robbery of customers, assault), and they frequently have pimps, individuals regarded with contempt by most organized crime members. When organized crime is involved in prostitution, it is usually in such forms as call girls, brothel trade, massage parlors, and encounter joints. Although organized crime takes a large share of the profits derived from prostitution and limits the prostitutes' independence, it also provides valuable services: housing, clients, and protection from the law.

Pornography

The pornography industry consists of films, magazines, books, sexual devices, and various "service" establishments. A number of recent studies indicate that pornography is organized crime's latest business. As with gambling and the drug trade, pornography is a prohibited product with a large market, requiring good organization, money, muscle, and lax law enforcement.

It is not known when organized crime became involved in pornography, but the Supreme Court decision in 1967, *Redrup v. N.Y.,* may have been a contributing factor. This case left unclear what constitutes pornography, making it difficult for law enforcement officers to build cases. Although organized crime's links to the pornography industry are documented as early as the 1950s, it did not become heavily involved until the late 1960s. By 1969 it is estimated that organized crime controlled 60 percent of the pornographic movies in New York.

The Task Force Report on Organized Crime (p. 227) notes that organized crime's pornography operations cover the country, and that although no accurate figures exist on what profits organized crime receives, it must be good money or organized crime would not be involved. One source put the gross profit from peepshows in Baltimore alone at about $10 million a year in 1973. Especially insidious is organized crime's involvement in and promotion of "kiddie porn."

Supreme Court decisions related to pornography have complicated the problem of law enforcement officers when dealing with the pornography industry. The Court has not extended First Amendment protections to pornography, so it is not automatically legal, but the Court's decisions have left unclear what constitutes pornography. At present three somewhat vague criteria exist *(Miller v. California):*

1. The dominant theme of the material must appeal to prurient interests;

2. The material must be utterly without redeeming social, political, literary, or scientific value; and

3. The material must be patently offensive in its depiction of sexual matters, in terms of contemporary standards.

Each state must pass its own legislation defining the standards, but a jury representing the community decides on individual cases.

The pornography issue was further complicated by a 1969 Supreme Court ruling (*Stanley v. Georgia*), which held that pornography for private use in one's home is legal.

Some pornography laws have successfully withstood legal challenge. However, public display of pornography, mailing unsolicited material, and sale or distribution to minors are banned nationally. Additionally, the federal government bans using the mails or interstate commerce facilities for conveying pornographic material.

The focus of attention in this relatively new area for organized crime has been on defining what is pornographic and how to control it; therefore, little attention has been paid to means of specifically controlling organized crime's involvement.

Loan-Sharking

Loan-sharking, lending money at higher than legally prescribed rates, is the second largest source of revenue for organized crime. Gambling profits often provide the initial capital for loan shark operations. Many types of individuals became involved with loan sharks: gamblers to pay off gambling debts, drug addicts to obtain needed drugs, businessmen to buy goods or to close deals.

Interest rates may vary from 1 percent to 150 percent a week, depending on the relationship between the lender and the borrower, the intended use of the money, and the size of the loan. A common rate for the small borrower is 20 percent a week. The payments are usually due at a certain hour on a certain day, and failure to make payment may result in a rise in interest rate and/or physical brutality.

According to the President's Commission on Law Enforcement and Administration of Justice (*Challenge of Crime*, p. 189): "No reliable estimates exist of the gross revenue from organized loan sharking; but profit margins are higher than for gambling operations, and many officials classify the business in the multi-billion dollar range."

Infiltration of Legitimate Business

Organized crime invests much of its money in legitimate business, thereby establishing a source of legal funds. Because business ownership is easily concealed, it is difficult to determine all the types of businesses which organized crime has penetrated. Control of businesses is usually acquired through one of four methods (*Challenge of Crime*, p. 190):

1. Investing concealed profits acquired from gambling and other illegal activities.
2. Accepting business interests in payment for the owner's gambling debts.
3. Foreclosing on usurious loans.
4. Using various forms of extortion.

The ordinary businessman can seldom compete with organized crime which has large amounts of ready cash, union connections, and "enforcers" to assure cooperation.

According to the Task Force Report: *(Organized Crime*, p. 25)

Organized crime tends to engage in those legitimate businesses that can profit from political influence. Its profits are made possible, to a large extent, by its corruption of the public officials charged with regulating those businesses. The opportunity for corruption exists in every instance where government regulates business. The public officials charged with such regulatory activities are open to bribery in exchange for disregarding, for example, character requirements in the area of liquor licensing, zoning laws in the issuance of construction permits, and fire and health violations in building inspection.

The Threat of Organized Crime

The primary goals of organized crime, whether through illegal enterprises such as gambling or legitimate businesses, are making money and maximizing profit. Organized crime has found it expedient to invest large amounts of money in corrupting political figures from the local level to the federal level as well as figures within the law enforcement field. Cressey has stated that the goal of organized crime is "the nullification of government." Organized crime can flourish only if it can control police investigation, prosecutions, judicial proceedings, and the corrections process.

> *The direct national threat is that organized crime seeks to corrupt and control police officers, prosecutors, judicial proceedings, and the corrections process.*

Police Corruption

Police officers' discretionary powers make them prime targets for corruption. (We will be discussing police discretion in depth later.) They can decide what laws to enforce, and organized crime may pay them handsomely not to enforce certain laws. Failure to arrest and prosecute those whom officers know have violated the law is only one form of police corruption. Goldstein (1975, pp. 16-18) lists several other forms of corruption:

■ Agreeing to drop an investigation prematurely.

- Agreeing not to inspect various locations where a violation may be occurring.
- Reducing the seriousness of a charge against an offender.
- Agreeing to alter testimony at a trial.
- Influencing departmental recommendations regarding the granting of licenses.
- Agreeing to alter departmental records of arrested persons.

When police officers are corrupt, the entire department becomes less effective and honest police officers do not know whom they can trust within the department. Police corruption also erodes the public's confidence in them.

Corruption in the Judicial System

A study done in cooperation with the New York City Police Department between 1960 and 1970 *(Organized Crime*, p. 25) covered 71 raids resulting in the positive identification of 99 persons who had a total of 356 arrests among them. Of these arrests, 198 were dismissed, 63 were acquitted, 12 were found guilty and given suspended sentences, 77 were fined, and 5 served jail sentences. The average fine was $113; the average jail sentence was 17 days. Although it is obvious from the preceding statistics that some judicial corruption exists, it is seldom proven.

Corruption in the Corrections System

Salerno and Tompkins (1969, p. 183) present convincing evidence that when organized crime figures do go to prison, they are usually quite comfortable:

Sam Giancana, for instance, frequently used the warden's office in the Cook County jail for business conferences, was permitted out of his cell after "lights out," and had easy access to liquor, special foods, and expensive cigars. And 3 weeks after Sam deStefano was moved by court order he was operating a loansharking business from his hospital room and enjoying fine foods, vintage wines, card games with underworld friends, and visits from women. Harold Koenigsberg, an enforcer and loan shark collector for Costa Nostra figures, was a Federal prisoner in Hudson County jail. Tracking down rumors, Federal authorities found that Koenigsberg lived in a special room with a telephone and women and food sent in. At one point in the ensuing flap, Koenigsberg sent his lawyer to court to try and recover $1,000 he had lent the warden.

The Pattern of Organized Crime— The Reality of the Threat

Refer back to Figure 5–1, which illustrates the seriousness of the threat organized crime presents to our society. The testimony of Joseph (The Baron) Barboza, syndicate crime enforcer, in hearings before the Select Committee on Crime, graphically demonstrates the seriousness of the threat posed by organized crime. (Excerpted from *Organized Crime in Sports* [Racing], Hearings before the Select Committee on Crime, House of Representatives, 1973.) After several of his friends and associates were killed, Mr. Barboza broke with the mob and testified against a number of racketeers. As a result of his testimony, four men were convicted of first degree murder and sentenced to death. While associated with the mob, Mr. Barboza was reported to be the most feared rackets enforcer in New England.

Mr. Nolde: Mr. Barboza. Will you please describe your first connection with the New England mob?

Mr. Barboza: It was around 1962, when I bundled a man that was running from the bakers union in Boston. I was given a thousand-dollar contract on him to bundle him. We got him during the hurricane, everybody was off the street and we hit him with sash weights. A Greek man, we popped his roots in, dislocated his shoulder blade, gave him 16 stitches in his knee, and he got thumped about the head with a sash weight from a window. It was about a 20-pound lead weight. I refused the $1,000 that was offered to me when it was over. It subsequently led to about $70,000 by refusing that thousand dollars through other channels.

Mr. Brasco: Okay. That $70,000 you made, was that for bundling people also?

Mr. Barboza: No. Primarily shylocking and shakedown and so forth.

Mr. Nolde: You mentioned shylocking or loan sharking. Would you describe the shylocking or loan sharking operation?

Mr. Barboza: Yes, I would take a hundred dollars and give it to a person and he would pay me $5 a week interest on this $100 that I would give him. In other words, I would say, "Give me $105 back next week. And the person would say, "Here's $5, I want to carry the $100 over till next week." As long as he paid that $5 interest every week he could hold on to that hundred dollars. Some guys hold on to it maybe 3 or 4 years and just pay $5, and $10 on $200, $15 on $300, $25 on $500, $50 on a thousand. So that in one year's time, with $2,000 I turned $200 into $25,000. And a couple of years later I had $5,500 coming in every week in the way of interest.

Mr. Nolde: How much money did you have on the street at the point?

Mr. Barboza: I had about $70,000.

Mr. Nolde: And you were getting a return on it every week?

Mr. Barboza: $5,500 a week. . . .

Mr. Brasco: Can we go back to the point as to why these men were killed? . . .

Mr. Barboza: Yes sir. At the time, anyway, the boss in the office was afraid of independent operators. They were making moves that the office wasn't used to. They were killing people at bus stops, walking into their houses, and killing them, walking in night clubs and killing them. People were found in backs of trunks with their heads sawed off. People were found in suitcases, dissected. Guys were found floating in the river. There was a lot of hits in

Boston and all different types of hits that put a lot of fear into these people that were connected with the office.

Mr. Phillips: You say there were other factors which led you to break with the office as you put it?

Mr. Barboza: Right.

Mr. Phillips: Was one of these factors the fact that they bombed your attorney?

Mr. Barboza: Well, they blew up my attorney's car and he lost his leg. He lost his right leg, and he lost chunks out of his left leg, and today he still picks pieces of steel that come out of his face and body.

Mr. Phillips: In addition to the lawyer and shooting up the fellow who worked with you, did they make a move on your wife or family?

Mr. Barboza: Crot went down to my house, where I lived at the time, took off the back screen window, and they terrified the family there. . . .

Chr. Pepper: Mr. Barboza, you have told us a lot of lurid and dramatic details about some of the methods of gang operations. How many people have you known of who were, according to your best knowledge, killed on account of gang action?. . .

Mr. Barboza: I would say from 1960 to 1966, maybe 75, and during, well more than that. It is pretty rough to estimate, Mr. Pepper.

Chr. Pepper: Roughly in a period of 10 years, maybe a hundred people?

Mr. Barboza: Yes.

Chr. Pepper: Has it been your observation that when people who are members of gangs, who derive their money from illegal operations by what is called a legitimate business, they generally carry over into the operation of the legitimate business the tactics they used in the illegal operation they carried on?

Mr. Barboza: Yes.

Chr. Pepper: So if gang members did infiltrate into horse racing, the chances are they would carry over into that operation some illegal activity; is that correct?

Mr. Barboza: Yes, sir.

Chr. Pepper: From having been on the other side of the table as it were, in your past operations, and now from the point of view of the public, would you think it desirable if we could set up more of the strike forces like they now have in New York where the federal, state, and local officials are all working in close integration together?

Mr. Barboza: Very much so.

Chr. Pepper: It would be helpful in fighting organized crime?

Mr. Barboza: Yes, sir. Mr. Pepper, organized crime is probably the worst threat to the United States. The Mafia in this country is the biggest. The trouble is, nobody wants to get involved with the politicians. And then at a certain point everybody lets it slide. So my concern is this: As I was on the other side of the fence, and right now I am doing everything in my power to try and do something for my children, because I don't want to leave it for their children, and they are leaving something for their generations. Would you want your great-grandchildren to be part of the mob, as far as working in an office? That is what it is coming to, because little by little, they are swallowing everything in legitimate business. And those they can get, they brutalize and intimidate and front for them. So that it is up to people like you, and it is up to the news media, to make the public aware of the threat the Mafia is, and keep it in the public's eye all of the time, not just now and then.

Mr. Brasco: In terms of the fight against organized crime, it seems to me in any event, what you are dealing with is a combination of racketeers knowing or being rather astute in the basic weaknesses of individuals: money, cars, women. And also in some of the problems that we have in society. Take loan sharking. I am curious. Did many of the people you lent money to qualify for bank loans? I am talking about business people now.

Mr. Barboza: Yes, but some of them did, some them didn't. But the ones that did, needed the money right away, and couldn't get it right away.

Mr. Brasco: So it is fair to say they take, and you took, advantage of all the weaknesses you could see in society and in human nature?

Mr. Barboza: Yes. In regard to infiltration, in other words, like Al Capone started the scheme of investing illegitimate money into legitimate enterprises. Well, he pioneered it, but he looks like a nothing compared to the vast sums that are struck in now by the mob. Now, where the people make the mistake is that they will find out that the Mafia came into a factory. They bought a piece of the joint, so they say as long as I do my work, I don't have nothing to do with him. All of a sudden, months later, somebody comes flying down the stairs with his neck broken, and that person is there and all of a sudden he is involved, because if he says anything he is going to get killed . . . .

Chr. Pepper: Mr. Barboza, without excusing any illegal acts you may have committed in the past, I want to commend you for now doing what you can to break up this shocking menace of organized crime in this country. It is an almost unbelievable fact that such a thing could exist in this great free country. You can be very helpful to those in authority who are trying to do something about it. We appreciate your coming here, giving your testimony to the committee.

NOTE: On February 11, 1976, while a protected witness of the U.S. Marshal's Office and using a new identification furnished to him by the federal government, Joseph (The Baron) Barboza, age 40, was gunned down and killed on the streets of San Francisco—a victim of an enforcer for organized crime.

The Police Officer and Organized Crime

The problem of organized crime is everyone's problem. Unfortunately many people believe that sole responsibility rests with law enforcement—that it is up to the police officer to apprehend those involved in organized crime. Here, more than in any other area of law enforcement, the police officer needs the help of the citizen and a judicial and political system free of corruption.

Detectives inspect confiscated gambling equipment.

> *Among the special problems the law enforcement officer encounters when dealing with organized crime are:*
>
> ■ *The lack of citizen cooperation.*
> ■ *The code of ethics of organized crime members which prevents them from giving information.*
> ■ *The tremendous wealth, power, and organization behind them.*
> ■ *The corruption of other police officers, politicians, judges, jury members, and corrections officers.*

Perhaps one of the most serious of the problems is lack of citizen cooperation. Citizens not only do not want to get involved; many actually promote organized crime by engaging in illegal activities from which organized crime obtains its working capital, for example illegal betting, buying stolen goods from fences, buying drugs, and so on.

The challenge is clear; however, it is also clear that law enforcement cannot do the job alone. A large part of the challenge rests in enlisting public support.

Federal Legislation Regarding Organized Crime

Siegel (1983, p. 392) points out that one of the first directly anti-organized-crime measures was the Interstate and Foreign Travel or Transportation in Aid of Racketeering Enterprises Act (Travel Act—18 U.S. 1952 [1976]). This act prohibits travel in interstate commerce or use of interstate facilities for promoting, managing, establishing, carrying on, or facilitating any unlawful activity.

The Organized Crime Control Act

The Organized Crime Control Act was passed by Congress in 1970. It has several important provisions, including the following (*Organized Crime*, 1976, p. 18):

- It provides for establishing a special grand jury in cities having major organized crime operations.

- It establishes a federal "use immunity" whereby witnesses can be ordered to testify in return for immunity from prosecution using any information so derived. Witnesses who fail to testify can be jailed for up to eighteen months.

- It provides protection for witnesses in organized crime cases and members of their families.

- It provides for perjury prosecution.

- It provides for taking and using pre-trial depositions when because of "exceptional circumstances it is in the interest of justice."

- It expands federal jurisdiction over illegal gambling operations.

- It prohibits using illegal profit from racketeering activity to take over legitimate businesses and unions (RICO).

- It provides for extended sentences for persons convicted of participating in continuing illegal businesses or who are habitual criminals.

RICO. The most important measure of the Organized Crime Control Act is Title IX, The Racketeer Influenced and Corrupt Organization Act (RICO) (Pub. L. No. 91-452, Title IX, 84 Stat. 922 [1970]). This act defines racketeering activity as involvement in two or more acts prohibited by twenty-four existing federal and state statutes. Siegel (1983, p. 392) states that the offenses listed in RICO include state-defined crimes such as murder, kidnapping, gambling, arson, robbery, bribery, extortion, and narcotic violations, as well as federally defined crimes such as bribery, counterfeiting, transmitting gambling information, prostitution, and mail fraud. Siegel goes on to note that RICO is designed to limit patterns of organized crime activity by defining racketeering as an act intended to:

1. Derive income from racketeering or the unlawful collection of debts and to use or invest such income.

2. Acquire through racketeering an interest in or control over any enterprise engaged in interstate or foreign commerce.

3. Conduct business enterprises through a pattern of racketeering.

4. Conspire to use racketeering as a means of making income, collecting loans, or conducting business.

A person found guilty of violating RICO is subject to twenty years in prison and a fine of $225,000. In addition, the person so convicted forfeits to the United States government any investment in a business that violates RICO.

To enforce the legislation, the federal government created a Strike Force Program in eighteen cities. This program coordinates the efforts of several state and federal law enforcement officers and prosecutors to work as a team against racketeering and organized crime.

> *The Organized Crime Control Act was passed in 1970. Title IX of this act, the Racketeer Influenced and Corrupt Organization Act (RICO), created new categories of offenses in racketeering activity.*

Summary

Organized crime is a threat not only to its victims but to our entire society. Its two unique characteristics, use of corruption and strong-arm tactics, can destroy respectable citizens and eventually the country if allowed to go unchecked. Unfortunately, the severity of the threat is seldom recognized by the public and is sometimes not recognized by individuals within law enforcement. Until the elimination of organized crime becomes a priority for police departments and communities, it poses a direct threat to each of us and to our society.

Organized crime goes by many names including the mob, the syndicate, the rackets, the Mafia, and Cosa Nostra. It probably originated with the lawless, violent criminal bands who dominated nineteenth-century Sicily. They came to the United States in 1880 and continued their terrorism and extortion. By 1925 they were a wealthy, powerful, highly organized operation.

The structure of organized crime consists of a ruling body, the Commission, which oversees the activities of each "family" within the organization. Each organized crime family consists of a boss, an underboss, a consigliere, caporegime, and soldiers.

Organized crime is heavily involved in gambling, drugs, prostitution, pornography, loan sharking, and infiltration of legitimate businesses. Its largest source of revenue is sports betting, particularly wagers on football games. Loan sharking is its second largest source of revenue.

Not only does organized crime cost the nation billions of dollars annually and ruin hundreds of lives, it also poses a direct national threat because it seeks to corrupt and control police officers, prosecutors, judicial proceedings, and the corrections process. Nonetheless, many citizens actually promote organized crime by engaging in illegal activities, for example, buying stolen property, placing bets with bookies, and the like. Among the difficult problems the law enforcement officer encounters when dealing with organized crime are (1) lack of citizen cooperation, (2) the code of silence of family members, (3) their tremendous wealth, power, and organization, and (4) the corruption of other police officers, politicians, judges, jury members, and corrections officers.

In 1970 Congress passed the Organized Crime Control Act. Title IX of this act, the Racketeer Influenced and Corrupt Organization Act (RICO), created new categories of offenses in racketeering activity.

Although not a crime in itself, organized crime is truly a serious problem to be dealt with by law enforcement agencies.

Application

Many of the activities engaged in by organized crime are classified as victimless crimes, that is, all persons engaged in the activity are voluntary participants. Victimless crimes include such activities as gambling, viewing pornography, and prostitution. Many people argue that such activities should not be crimes; they should be legalized or decriminalized.

Read the following extracts (from *Organized Crime: Report of the Task Force on Organized Crime,* National Advisory Committee on Criminal Justice Standards and Goals, 1976, pp. 230-232) on the arguments for and against general reform and reform to combat organized crime. Formulate your own opinion on this topic.

General Arguments for Reform

It is not the proper function of government or the criminal justice system to regulate private morality or behavior through criminal laws; that is the role of nonlegal institutions.

The laws are ineffective. They do not deter involvement in the proscribed activities, either by organized crime or the public. Neither fines or jail rehabilitate or alter the behavior of offenders.

The laws are unenforceable. The volume of activity is too great, public support is lacking and criminal justice systems resources are inadequate.

There is no evidence that legalization/decriminalization will lead to a harmful increase in immoral behavior. The activities are already easily accessible to anyone who wants them.

The rights of individuals to live as they want, so long as they do not harm others, is a fundamental principle on which this Nation was founded.

There is no proof that the moral standards of the country are declining, or that the Nation as a whole is being negatively affected by victimless crimes.

The burden of proof that harm results from these crimes should rest with those wishing to impose sanctions, not with participants in the activities.

Society cannot morally declare persons to be victims when they do not see themselves as such.

Even if the law's function is to provide symbolic guidance for a correct standard of behavior, it is questionable that the laws against victimless crimes guide people in the right direction. Instead, they may engender cynicism and disrespect for the criminal justice and legal systems and for government in general.

The laws are hypocritical. They allow some activities while proscribing others that are comparable; they penalize some people involved in an activity, but not others.

More realistic and well-founded policies must be developed. Current policies are based on emotion, outdated moral norms and values, and inaccurate information. Using up-to-date information on the effects of an activity, and bearing in mind the many priorities to be met, policymakers must weigh the costs of an activity against the costs of ineffective laws. Goals and effective approaches must then be developed.

The laws have many hidden costs: creation of a class of criminals who would not otherwise be considered criminals; discriminatory, arbitrary, and selective application of the laws; unsavory and often degrading tactics employed by the police to obtain evidence or make arrests; increase in crime associated with victimless crimes; creation of subcultures of criminals who reinforce one another's behavior; overburdening the criminal justice system; creation of antagonism among minority youth toward police as a result of enforcement that hits the inner city hardest; and failure to afford constitutional rights to the accused because of efforts to process cases quickly.

There is a lack of public support for the laws.

Overemphasis on the law blunts efforts to find other solutions to abuses of the proscribed activities.

The basis on which the laws were originally promulgated no longer apply; social mores and values have changed, and new information on the effects of the activities contradicts previously held theories and assumptions.

General Arguments Against Reform

The activities known as victimless crimes are antithetical to Christian beliefs and the principles on which the Nation was founded.

Modification of the sanctions against these activities will result in a disastrous increase in their occurrence. This in turn will lead to a moral decline of society. The Nation will become a second class power. Both the Greek and Roman civilizations were destroyed by the decadence of their citizenry.

Because morality affects the viability of a nation, it is a proper function of government to regulate morality by the use of criminal laws.

Laws are a reflection of social values and should be used, even symbolically, as a guide to proper behavior.

There has never been a serious, sustained effort to enforce the laws, so it is inaccurate to say the statutes are ineffective. A reform government backed by the public can wipe out organized crime, vice, and corruption.

Better law enforcement in terms of other crimes will not necessarily result from freeing resources by modifying the victimless crime laws, for "There is no empirical evidence that the police do a better job of protecting persons and property."* Perhaps there is a limit to the amount of resources a police department can effectively spend.

There are better ways to combat corruption than eliminating the victimless crime laws. Legalization will not eliminate the temptation to corrupt, because it will involve new regulations.

---

*Goldberg, Williams I., "Victimless Crimes: Should Police Preserve Community Morals." *Tennessee Law Enforcement Journal*, p. 56, reprinted from Police Law Quarterly, 1 (April 1972).

It is traditional in this country for government to protect individuals from themselves. For example, the state requires motorcycle drivers and riders to wear helmets.

The fact that a law seems unenforceable is no reason to abolish it. For example, murder and theft laws are not 100 percent enforceable but are nevertheless needed. A preferable alternative to abolishing the victimless crime laws is providing more resources to implement them.

The laws do not serve as deterrents because they are not strictly enforced and the sanctions are not strong enough.

If the criminal justice system is overburdened, the answer is not to eliminate certain laws. It is to increase the resources available to it.

If the laws result in more related crime, enforcement efforts should be stepped up.

There are not enough hard facts on the impact of victimless crimes to justify modifying the laws.

Arguments for Reform to Combat Organized Crime

Laws create the conditions under which organized crime can thrive—namely, prohibition of a good or service for which there is large demand and whose supply requires capital, expertise, and continuous organization. The laws should be changed in order to deprive organized crime of these conditions.

Capital essential to organized crime's survival derives largely from its operations in victimless crimes. This capital is used to finance other illegal activities that are clearly detrimental to the public interest.

Given the unenforceability of the laws, criminal justice officials are too often cooperative targets for corruption. The source of temptation must be removed.

Reform of the laws would free valuable resources for a more concerted and effective attack on the upper levels of organized crime.

Arguments Against Reform to Combat Organized Crime

Decriminalization or legalization would allow organized crime to continue in the victimless crime activities, but on a legal basis. Because of its prior experience, organized crime would have an advantage over the competition. Even in legal games, organized crime can still find ways to increase its profits illegally.

Legalizing only selected activities or aspects of them will not affect organized crime overall. That element of society will still have other illegal and legal businesses and will in all likelihood find other activities to move into, as at the end of Prohibition.

Legalization, because it involves regulations and licenses, offers ample opportunity for corruption.

It will be difficult to establish legal activities that can compete with the services and advantages organized crime operations offer. Competitive legal activities may not be possible unless some Federal laws are changed, such as the tax on gambling winnings.

It is not certain that either private interests or the government will want to provide all goods and services—for example, prostitution and heroin.

1. Which position do you support and why?
2. As a citizen, what is your responsibility in supporting this view?
3. As a law enforcement officer, what is your responsibility?
4. Who is responsible for interpreting the laws regarding victimless crimes?

Answers

1. Answers will vary here. You should be familiar with both sides of the controversy.
2. As a citizen, you should make your views known to your legislators, the persons responsible for making the laws.
3. As a law enforcement officer, your responsibility, as an agent of the executive branch of government, is to enforce the existing laws, whether you personally agree with them or not.
4. Judges are responsible for interpreting the laws regarding victimless crimes.

Discussion Questions

1. Why would or could you blame a person for not testifying against organized crime?
2. A recent article described witnesses testifying against organized crime. After testifying they had their names changed and were moved with their families to a different location. After several moves and a promise of protection from the federal government, the witnesses were informed that due to lack of funds, they couldn't be protected any longer. How do you view this decision?
3. Why is it so difficult for the police to deal with organized crime on a local level?
4. Why is it dangerous to have the mob infiltrate legitimate businesses?
5. What are some ways the average citizen can help stop or slow down organized crime?
6. Should we fear organized crime? Is it truly a dangerous threat to our society?
7. Why isn't more being done to curb organized crime? What is being done?
8. Does our area have organized crime? If so, in what activities do they engage?
9. Is the disappearance of Jimmy Hoffa connected with organized crime?

References

Committee on Criminal Justice Standards and Goals. *Organized crime*. Washington, D.C.: U.S. Government Printing Office, 1976.

Conklin, J.E., ed. *The crime establishment: Organized crime and American society*. Englewood Cliffs, N.J.: Prentice-Hall, 1973.

Cressey, D.R. *Theft of the nation: The structure and operations of organized crime in America*. New York: Harper and Row, 1969.

Gage, N., ed. *Mafia, USA*. Chicago: Playboy Press, 1972.

Goldstein, H. *Police corruption*. New York: Police Foundation, 1975.

Legal gambling in New York: A discussion of numbers and sports betting. New York: Fund for the City of New York, 1972.

Maas, P. *The Valachi papers*. New York: G.P. Putnam's Sons, 1968.

National Advisory Committee on Criminal Justice Standards and Goals. *Organized crime: Report of the task force on organized crime*. Washington, D.C.: U.S. Government Printing Office, 1976.

Pace, D.F., and Styles, J.C. *Organized crime: Concepts and control*. Englewood Cliffs, N.J.: Prentice Hall, 1983.

President's Commission on Law Enforcement and Administration of Justice. *The challenge of crime in a free society*. Washington, D.C.: U.S. Government Printing Office, 1967.

Rhodes, R.P. *Organized crime: Crime control vs. civil liberties*. New York: Random House, 1984.

Salerno, R., and Tompkins, J.S. *The crime confederation: Cosa Nostra and allied operations in organized crime*. New York: Doubleday and Company, 1969.

Siegel, L.J. *Criminology*. St. Paul, Minn.: West Publishing Company, 1983.

Sondern, F. J. *Brotherhood of evil: The Mafia*. New York: Manor Books, 1972.

U.S. Congress. House. Hearings before the Select Committee on Crime. *Organized crime in sports (racing)*. 92d Cong., 2d sess. Part 2 of 4 parts (May-July 1972). Washington, D.C.: U.S. Government Printing Office, 1973.

Vetter, H.J., and Silverman, I.A. *The nature of crime*. Philadelphia: W.B. Saunders Company, 1978.

Law Enforcement

The Total Context

Police officers not only function within the context presented in Section One, they are part of a vast network of law enforcement agencies encompassing federal, state, county, local, public, and private agencies (Chapter 6). The structure of their specific law enforcement agency and its specific goals prescribe to a large extent their responsibilities (Chapter 7). The complex roles they are expected to fulfill in meeting these goals are challenging, sometimes frustrating, and always vital to the welfare of our citizens and our country.

The law enforcement network, the independent department structure and goals, and the roles to be fulfilled, complete the context in which the modern law enforcement officer functions.

*Law enforcement is a cooperative effort among
local, county, state, federal, and private law
enforcement officers.*

Law Enforcement Agencies

A Mutual Effort

Do You Know . . .

- What five levels of law enforcement are currently operating in the United States?

- Who the chief law enforcement officer at the federal and state level is?

- What agencies and bureaus are related to law enforcement in the Department of Justice? The Department of the Treasury?

- What primary functions are performed by the Federal Bureau of Investigation? The Drug Enforcement Administration? The U.S. Marshals? The Bureau of Customs? The Internal Revenue Service? The Secret Service? The Bureau of Alcohol, Tobacco, and Firearms Tax? The Immigration and Naturalization Service? The Bureau of Prisons? Postal Inspectors? The armed forces military police?

- What services the FBI provides to state and local law enforcement agencies?

- What the Law Enforcement Assistance Administration (LEAA) was and what it accomplished?

- What state agencies are involved in or offer assistance to law enforcement?

- What the two main types of county law enforcement are?

- What major differences exist between public and private law enforcement officers?

*Intelligence . . . Investigation . . .
Enforcement . . . Protection . . .*

Introduction

Although law enforcement is primarily a local responsibility, criminal activities frequently do not remain localized; they may extend throughout a county, a state, or across the country. This is particularly true of organized crime. In such instances local authorities benefit from the assistance of other law enforcement agencies. Conversely, since the actual crimes are committed in a specific place, federal and state officials rely upon the cooperation of local law enforcement officers. Each can provide valuable assistance to the other.

American police forces may be classified according to the level of government that each serves, but no uniform pattern of police administration exists at any of the five levels of government, and no mechanism exists to coordinate the activities and goals of the agencies which differ greatly in size, jurisdiction, and operational methods.

The five levels of government authorized to have law enforcement agencies result in the presence of (1) township and special district police, (2) municipal police, (3) county police, (4) state police, and (5) federal police.

Federal Agencies

Federal law enforcement agencies were created by Congress to meet the needs of a dynamic, rapidly growing democracy. Federal agents fulfill important responsibilities. Intelligence agents produce and disseminate information on foreign and domestic areas which affect national security. Investigative agents conduct investigations to determine compliance with federal laws. They carry guns, make arrests, and are usually enforcement-oriented. Most federal agencies are attached to specific departments of the executive branch of government and have duties confined to the interests of the parent department.

The Department of Justice

The Department of Justice is the largest law firm in the country, representing the citizens in enforcing the law. It plays a significant role in protecting citizens through its efforts for effective law enforcement, crime prevention, crime detection, and prosecution and rehabilitation of offenders. It also conducts all suits in the Supreme Court which concern the United States. The **attorney general** is head of the Department of Justice and is the chief law officer of the federal government. Its law enforcement agencies include the Federal Bureau of Investigation. The Drug Enforcement Administration, the United States Marshals, the Immigration and Naturalization Service, and the Bureau of Prisons.

The attorney general is head of the Department of Justice and the chief law officer of the federal government.

The department has several divisions including the Antitrust Division, the Civil Division, the Land and Natural Resources Division, the Civil Rights Division, the Criminal Division, and the Tax Division.

The *Civil Rights Division,* established in 1957 to secure effective federal enforcement of civil rights, is responsible for enforcing federal civil rights laws prohibiting discrimination on the basis of race, color, religion, or national origin in the areas of voting, education, employment, and housing, in the use of public facilities and public accommodations, and in the administration of federally assisted programs (*U.S. Government Manual,* p. 333).

The *Criminal Division* is responsible for approximately nine hundred federal statutes, including statutes relating to bank robbery; bank violations; kidnapping; extortion; loan sharking; illegal gambling; labor racketeering; aircraft hijacking; fraud against the government; mail fraud; bankruptcy fraud; election fraud; bribery of public officials; perjury; obstruction of justice; conflict of interest; theft and larceny of public property; counterfeiting; forgery; interstate transportation of stolen motor vehicles, securities, and other property; illegal interception of private communications; illegal trafficking in narcotics and other controlled substances; distribution of obscene materials; illegal transportation of firearms and explosives; crimes on the high seas and government reservations, and other territorial jurisdiction offenses (*U.S. Government Manual* pp. 333–334).

The *Tax Division* prosecutes tax evaders under the criminal laws of the United States and has played an important role in curbing organized crime through such tax prosecutions.

The Department of Justice's law enforcement agencies include the Federal Bureau of Investigation, the Drug Enforcement Administration, United States Marshals, the Immigration and Naturalization Service, and the Bureau of Prisons.

The Federal Bureau of Investigation (FBI). One of the best-known federal agencies is the Federal Bureau of Investigation—the FBI. The FBI is an investigative branch of the U.S. Department of Justice whose responsibilities are set by federal statutes. Created in 1908 as the Bureau of Investigation, it was renamed the Federal Bureau of Investigation in 1935. Its national headquarters in Washington, D.C., maintains field offices in strategic cities in the United States and its possessions.

The FBI is the primary investigative agency of the federal government. Its special agents have jurisdication over more than 170 federal crimes. They are responsible for general investigations, both criminal and civil, and for domestic intelligence dealing with the internal security of the nation. FBI agents are not subjected to the same demands for service that local police officers are: they don't handle drunks, answer domestic calls, respond to medical emergencies, or deal with deviant persons, which are the most frequent local problems of the community.

The Federal Bureau of Investigation's responsibilities include: investigating espionage, interstate transportation of stolen property, kidnapping, unlawful flight to avoid prosecution, confinement, or giving testimony, sabotage, piracy of aircraft and other crimes aboard aircraft, bank robbery and embezzlement, and enforcement of the Civil Rights Acts.

Espionage includes illegally obtaining or disclosing information affecting the national security, either for the benefit of a foreign power or to the detriment of the country.

Interstate transportation of stolen property includes transportation of stolen automobiles as well as counterfeit, altered, or forged securities with the intent to defraud.

Kidnapping includes the unlawful abduction of a person, transporting the person across a state line, and holding him or her for ransom, reward, or favors.

Unlawful flight to avoid prosecution, confinement, or giving testimony includes the interstate flight of a person to avoid giving testimony in any felony proceedings. Fugitives apprehended are usually released to local authorities for extradition and prosecution or confinement.

Sabotage generally includes the willful destruction or attempted destruction of national defense materials, premises, or utilities, or the manufacture or construction of the preceding in a defective manner.

Piracy (hijacking) of aircraft and other crimes aboard an aircraft includes assault, intimidation, or interference with aircraft personnel, the commission of various crimes such as murder, assault, rape, or robbery aboard an aircraft or the false reporting of any such activities.

Bank robbery and embezzlement include robbery, burglary, larceny, embezzlement, or misapplication of funds by an officer or employee and false entry in the books or records of any member bank of the Federal Reserve System or federal programs such as urban development funds, grants, and the like.

Enforcement of the Civil Rights Acts of 1960 and 1964 requires that the FBI deter anyone who seeks to obstruct federal court orders. They must also see that no discrimination occurs in public accommodations, public facilities, or public education institutions.

In addition to these numerous responsibilities, the FBI provides valuable services to law enforcement agencies throughout the country.

The *Identification Division* was established in 1924 as a result of the tremendous value of fingerprint identification data. The FBI is the central repository for fingerprint information; all police agencies in the country contribute to and may obtain information from it.

Data from the identification records are furnished to law enforcement and governmental agencies at the federal, state, county, and local levels for official use only. Wanted notices, periodically distributed by the FBI at the request of other law enforcement agencies, frequently result in the apprehension of dangerous criminals. However, the Identification Division is not restricted to criminal matters: many missing persons have been located, and vicitms of amnesia and homicides have been identified.

The Identification Division also maintains a disaster squad to assist in identifying victims of disasters such as explosions, storms, and plane crashes in which fingerprints are often the only means of identifying victims.

The *Crime Laboratory,* established in 1932, is the largest, most effective criminal laboratory in the world. Its facilities are available without cost to any city, county, state, or federal law enforcement agency in the country. Physical evidence obtained in a criminal investigation is examined not only to support evidence against a suspect, but also to establish the innocence of accused persons. Included in the laboratory's services are identification of firearms, shoe prints, and tire prints; mineral analyses; and examination of blood, documents, hairs, fibers, and poisons.

The *National Crime Information Center (NCIC),* established in 1967, is a complex, computerized, electronic data exchange network developed to complement computerized systems already in existence and those planned by local and state law enforcement agencies.

Technician inspects bomb components at the FBI crime laboratory.

The numerous law enforcement agencies serving as terminals in the system are directly linked to the control center of the NCIC at FBI headquarters. The system is adjusted so that each terminal can communicate directly and immediately with the control center.

Records on file in the NCIC concern wanted persons, stolen vehicles, vehicles used in the commission of felonies, stolen or missing license plates, stolen guns and other items of stolen property which are serially identifiable such as television sets, boat motors, and so on. The reservoir of scientifically stored data on criminal activities gathered by federal, state, and local law enforcement agencies gives the street officer of any law enforcement agency in any part of the country up-to-the-minute information upon request in a matter of seconds.

Uniform Crime Reports are another service provided by the FBI. Since 1930, by an act of Congress, the FBI has served as a national clearing house for United States crime statistics. States report their monthly crime statistics to the FBI, which in turn releases information quarterly and annually regarding all crimes reported to them.

Crimes are categorized by their seriousness and their frequency. Part I crimes consist of homicide, rape, assault, robbery, burglary, larceny/theft, arson, and motor vehicle theft. Part II crimes consist of forgery, prostitution, narcotics, and the like. Uniform Crime Reports give law enforcement administrators valuable information related to crime rates in similar communities, felony and misdemeanor arrests, and the clearances for crimes. The FBI reports are valuable in assessing needed manpower, equipment, and budget increases.

The FBI Uniform Crime Reports seek to: (1) measure the reporting trends of serious crime, (2) record the volume of crime, and (3) determine significant police matters related to crime such as number of employees per thousand capita, the number of officers assaulted each year, the number of officers killed each year, and the types of action which caused the assaults or deaths.

The diverse character of the bureau's work makes it necessary to have regular contact with police at every level of government.

> *The FBI has an Identification Division, a crime laboratory, and a National Crime Information Center (NCIC) which may be used by any law enforcment agency in the country. The FBI also complies statistics and releases Uniform Crime Reports annually.*

The numerical strength, powers, and scope of operation of the FBI has increased greatly in recent years. Its jurisdiction has often been enlarged by Congress, and the federal government regularly makes use of its broadened enforcement powers and personnel. These developments are the inevitable response to the ever-broadening scope of operations, the increased mobility, and the increasingly effective techniques of modern criminals to elude apprehension.

Some of the legal instruments fashioned by Congress to increase the efficiency and broaden the scope of the FBI's operation include: (1) the National Stolen Property Act, (2) the Fugitive Felon Law, (3) the National Bank Robbery

Act, (4) the Federal Kidnapping Statute—prompted by the Lindberg case of 1930 (The Mann Act), and (5) the White Slave Act—covering interstate prostitution.

Federal Drug Enforcement Administration (FDEA). Prior to 1973, many fragmented government agencies pursued various courses of action in combatting dangerous drugs. In 1973 the Bureau of Narcotics and Dangerous Drugs (BNDD), the Office for Drug Abuse Law Enforcement, the Office of National Narcotics Intelligence, and the drug and investigative and intelligence units of the Bureau of Customs were merged into the Federal Drug Enforcement Administration.

Narcotics agents seek to stop the flow of drugs at their source, both domestic and foreign, and to assist state and local police in preventing illegal drugs from reaching local communities. They become involved in surveillance, raids, interviewing witnesses and suspects, searching for evidence, and seizure of contraband goods.

To accomplish its goals, the FDEA has developed an overall federal drug strategy that includes planning, workable programs, evaluation, and intelligence. Charged with the full responsibility for the prosecution of suspected violators of federal drug laws, they have liaison with law enforcement officials of foreign governments. They have highly trained agents stationed in all major United States cities and in thirty countries throughout the world.

The FDEA is also responsible for the regulation of the legal manufacture of drugs and other controlled substances under the Controlled Substances Act of 1970. Since intelligence is an essential element in the success of any enforcement agency, the FDEA has an Office of Intelligence staffed by experienced criminal investigators and intelligence analysts. An important facet of this intelligence program is the continued exchange of information with other federal, state, local, and foreign law enforcement agencies.

The FDEA maintains six regional laboratories throughout the country to accumulate up-to-date information regarding drugs under its jurisdiction. This information is distributed to law enforcement agencies, allowing them to better cope with drug abuse problems and their related effects.

Since successful prosecution of controlled substances cases requires physical evidence, the laboratories provide definitive identification of such substances as well as expert testimony in court. The laboratories also have the capability of fingerprint processing and photographic printing and development.

The primary emphasis of the Federal Drug Enforcement Administration (FDEA) is apprehending the suppliers and distributors of illicit drugs rather than arresting drug abusers.

The federal government recognized the existence of a drug problem in this country nearly sixty-five years ago. Early government response, embodied in the Harrison Narcotic Act of 1914, was directed exclusively at controlling the supply of dangerous drugs. The Harrison Act established federal control over the supply, distribution, and use of narcotics. But almost no attention was given at the federal level to the treatment and rehabilitation of drug users until the early 1930s when the United States Public Health Service Hospitals at Lexington, Kentucky, and Fort Worth, Texas, were established to treat drug addicts.

The Special Action Office for Drug Abuse Prevention, established in 1971, placed further emphasis on treatment and rehabilitation of drug addicts. The mission of this office is twofold: (1) to reduce drug abuse in the United States and (2) to develop a comprehensive, long-term federal strategy to combat drug abuse.

The Special Action Office covers all federal programs or activities related to drug abuse education, training, treatment, rehabilitation, and research. It was the Special Action Office which assisted in a nationwide review of all methadone maintenance programs, and its recommendations were instrumental in changing the status of the drug to a recognized form of medical treatment, under strict governmental controls.

The United States Marshals. In 1789 Congress created the office of United States Marshal. The U.S. Marshals are appointed by the president with the approval of the Senate, as recommended by the attorney general, for a period of four years.

Each marshal's office has a staff of deputy marshals to carry out its functions and responsibilities. The functions of most deputy marshals are more enforcement than investigative. They are responsible for (1) seizing property in both criminal and civil matters to satisfy judgments issued by a federal court, (2) providing physical security for United States courtrooms and protection for federal judges, jurors, and attorneys, (3) transporting federal prisoners to federal institutions when transferred or sentenced by a federal court, and (4) protecting government witnesses whose testimony might jeopardize their safety. Such witnesses are protected by the government by being salaried, relocated in other cities, and provided with new identities.

> *The U.S. Marshal's Office is responsible for arresting persons for whom warrants are issued charging a federal crime, providing physical security for U.S. courtrooms and personal protection for federal judges, jurors, and attorneys, for transporting prisoners, and for protecting witnesses.*

Immigration and Naturalization Service (INS). The Immigration and Naturalization Service has border patrol agents who serve throughout the United States, Canada, Mexico, Bermuda, Nassau, Puerto Rico, the Philippines, and Europe. They conduct investigations, detect violations of immigrant and nationality laws, and determine whether aliens may enter or remain in the United States. It also has immigration inspectors who are responsible for detecting people who are in violation of immigration and nationality laws. They work with border patrol agents and other investigators in determining whether an applicant may enter the United States.

The service administers a variety of federal laws that pertain to the admission, exclusion, or deportation of aliens who have unlawfully come into the country and taken up residence. They are also responsible for the registration of all aliens in this country and make recommendations to the courts regarding persons applying for citizenship or citizens for whom the service is requesting deportation.

The Immigration and Naturalization Service conducts investigations, detects violations of immigration and nationality laws, and determines whether aliens may enter or remain in the United States.

The extensive activities of the border patrol have resulted in many arrests for smuggling contraband and aliens into the United States. Searches for smuggled aliens are often made of automobiles, airplanes, and boats. The border patrol primarily uses airplanes, boats, and vehicles to deter illegal smuggling. Air-to-ground operations and searches of freight trains traveling between the United States and Mexico are common.

The Bureau of Prisons. Correctional officers are responsible for supervising, safeguarding, and training inmates of federal prisons, reformatories, and camps. They act as foreman of work assignments, enforce rules and regulations within the institutions, and carry out plans developed for correctional treatment and modification of attitudes of the inmates.

The correctional officers of the Bureau of Prisons supervise, safeguard, and train inmates of federal prisons, reformatories, and camps.

The Bureau of Prisons is an integral part of the federal criminal justice system. It is responsible for the care and custody of persons convicted of federal crimes and sentenced to federal penal institutions. The Bureau operates a nationwide system of maximum, medium, and minimum security prisons, halfway houses, and community program offices.

The Department of the Treasury

The Department of the Treasury also has several agencies directly involved in law enforcement activities.

Law enforcement agencies under the jurisdiction of the Department of the Treasury include the Bureau of Customs, the Internal Revenue Service, the Secret Service, and the Bureau of Alcohol, Tobacco, and Firearms Tax.

The Bureau of Customs. The Bureau of Customs has agents stationed primarily at ports of entry to the United States, places where people and/or goods enter and leave, either by boat, plane, or car. Customs agents conduct investigations concerning the prevention and detection of frauds on the customs revenue and the smuggling of merchandise and contraband into or out of the United States.

Bureau of Customs agents enforce the Tariff Act, the Mutual Security Act, and the Narcotic Drug Import and Export Act. They have authority to conduct investigations and searches on all ships registered under U.S. laws.

Customs is active in suppressing the traffic in illegal narcotics and works in close cooperative with the Federal Drug Enforcement Administration. Customs patrol officers maintain uniformed and plainclothes surveillance at docks and airports.

> *Bureau of Customs special agents assure that property duty is paid on goods coming into the country and that narcotics, drugs, and defense materials do not enter or leave the country illegally.*

The Internal Revenue Service (IRS). The Internal Revenue Service, established in 1862, is responsible for the enforcement of all internal revenue laws. Special agents obtain facts in tax fraud cases, particularly for income tax, excise tax, and coin-operated gaming devices.

> *Internal Revenue Service agents investigate willful tax evasion, tax fraud, and the activities of gamblers and drug peddlers.*

The service has responsibility in the areas of social security taxes, federal stamp taxes, estate taxes, excise taxes, the filing of income tax reports, and the willful evasion by citizens to pay their taxes. The Intelligence Division has been actively engaged in the prosecution of gamblers, drug peddlers, and others committing fraud against the government and citizens through illegal stock transactions, nondisclosure of income, and the transfer of money out of the country.

Among the functions of its many offices throughout the country, the IRS assists the general public in preparing tax returns, collects internal revenue taxes, and determines delinquent and additional tax liability.

Internal security inspectors investigate charges against IRS employees involving criminal violations of the Internal Revenue Code or violations of the Criminal Code.

The United States Secret Services. The Secret Service was established in 1865 to fight currency counterfeiters. In 1901 it was given the responsibility of protecting the president of the United States, members of his family, the president-elect, and the vice-president.

> *The Secret Service investigates counterfeiting of U.S. currency and forged government checks and bonds. Secret Service special agents guard the president and vice-president and their families, the president-elect and the vice-president-elect, and former presidents upon request.*

The Secret Service has two major law enforcement functions: the suppression of counterfeiting and the suppression of forgery of government checks and bonds.

It has other duties, too, such as investigations of United States financial institutions. In their efforts to suppress counterfeiting and forgery, agents rely heavily on scientific investigation. To aid the agents, the Bureau of Engraving and Printing in Washington maintains a laboratory with modern scientific crime detection equipment. From the examinations conducted at the laboratory, the Secret Service gets valuable information which often leads its agents to the successful conclusion of cases.

The Secret Service is also responsible for the investigation of threats against the president, either by mail or verbally. In 1976 the Secret Service became responsible for the protection of presidential candidates as a result of threats against several of them and the actual shooting of a presidental candidate, Governor George Wallace of Alabama.

In addition to Secret Service special agents, two uniformed groups are under the control and direction of the service: the White House Police and the Treasury Guard Force.

The *White House Police* protect the executive mansion and its grounds. Officers assigned to the White House Police are highly trained in detecting subversive activities, techniques of identifying potential threats to the president, and in self-defense tactics.

The *Treasury Guard Force* protects the Treasury Building and the Treasury Annex in Washington. The Treasury Building has 475 rooms and covers the greater part of two city blocks. Beneath this building are safety vaults where the nation's money and valuable papers are kept. The Treasury Guard Force is assigned to the continuous protection of the immense sums in the U.S. Treasury.

The Bureau of Alcohol, Tobacco, and Firearms Tax (BATF).   The Bureau of Alcohol, Tobacco, and Firearms Tax, an enforcement arm of the Department of the Treasury, is primarily a licensing and investigative agency involved in federal tax violations.

The Firearms Division is responsible for enforcing the Gun Control Act of 1968 which deals with the manufacture, sale, transfer, and possession of restricted firearms in the United States including the illegal possession of automatic weapons, machine guns, and submachine guns by persons other than antique collectors.

U.S. Secret Service protecting President Reagan during inaugural parade.

The bureau also regulates interstate commerce in all types of guns and to or from foreign countries. In addition, they collect the taxes of U.S. importers, manufacturers, and dealers of firearms. The bureau maintains a close relationship with other federal, state, and local enforcement agencies so that gun control laws are rigidly enforced.

The objectives of its criminal enforcement activity are to eliminate illegal possession and use of firearms, destructive devices, and explosives; to suppress the traffic in illicit distilled spirits; to enforce the criminal violation and forfeiture aspects of the federal wagering laws; and to cooperate with state and local enforcement agencies to reduce crime and violence (*U.S. Government Manual*, p. 437).

> *Alcohol, Tobacco, and Firearms Tax inspectors enforce federal laws dealing with the manufacture, sale, and distribution of illegal alcoholic beverages, cigarettes, and firearms.*

Other Federal Law Enforcement Agencies

Although the majority of federal law enforcement agencies are within the Department of Justice and the Department of the Treasury, other federal agencies are also directly involved in law enforcement activities such as the U.S. Postal Inspectors, the Coast Guard, military police of the armed forces, and investigators and intelligence agents and security officers for other federal agencies.

U.S. Postal Inspectors enforce federal laws pertaining to the mailing of prohibited items such as explosives, obscene matter, and articles likely to injure or cause damage. Any mail that may prove to be libelous, defamatory, or threatening can be excluded from being transported by the postal service. The postal inspectors are responsible for protecting the mails and the recipients of mail. They also investigate any frauds perpetrated through the mails such as chain letters, gift enterprises, and similar schemes. The postmaster general is also authorized to prevent the delivery of mail to persons who might be using the mails to conduct a fraudulent business.

The *U.S. Coast Guard* assists local and state agencies which border the oceans, lakes, and national waterways. They have been actively involved in preventing the smuggling of narcotics into this country.

The *armed forces* also have law enforcement responsibilities. The uniformed divisions are known as the Military Police in the Army, the Shore Patrol in the Navy, and the Security Police in the Marine Corps and Air Force. Military police are enlisted personnel and officers; civilians do not serve in the uniformed military police units. Usually, these military police must not only meet all enlistment requirements of the service, but also must show an aptitude for police work, must score well on the entrance examination, and must meet certain physical requirements. The military police in each service are primarily concerned with the physical security of the various bases under their control. Within each operation, the security forces control criminal activity, court martials, discipline, desertions, and the confinement of prisoners. In time of war they are responsible for prisoners of war as well as custodial care and movement of refugees.

> *Other federal law enforcement agencies include the U.S. Postal Inspectors, the Coast Guard, the military police of the armed forces, and investigators and intelligence agents and security officers for numerous federal units.*

The Law Enforcement Assistance Administration (LEAA)

In 1968 Congress enacted the Omnibus Crime Control and Safe Streets Act; Title 1 of this Act established the Law Enforcement Assistance Administration. When the Act was amended in 1970 the LEAA program was expanded. The Crime Control Act of 1973 further strengthened the agency and extended its authorization through 1976. The Crime Control Act of 1976 extended the program through September of 1979.

Pursley (1984, p. 165) notes that: "Although the Law Enforcement Assistance Administration (LEAA) was never a federal law enforcement agency, it deserves special attention because it may well have brought about the most important developments in the annals of American criminal justice. During its relatively brief period of existence, no other American crime control agency appears to have produced the far-ranging improvements that LEAA brought to American criminal justice."

LEAA worked in partnership with state and local governments, which have historically assumed the primary responsibility for crime reduction and law enforcement. Congress affirmed this historical responsibility in the Omnibus Crime Control and Safe Streets Act: "Crime is essentially a local problem that must be dealt with by state and local governments if it is to be controlled effectively."

On the other hand, as noted by Richard W. Velde, former LEAA administrator: "Crime control is everyone's business. It is not just the business of the criminal justice system—of police, courts, and corrections—but of all citizens who want to live in harmony and peace."

Realizing the national significance of the crime problem, Congress created the LEAA to join state and local law enforcement agencies in their efforts to combat crime. Under the anticrime partnership, the federal government supplied financial resources, technical advice, and leadership. However, states and localities set their own crime control priorities, devised specific action programs, and allocated LEAA funds according to their carefully developed plans.

LEAA awarded more than $9 billion to state and local governments to improve police, courts, and correctional systems; to combat juvenile delinquency; and to finance innovative crime-fighting projects.

> *Created by the Omnibus Crime Control and Safe Streets Act of 1968, The Law Enforcement Assistance Administration (LEAA) provided financial resources, technical advice, and leadership to state and local law enforcement agencies. States and localities set their own crime control priorities, devised specific action programs, and allocated LEAA funds according to their approved plans.*

Block Action Grants.   The LEAA awarded the states block action grants to carry out specific improvement projects. Block grants were allocated according to population to fifty-five eligible jurisdictions: the fifty states, Washington, D.C., Purerto Rico, American Samoa, Guam, and the Virgin Islands. The State Planning Agency then subgranted these funds to cities, counties, and state agencies.

Major Achievements.   Every state and locality felt the impact of LEAA's nationwide anticrime program. Tens of thousands of programs and projects were supported with LEAA funds, and millions of hours were applied to identify effective, efficient, economical ways to reduce crime and improve criminal justice. Projects were developed to reduce crime and improve criminal justice, to improve the management and administration of courts, to deploy police officers more effectively, to find jobs for ex-offenders, to sharpen the skills of criminal justice personnel, to give prosecutors better tools to fight crime, and to break the jail-street-crime-jail cycle of the drug addict.

> *LEAA supported: victimization surveys; establishment of standards and goals; high-impact programs; surveys of jails, courts, private security industry, and juvenile correctional facilities; development of new equipment; in-service and preservice educational grants and loans (LEEP); as well as hundreds of state and local anticrime projects.*

National Institute of Law Enforcement and Criminal Justice. The LEAA created the National Institute of Law Enforcement and Criminal Justice, a research and evaluation agency, which continued on after LEAA was no longer in existence. This institute developed the National Criminal Justice Reference Service and the National Criminal Justice Statistics Center.

Law Enforcement Education Program. Another major contribution of LEAA was the Law Enforcement Education Program (LEEP) which gave money to colleges so they could make loans and grants to individuals "employed in or preparing for employment in criminal justice agencies." These grants and loans totaled more than $150 million and allowed 200,000 men and women to upgrade their criminal justice capabilities. As Pursley (1984, p. 170) states: "Were it not for the LEEP program, many in-service criminal justice practitioners would never have had the opportunity to obtain advanced education."

The Demise of LEAA.   Richard D. Lamm, Governor of Colorado (1978), notes that LEAA "endured a very troubled history," due in part to extremely unrealistic and high expectations which led to inevitable excesses and failures. In the program's early years, the Nixon "law and order" administration exerted great pressure to get money out into the field without allowing states sufficient time to properly plan for use of the funds. In addition, LEAA's management was unstable; it had five administrators in seven years, each with his own philosophy. Finally, frequent delays in publishing the guidelines for the annual planning cycle hampered the states' ability to plan properly. According to Pursley (1984, pp. 165–170):

The death knell for LEAA sounded shortly after the election of Ronald Reagan in 1980. Reagan's austerity efforts backed by congress ended LEAA . . . .

LEAA received a great deal of criticism in certain areas. It was criticized primarily for the excessive red tape involved in compliance with its guidelines, poor targeting of grant funds, insufficient local control over expenditures, and ineffective research and evaluation efforts.

Although the concept and the goals of LEAA and the legislation that created the agency were laudable, the history of this agency and its efforts serve as a vivid example of how broad social goals fare badly when transmitted from legislation to actual application. Like so many other social programs initiated at the federal level, federal crime policy under the Safe Street Act met ideological and structural barriers that limited its effectiveness. It was also severely hampered by lack of understanding of the crime problem and simple naivete about how to deal with it.

State Agencies

Many of the federal agencies have state counterparts.

State agencies with law enforcement responsibilities include state bureaus of investigation and apprehension and state fire marshal divisions as well as departments of natural resources, driver and vehicle services divisions, and departments of human rights.

Office of the State Attorney General

The attorney general is the chief legal counsel for the state. His office provides representation and advice to agencies in the executive branch of state government. The attorney general proposes and drafts legislation on a variety of subjects and assures that all state laws are adequately and uniformly enforced. His office also supervises district attorneys and sheriffs.

In addition to an antitrust division and a consumer protection division, the attorney general's office has a criminal division which conducts criminal appeals, advises local prosecutors on the conduct of criminal trials, and helps develop and prosecute certain criminal cases, particularly those of organized crime and white-collar crime.

The attorney general's opinions office provides information to state and local officials on effects and requirements of state laws when laws either appear to conflict or are unclear in their application.

The state attorney general is the chief law enforcement officer at the state level. His office usually includes an antitrust division, a consumer protection division, a criminal division, and an opinions office.

State Bureau of Investigation and Apprehension

States vary in their organizations and functions of agencies that offer support to other law enforcement agencies in the state. They usually are organized to assist local law enforcement officials. The Bureau of Investigation and Apprehension places investigators throughout the state to assist in investigations of major crimes and organized criminal activities; aids in investigating the illegal sale or possession of narcotics and prohibited drugs; conducts police science training courses for peace officers; provides scientific examination of crime scenes and laboratory analysis of evidence; and maintains a criminal justice information and tele-communications system. The Bureau also provides statistical information on crimes and crime trends in the state.

State Fire Marshal Division

Designated state fire marshals investigate suspicious and incendiary fire origins, fire fatalities, and large-loss fires; tabulate fire statistics; and provide education, inspection, and training programs for fire prevention.

The *Fire Prevention Section* provides information on the state's Uniform Fire Code, removal of combustible materials, correction of fire hazards, fire prevention, and general information on smoke/heat detectors, fire alarms, fire extinguishers, and other fire protection appliances.

The *Inspection and Investigation Section* organizes investigation of all fires of suspicious and incendiary origin, large-loss fires, and fire fatalities. The section also conducts ongoing inspection of public and private schools, state hospitals, convalescent and other special purpose homes, hotels, rooming houses and other multiple dwellings, dry cleaning establishments, motion picture theaters, places of assembly, and all installations where petroleum products, liquified petroleum gas and natural gas are manufactured, stored, or distributed.

The *Fire Prevention Awareness Section* identifies problem fire areas, inspects fires and buildings to guarantee fire safety standards, conducts public awareness programs, and maintains contact with local fire departments.

State Department of Natural Resources (Fish, Game, and Watercraft)

Some states combine fish, game, and watercraft under one division, a Department of Natural Resources, which enforces all laws and rules under its jurisdicition including hunting, fishing, and trapping laws and licenses, and laws on the operation of watercraft. In some states the department is responsible for the firearms training laws. The division may hold auction sales to dispose of furs, firearms, and hunting, fishing, and trapping equipment confiscated from violators of fish and game laws.

Conservation officers investigate complaints about nuisance wildlife, misuse of public lands and waters, violations of state park rules, and unlawful appropriation of state-owned timber. Conservation officers also dispose of big game animals struck by motor vehicles, assist state game managers on wildlife census projects, enforce wild-rice harvesting rules, and assist in identifying needed sites for public access to lakes and streams.

The department also issues resident and nonresident boat licenses and licenses for hunting, fishing, and trapping.

Driver and Vehicle Services Division

The *Motor Vehicle Section of the Driver and Vehicle Services Division* registers motor vehicles, issues ownership certificates, answers inquiries, returns defective applications received through the mail, licenses motor vehicle dealers, supplies record information to the public, and in some states, registers bicycles.

The *Driver's License Section* tests, evaluates, and licenses all drivers throughout the state; maintains accurate records of each individual driver including all violations and accidents occurring anywhere in the United States and Canada; interviews drivers whose record warrants possible revocation, suspension, or cancellation; records the location of every reported accident; assists in driver education efforts; and administers written and road tests to applicants.

The Department of Human Rights

The Department of Human Rights enforces the Human Rights Act which prohibits discrimination on the basis of race, color, creed, religion, national origin, sex, marital status, status with regard to public assistance or disability in employment, housing, public accommodations, public service, and education. It is also responsible for current affirmative action laws. It investigates and conciliates discrimination complaints. When conciliation is not possible, it settles the complaint through legal proceedings.

State Police and State Highway Patrol

The most visible form of state law enforcement is the state police who often have general police powers and enforce all state laws, and state highway patrols who focus their attention upon the operation of motor vehicles on public highways and freeways.

Each state differs from all others in its state police agencies, depending on its history and evolving law enforcement needs. From the Texas Rangers in 1835 to the present, new agencies have been formed and old agencies reorganized to meet the changing requirements of the states.

Some state police enforce all state laws; others enforce only traffic laws on highways and freeways and are usually designated as state highway patrol.

Usually *state police agencies,* although often having general police authority, do not work within municipalities which have their own forces, except upon request. These state forces generally do not enter local labor, political, or other mass disturbances or potentially disastrous situations unless asked by the local sheriff or police chief.

Most *highway patrol agencies* enforce state traffic laws and all laws governing operation of vehicles on public highways in the state. They usually operate in uniform, drive distinctively marked patrol cars and motorcycles, and engage in such activities as (1) enforcing laws regulating the use of vehicles, (2) maintaining preventive patrol on the highways, (3) regulating traffic movements and relieving congestion, (4) investigating traffic accidents, and (5) making surveys and studies of accidents and enforcement practices to improve traffic safety (Adams, 1980).

The Michigan State Police and the Pennsylvania State Police are examples of agencies which have general police powers. In contrast, Florida's Highway Patrol deals with traffic while the Florida Department of Law Enforcement conducts investigations. Similarly, the Minnesota Highway Patrol directs its primary attention to enforcement of traffic laws while the Minnesota Bureau of Criminal Apprehension limits its function to investigative and enforcement functions at the state level.

In California, the Department of the California Highway Patrol is responsible for enforcing the traffic laws, investigating traffic accidents, and rendering aid to motorists on the state and interstate highways. The California State Police are responsible for protecting only state property. They protect the state capital and grounds as well as other state government buildings located throughout the state.

Some state highway patrol organizations maintain a traffic safety section that coordinates traffic safety programs throughout the state to assure uniformity in adherence to the many traffic laws. They assist all organizations, both public and private, in planning and operating effective safety programs. They may assist local agencies by providing intensive enforcement training for traffic personnel. They may also maintain auto theft records more efficiently because of their statewide jurisdiction. They may also provide laboratory and invesitgative personnel to assist local agencies in the investigation of hit-and-run cases and auto theft.

In addition, some highway patrol agencies coordinate the activity and maintain records on commercial vehicle enforcement, maintain public scales on the highways, inspect all school buses, and investigate accidents involving school buses throughout the state. Licensing or registration of official smog-control devices or headlights and other safety equipment installations as well as inspection stations may also be functions performed by state highway patrol.

A governor may send state highway patrol or state police personnel to a locality to preserve the peace. This occurred in Mississippi and other southern states during mob actions prompted by efforts to racially integrate public schools. On two such occasions (Little Rock, Arkansas, in 1957 and Oxford, Mississippi, in 1962), National Guard units and regular U.S. Army military personnel were ordered by federal authorities to assist state and local police in maintaining civil order.

The increasing responsibilities of state police are considerable. They often work in cooperation with the National Guard to restore order in mass disturbances. They have assumed responsibility from county sheriffs for policing traffic on major highways, and they assist the sheriff or small-town police officer in solving crimes requiring the use of specialized equipment. Further, many state police or highway patrol organizations administer the duties of the state fire marshal's office.

County Agencies

The two main types of county law enforcement agencies are the county sheriff and the county police.

The County Sheriff

Many state constitutions have designated the sheriff as the chief law enforcement officer of the county. The sheriff is usually elected locally for a two- or four-year term. Qualifications are set by state law, and the salary is usually set by the legislature or the county board. As Folley (1980, p. 288) notes:

> The office of sheriff is probably the most obvious example of mixing police and politics. This office was integrated into the American police system with little change from what it was in England. Today the office of sheriff is subject to popular election in almost all counties throughout the United States . . . when a new sheriff is elected he will repay political debts by appointing new deputies and promoting others already employed. . . . This constant change of leadership and manipulation of the heirarchy has not been conducive to the provision of efficient police services.

The sheriff's powers and duties are also established by state law. Each sheriff is authorized to appoint deputies and, working with them, to assume responsibility for providing police protection as well as a variety of other functions including (1) keeping the public peace, (2) executing civil and criminal process throughout the county (such as serving civil legal papers and criminal warrants), (3) keeping the county jail, (4) preserving the dignity of the court, and (5) enforcing court orders.

The sheriff operates freely in the unincorporated portions of the county and works with the municipal police departments in incorporated areas. The sheriff also works closely with the state police or highway patrol and township personnel in unincorporated portions of the county.

The sheriff appoints deputy sheriffs to assist him in fulfilling his responsibilities. The hundreds of sheriff's departments vary greatly in organization and function. In some states the sheriff is primarily an officer of the court; criminal investigation and traffic enforcement are delegated to state or local agencies. In other states, notably in the south and west, the sheriff and his deputies perform both traffic and criminal duties.

The sheriff's staff ranges in size from one (the sheriff only) to several hundred including sworn deputies as well as civilian personnel. Likewise, a wide range of technical proficiency and expertise also occurs among sheriff's personnel. Some departments have little equipment; others have fleets of patrol vehicles, airplanes, helicopters, and lavishly equipped crime laboratories.

Holten and Jones (1978, p. 98) cite a major difference between sheriffs' offices and municipal police departments as "a greater emphasis by sheriffs on civil functions and operation of corrections facitilites. There are often, for example, separate divisions or bureaus within sheriffs' departments for performing the civil functions of process serving and/or operating the county jail and caring for prisoners."

There are an estimated 3,340 county sheriff departments in the United States.

The County Police

The county police, not to be confused with the county sheriff and his deputies, are often found in areas where city and county governments have been merged, such as in Florida. County police departments are headed by a chief of police, usually an administrator appointed from within the department, who is accountable to a county commissioner, prosecutor, manager, or director of public safety.

There are about seventy-five such county police departments in the United States. Pursley (1984, p. 169) states that: "Many counties that have adopted the county police department have given this agency full authority and responsibility to perform all law enforcement functions."

Overlap Between the County Sheriff and County Police

Pursley goes on to note that when county police departments are established, they are often forced to retain the sheriff. He cites.Georgia as an example of a state which recognizes the sheriff as a constitutional officer yet allows counties to establish independent police agencies. Pursley suggests that: "This duplication is costly, and people do not know whether to call the sheriff's department or the county police. A great deal of political acrimony has also been apparent between the heads of these two agencies as well as among political supporters and elected officials who either side with the sheriff or the county police. This results in charges and counter-charges of incompetence, poor service, corruption, and a host of other claims being leveled at one agency by supporters of the other."

The Coroner or Medical Examiner

Another officer of the county is the coroner or medical examiner. Adams (1980, p. 150) points out that the office of coroner has a history similar to that of the sheriff, coming to modern law enforcement from ancient times. The principal task of the coroner is to determine the cause of death and to take care of the remains and personal effects of deceased persons. According to Adams: "The coroner is required by law to investigate and sign the death certificate in all circumstances where a violent death has occurred, a sudden or unusual death, an unattended death, and any death that may have suspicious circumstances surrounding it whether it be associated with a crime, a public hazard, or a disease."

The coroner need not be a medical doctor or have any legal background to be elected; however, in some jurisdictions, the coroner has been replaced by the medical examiner who is a doctor of medicine, usually a pathologist who has studied forensic science.

In some states the coroner or medical examiner is, by statutory provision, the chief law enforcement officer of the county. When this occurs, a sheriff's department usually has the traditional combination of criminal and civil duties to perform. In Illinois, for example, the coroner is the only one who can serve subpoenas on the sheriff. If the sheriff becomes incapacitated and cannot function, or if the sheriff is arrested (which can be done only by the coroner), the coroner becomes sheriff until one is elected.

Local Agencies

Township and Special District Police

The United States has approximately 19,000 townships which vary widely in scope of governmental powers and operations. Most townships provide a very limited range of services for predominately rural areas. Some townships, often those in well-developed fringe areas surrounding a metropolitan complex, perform functions similar to municipal police.

Not all townships have their own police force. Many rural townships have few law enforcement problems and purposely avoid appropriating funds for local police protection, relying instead upon the sheriff or state police (or both) for preventive patrol and criminal investigation.

When small, essentially rural townships enter the policing field, a variety of difficulties arise. In addition to jurisdiction conflicts and the resulting diffusion of responsibility, a general lack of coordination results from having two or more government agencies, at different levels, actively policing the same area. The small township department, with its limited financial support, cannot offer complete police services, provide specialized services, nor police the area continually, but if there is a township police force, regardless of its adequacy, township residents and officials cannot exert as much pressure on the county governing body to expand the sheriff's force to being about better general county police protection.

Many townships have only a one-man police force similar to the resident deputy system frequently found in sheriff's departments in which one person must police vast, sparsely populated regions. This person serves as a "jack-of-all-trades" and is on emergency call day and night. His home may serve as headquarters.

The Constable

Approximately twenty states have established through their constitutions the office of constable, especially in New England, the South and the West. The constable is usually an elected official who serves a township, preserving the peace and serving processes for the local justice court. The constable may also be the tax collector or in charge of the pound, execute arrest warrants and transport prisoners. In some jurisdictions, the constable is under the direction of the sheriff.

Municipal Police

The United States has over 40,000 police jurisdictions and approximately 450,000 police officers, all with similar responsibilities, but with limited geographical jurisdictions. The least uniformity and greatest organizational complexity is found at the municipal level due to local autonomy, that is, the independence of local governmental units to control their own police departments.

The majority of these police forces consist of fewer than ten officers who provide resident duputy-type police service rather than emergency-oriented service. Some personnel of very small forces are appointed with little attention to their mental or physical fitness for the work, and many such personnel have never received any formal police training and lack proper supervision and discipline.

In contrast are police agencies in large metropolitan areas such as New York City, which have over 30,000 officers who are highly qualified and trained to perform demanding duties. Likewise, many suburban areas are now hiring career-minded, progressive police officers who bring with them dedication, education, and a high degree of competency in human relations and technical skills.

Suburban police departments have different policing problems than small towns and large cities, just as a small town police department is far different from that of a city of several million people in terms of organization, structure, and discipline.

The Marshal

In some parts of the United States, a marshal serves as an officer of the court, serving writs, subpoenas, and other papers issued by the court and escorting prisoners from jail or holding cells in the courthouse to and from trials and hearings. The marshal also serves as the bailiff and protects the municipal judge and people in the court. In some jurisdictions the marshal is elected; in other jurisdications the marshal is appointed.

Overlap

Police agencies of the five governmental levels can be found operating in any given spot in America. For example, you can find: (1) several federal police establishments operating as much as 4,000 miles from Washington, D.C., (2) one or more state-wide police services, (3) the county sheriff and county police force,

(4) the township constables and town police constables or marshals, (5) village police or marshals, (6) city police forces that range in size from 10 to 39,000 officers, (7) special park and turnpike police, (8) special district police, (9) independent state and county detectives, identification, communication, and records agencies, and (10) numerous others of less direct relationship to the official police function. Furthermore, efforts must sometimes be coordinated with private security forces.

The evils of overlapping jurisdictions and the pitfalls of competition when two (and often many more) forces find themselves investigating the same offense pose serious problems to law enforcement and highlight the need for education and professionalism.

Private Security Forces

Private security forces include watchmen, guards, patrols, investigators, armed couriers, central alarm respondents, and consultants. These private security officers perform many of the same functions as public law officers: controlling entrances and exits to facilities; preventing or reporting fires; promoting safety; safeguarding equipment, valuables, and confidential material; and patrolling restricted areas. Businessess, educational, industrial, and commerical organizations frequently hire private security guards to protect their premises and investments.

There are, however, important differences between private and public security forces. Public police officers are salaried with public funds. They are responsible to a chief of police and ultimately to the citizens of the community. Technically they are on-duty twenty-four hours a day and have full authority to uphold the law, including the authority to make arrests and to carry a concealed weapon.

Still, the public police officer cannot be everywhere at the same time. Therefore, many businesses and organizations have elected to hire special protection. Basically, two different types of private security may be hired: private partolmen and private watchmen.

As the name implies, private patrolmen operate both on and off the premises of their employer and may have several customers to check periodically during a specified time period. However, private watchmen stay on the property to safeguard the premises at all times.

A further distinction exists between the security officer employed by a large industrial concern and the night watchman employed by a small firm. The former are usually carefully screened, well paid, and trained to perform specific duties. In contrast, the night watchman is frequently retired from a regular job (sometimes as a public police officer), needs only temporary work, or is simply supplementing a regular income by taking on a second job.

From 200,000 plant watchmen in World War II, to over one million private security personnel today, the private security force is experiencing tremendous growth and has expanded to include private investigators, armed couriers, central alarm respondents, and consultants. Hemphill (1979, p. 279) notes that in the 1980s private security is a multibillion-dollar-a-year business that in the past decade has grown 10 to 12 percent annually.

Private security forces differ from public security forces in several ways:

- *They are salaried with private funds.*
- *They are responsible to an employer.*
- *They have limited authority and then only on the premises which they were hired to guard.*
- *They have no authority to make arrests except as a citizen's arrest, unless deputized.*
- *They have no authority to carry a concealed weapon.*
- *Their uniform and badge must not closely resemble that of the regular police officer.*

Table 6–1.   **Trends for Tomorrow's Security.**

	Significant Increase	Moderate Increase	No Change	Moderate Decrease	Significant Decrease
Use of contract guards and services	24%	34%	18%	13%	2%
Use of proprietary guard services	21	40	22	9	2
State controls of guard services	29	39	24	1	1
Use of polygraph tests	8	23	38	20	7
Use of psychological stress evaluators	9	30	35	13	8
State control of stress evaluators	18	35	34	3	2
Integration of security/energy management	35	44	12	1	.2
Terrorist attacks in the U.S.	18	47	27	3	1
Bomb threats in the U.S.	17	47	27	4	.2
Computer crime	49	39	7	1	2
White collar crime	50	39	6	.5	0
Corporate security/training programs	26	55	14	1	0
Corporate security budgets	20	54	14	5	.2
Use of CCTV	33	49	13	1	0
Use of perimeter protection equipment	23	52	20	1	0
Use of space protection equipment	17	51	25	.2	0
Use of central station equipment	19	55	19	2	1
User awareness of equip. manufacturers	23	52	21	0	0
User awareness of equip. brand names	19	49	26	.2	0
User direct contact with manufacturers	14	45	35	1	0
Consideration of manufacturer of equipment	22	46	26	.2	.2

Totals may be more than 100%

The Complementary Roles
of Private and Public Officers *

Private and public security forces frequently engage in similar activities and have similar goals, including prevention of crime. However, private security officers also perform functions that cannot be performed by public law enforcement officers, which makes their roles complementary. As noted by Kakalik and Wildhorn (1977, p. 90):

> With few exceptions guards perform work that the regular police cannot perform because of legal constraints or because of resource limitations. The public police typically can not be spared to prevent or investigate certain

---

PROFILE

The Average Security Director:

Retail/Wholesale	Institutional
Married male.	Married male.
Age: 39	Age: 45
Salary: $24,800	Salary: $23,500
Staff size: 19 persons	Staff size: 22
In security field: 10.2 years	In security field: 11.7 years
In current job: 4.8 years	In current job: 5.9 years
Education: 38% probability of bachelor's degree or better.	Education: 53% probability of bachelor's degree or better.

Reflecting growing public and corporate concerns with security, survey respondents saw increased activity among a number of issues and trends in the security industry. Leading the way was white collar crime, with 89% of the respondents saying it would increase over the next five years. Similarly, 88% of the respondents said computer crime would increase. Apparently as an answer to these and other threats, 81% said corporate security training programs would increase and 74% said corporate security budgets would increase.

Source: Security World Magazine, a Cahners Publication, copyright December, 1980.

---

*Reprinted by permission from *Introductions to Private Security*, Hess and Wrobleski, Copyright © 1982 by West Publishing Company. All rights reserved.

suspected crimes such as employee pilferage, and by law they must refrain from most crime-prevention activities on private property unless asked to do so by the owner. The public police are not legally charged with enforcing privately established rules and regulations. When specific private citizens, businesses, or institutions desire protection not offered by the public police, they must draw upon private sources. Typically, private guards perform functions that complement those of public police.

The International Association of Chiefs of Police (IACP) and the American Society for Industrial Security (ASIS) have been working together to improve the interactions of private and public officers so vital to successful crime prevention.

Unfortunately, however, friction often exists between private and public officers. The Law Enforcement/Private Security Relationship Committee of the Private Security Advisory Committee found the following barriers to an effective relationship between the two sectors: lack of mutual respect; lack of cooperation; lack of two-way communication; lack of knowledge by law enforcement of the function, mission, and problems of private security; the failure of private security to speak with a unified professional voice; and the need for better formulated and articulated standards of professionalism on both sides (*Private Security,* 1976, p. 19).

Because of the preceding factors, in 1974 the Private Security Council established a standing committee to study the law enforcement/private security relationship, to outline proposals to improve understanding and cooperation between them, and to develop guidelines for cooperation (*Private Security,* 1976, p. 207). Promoting cooperative interaction between private and public police officers is of utmost importance, as noted by a past LEAA administrator, Richard Velde:

> There is so much to be done in the area of crime prevention that I can think of no reason for competition between the police and private security in this area. In fact, I visualize a comprehensive program of modern, effective crime prevention in which private security and police departments cooperate with each other, exchange information, and utilize common bases of expertise and know-how. This will require, of course, mutual respect for each other's talents and capabilities.

Summary

Law enforcement in the United States is a cooperative effort among local, county, state, federal, and private law enforcement officers. Each has something to offer and to gain from the other.

At the federal level several law enforcement agencies are under the jurisdiction of the Departments of Justice and the Treasury. The U.S. Attorney General, as head of the Department of Justice, is the chief federal law enforcement officer. Within his department are the Federal Bureau of Investigation, the Federal Drug Enforcement Administration, United States Marshals, the Immigration and Naturalization Service, and the Bureau of Prisons.

The FBI, in addition to its numerous investigative responsibilities, provides assistance to law enforcement agencies throughout the country through its Identification Division, its crime laboratory, its National Crime Information Center, and its Uniform Crime Reports.

Law enforcement agencies within the Department of the Treasury include the Bureau of Customs, the Internal Revenue Service, the Secret Service, and the Bureau of Alcohol, Tobacco, and Firearms Tax.

Other federal law enforcement agencies include the U.S. Postal Inspectors, the Coast Guard, and the military police of the armed forces.

Although not itself a law enforcement agency, the Law Enforcement Assistance Administration (LEAA) provided financial resources, technical advice, and leadership to state and local law enforcement agencies during the 1970s.

State law enforcement agencies include state bureaus of investigation and apprehension, state fire marshals divisions, state departments of natural resources, driver and vehicle services divisions, departments of human rights, state police, and state highway patrol.

At the county level, the two main types of law enforcement agencies are the county sheriff and the county police.

In addition, private security officers provide special protection for businesses and educational, industrial, and commercial organizations. They perform many of the same functions as public law officers, but they also differ in several important ways.

You may rightly be wondering, what about the local law enforcement? This is the focus of the remainder of the book.

Application

1. For each of the agencies listed below, indicate whether they are a part of the Department of Justice (J), the Department of the Treasury (T), or some other governmental agency (O):

___ a. Bureau of Alcohol, Tobacco, and Firearms (BATF)

___ b. Bureau of Customs

___ c. Sheriff's Office

___ d. Federal Drug Enforcement Administration (FDEA)

___ e. Federal Bureau of Investigation (FBI)

___ f. Immigration and Naturalization Services (INS)

___ g. Internal Revenue Service (IRS)

___ h.   Postal Inspectors

___ i.   Secret Service

___ j.   State Police

___ k.   United States Marshal

___ l.   United States Attorney General

___ m.   United States military police

2. Using the preceding agencies, state which agency would have the responsibility for the problems and activities which follow:

___ a.   Piracy of an aircraft

___ b.   Kidnapping

___ c.   Distributing illegal drugs

___ d.   Protecting witnesses in federal court cases

___ e.   Arresting persons charged with federal crimes

___ f.   Apprehending smuggled aliens

___ g.   Protecting the president and his family

___ h.   Assuring payment of duty on goods coming into the country

___ i.   Investigating tax fraud

___ j.   Investigating counterfeiting of U.S. currency

___ k.   Espionage

___ l.   Regulating interstate commerce in firearms

___ m.   Enforcing traffic laws on highways and freeways

___ n.   Sabotage

___ o.   Bank robbery

3. Check the characteristics below which are typical of a private security officer (in contrast to a public peace officer):

___ a.   Has full authority to make arrests

___ b.   May wear a uniform and a badge

___ c.   Is on duty twenty-four hours a day

___ d.   Works for an employer

___ e.   Has authority to carry a concealed weapon

___ f.   Salaried from private funds

Answers

1. a. T   d. J   g. T   j. O   m. O
   b. T   e. J   h. O   k. J
   c. O   f. J   i. T   l. J

2. a. FBI　　　f. INS　　　　　　　　m. State Police (Highway Patrol)
　　b. FBI　　　g. Secret Service　　　n. FBI
　　c. FDEA　　h. Bureau of Customs　o. FBI
　　d. U.S.　　　i. IRS
　　　Marshal　j. Secret Service
　　e. U.S.　　　k. FBI
　　　Marshal　l. BATF

3. b, d, f should have been checked.

Discussion Questions

1. How do different law enforcement agencies relate to each other?

2. Which departments have jurisdiction over other departments?

3. Why aren't all the federal law enforcement agencies under the Department of Justice?

4. What major differences are there between a private security officer and a public law enforcement officer?

5. What state law enforcement agencies do we have? Which are of most importance in assisting our local law enforcement agency?

6. What form of county law enforcement do we have?

7. Where is our regional FBI office? What facilities and services does it offer?

References

Adams, T.F. *Introduction to the administration of criminal justice.* 2d ed. Englewood Cliffs, N.J.: Prentice-Hall, Inc., 1980.

Baker, J.L. *The history of the Secret Service.* Garden City, N.J.: Doubleday and Company, 1948.

Feeley, M.M., and Sarat, A.D. *The policy dilemma: Federal crime policy and the Law Enforcement Assistance Administration, 1968–1978.* Minneapolis: University of Minnesota Press, 1980.

Folley, V.L. *American law enforcement.* Boston: Allyn and Bacon, Inc., 1980.

Hemphill, C.F., Jr. *Modern security methods.* Englewood Cliffs, N.J.: Prentice-Hall, Inc., 1979.

Hess, K.M., and Wrobleski, H.M. *Introduction to private security.* St. Paul, Minn: West Publishing Company, 1982.

Holten, N.G., and Jones, M.E. *The system of criminal justice.* Boston: Little, Brown and Company, 1978.

Kakalik, J.S., and Wildhorn, S. *The private police.* New York: Crane Russak (The Rand Corporation), 1977.

Lamm, R.D., "Evaluating LEAA — is it worth continuing?" *Security management,* 22:1 (January 1978): 33–35, 66.

National Advisory Committee on Criminal Justice Standards and Goals. Report of the Task Force on Private Security. *Private security.* Washington, D.C.: U.S. Government Printing Office, 1976.

Office of the Federal Register, National Archives and Records Service, General Services Administration. *U.S. government manual: 1976–77.* (Revised 5-1-76.) Washington, D.C.

President's Commission on Law Enforcement and Administration of Justice. *The challenge of crime in a free society.* Washington, D.C.: U.S. Government Printing Office, February 1967.

Pursley, R.D. *Introduction to criminal justice.* New York: Macmillan, 1984.

Sullivan, J.L. *Introduction to police science.* New York: McGraw-Hill, 1966, 1971.

U.S. Civil Service Commission. *Law enforcement and related jobs with federal agencies.* Washington, D.C.: December 1975.

U.S. Department of Justice. LEAA. *The Law Enforcement Assistance Administration: A partnership for crime control.* Washington, D.C.: 1976.

Vetter, J.S., and Simonsen, C.E. *Criminal justice in America.* Philadelphia: W.B. Saunders Company, 1976.

Common goals of police departments include preserving the peace, protecting civil rights and civil liberties, enforcing the law, preventing crime, and providing services.

Local Law Enforcement
Police Goals, Organization, and Roles

Do You Know . . .

- What the basic goals of most local law enforcement agencies are?

- What two basic organizational categories in a typical police department are?

- Who is the chief law enforcement officer at the local level?

- What major functions are undertaken in administrative service? In field service?

- Why accurate records and communications are important in law enforcement?

- How officers receive their information?

- What is the primary method of receiving and sending information between headquarters and units in the field?

- Why centralization of records is encouraged?

- What types of reports are used in law enforcement?

- What the NCIC is?

- What is required by a data privacy act?

- What primary tasks are performed in routine patrol? In a traffic division? In investigation? In community relations programs?

- How the police officer's roles relate to the people?

- What five basic roles the police officer must play?

- What services can reasonably be expected from a police officer?

- What demands are placed upon a police officer in fulfilling these roles?

- What special physical, intellectual, and emotional skills are required to fulfill the roles professionally?

The will of the people is the best law.
—*Ulysses S. Grant*

Introduction

Crimes are committed in a specific place; therefore, they have most immediate impact upon local law enforcement. Although local law enforcement agencies vary greatly depending on their size, resources, and problems, most police departments work within basically similar organizational structures and toward similar goals.

The most important individual within the police department is the law enforcement officer whose basic function is to protect and assist the public. Most people have a general idea of what a police officer is and does. Many people also have very specific ideas about what a police officer should be and do. The clearly defined roles of enforcing the laws and preserving the peace, established centuries ago, have become more complex, and additional roles have been added to the traditionally accepted roles. According to James Q. Wilson (1968, p. 182), the heart of law enforcement is: "Using the law to achieve certain social objectives—order, peace, security, and liberty."

Goals, Objectives, and Tasks

An effective police department needs clearly specified goals, objectives, and tasks to fulfill its responsibility to the community. A **goal** is a broad, general, desired outcome. An **objective** is a specific, measureable means of achieving the goal. A **task** is a specific activity which contributes to reaching the objective. Goals, objectives, and tasks are interdependent; each alone can accomplish little, but in combination they can provide the needed direction to achieve whatever ends are sought by the department.

Goals

A goal is a general statement of direction, purpose, or intent. It is a desired outcome or end to be achieved. The goals of a police department often depend, in large degree, upon community attitudes and desires. Some communities feel that the primary function of the police is to prevent crime and to maintain order. Police intervention in family quarrels, racial disputes, threatened gang wars, or any situation which *may* lead to criminal acts is expected and supported. In other communities the emphasis is on law enforcement. A police officer who intervenes in a family quarrel may be criticized for not being "out catching criminals."

The suggestion has even been made that two separate types of police officers are needed: peace officers and law enforcement officers. However, such a separation seems neither realistic nor efficient. What is required is an "all-purpose" police officer who can perform both functions effectively.

> *Common goals of police departments include:*
> - *To preserve the peace.*
> - *To protect civil rights and civil liberties.*
> - *To enforce the law.*
> - *To prevent crime.*
> - *To provide services.*

It is usually quite easy to reach agreement on goals. For example, few people would argue with the value of the preceding goals. However, placing goals into a priority ranking and finding means to accomplish these goals is more difficult. Effective progress toward goal achievement depends on a plan, and that plan must include clearly stated objectives for meeting each goal.

Objectives

An objective is a statement of a specific activity which can be measured within a given time period and under specifiable conditions. Objectives facilitate planning, assignment of responsibility, and evaluation of progress toward goals.

For example, given the goal "preventing crime," we need to ask, how can it be accomplished? Opinions will vary, as will reasonable options. Budgetary constraints often limit what objectives might be set for reaching a specific goal. In spite of such constraints, however, specific objectives should be set for each department goal.

Returning to the goal of "preventing crime," objectives for achieving this goal might include: to educate the public, to institute operation identification procedures, to make police officers highly visible, to increase the number of police officers on patrol at a given time, or to assist offenders who are returning to society.

Although it is difficult to measure "prevented crime," it is less difficult to measure implementation of public education, institution of operation ID, visibility of officers, and the like. The accomplishment of broad goals can be evaluated by the successful accomplishment of objectives set for reaching the goal.

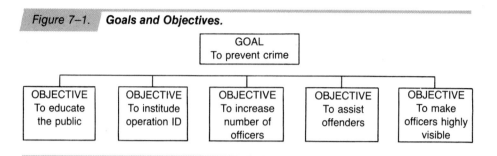

Figure 7–1.   **Goals and Objectives.**

The advantages of clearly stated objectives are numerous. They help to establish priorities; they provide direction for present activities and the assignment of responsibility; they assist in the evaluation of completed activities and in planning for the future; they enhance communication between the police department and the public—citizens can be informed of precisely what the department is trying to accomplish—and, perhaps most important, clearly stated objectives enhance communication within the police department. They make possible the precise specification of tasks to be accomplished to achieve the objectives. Police officers, supervisors, administrators, support personnel, all know what is expected and what outcomes are desired.

Tasks

Once the objectives have been stated, ways to achieve them must be determined. These are the tasks or activities which must be performed to meet the objective which will contribute to reaching the desired goal. When tasks are seen as ways of achieving objectives which lead toward realization of a department goal, they become more significant. Some tasks may seem unimportant, but if each task is looked upon as contributing to accomplishing an objective which in turn contributes to achieving a goal, each routine task becomes important in itself.

For example, while asking police officers "to educate the public" provides more direction than asking them "to prevent crime," the directive is still too general to be of much assistance. Specification of the tasks involved in "educating the public" is needed. Tasks identified might include talking to elementary school children about the seriousness of shoplifting, giving a speech to a community group about the importance of locking car doors, and so on.

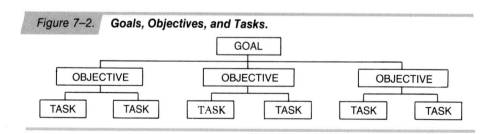

Figure 7–2.   **Goals, Objectives, and Tasks.**

If goals, objectives, and tasks are clearly stated, each person knows what is expected and can make a full contribution to the department's efforts to reach its goals. All police officers should be familiar with the goals and objectives of their department, with their role in working toward these goals (the focus of the next chapter), and with the specific tasks they are expected to perform to successfully fulfill their complex role (the focus of Section Three).

Organization of the Department

According to Arnold and Brungardt (1983, p. 232): "The organizational features of the United States police department exhibit a great deal of variation. The departments range from small, informally organized, small-town operations to highly bureaucratic metropolitan police departments with many subdivisions and thousands of employees."

Sullivan (1971, pp. 184–85) suggests that: "The biggest difference between the typical business organization and police organization is that business organizes for profit, while the police organize for public service." Sullivan goes on to suggest that the police are a semimilitary organization, with their uniforms, insignia, arms, special vehicles, and equipment being obviously military. He suggests that in a deeper sense, it resembles the military because it involves danger to life, requiring "a well-disciplined force, one high in morale and often subject, in crisis, to an absolute control by superiors. Consequently, the police's tighter, military type of organization is completely consistent with the nature of their law enforcement duties and responsibilities." Sullivan concludes by noting that: "Some features of this organization structure came into being by chance, some developed out of a long tradition of experience, and some were the outcome of careful planning and design."

The two basic organizational units within most police departments are field services (also called operations or on-line services) and administrative services (also called staff or support services).

> *Most police departments are organized into two basic units: field services and administrative services. Tasks and personnel are assigned to one or the other.*

Field services include patrol, traffic control, community services, and investigation. Administrative services include recruitment and training, planning and research, records and communications, crime laboratories, and facilities including the police headquarters and jail. Teamwork is essential within and between field services and administrative services.

The chief of police oversees the operation of the entire department and coordinates the efforts of field and administrative services. Under the chief of police, depending on the size of the department, are captains, lieutenants, sergeants, and police officers.

> *The chief law enforcement officer at the local level is the chief of police.*

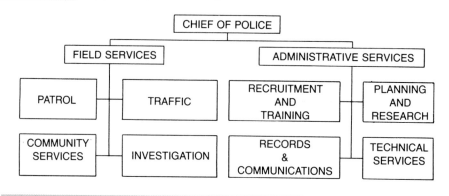

Figure 7–3.   Typical Department Organization.

A typical department might be organized as illustrated in Figure 7–3. The specific organization within a police department is influenced by the department's size, location, and the extent and type of crime with which it must deal. For example, a small police department often combines patrol, traffic, community services, and investigative tasks in a single division; a large police department usually has separate divisions for each. A community with a major freeway running through its business section faces different problems than a community located on a coast or on a border between the United States and Canada or Mexico. Communities with large groups of minorities face different problems than those which are homogeneous. For some communities, traffic control is a major problem; for others gambling, smuggling, or racial unrest may be priorities.

Administrative Services

Administrative services include records and communications, recruitment and training, and provision of special facilities and services.

Administrative services' two areas which most directly affect the efficient provision of field services are communications and records.

Communications

To properly serve the community, police officers must be kept currently and completely informed. They must know how much of each type of crime occurs, such as burglaries, car prowls, malicious destruction of property, and auto thefts. They also have to know where the crimes are occurring.

Current information is usually provided at roll call and by means of radio.

Roll Call. One of the most important functions of the administrative division in its support of the other units of the police department is keeping members informed of daily police operations and providing administrative instructions and special assignments and tasks to be performed. This is usually done at a **roll call** session before the officers on the next shift go out into the street.

Up-to-date information is usually contained in a daily bulletin which contains brief summaries of what has transpired in the previous twenty-four hours. Officers are given a synopsis of each complaint received and acted upon as well as descriptions of missing and/or wanted persons, descriptions of stolen personal property, and stolen autos.

Radio Communications. The information provided at roll call is continuously updated by radio. Data is available to officers in patrol cars or carrying portable radios. This immediate communication has improved the safety of law enforcement officers and has provided for better allocation of resources.

> *Radio is the primary method of transmitting and seeking information between headquarters and units in the field.*

The introduction of the small hand-carried portable police radio and the beeper have extended the communications system so that officers on foot may be reached to assist mobile patrol units and vice versa.

Many police departments operate on several radio frequencies assigned by the Federal Communications Commission (FCC). Police radio frequencies attempt to assure the dissemination of information to only the police officer and to maintain the confidentiality of that information. However, a large number of police monitors are sold to the general public, and many retail electronics stores publish lists of police radio frequencies. Therefore, some police jurisdictions have adopted a code transmitting message system which not only helps preserve confidentiality of information but which also conserves airtime and allows emergency calls to be transmitted without undue delay.

The dependability of radio transmissions has improved steadily over the years and has resulted in a great reduction in response time to calls for service or criminal activity.

A typical radio system has four channels providing the capability of (1) contacting car to car in its own jurisdiction, (2) contacting its own dispatchers, (3) contacting another officer patrolling in a different geographical subdivision through a repeater system, and (4) placing emergency calls. The fourth channel is reserved for such emergencies as roadblocks, disasters, and civil defense messages.

Communications is the lifeline of the police department. The police dispatcher, or in some cases the telephone operator, receives all citizens' requests for police service. In some instances the calls come directly to the dispatcher who must act upon them and determine their priority. Some agencies have telephone operators screen the calls prior to giving them to the dispatcher to segregate informational calls from service calls.

Dispatchers have the responsibility for dispatching patrol vehicles to requests for service and knowing what patrol vehicles are ready for assignment. They may also have some records responsibility, for example, making out the original incident complaint report, noting the time the call was received, the time the patrol vehicle was dispatched, the time it arrived, the time it cleared, and the disposition of the call.

In addition, dispatchers may have to handle any walk-in complaints. Some dispatchers also have the added responsibility of monitoring jails through a closed-circuit television hookup. Such a system exists in many smaller and medium-sized departments today.

In larger agencies several dispatchers handle the incoming calls and give them priority according to their seriousness and the availability of officers to respond. Larger agencies may also have direct and complete integration of police radio with regular telphone service. In this system any call to the police emergency number is automatically channeled to the dispatcher who controls squad cars assigned to the area from which the caller is telephoning.

Some cities have what is called the *911 system*. A person who wishes to call the police dials 911 on the telephone, and a central dispatching office receives the call directly. The 911 system has been implemented in many cities in the United States. The eventual goal is to have this number as the emergency number to call for police service in any city in the United States.

Dispatchers must be dependable, accurate when receiving information, and efficient so that a quick response can be made to police situations. They must be highly trained in the use of the radio system and the computer as well as familar with emergency plans, the geographic areas in which the officers work, disruptions in communications, and good public relations practices.

Records

The quality of records maintained is directly related to the quality of communications and field services provided. To give proper direction, a police agency must have a sound record system as well as an efficient communication system. Police departments throughout the country vary in their reporting systems and their needs in management control and effective operational control. The activities of a police department require keeping records, not only of criminal activity, but of all essential activities of the department.

The complexity of each department's records system is dictated by its needs and problems. Many different types of short transactions that police agencies must handle are continuously in process. Most of the information used to find the perpetrator of a crime would be useless unless it is integrated into a system of records. Unless the data received is recorded logically and systematically, it is impossible to coordinate the facts, especially when they are gathered by a number of persons. For example, uniform patrol may handle a preliminary investigation of a case while the investigative services division may follow up on the report.

Centralization.   Services divisions generally should not maintain separate records, as the tendency to operate independently makes coordination difficult. Situations may exist where space limitations do not allow complete centralization of records. However, normally records should be located near the point where complaints are received, radio squads controlled, and prisoners booked.

Centralization of records allows the various line functions to be coordinated.

In a small agency where a dispatcher or desk officer may handle all such duties alone, these functions can readily be observed and their close relationship noted. In a larger organization, the duties may be handled by a major division, with numerous employees performing specialized functions. For example, a radio dispatcher may handle only radio messages, another officer may handle only telephone complaints, and still another may handle over-the-counter information and complaints.

As smaller departments grow, the patterns remain the same, but with an increasing refinement of duties. Centralization fixes record-keeping responsibility and relieves the line-operating units from the responsibility of these administrative functions.

Types of Records.

Police records may be categorized as (1) administrative records, (2) arrest records, (3) identification records, and (4) complaint records.

Administrative records include inventories of police equipment, department memorandums, personnel records, evaluation reports, and all general information which reflects correspondence or services rendered.

Arrest records contain information obtained from arrested persons when they are booked as well as information about the control and/or release of prisoners and court procedures.

Identification records contain fingerprints, photographs, and other descriptive data obtained from arrested persons.

Complaint records usually contain information related to complaints and reports received by the police from citizens or other agencies as well as any actions initiated by the police. Since police work is public business, it requires accurate records of complaints received and the action taken by the police. Complaints may be criminal or noncriminal in nature; they may involve lost property, damaged property, traffic accidents, medical emergencies, or a missing person. Requests for police assistance may also involve robberies, murders, burglaries, vandalism, or children playing in the streets or cats up in trees. Although most complaints are minor, each must be treated with personal concern to the complainant and as a matter of importance to the police.

Most police agencies have a procedure for recording complaint information either on sheets or data processing cards. Initial complaint records are filled out on all complaints or requests for service received by the dispatcher or a police officer.

Information on the initial complaint record normally shows the complainant, victim, address of each, type of complaint, time of day, day of week, the officer handling the complaint or request, the area of the community where it occurred, the disposition, whether there was an arrest, and whether further follow-up reports or further investigation is justified by the investigative services division.

In the case of auto thefts, missing persons, recovered property, or an arrest, further reports will be made separately such as missing persons report, property recovered report, or the fingerprinting and booking of an arrested suspect report.

To minimize records work, some police departments use a combined complaint form containing a variety of information such as the initial complaint report, a missing-persons report, a stolen property report, an arrest report, a juvenile report, a case report sheet, an auto theft report, and so on. The disadvantages of the combined complaint form far outweigh the advantages. The retrieval of one category of information is difficult. In addition, a combined report tends to limit the amount of information an officer puts in the report.

An efficient reporting system requires separate reports for the initial and the follow-up investigation as well as separate reports for accidents, missing persons, wanted persons, auto thefts, stolen and recovered property, arrests, juveniles involved in any type of incident, photographic files, fingerprint files, and reports of the confiscation of property from prisoners.

Benefits of Efficient Records System.   Efficient records systems are a vital management tool which aid in assessing department accomplishments, in developing budget justifications, in determining additional manpower needs, and in evaluating the performance of officers as well as the attainment of objectives and goals.

Evaluation of carefully kept records will generally reflect needs in training, recruitment, public relations, allocation of resources, and general effectiveness. The continual or periodic evaluation of records by management in planning and research has allowed police agencies to provide better service to the public and, in turn, they have gained public support.

> *Centralized, integrated, and accurate systems of communications and records increase the effectiveness and efficiency of field services.*

Computerized Information (NCIC).   Many informational tools available to police agencies today are the result of the introduction of random-access storage and retrieval systems and computers into the police field. In the future such information can connect all law enforcement agencies in the country in a vast communications network.

A step in this direction was taken in 1967 when the FBI implemented its computerized crime information storage system, the National Crime Information Center **(NCIC)**. Under this system, each state has a number of computer terminals which interface with the FBI master computer in Washington, D.C. The computer contains records of stolen property such as guns, stolen autos, and office machines, and, in some cases, persons who are wanted on warrants.

The NCIC computer receives its information from other federal law enforcement agencies and from state and local law enforcement agencies. The NCIC makes it possible for a law enforcement officer in Texas who stops a suspicious person or car from California, to contact the dispatcher by radio or teleprinter requesting information. The dispatcher can make an inquiry to the computer in Texas which, in a matter of seconds, makes an inquiry on the status of the individual and/or the car to the NCIC terminal in Washington. The police officer can be quickly informed if the car has been stolen or if an arrest warrant is outstanding on the individual in the car.

The great volume of information contained in various state and federal computers is another aid given to police officers in maintaining up-to-date records systems.

> *The National Crime Information Center allows all police agencies in the country to have access to the computerized files of the FBI.*

Privacy of Records. The most sensitive aspect of computerized or manual records on persons arrested and related information about them is the possibility of including in the file unsubstantiated information which might contain derogatory, incomplete, or incorrect information—information which disseminated to the wrong person could prove damaging and provide cause for a civil action against the police agency. In addition, police agencies often tend to retain information longer than necessary.

As a result, by authority of the Omnibus Crime Control and Safe Streets Act of 1968 which was amended by the Crime Control Act of 1973, the Department of Justice issued regulations to assure that criminal history record information, wherever it appears, is collected, stored, and disseminated in a way that insures the completeness, integrity, accuracy, and security of such information and that protects individual privacy. The regulations apply to all state and local agencies and individuals collecting, storing, or disseminating criminal history information processed either manually or automated.

> *A data privacy act regulates the use of confidential and private information on individuals in the records, files, and processes of a state and its political subdivisions.*

Some law enforcement agencies have expressed dissatisfaction with provisions relating to law enforcement records and with the dissemination of criminal history information, particularly for employment purposes.

Because states have been slow in passing privacy act legislation, a certain amount of confusion often occurs among those who try to abide by the Department of Justice regulations. The effect of some state legislation has been that in the absence of an emergency classification, almost all information or data a police agency has kept on individuals legally must be made available to anyone requesting it. This unfortunate situation has been avoided in other states.

Minnesota, a progressive state in handling private data, passed legislation in 1974 and 1976* to regulate the use of confidential and private information on individuals in the records, files, and processes of the state and its political subdivi-

---

*Data Privacy Act (Laws 1974), Ch. 479 as amended by Laws 1975, Ch. 401 and Laws 1976, Ch. 283, coded as Minnesota Statutes 15.162 to 15.169.

sions. The **Data Privacy Act** provides three categories of information (termed *data* in the law): private, confidential, and public. Various regulations have been set for each type of data.

Private data are data which by state or federal law or emergency classification of the state commissioner of administration are not public but are accessible to the person who is the subject of the information. Police probation records of juveniles are in this category and may not be disclosed to the public except by order of the juvenile court. The social security number of employees is also classified as private data.

Confidential data include data collected by a civil or criminal investigative agency as part of an active investigation for the purpose of commencing a legal action.

Public data include all information which is accessible to the public in accordance with the public records law. In effect, the term means all information excluded from the private and confidential data categories including (1) the name, age, and address of the arrested persons, (2) the nature of the charge, (3) the time and place of the arrest, (4) the identity of the arresting agency, and (5) information as to whether an individual has been jailed and the location of the jail.

Emergency classifications are also provided for by the law. Any police agency may apply to the commissioner of administration for permission to classify particular data or types of data (except arrest information) as private or confidential. An application may cover all types of confidential or private data. The application itself, however, is classed as public data. To receive an emergency classification as private or confidential, the information must meet three standards:

- No statute either allows or forbids classification of the data as private or confidential.

- The data has been treated as either private or confidential by custom and is recognized by other similar state agencies or other similar political subdivisions and by the public.

- A compelling need exists for immediate emergency classification which, if not granted, could adversely affect the public interest or the health, safety, well-being, or reputation of the subject of the data.

A police agency or a city violating the Data Privacy Act is liable, in Minnesota, to a person who suffers any resulting damage. The person damaged may bring an action against the police agency or the responsible authority to cover any damages sustained, plus costs and reasonable attorney's fees. If the violation is willful, the agency or responsible authority is also liable for exemplary damages of not less than $100 nor more than $1,000 for each violation (M.S. 466.03).

The gathering of information by law enforcement personnel facilitates the formulation of effective strategies against criminals whose operations often go interstate. However, both privacy and freedom of information legislation can severely restrict the flow of free information between law enforcement agencies. The Privacy Act of 1974, for example, requires the purging and sealing of records, thereby preventing different governmental agencies from collecting an inclusive criminal history on any one individual.

In addition, the federal privacy act restricts government surveillance activities and prevents the public, the actual victims of criminals, from knowing what the actual threats are. Freedom of information legislation also can impede law enforcement. Unless law enforcement data are specifically exempted, law enforcement files can be examined by persons under investigation who could then destroy evidence or otherwise neutralize an investigation.

Where law enforcement data are not specifically exempted by law, a request for emergency classification of certain information should be made either to the courts or the state's administration department. Emergency classification could be requested in the accumulation of evidence on organized crime, prostitution, or other related law violations prior to prosecution.

Field Services

Sometimes field services are performed by one division; sometimes they are performed by separate divisions. They may be further specialized by the type of individual involved: juveniles, gamblers, prostitutes, burglars, dope peddlers, and so on; by specific geographic areas (beats); or by specific times when the demand for service is highest, for example, holiday traffic or abnormal conditions such as strikes and protests.

Field services include patrol, traffic, investigation, and community services.

Traditionally, however, police departments have been generalist organization; that is, most of their personnel is assigned to routine patrol and each officer is responsible for providing basic law enforcement services of all types to a specified geographic area. This routine patrol has been and is the backbone of police work in smaller departments. Larger departments tend to be more specialist-oriented.

Patrol

Usually sixty to seventy percent of a department's police officers are assigned to patrol operations. Although other divisions may have more prestige, patrol officers are the first and primary contact between the public and the criminal justice system. They not only initiate the criminal justice system, they strongly influence the public's perception of this system.

Patrol accounts for a major portion of most departments' expenditures, activities, personnel, and visibility. Whether measured by the number of police officers involved, the number of dollars spent, or by the reality that the uniformed police officer is the most visible part of our law enforcement system, patrol is the most vital component of police work. All other units are supplemental to this basic unit.

Patrol provides both crime- and noncrime-related services including preventing or deterring crime, apprehending criminals, recovering stolen property, providing emergency assistance, and giving citizens a sense of community security and confidence in the police.

Patrol is normally performed by uniformed officers in marked vehicles, although some larger departments assign uniformed officers to motorcycle and foot patrol in heavily populated or congested areas. This visibility, in itself, is one way to deter and repress crime. In addition, because the officers are in their vehicles and already moving, patrol allows the officers to respond quickly to calls for crime- and noncrime-related services, for example, to apprehend suspects or to assist in medical emergencies.

> *Patrol is responsible for providing continuous police service and high visibility of law enforcement. Tasks include crime prevention, response to calls for service, self-initiated activity, and completing administrative functions.*

Reserve Officers.   Some police departments have reserve units to help achieve the department's goals. The reserve officers patrol in uniform and are visible symbols of law enforcement although they cannot write citations. The reserve officers also help in public education programs, informing the public about such things as operation identification, drugs, and bike safety. When a crime does occur, the reserves can guard the crime scene while the regular officers continue with their routine or specialized patrol.

Specific activities and responsibilities within the patrol function are the focus of Chapter 8.

Traffic

Traffic may be a responsibility of patrol, or it may be a separate function. A well-rounded traffic program involves many activities designed to maintain order and safety on streets and highways.

> *Traffic officers are usually responsible for enforcing traffic laws, directing and controlling traffic, providing directions and assistance to motorists, investigating motor vehicle accidents, providing emergency assistance at the scene of an accident, gathering information related to traffic, and writing reports.*

The most frequent contact between the police and the noncriminal public is through traffic encounters; consequently, the opportunity for improving public relations by how traffic violations are handled must be considered. Although the traffic responsibilities of a police officer may not have the glamour of a criminal investigation, they are critical not only to the safety of the citizens in a community but also to the police image. It should be noted that a great number of criminal arrests result from traffic stops, for example, wanted persons and discovery of contraband.

The primary objectives of most traffic programs are to obtain the best possible movement of vehicles and pedestrians consistent with safety and to reduce losses from accidents. Chapter 9 describes the functions performed by the traffic officer in more detail.

Investigation

Although some investigations are carried out by patrol officers, the investigation services division (also known as the detective bureau) has the responsibility for follow-up investigation. The success of any criminal investigation relies on the cooperative, coordinated efforts of both the patrol and the investigative functions. The primary responsibilities of the investigator are to make certain the crime scene is secure, interview witnesses and interrogate suspects, photograph and sketch the crime scene, obtain and identify evidence, and record all facts related to the case for future reference and testimony in court.

To accomplish a successful investigation, police officers must (1) take their time, (2) use an organized approach that is efficient and methodical, as this may be their only chance to observe the scene, (3) recognize the issues and find facts to settle these issues, and (4) determine if a crime has been committed, and if so, by whom and how. These topics are the focus of Chapter 10.

> *The primary responsibilities of the investigator are to make certain the crime scene is secure, interview witnesses and interrogate suspects, photograph and sketch the crime scene, obtain and identify evidence, and record all facts related to the case for future reference.*

Community Service/Community Relations

In essence, every action of a police officer has an effect on community relations—either positive or negative. Many larger departments have established separate community relations divisions or community service divisions to strength communication channels between the public and its police department and/or to stress public education programs and crime prevention programs.

> *Every action of a police officer is, in effect, a part of community relations. Specific community relations or community service divisions seek to improve communications between the police and the public and/or to promote public education and crime prevention programs.*

The importance of community relations and community service will be seen throughout the remainder of the book. Chapter 11 focuses on community relations and community service programs and approaches.

Specialized Officers

In addition to the basic divisions which may exist within a police department, larger departments frequently train officers to perform highly specialized tasks.

> *Specialized officers may include evidence technicians, identification officers, intelligence officers, juvenile officers, vice officers, canine-assisted officers, and tactical forces officers.*

Members of an underwater recovery unit, marking for evidence a weapon which was recovered from the bottom of a lake.

Evidence Technicians.   Some police agencies, such as suburban police departments with a complement of forty or more officers, have established the position of evidence technician. The evidence technician is usually a patrol officer who has received extensive classroom and laboratory training in crime scene investigation. In departments which have small detective bureaus and relatively inexperienced officers, this position fills a notable void. The officer has not been relieved of regular patrol duties, but may be called upon to conduct a crime scene investigation. Use of evidence technicians provides better coordination of the preliminary investigation of crimes and increases the probability that the investigation will be successful during the preliminary stage because other patrol officers work with the evidence technician as a team.

It is the evidence technician's responsibilities to photograph the scene, take all necessary measurements, search the scene for physical evidence, and interview any suspects or witnesses still at the scene.

Evidence technicians carry tools to collect, mark, and identify evidence found at the scene, including cameras, fingerprint equipment, recorders, sketching equipment, and casting or impression material. They may have a vacuum cleaner in the equipment van for gathering evidence from a carpet or the inside of a car.

Through their laboratory training, evidence technicians know precisely what the laboratory can determine from the evidence submitted and its limitations. They do not have the type of equipment a full-scale crime laboratory possesses, but they do have some equipment to conduct preliminary tests for blood and certain types of narcotics and to identify the classifications of fingerprints.

The evidence technicians' classroom and laboratory training make them valuable assets to the patrol force because when not busy investigating crime scenes, they do regular patrol work.

Identification Officers. Identification officers have had specialized training in taking, identifying, and filing fingerprints. Fingerprint identification is an extremely important form of positive identification used by the police in identifying persons who break the law. Identification officers are highly trained in using scanners and computers in their work.

Intelligence Officers. Most large cities have an intelligence division whose top officer reports directly to the chief of police and whose activities are kept secret from the rest of the police department.

Intelligence units work in two areas. The first area is long-term, ongoing investigations into such criminal activity as illegal sale of guns, payoffs to police officers or politicians, major drug cases, and activities of organized crime. They often work on the same case in cooperation with county, state, and federal investigators.

Intelligence officers obtain information, buy information, infiltrate criminal groups, solicit data, conduct surveillances, and develop sources of information to keep themselves updated on criminal activity in the community. Any factual information that could lead to an arrest is given to the chief of police who assigns it to another division of the police department for action.

The second area of intelligence work is investigation of fellow police officers in the department. For example, the intelligence unit may investigate a complaint of an officer drinking on duty, corruption, or other activities considered conduct unbecoming to police officers.

Intelligence officers do not wear uniforms or drive marked cars. They may even use assumed names and fictitious identities. To avoid identification problems, some large police agencies use officers who have just graduated from rookie school, as they are less known on the street.

Juvenile Officers. The police officer is often the first contact a child has when he is in legal trouble. Therefore, it is justifiable and logical to have juvenile police specialists to work primarily with juvenile offenders.

Because most juvenile work is informal and includes powers to release, refer, or detain, juvenile officers must be chosen from the most qualified officers in the department. Specialists in handling juveniles should know the goals and functioning of the juvenile justice system because, in reality, they sit as judges of a youngster's actions and also serve the functions of social workers. Officers who work primarily with juveniles should be highly concerned for the welfare of the child, highly trained in the law, and able to recognize the difference between a neglected, dependent juvenile, and a juvenile delinquent.

Juvenile officers can provide assistance to all other departments within their own agency when juveniles are involved. They are the training officers of the patrol division when it comes to juvenile procedures. Since juveniles commit more than

50 percent of local crimes, all officers are juvenile officers much of the time, and it is the uniformed patrol division which has the most contact with these juvenile offenders.

Juvenile officers can also represent the police department in the juvenile's home, school, church, and the juvenile courtroom. Since prevention and control of juvenile delinquency are usually among the objectives of a police department, juvenile officers are a definite asset. They can plan and implement programs through the various service organizations within the community.

The role of the juvenile officer in the community is that of a highly visible specialist who probably has more influence upon the juveniles in the community than any other single person in law enforcement.

Vice Officers.   Vice problems vary from community to community; for example, some sections of the country allow prostitution, but many sections of the country do not. Vice officers usually concentrate their efforts on illegal gambling, prostitution, pornography, narcotics, and liquor violations. Sometimes their work is coordinated with intelligence officers.

Vice officers often maintain an unconventional lifestyle, frequently assuming an appearance that does not identify them with the police department. Therefore, these officers frequently are isolated. For example, undercover officers, because of the dangerous atmosphere in which they work, cannot afford to call or be seen with other police officers. Their activities are completely removed from the mainstream of the police department.

Many communities tolerate gambling, but few tolerate prostitution or narcotics; consequently, many vice officers concentrate on removing pimps and prostitutes from circulation and arresting narcotics peddlers. A major problem is discovering who is the organizer of these operations. The narcotic peddler, pimp, and prostitute are highly visible and, therefore, more susceptible to arrest than the "brains" of the operation. Because of this situation, vice officers may allow narcotics peddlers, pimps, and prostitutes to operate—to the anger of many citizens—in the hopes of discovering who is responsible for the organization.

Once vice becomes established in a community, more criminals are frequently attracted to the community. They may either believe that the law enforcement is ineffective in the community or that the police already have so many problems with vice that their operations will go unnoticed. If left uncontrolled, vice operations can create other police problems such as embezzlement, burglary, robbery, and murder. A community that allows vice to flourish is often politically corrupt and frequently has corruption within the police department as well.

Canine-Assisted Officers.   Man has used dogs in a variety of ways for thousands of years. Dogs have been used in police work in the United States, Europe, and throughout the world for more than fifty years. Today canine units exist in more than three hundred towns and cities in the United States.

Today's police dog has had intensive schooling with one officer—his partner. Both spend many weeks under a special trainer. The dog works with only one partner and will respond to his commands only. The police dog's use in most cities falls into five categories: search, attack and capture, drug detection, bomb detection, and as a crime deterrent.

Search dogs are specialists, almost like precision instruments. Their highly developed sense of smell can be used for tracking or searching by direct scent. Good results have been obtained in searching large buildings and open areas either in daylight or darkness.

In the summer of 1970 the U.S. Customs Service began an experimental program using drug detection dogs in a drive against narcotics smuggling across the nation's borders. The experiment proved so immediately successful that it was increased as rapidly as the dogs could be trained at the U.S. Customs Dog Training Center in San Antonio, Texas.

The value of these dogs has been demonstrated on many occasions. In San Francisco, an anonymous phone call sent patrolman W.D. Langlois and his "partner," Bourbon, rushing into the main branch of the Crocker Bank where a live bomb cached in a safe-deposit box might have detonated at any moment. Ignoring scores of other boxes, the dog dashed straight to the one which contained the explosives. Minutes later the bomb was safely removed.

Tactical Forces Officers.   Special crime tactical forces are immediately available, flexible, and mobile officers used for deployment against any emergency or crime problem. Tactical units supplement the patrol force and may operate selectively in high frequency crime areas. They may suppress burglaries, robberies, or

Philadelphia Police Department SWAT team in field exercises.

auto thefts. They may be used in hostage situations and where persons have barricaded themselves. In such instances, the idea is to negotiate and reason with barricaded subjects, hostage takers, or the mentally disturbed rather than using force. Tactical forces are frequently deployed in sniper situations to protect police officers. In addition, they may perform rescue missions, provide security for visiting dignitaries, and rescue hostages.

Tactical forces are deployed when the regularly assigned patrol forces cannot effectively cope with an emergency situation, on the basis of current crime pattern analyses, or on information received regarding expected crime activity.

Chicago has been operating a special street crime force since 1956 to reduce crime in certain parts of the city. The Detroit Police Department has two distinct tactical forces, one a crime prevention unit, the other a low visibility unit designed to reduce street robbery and other violent street crimes. The latter unit specializes in decoy techniques. The Seattle Police Department also has a "decoy squad," a flexible group of officers operating primarily during nighttime hours in high-crime areas or in areas where certain types of specialized crimes are occurring.

The Kansas City, Missouri, Police Department uses its tactical force to provide investigative support. Its squads operate in various counties and cities. Los Angeles has a Special Weapons and Tactics Section (SWAT) which maintains a manpower pool available for activities ranging from directing traffic to suppressing riots.

Tactical forces officers receive special training in numerous areas including crowd control, patrol maneuvers, investigative techniques, and stakeout tactics. SWAT team members are highly trained in marksmanship, guerrilla tactics, patrolling, night operations, camouflage and concealment, and the use of chemical agents. They frequently have field exercises to develop discipline and teamwork.

What is Policing?

John Webster (n.d., p. 94) points out the difference between what people often think of as the police officer's role and what it is in most instances:

> The cover of a major city's annual police report dramatically shows two police officers reaching for their guns as they burst through the doors of a massive black and white police car which is screeching to a halt. . .the flashing red lights and screaming siren complete the illustration. A less dramatic scene on an inside page of the report shows a police officer talking to a grateful mother whose lost child was returned. Which one of these illustrations most accurately describes the police role? . . .The New York Times reports that policemen like to think of themselves as uniformed soldiers in an extremely dangerous war against crime . . . in fact the police are more social worker and administrator than crime fighter.

What is it about the police officer's role that makes the general public think of the law enforcement aspect of police work more often than the social service aspect when, in fact, approximately 90 percent of their time is spent in the social service function? According to Egon Bittner (1971), the police: "unlike you and me, bear a very broad right to use coercive force in all sorts of situations that may call for it." Klockars (1983, p. 227) expands on the police officer's role and the right to use coercive force:

> Whether it is catching criminals, enforcing laws, maintaining order, moving pedestrian or vehicular traffic, managing the scene at fires, accidents, deaths, and unanticipated births, picking up lost or runaway children, taking custody of drunk or deranged persons, handling domestic or neighborhood disputes, turning on a fire hydrant on an oppressively hot city summer day, the police officer does these things because doing them may require exercising the right to use coercive force. The work of policing appears to call far more often for the skills of a social worker or administrator than those of a crime fighter. How do we reconcile Bittner's concept of the right to use coercive force as the core of the police role with the finding that the vast majority of work police are called upon to do requires skills of a social service nature? Bittner's [1974] answer . . . is that while the core of the police role is the right to use coercive force, THE SKILL OF POLICING CONSISTS IN FINDING WAYS TO AVOID ITS USE.

The Police Officer and the People

You learned earlier that **police authority** comes from the people—their laws and institutions. Police officers are ultimately responsible to the public they serve, and they usually recruit their officers from among local citizens.

Although the Tenth Amendment reserves police power for state and local governments, these governments must adhere to the principles of the Constitution and the Bill of Rights as well as to federal and state statutes. Police officers are not only a part of their community, they are also part of the state and federal government that provides their formal base of authority as well as a part of the state and federal criminal justice system that determines society's course in deterring lawbreakers and rehabilitating offenders.

Note that in Figure 7–4 the arrows between the citizens, governments, and courts go two ways. Not only are the people ultimately responsible for the establishment of governments and courts, they also elect the representatives who serve there. The citizens also directly influence the police. To a large extent, the specific goals and priorities of the police are established by what the community wants. For example, a community might want more patrols at night, stricter enforcement of traffic regulations during rush hour, or reduced enforcement for certain violations such as speeding.

Priorities are often more influenced by the desires of the policed than by any other consideration. Because the success of the police depends heavily upon public support, the wishes of the citizens must be listened to and considered.

The people largely determine the role of the police and give them their authority to fulfill this role. Their support is vital.

Figure 7–4.   **Sources of Police Authority.**

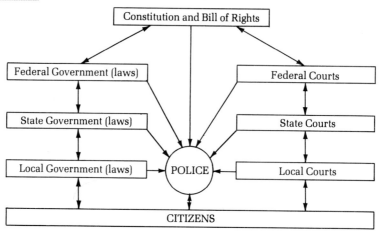

In addition, because the police are highly visible representatives of local government and are on duty twenty-four hours a day, people often call upon them for services which they are not, specifically, required to perform. Other agencies might be providing these services, but people do not know of them. For example, if a woman seeks help in dealing with a drunk husband (he is not abusing her; he is just drunk), a drug counselor, minister, or social worker might be the appropriate person to call. The woman, however, often doesn't know this. Since the police officers' reactions to requests for help affect the amount of respect received and promote a cooperative relationship with the public, police officers usually respond as helpfully as possible, even when the matter is technically civil and outside their responsibility (and sometimes their expertise).

Basic Roles of the Police Officer

Since the citizens of a community have such a great influence on the role of the police within the community, many differences exist in roles performed by police officers in different geographic localities. Generally, however, five basic roles are performed: enforcing laws, preserving the peace, preventing crime, protecting civil rights and civil liberties and providing services.

These roles often overlap. For example, officers intervening in a fight may not only enforce a law by arresting a suspect for assault, they may also maintain order, prevent others from becoming involved in the fight, protect the civil rights and civil liberties of the suspect, the victim, and the bystanders, and provide emergency service to an injured victim.

Success or failure in fulfilling each role directly affects the success or failure of fulfilling the other roles. Although we have listed five roles normally performed by police officers, in reality, it is a single role comprised of numerous responsibilities.

Five basic roles of most police officers are:

■ *To enforce laws*
■ *To preserve the peace.*
■ *To prevent crimes.*
■ *To protect civil rights and civil liberties.*
■ *Provide services.*

Law Enforcement—Crime Repression

The term law enforcement officer underscores the central importance of this long-accepted responsibility as does the quotation at the beginning of the chapter. Historically, enforcement of laws has been the prime responsibility of police officers. However, this long-accepted role has become increasingly complex. Not only must decisions be made as to what laws to enforce, but also the police have become an integral part of the criminal justice system, responsible not only for apprehending offenders, but for assisting in their prosecution as well.

Police officers are responsible for enforcing laws and for assisting in the prosecution of offenders.

The stereotype of the police officer emphasizes the role of "crime fighter," often to the exclusion of all others. In enforcing laws, police officers perform many functions: investigating offenses interrogating suspects, interviewing witnesses, conducting searches, acting upon leads, participating in stakeouts, apprehending suspects, recovering stolen property, testifying in court, suppressing riots, combatting organized crime, and patrolling to discover crimes in progress.

The patrol function is central to law enforcement. Not only may law enforcement officers encounter crimes in progress, they may also encounter "suspicious" circumstances which may be crime related. Questioning of a suspicious person might lead to arrests for outstanding warrants, possession of narcotics or concealed weapons, burglary, and other serious crimes.

Because each community and each state have numerous statutes to be enforced and limited resources, full enforcement of all laws is never possible. Even if it were, it is questionable whether full enforcement would be in keeping with legislative intent or the people's wishes. The police can, do, and must exercise discretion in which laws to enforce; that they cannot enforce all laws at all times must be accepted by both the police officer and the public.

Each police department must decide which reported crimes to actively investigate and to what degree, as well as which unreported crimes to seek out and to what degree. The law does not set priorities; it simply defines crimes, classifies them as felonies or misdemeanors, and assesses penalties for them. The police department sets its own priorities, based on citizens' needs.

Usually police departments concentrate law enforcement activities on serious crimes—those which pose the greatest threat to public safety and/or cause the greatest economic losses (the Part 1 Index Crimes). From that point on, priorities are usually determined by past police experience, the wishes and expectations of the citizens, and the resources available.

Engaging in law enforcement activities such as arresting armed robbers and using force when needed are sanctioned by statute and public opinion. On the other hand, if police become involved in conflicts which do not involve a crime, such as loud domestic arguments, their action may be viewed as interference. Even within the traditional role of enforcing laws, decisions must be made as to what is proper and what is not.

Further, the police officer's responsibility does not end with the enforcement of a law and the apprehension of a suspect. In effect, when the police arrest an offender, they have initiated the criminal justice process. The offender's guilt must then be determined in court. The police officer plays a key role in assisting the prosecutor in preparing the case and often is called upon to present evidence in court (the focus of Chapter 15). Unfortunately, since police are in the closest contact with the public, they are often blamed for failures in the criminal justice system. For example, an assault victim whose attacker is found innocent in court may feel resentment not only against the court, but against the police.

The release of a suspect from custody for lack of sufficient evidence, the failure of a prosecutor to take a case to trial, or the failure of the corrections system to reform a convict prior to parole or release, all directly affect the role police officers must play as well as their public image. And the public image of the police officer is critical when you consider that a large percentage of police work is in direct response to citizen complaints or reports. In fact, members of the community may be the single most important factor in the total law enforcement effort.

Preserving the Peace

The role of preserving the peace has also long been traditionally accepted by law enforcement officers. They have the legal authority to arrest individuals for disturbing the peace or for disorderly conduct.

> *Police are responsible for preserving the peace.*

Police are often called upon to intervene in noncriminal conduct such as that which occurs at public events (crowd control), in social relations (domestic disputes), and in traffic control (parking, pedestrians) to maintain law and order. They frequently help people solve problems that they cannot cope with alone.

Often such problems, if unresolved, could result in crime. For example, loud parties, unruly crowds, or disputes between members of a family, business partners, landlord and tenant, or a businessman and his customer might result in bodily harm—assault. Studies indicate that domestic violence frequently leads to homicide. In addition, responses to domestic disputes are a leading cause of serious injury and fatal assaults on police officers.

The police officer's effectiveness in actually preserving the peace will largely be determined by public acceptance of this role. Often if a police officer simply asks a landlord to allow a tenant access to his apartment or asks the host of a loud party to turn down the stereo, this is enough. Mere police presence may reduce the possibility of a crime—at least temporarily.

If the citizens respect the police and accept their suggestions, it is likely that police officers will be successful in preserving the peace. On the other hand, if the citizens do not accept this function and do not respect the police, the presence of police may provoke crime and violence. Here, as in the enforcement of laws, public support is vital.

Crime Prevention

Crime prevention is closely related to law enforcement and preservation of the peace. If the peace has been kept, crime has, in effect, been prevented. Crime prevention differs from peacekeeping and law enforcing in that it attempts to eliminate potentially dangerous or criminal situations.

A routine patrol might not only discover a crime in progress, but it might also deter or prevent crimes from being committed. If the police are very visible in a community, it is likely that many crimes will be prevented. However, this is extremely difficult to prove since we do not know what crimes might have been committed if the police were not present.

> *Police officers are responsible for attempting to prevent a crime.*

Notice the word *attempting*. These efforts will often be unsuccessful. Just as police officers cannot be expected to enforce all the laws at all times, they cannot be expected to prevent all crimes from occurring.

Crime prevention activities frequently undertaken by police officers include working with juveniles, cooperating with probation and parole personnel, educating the public, instigating operation identification programs, and providing visible evidence of police authority. In addition, many of the community services often provided by police departments (discussed in Chapter 11) aid considerably in crime prevention.

Protection of Constitutional Rights

Protection of Constitutional Rights.   The first paragraph of the *Law Enforcement Code of Ethics* (Figure 7–5) concludes with the statement that a law enforcement officer has a fundamental duty "to respect the Constitutional rights of all men to liberty, equality, and justice," the rights and liberties described in Chapter 13. Civil rights and civil liberties have gained increasing recognition within the last decade.

Figure 7–5.   **Law Enforcement Code of Ethics.**

SECTION VI
LAW ENFORCEMENT PERSONNEL

Law Enforcement Code of Ethics

As a Law Enforcement Officer, *my fundamental duty is to serve mankind; to safeguard lives and property; to protect the innocent against deception, the weak against oppression or intimidation, and the peaceful against violence or disorder; and to respect the Constitutional rights of all men to liberty, equality and justice.*

I will *keep my private life unsullied as an example to all; maintain courageous calm in the face of danger, scorn, or ridicule; develop self-restraint; and be constantly mindful of the welfare of others. Honest in thought and deed in both my personal and official life, I will be exemplary in obeying the laws of the land and the regulations of my department. Whatever I see or hear of a confidential nature or that is confided to me in my official capacity will be kept ever secret unless revelation is necessary in the performance of my duty.*

I will *never act officiously or permit personal feelings, prejudices, animosities or friendships to influence my decisions. With no compromise for crime and with relentless prosecution of criminals, I will enforce the law courteously and appropriately without fear or favor, malice or ill will, never employing unnecessary force or violence and never accepting gratuities.*

I recognize *the badge of my office as a symbol of public faith, and I accept it as a public trust to be held so long as I am true to the ethics of the police service. I will constantly strive to achieve these objectives and ideals, dedicating myself before God to my chosen profession . . . law enforcement.*

Source: Reprinted by permission of the International Association of Chiefs of Police.

As noted by the National Advisory Commission on Criminal Justice Standards and Goals (*The Police,* 1973, p. 9): "Any definition of the police role must acknowledge that the Constitution imposes restrictions on the power of the legislatures to prohibit protected conduct, and to some extent defines the limits of police authority in the enforcement of established laws."

The commission goes on to state, however, that (1973, p. 9): "Concern for the constitutional rights of accused persons processed by the police has tended to obscure the fact that the police have an affirmative obligation to protect all persons in the free exercise of their rights. The police must provide safety for persons exercising their constitutional right to assemble, to speak freely, and to petition for redress of their grievances."

Many citizens are angered when a suspect's rights prevent prosecution of the case. They begin to have doubts about the criminal justice system. However, should these same individuals find themselves in the position of being suspected of a crime, they, doubtless, would expect their rights to be fully protected. (Recall the Magna Carta and how these rights began.) It was Sir John Fortescue who said, "Indeed, one would rather twenty guilty persons should escape the punishment of death than one innocent person should be executed." Countries must guarantee all citizens, even those perceived as unworthy of such protection, their constitutional rights or there is danger of a police state.

The authority, goals, and methods of the police must promote individual liberty, public safety, and social justice. The role of protecting civil rights and civil liberties is perceived by some as the single most important role of the police officer. As a case in point, the National Advisory Commission on Criminal Justice Standards and Goals states (1973, p. 9): "If the overall purposes of the police service in today's society were narrowed to a single objective, that objective would be to preserve the peace in a manner consistent with the freedoms secured by the Constitution."

> *Police are responsible for protecting citizens' constitutional rights.*

Provide Services

In addition to enforcing laws, preserving the peace, assisting in preventing crime, and protecting civil rights and liberties, the police are often called upon to provide additional services to their community.

This role is acknowledged in the first sentence of the *Law Enforcement Code of Ethics*: "As a law enforcement officer, my fundamental duty is to serve mankind. . . ." Many police departments have as their motto: "Serve and Protect."

However, as society has become more complex, so have the types of service requested. Many new requests (often demands) are made upon the police because of their authority. Included among the numerous functions the police may perform in providing services are giving information, directions, and advice; counseling and referring; licensing and registering vehicles; intervening in domestic arguments; working with neglected children; rendering emergency medical or rescue services; dealing with alcoholics and the mentally ill; finding lost children; dealing with stray animals; and controlling traffic and crowds. In addition, many police departments provide community education programs regarding crime, drugs, safety, and the like.

> *Police may be responsible for providing services.*

Notice the word *may* in the boxed role definition. Considerable disagreement exists regarding what type and amount of services the police should provide.

On one hand, individuals like Bernard Garmire (1972, pp. 3–7) feel that this role should not be performed by police officers. He contends that to expect police to perform the two conflicting roles of law enforcement and community service is wrong:

> Even if the numbers of policemen were vastly increased, even if their training were improved, and even if their resources were expanded, I still submit that they could not perform both roles—so sharply do they conflict and so different are the skills required. One person simply cannot reasonably be expected to master both roles intellectually and jump psychologically from one to another in an instant's notice. . . . If we are to restore any semblance of faith in the police by the public—and the police themselves—we must begin first by defining the police role very carefully so that it does not distort reality . . . by fostering the belief that police . . . could function as a gigantic surrogate service agency to the community handling all the needs of the people all the time.

Garmire criticizes sharply the view that the police department is a "social agency of last resort—particularly after 5:00 P.M. and on weekends."

On the other hand, many contend that provision of social services is critical to perform effectively the other functions expected of police officers, a position supported in the Task Force Report of the President's Commission on Law Enforcement and Administration of Justice (1967, p. 14):

> Proposals to relieve the police of what are essentially social services have also been lacking in their consideration of the relationship of such services to the incidence of more serious crimes. Domestic disturbances, for example, often culminate in a serious assault or a homicide. The down-and-out drunk is almost a certain victim of a theft if he is left to lie on the street and has any article of value on him. The streetwalking prostitute may, in one sense, be primarily a social problem, but many streetwalkers engage regularly in arranging the robbery of their patrons as a supplement to their income.
>
> It might be desirable for agencies other than the police to provide community services that bear no relationship to crime or potential crime situations. But the failure of such agencies to develop and the relationship between the social problems in question and the incidence of crime suggest that the police are likely to remain, for some time, as the only 24-hour-a-day, 7-day-a-week agency that is spread over an entire city.

Between these two positions regarding the social service function of the police is that of the National Advisory Commission on Criminal Justice Standards and Goals (1973, pp. 14–15). It recognizes that police are often inappropriately asked to perform functions which might better be performed by another agency of the government—usually because they are the only government representatives available around the clock and because they have the resources and the authority to use force if necessary. It also notes, however, that in many small cities and towns, the police services provided (even though considered by some to be inappropriate "social services") could not be provided by any other agencies. It concludes:

> The concept of a flexible police role, adjustable to local conditions, does not require police agencies to accept submissively the imposition of duties basically unrelated to their essential purpose. On the contrary, effective and efficient policing requires that police agencies restrict themselves as far as possible to the provision of services that directly or indirectly serve to achieve their basic objectives of preserving the peace and protecting constitutional guarantees.
>
> Thus, while it may be appropriate in certain instances for a police agency to perform a nonpolice function, such as providing ambulance service or collecting stray animals, it may be undertaken only after a full public examination of its effect on other and more basic services provided by the agency. . . . Services have to be placed into perspective with all other services provided by the police, and considered as part of the local police role in determining objectives and priorities for the delivery of all police services.

Many police agencies have provided personnel with information to refer persons in need to the proper agency. For example, since New York City began using a citywide 911 emergency number, telephone calls for nonpolice municipal services have decreased dramatically. Police officers in Washington, D.C., use the *Referral Handbook of Social Services,* which indexes available governmental and private services by problem and agency. Police in Milwaukee, Wisconsin, have a comprehensive directory of almost five hundred community agencies and organizations.

What is of primary importance is that people who need help receive it; who provides the help is secondary. However, since many people are likely to turn first to the police for help, the police officer must be prepared either to provide the help or to refer the person to an agency which can provide it.

How the Roles Are Performed

Look again at the two middle paragraphs of the *Law Enforcement Code of Ethics:*

> I will keep my private life unsullied as an example to all; maintain courageous calm in the face of danger, scorn, or ridicule; develop self-restraint; and be constantly mindful of the welfare of others. Honest in thought and deed in both my personal and official life, I will be exemplary in obeying the laws of the land and the regulations of my department. Whatever I see or hear of a

confidential nature or that is confided to me in my official capacity will be kept ever secret unless revelation is necessary in the performance of my duty.

I will never act officiously or permit personal feelings, prejudices, animosities or friendships to influence my decisions. With no compromise for crime and with relentless prosecution of criminals, I will enforce the law courteously and appropriately without fear or favor, malice or ill will, never employing unnecessary force or violence and never accepting gratuities.

Not only are police officers expected to enforce laws, preserve the peace, prevent crimes, protect constitutional rights, and perform community services, they are also expected to do so in impeccable, professional manner. As noted by Dwight Dalbey of the FBI (James, 1968, p. 104):

We expect of a police officer the wisdom of Solomon in understanding the law, the strength of Sampson in arresting a criminal, the gentleness of St. Francis of Assisi in repelling a riot, the patience of Job in dealing with each of us, and the moral purity of Caesar's wife in a nation whose public and private morals in areas outside police work are sometimes open to legitimate questions.

In spite of these expectations, police officers are human, with emotions, biases, and weaknesses. Their work is sometimes dangerous. They see suffering, injustice, cruelty. They see people at their best and their worst. They are under constant pressure, even when things are momentarily calm. They must make rapid decisions, often without any guidelines. They frequently lack the necessary equipment and/or training. Their work is further complicated by people's conflicting expectations of them.

> Police roles must be carried out skillfully and professionally. This requires mental, intellectual, physical, and personal proficiencies.

To perform in the manner expected by the department and the community, the police officer needs numerous proficiencies. The following list summarizes the results of a University of Chicago study of the behavioral requirements needed to perform police patrol duties.*

Mental.   Police officers must:

Endure a long period of monotony in routine patrol yet react quickly (almost simultaneously) and effectively to problem situations observed on the street or to orders issued by the radio dispatcher (in much the same way that a combat pilot must react to interception or a target opportunity).

Have the facility to act effectively in extremely divergent interpersonal situations. A police officer constantly confronts persons who are acting in violation of the law, ranging from curfew violators to felons.

---

*Saunders, Charles B.,Jr. *Upgrading the American Police.* Brookings Institution, 1970, pp. 17–18.

Endure verbal and physical abuse from citizens and offenders (as when plac-ing a person under arrest or facing day-in-and-day-out race prejudice) while using only necessary force in the performance of their functions.

Tolerate stress in a multitude of forms, such as meeting the violent behavior of a mob, arousing people in a burning building, coping with the pressures of a high-speed chase or a weapon being fired at them, or dealing with a women bearing a child.

Personal.   Police officers must:

Relate to the people of their beat—businessmen, residents, school officials, visitors, etc. Their interpersonal relations must range up and down a continuum defined by friendliness and persuasion on one end, and firmness and force at the other.

Exhibit a professional, self-assured presence and a self-confident manner in their conduct when dealing with offenders, the public, and the court.

Take charge of situations, e.g.,a crime or accident scene, yet not unduly alienate participants or bystanders.

Be flexible enough to work under loose supervision in most of their day-to-day patrol activities and also under the direct supervision of superiors in situations where large numbers of officers are required

Exhibit personal courage in the face of dangerous situations which may result in serious injury or death.

Maintain objectivity while dealing with a host of special interest groups, ranging from relatives of offenders to members of the press.

Maintain a balanced perspective in the face of constant conflict, e.g., refrain from accepting bribes or "favors," provide impartial law enforcement, etc.

Intellectual.   Police officers must:

Exhibit initiative, problem-solving capacity, effective judgment, and im-agination in coping with the numerous complex situations they are called upon to face, e.g., a family disturbance, a potential suicide, a robbery in progress, an accident, or a disaster. Police officers themselves clearly recognize this requirement and refer to it as "showing street sense."

Make prompt and effective decisions, sometimes in life-and-death situations, and be able to size up a situation quickly and take appropriate action.

Demonstrate mature judgment, as in deciding whether an arrest is warranted by the circumstances or a warning is sufficient, or in assessing a situation where the use of force may be needed.

Demonstrate critical awareness in discerning signs of out-of-the-ordinary conditions or circumstances which indicate trouble or a crime in progress.

Adequately perform the communication and record-keeping functions of the job, including oral reports, preparation of formal case reports, and the completion of departmental and force forms.

Be capable of restoring equilibrium to social groups, e.g., restoring order in a family fight, in a disagreement between neighbors, or in a clash between rival youth gangs.

Be skillful in questioning suspected offenders victims, and witnesses of crimes.

Gain knowledge of their patrol areas, not only of its physical characteristics but also of its normal routine of events and the usual behavior patterns of its residents.

Physical.   Police officers must:

Exhibit a number of complex psycho-motor skills, such as driving a vehicle in normal and emergency situations, firing a weapon accurately under extremely varied conditions, maintaining agility, endurance, and strength, and showing facility in self-defense and apprehension, as in taking a person into custody with a minimum of force.

Few roles in modern society are as demanding as that of the police officer.

Discretion

As noted by Reiss (1971, p. 45), discretion is an integral of policing:

> It is incumbent upon a police officer to enter upon a variety of social stages, encounter the actors, determine their roles, and figure out the plot. Often, before they can act, the police must uncover the "plot" and identify the roles and behavior of the actors. This is true even in emergency situations where an officer is expected to assess the situation almost immediately and make judgments as to what he must do.

Sutherland and Cressey (1978, p. 389) call attention to the fact that "although police officers are expected to help make crime dangerous for all, they are to use discretion and to exercise certain judicial functions as they do so. They must decide whether a certain act is in violation of the law, and also whether it probably can be proved that the law has been violated.

Police officers, even those assigned to patrol duties in a large city, are confronted with few serious crimes in the course of a single tour of duty. They tend to view such involvement, particularly if there is some degree of danger, as constituting "real" police work. However , it is apparent that they spend considerably more time keeping order, settling disputes, finding missing children, and helping with medical emergencies than they do in responding to criminal conduct which is serious enough to call for arrest, prosecution, and conviction.

This does not mean that serious crime is unimportant to police officers. Quite the contrary is true. But it does mean that they perform a wide range of other functions which are of a highly complex nature and which often involve difficult social, behavioral, and political problems rather than major crimes.

Today's law enforcement officers need a broad background as well as broadening experiences to meet the complex challenges of a modern, changing, multiethnic and multiracial society. On that point there is near-unanimous agreement.

Summary

Although numerous federal and state agencies are directly involved in law enforcement, the ultimate responsibility is usually at the local level. It is here that the goals of law enforcement are initiated, based on what the citizens of the individual community perceive to be their most pressing needs.

Among the common goals of police departments are a commitment to preserve the peace, to protect civil rights and civil liberties, to enforce the law, to prevent crime, and to provide services.

Police officers work within the context of the goals, objectives, and tasks defined by their department. They also work within the basic organizational structure of their department which, most often, is divided into two sections: field services and administrative services. Tasks and personnel to accomplish them are assigned to one of these two sections.

Overseeing the entire police department is the chief of police, the primary law enforcement officer at the local level, who coordinates both the field services and the administrative services.

Administrative services provide support for field services, including records and communications, recruitment and training, and special facilities and services. Most current information is conveyed to police officers at roll call or by radio, the primary method of transmitting and seeking information between headquarters and units in the field.

In addition to direct communication, police officers also rely upon information contained in the department's records. Centralization of these records allows the various line functions to be coordinated. Among the types of records the police officer may use are administrative, arrest, identification, and complaint records. Further, the NCIC provides all police agencies in the country access to the computerized files of the FBI.

Access to information is not always unlimited, however. A data privacy act regulates the use of confidential and private information on individuals in the records, files, and processes of a state and its political subdivisions.

Within the field services provided in a police department are patrol, traffic, investigation and community service. Sometimes these are specialized departments; sometimes the services are provided by a single department. In addition, many police departments, particularly the larger departments, have specialized officers such as vice officers and juvenile officers.

The people largely determine the role of the police and give them their authority to fulfill this role. Their support is vital if any law enforcement effort is to succeed.

Police officers must *enforce laws,* federal, state, and municipal, to protect the health and welfare of the community. For example, they enforce highway laws to make the streets safe for driving; they arrest people who violate the privacy of another person's home, who unlawfully sell narcotics, or who otherwise break the law.

They *preserve the peace* in a professional manner by patrolling troubled areas, intervening in domestic disturbances, and advising people in community disputes, such as landlord and tenant disagreements.

They *prevent crime* by being highly visible in the community, by personally contacting people to show the police department's concern for them, by educating the public about crime and crime prevention, and by involving them in programs such as operation identification, in which valuables are marked for later identification in case of theft.

They *protect civil rights and civil liberties* by living and enforcing the principles contained in the Bill of Rights, such as respect for free speech, the right of privacy, and the right to due process under the law.

They also *provide necessary services* such as rendering first aid in medical emergencies, investigating traffic accidents, watching homes when people are on vacation, and assisting in community programs.

These roles must be carried out skillfully and professionally, and require numerous mental, intellectual, physical, and personal proficiencies as well as discretion.

Discussion Questions

1. How has communication between the officer in the field and headquarters changed in the last hundred years?
2. What affect does a data privacy act have on investigations of individuals involved in organized crime?
3. How do police relate to their community?
4. How have the roles of police officer changed over time?
5. What services should police officers provide? Which are provided in our community?
6. Why is the support of the people vital to the successful accomplishment of the responsibilities of the modern police officer?
7. Why does Garmire believe it is hard for an officer to change roles? Don't we all play many different roles in our lives? Isn't it harder to be the same all the time?
8. What aspects of the Code of Ethics seem most relevant to the 1980s?

References

Arnold, W.R., and Brungardt, T.M. *Juvenile misconduct and delinquency.* Boston: Houghton Mifflin Co., 1983.

Bittner, E. "Florence Nightingale in pursuit of Willie Sutton: A theory of the police," In *The potential for reform of the criminal justice system,* edited by Herbert Jacob. Beverly Hills: Sage, 1974.

Bittner, E. *The function of police in modern society.* Washington, D.C.: U.S. Government Printing Office, 1971.

Garmire, B.L. "The police role in an urban society." In *The police and the community,* edited by Robert F. Steadman. Baltimore: The Johns Hopkins University Press, 1972. (Copyright by the Committee for Economic Development.)

Gay, W.G., and Schack, S. *Prescriptive package: Improving patrol productivity.* Vol. 1, *Routine patrol.* Washington, D.C.: Office of Technology Transfer, National Institute of Law Enforcement and Criminal Justice, Law Enforcement Assistance Administration, U.S. Department of Justice (Grant Number 76–NI–00–0055), July 1977.

Iannone, N.F. *Principles of police patrol.* New York: McGraw-Hill, 1975.

James, H. *Crisis in the courts.* New York: David McKay Company, 1968. (Copyright by the Christian Science Publishing Society.) Based on a series of weekly articles in *The Christian Science monitor,* April to July, 1967.

Klockars, C.B. *Thinking about police: Contemporary readings.* New York: McGraw-Hill, 1983.

Leonard, V.A., and More, H.W. *Police organization and management.* 6th ed. Mineola, N.Y.: Foundation Press, 1982.

Martin, T.C. "Seattle police department's decoy squad." In *FBI law enforcement bulletin,* February 1978.

More, H.W., Jr. *Texting and readings: The American police.* Criminal Justice Series. St. Paul, Minn.:West Publishing Company, 1967.

Munro, J.L. *Administrative behavior and police organization.* Cincinnati: W.H. Anderson, 1974.

National Advisory Commission on Criminal Justice Standards and Goals. *The police.* Washington, D.C.: U.S. Government Printing Office (LEAA Grant Number 72–DF–99–0002, and NI 72–0200) 1973.

Nierderhoffer, A. *Behind the shield.* New York: Anchor, 1967.

President's Commission on Law Enforcement and Administration of Justice. *The challenge of crime in a free society.* Washington, D.C.: U.S. Government Printing Office, February 1967.

President's Commission on Law Enforcement and Administration of Justice. *Task force report: The police.* Washington, D.C.: U.S. Government Printing Office, 1967.

Reiss, A.J., Jr. *The police and the public.* New Haven, Conn.: Yale University Press, 1971.

Saunders, Charles B., Jr. *Upgrading the American police.* Washington, D.C.: The Brookings Institution, 1970.

Schack, S., and Gay, W.G. *Prescriptive package: Improving patrol productivity.* Vol. II, *Specialized patrol.* Washington, D.C.: Office of Technology Transfer, National Institute of Law Enforcement and Criminal Justice, Law Enforcement Assistance Administration, U.S. Department of Justice (Grant Number 76–NI–00–0055), July 1977.

Sullivan, J.L. *Introduction to police science*. 2d ed. New York: McGraw-Hill, 1971.

Sutherland, E.H., and Cressey, D.R. *Criminology*. 10th ed. Philadelphia: J.B. Lippincott, 1978.

Swanson, C.R., and Territo, L. *Police administration: Structure, processes and behavior*. New York: Macmillan, 1983.

Webster, J.A. "Police task and time study." In *Journal of criminal law, criminology, and police science,* Vol. 61. No date.

Wilson, J.Q. *Varieties of police behavior*. Cambridge, Mass.: Harvard University Press, 1968.

Police Operations

Getting the Job Done

By this point you should have a good understanding of the importance and complexity of being a law enforcement officer. The concepts from the preceding two sections should be kept in mind as you read about the day-to-day operations of the police officer. The citizens' civil rights and civil liberties, the laws to be enforced, the crimes to be dealt with, the other agencies that can lend assistance, the structure and goals of the individual police agency, the roles to be fulfilled, and the image of the police in the community all directly affect daily operations.

Despite a common conception that the police officer's routine is one of high-speed chases, shoot outs, and close calls with dangerous criminals, this is only a small part of a police officer's job. Some officers never draw their guns in twenty years of service. A great part of their time is spent in preventing crime and in providing services to the community.

Operations can be divided into four basic categories: patrol—the backbone of police operations (Chapter 8), traffic (Chapter 9), investigation (Chapter 10), and community service (Chapter 11). You have already been briefly introduced to each of these. In this section you will get a close-up view of each. Although discussed separately, the four categories have considerable overlap. In some smaller agencies all four functions are performed by a single field service division. In very small agencies they may be performed by a single police officer. Larger agencies, on the other hand, may have divisions within each of the four categories. In addition, larger agencies may have a separate division to deal with juveniles (Chapter 12).

Patrol is a vital part of police work, responsible for providing continuous police services and high visibility law enforcement.

Patrol

The Backbone of Police Work

Do You Know . . .

- What the primary responsibilities of patrol are?
- What four specific areas of responsibility are assigned to patrol?
- How specialized patrol differs from routine patrol?
- What methods of patrol may be used?
- What type of shift and beat staffing often lessens the effectiveness of preventive patrol?
- What approaches have been tried to improve preventive patrol effectiveness?
- What the central features of team policing are?
- What four basic types of team policing have been developed?
- What advantages and disadvantages accompany team policing programs?
- Whether it is preferable to have one or two officers assigned to a patrol car?

The execution of the laws is more important than the making of them.

—*Thomas Jefferson*

Introduction

Andrew Sutor (1976, pp. 85–86) vividly depicts what happened in Montreal, Canada, in October 1969 when the police went on strike and the city was without police:*

> Rioting, arson, and looting broke out. In parts of Montreal there were piles of broken glass, blocks of looted stores and burned-out vehicles.
>
> During the day there were twenty-three major holdups, including ten bank robberies. Armed men made off with $28,000 from the City and District Savings Bank on St. Denis Street. Four men with machine guns held up a finance company. Conditions became so bad that in a radio address Lucien Saulnier, Chairman of the Executive Committee of the City, advised citizens to stay home and protect their property. One householder who did, shot a burglar dead.
>
> Around 8 p.m. scores of taxis pulled up at the Murray Hill Limousine Company garage. Taxi drivers had long held a grudge against the company. Molotov cocktails were thrown, and buses and cars were set afire. Employees opened fire on the mob with shutguns. A provincial policeman was shot dead; other persons were wounded by gunfire.
>
> Passersby were caught up in the violence, and a mob, two to three hundred strong, left the Murray Hill garage and proceeded toward Montreal's main shopping and hotel district. With clubs, baseball bats and rocks the mob commenced an orgy of senseless destruction and looting....
>
> So extensive was the damage that a glass expert estimated that it would cost $2,000,000 merely to replace the broken windows. The total damage from fires, destruction and theft has been placed at millions more.
>
> . . . The extent of the lawlessness was amazing. One man reported: "I don't mean hoodlums and habitual lawbreakers, I mean just plain people committed offenses they would not dream of trying if there was a policeman standing on the corner. I saw cars driven through red lights. Drivers shot up the wrong side of the street because they realized no one would catch them. You wouldn't believe the number of car accidents I saw, because drivers took chances cutting corners and crossing traffic lanes against regulations. They knew there was no cop around to make a record of it.

In his summary Sutor concludes (p. 88): "You have often heard that crime prevention by police is hard to measure. For one long day Montreal had the scale and it measured 'anarchy.'"

Patrol is responsible for providing continuous police service and high visibility of law enforcement, thereby deterring crime. Patrol is the most vital component of police work. All other units are supplemental to this basic unit. Patrol can contribute to each of the common goals of police departments, including preserving the peace, protecting civil rights and civil liberties, enforcing the law, preventing crime, and providing services.

> *Patrol is responsible for providing continuous police service and high visibility of law enforcement, thereby deterring crime.*

In addition, patrol officers must understand the federal, state, and local laws they are sworn to uphold and use good judgment in enforcing them. As noted by the Task Force on the Police (1973, p. 192):

> The patrol officer is the first interpreter of the law and in effect performs a quasi-judicial function. He makes the first attempt to match the reality of human conflict with the law; he determines whether to take no action, to advise, to warn, or to arrest; he determines whether he must apply physical force, perhaps sufficient to cause death. It is he who must discern the fine distinction between a civil and a criminal conflict, between merely unorthodox behavior and a crime, between a legitimate dissent and disturbance of the peace, between the truth and a lie. As the interpreter of the law, he recognizes that a decision to arrest is only the first step in the determination of guilt or innocence. He is guided by, and guardian of, the Constitution.

Unfortunately, however, as noted by this same report (p.189): "The patrolman is usually the lowest paid, least consulted, most taken for granted member of the force. His duty is looked on as routine and boring."

Despite the lack of status within some police departments, patrol is the backbone of policing. Samuel Walker (1983, p.103) notes that the "majority of police officers are assigned to patrol and, in that capacity, deliver the bulk of police services to the public. The marked patrol car and the uniformed patrol officer are the most visible manifestations of the police in the eyes of the public."

Duties and Responsibilities

The Task Force on the Police (1973, p.191) notes that no matter what size a police department is, patrol officers have two basic responsibilities: (1) to prevent criminal activity, and (2) to provide day-to-day police service to the community. "The specific duties and responsibilities of the patrol officer are innumerable, as varied and complex as the society in which he works. In his multi-purpose role, the patrol officer serves as a protector of public safety, enforcer of law, controller of traffic, and investigator and interpreter of the law."

Patrol officers are responsible for:
- *Preserving the peace.*
- *Protecting and serving the community.*
- *Enforcing the laws.*
- *Directing traffic.*
- *Investigating crimes.*

As protectors, patrol officers promote and preserve order, respond to requests for services, and attempt to resolve conflicts between individuals and groups. Specific aspects of community service are covered more fully in Chapter 11.

As law enforcers, the first duty of patrol officers is to protect constitutional guarantees (as described more fully in Chapters 13 and 14); the second duty is to enforce federal, state, and local statutes. Patrol officers not only encourage voluntary compliance with the law, but also seek to reduce the opportunity for crimes to be committed.

Patrol officers also serve important traffic control functions, described in detail in Chapter 9, and important investigative functions, described in detail in Chapter 10.

Finally, as also noted in the Task Force on the Police, patrol officers in any community are the most visible representatives of government, and although they are not supervisors in the organizational sense, they are responsible for the safety and direction of hundreds of people each day.

Types of Patrol

Patrol is frequently categorized as being either routine or specialized. Both routine and specialized patrol seek to deter crime and apprehend criminals as well as to provide community satisfaction with the services provided by the police department. Routine patrol does so by providing rapid response to calls for service; specialized patrol by focusing its efforts on already identified problems. Whether routine or specialized patrol is used depends on the nature of the problem and the tactics required to deal with it most effectively.

Routine Patrol

There is nothing "routine" about routine patrol. Its demands and challenges change constantly; the patrol officer may be pursuing an armed bank robber in the morning and rescuing a cat from a tree in the afternoon. It has been said that patrol consists of seven hours and fifty–nine minutes of boredom followed by one minute of sheer panic. As noted previously, routine patrol is the most basic unit of the police department. It is the primary means by which the police department fulfills its responsibility to the community. The workload of routine patrol is illustrated in Figure 8–1.

Figure 8–1.   **Routine Patrol.**

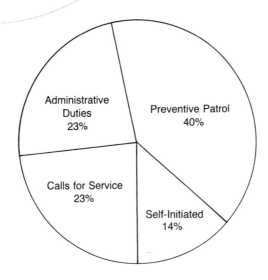

Source: National Institute of Law Enforcement and Criminal Justice, *Improving Patrol Productivity*. Vol. I, *Routine Patrol,* Washington, D.C.: U.S. Government Printing Office, 1977, p. 3.

Crime Prevention.   The theory behind preventive patrol is that the presence of highly visible mobile patrol units will help prevent crime. As noted by the President's Commission on Law Enforcement and Administration of Criminal Justice (*Challenge of Crime*, 1967): "Preventive patrol, the continued scrutiny of the community by visible and mobile policemen, is universally thought of as the best method of controlling crime that is available to the police." The Montreal experience would seem to support this contention.

Preventive patrol is generally accomplished by uniformed officers moving at random through as assigned area. Since officers usually decide for themselves what they will do while on preventive patrol, this time is sometimes referred to as "noncommitted" time. It comprises between thirty and forty percent of patrol time, but it is often broken into small segments due to interruptions by self-initiated activities, service calls, and administrative duties.

Often priorities for preventive patrol are identified and/or assigned during roll call. For example, patrol officers may be alerted to the presence of a known escaped criminal sighted in the area to watch for while on patrol.

Although patrol is commonly thought to have a deterrent effect on crime, one important study, the *Kansas City Preventive Patrol Experiment,* suggests this is not the case. Funded by a grant from the Police Foundation, this study was conducted in 1972 and is often referred to as the most comprehensive study of routine preventive patrol ever undertaken. The basic design divided fifteen beats in Kansas City into three different groups:

- Group 1 Reactive Beats— five beats in which no routine preventive patrol was used. Officers responded only to calls for service.
- Group 2 "Control" Beats— five beats maintained their normal level of routine preventive patrol.
- Group 3 Proactive Beats— five beats doubled or tripled the level of routine preventive patrol.

According to Kellings, et al, (Klockers, 1983, p.160): "Given the large amount of data collected and the extremely diverse sources used, the overwhelming evidence is that decreasing or increasing routine preventive patrol within the range tested in this experiment had no effect on crime, citizen fear of crime, community attitudes toward the police on the delivery of police services, police response time or traffic accidents."

Klockers (1983, p.130) asserts that the results of the Kansas City Patrol Experiment indicate that "it makes about as much sense to have police patrol routinely in cars to fight crime as it does to have firemen patrol routinely in fire trucks to fight fire."

Self-Initiated Tasks.   Officer-initiated activities usually result from officers' observations while on preventive patrol; that is, they encounter situations which require their intervention. For example, an officer may see a crime in progress and arrest the suspect. Usually, however, officer-initiated activities involve community relations or crime prevention activities such as citizen contacts or automobile and building checks. Officers may see a large crown gathered and decide to break it up, thereby, preventing a possible disturbance or even a riot. Or they may see a break in a store's security, take steps to correct it, and thus prevent a possible burglary later.

Such self-initiated activities occupy about fourteen percent of an officer's patrol time. Officers are sometimes hesitant to get involved in community services and preventive activities because such duties make the officers unavailable for radio dispatches and interfere with their ability to respond rapidly to service calls. Hand-held radios and beepers have allowed patrol officers more freedom of movement and have allowed them to initiate more activity.

Call for Service.   The two-way radio has made the service call an extremely important element of patrol. It has also made it necessary to prioritize calls. A radio dispatch almost always takes precedence over other patrol activities. For example, if an officer has stopped a traffic violator (a self-initiated activity) and receives a call of an armed robbery in progress, most departments' policy requires the officer to discontinue the contact with the motorist and answer the service call.

Too often little attention is paid to the officer's use of noncommitted time, which is often regarded as having no function other than to ensure the availablity of officers to quickly respond to service calls. Frequently noncrime service calls interrupt a patrol officer's self-initiated activity that could prevent or deter crime. Emphasis on rapid response to all service calls has sometimes retarded the development of productive patrol services. Obviously, not all service calls require a rapid response.

Calls for service account for approximately one-fourth of the officer's workload.

Administrative Duties. Accounting for another one-fourth of patrol time is administrative work, including preparing and maintaining the patrol vehicle, transporting prisoners and documents, writing reports, and testifying in court. Efforts to make patrol more cost-effective have often been aimed at cutting time spent on administrative duties. Some departments have greatly reduced the time officers spend maintaining their vehicles. Other departments have drastically reduced the amount of paperwork required of the patrol officers by allowing them to dictate reports which secretaries then transcribe.

The types of reports police officers frequently use include: Motor Vehicle Report, Vehicle Recovery Report, Offense Report, Continuation Report, Juvenile Report, Juvenile Report Summary, Missing Persons Report, Arrest/Violation Report, and Record Check.

Specialized Patrol

Specialized patrol is designed to handle problems and situations that require concentrated, coordinated efforts. Some patrol officers receive special training to deal with specific problems such as hostage and sniper situations, VIP protection, riot or crowd control, rescue operations, and control of suppressible crimes.

Suppressible crimes are crimes which commonly occur in locations and under circumstances which provide police officers a reasonable opportunity to deter or apprehend offenders. Included in the category of suppressible crimes are robbery, burglary, car theft, assault, and sex crimes. Such problems frequently involve a need for covert surveillance and decoys, tactics which cannot be used by uniformed patrol officers.

Specialized patrol operations are often used to saturate particular areas or to stake out suspects and possible crime locations. Countermeasures to combat street crimes have included police decoys to catch criminals—one of the most cost-effective and productive apprehension methods available. Officers have posed as cab drivers, old women, truck drivers, money couriers, nuns, and priests. They have infiltrated drug circles as undercover agents. Usually operating in high-crime areas, decoy officers are vulnerable to violence and injury. However, the results are considered worth the risk; an attack upon a decoy almost always results in a conviction of the attacker.

Some patrol officers receive special training to deal with specific problems such as hostage and sniper situations, VIP protection, riot or crowd control, rescue operations, and control of suppressible crimes.

Methods of Patrol

Williams, Formby, and Watkins (1982, p.100) note that: "Patrol usually refers to the random movement of uniformed officers within a defined area. This random movement may be done on foot, in or on some type of vehicle, or, in some areas, on horseback."

> *Patrol may be accomplished via foot, automobile, motocycle, bicycle, horseback, aircraft, and boat. The most commonly used and most effective patrol is usually a combination of automobile and foot patrol.*

Foot Patrol.   Foot patrol, the oldest form of patrol, has the advantage of close citizen contact. Most effective in highly congested areas, it may help to deter burglary, robbery, purse-snatching, and muggings. The 1980s have seen a significant trend back to foot patrol. Foot patrol is relatively expensive and does limit the officer's ability to pursue suspects in vehicles and to get from one area to another rapidly. Used in conjunction with motorized patrol, foot patrol is highly effective.

Automobile Patrol.   Automobile patrol offers the greatest mobility and flexibility and is usually the most cost-effective method of patrol. It allows wide coverage and rapid response to calls—the vehicle radio provides instant communications with headquarters. The automobile also provides a means of transporting special equipment and prisoners or suspects. The obvious disadvantage of automobile patrol is that access to certain locations is restricted, for example, inside buildings. Therefore, officers may have to leave their vehicles to pursue suspects on foot.

Another disadvantage of automobile patrol is a lack of community contact between the police and the citizens. As a result, the President's Commission on Crime urged that officers in patrol cars should be considered foot officers who use cars for transportation from one point to another. Many officers, however, do not see it that way.

Many officers resist getting out of their cars to talk to citizens; some even feel it is a degrading type of appeasement. In addition, the practice contradicts the tactical principle of preventive patrol which requires the continual presence of moving, motorized street patrol. Some departments stress this principle to the extent that department regulations forbid unnecessary or unofficial conversations with citizens.

However, recent research on the effectiveness of preventive patrol indicates that a crime prevented by a passing vehicle can, and usually is, committed as soon as the police are gone. In effect, police presence only prevents street crime if the police can be everywhere at once.

Motorcycle Patrol.   Motorcycle patrol is similar to automobile patrol; however, it foregoes the advantage of transporting special equipment and prisoners to overcome the disadvantage of limited access presented by automobile. The motorcycle is also better suited to maneuver easily through heavy traffic or narrow alleys.

Bicycle Patrol.   Bicycle patrol is sometimes used in parks and on beaches, or in conjunction with stakeouts and surveillance. Although used infrequently, it adds another dimension of patrol available in special circumstances.

Mounted Patrol.   Mounted patrol is decreasing in the United States, but it is still used effectively in larger cities such as New York to quell civil disorders and riots, to patrol bridle paths and parks, and to control traffic. Although expensive, this method of patrol has a unique advantage—the size and mobility of the horse is more effective in an unruly crowd than an officer on foot or in a vehicle.

Air Patrol.   Air patrol is another expensive yet highly effective form of patrol, especially when large geographic areas are involved, for example, a widespread search for a lost person, a downed plane, or an escaped convict. Helicopters and small aircraft are generally used in conjunction with police vehicles on the ground in criminal surveillance and in traffic control, not only to report tie-ups, but to clock speeds and radio to ground units. Helicopters have also been used to rescue persons from tall buildings on fire, and in other situations such as floods. In addition aircraft is a cost-effective means of transporting prisoners over long distances.

Boat Patrol.   Boat patrol is used extensively on our coasts to apprehend gun and narcotics smugglers. Inland, boat patrols are often used to control river and lake traffic.

Sheriff's water patrol submersing a water pump preparatory to fighting a fire on a launch.

Canine-Assisted Patrol.   Canine-assisted patrol is a specialized method of patrol usually found only in larger departments. It has been used in crowd control, in searching out concealed suspects, and in identifying hidden narcotics. Dogs have also been trained and used extensively in major airports to locate bombs or narcotics on planes. Although expensive, canine-assisted patrol may be cost-effective by diminishing the number of officers required for a search.

Combination Patrol.   Combination patrol provides the most versatile approach to preventing or deterring crime and apprehending criminals. The combination used will depend not only on the size of the police department but also upon the circumstances which arise.

Table 8–1.   **Summary of Patrol Methods.**

METHOD	USES	ADVANTAGES	DISADVANTAGES
Foot	Highly congested areas Burglary, robbery, theft, purse snatching, mugging	Close citizen contact High visibility Develop informants	Relatively expensive Limited mobility
Automobile	Respond to service calls Provide traffic control Transport individuals, documents, and equipment	Most economical Greatest mobility and flexibility Offers means of communication Provides means of transporting people, documents, and equipment	Limited access to certain areas Limited citizen contact
Motorcycle	Same as automobile except for transporting individuals and limited equipment	Maneuverability in congested areas and areas restricted to automobiles	Inability to transport much equipment Not used during bad weather Hazardous to operator
Bicycle	Stake-outs Parks and beaches Congested areas	Quiet and unobtrusive	Limited speed
Mounted	Parks and bridle paths Crowd control Traffic control	Size and maneuverability of horse	Expensive
Aircraft	Surveillance Traffic control Searches and rescues	Covers larger areas easily	Expensive
Boat	Deter smuggling Water traffic control Rescues	Access to activities occurring on water	Expensive
Canine-Assisted	Locating bombs, drugs, and concealed suspects	Minimizes officers' risks	Expensive

Structure and Management of Patrol

Traditionally, patrol officers have been assigned a specific time and a specific geographic location to patrol. Typically, a three-shift structure is implemented and the beats are set up to be of equal geographic size. Such a structure poses obvious problems, because the workload is not the same at all hours of the day or in all areas. For example, as noted by Williams, Formby, and Watkins (1982, p. 101): "Statistics show that the 4 p.m. to midnight shift workload, in terms of calls for service and crimes committed, is about twice as high as that for the midnight to 8 a.m. shift. Where equal shift staffing is used, the amount of preventive patrol time and the workload per officer are doubled, resulting in less preventive patrol to deter crime during times when the crime occurrence is highest." Likewise, some areas of a city or town are likely to have a higher demand for police service than others.

> *Equal shift and beat size staffing creates major problems and lessens the effectiveness of preventive patrol during certain times and in certain areas.*

Several attempts have been made to overcome the problems inherent in equal shift and beat size staffing. Some departments, usually larger ones, assign officers according to the demand for services, concentrating the officer's time where it is most needed. However, union contracts sometimes make this difficult.

Another problem with traditional approaches to organizing patrol is how the officer's time is structured. Recall that preventive patrol occupies approximately 40 percent of an officer's time, but it is usually broken up into short intervals of twenty to thirty minutes. Lack of a concentrated effort reduces the effects of preventive patrol.

Several attempts to improve the use of preventive patrol time have been implemented. Four such nontraditional preventive patrol strategies are described by Williams, Formby, and Watkins (1982, p.101).

Their first example involves the Community-Oriented Policing concept and the Community Manager concept. Both approaches allow an officer to plan ahead for use of noncommitted time through the use of statistics on crime in the officer's allotted time and area. Officers are to use such crime analysis information to work with the community to devise methods to deter crime. Although such programs might be perceived as basically community relations, they do provide one approach to planning for more effective use of preventive patrol time.

A second approach, used primarily in and around New Haven, Connecticut, is the Directed Deterrent Patrol (DDP). Like the preceding example, DDP uses crime analysis information to organize the route and timing of preventive patrol. Officers are given the exact time, route, and duration of each preventive patrol activity, known as a D. run. When a D. run begins, the officers notify the dispatcher. From then until the run is completed, these officers do not receive any routine calls. Upon completion of the D. run, the officers again notify dispatch. This approach provides substantial time to be used for only preventive patrol.

A third example is the approach used in Wilmington, Delaware, called the Directed Apprehension or the Split-Force Patrol. In this approach, part of the patrol force undertakes only directed patrol activities; the remainder of the patrol force answers calls for service and performs traditional patrol activities.

The fourth example is the New York City Street Crime Unit, a unit of specially trained patrol officers using plainclothes surveillance and decoy tactics to apprehend offenders in the act of committing crimes. The officers, disguised as potential victims, patrol high-crime areas, watched by a back-up team, also in disguise. Such specialized patrol teams were described earlier in this chapter.

> *Preventive patrol has used crime statistics to plan shift and beat staffing, providing more coverage during times of peak criminal activity and in high-crime areas.*

Other approaches to enhance the effectiveness of patrol include team policing and use of volunteers from the community.

Team Policing

Team policing in the United States, patterned after a unique patrol experiment in Aberdeen, Scotland, in 1948, is designed to deliver patrol, investigative, and community services on a more informal basis. In other words, neighborhood team policing combines the specialized services and equipment of large urban departments with the more personal community contact of small departments.

Police services are decentralized, with a team of officers assigned around-the-clock responsibility for crime control and police services in a specific area. In many programs the officer's responsibilities are expanded to include investigative work as well as community relations services. As departments become decentralized, decision-making becomes a product of teamwork, giving officers a voice in planning actions and policies which directly affect them. These features not only increase officer job satisfaction, but they also frequently improve the quality and quantity of police service delivered to the community.

> *Central features of team policing include:*
> - *Combining patrol, investigative, and community relation services.*
> - *Decentralization.*
> - *Cooperative decision making.*
> - *Permanent assignment to a team and a geographic area.*

Although team policing means different things to different departments, a 1973 study of team policing suggests that most programs have three basic operational elements (Sherman, et al. 1973, pp. 3–5):

- Geographic stability of patrol.
- Maximum interaction among team members.
- Maximum communication among team members and the community.

The authors identify the most basic operational element as geographic stability of patrol. This same study identified common organizational supports in addition to the three basic operational elements: unity of supervision, lower-level flexibility in policy making, unified delivery of services, and combined investigative and patrol functions.

The teams are organized in two different ways: shift teams and area teams. A shift team usually has no formal coordination of the various shifts serving a single area. The supervisor of the shift team reports to a watch commander who is responsible for only a single shift within a twenty-four hour period. This approach provides less continuity of service.

Area teams, in contrast, provide law enforcement services twenty-four hours a day. This around-the-clock responsibility allows a single team leader to coordinate all patrol activities in the same area and provides considerable flexibility in deploying officers to meet changing levels of service demands throughout the day.

Area teams have three distinct advantages over shift teams. First, they provide continuity of service to citizens; second, they allow for alteration of schedule; and third, they have a larger manpower pool from which to draw.

Team policing is found in small, medium, and large cities in equal numbers, not just in the big cities. It is found in both urban and suburban communities and in all parts of the country. Most team programs have replaced random roving patrol with objective-based patrol activities. Teams are assigned crime prevention, investigative, and community relations activities to perform when not responding to calls. Some departments place more emphasis on one of these activities than the others, and hence can be classified by their primary focus.

Basic patrol teams are synonymous with routine patrol in most respects. In routine patrol, the simplest form of team policing, the department is organized into teams responsible for basic preventive patrol, radio dispatch service, and traffic duties. The officers do not have investigative or community relations responsibilities, and specialists such as evidence technicians are not usually assigned to the team. The primary objectives of basic patrol teams are improved manpower allocation, reduced response time, and the clearance of service calls.

The *patrol-investigative team* combines the basic patrol and follow-up investigative responsibilities. Some departments have transferred almost half of their detectives to the team. Although the detectives perform most of the follow-up investigations, patrol officers are responsible for conducting more complete preliminary investigations and are occasionally assigned to investigative follow-ups. According to a national evaluation of the investigative effectiveness of teams (Gay, Day, and Woodward, 1977, pp. 23–27), "at the very least, teams with investigative functions have performed as well as, and in some cases, better than, non-team control units." This same evaluation suggested two advantages of combining patrol and investigative functions: (1) team policing contributes to the breakdown of officer-investigator isolation and hostility existing in many traditionally organized departments and provides an organizational context in which officers and investigators can coordinate their activities; and (2) since most crime is committed locally, it is natural for officers and investigators who are permanently assigned to a small number of beats to acquire knowledge of the assigned area and its people, thus increasing their investigative effectiveness.

The *patrol-community service team* combines basic and community relations responsibilities. It may also include traffic responsibilities. The assignment of community responsibilities to team officers is hoped to increase both the level and kinds of service delivered to the community. Many patrol community service teams have increased their attention to noncrime services such as interpersonal disturbances, auto accidents, missing persons, and referrals to social agencies for assistance.

Full-service teams are the most complex team policing programs, combining patrol, investigative, and community relations responsibilities. They also sometimes include traffic responsibilities. The decentralization of these functions usually involves transfer of detectives, community relations, and traffic personnel. Frequently three to four detectives are assigned to each team, thereby having a significant impact on the detective bureau of most departments. Most full-service teams are organized as area teams.

Full-service teams may be classified further as either multispecialist or generalist. A *multispecialist team*, as the name implies, combines patrol officers and specialists (detectives and community relations officers) under the direction of a team leader. The patrol officers participate in investigative and community relations activities, but the team specialists have primary responsibility.

In contrast, *generalist teams* expect each team officer to perform both basic patrol and specialist duties. The generalist approach severly reduces the number of personnel and functions assigned to centralized bureaus within a police department.

> *Four basic categories of team policing are:*
> - *Basic patrol teams.*
> - *Patrol-investigative teams.*
> - *Patrol-community service teams.*
> - *Full-service teams.*

Each department using team policing has a slightly different organization, slightly different goals, and slightly different achievements. Yet each shares common goals with other police departments: perserving the peace, preventing crime, enforcing laws, preserving civil rights and civil liberties, and providing community services. A brief review of some team policing programs in various parts of the country illustrates the variety of approaches taken in implementing team policing.

Syracuse: Crime Control Team.   Syracuse, N.Y., was the first city to combine patrol and investigative functions into a single unit with geographic responsibility for crime control. The crime control team consisted of eight police officers; a deputy leader; and a team leader, a lieutenant with considerable discretion in directing the team's activities and operations. The team was relieved of routine, noncriminal duties and given responsibility for controlling serious crime, apprehending offenders, and conducting investigations in a small area of the city. The decentralized crime control team operated independently of the rest of the agency and achieved considerable success in reducing crime and increasing crime clearance rates. The team concept has been extended to other agency operations.

Los Angeles: Basic Car Plan.   The objectives of the Basic Car Plan are to prevent crime by improving community attitudes toward the police, to provide stability of assignment for street police officers, and to give each team a proprietary interest in its assigned area. The plan was first tested in two divisions and then expanded city-wide in 1970. Each police division has geographic areas of varying size determined by workload and crime frequency data. A team consists of nine officers per shift assigned to a specific area and responsible for providing police service twenty-four hours a day. Specialized personnel are not assigned to the basic car teams. Each team is headed by a senior lead officer. The patrol watch commander and field sergeant's supervisory responsibilities remain unchanged. The team and citizens in each area hold formal meetings monthly. Informal meetings occur more frequently.

Detroit: Beat Commander System.   The Beat Commander System began in 1970 in two scout car areas in Detroit's 10th Precinct. The beat commander, a sergeant, commands approximately twenty men, including three detectives who investigate only cases originating in the beat command area. Two additional sergeants provide around-the-clock supervision. The primary element of the system is stability of the team's assignment to a specified neighborhood. The goals are to improve police-community understanding, cooperation in crime control, police efficiency, and job satisfaction.

New York City: Neighborhood Police Team.   New York City began operations in one radio motor patrol sector with a team consisting of a sergeant and eighteen officers. The system was later expanded throughout the department. Although similar in structure to the Detroit system, neighborhood team policing officers have greater investigative responsibilities because detectives are not directly involved in the program. The principal goals of the project are crime control and improved community relations. Benefits resulting from the program include improved supervision and motivation, resulting in increased productivity and efficiency as well as substantial reductions in response time to calls.

Dayton: Team Policing.   Dayton, Ohio, decentralized authority and functions and concentrated upon community participation. The system used a generalist team approach to produce a community-based police structure, changing the traditional military structure of the police organization to a neighborhood-oriented professional organization. The experiment began in a district comprising one-sixth of the city. The personnel included thirty-five to forty officers, twelve community service officers, four sergeants who acted as leaders for teams of ten to twelve men, and a lieutenant in charge, selected by the chief of police and approved by neighborhood groups. Team leaders were selected from a slate of sergeants by vote of the officers. Team members made most decisions democratically.

Advantages and Disadvantages of Team Policing

Team policing in any form attempts to strengthen cooperation and coordination of effort between the police and the public to prevent crime and to maintain order. The decision to institute team policing depends on officer expectations, department expectations, community expectations, manpower, budget, and numerous other factors. Ironically, many citizens want their police officers to be friendly, warm, and caring, but they also expect them to keep the streets safe and "crack down" on lawbreakers. Fulfilling both expectations simultaneously is no easy task.

Unfortunately, no hard data supports or discredits team policing. Since departments vary so greatly in their approach, the data that does exist is inconclusive. However, certain advantages and disadvantages or potential hazards have been tentatively identified.

According to Ralph Olmos (1977, p. 33): "While team policing appears to present a viable alternative to the traditional staff and line organization, it does entail certain risks. One drawback is that it is substantially more costly than line patrol due to increased manpower requirements. Additionally, it places great demands upon supervisory personnel and requires intensive retraining of patrol officers and specialists as well. There is also the included risk of added opportunity for graft." However, he goes on to state that evidence strongly indicates that properly implemented neighborhood team policing greatly improves police-community relations, employee job satisfaction, and causes reduction in crime as well.

Possible advantages of team policing:
- *Improves police-community relations.*
- *Improves job satisfaction.*
- *Reduces crime.*

Possible disadvantages of team policing:
- *More costly.*
- *Places great demands upon supervisory personnel.*
- *Requires intensive retraining of officers.*
- *Added opportunity for graft and corruption.*

The advantages and disadvantages must be carefully weighed in arriving at a decision regarding implementation of team policing. If the decision is made to implement, precautions must be taken to assure success.

Factors Contributing to Success or Failure of Team Policing

A study supported by the Police Foundation (Sherman, et al. 1973, pp. 107–108), examined seven programs in depth. The study identified three principle reasons team policing either failed or reached only partial success:

1. Middle managers in the departments, seeing team policing as a threat to their power, subverted, and, in some case, actively sabotaged the plans.

2. Teams were dispatched by radio too often to permit their stay in a particular neighborhood.

3. The patrols never received a sufficiently clear definition of how their behavior and role should differ from that of a regular patrol; at the same time, they were considered an elite group by their peers, who often resented not having been chosen for the project.

According to the authors of this study, "whether a specific community should adopt team policing . . . depends first on that community's goals, and second on that community's judgment of team policing's effectiveness within its own situation. Most of all, it depends on both the commitment and the available resources to manage a complex process of institutional and community change."

Volunteer Patrols

The use of volunteer patrols is described in depth by Lawrence W. Sherman in *Crime and Public Policy* (1983). According to Sherman (p. 147):

> Few developments are more indicative of public concern about crime, and declining faith in the ability of public institutions to cope with it, than the burgeoning growth in private policing. According to a recent Gallup poll, 17% of Americans surveyed nationally reported some sort of organized volunteer crime prevention effort in their neighborhoods. The upsurge in private policing bears witness to the persistence in modern life of an age-old, commonsensical conviction about public safety, namely, that "watching" is one key to preventing crime. At the same time, the recent emphasis on voluntary watching efforts suggests a diminishing public confidence in the ability of publicly empowered police to perform this traditional task.

Sherman goes on to note that questions related to "watching" raise very difficult public policy questions such as how much watching do we need? Who should pay for it? How effective is watching by volunteers? Watching as a crime prevention strategy consumes a vast amount of public financing and, in addition, is a controversial strategy because it is reminiscent of dictatorships and oppression.

Nonetheless, the growth of private watching has been resisted by many police executives who view such watchers as lacking competence. In some instances, incidents of volunteer "vigilantism" have reinforced such concerns. It may also be that police executives view such private watchers as a threat to their own job security. In fact, according to Sherman (p. 147): "Public police unions have been called auxiliary police 'scab labor.'. . .The more the police can discourage private watching, the larger the market share they may be able to retain."

One key question yet to be answered is just how effective private watching is. Sherman states that: "There is virtually no systematic evidence about the crime prevention effectiveness of private watching in uniform, by commercial uniformed private security guards, uniformed volunteer auxiliary police, or uniformed volunteer patrols such as the Guardian Angels."

The limited research on the effectiveness of watching by citizen volunteers from within their own homes is somewhat more encouraging. Numerous volunteer programs have claimed dramatic reduction in crime. However, the tendency is for interest in such voluntary watching to gradually decrease, and as citizen interest decreases, crime increases.

One-Officer Versus Two-Officer Patrol Units

Another controversial organizational decision is whether patrol units should be one-officer or two-officer units. According to Charles D. Hale (1981, p. 97): "It is a very emotional subject since officer safety is an overriding concern. At the same time, the police administrator must be concerned with the economic aspect of the issue as a result of scarce resources and limited appropriations. . . .It is safe to say that there are a number of valid arguments for both one-officer and two-officer patrol units." Hale points out that sometimes it is necessary to use two-officer units to ensure the officers' safety and to satisfactorily resolve the problem involved. However, usually officer productivity and operational efficiency can be increased by using one-officer patrol units.

> *Circumstances should determine whether a one-officer or a two-officer unit is more appropriate.*

Hale contends that the single-officer unit is the "rule rather than the exception," and that most incidents can be handled by one officer. If two officers are required, two one-officer units can be dispatched to the scene. He feels two-officer units should be restricted to those areas, shifts, and types of activities most likely to threaten the officers' safety, for example during the evening or in high-crime areas.

Several advantages are obtained by the one-officer unit including cost effectiveness in that the same number of officers can patrol twice the area, with twice the mobility, and twice the powers of observation. In addition, officers working alone are generally more cautious in dangerous situations, recognizing that they have no back-up. And officers working alone are generally more attentive to patrol duties, since they do not have a conversational partner. However, the expense of two cars compared to one is often a mitigating factor.

In addition, a study conducted by Chapman (1974, p. 145) found that two-officer patrol units did not enhance officer safety; nearly two-thirds of the officers suffering on-duty assaults were assigned to two-officer units; less than 15 percent of the reported assaults occurred with only one officer present.

Another study conducted in the San Diego Police Department (Boydstun, 1977), comparing one-officer and two-officer patrol units on several criteria, found that:

- While overall performance for calls for service and officer-initiated activities were judged to be equal, more traffic citations were issued by two-officer units.
- Overall efficiency of one-officer units was judged to be higher than that of two-officer units, even though the former required most back-up support.
- While citizens resisted arrest less frequently when dealing with one-officer units, overall safety was judged to be equal between both types of units. Assaults on officers, officer injuries, and vehicle accidents occurred at the same rate for both single-officer and two-officer units.

Such findings strongly support use of the single-officer patrol unit in most circumstances.

Summary

Of all the operations performed by the police, patrol is the most vital. Patrol is responsible for providing continuous police service and high visibility of law enforcement, thereby deterring crime. Patrol officers are responsible for protecting and serving the community, enforcing the laws, directing traffic, and investigating crimes. Specialized patrol officers concentrate on specific problem such as hostage and sniper situations, VIP protection, riot and crowd control, rescue operations, and control of suppressible crimes.

Patrol can be accomplished via foot, automobile, motorcycle, bicycle, horseback, aircraft, and boat. The most commonly used and most effective patrol is usually a combination of automobile and foot patrol.

Several factors are important in the structure and management of patrol. Equal shift and beat size staffing creates major problems and lessens the effectiveness of preventive patrol during certain times and in certain areas. Preventive patrol has used crime statistics to plan shift and beat staffing, providing more coverage during times of peak criminal activity and in high-crime areas.

Another approach to enhancing the effectiveness of patrol is use of team policing, especially popular during the 1970s. The central features of team policing include combining patrol, investigative, and community relation services; decentralization; cooperative decision-making; and permanent assignment to a team and a geographic area. The four basic categories of team policing are basic patrol teams, patrol-investigative teams, patrol-community service teams, and full-service teams. Possible advantages of team policing are that it improves police-community relations, improves job satisfaction, and reduces crime. Possible disadvantages of team policing are that it is more costly, places great demands upon supervisory personnel, requires intensive retraining of officers, and provides added opportunity for graft and corruption.

Use of volunteers to patrol is another approach to preventing crime, but its effectiveness has not been clearly established.

An additional factor of importance in the management and structure of patrol is whether one-officer or two-officer patrol units are more appropriate. This is determined by individual circumstances.

Application

As a supervisor, you are responsible for new police officers who are assigned to your shift. The chief of police has instructed you to emphasize to these new officers the value of patrol. "Patrol," he states, "is charged with executing the total police function." Explain to these new police officers how patrol achieves the following:

- Crime prevention
- Protection of life and property
- Preservation of the peace

- Enforcement of all laws and ordinances
- Detection and arrest of law violators

Answer

Answers will vary from police department to police department.

Discussion Questions

1. What type of patrol is used in our community?
2. What would happen if our police officers went on strike?
3. Why doesn't patrol have as much prestige as investigation?
4. Why is patrol considered a hazardous assignment by some and a "drag" by others?
5. What is the reason for team policing? How did it come about?
6. What are the advantages of team policing to the officer? What are the disadvantages?
7. Who decides whether team policing will be implemented?
8. Is team policing used anywhere in our state? If so, has it been successful? If not, what were the problems?
9. Are volunteers used in our police department? If so, how?
10. Which do you support, a one-officer or two-officer patrol unit? Why?

References

Adams, T.F. *Police field operations*. Englewood Cliffs, N.J.: Prentic-Hall, 1985.

Boydstun, E. et al. *Patrol staffing in San Diego: One- or two-officer units*. Washington, D.C.: Police Foundation, 1977.

Brown, M.K. *Working the street*. New York: Russell Sage Foundation, 1981.

Chapman, S.G. et al. *Perspectives on police assaults in the south central United States*. Vol. 1. Norman, Okla.: The University of Oklahoma Press, 1974.

Eastman, G., and Eastman, E., eds. *Municipal police administration*. Washington, D.C.: International City Management Association, 1982.

Gay, W.G.; Day, H.T.; and Woodward, J.P. *Neighborhood team policing*. National Evaluation Program, Phase 1 Summary Report, National Institute of Law Enforcement and Criminal Justice, Law Enforcement Assistance Administration, U.S. Department of Justice, February 1977.

Gay, W.G., and Schack, S. *Prescriptive package: Improving patrol productivity*. Vol. 1, *Routine patrol*. Washington, D.C.: Office of Technology Transfer,

National Institute of Law Enforcement and Criminal Justice, Law Enforcement Assistance Administration, U.S. Department of Justice (Grant Number 76–NI–00–0055), July 1977.

Hale, C.D. *Police patrol operations and management.* New York: John Wiley and Sons, 1981.

Iannone, N.F. *Principles of police patrol.* New York: McGraw-Hill, 1975.

Klockars, C.B., ed. *Thinking about police: Contemporary readings.* New York: McGraw-Hill, 1983.

More, H.W., Jr. *The American police: Text and readings.* Criminal Justice Series. St. Paul, Minn.: West Publishing Company, 1976.

National Advisory Commission on Criminal Justice Standards and Goals. Task Force on the Police. *The police.* Washington, D.C.: U.S. Government Printing Office, 1973.

The Newark foot patrol experiment. Washington, D.C.: Police Foundation, 1981.

Olmos, R.A. "Team policing." *Minnesota police journal* (October 1977): 32–33.

President's Commission on Law Enforcement and Administration of Justice. *The challenge of crime in a free society.* Washington, D.C.: U.S. Government Printing Office, 1967.

Schack, S., and Gay, W.G. *Prescriptive package: Improving patrol productivity.* Vol. II, *Specialized patrol.* Washington, D.C.: Office of Technology Transfer, National Institute of Law Enforcement and Criminal Justice, Law Enforcement Assistance Administration, U.S. Department of Justice (Grant Number 76–NI–00–0055), July 1977.

Sherman, L.W. "Volunteer patrols." In *Crime and public police,* edited by James Q. Wilson. San Francisco: Institute for Contemporary Studies, 1983.

Sherman, L.W.; Milton, C.H.; and Kelly, T.V. *Team policing: Seven case studies.* Mineola, N.Y.: Police Foundation, 1973.

Sutor, A.P. *Police operations: Tactical approaches to crimes in progress.* St. Paul, Minn.: West Publishing company, 1976.

Walker, S. *The police in America: An introduction.* New York: McGraw-Hill, 1983.

Williams, V.L.; Formby, W.A.; and Watkins, J.C. *Introduction to criminal justice.* Albany, N.Y.: Delmar Publishers, 1982.

Wilson, J.Q. *Thinking about crime.* rev. ed. New York: Basic Books, 1983.

Wilson, J.Q., and Boland, B. *The effect of police on crime.* Washington, D.C.: U.S. Government Printing Office, 1980.

Wilson, O.W., and McLaren, R.C. *Police administration.* 4th ed. New York: McGraw-Hill, 1977.

The traffic officer does not have a glamorous job, but it is a job that is critical to the safety of citizens in the community.

Traffic

Law Enforcement in a Mobile Society

Do You Know . . .

- What the responsibilities of the traffic officer are?
- What the primary goal of traffic law enforcement is?
- What five actions are included in effective traffic enforcement?
- What the Enforcement Index is and how it is used?
- What selective enforcement is and what purpose it serves?
- What specific tasks are performed by the police officer when responding to a traffic accident?
- What should be included in a traffic accident report?
- What the most basic causes of motor vehicle accidents are?
- How frequently alcohol is related to automobile accidents?
- What purposes are served by traffic reports? Who makes use of them?
- What Scandinavian-type drunken driving laws are and when they are effective?

Motor vehicle accidents are the leading cause of death for people between the ages of one and forty-five!

—Accident Facts

Introduction

Traffic is a complex responsibility, involving not only investigation, but also service and interrelation with other agencies such as traffic engineering.

The Responsibilities of the Traffic Officer

As noted by the National Advisory Commission on Criminal Justice Standards and Goals (*The Police,* 1973, p. 226):

> The role of the police in motor vehicle transportation systems has undergone significant changes through the years. The traditional police function has centered around traffic law enforcement, accident investigation, and traffic direction and control processes. In today's highly complex and mobile society, the police officer's responsibilities have been expanded beyond the restrictive area of traffic supervision and evolved into a more comprehensive service that includes motorist service, public information, motor theft prevention, and other activities vital to the safe and efficient movement of traffic.

A well-rounded traffic program involves many activities designed to maintain order and safety on streets and highways. Although the traffic responsibilities of a police officer may not have the glamour of a criminal investigation, they are critical not only to the safety of the citizens in a community but also to the police image. Traffic is the most frequent contact between police and law-abiding citizens.

Traffic officers are usually responsible for:
- *Enforcing traffic laws.*
- *Directing and controlling traffic.*
- *Providing directions and assistance to motorists.*
- *Investigating motor vehicle accidents.*
- *Providing emergency assistance at the scene of an accident.*
- *Gathering information related to traffic and writing reports.*

All uniformed officers should be responsible for enforcing traffic laws and regulations because of the close interrelationship between traffic activity and all other police activities. It is not uncommon, for example, for a routine stop for a traffic violation to result in the arrest of the driver for a serious nontraffic offense. Abandoned vehicles may have served as getaway cars in a robbery or have been stolen for joyriding by teenagers.

The primary objectives of most traffic programs are to obtain the smoothest possible movement of vehicles and pedestrians consistent with safety and to reduce losses from accidents.

Enforcing Traffic Laws.   Police officers seek to obtain the compliance of motorists and pedestrians with traffic laws and ordinances as well as driver license regulations and orders. They issue warnings or citations to violators. Traffic officers provide law enforcement action related to operating and parking vehicles, pedestrian actions, and vehicle equipment safety.

Directing and Controlling Traffic.   Police officers frequently are called upon to direct traffic flow, to control parking, to provide escorts, and to remove abandoned vehicles. They frequently are asked to assist in crowd control at major sporting events. They also are responsible for planning traffic routing, removal of traffic hazards, and emergency vehicle access for predictable emergencies.

Providing Directions and Assistance to Motorists.   Police officers provide information and assistance to motorists and pedestrians by patrolling, maintaining surveillance of traffic and the environment, conducting driver-vehicle road checks, and being available when needed.

Investigating Motor Vehicle Accidents.   Police officers gather and report the facts about accident occurence as a basis for preventing accidents and providing objective evidence for citizens involved in civil settlements of accident losses. Police officers investigate accidents, including gathering facts at the scene and reconstructing the accident. They may also prepare cases for court and appear as prosecution witnesses when there has been a violation such as drunk driving.

Providing Emergency Assistance at the Scene of an Accident.   At an accident scene the police officer may assist accident victims by administering first aid, transporting injured persons, protecting property in the victim's vehicle, and arranging for towing of disabled vehicles.

Gathering Information Related to Traffic and Writing Reports.   The police officer reports on accidents, violations, citations and arrests, disposition of court actions, drivers' cumulative records, roadway and environmental defects, and exceptional traffic congestion. The reports assist the traffic engineer and traffic safety education agencies by providing information useful in their accident prevention programs as well as in planning for traffic movement or vehicle parking. Furthermore, traffic-related records, including registration records, drivers' licenses, traffic citations, and collision reports, may play an important role not only in traffic management, but also in criminal investigations.

Sometimes police officers serve unofficially as the city's road inspectors as they discover problems in either road conditions or traffic flow. They may propose corrections to achieve safer, more effective motor vehicle and pedestrian travel and vehicle parking.

Traffic Law Enforcement

The National Advisory Commission on Criminal Justice Standards and Goals (*The Police*, 1973, p. 227) defines the traffic law enforcement function as "the total police effort directed toward obtaining compliance to traffic regulations after programs of traffic safety education, driver training, traffic engineering, and similar activities have failed to reach this objective. This function involves all levels of operation within a police organization."

The commission points out that violating traffic laws does not carry the social stigma attached to violation of other laws such as laws against murder and rape. Running a stop light or speeding is not considered a crime, and people "regularly and without any natural consciousness of wrongdoing violate laws designed to insure safe use of the streets and highways." Recall the distinction made in Chapter 2 between crimes which are *mala in se* (bad in themselves) and *mala prohibita* (bad because they are forbidden). Traffic laws are excellent examples of *mala prohibita* crimes. The commission also states that: "The ultimate aim of traffic law enforcement is to produce voluntary compliance with traffic regulations and to provide maximum mobility with minimum interruption."

> *The primary goal of traffic law enforcement is to produce voluntary compliance with traffic laws while keeping traffic moving safely and smoothly.*

A properly administered and executed police traffic law enforcement procedure is probably the most important component of the overall traffic program. If people obey the traffic laws, traffic is likely to flow more smoothly and safely, with fewer tie-ups and accidents. Effective traffic law enforcement usually consists of at least five major actions: on-the-spot instructions to drivers and pedestrians, verbal warnings, written warnings with proper follow-up, citations or summonses, and arrests.

Each of these actions has importance to traffic law enforcement. The circumstances of each individual incident will determine which action is most appropriate. It is up to the traffic officers to decide which action to take, but their decisions will be more impartial and consistent if they have guidelines on which to base them.

> *Traffic law enforcement may take the form of:*
> - *On-the-spot instructions to drivers and pedestrians.*
> - *Verbal warnings.*
> - *Written warnings with proper follow-up.*
> - *Citations or summonses.*
> - *Arrests.*

The question inevitably arises as to how much enforcement is needed to control traffic and reduce accidents. How many traffic citations will constitute the right amount to meet enforcement requirements and still retain public support for the police department? This is a local issue which must be determined for each jurisdiction. However, a nationally approved guide, called the *Enforcement Index,* has been developed to assist in this determination.

The Enforcement Index

The Enforcement Index is calculated by dividing the number of convictions with penalty for hazardous moving traffic violations during a given period by the number of fatal and personal injury accidents occurring during the same period.

For example, if during January a city had 25 fatal or personal injury accidents and the police departments had 300 convictions for hazardous moving traffic violations, you would divide 300 by 25 and arrive at an index figure of 12—below the recommended level. This city should have from 500 to 625 convictions for hazardous moving violations rather than 300.

$$\text{Enforcement Index} = \frac{\text{number of convictions for hazardous moving traffic violations}}{\text{number of fatal and personal injury accidents}}$$

Recommended Index Figure: 20 to 25

While not conclusive, this index provides one means of measuring the quantity of enforcement. The International Association of Chiefs of Police and the National Safety Council, through statistical research, have suggested that an index of 20 to 25 is both obtainable and effective for most cities. In other words, for each fatal and personal injury accident there should be twenty to twenty-four convictions for hazardous moving traffic violations.

To attain an effective traffic program, the index value may have to be raised in some cities and lowered in others. The index is simply a management tool designed to measure general compliance of the motorists in the community.

In addition, any strategy that makes use of indexes or quotas must also take into account the "human equation," that is, the possibility that officers may fill the quota as quickly as possible and then do no more until the next period of evaluation. Effective supervision can eliminate this problem of substituting quantity for quality.

Selective Traffic Law Enforcement

Because numerous traffic violations occur every hour of every day, police departments cannot enforce all traffic regulations at all times. It is impossible to achieve 100 percent and almost always unwise to try to do so. Selective enforcement emphasizes giving citations for hazardous violations that cause accidents, for example, excessive speed around a schoolyard or playground where young children are present.

Selective enforcement is not only logical, it is practical, since most police departments' limited manpower requires them to spend time on violations that contribute to accidents. Enforcement personnel, such as officers on motorcycles or assigned to a radar unit, are usually the officers assigned to selective traffic enforcement. The officers' activity is directed to certain high-accident areas, during certain days of the week and certain hours of the day or night.

> *Selective enforcement places officers in preselected locations where high rates of vehicle and pedestrian accidents and traffic law violations require patrol saturation.*

Studies in city after city have proven a definite relationship between accidents and enforcement. In analyzing accident reports, one finds at the top of the list year after year the same traffic violations contributing to accidents and the same group of drivers being involved. Accidents will be discussed in greater detail in a few pages.

Selective enforcement is based upon thorough investigation of accidents, summarization, and careful analysis of the records. Adequate records are essential to the overall effectiveness of the selective enforcement program.

Quantity and quality of traffic law enforcement go hand in hand in any community. Many police departments have found that without quality, selectivity, or

Directing traffic is a major responsibility of the police.

direction, their desired objectives in traffic supervision programs simply will not work. The public resents quantity goals that cause a police officer to issue many traffic citations and the court dockets to become overloaded with ''not guilty'' pleas. In departments where quality is emphasized, the public usually complies with safe driving techniques and acknowledges and supports safety programs.

Almost everyone has heard in exhaustive detail a friend's version of getting an ''unfair'' speeding ticket. The person will tell several people about it. In terms of quality and selective enforcement, this has the effect of informing the general public that the police are doing their job. It may also prevent others from speeding.

High-quality enforcement is not only supported by the public, it has an important effect on the would-be traffic violator. When the public is informed of the police department's enforcement program and it is understood and believed to be reasonable and fair, the public will usually accept and support it.

Traffic and Patrol

Detecting traffic violations is no different for a patrol officer than detecting vandalism, auto theft, burglary, or trespassing. The officers know general police methods, they appreciate the functions they have to perform while on patrol, and they know traffic laws and the department's traffic policies. A thorough knowledge of the department's overall traffic program, its objectives and operations, will make the patrol officers assigned to traffic responsibilities more effective.

While on patrol, police officers may also inspect buildings, detect hazardous road situations, and note locations where traffic control signs may be needed. In addition, they are readily available to respond to accident calls.

Traffic Accidents*

According to *Accident Facts* (1983, p. 71): ''The first motor-vehicle death in the United States is reported to have occurred in New York City on September 14, 1899. Since the first motor-vehicle death in the United States, about 2,450,000 persons have died in motor-vehicle accidents through the end of 1982. . . . Based on historical figures, the 1,000,000th motor-vehicle death occurred some time during 1952. The 2,000,000th motor-vehicle death occurred in early 1974. If the current annual trend in motor-vehicle deaths continues, the 3,000,000th motor-vehicle death will probably occur in the mid 1990s.''

As noted at the beginning of this chapter, motor vehicle accidents are a leading cause of death for people ages one to forty-four. During the hour in which you are reading this chapter there have probably been two hundred traffic accidents

---

*Unless otherwise noted, all statistics, tables, and figures in this section are from *Accident Facts*, 1984 edition, a National Safety Council Publication.

Table 9–1.   *Motor Vehicle Deaths per Registered Vehicles.*

Between 1912 and 1983, motor vehicle deaths per 10,000 registered vehicles were reduced 91 per cent, from 33 to about 3. (Mileage data were not available in 1912.) In 1912, there were 3,100 fatalities when the number of registered vehicles totalled only 950,000. In 1983, there were 44,600 fatalities, but registrations soared to almost 168 million.

The 1983 mileage death rate is the lowest on record. Motor vehicle deaths decreased in 1982 and 1983, while vehicle miles increased in 1982 and 1983.

Deaths 44,600
Disabling injuries 1,600,000
Cost . . . . $43.3 billion
Motor vehicle mileage . . . . 1,651 billion
Death rate per 100,000,000 vehicle miles 2.70
Registered vehicles in the U.S. 167,700,000
Licensed drivers in the U.S. 152,000,000

Accident totals

	Number of Accidents	Drivers (Vehicles) Involved
Fatal	39,500	58,000
Disabling injury	1,100,000	1,800,000
Property damage and nondisabling injury	17,200,000	28,800,000
Total (rounded)	18,300,000	30,700,000

resulting in injury and five resulting in death. Billions of dollars are lost annually through motor vehicle accidents, and the cost in human suffering and loss is impossible to estimate.

Of the vehicles involved in fatal accidents in 1983, approximately 60 percent were passenger cars, 25 percent were trucks, and only 8 percent were motorcycles.

Motor vehicle deaths and the mileage death rates are sharply higher at night. In fact, in both urban and rural areas, the mileage death rates at night are about three times the day rates. The highest death rate occurred at 1:00 A.M., followed by midnight. Motor vehicle death totals also differ sharply for different days of the week and different months of the year. The day with the highest death rate is Saturday, followed by Sunday, Friday, Thursday, Wednesday, Tuesday, and Monday. Motor vehicle deaths are at their lowest levels in January and February and increase to their highest level in July and August, remaining at this general level the rest of the year.

Almost two out of three deaths in 1983 occurred in places classified as rural. In urban areas, more than one third of the victims were pedestrians; in rural areas, the victims were mostly occupants of motor vehicles. Almost three fifths of all deaths occurred in night accidents, with the proportion somewhat higher in urban areas.

Causes of Motor Vehicle Accidents

"In most accidents, factors are present relating to the driver, the vehicle, and the road, and it is the interaction of these factors which often sets up the series of events which culminates in the mishap." (*Accident Facts*, 1984, p. 48)

Table 9–2.	How People Died in Motor Vehicle Accidents, 1983.			
Type of accident	**Urban**	**Rural**	**Total**	**Death Rate***
All motor vehicle accidents	16,600	28,000	44,600	19.1
Collision between motor vehicles	5,700	13,600	19,300	8.2
Noncollision accidents	2,800	9,700	12,500	5.3
Pedestrian accidents	5,800	2,200	8,000	3.4
Collision with fixed object	1,500	1,500	3,000	1.3
Collision with pedalcycle	500	600	1,100	0.5
Collision with railroad train	300	300	600	0.3
Other collisions (animals, street cars)			100	less than 0.5

*Deaths per 100,000 population

The basic causes of motor vehicle accidents are: human faults, errors, violations, and attitudes; road defects; and car defects.

Vehicle defects account for approximately 5 percent of all accidents. The most common defect is worn or smooth tires. The second most common defect is faulty brakes.

The National Safety Council notes that improper driving is the most common factor by far in fatal and nonfatal accidents. The most common type of improper driving is speeding. The second most common type of improper driving is failing to yield the right of way. Drinking is indicated to be a factor in at least half of the fatal motor vehicle accidents. Problems mount when the drinking age varies from state to state. In such instances, some teenagers may drive to neighboring states with lower drinking ages than their own and come home, usually during the late night hours, driving under the influence of alcohol. Overall, however, a study by the Insurance Institute of Highway Safety *Status Report,* September 23, 1981, reports that, on the average, a state that raises its drinking age can expect about a 28 percent reduction in nighttime fatal crash involvement among drivers to which the law change applies.

Alcohol is a factor in at least 50 percent of fatal motor vehicle accidents.

Another driver-related factor is failure to wear seat belts. The National Highway Traffic Safety Administration studies show that safety belts are 50 percent to 65 percent effective in preventing fatalities and injuries, meaning 12,000 to 16,000 lives could be saved annually if all passenger car occupants used safety belts at all times. Although only New York currently has adult safety belt laws, as of July 31, 1983, forty-one state legislatures and the District of Columbia have mandated child safety-seat usage. Such usage is estimated to be 80 percent to 90 percent effective in preventing fatalities and injuries.

Good driving attitudes are more important than driving skills or knowledge, a fact frequently overlooked in driver education programs. Drivers who jump lanes, try to beat out others as they merge from cloverleafs, race, follow too closely, or become angry and aggressive account for many of our serious motor vehicle

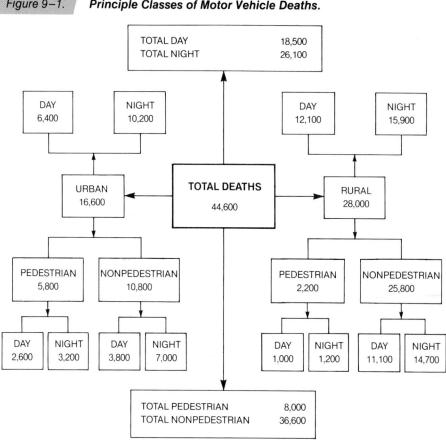

Figure 9–1. **Principle Classes of Motor Vehicle Deaths.**

accidents. Negative driver behavior, such as illegal and unsafe speed, failure to yield the right of way, crossing over the center line, driving in the wrong lane, and driving while under the influence of alcohol, increases the number of accidents and causes traffic statistics to rise year after year.

And year after year the same group of drivers cause the most frequent accidents: male drivers ages twenty to twenty-nine. Although males are involved in more accidents than females, males also do more driving.

Thus far, causes of motor vehicle accidents resulting in personal injury or fatality have been discussed. Also of concern, however, are those accidents which involve property damage. The U.S. Department of Transportation undertook an extensive study of traffic accidents from 1972 through 1977 (*Tri-Level Study of the Causes of Traffic Accidents, Executive Summary,* May 1979). This $1.5 million project found that human factors were cited by the in-depth team as probable causes in 92.6 percent of the accidents investigated. The major human direct causes were improper lookout, excessive speed, inattention, improper evasive action, and internal distraction.

Table 9–3.	Accident Rates per Age and per Sex.

Age of Driver

There were about 152,000 drivers in the nation in 1983. The approximate number in each group is shown in the table below, along with each group's accident experience for the year. The figures in the last two columns at the right indicate the frequency of accident involvement; the higher the number, the higher the involvement in each age group.

Age of Drivers—Total Number and Number in Accidents, 1983

Age Group	All Drivers Number	All Drivers %	Fatal Number	Fatal %	Drivers in Accidents All Number	Drivers in Accidents All %	Per No. of Drivers Fatal[a]	Per No. of Drivers All[b]
Total	152,000,000	100.0%	58,000	100.0%	30,700,000	100.0%	38	20
Under 20	14,400,000	9.5	7,800	13.5	4,400,000	14.3	54	31
20-24	18,000,000	11.8	12,900	22.2	6,700,000	21.8	72	37
25-29	18,600,000	12.3	8,400	14.5	4,500,000	14.7	45	24
30-34	17,800,000	11.7	7,200	12.4	3,600,000	11.7	40	20
35-39	14,900,000	9.8	4,300	7.4	2,400,000	7.8	29	16
40-44	12,900,000	8.5	4,200	7.3	2,200,000	7.2	33	17
45-49	11,200,000	7.4	2,900	5.0	1,600,000	5.2	26	14
50-54	11,300,000	7.4	2,200	3.8	1,200,000	3.9	19	11
55-59	10,400,000	6.8	2,100	3.6	1,300,000	4.2	20	13
60-64	8,000,000	5.3	1,800	3.1	9,000,000	3.0	23	11
65-69	6,700,000	4.4	1,400	2.4	1,000,000	3.2	21	15
70-74	4,700,000	3.1	1,100	1.9	300,000	1.0	23	6
75 and over	3,100,000	2.0	1,700	2.9	600,000	2.0	55	19

Source: Drivers in accidents based on reports from 14 state traffic authorities. Number of drivers by age are National Safety Council estimates based on reports from state traffic authorities and research groups.

[a]Drivers in Fatal Accidents per 100,000 drivers in each age group.
[b]Drivers in All Accidents per 100 drivers in each age group.

Sex of Driver

Of the estimated 152,000 drivers in 1983, about 79,000,000 are males and 73,000,000 are females. Males are involved in more accidents than are females, as shown in the table below. The difference is due at least partly to differences in the amount of driving done by the members of each sex, and to differences in time, place, and circumstances of the driving.

Sex of Driver Involved in Accidents, 1969–1983

Year	Drivers in Fatal Accidents Male No.	Drivers in Fatal Accidents Male Rate[a]	Drivers in Fatal Accidents Female No.	Drivers in Fatal Accidents Female Rate[a]	Drivers in All Accidents Male No.	Drivers in All Accidents Male Rate[b]	Drivers in All Accidents Female No.	Drivers in All Accidents Female Rate[b]
1969	59,800	80	10,900	33	20,000,000	268	6,800,000	209
1970	57,800	75	10,700	31	20,500,000	265	7,200,000	209
1971	56,700	70	11,100	30	20,900,000	256	7,400,000	199
1972	59,000	68	11,900	28	21,000,000	243	8,100,000	201
1973	55,900	63	11,400	27	20,200,000	227	7,900,000	189
1974	48,000	55	9,800	24	17,800,000	205	7,300,000	177
1975	46,500	52	9,600	22	19,100,000	212	8,400,000	195
1976	48,100	51	10,900	24	19,600,000	206	8,800,000	191
1977	51,900	53	11,800	25	20,600,000	209	9,300,000	193
1978	51,500	50	15,500	30	21,700,000	209	9,800,000	192
1979	52,700	52	12,500	25	20,600,000	202	9,100,000	180
1980	56,100	56	12,200	24	20,100,000	200	9,700,000	192
1981	53,200	52	11,800	23	20,500,000	200	9,500,000	183
1982	48,800	47	11,500	22	20,600,000	198	9,900,000	186
1983	46,300	43	11,700	21	20,400,000	187	10,300,000	184

Source: Accidents and Drivers—National Safety Council estimates based on reports from state motor-vehicle departments and Federal Highway Administration Mileage—National Safety Council estimates based on survey data from National Family Opinions, Inc.
[a]Number of drivers in fatal accidents per 1,000,000,000 miles driven.
[b]Number of drivers in all accidents per 10,000,000 miles driven.

Environmental factors were cited as probable causes in 33.8 percent of the accidents, with view obstructions and slick roads leading the list of causes.

Vehicular factors were identified as probable causes in 12.6 percent of the accidents with brake failure, inadequate tread depth, side-to-side brake imbalance, underinflation, and vehicle-related vision obstructions being among the leading causes.

Vision and personality (especially poor personal and social adjustment) were also found to be related to accident involvement. Interestingly, knowledge of the driving task was not shown to be related.

A summary of the findings of this study is contained in Figure 9–2.

Law Enforcement and the Drunk Driver

Ross (1981, p. 632) contends that:

> The problem of crashes caused by drivers influenced by alcohol has pre-occupied public opinion and the law ever since the invention of the automobile in the late nineteenth century. . . . Vehicle codes initially forbade driving "while under the influence of intoxicating liquor," driving in an "intoxicated condition," or simply "drunk driving." These "classical" laws were directed against obviously blameworthy conduct and prescribed traditional criminal penalties and procedures.

Such laws were extremely difficult for police officers to enforce unless an accident resulted, and even then obtaining a conviction was difficult.

In the 1930s a new approach to drinking and driving emerged as a result of widespread dissatisfaction with existing laws. This approach, called the **Scandinavian-type law,** reflected the Scandinavian tendency at that time toward temperance. The Scandinavian-type laws prohibited driving with blood alcohol concentrations exceeding specific levels relative to body weight. According to Ross (1975, p. 633):

> Enforcement required chemical tests: a preliminary breath test that could be demanded by a policeman who suspected a driver of committing the offense, and an evidentiary quantitative blood test for those failing the first test. Penalties for violating the laws included license suspension and confinement in prison; the latter was made mandatory for blood alcohol concentration exceeding .05 percent in Norway and .15 percent in Sweden. In short, the Scandinavian laws introduced objective, nonclinical definitions of the drinking-and-driving offense, employing novel scientific criminal procedures and severe penalties. After World War II these laws were widely adopted throughout the developed, automobile-dependent world.

The effectiveness of Scandinavian-type laws in deterring drunk driving has been studied in England, France, and Canada, with the conclusion usually being that such laws are initially effective in deterring drunk driving, but that the effect eventually dissipates. The United States Department of Transportation conducted several campaigns called Alcohol Safety Action Projects which all found that

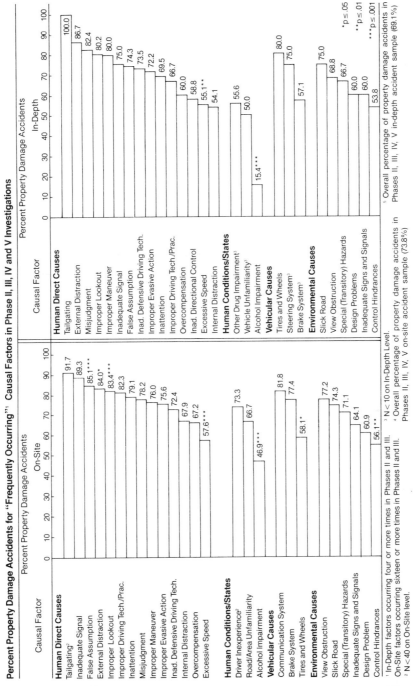

Figure 9–2. *Percent Property Damage Accidents for "Frequently Occurring"*
Causal Factors in Phase II, III, IV and V Investigations.

Source: Tri-level Study of the Causes of Traffic Accidents, Executive Summary. U.S. Department of Transportation. May 1979.

declines in the frequency of drinking and driving were limited to the period covered by the campaigns.

In addition to enforcement campaigns, punishment campaigns have also been attempted, greatly increasing the severity of the penalty for driving under the influence of alcohol. Such campaigns have been largely unsuccessful. However, an increased public perception of the likelihood of punishment *does* appear to deter drinking and driving. Unfortunately, it has been estimated that the chances of a drunk driver being apprehended in the United States under a Scandinavian-type law are between 1 in 200 and 1 and 2,000 (Beitel, Sharp, and Glauz, 1975).

> *Scandinavian-type drinking and driving laws prohibit driving with blood alcohol concentrations exceeding specific levels and establish severe penalties for doing so. Such laws are effective if they are widely publicized and if the likelihood of punishment for noncompliance is high.*

Ross (1981, p. 635) concludes that:

The deterrent effect on drinking and driving that is apparently achieved by the adoption and enforcement of Scandinavian-type laws affords some encouragement to those who advocate deterrence as a means of dealing with this problem. However, the universal experience of a declining and vanishing deterrent effect suggests the need for great caution. In the future, policies using deterrence to control drinking and driving might aim at increasing the genuine likelihood of punishment to such an extent that important and permanent changes in public perception are achieved.

Responsibilities of the Officer Called to the Scene of an Accident

Frequently police officers are the first persons arriving on the scene of a traffic accident who are equipped, trained, and legally responsible for providing services, perhaps lifesaving services if they act quickly and effectively. In addition to rendering first aid to accident victims, police officers have several other duties to perform such as protecting victims from further harm, reducing to the extent possible the involvement of other cars as they arrive on the scene, summoning emergency service for victims and, if needed, towing services for the vehicles involved, protecting the victims' personal property, locating witnesses, securing evidence, and in other ways investigating the accident, and keeping traffic moving as though no accident had occurred.

> *The officer called to the scene of an auto accident should:*
> - *Proceed to the scene rapidly but safely.*
> - *Park safely and conveniently.*
> - *Administer emergency first aid if required.*
> - *Interview all persons involved as well as all witnesses.*
> - *Provide needed assistance to victims.*
> - *Accurately observe and record all facts related to the accident.*
> - *Clear the scene as soon as possible to restore traffic flow.*

It is important that all facts related to the accident are accurately observed and recorded. The time of day should be noted, as a setting or rising sun might have temporarily blinded one of the drivers. All marks on the road should be measured and recorded. The condition of the road should be noted: wet or dry; muddy, dusty, or sandy; dirt, asphalt, or cement. The width of the street and any obstruction to vision should also be noted.

> *Traffic accident reports should include all relevant details, including information about the drivers, their actions, their vehicles, the type of accident, the manner of collision, the type of street, weather conditions, road conditions, light conditions, and existing traffic control.*

Importance of Accident Reports

Accident reports provide important information for enforcement of laws, traffic engineering, and educational activities. Report writing is critical to a good traffic program. The best possible investigation serves little purpose if it is not accurately and completely reported.

Accident reports by police officers provide a guide for many other department activities as well as a guide for other agencies involved in traffic and safety.

> *Accident reports provide important information for:*
> - *Enforcement of laws.*
> - *Traffic engineering.*
> - *Educational activities.*

In addition, a host of other agencies involved in traffic make use of the information contained in traffic accident reports. Public information agencies such as newspapers, television, and radio disseminate information about traffic, traffic conditions, road conditions, and traffic accidents. Attorneys and the courts use traffic accident reports in determining the facts in traffic accidents which result in lawsuits. The state motor vehicle department or state department of public safety, which has the power to suspend or revoke drivers' licenses, also uses information contained in these reports. Legislative bodies in each state may rely on traffic accident reports when they plan for providing funds, equipment and personnel to effectively enforce traffic safety programs and when they determine what laws must be passed to control traffic.

Traffic accident reports may be used by engineers, both federal and state, who research ways to improve highway systems and by the National Safety Council and state safety councils which compile statistics related to accidents: Who is having them? Where? When? How? The reports may be used by insurance companies which base their automobile insurance rates upon the accident record of the community.

> *Traffic accident reports serve as the basis of traffic law enforcement policy, accident prevention programs, traffic education, legislative reform of traffic laws, traffic engineering decisions, and motor vehicle administration decisions.*

In addition to effective reporting, police departments need an efficient traffic accident records system to evaluate the effectiveness of highway safety measures. Compilation of traffic statistics and records on major moving violations and frequent locations and causes of traffic accidents is also critical if a department is going to institute selective patrol and enforcement techniques.

In some smaller police departments, a police officer might be assigned to work with public works departments or city engineers in traffic engineering. Although not involved in the technical design, construction, or maintenance decisions and problems, the officer contributes information beneficial to mechanical operations such as routine maintenance by calling in hazardous road situations encountered while on routine patrol; inspecting facilities and making recommendations for the erection of traffic control signs, needed painting of street lines, crosswalks, and curbs; and performing similar activities of a nontechnical nature.

Although large cities usually have special traffic engineers, police officers still contribute expertise to those who make the final decisions. Police officers' most important contribution to traffic engineering is the research they compile related to accidents and congested streets. They further report hazardous conditions which need attention. In return, traffic engineers often furnish the police with advice and information to further their traffic supervision policies. This relationship can result in increased accident prevention and attainment of traffic control goals and objectives.

Public Education Programs

The police also seek to educate the public in traffic safety. Although it is not one of their primary functions, they often participate in local school programs, private safety organizations, local service clubs, and state safety councils, as we will discuss in more depth in Chapter 11. The police are in a position to know why these programs are important and how they can contribute to the good of the community.

Traffic safety education also has high public relations value. An officer on the school grounds supervising the school crossing guards (patrols) or teaching youngsters bicycle safety contributes much to the police officers' image. It reflects their concern for the safety and welfare of the community's youth. However, since safety education is a community responsibility, community agencies should assume their share of work and not rely solely upon the police department for the entire effort.

Summary

Traffic is a major problem in most cities. Many man-hours are spent in traffic-related police work. Traffic officers have numerous responsibilities to fulfill and specific tasks to perform including enforcing traffic laws, directing and controlling traffic, providing directions and assistance to motorists, investigating motor vehicle accidents, providing emergency assistance at the scene of an accident, gathering information related to traffic, and writing reports.

The laws the officers enforce, the services they provide, and the information they compile are important to the total police department traffic program as well as to the image conveyed to the public.

The primary goal of traffic law enforcement is to produce voluntary compliance with traffic regulations and to provide maximum mobility with minimum interruption. Traffic law enforcement may take the form of on-the-spot instructions to drivers and pedestrians, verbal warnings, written warnings with follow-up, citations or summonses, or arrests. The type of enforcement may be guided by the Enforcement Index and by use of selective enforcement principles.

In spite of a highly effective traffic program, motor vehicle accidents will occur. The three basic causes of such accidents are (1) human faults, errors, violations, and attitudes, (2) road defects, and (3) car defects.

Drinking alcohol is indicated to be a factor in at least half of the fatal motor vehicle accidents. One attempt at reducing the problem of the drunk driver has been establishing Scandinavian-type drinking and driving laws that prohibit driving with blood alcohol concentrations exceeding specific levels and establishing severe penalties for doing so. Such laws are effective if they are widely publicized and if the likelihood of punishment for noncompliance is high.

An officer called to the scene of an accident must proceed to the scene rapidly but safely, park safely and conveniently, administer emergency first aid if required, interview all persons involved as well as all witnesses, provide needed assistance to victims, accurately observe and record all facts related to the accident, and then clear the scene as soon as possible to restore normal traffic flow. The accident report should include all relevant details including information about the drivers, their actions, their vehicles, the type of accident, the manner of collision, the type of street, weather conditions, road conditions, light conditions, and existing traffic conditions.

It is important that accident reports be accurate and complete as they provide information for enforcement of laws, traffic engineering, and educational activities. They may also serve as the basis of traffic law enforcement policy, accident prevention programs, traffic education, legislative reform of traffic laws, traffic engineering decisions, and motor vehicle administration decisions.

The responsibilities of the traffic officer in a mobile society are numerous, demanding, and vital.

Application

A police department has just released its statistics on accidents for the year. There appears to be a 20 percent increase in personal injury accidents and a 10 percent increase in property damage accidents. The chief of police has instructed all officers to report any ideas they have to reduce the accident rate. One officer, after two months on patrol, has made the following observations and recommendations for reducing the traffic accident rate.

He has noted that accidents involving drinking drivers are happening late Friday night, early Saturday morning, late Saturday night, and early Sunday morning. He suggests that liquor lounges set up breathalyzer tests so patrons may test themselves before leaving to see if they are under the allowable blood alcohol level to legally drive a motor vehicle.

He has observed many drivers disobeying the 55 mph speed limit and recommends establishing some tolerances and guidelines and then issuing citations. To do this, he recommends that a speed survey be made on the major highways.

He also has observed that a large number of accidents are caused by drivers of all ages when they make improper or erratic lane changes. He suggests selective enforcement to cope with this problem.

Although not directly involved in any bicycle accident investigations, he has observed an increasing proportion of young adults and adults riding bicycles improperly and causing hazardous conditions for both pedestrians and automobile drivers. He recommends that the police department establish a bicycle safety program, that bicycle patrols be used to educate bicyclists, and that citations be issued to bicyclists who disobey the law.

1. Which of the above recommendations has the most potential for reducing the accident rate? Why?
2. What type of traffic enforcement is more productive, general or selective? Why?

Answers

1. The recommendation that tolerances and guidelines be used in issuing citations to enforce the 55 mph speed limit is the best recommendation for reducing the accident rate because excessive speed is the major cause of personal injury accidents.
2. Selective enforcement is most productive because it most directly affects the citizens who are given citations. Good selective enforcement is usually supported by the public (except those who get the citations).

Discussion Questions

1. How should an officer approach an accident scene and what should be done first?
2. Have you ever been involved in a traffic accident? How would you evaluate the performance of the officer(s) responding to the call?
3. What can the public do to make the traffic officer's job easier?
4. Does our police department use an Enforcement Index?
5. How does an officer determine who gets a verbal or written warning and who gets a ticket (citation)?
6. Is the idea of selective enforcement a good one? When and where should it be used?

References

Accident facts. 1983 and 1984 eds. Chicago: National Safety Council, 1983, 1984.

Adams, T.F. *Police field operations.* Englewood Cliffs, N.J.: Prentice-Hall, 1985.

Andenaes, Johannes. "The effects of Scandinavia's drinking-and-driving laws: Facts and hypotheses." *Scandinavian studies in criminology* 6 (1978).

Beitel, G.A.; Sharp, M.C.; and Glauz, W.D. "Probability of arrest while driving under the influence of alcohol." *Journal of studies of alcohol* 36 (1975): 109–16.

Eastman, G.D., ed. *Municipal police administration.* Washington, D.C.: International City Management Associations, 1971.

Insurance Institute for Highway Safety. *Status report.* Vol. 16, No. 14 (September 23, 1981).

International Association of Chiefs of Police. *The patrol operation.* Washington, D.C.: 1970.

McCready, K. *Theory and methods of police patrol.* Albany, N.Y.: Delmar Publishers, 1974.

National Advisory Commission on Criminal Justice Standards and Goals. *The police.* Washington, D.C.: U.S. Government Printing Office, 1973.

President's Committee for Traffic Safety. *The action program.* Washington, D.C.: U.S. Government Printing Office, 1964.

Ross, H.L. *Deterrence of the drinking driver: An international survey.* National Highway Traffic Safety Administration Technical Report, DOT HS-805 820. Washington, D.C.: U.S. Government Printing Office, 1981.

Ross, H.L. "Drinking and driving." *Encyclopedia of crime and justice.* New York: The Free Press, 1983.

Treat, J.R. et al. *Tri-level study of the causes of traffic accidents: Executive summary, final report.* National Highway Safety Administration Technical Report, DOT HS-805 099. Washington, D.C.: U.S. Government Printing Office, 1979.

Waters, J.R., and McGarth, S.A. *Introduction of law enforcement.* Columbus, Ohio: Charles E. Merrill Publishing Company, 1974.

Identifying photographs for presentation in court. An investigator's goal is to answer the questions: who? what? where? when? how? and why?

CHAPTER 10

Investigation

An Objective Quest for Truth

Do You Know . . .

- What the primary characterisitc of an effective investigator is?
- What the primary responsibilities of the investigator are?
- Why both sketches and photographs of a crime scene are usually needed?
- What questions the investigator must seek answers to?
- How the investigators must deal with evidence?
- What types of evidence are likely to be found at the scene of a crime?
- What the Miranda warning is?
- Why two people may see the same event yet report it differently?
- How witnesses may be aided in making an identification?
- What the three basic types of identification are? When each is appropriate?
- What rights the suspect has during the identification process?
- What instructions and precautions should be taken to assure the legality and admissibility of an identification in court?
- What relevance the *Wade* decision has to identification of a suspect?
- What should be done if a suspect refuses to participate in a lineup?

When you have eliminated the impossible, whatever remains, however improbable, must be the truth.
                                        —Sir Arthur Conan Doyle

Every fact that is learned becomes a key to other facts.
                                        —E.L. Youmans

Introduction

On January 10, while on patrol, Officers James and Fisher received a call to a silent burglary alarm at the Kwik Stop Super Market. As they approached the building, they saw two burglary suspects entering the back door. James and Fisher called for a back-up unit and then entered the supermarket. They found the two suspects hiding in the office and took them into custody. They then searched their vehicle where they found a large screwdriver which they submitted to the crime laboratory. At headquarters the suspects' clothing was taken as evidence and submitted to the crime laboratory for comparison purposes as they were suspects in other burglaries in the area.

The suspects were charged with burglary of the Kwik Shop Super Market. Several days later, the crime laboratory report of analysis and comparison of evidence seized from the suspects showed the following:

■ The casting of the identifications found on the doors at the Lakeside Super Market indicated that they were made by the same size screwdriver found in the vehicle on January 10.

■ The metal and paint samples matched those on the sledge hammer and the crowbar found at the scene of the Lakeside Super Market.

■ The insulation on the pry bar also matched the insulation of the steel cabinets at the Lakeside Super Market.

■ Samplings of metal, paint, glass, and insulation found in the two suspects' pants cuffs were identical in composition to those submitted to the crime laboratory.

Faced with the evidence, the suspects confessed to the burglary of the Lakeside Super Market and to several others in the area.

This case was successfully solved because the officers understood their functions at the crime scene and performed them skillfully. They knew that both in science and law they must observe strict rules of procedure for physical evidence integrity. They took adequate samplings of the evidence representative of the crime as well as samples for control purposes.

A large part of an investigator's role centers around obtaining information and **evidence.** The successful investigator obtains proof that a crime has been committed as well as proof that a particular person (the suspect) committed the crime. In the preceding case, the suspects confessed because of the sufficient evidence against them. However, the investigators did *not* determine the suspects to be guilty; they remained objective in their investigation.

> *A primary charcteristic of an effective investigator is objectivity.*

The investigator seeks to find the truth, not simply to prove suspects guilty As stated in Article 10 of the *Canons of Police Ethics:*

> The law enforcement officer shall be concerned equally in the prosecution of the wrong-doer and the defense of the innocent. He shall ascertain what constitutes evidence and shall present such evidence impartially and without malice. In so doing, he will ignore social, political, and all other distinctions among the persons involved, strengthening the tradition of the reliability and integrity of an officer's word.
>
> The law enforcement officer shall take special pains to increase his perception and skill of observation, mindful that in many situations his is the sole impartial testimony to the facts of a case.

Walton (1979, p. vii) points out that investigation is a line function and traditionally a task for patrol, but at times the type and frequency of crimes may require a specialized organization component, commonly called the investigative or detective division. He goes on to note, however, that: ''In a sense, the investigation of a case is the responsibility of the entire department, and not just a single investigator. Effective investigation often depends on many people and on the organizational structure that governs what they do.''

In this chapter, when the term ''investigator'' is used, it may be interpreted as referring to either a patrol officer performing investigative duties or to a specialist assigned only investigative duties.

The Rand Corporation undertook an extensive study of the role of detectives in solving crimes. Waldron (1984, pp. 194–195) says of this study that: ''The single most important determinant of whether or not a case will be solved is the information the victim supplies to the immediately responding patrol officer. If information that uniquely identifies the perpetrator is not presented when the crime is reported, the perpetrator usually will not be subsequently identified. Of those cases that are ultimately cleared but in which the perpetrator is not identified at the time of the initial police incident report, almost all are cleared as a result of routine police procedures. Differences in investigative training, staffing, workload, and procedures have no appreciable effect on crime, arrest, or clearance rates.''

This same interpretation of the Rand Study of Detectives is made by Klockars (1983, p. 131) who says the study shows that "All but about 5 percent of serious crimes that are solved by detectives are solved because a patrol officer has caught the perpetrator at the scene, because a witness tells the detective whodunit, or by thoroughly routine clerical procedures."

Police Response Time

The Rand Study would seem to suggest that rapid response to a report of crime is extremely important. However, a study conducted by the Forum (Spelman and Brown, 1981, pp. iii-xx) in Florida, Illinois, New York, and San Diego found that, in the cities studied, arrests could be attributed to fast police response in only 2.9 percent of reported serious crimes. Spelman and Brown indicate this is so because about 75 percent of all serious crimes are discovery crimes, crimes discovered after they have been committed. It is in only the remaining 25 percent, the involvement crimes, that rapid response is critical. Klockars (1983, p. 130) rather humorously suggests that: "Police currently make on-scene arrests in about 3 percent of the serious crimes reported to them. If they traveled faster than a speeding bullet to all reports of serious crimes, this on-scene arrest rate would rise no higher than 5 percent."

Responsibilities of the Investigator

To accomplish a successful investigation, police officers must (1) take their time, (2) use an organized approach which is efficient and methodical, because this may be their only chance to observe the scene, (3) recognize the issues and find facts to settle these issues, and (4) determine if a crime has been committed, and, if so, by whom and how.

Each of these investigator's responsibilities will be discussed in a few pages, but first a distinction should be made between the preliminary investigation and the follow-up investigation.

The *preliminary investigation* consists of actions performed immediately upon receiving a call to respond to the scene of a crime. This preliminary investigation is usually conducted by patrol officers. When patrol officers receive a call to proceed to a crime scene, they must proceed to the scene promptly and safely; render assistance to anyone who is injured; arrest the suspect if he is still at the scene; secure the crime scene and protect any evidence; interview complainants, witnesses, and suspects; collect evidence; and make careful notes of all facts related to the case.

The International Association of Chiefs of Police (1970, p. 13) has developed an acronym around the meaning of PRELIMINARY as follows:

P   Proceed to the scene promptly and safely.

R   Render assistance to the injured.

E   Effect the arrest of the criminal.

L   Locate and identify witnesses.

I   Interview the complainant and the witness.

M   Maintain the crime scene and protect the evidence.

I   Interrogate the suspect.

N   Note conditions, events, and remarks.

A   Arrange for collection of evidence (or collect it).

R   Report the incident fully and accurately.

Y   Yield the responsibility to the follow-up investigator.

The *follow-up investigation* may be conducted by the investigative services division, sometimes also known as the detective bureau. Therefore, the success of many criminal investigations relies on the cooperative, coordinated efforts of both the patrol and the investigative functions. In most smaller departments, however, the same officer handles both the preliminary and the follow-up investigations.

> *The primary responsibilities of the investigator are to:*
> - *Assure that the crime scene is secure.*
> - *Record all facts related to the case for further reference.*
> - *Photograph and sketch the crime scene.*
> - *Obtain and identify evidence.*
> - *Interview witnesses and interrogate suspects.*
> - *Assist in the identification of suspects.*

Securing the Crime Scene

Any area that contains evidence of criminal activity is considered a crime scene, and it must be secured to eliminate contamination of the scene and outlying areas. The investigator in charge should limit the number of officers assigned to the crime scene, using only those required to do the work. Although some crimes do not have identifiable scenes, (for example, embezzlement) or known scenes, the majority of crimes do; for example, bank robberies, burglaries, homicides, assaults, and bombings.

The suspect may have left evidence such as fingerprints, blood, footprints, a weapon, a tool, strands of hair, fibers from clothing, or some personal item, such as a billfold which may contain identification. No evidence should be touched or moved until photgraphing, measuring, and sketching of the scene are complete.

Walton (1979, p.vii) emphasizes that: "In both large and small communities, the first officer on the scene must know enough to protect the crime scene from further change. Although this officer may have little or nothing further to do with the case, this single responsibility is a large one and may have far reaching effects on a final solution of the crime. It is essential that physical evidence be properly protected if it is to have legal and scientific validity.''

Recording Relevant Information

Investigators do not rely upon memory; they record all necessary information by photographing, sketching, and taking notes to be used later in a written report of the investigation. Photographs, sketches, and notes are a permanent aid to memory and may be helpful not only in investigating the case and writing the report, but also in testifying in court.

The notes should be written in a notebook, not on scraps of paper that might be lost or misplaced. They should be written in ink because they are a permanent record and also because pencil may smear and become unreadable over time. The notes should be written legibly and be identified by the investigator's name, the date, and the case number. They should contain all relevant facts, especially the names and addresses of victims, witnesses, and possible suspects.

Although each specific type of crime requires somewhat different information, most investigations require answers to such questions as the following:*

When: did the incident happen? was it discovered? was it reported? did the police arrive on the scene? were suspects arrested? will the case be heard in court?

Where: did the incident happen? was evidence found? stored? do victims, witnesses, and suspects live? do suspects frequent most often? were suspects arrested?

Who: are suspects? accomplices?
        Complete descriptions would include the following information: sex, race, coloring, age, height, weight, hair (color, style, condition), eyes (color, size, glasses), nose (size, shape), ears (close to head or protruding), distinctive features (birthmarks, scars, beard), clothing, voice (high or low, accent), other distinctive characterstics such as walk.

Who: were the victims? associates? was talked to? were witnesses? saw or heard something of importance? discovered the crime? reported the incident? made the complaint? investigated the incident? worked on the case? marked and received the evidence? was notified? had a motive?

What: type of crime was committed? was the amount of damage or value of the property involved? happened (narrative of the actions of suspects, victims, and witnesses; combines information included under

---

*Hess and Wrobleski. *For the Record: Report Writing in Law Enforcement, Innovative Publications, Co., 1985, Revised.*

''how'')? evidence was found? preventive measures had been taken (safes, locks, alarms, etc.)? knowledge, skill, or strength was needed to commit the crime? was said? did the police officers do? further information is needed? further action is needed?

How: was the crime discovered? does this crime relate to other crimes? did the crime occur? was evidence found? was information obtained?

Why: was the crime committed (was there intent? consent? motive?) was certain property stolen? was a particular time selected?

> *The investigator must obtain answers to the questions: who? what? where? when? how? and why?*

Answers to these questions are obtained by observation and by talking to witnesses, complainants, and suspects. They are recorded in notes, photographs, sketches, or are in the form of actual physical evidence.

Photographing, Measuring, and Sketching the Crime Scene

In addition to taking notes, the investigator or crime-scene technician should photograph, measure, and sketch the crime scene. Photographic coverage of the scene must be done carefully. In addition to being technically competent and well equipped, the photographer must photograph objects which are related to the case and in such a way that no distortion occurs. The photographs should show the scene as it was found. They are usually taken in a series and ''tell a story.'' In addition, they usually are taken from general to specific, that is, first an entire room, then one area of the room, then specific items within that area.

The evidence and location should be in their proper relationship and in a sequence that will orient a person unfamiliar with the scene. If a photograph is intended to show dimensional relationships, a suitable scale should be included. Photographs of evidence such as shoe prints, tire tracks, and tool marks must be done using close-up photography.

In addition to photographs, a sketch should be made of the crime scene before any evidence is moved. Sketches supplement photographs. They can be selective, and they can also show entire areas, for example, an entire layout of a home or business. The sketch need not be an artistic masterpiece as long as it includes all relevant details and is accurate and clear. The sketch should show the locations of all important evidence found during the crime-scene search. See Figure 10–1 for some common types of sketches.

> *Both photographs and sketches are usually needed. The photographs include all detail and can show items close up. Sketches can be selective and can show much larger areas.*

Figure 10–1.   *Types of Crime-Scene Sketches.*

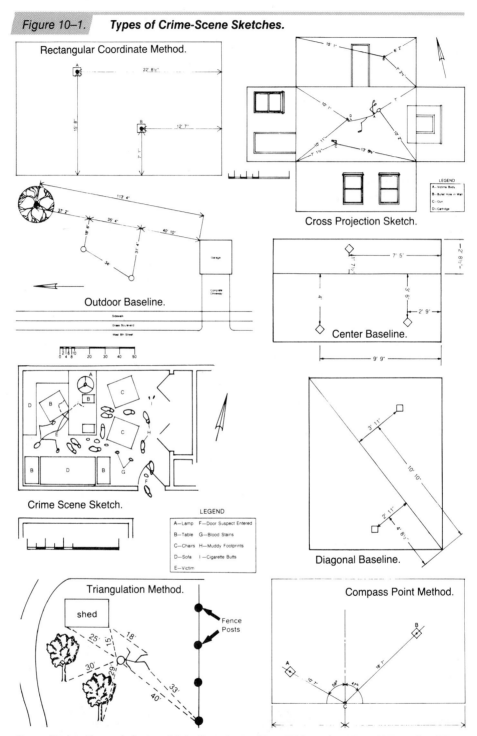

Source: Reprinted by permission from *Criminal Investigation.* Wayne W. Bennett and Karen M. Hess. Copyright ©
1981 by West Publishing Company. All rights reserved.

Obtaining and Identifying Physical Evidence

A primary responsibility of the investigator is to obtain and identify physical evidence. All important decisions will revolve around the available evidence and how it was obtained.

Effective investigators understand their functions as finders of facts and suppliers of proof which have both a scientific and a legal basis for presentation in court. Items of evidence found at the crime scene are usually routinely taken and held pending apprehension of a suspect. Frequently evidence is sent to a crime laboratory for analysis and comparison.

In the preface to the *Laboratory Manual for Introductory Forensic Science,* Walton (1979, p. vii) notes that: "Today, the successful prosecution of criminal cases rests less upon confessions or eyewitness accounts and more upon the use of physical evidence. Even so, it is commonly conceded that a pitifully small fraction — two percent or less — of available evidence is properly recognized, collected, evaluated, and brought into court to tell its story to judge and jury." Walton contends that this is a "sorry situation" and that it must be corrected at the source, that is the crime scene, "with properly trained and qualified personnel who know what to look for and how to collect, handle, and transport evidence so as to keep intact its legal and scientific integrity. At the crime laboratory the *criminalist* must evaluate what facts may be obtained from the evidence and be prepared to support his or her findings in a court of law."

> The investigator must recognize, collect, mark, preserve, and transport physical evidence in sufficient quantity for analysis and without contamination.

Walton sees physical evidence as being the primary responsibility of two law enforcement agents: the crime-scene investigator (who may be a patrol officer, remember) and the criminalist. And he sees the single most important question in **criminalistics** as being related to identity: "Did this blood stain come from this victim? Did this automobile hit this pedestrian? Was this slug fired from this handgun?" Such questions are often answered by comparing one item to another, for example, fingerprints left at a crime scene with those taken from a suspect.

The kind of evidence to be anticipated is often directly related to the type of crime committed.

Crimes against the person include homicide, forcible rape, robbery, assault, kidnapping, and sex crimes. These crime scenes frequently contain evidence such as blood, hair, fibers, fingerprints, footprints, and weapons.

Crimes against property include burglary, larceny, arson, and auto theft. These crime scenes are commonly characterized by forcible entry with tools leaving marks on doors, windows, safes, money chests, cash registers, and desk drawers.

> Among the more common types of evidence found at the crime scene are: fingerprints, blood, hair, fibers, documents, footprints or tire prints, tool fragments, tool marks, broken glass, paint, insulation from safes, firearms, and explosives.

Specific Evidence and Scientific Aids

Fingerprints are often found at crime scenes. Fingerprint identification is currently the most positive form of identification because the ridge arrangement on every finger of every person is different and unchanging, although as a person grows, the patterns enlarge slightly. According to Allison (1973, p. 123): ''A temporary scar will alter the print during the time of healing, but when the healing process is completed, the pattern on the print will return to its former structure. Permanent scars may change the appearance of the print, but this is not to say that it cannot be identified.'' Experts in fingerprints look for nine basic patterns which can occur in any combination (see Figure 10–2).

Figure 10–2.   **Fingerprint Chart.**

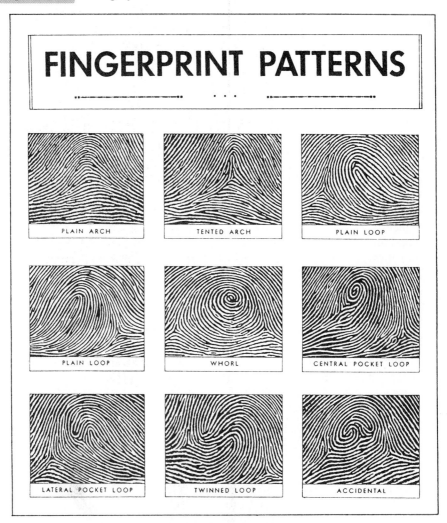

Source: Courtesy of Faurot, Inc. 26 Nepperhan Avenue, Elmsford, N.Y. 10523.

Latent fingerprints are made by sweat or grease which oozes out of the pores from little wells situated under the ridges at the ends of the fingers. When a person grasps an item with reasonable pressure, this grease takes the pattern of the person's fingerprints. This usually happens if the item grasped has a highly polished surface such as glass, polished metalware, highly glazed fabrics, or paper. It usually will not occur if the item grasped is soft, spongy, or has a rough surface.

Fingerprints may be found in an infinite number of places and under varied circumstances. Most crime scenes contain fingerprints of the suspect. Usually articles such as weapons, tools, documents, glass, metal, or any other objects which could have been touched or handled by the perpetrators may have latent fingerprints on them.

Finding fingerprints is only half the job; they must be matched with the actual (inked) fingerprints of a suspect to be valuable as evidence.

Also, DeAngelis (1980, p. 41) notes that friction ridges occur not only on the tips of the fingers, but also on the palms of the hands and the soles of the feet.

Blood can be classified as having come from humans or animals. Human bloodstains can be classified into one of the four international blood groups: A, B, AB, or O. Bloodstains may be valuable as evidence in assaults, homicides,

Figure 10–3. *Positive Identification of a Fingertip.*

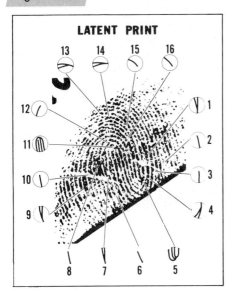 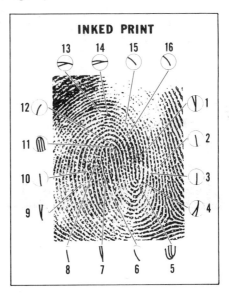

Three men checked into a motel at 11:00 p.m. Shortly after midnight when a new desk clerk came on duty, the men went to the office and committed an armed robbery. Police investigating the scene went to the room occupied by the three men and found the latent fingerprint on an ash tray. This print was later matched up to one of the suspects whose fingerprints were on file with the police department.

burglaries, hit-and-run, and rape. Although blood cannot be identified as having come from a particular individual, race, or sex, it can be helpful in eliminating suspects.

Hair can also be classified as having come from humans or animals. It is not possible except in very unusual cases to determine definitely that a questioned hair sample came from a particular person. It can be determined, however, that the hair of unknown sources matches a known hair sample from a certain individual in all microscopic characteristics and, accordingly, could have originated from the same source. It can be established that the hair was pulled out forcibly if the root end is present. In addition, the region of the body from which the hair was removed can be determined with considerable accuracy from the length, size, color, stiffness, and general appearance. Hair from the scalp, beard, eyebrows, eyelid, nose, ear, trunk, and limbs all have different characteristics. Hair from each racial group can be identified by its shape. The sex and age of a person cannot be determined from a hair examination with any degree of certainty except in the case of infant hair.

The possibility of hair evidence in any crime should never be overlooked. Hair is often valuable as a means of personal identification or as an investigative aid in cases such as hit-and-run, unusual death, and rape. Hair may be found from both the victim and the suspect on clothing, weapons, undergarments, blankets, sheets, seat covers, and the undercarriage of vehicles.

Fibers are excellent aids to investigators. It is possible to identify fibers as to type, such as wool, cotton, rayon, nylon, and so on. Sometimes it is possible to determine the type of garment from which the fibers came. In assault and homicide cases some contact usually occurs between the victim and the suspect causing clothing fibers to be interchanged. Fingernail scrapings and weapons may also contain fiber evidence. In burglaries, clothing fibers are frequently found where the burglar crawled through a window or opening. In hit-and-run cases, clothing fibers are often found adhering to the fenders, grill, door handle, or parts of the undercarriage of the automobile.

Document examination consists of a side-by-side comparison of handwriting, typewriting, or other written or printed matter. Age, sex, and race cannot be determined with certainty. However, in cases such as check forgery and alteration of wills, stocks, and bonds, conclusions based on examinations conducted by competent experts are positive and reliable. Such handwriting testimony has been accepted in our courts for many years. Typewriter samples may also identify the manufacturer, make, model, and age of a typewriter.

A *shoe or tire impression* can be a "material witness" in locating a criminal and placing him at the scene of a crime. Such evidence is sometimes more reliable than an eyewitness. Impressions from shoes or tires are often found where the perpetrator of the crime hastily entered or left the scene of the crime and overlooked the impressions. After photgraphing, measuring, and sketching, investigators carefully preserve such evidence by making a plaster cast of it. It often serves as a vital link to a criminal.

Tool fragments may be found at the crime scene. These pieces may later be matched to a broken tool in the possession of a suspect.

Pry tool used to open the rear door of a hardware store. Items 2 and 4 were found at the scene of the burglary. Item 3 was found in the suspect's car. This evidence led to the suspect's conviction for burglary.

Tool marks may be left where windows have been forced with screwdrivers, or pry bars, locks snipped with bolt cutters, or safes attacked with hammers, chisels, and/or punches. All these tools leave marks which, under favorable conditions, can be identified as definitely as fingerprints. Tool marks are most commonly found in the crime of burglary and malicious destruction of property. They may be found on window sills, frames, doors, door frames, cash register drawers, file cabinets, or cash boxes.

Glass is also an aid to the laboratory crime investigator. Glass is an excellent source of positive identification because two pieces of glass rarely contain the same proportions of sand, metal, oxides, or carbonates. Police officers frequently encounter glass from windows, automobiles, bottles, and other objects as evidence in burglaries, murders, assaults, and a large variety of other crimes.

When a criminal breaks a window, minute pieces of glass are usually found in his clothing, for example in his pant cuffs, breast pockets, or, to a lesser extent, on the surface of his clothing. Since these fragments are so small they should be removed with a vacuum sweeper. Larger fragments should be carefully collected. The area adjacent to the actual break in a glass is critical in the examination. Fragments should not be overlooked.

Microscopic examination of glass fragments by an expert can determine:

◾ Whether a tiny glass fragment probably or definitely came from a particular broken glass object.

- If a large fragment came from a particular glass object which was broken.
- If a fragment came from a particular kind of glass object such as a window pane, a spectacle lens, a bottle, etc.
- The origin of a fracture, its direction, and the direction of the force producing it.
- The order of occurrence of multiple fractures.

An investigator can determine whether glass was broken from the inside of a building by noticing where the fragments are.

Paint frequently is transferred from one object to another during the commission of a crime. Paint is often smeared on tools during unlawful entry. It may be chipped off surfaces during burglaries. It may flake off automobiles during hasty getaways following impacts. Paint has often proved to be a strong link in the chain of circumstantial evidence. It may have sufficient individual and distinct characteristics for significant examination or comparison. It often associates an individual with the crime scene, or it may eliminate innocent suspects.

Insulation from safes may also prove valuable as evidence. Insulations can be identified microscopically by composition, color, mineral content, and physical charcteristics. Since few laymen normally come into contact with this type of material, particles of safe or fireproof insulation material on the clothing or shoes of a suspect are a strong indication of guilt.

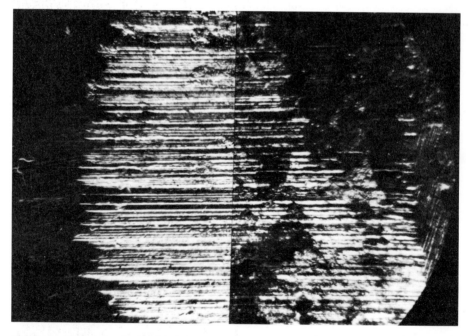

Striation pattern of a sledge hammer used to open a safe. The white marks are safe insulation. The left half of the photograph is evidence obtained at the scene of the crime; the right half shows the actual hammer seized from the suspect. The marks were matched up under a comparison microscope and magnified.

Firearms left at a crime scene may be traced to their owner through the serial number, the manufacturer's identification, or the dealer who sold the gun. The firearm might also contain the suspect's fingerprints or other marks which could lead to his identification.

The make of the weapon is usually determined by the riflings in the barrel, which are spiral grooves cut into the barrel of a gun in its manufacture. The riflings vary considerably from manufacturer to manufacturer.

In addition, the entry of a bullet can be determined by the hole it makes; the bullet produces a cone-shaped hole, entering from the small point of the hole and emerging through the large end.

Explosives may be of value as evidence in burglary; malicious destruction of property such as school buildings, churches, or public buildings; murder; or murder attempted by an explosive placed in an automobile or a home. The area around an explosion may contain such items as blasting caps, cap fragments, detonating wire, safety fuse, dynamite paper, cotton, soap, masking tape, prima-cord, or steel fragments. In some cases it is possible to find samples of unexploded materials.

Interviewing Witnesses and Interrogating Suspects

The investigator must gain information by talking with victims, witnesses, friends, co-workers, neighbors, or immediate members of the family, as well as by talking with suspects in the case.

Witnesses

A **witness** is a person other than a suspect who has helpful information about a specific incident or a suspect. A witness may be a **complainant,** an accuser, a victim, an observer of the incident, a confidential or reliable **informant,** an expert, or a scientific examiner of physical evidence.

Most evidence at a trial is presented through witnesses. A person who is a qualified witness, who can perceive what was seen firsthand and can relate this experience, is an invaluable aid in the prosecution of a defendant.

Witnesses are valuable because they may have seen:

- The suspect actually committing the crime.
- A tool, gun, or instrument used in the commission of the crime in the suspect's possession subsequent or prior to the crime's commission.
- Property that was stolen in the suspect's possession subsequent to the crime's commission.
- The suspect making preparations to commit the crime, or heard him threatening to commit the crime, or knew that he had a motive for committing it.

■ The suspect going to or leaving the scene of the crime about the time the crime was committed.

In cases such as robbery, assault, or rape, the eyewitness testimony of the victim or a witness may be all that is necessary for a conviction. It is always preferable, however, to have physical evidence to corroborate the eyewitness testimony.

Suspects

Before interrogating any suspect, the police officer should give the Miranda warning, as established in *Miranda v. Arizona* when the United States Supreme Court asserted that suspects must be informed of their rights to remain silent, to have counsel present, to a state-appointed counsel if they cannot afford one, and to be warned that anything they say might be used against them in a court of law. Many investigators carry a card which contains the Miranda warning to be read before interrogating a suspect.

On the evening of March 3, 1963, an eighteen-year-old girl was abducted and raped in Phoenix, Arizona. Ten days after the incident, Ernesto Miranda was arrested by Phoenix police, taken to police headquarters, and put in a lineup. He was identified by the victim and shortly thereafter signed a confession admitting the offenses. Despite objections to the statement by the defense attorney, the trial court admitted the confession. Miranda was convicted and sentenced to from twenty to thirty years on each count.

Figure 10–4.   *Miranda Warning Card.*

MIRANDA WARNING
1. YOU HAVE THE RIGHT TO REMAIN SILENT.
2. IF YOU GIVE UP THE RIGHT TO REMAIN SILENT, ANYTHING YOU SAY CAN AND WILL BE USED AGAINST YOU IN A COURT OF LAW.
3. YOU HAVE THE RIGHT TO SPEAK WITH AN ATTORNEY AND TO HAVE THE ATTORNEY PRESENT DURING QUESTIONING.
4. IF YOU SO DESIRE AND CANNOT AFFORD ONE, AN ATTORNEY WILL BE APPOINTED FOR YOU WITHOUT CHARGE BEFORE QUESTIONING.

WAIVER
1. DO YOU UNDERSTAND EACH OF THESE RIGHTS I HAVE READ TO YOU?
2. HAVING THESE RIGHTS IN MIND, DO YOU WISH TO GIVE UP YOUR RIGHTS AS I HAVE EXPLAINED TO YOU AND TALK TO ME NOW?

Miranda appealed on the grounds that he had not been advised of his constitutional rights under the Fifth Amendment. The Arizona Supreme Court ruled in 1965 that because Miranda had been previously arrested in California and Tennessee, he knowingly waived his rights under the Fifth and Sixth Amendments when he gave his confession to the Phoenix police. Justice McFarland of the Arizona Supreme Court ruled that because of Miranda's previous arrests, he was familiar with legal proceedings and individual rights and made an intelligent waiver.

In 1966, upon appeal, the United States Supreme Court reversed the Supreme Court of Arizona in a 5–4 decision and set up precedent rules for police custodial interrogation. Chief Justice Warren stated: "The mere fact that he signed a statement which contained a typed-in clause stating that he had 'full knowledge of his "legal rights" ' does not approach the knowing the intelligent waiver required to relinquish constitutional rights."

The United States Supreme Court mandated that any time a person was in police custody police officers must give the Miranda warning so that persons being questioned can intelligently waive their right not to incriminate themselves as provided by the Fifth Amendment. If the warnings are not given, the prosecution cannot prove an intelligent waiver against self-incrimination, and any statement or confession will not be admissible against the suspect.

The Miranda rule applies not only to in-custody situations, but to any instance in which a suspect is questioned and the questioning results in the individual being deprived of a substantial portion of his liberty. When police officers attempt to obtain a statement or confession from a suspect, they should usually first advise that person of the Miranda warning. This applies whether a suspect is questioned in the police station, in a police car, or on a street corner.

When the probable cause builds to such a point that no reasonable person could deny that an arrest would be imminent, the police officer should at that point, give the Miranda warning to the suspect if it has not already been given.

When the *Miranda* decision was handed down in 1966, there was much controversy. Many police officers and citizens complained that the court was "handcuffing the police," hampering them in their duties. However, the Federal Bureau of Investigation had been advising suspects of their constitutional rights for several years before the *Miranda* decision.

The Public Safety Exception is an important consideration when discussing the *Miranda* decision. On June 12, 1984, in a landmark 5–4 decision in *New York v. Quarles,* the United States Supreme Court announced that in certain cases police may question a suspect in custody without first advising him of his right not to incriminate himself. Writing for the Court's majority, Justice Rehnquist cited the Supreme Court decision in *Michigan v. Tucker* and made the distinction that the Miranda warnings are: "Not themselves rights protected by constitution, but are measures to insure that the right against compulsory self-incrimination is protected. . . . On some facts there is a 'public safety' exception to the requirement that Miranda warnings be given before a suspect's answers may be admitted into evidence, and that the availability of that exception does not depend upon the motivation of the individual officers." Although the court set forth the "public safety exception,'' no attempt was made to determine in what situations this exception might apply.

Interviewing and Interrogating Techniques

Witnesses who are pressured to give information may become antagonistic and refuse to cooperate. The following simple procedures may help make an **interview** with a witness or an **interrogation** of a suspect more productive:*

- Prepare for each interview in advance if time permits. Know what questions you need to have answered.

Table 10–1. **Interviewing Subjects.**

Types of Individuals	Police Interviewing Behavior
Hostile Witness	Relieve anxiety and stress. Indicate what can and cannot be said. State the purpose of the interview. Exert control (nonthreatening). Develop trust and cooperativeness. Indicate potential outcomes of noninvolvement or silent behavior.
Nonhostile Witness	Listen closely to disclosures. Double-check all observations and perceptions. Avoid angering, confusing, frustrating, or silencing the interviewee. Record all descriptions. Seek specific details.
Victims	Check their mental and physical health. Conduct the interview when the victim has stabilized from shock or trauma. Be patient. Forgotten or confused recall may be brought out with careful questions. Reassure, calm, relax, protect victim. Seek appropriate help where necessary. Keep initial questions to a minimum. Encourage cooperation.
Indirectly Involved or Uninvolved Subject	Be polite, patient, understanding. Thoroughly canvas frequented locales. Listen carefully. Be perceptive. Observe nonverbal signals. Avoid antagonizing the general public. Persuade reticent individuals to disclose.
Suspects	Safety first. Monitor the suspect's behavior and likelihood of possessing a weapon. Gather information; avoid initial interrogation. Inform a suspect of appropriate rights. Avoid forming prejudgments. Avoid giving a suspect cause for alarm. Avoid signaling nervousness or anxiety. Be honest. Do not make false promises. Do not bully or ridicule. Never underestimate a suspect's behavior or testimony.

*From Hess and Wrobleski. *For the Record: Report Writing In Law Enforcement.* Innovative Publications Co., 1985 Revised. Reprinted by permission.

■ Obtain your information as soon after the incident as possible. A delay may result in the subject's not remembering important details.

■ Be considerate of the subject's feelings. If someone has just been robbed, or seen an assault, or been attacked, the individual may be understandably upset and emotional. Allow time for the person to calm down before asking too many questions. Remember that when emotions increase, memory decreases.

■ Be friendly. Try to establish rapport with the subject before asking questions. Use the person's name; look at the person as you ask questions; respond to the answers.

Types of Individuals	Police Interviewing Behavior
Angry Witness	Assess the interviewee's mental stability. Check for weapon. Call for assistance where necessary. Gain control of the interview. Demonstrate neutrality. Never argue or disagree. Defuse anger with questions. Do not allow a shouting match to develop.
Excessively Verbal Subject	Redirect the interviewee's responses. Remind interviewee of the interview's purpose. Interrupt and ask closed-ended questions. Indicate specific topic areas for discussion.
Reticent Interviewee	Establish rapport. Compliment the interviewee. Reassure, reduce anxiety. Establish pleasant demeanor. Encourage talk. Avoid limiting response choices.
Uncooperative Interviewee	Exercise control. Remind interviewee of penalty for noncooperation. Reduce apprehension. Clarify unfounded fears. Provide incentives for disclosing.
Anxious and Stressed Interviewee	Direct stressed interviewee, when necessary, to professional counseling. Release tension in face and body. Establish a conversational climate. Clarify the nature of the interview. Allow opportunity for thinking. Do not rush responses. Double-check responses.
Interviewee of Different Race, Culture, Sex, or Ethnic Background	Be cognizant of how others communicate in interview situations. Understand the unique or specific verbal and nonverbal behaviors of people who differ from yourself. Repeat, reiterate, re-explain. Translate your meanings into the language of the interviewee.

Source: The Police Officers Guide to Better Communication by T. Richard Cheatham and Keith V. Erickson. Copyright © 1984 by Scott, Foresman and Company. Reprinted by permission.

- Use a private setting if possible. Eliminate as many distractions as you can, so that the subject can devote full attention to the questions you ask.
- Eliminate physical barriers. Talking across a desk or counter, or through a car window, does not encourage conversation.
- Sit rather than stand. This will make the subject more comfortable and probably more willing to engage in conversation.
- Encourage conversation. Keep the subject talking by:
  Keeping your own talking to a minimum.
  Using open-ended questions, such as "Tell me what you saw."
  Avoiding questions that call for only a "yes" or "no" answer.
  Allowing long pauses. Pauses in the conversation should not be uncomfortable. Remember that the subject needs time to think and organize his thoughts. Give the subject all the time needed.
- Ask simple questions. Do not use law enforcement terminology when you ask your questions. Keep your language simple and direct.
- Ask one question at a time. Allow the subject to answer one question completely before going to the next question.
- Listen to what is said, and how it is said.
- Watch for indications of tension, nervousness, surprise, embarrassment, anger, fear, or guilt.
- Establish the reliability of the subject by asking some questions to which you already know the answers.
- Be objective and controlled. Recognize that many persons are reluctant to give information to the police. Among the several reasons for this reluctance are fear or hatred of police, fear of reprisal, lack of memory, or unwillingness to become involved. Keep control of yourself and your situation. Do not antagonize the subject, use profanity or obscenity, lose your temper, or use physical force. Remain calm, objective, and professional.

The basic objective of an interview is to get the facts from a witness to eventually prove to the court that the suspect in question did, in fact, commit the crime. The interview itself must be carefully planned by the officer, with only relevant questions asked. In addition to seeking facts and evidence, the investigator is looking for honest witnesses, witnesses who demonstrate concern and cooperativeness.

Some witnesses are fearful, uninterested, or unwilling to get involved. With such witnesses, investigators must develop a rapport: be tolerant of the witness's position and thinking; eliminate misunderstanding, mistrust, and suspicion; and induce confidence. They must recognize that each individual will have a somewhat different view of the same incident.

Tables 10–1 and 10–2 summarize interviewing techniques and the types of questions that might be asked.

Table 10–2. **Interview Questions.**

Type of Question	Purpose	Characteristics	Example
Open-Ended	To elicit a variety of responses To provide interviewee response choices To break the ice To reduce apprehension	No set response expected of interviewee No specific topic Found in nondirected inverviews Interviewee-centered Nonthreatening	"How is the weather today?" "How have you been?" "Will it be a good football year?" "Life treating you well?" "What do you think of politics?" "How is the economy affecting you?"
Closed-Ended	To limit interviewee response choices To gather specific information from subject To facilitate use of time To control	One- to three-word replies Specific answers sought Authoritarian Frequently appears in a series of closed-ended questions Brusque	"What did he say?" "Did you do it?" "What is your name?" "Where do you work?" "What time is it?" "What did she wear?" "Was it red or green?"
Probing	To force replies Explanatioin Clarification Elaboration Confrontation Repetition	Seeks additional information Requires respondent to be responsive to interviewer Clears up misunderstandings Reveals sensitive/disguised information	"Explain what you mean?" "Tell me again what you said?" "How is that possible?" "You don't believe that do you?" "Why did you do that?" "More details, please."
Mirror	To keep interviewee talking Clarification Explanation	Repeats or paraphrases interviewee's remarks Places burden of talk on interviewee	"So, you took the bike, huh?" "And then you left town?" "You say you like it?" "Which job are you talking about?"
Leading	To lead interviewee to particular response To reveal discrepancies in testimony To facilitate admissions To force a stand	Suggests or implies an appropriate answer Places words in respondent's mouth Leaves little room for interviewee explanation of responses Placed in a series of questions	"You didn't like her, did you?" "Do you think that was right?" "Can you really say that was the correct thing to do?" "You won't act like that again, will you?"

Witness Perception

Experience has illustrated time and again that no two people will view the same situation in exactly the same way. How a witness describes what has happened is affected by many factors, some subjective (within the individual) and some objective (inherent in the situation). Because these factors vary from person to person, two people looking at the same thing may see something different. Take, for example, the following illustration:

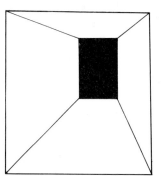

Whether the black surface projects toward the viewer or away depends completely upon the viewer's perception. In fact, the same person may see the black surface as projecting on first viewing, yet as receding on a second viewing.

Context, too, can alter how an object or event is perceived. For example, how do you ''interpret'' the following: 13

Now how do you interpret it? A 13 C   12 13 14

Another factor affecting perception is the amount of attention which is focused on an incident. When an incident barely catches the attention of a witness, perception is liable to be faulty. One reason for this is the human tendency to complete comprehension of a situation to make it meaningful. That is, people tend to organize their observations into a complete, meaningful picture. A witness may see a man with a mask on and his right hand extended as if holding a gun, and the witness may mentally *add* the gun in his perception of the incident, even though it did not actually exist. To overcome this tendency and obtain valid information, police officers must be aware of how and why people think and act in given situations. In other words, they should try to put themselves in the other person's position and use what is called ''street sense'' and empathy.

> *Perception of an incident is affected by the viewer's accuracy of observation, interpretation of what is seen, and attention paid to the incident.*

As noted in the *Encyclopedia of Crime and Justice* (Yarmey, pp. 749–755):

Eyewitness identification is frequently much less reliable than the courts would generally believe. . . . Researchers have extensively investigated the perception and memory of faces. What is the application of this work to the criminal identification of suspects through the viewing of mug shots, artists' drawings, commercial composites, and corporeal lineups? Laboratory studies have indicated that subjects asked to identify faces in a recognition memory test did so accurately in about 75 percent of their selections. . . . More significantly, research is increasingly being conducted outside the laboratory in more naturalistic settings, for example, testing persons who witnessed mock crime performed in supermarkets and banks. . . . As indicated in the *United States v. Nobles,* it is now for the courts to decide whether expert testimony on eyewitness identification should be taken to assist the jury in understanding the evidence, or whether such evidence should be excluded on the ground that it invades the province of the jury.

The Noncooperative Witness

A Witness Cooperation Study ("Witness Responses Misunderstood by Prosecutors," 1976) of almost 3,000 randomly selected witnesses indicated that many citizens are incorrectly perceived as noncooperative. According to this study (p. 6): "Prosecutors were apparently unable to cut through to the true intentions of 23% or more of those regarded as noncooperative and recorded the existence of witness problems when this was a premature judgment at best and an incorrect decision at worst." The primary cause for this problem was attributed to faulty communication between police, prosecutor, and witness. Problems arise when witnesses are not contacted, when their role is not explained, when they are not told when and where to appear, when their participation is discouraged, and when they are given vague instructions.

The study showed that the police did not obtain the correct addresses for 23 percent of the witnesses at the time of the crime, that the prosecutors often did not ensure that witnesses knew when and where to appear, that police sometimes asked for witness identification within hearing of suspects, and that witnessess often had no understanding of their role in the judicial process.

Obtaining Identification of a Suspect

If police officers do not actually witness the commission of the crime, eyewitness identification plays an important part in the arrest as well as in the trial proceedings.

Aids to Witness Identification of Suspects

Rather than simply asking a witness to describe a suspect, it is often helpful if the investigator asks specifically about such items as the following:

Sex

Race

Age

Height

Weight

Build—Stout, medium, slim, stooped, square-shouldered

Complexion—Flushed, sallow, pale, fair, dark

Hair—Color, thick or thin, bald or partly bald, straight, kinky, wavy, style

Eyes—Color, close or far apart, bulgy or small

Eyebrows—bushy or normal

Nose—small, large, broad, hooked, straight, short, long, broken

Beard—Color, straight, rounded, chin whiskers only, goatee, long sideburns

Mustache—Color, short, stubby, long, pointed ends, turned-up ends

Chin—Square, broad, long, narrow, double and sagging

Face—Long, round, square, fat, thin, distinctive pimples or acne

Neck—Long, short, thick, thin

Lips—Thin, thick

Mouth—Large, small, drooping or upturned

Teeth—Missing, broken, prominent, gold, conspicuous dental work

Ears—Small, large, close to head or extended outward, pierced

Forehead—High, low, sloping, bulging, straight

Distinctive marks—Scars, moles, amputations, tatto marks, peculiar walk or talk

Peculiarities—Twitching of features, rapid or slow gait, eyeglasses or sunglasses, stutter, foreign accent, gruff or feminine voice, nervous or calm

Clothing—Mask: if so, color; did it have eye slits, ear openings, mouth openings? Did it cover the whole face, have any designs on it? Did the suspect wear a hat or cap (baseball, golf, etc)? Any markings on the hat? Shirt and tie, sport shirt only, scarf, coat or jacket? Gloves, color of trousers, shoes, stockings, dressed well or shabbily, dressed neatly or carelessly? Any monogram on shirt or jacket?

Weapon used (if any)—Shotgun, rifle, automatic weapon, hand gun. Was weapon readily shown or concealed? Taken with or left at scene?

Jewelry—Any noticeable rings, bracelets, or necklaces, earrings, watch?

In addition to questions related to the suspect's appearance, the investigator might also assist the witness by using a description sheet such as the one in Figure 10–6.

Other information related to the suspect must also be obtained by the investigator. It is important to know how the suspect left the scene—running, walking, in a vehicle—and in what direction.

If the suspect escaped in a vehicle, the investigator should obtain information about the license number, make of the vehicle, number of passengers, direction of travel, the color and size of the car, as well as any other identifiable features such as racing stripes, hood ornaments, customized features, broken taillights or headlights, body damage, and so on. The car, if identified, may lead the investigator to the suspect.

If the witness knows the suspect, the investigator should ask about the suspect's personal associates, his habits, and where he is likely to be found.

Very specific questions and use of an identification diagram may aid witnesses in their identification of suspects.

Figure 10–6.   **Witness Identification Diagram.**

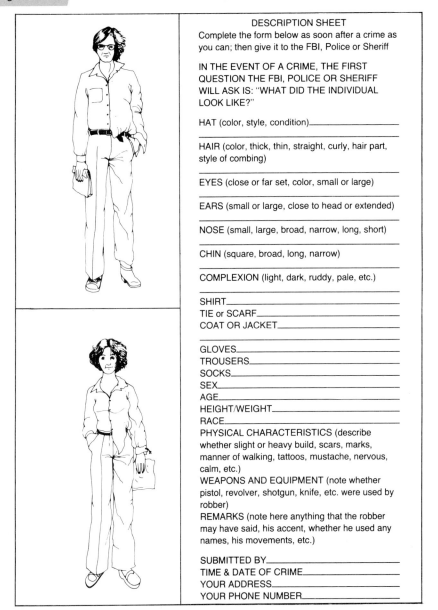

DESCRIPTION SHEET

Complete the form below as soon after a crime as you can; then give it to the FBI, Police or Sheriff

IN THE EVENT OF A CRIME, THE FIRST QUESTION THE FBI, POLICE OR SHERIFF WILL ASK IS: "WHAT DID THE INDIVIDUAL LOOK LIKE?"

HAT (color, style, condition)_____

HAIR (color, thick, thin, straight, curly, hair part, style of combing)

EYES (close or far set, color, small or large)

EARS (small or large, close to head or extended)

NOSE (small, large, broad, narrow, long, short)

CHIN (square, broad, long, narrow)

COMPLEXION (light, dark, ruddy, pale, etc.)

SHIRT_____
TIE or SCARF_____
COAT OR JACKET_____

GLOVES_____
TROUSERS_____
SOCKS_____
SEX_____
AGE_____
HEIGHT/WEIGHT_____
RACE_____
PHYSICAL CHARACTERISTICS (describe whether slight or heavy build, scars, marks, manner of walking, tattoos, mustache, nervous, calm, etc.)
WEAPONS AND EQUIPMENT (note whether pistol, revolver, shotgun, knife, etc. were used by robber)
REMARKS (note here anything that the robber may have said, his accent, whether he used any names, his movements, etc.)

SUBMITTED BY_____
TIME & DATE OF CRIME_____
YOUR ADDRESS_____
YOUR PHONE NUMBER_____

Usually, however, the witness does not know the suspect. If investigators can identify a suspect based on information given by the witness or on their own intuition as to who might be responsible for the crime, they must follow strict procedures in establishing that the individual is identified by the witness.

Basic Types of Identification

The three basic types of identification are field identification, photographic identification, and lineup identification. Each type of identification is used in specific circumstances, and each must meet certain legal requirements to be admissible in court. Frequently more than one type of identification is used.

> *The three basic types of identification are:*
> - *Field identification*
> - *Photographic identification*
> - *Lineup identification*

Field Identification

Field identification is at-the-scene identification that must be made within a reasonable time after a crime has been committed. Generally the suspect is returned to the crime scene for possible identification, or the witness may be taken to where the suspect is being held.

> *Field identification is generally used when a suspect matches the description given by a witness and is apprehended close to the scene of the crime. The critical element in a field identification is time.*

Field identification is based on a totality of circumstances in which a witness identifies a suspect as being the person who committed a crime. Totality of circumstances takes into consideration the concentration a witness had upon the suspect at the time the crime was committed, the accuracy of the witness's description of the suspect, the certainty of the witness at the time of the confrontation, and the length of time between commission of the crime and the field identification.

Studies have shown a 60 percent probability of arrest if response time to crime calls was within one minute. However, the probability of arrest was considerably less when response time was longer. Rapid response greatly improves the officer's chances of apprehending suspects still at the scene. In such cases field identification is obviously justified. Even when the suspects have left the scene, however, if they are apprehended within a reasonable time (up to approximately fifteen minutes) after commission of the crime, immediate identification is justified. A reasonable basis for believing that immediate identification is needed must exist before using field identification, since the suspect does not have the right to have counsel present *(United States v. Ash, Jr.)*.

> *The suspect does not have the right to have counsel present at a field identification.*

Photographic Identification

Most people are familiar with the procedure of having victims and witnesses go through mug books in hopes of finding a picture of the person they saw commit a particular crime. This type of identification is time-consuming and is profitable only if the suspect has a record.

> *If a suspect is not known, witnesses may make identification through mug shots.*

Mug shots are not the only types of photographs used in suspect identification. Frequently officers know, or have a strong suspicion about, who committed a given crime. If the suspect is not in custody, or if it is not possible to conduct a fair lineup, officers may present photographs of people of similar general description to victims or witnesses, who may identify the suspect from among the photographs.

> *Photographic identification is reserved for times when the suspect is not in custody or it is not possible to conduct a fair lineup. Photographic identification should use people of comparable race, height, weight, and general description.*

Photographs used for suspect identification should not contain labels which reveal that a certain suspect has a criminal record. The identification is to be impartial, based on the witness's view of the suspect, and untainted by the suspect's past record. Witnesses should be instructed that they are not obliged to identify anyone from the photographs.

Both the United States Supreme Court and several state supreme courts have issued decisions recognizing the hazards in identification from photographs. Some state prosecutors require a minimum number of photos. However, each has stated that every case must be considered on its own facts. Admissibility in court is more probable if the witness was shown the photographs when he was alone and had had no communications with any other witnesses.

Lineup Identification

The basic idea of the lineup is to provide the opportunity for witnesses to observe several individuals, one of whom is the suspect, to see if he can be identified. As with photographic identification, the prosecutor may require a minimum number of participants in the lineup.

The witnesses not only can see the persons in the lineup, they also can hear them speak. A suspect may be asked to speak, walk, turn, assume a stance or a gesture, or put on clothing. If witnesses have described the suspect's clothing, then all persons in the lineup or none should wear that type of clothing. Obviously if only one dressed the way witnesses described, the tendency would be to pick him. Some police departments have a small inventory of clothing and personal effects such as sunglasses, masks, scarves, gloves, and coats which they have the participants in a lineup wear, depending upon the description of the witness(es).

A lineup is used when a suspect is in custody. It should contain persons of similar race, height, weight, and general description. Witnesses must be instructed that no identification need be made.

A number of important court decisions have been made regarding lineup identification. One of the most important is *United States v. Wade,* which affirms a suspect's right to have counsel present when participating in a lineup.

Although requesting participation is not considered a form of self-incrimination under the Fifth Amendment, the lineup is considered a "critical stage" in the legal process. The *Wade* decision was based on a case in which Wade was convicted of robbing a Texas bank. His case went to the United States Supreme Court, which reviewed the proceedings and then sent the case back to an appeals court. In its review, the Supreme Court said: "The Sixth Amendment of the Constitution guarantees that every citizen shall have the right to counsel in criminal prosecution. When a citizen is suspected of a crime and required to participate in a lineup where witnesses attempt to identify him, then he has a constitutional right to have his lawyer present." The United States Supreme Court stated that "a lineup is just as critical a stage of the prosecution as the trial itself." It should be noted, however, that this particular constitutional right does *not* apply to field identification or to photographic identification.

The Wade decision states that "prior to having a suspect participate in a lineup, the officer must advise the suspect of his constitutional right to have his lawyer present during the lineup." Requesting a suspect to participate in the lineup is not a violation of the person's civil rights.

When using lineup identification, the officer must know the legal requirements accompanying such an identification as well as the composition of the lineup itself. A legal lineup should assure that:

- The suspect has been advised of his right to a lawyer.
- A lawyer has been secured if requested.
- The witnesses have been given impartial pre-lineup advice.
- The lineup is conducted fairly.
- The individuals in the lineup meet the requirements previously specified.

Generally when an officer talks about "reading a suspect his rights," he means the Miranda rights protecting the suspect from self-incrimination. For a lineup, however, the officer is talking about the suspect's Sixth Amendment right to have a lawyer present as specified in the *Wade* decision. The *Miranda* decision is not relevant here.

When a suspect is in custody a lineup should be used as long as it can be done without force and in a fair manner. If these conditions cannot be satisfied, photographic identification should be used.

If for any reason a suspect refuses to cooperate in a lineup, photographic identification may be used. The suspect's refusal to participate may be used against him in court.

If a lineup can be held, there is no reason to show pictures. If both are done in a short period of time, the officer destroys any doubt the witness might have that the person in the picture is the guilty party. A recent Midwest supreme court ruling reversed a guilty decision because a photo identification and lineup were held within minutes of each other.

Witnesses should not make photographic identification and then lineup identification within a short period of time.

Summary

A large part of an investigator's role centers around *objectively* obtaining and presenting information and evidence. The primary responsibilities of the investigator are to (1) assure that the crime scene is secure, (2) record all facts related to the case for future reference, (3) photograph, measure, and sketch the crime scene, (4) obtain and identify evidence, (5) interview witnesses and interrogate suspects, and (6) assist in the identification of suspects.

Investigators, be they patrol officers or detectives, are responsible for securing the crime scene, which includes any surrounding area that contains evidence of criminal activity. They must obtain answers to the questions: who? what? where? when? how? why? Usually they must obtain both photographs and sketches because although photographs include all details and can show items close up, sketches can be selective and can show much larger areas.

A primary responsibility of investigators is to recognize, collect, mark, preserve, and transport physical evidence without contamination in sufficient quantity for analysis. Such evidence may consist of fingerprints, blood, hair, documents, footprints or tire prints, tool fragments, tool marks, broken glass, paint, insulation from safes, firearms, and explosives.

In addition, investigators must interview witnesses and interrogate suspects. A witness may be a complainant, an accuser, a victim, an observer of the incident, a confidential or reliable informant, an expert, or a scientific examiner of physical evidence. A suspect, the person believed to have committed the crime, should not be interrogated without first being given the Miranda warning which advises him that he has the "right to remain silent . . . the right to speak with an attorney and to have the attorney present during questioning."

Information obtained from witnesses is usually critical to resolution of a case. Unfortunately, witnesses' perception of what happened often varies because perception is affected by the viewer's accuracy of observation, interpretation of what is seen, and attention paid to the incident.

In addition to physical evidence, eyewitness identification plays an important part in the arrest and in the trial proceedings. Very specific questions and use of an identification diagram may aid witnesses in their identification of suspects. Once this information has been obtained, the investigator may use three basic types of identification: (1) field identification, (2) photographic identification, or (3) lineup identification. Sometimes more than one type of identifcation is used.

Field identification is used when a suspect is temporarily detained or arrested. It is usually "at-the-scene" identification. Field identification is based on totality of circumstances in which a witness identifies a suspect as being the person who committed the crime. The suspect does *not* have the right to have counsel present at a field identification. The critical element in a field identification is time — it should usually occur within approximately fifteen minutes of the commission of the crime to be legally admissible.

Photographic identification may be of two types — mug shots or ordinary photographs. Mug shots are usually used when the suspect is not known to the witness or the police. Ordinary photographic identification is used when the police have a fairly good idea of who is involved in the crime and the suspect is not in custody or it is not possible to conduct a fair lineup. Photographic identification should use people of comparable race, height, weight, and general description.

A lineup is used when a suspect is in custody. The same legal requirements exist as for photographic identification: the lineup should contain persons of similar race, height, weight, and general description. Witnesses must be instructed that no identification need be made.

The *Wade* decision states that "prior to having a suspect participate in a lineup, the officer must advise the suspect of his constitutional right to have his lawyer present during the lineup." Requesting a suspect to participate in a lineup is not a violation of the person's civil rights. However, if for any reason the suspect refuses to cooperate in a lineup, photographic identification may be used and the suspect's refusal to participate may be used against him in court. If both photographic identification and lineup identification are used, they should not be done within a short period of time.

Discussion Questions

1. If there was a crime and the suspect was unusually tall or was a member of a minority group not common in the area, how could you hold a fair lineup?

2. In what crimes is eyewitness testimony all that is required for conviction?

3. Why wouldn't people want to help put a stop to crime by being witnesses?

4. How do you convince witnesses to get involved when they really don't want to?

5. Can you force a witness to answer questions?

6. If two witnesses disagree on an identification, what happens?

7. If five witnesses are to identify a suspect in a lineup and four of them pick one person and one picks another, is it assumed that the majority are right, or is the lineup inconclusive?

8. How are participants in a lineup chosen?

9. Is it legal to put other suspects in a lineup with the prime suspect?

10. Why does the suspect not have the right to counsel at a field identification?

References

Allison, H.C. *Personal identification*. Boston: Holbrook Press, 1973.

Bennett, W., and Hess, K.M. *Introduction to criminal investigation*. St. Paul, Minn.: West Publishing Company, 1981.

Bloch, P.B., and Weidman, D.R. *Managing criminal investigation*. Washington, D.C.: U.S. Government Printing Office (LEAA Grant Number 72-TA-99-1077), 1975.

Cheatham, R.T., and Erickson, K.V. *The police officer's guide to better communication*. Gleview, Ill.: Scott, Foresman, and Company, 1984.

DeAngelis, F.J. *Criminalistics for the investigator*. Encino, Cal.: Glencoe Publishing Company, 1980.

Dowling, J.L. *Criminal investigation*. New York: Harcourt Brace Jovanovich, 1979.

Federal Bureau of Investigation. *Handbook of forensic science*. Washington, D.C.: U.S. Government Printing Office, 1981.

Hanley, J.R., and Schmidt, W. *Introduction to criminal evidence*. Berkeley, Cal.: McCutchan Publishing Corporation, 1982.

Hess, K.M., and Wrobleski, H.M. *For the record: Report writing in law enforcement*. Eureka, Cal.: Innovative Publications Company, 1985.

International Association of Chiefs of Police. *Criminal investigation*. 2d ed. Gaithersburg, Md.: 1970.

Klockars, C.B. *Thinking about police: Contemporary readings*. New York: McGraw-Hill, 1983.

The prosecution function and defense function. New York: Standards for the Administration of Criminal Justice, American Bar Association, 1971.

Saferstein, R. *Criminalistics: An introduction to forensic science*, 2d ed. Englewood Cliffs, N.J.: Prentice-Hall, 1981.

Spelman, W.G., and Brown, D.K. *Calling the police: A replication of the citizen reporting component of the Kansas City response time analysis*. Washington, D.C.: The Police Foundation, 1981.

Swanson, C.R., Jr.; Chamelin, N.C.; and Territo, L. *Criminal investigation*. 2d ed. Santa Monica, Cal.: Goodyear Publishing Company, 1981.

Waddington, L.C. *Criminal evidence*. Encino, Cal.: Glencoe Publishing Company, 1978.

Waldron, R.M. *The criminal justice system,* 3d ed. Boston: Houghton Mifflin Company, 1984.

Walton, G. *Laboratory manual for introductory forensic science*. Encino, Cal.: Glencoe Publishing Company, 1979.

Weston, P.B., and Walls, K.M. *Criminal investigation: Basic perspectives*. Englewood Cliffs, N.J.: Prentice-Hall, 1980.

"Witness responses misunderstood by prosecutors." *Target* (LEAA Newsletter) 5:1 (January 1976): 6.

Yarmey, A.D. "Eyewitness identification." *Encyclopedia of crime and justice*. New York: The Free Press, 1983.

Police community service programs emphasize helping citizens to learn to help themselves in preventing crime and preserving individual safety and well-being.

CHAPTER

11

Community Service

Helping Citizens Help Themselves

Do You Know . . .

- What community services the police department may provide its citizens?

- What most public relations programs emphasize?

- What most community relations programs emphasize?

- What factors interfere with good community relations and two-way communications?

- What single element is critical for any successful community relations program?

- What types of community service programs have been instituted to deter crime?

The vocation of every man and woman is to serve other people.
—*Leo Tolstoi*

The highest and best form of efficency is the spontaneous co-operation of a free people.
—*Woodrow Wilson*

Introduction

''Police . . . and the communities they serve need to be reminded that police are people dealing with people, that it is people who commit crimes, and it is people who need police assistance'' (Radelet, 1970, p. 62).

The types of assistance provided by the police take a variety of forms. We discussed earlier (Chapter 7) the types of service which might be expected from a police department and the controversy as to how much and what types of service are justified.

Police departments provide a wide variety of services including giving information, directions, and advice; counseling and referring; licensing and registering vehicles; intervening in domestic arguments; working with neglected children; rendering emergency medical or rescue services; dealing with alcoholics and the mentally ill; finding lost children; dealing with stray animals; controlling crowds; and providing community education programs on crime prevention, drug abuse, safety, and the like.

Although some police departments have a separate division assigned the responsibilities of community service and some have made community service a responsibility of a patrol team, in reality, community service is a vital part of every police officer's job.

In the interest of economy and professionalism, several departments have turned to the use of civilians for such duties as monitoring parking meters, dispatching, and doing clerical jobs. However, certain types of community service are important not only because they fulfill community needs, but also because they allow the public to see police officers functioning in a helping way rather than only performing acts related to criminal activity.

According to Brandstatter and Hyman (1971, p. 299):

It is true that all police departments engage in service activities and will continue to do so for some time to come. Even those who want to eliminate certain such activities cannot always do so. A department which perfers not to provide ambulance service, for example, must make exceptions when police vehicles are the only available means of transporting a traffic accident victim to the medical facilities that can save his life. . . . Accordingly, all police officers should know and understand the principles and techniques of the more common of these service functions. Whether engaging in such activities happens to be unavoidable or whether it happens to be in accord with the regular policy of the department, it must be done well.

Providing Emergency Services

Frequently patrol officers are the first on the scene of a situation requiring emergency services.

Emergency First Aid

As noted in the chapter on traffic, police officers are often the first on the scene of a traffic accident and are responsible for providing first aid to any persons injured in the accident. They may also be called on to assist persons who have been injured in other ways or who become seriously ill. Police officers should be thoroughly trained and certified in CPR as well as in advanced first aid, including measures to stop bleeding, to deal with fractures, shock, burns, and epileptic convulsions. They should also recognize insulin coma and know how to treat it.

Ambulance Service

Closely related to providing emergency first aid, police officers may be required to transport accident victims or other persons who are gravely ill or injured to the nearest medical facility. In fact, in some communities, the police department is the sole ambulance service, and patrol cars are specially equipped to serve as ambulances. This policy of providing ambulance service tends to make the public more appreciative of the police department and may foster citizen cooperation. However, this can place a drain on a police department's resources. Local conditions should determine whether this service is routinely provided.

Fire Control Service

In some departments, police and firefighting are combined into a public safety department. In such instances, obviously, police officers must be trained in fire suppression techniques. In departments where the police are not primarily responsible for fire suppression activities, they may still be the first to arrive at the scene of a fire and can lend valuable assistance to the firefighters.

The first action of police officers who come upon an uncontrolled fire is to call the fire department. Only then should any attempts be made to control or suppress the fire. Other functions the police may serve include traffic control, assuring that firefighting equipment can arrive quickly at the scene, and helping search for and rescue persons trapped by the fire. If children are trapped in a home that is burning, rescuers should check under beds and in closets because children frequently try to hide from the smoke and flames. Police officers can also provide crowd control, assist with first aid, transport injured persons to the nearest medical facility, and guard any personal property removed from the burning structure.

Bomb Threats or Incidents

If a bomb threat is made or a bomb is actually found, the police are usually the ones to be notified. In such instances the main responsibility of the police is to assure the safety of persons in the vicinity of the bomb and to call in experts to actually dispose of the bomb. Frequently a bomb disposal unit of a military installation is called in. Larger departments, however, may have their own bomb disposal teams.

In the event of an actual explosion, be it intentional or accidental as in an explosion at an industrial site, the police are usually responsible for crowd control and for investigating the incident.

Natural Disasters

Floods, tornadoes, hurricanes, fires, and earthquakes can produce emergency conditions requiring action on the part of the police officers. They may need to provide first aid to victims, provide crowd control, and protect the property of those involved.

Search and Rescue

Many departments are also actively involved in search and rescue operations which may or may not be necessitated by natural disasters.

Preserving the Peace and Safety of the Public

As part of their role to preserve the peace and safety of the public, police officers may be called to handle disputes and disturbances, to quell civil disturbances, and to maintain order in labor/management disputes and strikes.

Disputes and Domestic Quarrels

One of the most common and most dangerous calls made to the police department is for assistance in settling a dispute, for example a fight in a bar, or for resolving a domestic situation, for example, a husband beating his wife (or vice versa). Frequently alcohol is involved in such situations. Tempers are short, and the potential for violence is ever present.

As noted by Levine, Husheno, and Palumbo (1980), p. 23):

Diversity within cities creates the potential for all kinds of disputes and disturbances. Parties to traffic accidents get angry with one another; people imbibing at taverns get into fights; young people blasting stereos disturb neighborhood residents. One purpose of the criminal justice system is to moderate these tensions and keep hostilities from escalating. Indeed peace-keeping is one of the primary missions of the police and as important as this goal is, if it is pursued too zealously, the right of the people to be different may be impaired. There is a fine line between obnoxious conduct that intrudes into other people's lives and harmless behavior that merely defies common standards of propriety. Thus, neighbors may be annoyed when teen-agers ''hang out'' on the streets and use vulgar language, but it is arguable that they have a right to do so if they do not interfere with passers-by. Likewise, demonstrators passing out political fliers often disturb people who disagree with their views, and the discarded sheets of paper can cause a mess, but to prohibit such activities would invade the constitutional right of freedom of speech. Too much emphasis on public peace can lead to social repression and an insistence on mass conformity.

Civil Disturbances

The civil disturbances on campuses throughout the country in the 1960s high-lighted the role of the police in controlling civil disturbances. Although civil disturbances are not as prevalent in the 1980s, protest demonstrations continue throughout the country, for example, strong antiwar sentiment, disagreement with legislative decisions, strong sentiments for or against abortion, or protests against industries engaged in manufacturing war materials.

In dealing with civil disturbances, police officers must always remember that our Constitution guarantees its citizens the right to *peacefully* assemble. This right must be protected. It is only when the assembly is no longer peaceful that officers have the responsibility to intervene. Determining what constitutes peaceful assembly places a large amount of dicretionary power in the hands of the police officers.

The primary responsibilities of police officers are to maintain order and to protect lives and assets. In the event of sit-in demonstrations, it may be necessary to forcibly remove participants. In such instances, the minimum amount of force necessary should be used.

Labor/Management Disputes and Strikes

Strikes are legal, but, as with the right to assemble, the strike must be peaceful. If strikers physically restrict others from crossing the picket line, they are acting illegally, and the police may be called to intervene. In such instances, police officers must remain neutral. Their only responsibility is to prevent violence and property damage or loss.

Escort Services

Police may be called upon to provide escort service to individuals who are extremely popular, for example, rock stars, or for those who are extremely unpopular, for example, a politician the public greatly dislikes. They may also provide escort services for dangerous cargoes such as those containing highly inflammable materials, hazardous wastes, and the like, or for oversized cargoes.

In addition, police may be asked to provide escort services for funeral processions or for very valuable cargoes such as large sums of cash.

Little agreement exists on when escort services are appropriate or on how they should be provided, that is, should they go with red flashing lights and siren, or proceed as though on routine patrol? Local circumstances will largely determine the answers to these questions. The important thing in the area of escort services is that the department have a clearly established policy on the use of police escorts to avoid any charges of favoritism should a request for such services be denied.

Licensing

The police department is frequently involved in the licensing of handguns, and understandably so since it is to their advantage to know who owns what kind of weapons in their locality. In addition, they are in a position to investigate the applicant for a license and to determine if such a license should be granted. They may also do background investigations on applicants for liquor licenses, for taxi licenses, and for tow truck licenses.

The police department is also frequently involved in other types of licensing such as licenses for holding a parade or for blocking off a street for a community function. When such licensing is provided by the police department, it is also responsible for such activities as blocking off streets and setting up detours, rerouting traffic, and the like.

Inspections

Because patrol officers routinely cover the entire area over which the police department has jurisdiction, many decision makers believe they should be responsible for inspections, seeing that fire codes, health codes, building codes, and the like are being adhered to. This is another area of controversy because such activities are extremely time consuming. They do present the advantage of familiarizing the patrol officers with the people and buildings on their beats. On the other hand, such activities do take the patrol officers off the street and into buildings where they are no longer on preventive patrol but are rather serving a function that could as easily be carried out by an inspector specifically hired for the job, and usually at less cost.

In many areas, police are also responsible for checking the weight of trucks. Police are used in this capacity because they must be on the scene anyway to be readily available to issue tickets to overweight trucks or to stop trucks who bypass the scales completely. Others contend, however, that the patrol officers in the vicinity could be called in for either of the preceding situations and that it might be more practical not to use patrol officers in this capacity.

Other Community Services

Several other services may or may not be provided by police departments, depending on local policy.

Transporting Civilians in Police Cars

As a general rule, most police officers are not allowed to transport civilians in their patrol cars unless they are on official business, for example, transporting a prisoner from one jail to another, a defendant to court for trial, or a witness to view a suspect.

In some departments, police officers are responsible for chauffeuring public officials and for transporting economically disadvantaged people to the welfare office to obtain assistance. Use of police vehicles for such purposes is usually not good practice. However, instances may arise when the police may have to transport civilians in their squads. For example, a patrol officer may come upon a motorist whose car is totally disabled and the weather is extremely inclement. The patrol officer may, in such instances, give the civilian a ride to a service station or home, depending on the circumstances. In such instances, the patrol officer should notify headquarters of the situation.

Persons Locked Out

The police are frequently called to assist someone who has locked himself out of his car or his home. In such instances it is usually preferable to have the civilian call a locksmith. If this is not possible, however, police officers should check the identity of the person requesting assistance. Imagine the predicament of a police officer who assists a burglar in breaking and entering.

If the police do assist in gaining entry to a car or home, headquarters should be fully informed prior to the action.

Damage to Property

Citizens who experience damage to their property are very likely to call the police. The first action of officers responding to such calls is to determine if any danger is inherent in the situation. If danger does exist, the police officers must take action to remove the danger. For example, if a tree has fallen on power lines and hot wires are on the ground, the police should rope off the area and call the power company. If no danger is inherent in the situation, the police officers should determine if the damage is the result of criminal or noncriminal actions. If it is criminal property damage, for example, the work of vandals, the officers should conduct a thorough investigation. If it is a noncriminal (and nondangerous) situation, for example, a tree has fallen on a home, the police officers should advise the complainant of alternatives in taking care of the damage. The complainant should usually also be advised to notify his or her insurance agent.

Missing Persons

Television programs have made the missing persons function of the police department seem a routine activity. In actuality, however, unless foul play is suspected or the person missing is retarded, mentally incompetent, or in need of medication, the police do not become involved in missing person cases. If no crime has been committed and the safety of the missing person is not in jeopardy, the police department performs an administrative function, recording the information to be used in helping to identify individuals who are unconscious, who are found wandering (senility), or who are found dead and who have no identification on them.

McCreedy (1974, p. 140) suggests that although adults are often reported missing from their jobs or homes, some such absences are voluntary and do not require police action. Consequently, most police departments will not take a missing adult report until the person has been missing more than twenty-four hours. According to McCreedy, more than 90 percent of the adults reported missing return within twenty-four hours. He also suggested that a large number of adults who are reported missing are suicidal, frequently despondent over family or business pressures or from failure. In addition, senile, elderly people frequently become disoriented and wander away from their homes or from nursing homes. Although such people are seldom dangerous to others, they may be attacked, become lost, or be hit by a vehicle.

Because of the mobility of individuals in our society, the need for a centralized, computerized system for recording information about missing persons was recognized and acted upon over a decade ago when the National Crime Information Center (NCIC) Advisory Policy Board approved establishing a Missing Person File. This file was added to the nationwide NCIC system in October 1975. The file has four specific categories and criteria for entry (Bishop and Schuessler, 1982, p. 21):

- Disability—A person of any age who is missing and under proven physical and/or mental disability or is senile, thereby subjecting himself or others to personal and immediate danger.

- Endangered—A person of any age who is missing and is in the company of another person under circumstances indicating that his physical safety is in danger.

- Involuntary—A person of any age who is missing under circumstances indicating that the disappearance was not voluntary, i.e., abduction or kidnapping.

■ Juvenile—A person who is missing and declared unemancipated as defined by the laws of his state of residence and who does not meet the entry criteria of the other three categories.

The police's role in helping to locate missing children is discussed in the next chapter.

Lost and Found

People who find valuable property are likely to turn it in to the police department. Conversely, people who have lost items of value are likely to request assistance from the police department. In this situation, also, the police department plays primarily an administrative function, maintaining accurate records of property that has been found or lost. The department is responsible for protecting all found property and for attempting to locate the rightful owners. Of course, the owner also is responsible for checking with the police to see if the property has been found. Any unclaimed property is frequently disposed of through an open auction.

Missing and Stray Animals

Some police departments also have the responsibility to handle stray animals, especially unlicensed dogs. They may also be called upon to deal with dangerous animals such as bears or with trapped animals such as a raccoon up a chimney of a home. Department policy will determine whether such calls are responded to by the police department. If the department policy is not to handle animal problems other than unlicensed stray dogs (usually in violation of a leash law), officers should be prepared to offer advice to the person seeking assistance, for example, that the person should call the humane society.

Public Relations Programs

Public relations programs frequently seek to enhance the image of the police officer, to gain understanding and acceptance of their role in the community. The programs are directed to groups or the entire community. The police officer may be portrayed as the friend of the young and the old, may appear at school and church programs, sponsor little league teams or law enforcement days, or hand out bumper stickers encouraging people to support their local police.

> *The primary emphasis of most public relations programs is to raise the image of the police agency and its officials.*

Such programs are usually geared to the needs of the police. Sometimes they are only cosmetic or token efforts to gain community approval. However, public relations is an accepted and healthy form of advertising used very successfully by major corporations and by many law enforcement agencies. There is nothing wrong with a police department employing such tactics. The problem arises when a department institutes a special unit to "take care of the public image" and assumes that this is all that is required. No amount of bumper stickers or sponsorships will counteract negative actions by police officers. Respect must be earned; it cannot be bought or commanded. It must always be remembered that the police image is primarily the result of daily contacts between the police officer and citizens of the community.

The President's Task Force Report (1967) outlines three types of programs that were conducted in several police agencies. Most programs concentrated on attempting to teach the police officers how to improve the image of the police and how to conduct themselves so as not to alienate the public — how to talk courteously to citizens, and how and why to avoid physical or verbal abuse and discrimination. A second type of training gave police officers an understanding of the various kinds of individuals with whom they would come in contact and the various neighborhoods of the city. The third type of training was aimed at changing attitudes and prejudices of recruits and police officers. Role-playing and small discussion groups helped the officers to think through their own emotions and beliefs to see how these might influence their actions as police officers.

Any public relations program should be realistic in the image it hopes to convey to the public. As Garmire (1972, p. 11) puts it:

> I do not believe that police officers and the police service can become objects of love and endearment; it is not in the nature of men, particularly Americans, to give such affection to those representatives of authority who directly control their lives. And, no matter how we describe the activities of the police, the business of police is policing. The most we can hope for . . . is respect for the police as professionals, confidence in their integrity, and public conviction that the police will perform their mission.

Conveyance of such an understanding requires more than public relations programs. It requires, first and foremost, appropriate actions by police officers, and second, sound community relations programs.

Police-Community Relations Programs

While public relations programs are a one-way effort directed at raising the image of the police, police-community relations programs seek to provide means for police and citizens to work together to achieve their mutual goal of law and order.

The primary emphasis of police-community relations programs is to provide two-way communication between police and citizens to work toward achieving law and order in the community.

Almost twenty years ago the President's 1966 Crime Commission, in *The Challenge of Crime in a Free Society* (1967, p. 100), stated: "A community relations program is not a public relations program 'to sell the police image' to the people. It is not a set of expedients whose purpose is to tranquilize for a time an angry neighborhood by, for example, suddenly promoting a few Negro officers in the wake of a racial disturbance. It is a long-range, full-scale effort to acquaint the police and the community with each other's problems and to stimulate action aimed at solving those problems.''

This same notion is reiterated by Radelet (1980, p. 21) when he states:

Police-community relations simply is the reciprocal attitudes of police and civilians. We are interested in the sum total of activities by which it may be emphasized that police are an important part of—not apart from—the communities they serve. . . . Properly understood, the principle is one for *total orientation* of a police organization. It is an attitude and an emphasis for all phases of police work, not merely for a specialized unit in the department. It is a way for a police officer to view his work in dealing with citizens. For citizens, it is a way of viewing the police officer: what he does and how he does it. Ideally, it is a matter of striving to achieve mutual understanding and trust, as with any human relationship. Every problem in police work today is in some sense a problem of police-community relations. Its solution depends to some extent upon police and community cooperation.

Many people are concerned about the relationship between the police and the citizens. Many people think they know the answer to the problem. Police officers feel that if citizens would only understand the responsibilities of law enforcement officers and would obey the law themselves, there would be no problem. Citizens, on the other hand, frequently believe that if the police would be more human and understanding, the problem would be solved. Both sides are partly right and partly wrong; however, their attitudes toward one another frequently interfere with working together to find answers to their mutual problems.

Factors Interfering with Communication*

Several factors including negative attitudes and unwillingness to listen, interfere with two-way communication between police officers and citizens. The following comments are indicative of attitudes which block two-way communication:

From the Police:

People just don't respect the police any more.

We can't get cooperation. People just don't care.

Yeah, you walk into the kind of situations I face, and have people call you obscene names and threaten you, and then see if you can keep your temper.

Talk about police brutality. What about citizen brutality against the police? We're in danger of attack every minute of the day.

You hear some mother tell her kid that if he isn't good she'll turn him over to a cop. Just a little kid. Man, that really chills you.

---

*Adapted from *Police and Community Relations . . . is a Two-Way Street.* Written by Don McEvy for the National Conference of Christians and Jews.

Folks these days think they can choose the laws they want to obey or disobey. That's the real problem.

Even when you want to make an arrest, for disorderly conduct or DWI or anything, first thing you know you're surrounded by an angry mob wanting to fight.

With all the new court decisions and departmental policies an ordinary police officer is expected to be a constitutional lawyer. One little mistake and the judge turns a criminal loose, and a conscientious police officer gets a reprimand. How can we do our job under those conditions?

One police officer gets out of line and it's smeared all over the newspapers for a week. A hundred guys do a good job and nobody notices. Sure, we have some bad apples on the force, but I resent all of us being condemned just because of those few.

People sweep floors and make more money than I do. If the public wants professional police, they're going to have to pay them. I like police work, but I'm getting out if they don't do something about salaries.

From the Community:

Why do they have to be so arrogant? A little common courtesy would go a long way.

We haven't got a chance. The police act like it was a federal crime to be a teenager.

A bunch of guys are just hanging around the corner, not doing nothing wrong, and they come along and yell, "Okay, you guys, move along."

They act like we don't belong in America just because we speak Spanish. We're just as much citizens as anybody else.

I know I should cooperate more. But it just doesn't pay to get involved.

They expect us to obey the law. Let's see them start doing it themselves. They know every pusher and prostitute on the street, but they don't do a thing as long as they get their kickback.

I heard a cop call my daddy "Boy." They're not going to get by with that stuff with me.

A police officer raps you around real good. Then you make a complaint and that's the end of it. They never investigate those things, so what's the use? Just because we don't dress like people on Madison Avenue or wear our hair to suit them, they treat us like animals. It's not brutality so much as constant harassment.

The things that bugs me is that if you run a red light, the police officer will drag you out of the car and throw you across the hood and frisk you. There ain't no cause for that.

Why can't a cop explain to you what he is detaining you for? If you ask "What for?" they threaten you with resisting arrest.

The police in my town are supposed to wear identification badges, but the names are never in sight when you want to see one. They must put them in their pockets every time things get a little rough.

Just try and find one when you need him. They're all up at the diner drinking coffee . . . and then walk out without paying for it, too.

You've probably heard many of the comments, or similar ones, before. You may even have made some of them yourself. When the two lists are placed side by side, several interesting similarities are evident. Whether the sentiments of a hostile citizen or an embittered police officer, the pride, fear and isolation, the need for understanding, and the demand for respect are strikingly similar.

Important factors limiting two-way communication between police and community are negative attitudes toward each other and unwillingness to listen to the other's side.

Police resent being the targets for obscene epithets. Nor do they like being called *the fuzz, flatfoot, honkie cop, fascist pig* any more than private citizens like being referred to as *animals, young punks, scum, niggers, spikes, dorks,* and an endless variety of other racial or degrading slurs. Words have the power to inflame and incite to violence. Classifying all members of a group into one negative category is immature and ignorant. Each group has good and bad individuals within it. It is individuals who should be considered, not the group to which they happen to belong.

Stereotypes interfere with communication and good relations.

People tend to think in terms of the "in-group" — the group to which they belong — and the "out-group." The out-group is everyone else and usually is perceived as being "bad." If citizens perceive police as members of the out-group, they will be uncooperative and perhaps even hostile. Nobody wants to tell on a friend or sometimes even a total stranger who is a private citizen like himself. Similarily, group protectiveness may make it difficult for a police officer to "blow the whistle" on a fellow officer.

Group protectiveness interferes with communication and good relations.

Today it is more difficult to get a case through court, more dangerous to walk the streets at night, and more of a strain to get along with neighbors crowded in on all sides. Living in this generation requires more skill, knowledge, patience, and good will.

Police work also requires better training and more self-discipline than ever before. Law enforcement is no longer a job. It is a profession. Likewise, the citizen must be willing to pay the price for living in this generation. One of the costs is personal involvement. To stand aside and expect others to carry the load is to default in one of the primary obligations of citizenship. As Seneca (Troades) noted: "He who does not prevent a crime when he can, encourages it."

The police and public are bound together in a common destiny. What is good for one is inevitably good for the other. What is bad for one, is bad for the other. If police work for low salaries, with inadequate training, in hostile communities that provide little cooperation and frequent danger, they are not going to operate effectively. Citizens can do something to alleviate these conditions and thereby assure themselves of better and more professional police services.

As long as citizens live in fear of the police, believing them to be unfriendly mercenaries at best and brutal oppressors at worst, they will not provide the environment essential for effective law enforcement. R. F. Kennedy once said: ''Every society gets the kind of criminal it deserves. What is equally true is that every community gets the kind of law enforcement it insists upon.''

> *Societal factors interfere with communication and good relations.*

Approaches to Police-Community Relations

Several approaches have been taken to police-community relations programs. Bureaus have been established within police agencies. Community-wide citizen groups have been formed. Civilian review boards or advisory committees have worked with police agencies in establishing goals and priorities. Large-scale educational programs have been successful when they have promoted dialogue rather than simply conveying information (public relations). As noted by the President's Commission on Law Enforcement and the Administration of Justice (*The Police,* p. 159):

> Citizens who distrust the police will not easily be converted by information programs they consider to come from a tainted source. However, even for these groups, long-term education based upon honest and free DIALOGUE between the police and the public can have an effect. Indeed, this is one of the basic goals of the citizen advisory committees. On the other hand, citizens who are neutral or supportive can benefit from increased understanding of the complicated problems and tasks of the police. Informational programs can also generate support for more personnel, salary increases, sufficient equipment, and other resources to improve the efficiency of police work. It can help the cooperative citizen to avoid becoming a victim of crime and show him how to work more effectively with the police. And, to the extent that the police department is genuinely working at improved community relations, dissemination of this information to the press and other media does have a positive effect on community relations.

The police officer on the street is the community-relations officer of the department. The officer's actions, demeanor, appearance, and empathy for people are all accountable for positive or negative community relations.

Community acceptance of crime prevention programs initiated depends on the overall effectiveness of all police operations. Hundreds of programs have aided the police in their efforts toward not only community relations, but also improved law enforcement. As police officers' knowledge of the community and its citizens increases, so does their effectiveness as law enforcement officers. Their street contacts and sources of information are also vastly improved.

> *The police officer on the street is ultimately responsible for the success of police-community relations programs.*

Community relations is a responsibility of both the police and the citizen. The police may contribute to improving two-way communication by:

- Understanding the problems of the citizen and keeping an open mind, using good judgment.
- Paying attention rather than displaying a casual attitude. Police officers should listen attentively. If they disagree on a point, they should do so politely. They should show consideration rather than ignoring the citizen. The problem the citizen conveys to the police officer may be of utmost importance to him or her.
- Using courteous words. Sarcasm in either words or attitude is readily apparent to the citizen and hampers communication. Tone of voice can be as important as the words used. Tone can incite anger or instill confidence.
- Being patient. Police officers must exercise self-command and self-discipline. Although patience and kindness may be misperceived by some as a sign of weakness, this is not true.
- Giving time. Give citizens time to air their problems. Do not rush them.
- Showing enthusiasm. Officers should approach each contact with enthusiasm, believing in themselves and their communities. A lackadaisical attitude will thwart the objectives of any contact.
- Being helpful instead of hindering. Rendering aid is one of the most important functions of a police officer.
- Showing sincerity. Mere words, in themselves, are not proof of sincerity. Police officers must be honest and straightforward in their citizen contacts.
- Being polite and friendly. A smile at the opportune moment is an asset to a police officer. It is hard for anyone to ignore a friendly smile.

Community Service Programs to Deter Crime

Many police departments have instituted programs aimed at preventing crime in the community.

> *Crime prevention programs include store security, home security, car security, operation identification, and neighborhood or block watch programs*

Store Security

Police departments may assist store owners in their efforts to reduce losses from shoplifting by studying their stores and then recommending action, such as hiring store detectives, implementing educational campaigns, installing convex, wide-angle mirrors in isolated areas, installing closed-circuit television cameras to watch shoppers from observation booths, or installing electronic systems using special magnetic or microwave-sensitive tags. The tags require a deactivating device or a special tool to be removed without damaging the merchandise. If a customer leaves an area of the store before a salesperson removes the tag or deactivates it, a sensor sounds an alarm and store personnel apprehend and detain the suspect for the police.

Home Security

Police departments may also provide home security inspections in which an officer goes to a citizen's home, evaluates its security, and suggests methods for making the home a less inviting target for crime. Recommendations may be made to install deadbolt locks, improve lighting, and so on. In some communities a subsidy is available for half the cost of making recommended changes.

An officer teaches home safety.

Automobile Security

Because of the vulnerability of autos to theft, many antitheft programs and devices have been introduced to make it more difficult for a person to steal a car and more difficult for that person to use or sell it without its stolen nature being detected.

Automobile manufacturers have contributed by making the mechanism of the ignition switch lock the steering wheel and by having a separate steering post lock key and door lock key. Some police agencies have placed on every parking meter a sticker stating: "Have you locked your car?" and provided dashboard stickers which remind motorists: "Have you taken your keys and locked your car?"

Some cities have encouraged their used-car dealers to fence in their lots or chain their entrances and exits. Public education campaigns have also been instituted using newspaper, radio, television, and placard publicity as well as bumper stickers with slogans reminding motorists to lock their cars.

Because 72 percent of the autos stolen are taken by persons under the age of twenty-one, extensive educational campaigns have been launched to educate youth about the seriousness of car theft and its consequences. Law enforcement agencies have also taken stronger measures to assure the immediate processing of persons apprehended.

Law enforcement agencies constantly have stressed the need for a uniform title law throughout the country. It is possible in some states for an applicant to appear before a licensing agent and obtain a title for a car without the agent seeing the car for which the title is being issued. However, many states are considering legislation requiring that before a vehicle is licensed, it must be taken before a commissioned officer who would personally check the motor and verify the serial numbers.

Operation Identification Programs

Police have also implemented operation identification programs in which citizens are provided tools and loaned markers to identify their property with a permanent

Figure 11–1. Operation I.D. Sticker.

Source: Courtesy of Minnesota Crime Watch—Department of Public Safety.

identification number. If these items are lost or stolen and recovered by the police, the identification number provides a positive method of identifying the rightful owner. If the items are found in the possession of a burglar or thief, the number can aid the police in prosecuting and convicting the suspect.

Stickers and decals are furnished those citizens participating so that they can place a warning on their doors and window.

The warning labels and the marking of personal property with a permanent identification number are positive approaches to deter a burglar or thief from attempting to steal that property.

Neighborhood or Block Watch Programs

Block watch programs have been initiated, instructing homeowners to form co-operative block groups to deter burglaries and thefts during the absence of home-owners and to provide places of safety for children who might be threatened on their way to or from school. Such neighborhood watch programs bring neighbors together in an effort to reduce the incidence of crime in their neighborhood. The program involves being aware of who your neighbors are, what their daily routines are, and being aware of suspicious activities or persons in the neighborhood and reporting anything unusual to the police.

With cooperation and involvement of all citizens, such as sharing the responsibility of checking each other's homes when they are on vacation, the neighborhood is a safer place in which to live. Most programs emphasize that residents should *not* try to apprehend suspects, so the program should not be in danger of creating "vigilante" actions.

Other Programs

Programs in the schools, such as lectures and video aids in "Children and the Law," have aided police in their fight against vandalism and shoplifting. They reach a segment of society that represents future citizens, informing children of the problem of crime in our society and how they might help reduce this problem.

In addition to community programs to help combat crime, many police departments have instituted programs to promote safety and the general welfare of the public. Most such programs are aimed at children, for example, bike safety programs, drug abuse program, "officer friendly" programs for elementary school children, and school-police liaison programs. These efforts are discussed in the next chapter.

Summary

Although the type and amount of community service provided by a police depart-ment varies from city to city, a certain level of community service is expected everywhere. The services provided include giving information, directions, and advice; counseling and referring; licensing and registering vehicles; intervening in domestic arguments; working with neglected children; rendering emergency medical or rescue services; dealing with alcoholics and the mentally ill; finding lost children; dealing with stray animals; controlling crowds; and providing community education programs on crime prevention, drug abuse, safety, and the like.

Community service should be differentiated from public relations and community relations. Public relations emphasizes building a positive image of the law enforcement officer. Community relations emphasizes improving two-way communication between citizens and the police, with the raising of image being an anticipated side effect. Community service, in contrast, emphasizes actual police assistance or efforts to help citizens learn to help themselves in preventing crime and preserving individual safety and well-being.

Some police departments attempt to improve their image by instituting public relations programs — programs which emphasize raising the image of the police officer rather than opening channels of communications. Other departments concentrate on community relations programs to provide two-way communication between police and citizens to work toward achieving law and order in the community.

Communication may be limited by such factors as negative attitudes toward each other and unwillingness to listen to the other's side.

No matter what type of program is instituted, however, the fact remains that the police officer on the street is ultimately responsible for the success of the police-community relations program and for the image of the police held by the citizens of the community.

Several community service programs focus on crime prevention, including store security, home security, car security, operation identification, and neighborhood or block watch programs.

Application

The following activities are engaged in by a typical police department. Identify each as being primarily public relations, community relations, or community service oriented. Then select one activity from each category which you feel has the most potential benefit for the community and the department.

  A. Informational pamphlets
     1. How To Make Your Home Secure
     2. What To Do Before Going on Vacation
     3. Know Your Police Department
  B. Speeches on drug abuse to service organizations, schools, and businesses
  C. Press releases
     1. Release of local crime statistics
     2. Interviews with local police officers
     3. Public warnings of fraud schemes, stolen checks, and so on

D. Operation Smile (distribute buttons with the slogan and actually "smile")

E. Law Enforcement Week
   1. Public display of police equipment
   2. Slide show on burglary prevention
   3. Demostration of lifesaving techniques

F. School-oriented activities
   1. Distribute "Schools Open, Drive Carefully" bumper stickers
   2. Assist school crossing guards
   3. Instruct children in safe street crossing

G. Operation Identification
   1. Assist public in marking their valuables
   2. Distribute decals for doors

H. Business and residential security checks

I. Public tours of the police department
   1. Demonstrate facilities and equipment
   2. Coffee and cookies and an informal interchange between police officers and citizens.

J. Neighborhood meetings
   1. Discuss problems common to the neighborhood and the police
   2. Formulate a plan with cooperation of citizens
   3. Implement the plan of action

K. Minority group relations
   1. Set up meetings with leaders of minority community
   2. Work with leaders on mutually agreed upon programs
   3. Implement a ride-along program

L. Bicycle Safety Program
   1. Inspect bicycles for safety at parks, playgrounds, and schools
   2. Distribute reflective safety materials for bicycles
   3. Demonstrate bicycle safety throughout the community

M. Sponsorship of little league teams

Answers

A. 1. Community service
   2. Community service
   3. Community relations
B. Community service
C. 1. Community relations
   2. Public or community relations
   3. Community service
D. Community relations

E. 1. Public relations
   2. Community service
   3. Community service
F. 1. Community service
   2. Community service
   3. Community service
G. 1. Community service
   2. Community service

H. Community service
I. 1. Public relations
    2. Community relations
J. 1. Community relations
    2. Community relations
    3. Community relations

K. 1. Community relations
    2. Community relations
    3. Community relations
L. Community service
    2. Community service
    3. Community service
M. Public relations

Discussion Questions

1. What community services are available in our community? Which are most important? Which might be frivolous? Are any necessary services *not* provided?

2. What types of crime prevention programs are used in our community?

3. What types of safety promotion programs are used in our community?

4. Which is the most important: public relations programs, community relations programs, or community service programs? Why?

5. Can you imagine a situation in which a police department placed so much emphasis on public relations that it had the opposite effect than intended, that is, the image of the police was lowered rather than raised?

6. Have you ever personally received service from a police officer? What were the circumstances? How would you evaluate the officer's performance? Have you ever needed a service which was not provided?

7. How might one event serve all three purposes: public relations, community service, and community-police relations?

References

Bent, A.E., and Rossum, R.A. *Police, criminal justice, and the community*. New York: Harper and Row, 1976.

Bishop, D.R., and Scheussler, T.J. "The National Crime Information Center's missing person file." *FBI law enforcement bulletin*. (August 1982): 20-24.

Brandstatter, A.F., and Hyman, A.A. *Fundamentals of law enforcement*. Beverly Hills, Cal.: Glencoe Press, 1971.

The challenge of crime in a free society. President's Commission on Law Enforcement and the Administration of Justice. Washington, D.C.: U.S. Government Printing Office, 1967.

Cohn, A.W., and Viano, E.C. *Police community relations: Images, roles, realities*. Philadelphia: J.B. Lippincott Company, 1976.

Duncan, J.T. *Citizen crime prevention tactics: A literature review and selected bibliography*. Washington, D.C.: U.S. Government Printing Office, 1981.

Garmire, B.L. ''The police role in an urban society.'' In *The police and the community,* edited by R.F. Steadman. Baltimore: Johns Hopkins University Press, 1972.

Levine, J.P.; Husheno, M.C.; and Palumbo, D.J. *Criminal justice: A public policy.* New York: Harcourt Brace Jovanovich, 1980.

McCreedy, K.R. *Theory and methods of police patrol.* Albany, N.Y.: Delmar Publishers, 1974.

More, H.W., Jr. *The American police.* Text and readings. Criminal Justice Series. St. Paul, Minn.: West Publishing Company, 1976.

The police. President's Commission on Law Enforcement and Administration of Justice. Task Force Report. Washington, D.C.: U.S. Government Printing Office, 1967.

Police and community relations . . . is a two-way street! New York: National Conference of Christians and Jews, 1969.

Radalet, L.A. *The police and the community.* 3d ed. Encino, Cal.: Glencoe Publishing Company, 1980.

Radalet, L.A. ''Who's in charge of law and order?'' In *Police-community relations: An anthology and bibliography,* edited by W.H. Hewitt and C.L. Newman. Mineola, N.Y.: Foundation Press, 1970.

Vandalism or art? The attitudes of the community may sometimes affect whether or not certain behavior is considered delinquent.

Juveniles

Shaping Our Future Generations

Do You Know . . .

■ How much discretionary power the police have when dealing with juveniles?

■ What procedural safeguards should be followed if detaining or arresting a juvenile?

■ What significance the *Gault* case has for the police officer dealing with a juvenile offender?

■ Whether juveniles can be fingerprinted or photographed?

■ What factors related to juvenile delinquency a police officer should learn to recognize?

■ What a school liaison program is and how effective some have been?

■ What kinds of police-community relations programs have been implemented to promote the safety and general welfare of juveniles?

■ What other services are frequently provided that involve juveniles?

> *The childhood shows the man,*
> *As morning shows the day.*
>
> —*Milton*

Introduction

Chapter 3 introduced you to the seriousness of the problem of juvenile delinquency. This chapter presents concepts related to how patrol officers or, in larger departments, officers assigned to the juvenile division deal with not only juvenile delinquents, but also law-abiding juveniles. The Constitution guarantees that all citizens be presumed innocent until proven guilty. This applies to juveniles as well. The majority of the juveniles in our country are not delinquents and do not deserve to be treated as such merely because they are underage. If good relations can be established between the police and our youth, everyone will benefit.

Enforcing the Laws

One of the most important aspects of the juvenile justice system is the initial contact with the law. Trojanowicz (1978, pp. 175–76) feels that:

> The intake and screening process is an important aspect of the juvenile justice system. When used properly, it can effectively curtail or interrupt much delinquent behavior before it becomes serious. The intake process can also stimulate community agencies to help parents to better understand their children's behavior and the measures needed to prevent further delinquent acts.
>
> If the child is released at intake and no further processing takes place, there should still be a follow-up after any referral to a community agency by either the police or the intake unit. Follow-up facilitates not only the rendering of services to the child, but also promotes closer cooperation between the agencies involved. . . . The police have a great deal of discretionary power, ranging all the way from the option of releasing the juvenile at initial contact in an unofficial manner to referring him to the juvenile court, which may result in detention.

Within this range are other options such as referring the juvenile to a community agency.

Whether a juvenile is actually arrested usually depends on a number of factors, the most important of which is how serious the offense is. Other factors that enter into the decision include (Trajanowicz, 1978, p. 419):

> . . . the appraised character of the youth, which in turn is based on such facts as his prior police record, age, associations, attitude, family situation, the conduct of his parents, and the attitude of other community institutions such

as his school. The external community may exert pressure on the police department which may affect the disposition of any case. Here attitudes of the press and the public, the status of the complainant or victim, the status of the offender, and the conditions which prevail in the available referral agencies (the length of the waiting list, the willingness of the social agencies to accept police referrals) are all of consequence. Internal police department pressure such as attitudes of co-workers and supervisors and the personal experience of the officer may also play an important part in determining the outcome of any officially detected delinquent offense. These factors also indirectly determine the officially recorded police and court delinquency rates.

The amount of discretion available to police officers and the lack of criteria by which to make a decision were noted several years ago by the President's Commission on Law Enforcement and Administration of Justice, Task Force on Juvenile Delinquency and Youth Crime, when it stated (1967, p. 14):

> In sum, the range of police dispositions is considerable, and the criteria for selection of a disposition are seldom set forth, explicitly, ordered in priority, or regularly reviewed for administrative purposes. Inservice training designed to assist police in exercising their discretionary functions is unusual.

The police have a considerable amount of discretionary power when dealing with juveniles.

Detaining or Taking into Custody

If police officers determine that the offense is serious enough to warrant detention or that the juvenile is a threat to himself or the general public, they should exercise certain safeguards.

In most jurisdictions it is mandatory that the parents of a juvenile who is detained be notified as soon as possible and that questioning of the juvenile be delayed until the parents are present.

In addition to notifying the parents, police officers are also required to notify juveniles of their rights, the direct result of the *Gault* decision.

If a juvenile is detained or taken into custody the parents should be notified. In addition, as a result of the Gault *decision, the juvenile must be told of his rights.*

After questioning the juvenile, the police officers must determine whether the juvenile should be referred to the court or returned to his parents. Usually, if the offense is relatively minor, the juvenile's attitude and past record are good, and the parents are willing to provide adequate supervision and guidance, the juvenile will be returned to his parents with no further legal action taken.

If the offense is judged to be serious, if the youth has a past record of criminal activity, or if the parents appear unconcerned or nonsupportive of the police's position, the juveniles may be taken to a detention facility and may be referred to the court for a hearing. In such instances all records related to the case should be provided to the judge.

Fingerprinting and Photographing

Whether juveniles should be fingerprinted or photographed is an important issue. Some states allow one or the other, but not both. Questions are often raised as to who should have access to these records and for how long. Some states have laws that require the police to purge all juvenile records when the youngster reaches age eighteen.

Some states prohibit fingerprinting or photographing of juveniles. Others permit fingerprinting and photographing, but the records are kept by the department and not released to any other agency.

Reducing Juvenile Delinquency

Traditionally the police officer's role was clearly defined: arrest lawbreakers and preserve the peace. Although historically the police have been viewed as punitive

Police seek to educate children and promote cooperation.

and authoritarian, this view is changing. Rather than simply apprehending and punishing offenders, police officers now also seek to educate and to promote prevention of crime. Modern approaches to juvenile delinquency take several forms, but all have in common a goal of preventing juvenile delinquency.

Knowledge of Indicators of Potential for Delinquent Behavior by Juveniles

Certain factors may indicate that a youngster has the potential for or actually is involved in delinquent behavior. Police should learn to recognize these factors and take appropriate actions, considering community resources and school and police department policies.

Police officers are in a unique position to help juveniles because they are usually the first persons of authority to confront the juvenile offender during or following a delinquent act. Additionally, police officers are often familiar with the youngsters in their patrol area whose behavior marks them as potential delinquents, and they have the authority to reprimand, release, or refer youngsters to court.

> *The police officer can learn to recognize the environmental and personal factors contributing to or indicative of delinquency.*

Environmental factors potentially contributing to delinquency include broken homes, criminal parents, incompetent parents, erratic discipline, economic insecurity, impoverished neighborhoods, transient populations, and racial and other tensions.

Personal factors or behavior indicating potential delinquency include unsociability, cheating, lying, fighting, temper tantrums, anxiety, guilt feelings, hostility and aggression, laziness, truancy, running away from home, and a rebellious attitude.

The environmental and personal factors may be complicated by misuses of alcohol, narcotics and drugs, by economic factors, by physical disabilities, by sexual problems, or by numerous other factors. The result is frequently youths who show overwelming symptoms of weakness and inadequacy. They cannot accept life as it is, cannot conform, cannot get along, cannot compete, or cannot exercise self-control.

The sooner a police officer recognizes such youngsters and attempts to work with them, the greater the chance that the juveniles will not become delinquents.

Police-School Liaison Programs

Prevention programs in juvenile delinquency began in the early twentieth century when a wave of social reform swept through the western world. The earliest documented program, established in 1905 in Portland, Oregon, was designed to protect young girls. In 1918 New York City assigned ''welfare officers'' to each precinct, the beginning of a program which expanded into a comprehensive community program called "The Juvenile Aid Bureau," a forerunner of the more modern police-school liaison programs.

Although police participate in many different types of school programs, such programs do not exist in a large number of police jurisdictions. Where they do exist, they have evolved gradually in response to community requests. Formal programs frequently result from surveys conducted by forward-looking police departments.

The need for specialized training of juvenile officers in understanding children and their problems has also been recognized. The importance of special training for officers appointed to juvenile units and the need for close police-school relationships is supported by the Flint Michigan Program, the first publicized, comprehensive, formalized police-school liaison effort in the United States (Morrison, 1968, p. 62). Cooperatively developed between 1958 and 1960 by school, police, court, social agency, and community personnel interested in decreasing juvenile delinquency in Flint, the program has been a model for many police-school programs.

The police officer (called police counselor) is assigned to a junior or senior high school and is also responsible for the feeder elementary school(s). The officer does not wear a uniform and is not responsible for enforcing school rules and regulations; rather, he deals with predelinquent or actual delinquent behavior problems around the school, keeps records of student contacts, and uses this information for counseling the students.

A counseling team composed of a dean of counseling, dean of students, visiting teacher, police counselor, and nurse counselor may recommend that a student be referred to other individuals or agencies for help. The functions of the counseling team include the following (Flint Public Schools, 1965, p. 2):

- Identifying pupils with specific problems.
- Collecting, studying, and evaluating data.
- Relating and interpreting information.
- Planning a course of action.
- Serving as resource person in the area of specialization.
- Accepting responsibility for analysis and treatment in the area of specialization.
- Cooperating and communicating with other team members, school personnel, and outside agencies.
- Conducting in-service education for staff, parents, and community agencies.
- Making progress reports when specific responsibilities have been assigned.

Before this program, one in every thirty-six children in a certain area of Flint were involved in delinquency. One year later the ratio had dropped to one in every two hundred eighty (Brandstatter and Brennan, 1967, p. 200). The Flint Program was so successful that it was instituted as a permanent part of the police department's public service.

Another program which has achieved nationwide prominence is the Tucson Arizona Police Department School Resource Officer Program whose purpose statement you read earlier. Patterned after the Flint Program, the Tucson Program has made several modifications, the most noticeable and perhaps most important being that the officer wears full police uniform. The rationale for this change is that students learn to see that the uniformed police officer's primary function is to help. This fosters the traditional ''beat cop'' personalized approach where the police officer was a familiar and welcome part of a neighborhood, knowledgeable of the residents and their problems. Like the Flint Program, the Tucson Program uses the team approach, but the police officer makes the final decision about referrals (*School Resource Manual*).

Almost all programs in the United States today started with placement of an officer in a junior high school who was also responsible for the feeder elementary school(s). Most police-school liaison programs are similar to the Flint and Tucson Programs.

> A police-school liaison program places a police officer within a school as a cooperative effort of the schools and the law enforcement agencies to develop an understanding of law enforcement functions and to prevent juvenile delinquency and crime.

Although school administrators are usually enthusiastic about police-school liaison programs and believe that programs help to reduce delinquency, many citizen groups are strongly opposed to such programs. The Southern Chapter of the Arizona Civil Liberties Union (1966) has listed eight objections to the police-school liaison program:

1. The invasion of the privacy of the home.
2. The indiscriminate interrogation of students who are neither suspects nor offenders concerning offenses committed both inside and outside the school precincts, related and unrelated to school activities.
3. The interrogation of students without the supervision or presence of school authorities or parents.
4. The establishment of a network of informers among junioir high and elementary students.
5. The use of police officers, rather than trained school personnel, as disciplinarians.
6. The use of unprotected minors as a source for data regarding the activities and opinions of parents, neighbors, and other adults in the community.
7. The harassment of juveniles with a history of delinquency, through continual surveillance and frequent questioning, a harassment which has led to dropouts.
8. The misuse of the educational process for police purposes.

Objections have also been raised by individuals within law enforcement (Shephard and James, 1967, pp. 2–3):

1. The primary objective of police-school liaison programs is to change the attitudes of the students toward police. It is believed that even highly trained and skilled professionals may not be effective in changing attitudes. Further, since attitudes can be positive or negative, the end results of such efforts by police may be self-defeating.

2. Few officers have the training or experience to prevent delinquency in a school setting.

3. These programs take manpower from regular police efforts. There is a serious shortage of police manpower in the cities, and police departments can ill afford to assign officers to a police-school program.

4. Possible legal complications that result from the school authorities, who stand in *loco parentis* (in place of the parents) to the child, delegating the right to inspect and interrogate students in the school.

5. The possibility that some stigma might be attached to the school that is chosen for an experimental program.

6. The possibility that the police officer may be used as a school disciplinarian.

These objections were raised over a decade ago, and many of them have since been eliminated by changes in the program. The ultimate decision as to whether such programs will be implemented rests with the citizens of each community, for without their support, there is little chance of success. Where community support has existed, however, such programs have made a significant impact not only on prevention of juvenile delinquency but also on attitudes toward police officers and our system of law enforcement.

Programs To Promote Safety and General Welfare

In addition to programs which seek citizen cooperation in reducing juvenile delinquency, many police departments have implemented community service programs to provide juveniles with information and guidance in protecting their general safety and welfare.

Community service programs emphasize drug abuse prevention, bike safety, or general safety.

Drug Abuse Prevention

Drug abuse prevention is a responsibility of local law enforcement agencies. They have attacked the problem of drug abuse and narcotics by attempting to apprehend the illegal distributor, by educating and seeking voluntary compliance by industries producing and distributing narcotics and dangerous drugs, and be educating the public on the hazards of drugs and narcotics.

Through various programs with civic groups and the schools, law enforcement officers can make citizens aware of the hazards of narcotics and dangerous drugs. By presenting factual information through pamphlets, speeches, films, and displays to a variety of organizations, especially the schools, law enforcement personnel may heighten the local citizen's concern and install cooperation in combatting the problem of drug abuse in the community.

Bike Safety

Bike safety programs are found throughout the country. The Minnesota Highway Department, for example, has a "talking" bike that presents safety rules to the children through a tape-recorded message.

Mike the Talking Bike has all the necessary safety features for a bike to be used in traffic: reflectors on the spokes and the sidewalls of the tires are a luminous white, the new pedals reflect, and a tall yellow flag is on the rear. Throughout the presentation the children are reminded to be visible when riding bicycles, to ride on the proper side of the road, and to stop and yield the right-of-away before crossing streets. They are cautioned always to be careful—to watch for traffic and to drive defensively. Even if the bike rider is in the right, he usually is the loser if an accident occurs.

An earlier version of the Minnesota Highway Patrol talking bike was Spike, an old battered bike that told the children all the bad things he did to get into trouble. He also told them about the little boy who was riding him and was killed when he was hit by a car. A combination of these two bikes might make a very effective presentation for youngsters.

Other bike safety programs include police officers going into grade schools, conducting safety inspections of the children's bicycles, licensing them, and sponsoring bike rodeos which concentrate on both knowledge about bike safety and demonstration of safe bike-riding skills.

General Safety

Some community service programs emphasize general safety and welfare. An example of one such program is the Safety City program in Eden Prairie, Minnesota.

Safety City is a scaled-down city with houses, businesses, church, school, park, movie theater, fire station, and police station. Twice a year Safety City is set up for one week to give area school children ages five to nine a controlled, realistic environment in which to learn or review community safety rules. The cost of materials and labor is furnished by Homart Company, a local firm. Staffing consists of public safety officers, community service officers, reserves, and Homart employees. The program is administered by the Shopping Center and Juvenile Division of the Eden Prairie Crime Prevention Unit.

Safety City.

The purpose of Safety City is to teach area children how to be safe within their own environment. In addition to the buildings, this miniature city includes streets, sidewalks, stop signs, street semaphores, and a railroad crossing, each constructed so it is easily recognizable to children.

The children enter the gates of Safety City and follow a specific route. They can be led by a community service officer, but a public safety officer is in Safety City at all times to handle difficult questions and to oversee the entire operation. The city has two public safety officers, four community service officers or reserves, and one or two firefighters. The community service officers lead groups and miniclasses at the individual stops. One public safety officer from the patrol unit conducts the pedestrian and bike safety classes. He takes individual children through a series of learning exercises to increase their skills in pedestrian and bicycle safety, specifically sidewalks, sign knowledge, stoplights, railroad tracks, and the use of school crossings.

At the first stop, the city park, safety in the park is explained. An animated figure of a stranger handing out candy teaches children what to do in such situations, that is, the do's and don'ts with strangers. Safety on playground apparatus is also briefly explained. Beginning with this stop and continuing throughout the tour, the merits of vandalism prevention are explained.

The next stop is a nondenominational church used to demonstrate that when crisis erupts in the family, there is always a place to seek help. This counseling help can also be found in police, school, and county agencies. As the tour proceeds through the first intersection, children learn to cross a semaphore-controlled intersection safely.

The police station (public safety building) is the next stop on the tour. Here children learn the purpose of police and laws, who police officers are, and what they do. This stop also includes a reminder to all children that they should know their telephone number and address. The whens and hows of calling on the telephone are included. A crime prevention display in the rear of the public safety building is geared to the younger set and includes such things as bicycle theft prevention.

The next stop on the tour is the retail shopping center where children are told the impact of shoplifting and its effect on their lives. The tour is then assisted by a patrol officer who instructs the children in how to cross the railroad tracks safely. After crossing the tracks, the partrol officer instructs the children in pedestrian safety. The children then use the school crossing aided by the school patrol.

The next stop is the fire department where a firefighter explains to the children fire prevention and what to do in case of a fire. Behind the fire station is a display on fire prevention set up by the Fire Prevention Bureau.

Next the children pass a house and are reminded that they can call the police from their homes when they are frightened or when an accident occurs. They are also instructed on the proper respect for other people's property.

The last stop in Safety City is the movie theater where short crime prevention films are shown—one movie per group, less than five minutes each. Upon leaving the gates of Safety City, each child receives a ''Safety City Certificate'' showing that he or she has visited Safety City.

Other Services for Juveniles

In addition to instituting programs to reduce juvenile delinquency, the police are also responsible for some specific services involving children.

> *Other services involving children include helping to locate missing or runaway children, conducting fingerprinting progams, and investigating reports on neglected or abused children.*

Missing Children

A missing child is an extremely traumatic experience for parents. In contrast, police officers know that the vast majority of missing children show up safe and well. Frequently they have stopped at a friend's home and have forgotten about the time. Despite the fact that most missing children do show up or are found, police officers must not be casual about the situation. It is a critical circumstance in the eyes of the parents.

A complete description of the child and the clothing worn should be obtained, as should a recent picture. Details regarding where the child was last seen and favorite hideaways should also be obtained.

Sometimes it is necessary to call in additional help, for example, if a child wandered off into a forest. Local Boy Scout troops can sometimes be called on to assist in such situations. Dogs may also be of help.

Time is an important factor because the more time that elapses, the more likely it is that the child will wander farther away or come to harm.

On October 12, 1982, President Reagan signed into law the Missing Children Act, requiring the attorney general to: ''Acquire, collect and preserve any information which would assist in the location of any missing person (including children . . .) and provide confirmation as to any entry (into FBI records) for such a person to the parent, legal guardian or next of kin. . . .'' What this means, in effect, is that parents, legal guardians, or the next of kin may have access to the information in the FBI National Crime Information Center's (NCIC) Missing Person File.

The law does not, however, require that the FBI investigate the case. It can undertake a preliminary inquiry if an indication exists that a crime has been committed and the child has been transported out of the state.

Because of this law, it is even more important that children be fingerprinted. Many schools have instituted such a program in conjunction with the local police department.

Runaway Children

The same procedures used to search for a missing child might be used to locate a runaway child. Here much depends on the child's age and reason for running away. If the child is a teenager with good reasons for running away, it may be futile to conduct a search.

Runaway children who are found should not automatically be returned to their homes. An investigation should be conducted to see if conditions there are such that they led to the youth leaving. It may be that the youth would be better off in a foster home or even staying with friends for a time.

Neglected or Abused Children

Police are sometimes called upon to investigate reports of neglected or abused children. Eldefonso (1983, p.12) notes that: ''Most jurisdictions define as a crime parental abuse or neglect of children, but vary in their criteria for defining what constitutes abuse or neglect. In general, some degree of failure to feed and clothe a child is usually defined as a crime, along with some degree of failure to provide adequate shelter. Most jurisdictions establish discretionary or judgmental statutes with respect to the degree of cleanliness required in homes for children.'' He lists five conditions that indicate, separately or collectively, the need for action (p. 388):

- Lack of physical care and protection
- Lack of supervision, guidance, and discipline

- Exploitation
- Lack of protection from degrading conditions
- Abuse and fear of physical cruelty

Eldefonso (p. 392) suggest that: "The line between neglect and abuse is sometimes difficult to draw, but the two can generally be distinguished in the following way: neglectful parents usually do not consciously intend to harm their children, but through failure to meet children's health, nutritional, comfort and emotional needs, they expose their children to severe risk."

When a law enforcement agency receives a report of child neglect or abuse it may investigate on its own or with personnel from the Welfare Department. No matter what the source of the report or who does the investigating, the primary responsibility of those investigating is the welfare of the child. Any child who appears to be in danger should be removed to protective custody.

Summary

When dealing with juveniles, the police have a great deal of discretionary power, ranging from the option of releasing the juvenile at initial contact in an unofficial manner to referring him to the juvenile court, which may result in detention. If a juvenile is detained or taken into custody the parents should be notified. In addition, as a result of the *Gault* decision, the juvenile must be told of his rights. An additional precaution is that in some states, fingerprinting or photographing juveniles is prohibited.

One means to deter juvenile delinquency is through a police-school liaison program. Such programs place a police officer in a school as a cooperative effort of the schools and the law enforcement agencies to develop an understanding of law enforcement functions and to prevent juvenile delinquency and crime.

Community service programs may emphasize drug abuse prevention, bike saftey, or general safety, such as the Safety City program.

In addition, police are often responsible for providing other services involving children, including helping to locate missing or runaway children, conducting fingerprinting programs, and investigating reports of neglected or abused children.

Application

There is much controversy today regarding the possession of marijuana by juveniles and whether this type of offense ought to be handled through a diversionary program or by the juvenile court of jurisdiction.

Contact either the local police department or the juvenile court in your jurisdiction to see how policies may coincide or conflict in handling this type of offense. Also find out if there is a difference in policy regarding the possession of marijuana for one's own personal use and the possession of marijuana for sale.

Answers

Answers will vary depending on the laws prevailing in individual communities.

Discussion Questions

1. What is the policy in our police department regarding photographing and fingerprinting juveniles?
2. Should police officers have as much discretionary power as they have with juveniles? Why or why not?
1. Does our community have a police-school liaison program? If so, how effective does it seem to be? How popular does it seem to be?
4. What other community relations programs are offered by our police department for juveniles?
5. What community services do our police officers provide?
6. Does our police department have a separate juvenile division or do police officers have the responsibility for dealing with juveniles?

References

Arizona Civil Liberties Union, Southern Chapter, Tucson, Arizona. Release dated June 2, 1966 (mimeographed).

Brandstatter, A.F., and Brennan, J.J. "Prevention through the police." In *Delinquency prevention*, edited by W.E. Amos and C.F. Wellford. Englewood Cliffs, N.J.: Prentice-Hall, 1967.

Davis, S.M. *Rights of juveniles: The juvenile justice system*. 2d ed. New York: Clark Boardman Company, Ltd., 1980.

Eldefonson, E. *Law enforcement and the youthful offender*. 4th ed. New York: John Wiley and Sons, 1983.

Finckenauer, J.O. *Juvenile delinquency and corrections: The gap between theory and practice*. Orlando, Fla.: Academic Press, 1984.

Flint public schools regional counseling teams, October 1965 (mimeographed). Haskell, M.R., and Yablonsky, L. *Crime and delinquency*. Chicago: Rand-McNally, 1970.

"Missing children act." *Minnesota sheriff* (Spring 1984): 21-23.

Morrison, J. "The controversial police-school liaison programs." *Police* (November-December 1968): 60-64.

Murrell, M.E., and Lester, D. *Introduction to juvenile delinquency*. New York: McMillian Publishing Company, Inc., 1981.

President's Commission on Law Enforcement and the Administration of Justice. *The challenge of crime in a free society*. Washington, D.C.: U.S. Government Printing Office, 1967.

Radelet, L.A. "Who's in charge of law and order?" In *Police-community relations: An anthology and bibliography,* edited by W.H. Hewitt and C.L. Newman. Mineola, N.Y.: Foundation Press, 1970.

School resource manual. Adopted by Tucson District #1 School Board, June 21, 1966. Revised and accepted February 21, 1967.

Shephard, G.H., and James, J. "Police—Do they belong in schools?" *American education* (September 1967): 2-3.

Tappan, P. *Juvenile delinquency.* 3d ed. New York: McGraw-Hill, 1969.

Trojanowicz, R.C. *Juvenile delinquency: Concepts and controls.* Englewood Cliffs, N.J.: Prentice-Hall, Inc., 1978.

U.S. Department of Justice, Law Enforcement Assistance Administration, National Criminal Justice Information and Statistics Service. *Children in custody.* (Advance Report on the Juvenile Detention and Correctional Facility Census of 1972-1973), May 1975.

FOUR

In Search of Justice

The Police Officer and the Criminal Justice System

According to Waldron: "Our system of criminal justice has three interrelated components staffed by more than 1.0 million people: *The law enforcement community*, . . . the *judicial community* . . . and the *corrections community*. . . . Each of these components and its respective personnel in turn contributes to the criminal justice *process*, which is a well-defined legal continuum through which each offender may pass from detection and investigation of the criminal act; to arrest and accusation; to trial, conviction, sentencing, and possible incarceration; to eventual release."*

Having looked at the day-to-day operations in which law enforcement officers become involved, it is time to turn attention to their importance within the criminal justice system. All law enforcement officers must understand the constitutional safeguards provided by the Constitution and the Bill of Rights and also the limitations they impose (Chapter 13). Police officers must be thoroughly familiar with what constitutes a lawful arrest and a lawful search (Chapter 14). The role officers play in cooperation with the judiciary and corrections will be examined in Section Five.

---

*Ronald J. Waldron, *The Criminal Justice System, An Introduction*. 3rd ed. (Boston: Houghton Mifflin Company, 1984), p. 57.

The Supreme Court Building in Washington, D.C. The
Constitution guarantees many rights and liberties to
the people of the United States.

Equal Justice Under the Law

Civil Rights and Civil Liberties

Do You Know . . .

- What civil rights and civil liberties are?

- What contributions the Magna Carta made to our Constitution and our system of justice?

- What the Declaration of Independence says about civil rights and civil liberties?

- What the basic instrument of government and the supreme law of the land is?

- What the Bill of Rights is?

- What specific rights are guaranteed by the First, Second, Fourth, Fifth, Sixth, Eighth, and Fourteenth Amendments?

- What four guarantees are included in due process?

- What the difference is between the Fifth and the Fourteenth Amendments?

- Where police get their power and authority and what restrictions are placed on this power and authority?

- When changes in our institutions and statutes are necessary?

> *The welfare of the people is the chief law.*
>
> —Cicero

Introduction

My country 'tis of thee, sweet land of liberty . . .
From every mountain side, let freedom ring.

U.S. Supreme Court Censures Government on Illegal Wiretap

One nation, under God, with liberty and justice for all.

Discrimination Claimed in Job Firing

We hold these truths to be self-evident: that all men are endowed by their creator with certain unalienable rights; that among these are life, liberty and the pursuit of happiness.

Police Embarrassed as a Result of False Arrest

Between the idea and the reality . . . falls the shadow . . .

T.S. Eliot

We are surrounded by symbols of freedom, liberty, and justice. The Statue of Liberty, a gift from France to celebrate the central theme in American development, our money, our coins, our stamps, our patriotic songs, our oaths of office, all echo our belief in freedom, liberty, and justice. Yet sometimes what we believe does not match reality. We are still striving to achieve civil rights and civil liberties for all Americans. **Civil rights** are those claims which the citizen has to the affirmative assistance of government. **Civil liberties** are an individual's immunity from governmental oppression.

> Civil rights are those claims which the citizen has to the affirmative assistance of government. Civil liberties are an individual's immunity from governmental oppression.

Although we have not completely achieved our ideals of freedom, liberty, and justice for all, we are far ahead of other countries and have come a long way since the founding of the United States. Much of our progress can be traced to developments in England, as was seen in Chapter 1. Of special significance is the historic Magna Carta.

The Magna Carta

Our modern system of justice owes much to the Magna Carta, a decisive document in the development of constitutional government in England.

The Magna Carta contained sixty-three articles, most requiring the king to uphold feudal law. The articles initially benefited only the barons and other members of the feudal class, but they later became important to all people. Some articles granted the church freedom from royal interference, and a few guaranteed the rights of the rising middle class. Ordinary freemen and peasants, although making up the great majority of England's population, were hardly mentioned in the charter.

The charter required the king to seek the advice and consent of the barons on all matters important to the kingdom, including taxation. Later such articles supported the argument that no law should be made nor tax raised without the consent of England's Parliament. Article 13 restored local control to cities and villages, a fundamental principle of American law enforcement.

Other articles of the Magna Carta became foundations for modern justice. One article, for example, required that no freeman should be imprisoned, deprived of property, sent out of the country, or destroyed except by the lawful judgment of his peers or by the law of the land. The concept of due process of law, including trial by jury, developed from this article.

During the 1500s, members of Parliament viewed the charter as a constitutional check on royal power and cited it as legal support for the argument that there could be no laws or taxation without the consent of Parliament. They also used the charter to demand guarantees of trial by jury, safeguards against unfair imprisonment, and other rights.

In the 1700s, colonists carried these English ideals regarding legal and political rights to America where they eventually became part of the framework of the United States Constitution.

> The Magna Carta, a precedent for democratic government and individual rights, laid the foundation for:
>
> - Requiring rulers to uphold the law.
> - Forbidding taxation without representation.
> - Requiring due process of law, including trial by jury.
> - Providing safeguards against unfair imprisonment.

The Quest for Civil Rights and Civil Liberties in the United States

The Europeans' original immigration to the new world was heavily motivated by a desire to escape the religious, economic, political, and social repressions of traditional European society. North America was seen as a land where individuals could get a new start, free to make of themselves what they chose.

Sometimes, however, reality did not fully coincide with the **American creed** of individual freedom, as seen in the treatment of the American Indian, the importation of slaves, the establishment of state churches, and the repressiveness involved in episodes such as the Salem witchcraft trials. Nevertheless, the spirit of liberty and justice remained strong. As noted by Gunnar Myrdal (1944): the American creed is the national conscience; a body of beliefs about equality, liberty, and justice which most Americans believe in, in spite of the fact that America has, and always has had, multiple wrongs.

In the 1760s the British began taking away rights which Americans had come to feel were naturally theirs, and the American Revolution resulted. In effect, the United States was born out of a desire for—indeed, a demand for—civil rights and civil liberties.

Civil rights and civil liberties are recurring themes in America's development. Our initial institutions reflected an intense concern for the individual human spirit. Our founding fathers showed strong commitments to postively guarantee those rights which Americans had fought and died to protect in the American Revolution. These values were forcefully stated in our most basic document: The Declaration of Independence.

The Declaration of Independence

The Declaration of Independence is not only a statement of grievances against England, but is also a statement of alternative basic premises underlying man's freedom. As Thomas Jefferson phrased it in the Declaration, the United States was demanding ''the separate and equal station to which the laws of nature and of nature's God entitle them.'' In powerful rhetoric, Jefferson asserted:

> We hold these truths to be self-evident: —That all men are created equal; that they are endowed by their Creator with certain unalienable rights; that among these are life, liberty, and the pursuit of happiness. That, to secure these rights, governments are instituted among men, deriving their just powers from the consent of the governed; that, whenever any form of government becomes destructive of these ends, it is the right of the people to alter or to abolish it, and to institute new government.

In other words, the purpose of government is to secure the people's unalienable rights, including life, liberty, and happiness—on an equal basis, since ''all men are created equal.''

> *The Declaration of Independence asserts that all men are created equal and are entitled to the unalienable rights of life, liberty, and the pursuit of happiness. It further asserts that governments are instituted by and derive their power from the governed.*

The Declaration, however, was principally a statement of ideals and intentions; its importance, therefore, is more as a philosophy than as a concrete governing mechanism. The Constitution afforded the mechanism for achieving the goals of the Declaration. The Declaration and the Constitution are two parts of one whole, one breaking away from old government and calling for a new one, and the other creating that government, a carefully developed mechanism for the achievement of the principles contained in the Declaration.

The United States Constitution

The **Constitution** was drafted by the Constitutional Convention of 1787 and, following its ratification by conventions in two-thirds of the states, became effective in 1789. It is the basic instrument of government and the supreme law of the United States.

The Constitution states that the legislative, executive, and judicial departments of government should be separated as far as is practicable, and that their respective powers should be exercised by different men or groups of men. The legislature makes the laws, the executive branch, of which law enforcement is a part, enforces the laws, and the judicial branch determines when laws have been violated. The United States Constitution does not require that the three branches of government be separated on the state level, but all state constitutions require it in varying degrees.

> *The Constitution is the basic instrument of government and the supreme law of the United States.*

The Constitution is divided into seven major articles:

- Article I—Sets forth the structure and functions of Congress.
- Article II—Establishes the executive branch of government.
- Article III— Delineates the judicial power of the United States Supreme Court and other courts that Congress may establish.
- Article IV—Describes the duties of the states to the federal government and to each other.
- Article V—Provides for amendments to the Constitution and describes the procedures which must be followed.
- Article VI—Provides for the taking of the oath of office for all federal and state legislative, executive, and judicial officers. It also contains the Supremacy Clause which provides that the Constitution, laws, and treaties of the United States are the supreme law of the land and that all states are bound by them.
- Article VII—Deals primarily with the method of ratification of the Constitution which was completed in 1789.

When the first Congress of the United States convened on March 4, 1789, it had before it 103 amendments to the Constitution submitted by the states, forty-two amendments proposed by minority groups within the states, and bills of rights submitted by two states. After deliberating on these proposed amendments, Congress reduced them to twelve to submit to the states for ratification. Two failed to be ratified; the others became the first ten amendments. They went into effect on December 15, 1791, and are known as the Bills of Rights.

The Bills of Rights

The Constitution, adopted in 1789, organized the government of the new nation, but it contained very few personal guarantees, and, consequently, some states refused to ratify it without a specific bill of rights. In 1791 the ten amendments, with personal guarantees included, came into effect. They became known as the **Bill of Rights,** a fundamental document describing the liberties of the people and forbidding the government to violate these rights.

> *The Bill of Rights protect a person's right to "life, liberty, and the pursuit of happiness." It forbids the government to violate these rights.*

Man is considered to have inborn rights of which a government may not deprive him. Government has only limited powers which are delegated by the people.

Initially the Bill of Rights applied only to the federal government. It was not until the Fourteenth Amendment was adopted that it became possible for the United States and Congress to end state actions which violated the human rights of its citizens, as will be discussed shortly.

Individual constitutional rights are clearly specified in each amendment. Some are of more relevance to individuals in law enforcement than others. Of special importance are the First, Second, Fourth, Fifth, Sixth, Eighth, and Fourteenth Amendments.

The First Amendment

Congress shall make no law respecting an establishment of religion, or prohibiting the free exercise thereof; or abridging the freedom of speech or of the press; or the right of the people peaceably to assemble and to petition the government for a redress of grievances.

The First Amendment guarantees:

- *Freedom of religion.*
- *Freedom of speech.*
- *Freedom of the press.*
- *Freedom of peaceable assembly.*
- *Freedom of petition.*

Freedom of Religion.   Two guarantees of religious freedom are provided: (1) No law may be enacted which establishes an official church that all Americans must accept and support, or to whose tenets all must subscribe, or that favors one church over another, and (2) no law is constitutional which prohibits the free exercise of religion. In short, citizens are guaranteed freedom to worship as they see fit.

The First Amendment clearly separates church and state and requires that the government be neutral on religious matters, favoring no religion above another. The first guarantee of this amendment, called the Establishment Clause, was made applicable to the states in *Cantwell v. Connecticut* (1940) and *Murdock v. Pennsylvania* (1943). The Establishment Clause is governed by the following principles (Lewis and Peoples, 1978, p. 1093):

- A state law that protects a valid secular interest is not invalid simply because it also incidentally benefits one or more (or all) religions—the "incidental benefit" rule.

- The government need not be hostile to religious institutions, only neutral, and the required neutrality need not result in a callous indifference to religion—the "government neutrality" rule.

- The government may "accommodate" religion as long as the end result does not excessively entangle government in the affairs of religion—the "excessive entanglement" rule.

- Religious organizations may use the civil courts to decide disputes.

The second guarantee of the First Amendment is called the Free Exercise Clause and is very closely related to the freedom of speech portion of the First Amendment. Important cases related to this law are as follows (Pritchett, 1977, p. 391):

- *Pierce v. Society of Sisters* (1925) struck down an Oregon law requiring all children to attend only public schools for the first eight grades.

- *Lovell v. Griffin,* (1938) protected the right of Jehovah's Witnesses to sell the sect's literature door to door without a permit, on free press grounds.

- *Cantwell v. Connecticut* (1940) held that a state statute requiring approval of a county official for any person to solicit from house to house for religious or philanthropic causes amounted to "a censorship" of religion.

- *Murdock v. Pennsylvania* (1943) ruled that municipal license fees on transient merchants or book agents could not be applied to Jehovah's Witnesses who went door to door offering religious tracts for sale.

- *Niemotko v. Maryland* (1951) reversed the conviction of some Jehovah's Witnesses who had been arrested for making speeches in a public park without a permit.

- *Kunz v. New York* (1951) invalidated a New York ordinance requiring a police permit for public worship meetings on city streets.

Freedom of Speech.   The Supreme Court has ruled that the protections afforded by the First Amendment do not extend to all forms of expression. Highly inflammatory remarks spoken to a crowd, which advocate violence and clearly threaten the peace and safety of the community, or present a "clear and present danger" to the continued existence of the government are not protected.

Schneck v. United States (1919) established the "clear and present danger" doctrine and serves as a guide to the constitutionality of government restrictions on free speech (and free press). In this case the Court held that: "The most stringent protection of free speech would not protect a man in falsely shouting fire in a theatre causing a panic. . . . The question in every case is whether the words are used in such circumstances and are of such a nature as to create a clear and present danger that they will bring about the substantive evils that Congress has a right to prevent."

Chaplinsky v. New Hampshire (1942) also established that use of "fighting words" likely to cause violence will not be tolerated. The Court ruled in this case that the states can ban the use of those "personally abusive epithets which, when addressed to the ordinary citizen, are, as a matter of common knowledge, inherently likely to provide violent reaction" (Lewis and Peoples, 1978, p. 1074).

The ban on "fighting words" and words presenting a "clear and present danger" is counterbalanced by the concept of "pure speech," a theory created by the Supreme Court. Pure speech is speech without any accompanying action. In *Watts v. United States* (1969) the Court reversed the conviction of a defendant who told a discussion group that he was not going to report for military induction and that: "If they ever make me carry a rifle, the first man I want to get in my sights is L.B.J." Watts was originally convicted under the federal law against knowingly and willfully threatening the president. When it was proved that Watts had no real intention of killing the president, the Court held Watts was exercising his right to free speech and that his statement was "political hyperbole" rather than a true threat. Another example of pure speech is the Americanism "Kill the umpire," heard throughout the country during the baseball season.

Unlike pure speech, a second type of speech called "speech plus" is not protected by the First Amendment. An example of speech plus is the action taken by people in a labor strike picket line. If the striking employees physically prevent other people from entering or leaving a commercial building, the police may be called upon to assure that those who wish to enter or exit the building are allowed to do so.

Courts have also recognized that "symbolic speech," involving tangible forms of expression such as wearing buttons or clothing with political slogans or displaying a sign or a flag, is protected by the First Amendment.

Tinker v. Des Moines School District (1969) upheld the right of an individual to wear a black armband as an antiwar emblem. *Stromberg v. California* (1931) held the burning of a red flag as symbolic opposition to organized government to be an activity protected under the First Amendment. In contrast, *United States v. O'Brien* (1968) held that burning a draft card in protest of the Vietnam War violated a constitutional statute and was not permissible. The Court reasoned here that the government had a substantial interest unrelated to the free speech issue and that this issue far outweighed the defendant's right to freedom of speech. As noted by Klein (1980, p. 131): "The relative weights of the individual's constitutional rights are thus placed theoretically on a scale of values. The right which the Supreme Court holds to be the most weighty at a given time becomes the law of the land."

Finally, the courts have frequently condemned censorship by requirement of official approval or a license in advance of speaking. While citizens are free to make speeches on the public streets, they may be prevented from doing so when they use a loud, raucous amplifier in a hospital zone, or when the location chosen for the address is likely to interfere with traffic. Thus, freedeom of speech is not an absolute.

Freedom of the Press.   The First Amendment also guarantees the right to express oneself by writing or publishing one's views. The founding fathers recognized the importance of a free interplay of ideas in a democratic society and sought to guarantee the right of all citizens to speak or publish their views, even if they were contrary to those of the government or the society as a whole. Accordingly, the First Amendment generally forbids censorship or other restraint upon speech or the printed word.

As with speech, freedom to write or publish is not an absolute right of expression. The sale of obscene or libelous printed materials is not protected. The Supreme Court has ruled, however, that public figures cannot sue for defamation unless the alleged libelous remarks were printed with knowledge of their falsity or a reckless disregard for the truth.

Broadcasting, including radio, television, and motion pictures, receives the protection of the free press guarantee and is subject to its limitations.

As Klein (1980, p. 141) notes: "The right of freedom of expression has come to a head-on collision with those proponents of pornographic literature, movies, and photos. The police are in a dilemma in enforcing statutes designed to inhibit or control this activity. . . . The Supreme Court has not been too helpful in offering precise guidelines as to what is constitutional and what is unconstitutional behavior." Several Supreme Court decisions have attempted to define obscenity.

Roth v. United States (1957) held that obscenity is not within the area of constitutionally protected freedom of speech or press and that the standard to be employed is "whether to the average person, applying contemporary community standards, the dominant theme of the material, taken as a whole, appeals to prurient interest, that is, having a tendency to excite lustful thoughts."

In *Memoirs v. Attorney General of Massachusetts* (1966) the Court stated that for material to be obscene it must be shown that (1) the dominant theme of the material taken as a whole appeals to a prurient interest in sex, (2) the material is patently offensive because it affronts contemporary standards for the description or representation of sexual matters, and (3) the material is utterly without redeeming social value.

Mishkin v. New York (1966) held that the First Amendment was not violated by a state criminal obscenity statute which covered only "hard-core pornography"—that definition being more stringent than the definition required by federal constitutional standards. The case of *Miller v. California* (1973) set forth the following guidleines to determine whether a particular material was obscene: (1) whether the average person, applying contemporary community standards, would find the work, taken as a whole, as appealing to prurient interests; (2) whether the work depicted or described, in a patently offensive way, sexual conduct specifically prohibited by the applicable state law; and (3) whether the work, taken as a whole, lacked serious literary, artistic, political, or scientific value. This case held that the "utterly without redeeming social value" test and the "national standards" test were no longer applicable. In essence, the Court held that local community standards determine what is obscene, and that a work having "some redeeming social value" could no longer be used as a defense.

Finally, *Jenkins v. Georgia* (1974) stated that in state obscenity prosecutions, juries could properly be instructed to apply "community standards" of obscenity without specifying which community.

Other Supreme Court cases have dealt with private use of obscene materials, using the mails to send obscene materials, and laws protecting minors from obscene material. Among the most important such cases are the following:

Bantam Books v. Sullivan (1963) stated that it was unconstitutional for a commission created by a state legislature to notify distributors that certain books and magazines were obscene or objectionable for youths under age eighteen.

Freedman v. Maryland (1965) found a state motion picture censorship statute to be unconstitutional because it failed to provide adequate safeguards against undue inhibition of expression protected by the First Amendment.

Ginzburg v. United States (1966) affirmed the conviction for mailing obscene materials even though the literature was not obscene on its face.

Ginzburg v. New York (1968) stated that it was constitutional for state criminal statutes to prohibit the sale of obscene material to minors.

Stanley v. Georgia (1969) held that an individual possessing and viewing an obscene film in the privacy of his or her home is protected by the First Amendment.

Hamling v. United States (1974) found that a federal statute prohibiting use of the mails for sending obscene material or advertisements was not in violation of the First Amendment.

One other area in which police officers may confront problems related to freedom of the press is during political elections. *Branton v. State* (1949) held that a statute forbidding candidates to distribute ballots used in the election to instruct voters to vote for them was constitutional. This problem should diminish, however, as use of voting machines becomes more common.

Freedom of Peaceable Assembly.   Americans have the right to assemble peaceably for any political, religious, or social activity. Public authorities cannot impose unreasonable restrictions on such assemblies, but they can impose limitations reasonably designed to prevent fire, health hazards, or traffic obstructions. The Supreme Court has emphasized that freedom of assembly is just as fundamental as freedom of speech and press. Thus, while no law may legitimately prohibit demonstrations, laws or governmental actions may legitimately restrict demonstrations to certain areas or prohibit the obstruction and occupation of public buildings.

Picketing has also been protected under the free speech guarantee; however, it may be reasonably regulated to prevent pickets from obstructing movement onto

Officers on horseback maintain order at a demonstration.

and from the involved property. Picketing on private property has been upheld, but only where the property is open to the public and the picketing relates to the business being conducted on the property. Klein (1980, p. 137) points out that:

> Police problems involving labor disputes are similar in some respects to that of the Parade Regulation. There are two competing constitutional rights that the police officer is confronted with: those who are on strike have a constitutional right to peacefully picket and those who may wish to go to work who have a constitutional right to peacefully conduct their business. . . . The police administrator is often confronted with the problem of maintaining order when groups unlawfully and without applying for a permit take over the streets, parks, or public buildings. . . . The prevailing rule now appears to be that so long as the gathering is reasonably orderly, notwithstanding the fact that the police may validly enforce a constitutional limitation, the demonstration is permittted in order to avoid a confrontation which might result in loss of life or injury to persons or property.

Supreme Court decisions related to balancing the rights of people who wish to assemble and those who want to pursue their normal routine include *Poulos v. New Hampshire* (1953). This case stated that a group of demonstrators cannot insist on the right to blockade a street or entrance to a public or private building and allow no one to pass who did not agree to listen to their exhortations. *Walker v. Birmingham* (1967) stated that the First Amendment does not give people the right to trespass and disrupt the normal operations of business and government during the course of social protest, while *Cameron v. Johnson* (1968) held that taking over buildings for the purpose of demonstration is not protected by the First Amendment.

Freedom to Petition. The right of petition is designed to allow citizens to communicate with their government without obstruction. When citizens exercise their First Amendment freedom to write or speak to their senator or congressman, they partake of "the healthy essence of the democratic process."

The Second Amendment

A well-regulated militia being necessary to the security of a free state, the right of the people to keep and bear arms shall not be infringed.

The Second Amendment guarantees the right to bear arms.

Citizens are guaranteed the right to protect themselves from disorder in the community and attack from foreign enemies. This right to bear arms has become much less important in recent decades as well-trained military and police forces have been developed to protect citizens. No longer do they need to rely on having their own weapons available, yet attempts to limit this right are strenuously opposed by many citizens, as evidenced in the current gun control controversy. No matter what police officers' views are on gun control, they are obliged to enforce the laws passed by Congress.

The Supreme Court has ruled that state and federal governments may pass laws prohibiting the carrying of concealed weapons, requiring the registration of firearms, and limiting the sale of firearms for other than military use. Thus, it is illegal to possess certain types of "people-killing" weapons such as operable machine guns and sawed-off shotguns of a certain length.

The right of the states to pass laws regulating firearms rests in the interpretation of the Second Amendment by the Supreme Court. In *United States v. Cruickshank* (1876) the Court stated that the amendment protected only the right of the states to maintain and equip a militia, and that unless a defendant could show that his possession of a firearm in violation of federal statutes had "some reasonable relationship to the preservation or efficiency of a well-regulated militia," he could not challenge a gun control statute on Second Amendment grounds. The American Bar Association has stated: "Every Federal court decision involving the amendment has given the amendment a collective, militia interpretation and/or held that firearms control laws enacted under a state's police power are constitutional" ("Handgun Facts").

Many people are in favor of strict gun control laws, especially laws controlling handguns. According to Handgun Control, Inc., the public strongly favors such controls, as attested to by the results of the following public opinion polls:

■ April 1981 Washington Post/ABC Poll, 65% favored stronger legislation controlling distribution of handguns.

- April 1981 Associated Press/NBC News Poll, 71% favored a law requiring a person to obtain a permit before he or she could buy a handgun.

- July 1981 Gallup Poll, 91% favored a law requiring a 21-day waiting period before a gun could be purchased to give authorities time to see if the prospective owner had a criminal record or had been in a mental institution.

- August 1982 Harris Survey, 66% favored a federal law requiring that all handguns people own be registered by federal authorities.

Research on the effects of gun control laws has been done, with mixed results. For example, after Massachusetts law mandated a minimum one-year sentence for any person convicted of carrying a gun without proper authorization, research concluded that the law had reduced the number of assaults with a gun and armed robbery, but not homicide (Binder and Geis, 1983, p. 147). According to Siegel (1983, p. 280): "Though the existence of a direct causal link between gun ownership and murder is still a matter for investigation, there is little question that in some major urban areas rising homicide rates are closely associated with the use and possession of handguns."

Other statistics cited by Handgun Control, Inc., also seem compelling. For example, it states that in 1980 handguns killed: 4 in Australia, 8 in Canada, 8 in Great Britain, 18 in Sweden, 23 in Israel, 24 in Switzerland, 77 in Japan, and 11,258 in the United States. In addition, during the peak seven years of the Vietnam War, more than 40,000 American soldiers were killed in action, and during that same period more than 50,000 American civilians died right here at home—murdered with handguns.

Despite such statistics, opposition to gun control laws is strong. As noted by Levine, et al. (1980, p. 374): "Ironically, Governor George Wallace of Alabama, who was permanently paralyzed from the waist down by the bullets of an attempted assassin, continued to oppose tough gun laws because so much of his political support came from groups that favored the use of firearms." In addition, "Many voting analysts contend that Senator Joseph Tydings of Maryland, a popular politician from a prominent Maryland family, was defeated for reelection largely because of the mail campaign conducted by gun groups offended by his support of a federal gun registration law. Such ominous results may deter legislators from advocating similar measures—even though they seem to work."

Those who argue against gun control include the National Rifle Association which contends that "Guns don't kill—people do," and that we should "Control criminals, not guns." Other common concerns are voiced in such phrases as "When guns are outlawed, only outlaws will have guns." "Handgun control will leave the citizens defenseless," and "God created man, but Colonel Colt* made them equal."

A defense of the "right to bear arms," and a refusal to accept the Supreme Court's interpretation of the Second Amendment has been made by Don Feder (1980):

---

*Inventor of the Colt .45 pistol.

For the past 20 years, gun prohibitionists have been telling us that the 2nd Amendment is only a collective right. . . . This argument doesn't stand up to scrutiny. The term "militia" was well founded in Colonial usage. To the drafters of the Constitution it meant not only the organized militia, such as the Minute Men of Lexington and Concord, but every able-bodied man who could bear arms in defense of his liberty. . . .

Webster's dictionary defines militia as: ". . . 2. the whole body of able-bodied male citizens declared by law as being subject to call for miliary service."

In fact, the U.S. Code, Title 10, Section 311, militia: composition and classes (enacted in 1970) reads in parts as follows: "The militia of the United States consists of all able bodied males at least 17 years of age . . ."

What about the term "people" in the 2nd Amendment? If you'll recall, the same expression is used elsewhere in the Bill of Rights. The 1st Amendment refers to ". . . the right of the *people* to assemble peaceably."

Our Founding Fathers had an abiding fear of government. The 2nd Amendment was written to guarantee the people that they, the militia would always have arms to oppose governmental tyranny.

Feder goes on to note that: "In his Virginia Constitution of 1776 Jefferson provided 'no freeman shall ever be debarred the use of arms,' " and that George Washington had stated, "Firearms stand next in importance to the Constitution itself. They are the American people's liberty teeth and keystone under independence."

The controversy continues.

The Third Amendment

No soldier shall, in time of peace, be quartered in any house without the consent of the owner, nor in time of war but in a manner to be prescribed by the law.

Before the Revolution, American colonists were frequently forced to provide food and lodging for British soldiers. The Third Amendment prohibited continuing this practice.

The Fourth Amendment

The right of the people to be secure in their persons, houses, papers, and effects, against unreasonable searches and seizures, shall not be violated, and no warrants shall issue but upon probable cause, supported by oath or affirmation, and particularly describing the place to be searched, and the persons or things to be seized.

The Fourth Amendment requires probable cause and forbids unreasonable searches and seizures.

In some countries, even today, police officers may invade citizens' homes, seize their property, or arrest them whenever they see fit. In the United States such actions are prohibited by the Fourth Amendment which protects individuals and their property from unreasonable search and seizure by law officers.

In most instances a police officer is not allowed to search the homes of private citizens, seize any of their property, or arrest them without first obtaining a court order—a **warrant.** Before a warrant will be issued, the police officer must convince a magistrate that he has **probable cause**—good reason—to believe either that the individual involved has committed a crime, or that he has in his possession evidence related to a crime. Even with a warrant, police cannot typically break into a private home without first demanding entrance, unless such action is permissible under a ''no-knock'' statute which authorizes such entry if it is reasonable to expect the evidence will be destroyed.

The courts have ruled that in some instances it is permissible to arrest a person or conduct a search without a warrant. For example, if a felony is committed in the presence of a police officer, the officer has the right to arrest the criminal immediately, without an arrest warrant. If the police officer makes such an arrest, he may search the suspect and a limited area surrounding him to prevent the suspect from seizing a weapon or destroying evidence. Any evidence in plain view may also be seized.

The courts have permitted the police to search certain vehicles without a warrant on the grounds that the vehicle may be miles away by the time a police officer returns with a warrant.

The courts have frequently faced the problem of determining what constitutes probable cause for a search or an arrest. Generally speaking, the criterion has been common sense: On the available evidence, would a reasonable person consider there was a good basis to believe that the person to be arrested had committed a crime or that the place to be searched contained evidence of a crime?

The Supreme Court, in considering whether a police officer who stopped and frisked a citizen with reason to believe the individual concerned had committed a particular crime, ruled that the Fourth Amendment did not prohibit such a search if it was reasonable on the basis of the police officer's experience and the demeanor of the individual who was frisked.

Listening in on a telephone conversation by mechanical or electronic means and electronic bugging are considered search and seizures under the Fourth Amendment, and, therefore, they also require probable cause, reasonableness, and a warrant for their use. Congress has passed legislation which limits the use of wiretapping and bugging to the investigation of specific crimes and restricts those officials permitted to authorize them. *Berger v. New York,* (1967) established that electronic evesdropping was prohibited by the Fourth Amendment, but that under specific conditions and circumstances it could be permitted. *Katz v. United States* (1967) also established that evidence of conversations overheard through electronic surveillance of a telephone booth was inadmissible because the proper authorization had not been obtained.

Evidence secured by means of an unlawful search and seizure cannot be used in either a state or federal prosecution. Thus, the phrase ''innocent until proven guilty'' in practice means ''innocent until proven guilty by evidence obtained in accordance with constitutional guarantees.''

Numerous Supreme Court cases have interpreted restrictions imposed by the Fourth Amendment. For example, in *Boyd v. United States* (1886), the Court held that the Fourth Amendment applied "to all invasions on the part of the government and its employees of the sanctity of a man's home and the privacies of life. It is not the breaking of his doors, and the rummaging of his drawers, that constitutes the essence of the offense; but it is the invasion of his indefensible right of personal security, personal liberty and private property." The findings in *Boyd* clearly suggest that evidence gathered in violation of the Fourth Amendment should be excluded from federal criminal trials and, consequently, contributed to the development of the Exclusionary Rule some thirty years later.

In *Weeks v. United States* (1914) the Court, considering evidence seized unconstitutionally, concluded:

> If letters and private documents can thus be seized and held and used in evidence against a citizen accused of an offense, the protection of the Fourth Amendment declaring his right to be secure against such searches and seizures is of no value, and, so far as those thus placed are concerned, might as well be stricken from the Constitution. The efforts of the courts and their officials to bring the guilty to punishment, praiseworthy as they are, are not to be aided by the sacrifice of those great principles established by years of endeavor and suffering which have resulted in their embodiment in the fundamental law of the land.

The Weeks case established that "in a federal prosecution the Fourth Amendment bars the use of evidence secured through an illegal search and seizure."

Mapp v. Ohio (1961) established that the Exclusionary Rule must be applied at the state level as well as the federal level—that any evidence seized in violation of the Fourth Amendment guarantees was not admissible in state criminal prosecutions.

Other important Supreme Court cases related to the Fourth Amendment include several related to searches:

- *Burdeau v. McDowell* (1921) held that evidence obtained by a government agency from an unlawful search and seizure conducted by a private citizen can be used in government prosecution, provided the government had not "connived" in the unlawful search and seizure.

- *Abel v. United States* (1960) found that there was no invasion of privacy if an abandoned room or property was searched.

- *Stoner v. California* (1964) established that a guest in a hotel room was entitled to constitutional protection against unreasonable search and seizure, and that evidence obtained without a warrant, even with the consent of the desk clerk, was not admissible.

- *Michigan v. Tyler,* (1978) held that entry by police and fire officials to investigate fire-damaged private property was subject to the Fourth Amendment, but that no warrant was required in an emergency to enter a burning structure to extinguish the fire.

■ *Nix v. Williams* (1984) adopted what is now known as the ''inevitable discovery exception to the Exclusionary Rule.''

Supreme Court cases concerning searches related to arrests include *Henry v. United States* (1959), which found that if police did not have reasonable cause to believe a crime had been committed at the time they stopped a defendant, any search incidental to arrest was not legal. *Beck v. Ohio* (1964) held that in determining the validity of a warrantless arrest, the court must first determine if the facts available to the officer at the time would cause a man of ''reasonable caution'' to believe a crime had been committed.

In *Terry v. Ohio* (1968) it was established that if police officers believe a suspect is armed, they can stop and frisk him as a safety precaution, and *Chimel v. California* (1969) held that a warrantless search incidental to lawful arrest must be limited to the suspect's immediate surroundings to prevent the suspect from obtaining a weapon or destroying evidence. Any search beyond this limit was unconstitutional.

Five other Supreme Court decisions relate directly to searches of automobiles:

■ *Carroll v. United States* (1925) established that since automobiles and other conveyances were highly mobile, they could be searched without a warrant if they were suspected of containing contraband.

■ *Chambers v. Maroney* (1970) held that police could search a vehicle at the police station after they had arrested the driver. They did not have to search it at the time of the arrest.

■ *Coolidge v. New Hampshire* (1971) found that a warrantless search of a suspect's car parked in his driveway at the time the suspect was arrested inside his house was not constitutional; a warrant should have been obtained.

■ *South Dakota v. Opperman* (1976) established that a routine search of vehicles impounded for traffic violations was constitutional.

■ *United States v. Ross* (1982) held that the police may search a car, including containers, without a warrant as long as they have probable cause to believe contraband is somewhere in the car.

Strict interpretation of the Fourth Amendment frequently results in evidence being excluded from a trial and may greatly limit the police's investigatory powers. Consequently, support for the strict interpretation of the amendment has declined. In *Go-Bart Import Company v. United States* (1931), and in *United States v. Rabinowitz* (1950), the Court held that ''What is a reasonable search must be resolved in the facts and circumstances of each case.'' In effect, the Court assumed the responsibility of deciding on a case-by-case basis whether the Fourth Amendment was violated. This has resulted in numerous exceptions to the warrant requirement implied by the Fourth Amendment.

The search and seizure provisions of the Fourth Amendment are critical to law enforcement officers and will be discussed in depth in Chapter 14.

The Fifth Amendment

No person shall be held to answer for a capital or otherwise infamous crime unless on a presentment or indictment of a grand jury, except in cases arising in the land or naval forces, or in the militia, when in actual service, in time of war or public danger; no shall any person be subject for the same offense to be twice put in jeoparty of life or limb; nor shall be compelled in any criminal case to be a witness against himself; nor be deprived of life, liberty, or property, without due process of law; nor shall private property be taken for public use without just compensation.

The Fifth Amendment guarantees:

■ *Due process: notice of a hearing, full information regarding the charges made against him, the opportunity to present evidence in his own behalf before an impartial judge or jury, and to be presumed innocent until proven guilty by legally obtained evidence.*

■ *Just compensation when private property is acquired for public use.*

The Fifth Amendment prohibits:

■ *Double jeopardy.*

■ *Self-incrimination.*

Grand Jury.   The Fifth Amendment requires that before individuals are tried in federal court for an "infamous" crime, they must first be indicted by a **grand jury**. The grand jury's duty is to assure that there is probable cause to believe the accused person is guilty. This prevents a person from being subjected to a trial when insufficient proof exists that he has committed a crime.

An "infamous" crime is a felony (a crime for which a sentence of more than one year's imprisonment can be given) or a lesser offense which can be punished by confinement in a penitentiary or at hard labor.

An indictment is not required for a trial by court-martial or by other military tribunals. Also, the constitutional requirements of grand jury indictment do not apply to trials in state courts.

Due Process.   The words *due process of law* express the fundamental ideas of American justice. A due process clause is found in both the Fifth and Fourteenth Amendments as a restraint upon the federal and state governments respectively.

The due process clause protects against arbitrary, unfair procedures in judicial or administrative proceedings which could affect a citizen's personal and property rights. Due process requires notice of a hearing or trial which is timely and which adequately informs the accused persons of the charges against them. It also requires the opportunity to present evidence in one's own behalf before an impartial judge or jury, to be presumed innocent until proven guilty by legally obtained evidence, and to have the verdict supported by the evidence presented.

The due process clauses of the Fifth and Fourteenth Amendments provide other basic protections to prevent the state and federal governments from adopting arbitrary, unreasonable legislation or other measures which would violate individual rights. Thus, constitutional limitations are imposed on governmental interference with important individual liberties such as the freedom to enter into contracts, to engage in a lawful occupation, to marry, and to move without unnecessary restraints. Governmental restrictions placed on one's liberties must be reasonable and consistent with due process to be valid.

The United States Supreme Court has not given a precise definition of due process. Justice Frankfurter, in *Rochin v. California* (1952), stated: "Due process of law, as a historic and generative principle, precludes defining, and thereby confining, these standards of conduct more precisely than to say that convictions cannot be brought about by methods that offend a sense of justice."

Lewis and Peoples (1978, p. 19) suggest that: "Due process can be operationally defined as law in the regular course of judicial proceedings that is in accordance with natural inherent and fundamental principles of justice. Thus one could argue that due process simply means that a defendant must receive all the substantive and procedural protections that the law presently provides." They note that: "In general, substantitive due process protects all persons against unreasonable, arbitrary, or capricious laws and acts as a limitation against arbitrary governmental actions so that no court or governmental agency may exercise powers beyond those authorized by the Constitution."

In contrast, procedural due process deals with notices, hearings, and gathering of evidence. The vast majority of due process cases are in the area of procedural due process. Because the Fifth Amendment is so vague, hundreds of cases have been heard. Important Supreme Court cases involving due process include *Brady v. Maryland* (1963), which held that the suppression of evidence favorable to an accused by the prosecution violates due process. *In Re Gault* (1967) established that juvenile court proceedings must also meet the requirements of due process, and *United States v. Russell* (1973) found that it was not entrapment for an undercover agent to have supplied the defendant with a scarce ingredient required to manufacture an illicit drug.

In *Hampton v. United States* (1976) the Court held that it was not entrapment for undercover agents to be both providers and purchasers of drugs involved in the case. *Manson v. Brathwaite* (1977) established that eyewitness identification could be made from a single photograph if "the totality of circumstances" made it reliable.

Double Jeopardy.   The Fifth Amendment also guarantees that citizens will not be placed in double jeopardy; that is, they will not be tried before a federal or state court more than once for the same crime. A second trial can occur, however, when the first trial results in a mistrial, for instance, when the jury cannot agree on a verdict, or when a second trial is ordered by an appellate court.

Double jeopardy does not arise when a single act violates both federal and state laws, and the defendant is prosecuted in both federal and state courts. Nor does a criminal prosecution in either a state or federal court exempt the defendant from being sued for damages by anyone who is harmed by the criminal act. Further, a defendant may be prosecuted more than once for the same conduct if it involves the commission of more than one crime. For instance, if a person kills three victims at the same time and place, he can be tried separately for each slaying. *Benton v. Maryland* (1969) stated that the double jeopardy clause also applies to state prosecutions.

Self-Incrimination.   In any criminal case every person has the right not to be a witness against himself; that is, no one is required to provide answers to questions which might convict him of a crime. Such questions may be asked at the very earliest stages of an investigation; therefore, the Supreme Court has ruled that when an individual is interrogated in the custody of the police, the guarantees of the Fifth Amendment apply. Custodial interrogation can extend to questioning outside the police station and has even included police questioning of a defendant in his own bed.

To insure against self-incrimination the Court ruled, in the well-known *Miranda* decision, that citizens must be warned prior to custodial interrogation of their right to remain silent, that what they say may be used against them in court, and that they have a right to counsel which will be furnished them. If these warnings are not given, any statements obtained by the questioning are inadmissible in later criminal proceedings.

Although accused persons may waive their rights under the Fifth Amendment, they must know what they are doing and must not be forced to confess. Any confession obtained by force or threat is excluded from the evidence presented at the trial. Further, if defendants or witnesses fail to invoke the Fifth Amendment in response to a question when on the witness stand, such a failure may operate as a waiver of the right, and they will not be permitted to object to a court's admitting their statement into evidence.

Courts have ruled that the guarantee against self-incrimination applies only to testimonial actions. Thus, handwriting samples, blood tests, and appearance, including repeating words in a police lineup, do *not* violate the Fifth Amendment.

Courts have also ruled that the Fifth Amendment prohibits both federal and state prosecutors and judges from commenting on the refusal of defendants to take the witness stand in their own defense. The refusal of witnesses to testify to matters which could subject them to criminal prosecutions at a later date has also been upheld. The courts have recognized, however, a limited right of the government to question employees about the performance of official duties and have upheld the dismissal of employees who refuse to answer such questions.

Important Supreme Court cases regarding self-incrimination include the following:

- *Rochin v. California* (1952) held that pumping a defendant's stomach without a search warrant to obtain contraband was a denial of due process.
- *Escobedo v. Illinois* (1964) said that when the investigative process shifts to accusatory, the adversary system starts to operate and the suspect must be allowed to consult with his attorney.
- *Schmerber v. California* (1966) established that taking physical evidence such as blood samples despite the accused's objections did not violate the Fifth Amendment, and that the evidence was admissible.

- *Miranda v. Arizona* (1966) held that any suspect must be told of his right to remain silent, of the possibility of using what is said against him in court, and his right to a lawyer. Unless the suspect is advised of these rights, any statements, admissions, or confessions are not admissible in court.

- *Gilbert v. California* (1967) established that requiring a suspect to give a sample of his handwriting without his attorney present did not violate the Fifth Amendment.

- *Cupp v. Murphy* (1973) held that police may take incriminating samples from the fingernails of a suspect without a warrant where there was probable cause to arrest.

- *Carter v. United States* (1981) stated that a defendant who does not choose to testify in his own defense has the right to ask the judge to instruct the jury not to infer guilt because of this refusal to testify.

- *New York v. Quarles* (1984) established a new public safety exception to the Exclusionary Rule in that in certain cases police may question a subject in custody without first advising him of his right not to incriminate himself.

Creamer (1980, p. 367) contends that:

The public sees the Fifth Amendment invoked by people they don't like and who they presume are dishonest—or worse. People perceive that crime by government officials and other white-collar types is a serious problem, and they assume that too many such criminals are hiding behind the Fifth Amendment. The rising use of the Fifth Amendment has brought with it a rising outcry that the Fifth isn't worth the trouble it causes. This shallow notion is appealing on the surface, but in substance it is a dangerous idea, much like setting fire to one's home in order to rid the house of termites.

No principles of law are more misunderstood by Americans than those which encompass the Fifth Amendment. From the old Red-baiting days through the postwar anti-racketeering era and the anti-war dissent period and the Watergate age, the myth has grown that justice and virtue have been continually frustrated by public enemies hiding behind the Fifth.

To the contrary, the history of the Fifth Amendment is the history of humankind's attempts to become civilized. In its origins it was a rejection of government torture as a means of solving governmental problems. Today it is all that stands between a citizen and our government's unlimited right to ask questions and demand answers.

The Fifth Amendment serves as a declaration of our centuries-old American distrust of public officials. That this distrust has been well founded is especially evident now, when we are still recovering from overzealous governmental assaults on war protesters, black militants and political dissidents coupled with government-sponsored burglaries, illegal wiretaps and illegal mind control experiments, all committed in the name of law and order. . . . The right to silence has long been with us. It stands for human dignity and self-respect. It prevents the government from probing the secrets of our conversations or our innermost thoughts. Former Supreme Court Justice William O. Douglas once observed, "The crucial point is that the Constitution places the right of silence beyond the reach of government."

The Sixth Amendment

In all criminal prosecutions, the accused shall enjoy the right to a speedy and public trial, by an impartial jury of the state and district wherein the crime shall have been committed, which districts shall have been previously ascertained by law, and to be informed of the nature and cause of the accusation; to be confronted with the witnesses against him; to have compulsory process for obtaining witnesses in his favor, and to have the assistance of counsel for his defense.

> *The Sixth Amendment establishes requirements for criminal trials. It guarantees the individual's right:*
> - *To have a speedy public trial by an impartial jury.*
> - *To be informed of the nature and cause of the accusation.*
> - *To be confronted with witnesses against him.*
> - *To subpoena witnesses for his defense.*
> - *To have counsel for defense.*

The right to speedy and public trial requires that the accused be brought to trial without unnecessary delay and that the trial be open to the public. Intentional or negligent delay by the prosecution has been grounds for dismissal of charges. The Supreme Court has ruled that delay in prosecution is not justified by the defendant's confinement on an earlier conviction; he should be temporarily released for trial on the later charge.

Trial by an impartial jury supplements the guarantee contained in Article III of the Constitution. The requirement that the jury have twelve members and that the twelve members must reach a unanimous verdict was derived from common law, not from the Constitution. The Supreme Court has ruled that state juries need not have twelve members and has approved state statutes which require only six. Moreover, the Court has ruled that jury verdicts in state courts need not necessarily be unanimous.

The right to jury trial does not apply to trials for petty offenses, which the Supreme Court has suggested are those punishable by six months' confinement or less, for example, shoplifting or some traffic violations.

In all jury trials the jury members must be impartially selected. No one can be excluded from jury service because of race, class, or sex.

The Sixth Amendment requires that accused persons must be told how it is claimed they have broken the law so they can prepare their defense. The crime must be established by statute beforehand so all persons know it is illegal before they act. The statute must clearly inform people of the exact nature of the crime.

Generally, accused persons are entitled to have all witnesses against them present their evidence orally in court. Hearsay evidence cannot be used in federal criminal trials except in certain instances. Moreover, those accused are entitled to the court's aid in obtaining their witnesses. This is usually accomplished by **subpoena,** which orders into court as witnesses persons whose testimony is desired at the trial.

Finally, the Sixth Amendment provides a right to be represented by counsel. For many years this was interpreted to mean that defendants had a right to be represented by a lawyer only if they could afford one. However, the Supreme Court held in 1963, in *Gideon v. Wainwright,* that the amendment obligated the federal and state governments to provide legal counsel at public expense for those who could not afford it. This right extends even to cases involving petty offenses if a jail sentence might result. The indigent have such a right at any "critical stage of the adjudicatory process," including the initial periods of questioning, police lineups, and all stages of the trial process.

In addition, indigents have the right to a free copy of their trial transcript for purposes of appeal of their conviction. Congress enacted the Criminal Justice Acts of 1964 and 1970 to implement this right to counsel by establishing a federal defender system to represent those defendants who could not afford legal counsel. Most state legislatures have enacted similar measures.

The Supreme Court's first modern ruling on the right to counsel was *Powell v. Alabama* (1932), a case involving nine young blacks, ages thirteen to twenty-one, charged with raping two white girls. The trial was held in Scottsboro, Alabama, where community sentiment was extremely hostile toward the defendants. Although the trial judge appointed a member of the local bar to serve as defense counsel, no attorney appeared on the day of the trial, so the judge appointed a local lawyer who reluctantly took the case. The defendants challenged their conviction on the grounds that they did not have a chance to consult with their lawyer or prepare a defense, and the Supreme Court concurred.

Another Supreme Court case seems to fly in the face of the Sixth Amendment right to a lawyer. That is the case of *Faretta v. California* (1975) in which the Supreme Court held that defendants could reject counsel appointed to represent them and could, instead, represent themselves. Justice Potter Steward stated: "It is one thing to hold that every defendant, rich or poor has the right to the assistance of counsel, and quite another to say that a state may compel a defendant to accept a lawyer he does not want."

Other important Supreme Court cases related to the Sixth Amendment include the following:

Right to a Speedy Trial.

- *Klopfer v. North Carolina* (1967) held that the right to a speedy public trial applies to the states.
- *Barker v. Wingo* (1972) found that whether or not a defendant has been denied the right to a speedy trial must be determined by considering the length of delay, the reason for the delay, and any prejudice resulting from the delay.

Right to an Impartial Jury.

- *Parker v. Gladden* (1966) stated that the right to trial by an impartial jury applies to the states.
- *Duncan v. Louisiana* (1968) held that the states are bound by the Sixth Amendment requirement of a jury trial in criminal cases but not in cases involving petty offenses.

Right to Confront Witnesses.

- *Pointer v. Texas* (1965) found that the right to confront witnesses applies to the states.
- *Illinois v. Allen* (1970) stated that the Sixth Amendment right to be present during the trial can be lost by a defendant who, despite warnings, disrupts the trial.

Right to Counsel.

- *Massiah v. United States* (1964) stated that an indicated person cannot be questioned or otherwise persuaded to make incriminating remarks without the presence of counsel.
- *United States v. Wade* (1967) found that an accused's right to counsel included having counsel present during a lineup identification because the suspect had been indicted and it was a critical stage in the prosecution.
- *Kirby v. Illinois* (1972) held that there is no right to counsel during a police lineup for identification if a suspect has not been formally charged with a crime.
- *Argersinger v. Hamlin* (1972) stated that no person can be imprisoned for any offense, even a misdemeanor, unless represented by counsel at his trial, or unless this right was knowingly and intelligently waived.
- *United States v. Ash, Jr.* (1973) found that a suspect is not entitled to counsel during postindictment display of photographs used for identification.
- *Brewer v. Williams* (1977) reaffirmed the Massiah rule that once a defendant is formally charged with a criminal offense, he has the right to have a lawyer present when being interrogated.
- *Scott v. Illinois* (1979) held that a state defendant has the right to a state-paid attorney, if necessary, only in cases that lead to imprisonment, not in all cases where imprisonment is possible.

The Seventh Amendment

In suits at common law, where the value in controversy shall exceed twenty dollars, the right of trial by jury shall be preserved, and no fact by a jury shall be otherwise re-examined in any court of the United States than according to the rules of the common law.

The Eighth Amendment

Excessive bail shall not be required, nor excessive fines imposed, nor cruel and unusual punishments inflicted.

The Eighth Amendment forbids excessive bail, excessive fines, and cruel and unusual punishments.

Bail. Bail has traditionally meant payment by the accused of an amount of money, specified by the court based on the nature of the offense, to insure the presence of the accused at trial. An accused released from custody and subsequently failing to appear for trial forfeits his bail to the court.

The Eighth Amendment does not specifically provide that all citizens have a right to bail, but only that bail will not be excessive. A right to bail has, however, been recognized in common law and in statute since 1791. In 1966 Congress enacted the *Bail Reform Act* to provide for pre-trial release from imprisonment of indigent defendants who could not afford to post money for bail, and who were, in effect, confined only because of their poverty. The act also discouraged the traditional use of money bail by requiring the judge to seek other means as likely to insure that defendants would appear when their trial was held.

The leading Supreme Court decision on excessive bail is *Stack v. Boyle* (1951) in which twelve community leaders were indicted for conspiracy and bail was fixed at $50,000 per defendant. The defendants moved to reduce this amount on the ground that it was excessive, and the Supreme Court agreed. Chief Justice Fred M. Vinson stated that in the opinion of the Court:

> This traditional right to freedom before conviction permits the unhampered preparation of a defense, and serves to prevent the infliction of punishment prior to conviction. . . . Unless this right to bail before trial is preserved, the presumption of innocence, secured only after centuries of struggle, would lose its meaning.
>
> The right of release before trial is conditioned upon the accused's giving adequate assurance that he will stand trial and submit to sentence if found guilty. . . . Bail set at a figure higher than an amount reasonably calculated to fulfill this purpose is "excessive" under the Eighth Amendment.

The following spring, in *Carlson v. Landon* (1952), the Court held that the Eighth Amendment did not guarantee the right to bail.

Cruel and Unusual Punishment. Whether fines or periods of confinement are cruel and unusual must be determined by the facts of each particular case. Clearly excessive practices such as torture would be invalid. The Supreme Court has held the death penalty itself to be cruel and unusual in certain circumstances if it is not universally applied.

The clause also applied to punishment for a condition which the criminal had no power to change. For example, a law making narcotics addiction illegal was struck down by the Supreme Court as cruel and unusual since it punished a condition beyond the accused's control. Some courts have held laws punishing public drunkenness to be cruel and unusual when applied to homeless alcoholics, since they cannot usually avoid public places.

The Supreme Court has heard numerous cases concerning cruel and unusual punishment, including the following:

- *Furman v. Georgia* (1972) stated that the death penalty does violate the Eighth Amendment if the sentencing authority has the freedom to decide between the death penalty and a lesser penalty.
- *Gregg v. Georgia* (1976) held that the death penalty for murderers is not per se cruel and unusual punishment.
- *Proffitt v. Florida* (1976) reaffirmed the *Gregg* decision.
- *Jurek v. Texas* (1976) also reaffirmed the *Gregg* decision, refusing to declare the death penalty unconstitutional in all circumstances.
- *Roberts v. Louisiana* (1977) ruled that the statute requiring the death penalty for murdering a police officer engaged in performing his duty, with no consideration of mitigating circumstances, was unconstitutional.
- *Coker v. Georgia* (1977) stated that the death penalty for a person convicted of rape was cruel and unusual punishment.
- *Lockett v. Ohio* (1978) invalidated Ohio's death penalty for murder because it limited too strictly the factors that could be considered in the decision whether or not to impose the death penalty.
- *Rummel v. Estelle* (1980) ruled that a mandatory life sentence required by a state habitual offender statute was not cruel and unusual punishment.

The Ninth Amendment

The enumeration in the Constitution of certain rights shall not be construed to deny or disparage others retained by the people.

The Ninth Amendment emphasizes the founding fathers' view that powers of government are limited by the rights of the people, and that it was *not* intended, by expressly guaranteeing in the Constitution certain rights of the people, to recognize that government had unlimited power to invade other rights of the people.

Griswold v. Connecticut (1965), a case involving the Ninth Amendment, addressed the issue of whether the right to privacy was a constitutional right, and, if so, whether the right was reserved to the people under the Ninth Amendment or was only derived from other rights specifically mentioned in the Constitution.

Courts have long recognized particular rights to privacy which are part of the First and Fourth Amendments. Thus, freedom of expression guarantees freedom of association and the related right to be silent and free from official inquiry into such associations. It also includes the right not to be intimidated by the government for expressing one's views. The Fourth Amendment's guarantee against unreasonable search and seizure confers a right to privacy because its safeguards prohibit unauthorized entry onto property and tampering with a citizen's possessions or property including his very person.

The Court in *Griswold* ruled that the Third and Fifth Amendments, in addition to the First and Fourth, created "zones of privacy" safe from governmental intrusion, and, without resting its decision upon any one of these or on the Ninth Amendment itself, simply held that the right of privacy was guaranteed by the Constitution.

The Tenth Amendment

The powers not delegated to the United States by the Constitution, nor prohibited by it to the states, are reserved to the states respectively, or to the people.

The Tenth Amendment embodies the principle of federalism which reserves for the states the residue of powers not granted to the federal government or withheld from the states.

Additional Amendments

Since the ratification of the first ten amendments (the Bill of Rights), other amendments have been passed. Of special importance to civil rights and civil liberties is the Fourteenth Amendment, passed in 1868.

The Fourteenth Amendment

1. All persons born or naturalized in the United States, and subject to the jurisdiction thereof, are citizens of the United States and of the state wherein they reside. No state shall make or enforce any law which shall abridge the privileges or immunities of citizens of the United States; nor shall any state deprive any person of life, liberty, or property without due process of law, nor deny to any person within its jurisdiction the equal protection of the laws. . . .
5. The Congress shall have power to enforce by appropriate legislation the provisions of this article.

The Fourteenth Amendment requires each state to abide by the Constitution and the Bill of Rights. It guarantees due process and equal protection under the law.

Due Process. The Fourteenth Amendment limits the states' infringement upon the rights of individuals. The Bill of Rights does not specifically refer to actions by states, but applies only to actions by the federal government.

Thus, state and local officers could proceed with an arrest without any concern for the rights of the accused. The Fourteenth Amendment, in essence, duplicates the Fifth Amendment, except it specifically orders state and local officers to provide the legal protections of due process.

Some important Supreme Court cases related to the Fourteenth Amendment include *Brown v. Mississippi* (1936), which stated that a criminal conviction based on a confession obtained by brutality was not admissible under the Fourteenth Amendment due process clause. In *Gideon v. Wainwright* (1963) the Court held that the Fourteenth Amendment requires states to provide indigent defendants with counsel in criminal cases, whether the offense is capital or noncapital. Finally, *Malloy v. Hogan* (1964) found that the Fourteenth Amendment gives state prosecutors the same privileges against self-incrimination as provided to federal prosecutors under the Fifth Amendment.

Equal Protection.   The Fourteenth Amendment also prohibits denial of the "equal protection of the laws." A state cannot make unreasonable, arbitrary distinctions between different persons as to their rights and privileges. Since "all people are created equal," no law could deny red-haired men the right to drive an automobile, although it can deny minors the right to drive. The state can make reasonable classifications; however, classifications such as those based on race, religion, and national origin have been held to be unreasonable. Thus, racial segregation in public schools and other public places, laws which prohibit sale or use of property to certain races or minority groups, and laws prohibiting interracial marriage have been struck down.

The Supreme Court has further held that purely private acts of discrimination violate the equal protection clause if such acts are customarily enforced throughout the state, whether or not there is a specific law or other explicit manifestation of action by the state.

The equal protection clause also means that citizens may not arbitrarily be deprived of their right to vote, and that every citizen's vote must be given equal weight. Therefore, state legislatures and local governments must be apportioned strictly in terms of their populations in a way that accords one person one vote.

Section 5 of the Fourteenth Amendment provides the authority for much of the civil rights legislation passed by Congress in the 1960s.

Police Power

Without means of enforcement, the great body of federal, state, municipal, and common law would be empty, meaningless. Recall that the term *law* implies not only the rule, but also enforcement of that rule. It has been said that: "Common to all forms of society are the requisites of authority and power. *Authority* is the right to direct and comand. *Power* is the force by means of which others can be obliged to obey" (Germann, Day, and Gallati, 1969, p. 9).

Police power is a term used to describe the power of the federal, state, or municipal governments to pass laws regulating private interests, to protect the health and safety of the people, to prevent fraud and oppression, and to promote public convenience, prosperity, and welfare.

Police power is derived from the U.S. Constitution, U.S. Supreme Court decisions, federal statutes, state constitutions, state statutes, state court decisions, and various municipal charters and ordinances.

Police power was defined by the United States Supreme Court in 1887 as ''embracing no more than the power to promote public health, morals, and safety'' (*Mulger v. Kansas*). Others have defined police power as the force used by the state to preserve the general health, safety, welfare, and morals.

For example, narcotics laws are passed to preserve the people's health. Any person who abuses narcotics or drugs by taking them without medical prescription and in proper dosage jeopardizes his mental and physical health. Traffic laws are passed to preserve the general safety and to make the highways safe for the motoring public. Gambling laws are passed by the legislature to protect the individual and the family from financial loss. Likewise, juvenile laws are passed to protect the juvenile from his parents, guardians, relatives, or other people who would place his physical and mental welfare in danger. Finally, legislation prohibiting prostitution and obscenity is passed to protect the public's morals.

All levels of government grant their legislative branches the right and power to make laws. The executive branches of government are created to enforce these laws, while the judicial branches interpret what the laws mean and how they are to be enforced.

The police power of the federal government is based on authority granted by the United States Constitution. The general grants of power, such as the power of Congress, the legislative branch of government, to provide for the general welfare of the United States by law, are restricted by other provisions of the Constitution taken from the English Bill of Rights or from the political experience of England and America.

The police power of the states is delegated to them by the federal government in the Bill of Rights. The Tenth Amendment of our Bill of Rights gives the states those powers not delegated to the federal government. Since the power to organize police forces is not delegated to the federal government, this authority is given to the individual states and their subdivisions, that is, their cities, counties, and townships. Therefore, police power ultimately rests with the people, since their elected representatives create the laws which the police enforce.

Because each state is responsible for its citizen's health, safety, and general well-being, the usual procedure has been to assign these functions to municipal police departments in the cities and to sheriffs and constables in the rural areas of the state. Within the limits established by state constitutions, state legislatures may define the powers and duties of police officers in the state. However, police officers' authority and powers cannot conflict with the provisions in the Fourteenth Amendment of the Constitution which guarantee citizens equal protection by due process of law. Therefore, police officers can exercise only the powers and authority specifically granted by legislative enactment.

The authority, powers, duties, and limits of the police officer are usually determined by each state for all police officers—state, municipal, and rural. Most states fulfill their responsibility for preserving the public peace, detecting and arresting offenders, and enforcing the law by giving cities the authority to appoint municipal police officers. Although these municipal officers are concerned with enforcing city ordinances, enforcing state statutes is their most important job.

Police authority and power are broad in scope and include maintaining the peace, licensing trades and professions, regulating public service corporations' rates, and enforcing health regulations such as quarantines, compulsory vaccinations, and segregation of people with contagious diseases. State laws and judicial decisions also determine the civil and criminal liability of police officers who step beyond their legal powers in discharging the duties of their office.

Although the state legislature passes laws, the courts, the judicial branch of government, decide the purpose and character of the statutes as well as whether or not these statutes conflict with the Constitution or are contrary to proper public policy. Since the courts continuously review laws, police authority and power cannot easily be corrupted or controlled by private interests.

The courts determine what police authority and power is appropriate. Acceptable police power requires that the regulations are (1) reasonable, (2) within the power given to the states by the Constitution, and (3) in accord with due process of law.

Police power is restricted by the Constitution, by the Fourteenth Amendment, and by the courts.

Principle Versus Practice

There is a vast difference between stating ideals and goals and achieving them. Our forefathers wrote our Constitution and the Bill of Rights on the premise that all people would obey the law. Time has shown that this is not always true. The ideals set forth in our Declaration of Independence, our Constitution, and our Bill of Rights have not been achieved automatically.

Civil rights and civil liberties must be consciously and actively sought and protected if the documents on which our government is founded are to be more than elegant words. Laws and institutions must parallel our goals and ideals of liberty, freedom, equality, justice, human dignity, individual self-determination, freedom from tyranny, and freedom of conscience.

These goals have motivated Americans since they first came to the New World. These same goals carried American pioneers west, looking for a new life, an El Dorado. These goals have led men and women of all races and creeds, from all parts of the country, to invest tremendous energy in the civil rights movement, to risk their lives confronting violently irate traditionalists, in an effort to obtain new levels of human decency and equality, new levels of freedom and justice for millions of Americans who belong to minority groups.

In many respects the history of civil rights and civil liberties in the United States has been a fight for the attainment of the abstract values which our nation claims it is committed to achieving.

The history of civil rights and civil liberties is not simply struggle, confrontation, marching, picketing, and demanding; it is holding the government responsible for the principles which are its central purpose for existence. From the beginning, our institutions, our statutes, our legal process were means to obtain fundamental civil liberties central to the American purpose: freedom of speech, freedom of the press, freedom of assembly, freedom of religion, due process of law, the right to privacy, the right to a fair trial, the right to vote and have that vote counted fairly, the right to equal opportunity, education, housing, and employment.

The history of civil rights and civil liberties has been dynamic, reflecting constant change as new challenges emerged in the shift from a simple, homogenous, agrarian, rural society to an advanced, highly complex, industrial, urban society. Although our principles have remained the same, our institutions and laws have continually changed. Thomas Jefferson recognized the necessity for such change in a letter he wrote in the nineteenth century:

> I am certainly not an advocate for frequent and untried changes in laws and constitutions. I think that moderate imperfections had better be born with because we accommodate ourselves to them and find practical means to correct their ill effects, but I know also that laws and institutions must go hand in hand with the progress of the human mind, as that becomes more developed, as more discoveries are made, new truths disclosed, and manners and opinions change with the changing circumstances, institutions must advance also, and keep pace with the times. We might as well require a man to wear still the coat which fitted him as a boy as civilized society to remain ever under the regiment of their barbarous ancestors.

Our institutions and laws must change as our society changes.

We may not think of our ancestors as "barbarous," yet our early treatment of black Americans, native Chinese-Americans, and women can hardly be considered "enlightened."

Changes have occurred. For example, at one time imprisonment was considered a constructive solution to social problems. Until recently, daily devotional services in public schools were considered a way to achieve proper public values. Eighteen-year-olds were not considered mature enough to vote in most states. Progress has been made in all these areas.

Still, the history of civil liberties is not always a pleasant one, nor does it show Americans in their best light. It is painfully clear in American history that at certain times and under certain circumstances individuals and groups have been deprived of their liberties and denied fundamental freedoms under the rationalization that such denial was in the public interest.

Granted, liberty is not license; if an individual abuses his freedom, takes advantage of society, corrupts justice, or poses a threat to law and order, society has the right to take action on its own behalf. The problem is to know when and where to draw that line. When have the limits of freedom been exceeded? Conversely, when have the essential social controls of free society been imposed too arbitrarily? Does the majority have the right to temporarily suspend the rights of the minority in order to preserve liberty?

Examples of attempts to suspend the rights of members of minority groups are, unfortunately, recurrent in our history. Aliens, for example, have faced this problem since the Alien and Sedition Acts of 1798. In the turbulent years of the 1840s, Catholic immigrants were often treated with intolerance and as second-class citizens. The lack of equality in the treatment of Indians, slaves, free blacks following the Civil War, and women is also evident in the treatment of labor agitators and political and economic radicals with allegedly dangerous ideas. Pacifists and conscientious objectors encounter great difficulties during war years. And we have had not only arguments for, but also public policy which calls for placing American Communists in a deprived legal status.

The treatment of the Japanese-Americans during World War II is an example of the complexity of civil rights and civil liberties. After the attack on Pearl Harbor many Americans honestly believed the Japanese-Americans posed a serious national threat; yet, in retrospect, we must ask ourselves if they were not victims of temporary national hysteria and if their rights were not unjustifiably sacrificed.

The Japanese began appearing on the United States West Coast in the late nineteenth century and were used as cheap, reliable, highly effective labor. The Japanese, on the whole, were ambitious, aggressive, thrifty, and quick to accept the American work ethic. As they realized their importance to the system, they began to demand more wages. In 1891 the first of several strikes by Japanese agricultural workers occurred, causing considerable criticism of these "undesirable aliens," these "overaggressive, insolent, money-graspers."

By World War I the Japanese had acquired nearly 75,000 acres of California land and were leasing nearly half a million acres more. Many Californians saw them as alien landlords and tried to stop their progress. But the Japanese, anxious to become part of the American system, saved their money, went to school, obtained good training, and demanded jobs commensurate with that training. However, the unions refused and few were hired, so the Japanese went into business for themselves.

Soon several thousand Japanese men were successfully operating small businesses, acquiring wealth, and seeking the benefits of American life. Many looked for property outside the Japanese ghetto. The hostile American reaction resulted in the formation of the Asiatic Exclusion League, and technical laws preventing naturalization were rigidly enforced. By this time, however, a generation of American-born Japanese with proper claim to the full rights of American citizenship had been born. As hardworking, enterprising, and thrifty as their parents, they continued to play an important but resented role in the American economy. The growing tension with Japan added to many Americans' resentment of the Japanese.

The attack on Pearl Harbor brought the situation to a climax. Some 110,000 Japanese, the majority of whom were American-born citizens, were forced by government order to sell their homes and businesses and were herded into temporary barracks (in essence, benign concentration camps).

Although at the time it was claimed that the American-Japanese were a threat to national security, if one group of citizens can be so treated during a period of national emergency, a precedent is created which should disturb every American.

From the standpoint of civil liberties, the episode has long-range implications, for the denial of one individual's rights is a direct threat to the rights of all Americans.

In the 1930s the United States Supreme Court began to question whether justice was being attained for large numbers of Americans as a result of the federal policy of keeping "hands off" local law enforcement. After careful examination, begun in 1932 and continuing for forty years, it was gradually and consistently concluded that local justice was *not* true justice. Often local courts offered no true justice for a black man in the South. Likewise, there was often little justice for a stranger accused of a crime in a community. Local standards were often biased, prejudiced, and intolerant. Therefore, the Court came to insist that uniform national standards be applied in local courts and in police procedures. The Supreme Court, charged with interpreting our laws, established uniform national standards to be applied to local justice.

Unfortunately, however, value systems such as prejudices and resistance to change cannot be legislated out of existence.

Summary

The history of civil rights and civil liberties reflects our values, national purpose, the American experience with government, and the need for flexibility within stability. If the fundamental values of our society are to be preserved and extended, citizens must understand and support those institutions and statutes which, in practice, reflect the principles set forth in the Declaration of Independence, the Constitution, and the Bill of Rights.

These documents established not only each citizen's civil liberties—freedom from government oppression—but also each citizen's civil rights—claims to affirmative assistance from the government.

Many of our basic principles relating to civil rights and civil liberties are derived from the Magna Carta. Signed in England in 1215 by King John, the Magna Carta became a precedent for democratic government and individual rights, laying the foundation for requiring rulers to uphold the law, forbidding taxation without representation, requiring due process of law, and providing safeguards against unfair imprisonment.

The colonists brought these ideals to America, and when they were again faced with oppression by the English king they rebelled. Their belief in and desire for civil rights and civil liberties were stated in the Declaration of Independence which asserted that all men are created equal and are entitled to the unalienable rights of life, liberty, and the pursuit of happiness. It further asserted that governments are instituted by and derive their power from the governed.

To achieve the goals set forth in the Declaration of Independence, our forefathers drafted the United States Constitution, the basic instrument of our government and the supreme law of the land, which was signed in 1789.

Some states refused to ratify the Constitution if it did not contain personal guarantees. Ten amendments to the Constitution containing such guarantees were passed in 1791 and became known as the Bill of Rights. The Bill of Rights protects a person's right to "life, liberty, and the pursuit of happiness" and forbids the government to violate these rights:

- The First Amendment guarantees freedom of religion, freedom of speech, freedom of the press, and freedom of assembly and petition.
- The Second Amendment guarantees the right to bear arms.
- The Fourth Amendment forbids unreasonable searches and seizures and requires probable cause.
- The Fifth Amendment guarantees due process and just compensation when private property is acquired for public use; it prohibits double jeopardy and self-incrimination.
- The Sixth Amendment guarantees the individual's rights in a criminal trial.
- The Eighth Amendment forbids excessive bail, excessive fines, and cruel and unusual punishments.

Since the Fifth Amendment was directed to federal officials, an additional amendment was later ratified, the Fourteenth Amendment, which requires each state and locality to abide by the Constitution and the Bill of Rights.

Without means of enforcement, the great body of federal, state, and municipal law would be meaningless. To ensure enforcement, police have been given power and authority from local, state, and federal sources; but they are also restricted in their use of this power by the Constitution, the Fourteenth Amendment, and the courts. They have the power to enforce the laws so long as they do not violate the civil rights and liberties of any individual.

Although the principles of civil rights and civil liberties do not always prevail in practice, they remain the cornerstone of our democracy, our American creed. These principles directly affect how law enforcement officers fulfill their responsibilities. In addition, as our society changes, our institutions and laws must change accordingly.

Application

Read the following case studies and answer the questions following each.

A. Liberty Jones was standing on a street corner speaking to a crowd that had gathered. Incensed about violence on television, he was advocating the destruction of all television sets. The crowd began to chant remarks as Jones accelerated his feelings about violence. Jones then led the crowd down Main Street, demonstrating peacefully with banners and shouts of "Down with television violence." As they passed a television service store, Liberty picked up a rock and threw it at the display window, shattering it. Others followed, and considerable damage was done to the store and its merchandise. Liberty was arrested and charged by the police. His defense in court was the First Amendment to the Constitution.

1. Would the First Amendment protect Liberty in this case?
2. What would be the arguments for and against whether Liberty was guilty of breach of peace?

B. Herman Remington was sitting in his car in his driveway, looking over a pistol he had just purchased from a local gun store. As Officer Willie Ketcham drove by, he observed Herman's actions and arrested him for possessing a firearm. When in court, Herman pleaded not guilty and stated that his arrest was a constitutional violation.

1. Does Remington have a justifiable defense? Why or why not?

C. Detective Mary O'Brien saw Sam Newstart walking down the street and remembered that she had arrested Sam a month ago for possession of narcotics. Detective O'Brien felt very strongly that Sam would have narcotics in his possession again and decided to stop and search him. She found heroin in Sam's possession and charged him. In court Sam pleaded not guilty and claimed that his constitutional rights had been violated.

1. What amendment would apply to this case?
2. Will Sam's contention of violation of this amendment be upheld in court?
3. What are the issues?

D. Officer James Strongbow arrested fourteen-year-old Billie Akerson who was riding a stolen bicycle. At the station house, Officer Strongbow advised Billie that if he wanted to relieve his conscience, he should give a written statement admitting the theft. Billie did so. At the court hearing, the judge stated that he would handle the case as a moral issue and that, in view of the confession, Billie didn't need a lawyer. The parents agreed, and Billie was sent to the home school for boys for six months. While there he met Rodney Harcourt, a public defender who felt Billie was a victim of a miscarriage of justice. He appealed the case to a higher court.

1. What amendment(s) would the lawyer base his case on?
2. What are the issues?
3. Do you think the appeal should be granted?

Answers

A. 1. The First Amendment would protect Liberty's right to express his opinions publicly. It would not protect his right to incite the crowd to violence nor his own violent act.
   2. Liberty was not guilty of breaching the peace when he spoke to the crowd, nor when he led the peaceful demonstration, provided they were not obstructing traffic and there was no ordinance against peaceful street marches. (A license is required in many cities.) Liberty was

guilty of breaching the peace when he threw the rock through the television service store window and when he incited others to follow suit.

B. 1. Remington has a justifiable defense under the Second Amendment which guarantees the right to bear arms.

C. 1. The Fourth Amendment applies to the case of Sam Newstart.

   2. The contention of violation of constitutional rights will probably be upheld.

   3. The issues are: (1) Did the officer have probable cause to suspect that a crime had been committed and that the individual stopped and searched had committed the crime? (2) Was a warrant issued? In both instances, the answer is *no*. The officer had no probable cause to believe that a crime had been committed, and she had no warrant.

D. 1. The lawyer would base his case on the Fifth Amendment which guarantees due process of law and on the Sixth Amendment which governs criminal prosecutions.

   2. The issues are: (1) Was Billie informed of his right to remain silent, to refrain from self-incrimination? (2) Was Billie provided with counsel for his defense?

   3. The appeal should be granted since Billie was *not* informed of his right to remain silent nor was he provided with counsel for his defense.

Discussion Questions

1. What specific restrictions are placed on the police officer by the Bill of Rights?

2. Why has the Supreme Court said that state and federal governments can pass laws against carrying weapons when the Second Amendment specifically guarantees the right to bear arms?

3. Why were blacks considered ''unequal'' until Lincoln was president? The Constitution existed; why did it not apply to blacks?

4. What is the basic difference between civil rights and civil liberties?

5. In what well-known cases has the Fifth Amendment been repeatedly used?

6. What does police power and authority consist of?

References

Binder, A., and Geis, G. *Methods of research in criminology and criminal justice.* New York: McGraw Hill, 1983.

Creamer, J.S. *The law of arrest, search and seizure.* 3rd ed. New York: Holt Rinehart and Winston, 1980.

Feder, D. ''What does the 2nd amendment really mean?'' *Human events* (May 17, 1980): 8-11.

Felkenes, G.T. *Constitutional law for criminal justice.* Englewood Cliffs, N.J.: Prentice-Hall, Inc., 1978.

Frankel, L.H. *Law, power and personal freedom.* St. Paul, Minn.: West Publishing Company, 1975.

Germann, A.C.; Day, F.D.; and Gallati, R.B. *Introduction to law enforcement and criminal justice.* Springfield, Ill.: Charles C. Thomas, 1969.

"Handgun facts." A pamphlet distributed by Handgun Control, Inc. (n.d.).

Klein, I.J. *Constitutional law for criminal justice professionals.* North Scituate, Mass.: Duxbury Press, 1980.

Levine, J.P.; Musheno, M.C.; and Palumbo, D.J. *Criminal justice: A public policy approach.* New York: Harcourt Brace Jovanovich, 1980.

Lewis, P.W., and Peoples, K.D. *The Supreme Court and the criminal process: Cases and comments.* Philadelphia: W.B. Saunders Company, 1978.

Miller, F.W.; Dawson, R.O.; Dix, G.E.; and Parnas, R.I. *The police function.* Mineola, N.Y.: The Foundation Press, 1971.

Myrdal, G. *The American dilemma.* New York: Harper and Brothers, 1944.

Pritchett, C.H. *The American Constitution.* New York: McGraw-Hill, 1977.

Siegel, L.J. *Criminology.* St. Paul, Minn.: West Publishing Company, 1983.

Subcommittee to the Constitution. *The layman's guide to individual rights under the United States Constitution.* Washington, D.C.: U.S. Government Printing Office (n.d.).

"The Supreme Court and individual rights." *Congressional quarterly,* (December 1979).

Waldron, R.J. *The criminal justice system.* 3rd ed. Boston: Houghton Mifflin Co., 1984.

Weglyn, M. *Years of infamy.* New York: Wm. Morrow and Company, 1976.

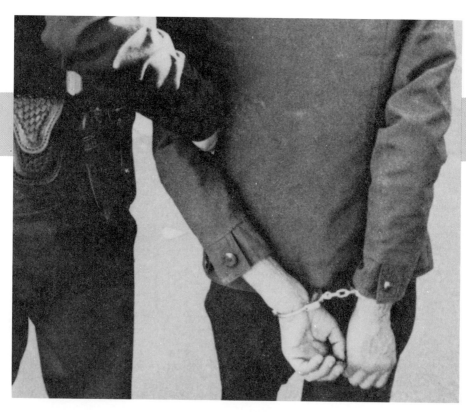

*The Fourth Amendment requires that a search or
arrest be reasonable and based on probable cause.*

Lawful Search, Seizure, and Arrest

Reliance Upon Reason and Probable Cause

Do You Know . . .

- The major provisions of the Fourth Amendment?
- How to define seizure, reasonable, arrest, and stop and frisk?
- On what major sources probable cause can be based?
- What the major categories of informational probable cause are?
- What is established by the Exclusionary Rule?
- What the principal justifications (preconditions) for a reasonable search are?
- What authorities and restrictions are provided by the following cases: *Chimel, Weeks, Mapp, Carroll, Chambers, Coolidge?*
- What limitations are placed on searches?
- What a search warrant is and what it must contain?
- When forcible entry is legal?
- When nighttime and no-knock warrants are justified?
- What challenges might be made to a warrantless search?
- What special conditions apply to search of automobiles?
- What is meant by plain view evidence and what qualifies an item as such?
- What the authorities for lawful arrest without a warrant are?
- What basic principles underlie stop and frisk?

- What the differences are between an arrest and stop and frisk?

- What significance the *Terry* case has in relation to the Fourth Amendment?

> *Reason never has failed men. Only force and oppression have made the wrecks in the world.*
>
> —*William Allen White*
>
> *Common sense is instinct and enough of it is genius.*
>
> —*W.H. Shaw*

Introduction

Detective Martin McFadden of the Cleveland Police Department liked to walk the streets of Cleveland, watching and meeting people. Sometimes he would just stand for a while, letting the people walk past. It wasn't his hobby; it was his job. For thirty years he had spotted criminal activity such as pickpocketing and shoplifting, and he was good at his job. McFadden's success was attributable not just to the years of experience or the knowledge of criminal activity he had gained, but to his patience. The average criminal couldn't wait the way McFadden could.

One afternoon in 1963 Detective McFadden saw two men standing near a jewelry store. For all practical purposes they just seemed to be talking to each other, but to McFadden, a man of thirty years of detective work (thirty-nine years of police experience), "they just didn't look right." He had never seen the two before and couldn't say what first drew his attention to them, but he decided to take a post in a nearby store entrance and watch for a while.

The two men repeated a ritual nearly a dozen times. One man would walk to the window, pause, look into the window for a while, and then walk toward the corner. He would come back to look into the same window and then rejoin his companion. After a short conference, the man would repeat the entire pattern: walk to the store window, up to the corner, back to the store, and then back to rejoin the first man.

While this was going on, Detective McFadden continued to watch the two. At one point a third man joined them, talked with them briefly, then left. When he left, the other two spent several more minutes repeating the routine.

By this time McFadden suspected they were casing the store for a "stick-up." As he made this decision, he also feared they might have a gun. He had already decided to investigate their activity further when the two men walked toward the store where the third man was waiting. At this point, the detective's knowledge was confined to what he had observed. He didn't know any of the three men by name or sight, and he had received no information on them from any other source.

McFadden approached the three, identified himself as a police officer, asked for their names, and then decided to act. He turned one man, later identified as John Terry, around, putting Terry between himself and the other two men. McFadden then made a quick ''pat down'' of Terry's outer clothing. He could feel a pistol in one of Terry's pockets but was unable to remove the gun. Keeping Terry between himself and the others, he ordered all three men to enter the store. As they obeyed him, McFadden removed Terry's coat and took a .38 caliber revolver from the pocket. Inside the store McFadden asked the owner to call for a police wagon while he patted the outer clothing of the others, taking another revolver from the coat of a man named Chilton. At the station Terry and Chilton were formally charged with carrying concealed weapons.

When Terry and Chilton were brought to court, their lawyers moved that the guns could not be used as evidence, claiming they were illegally seized. If the guns couldn't be used as evidence, there was no evidence and there was no charge or case.

The trial judge heard the two cases at the same time. He made two decisions which, at first, seemed to contradict each other. First, he rejected the defense motion that the evidence had been illegally seized. Then he rejected a prosecution contention that McFadden had established probable cause to arrest, and therefore, that officer had taken the guns in a search which was incidental to a lawful arrest. If neither theory applied, what did?

The judge said that on the basis of McFadden's experience, he had reasonable cause to believe that the defendants were conducting themselves suspiciously and some interrogation should be made of their actions. Purely for his own protection, the court added, McFadden had the right to frisk the men whom he believed to be armed. The judge said McFadden had stopped the suspects for the purpose of investigation, no arrest occurred at that point, and the ''frisking of the outer clothing for weapons'' was *not* a full search.

Both men appealed their conviction to the United States Supreme Court, but before the Court's decision was handed down in 1968, Chilton had died. Therefore, its review applied only to Terry.

The Court recognized Detective McFadden as a man of experience, training, and knowledge. McFadden was certainly ''a man of reasonable caution.'' And, as a man of ''**ordinary care** and prudence,'' he waited until he had strengthened his suspicions, making his move just prior to what he believed would be an armed robbery.

The United States Supreme Court upheld the Ohio court verdict; it said that McFadden had ''acted reasonably'' because (1) Terry and Chilton's actions were consistent with McFadden's theory that they were contemplating a daylight robbery, (2) such a robbery would most likely involve the use of guns, and (3) nothing in the men's conduct, from the time the officer first noticed them until he confronted them, gave him any reason to doubt his theory.

The Court went on to say that McFadden had to make a quick decision when he saw the three gathered at the store and his actions were correct.

The Fourth Amendment

Arbitrary searches and/or seizures have no place in a democratic society. In fact, colonial grievances against unreasonable searches and seizures, in part, led to the revolt against English authority. The Fourth Amendment of the Constitution guaranteed the right of citizens to be secure from such arbitrary searches and seizures.

> *The constitutional standards for searches and seizures, including arrests, are contained in the Fourth Amendment which requires that searches and seizures be reasonable and based on probable cause.*

The terms *reasonable* and *probable cause* provide a very fine, but significant, weight to balance the scales of justice which measure the conduct of all people. Without what is referred to as probable cause, the laws that govern us might easily become unbalanced, that is, too permissive or too restrictive.

The second part of the Fourth Amendment, called the "warrant clause," states: "No warrant shall issue but upon probable cause. . . ." In other words, all warrants (search and arrest warrants) must be based on probable cause.

Reasonable

The rules for determining what constitutes a reasonable search or seizure result from interpretation of the first part of the Fourth Amendment, called the "reasonable search and seizure clause," which states in part: "The right of the people to be secure in their persons, houses, papers, and effects, against unreasonable searches and seizures shall not be violated."

Reasonable means sensible, just, logical, possessing good sound judgment, well balanced. "Possessing good judgment" implies making decisions. Each case and situation is different from other cases and other situations; therefore, police officers must use their personal judgment as to what action to take. "Well balanced" applies to a built-in stability for justice. On the one hand there is the justification for an action, whether it be an arrest based on probable cause, or an arrest warrant, or stopping and frisking someone. On the other hand, the justification for the action must be balanced by observing the limitations on each action. When the limitations for any action are exceeded, we have gone beyond the reasonableness that made the action legal. Justification and limitation must always be considered together.

> Reasonable *means sensible, justifiable, logical, based on reason.*

Probable Cause

According to Creamer (1980, p. 9):

> Probable cause for an arrest is defined as a combination of facts or apparent facts, viewed through the eyes of an experienced police officer, which would lead a man of reasonable caution to believe that a crime is being or has been committed.
>
> Probable cause for the issuance of a search warrant is defined as facts or apparent facts, viewed through the eyes of an experienced police officer, which would lead a man of reasonable caution to believe that there is something connected with a violation of law on the premises to be searched.

Probable cause requires more than mere suspicion; it requires facts or proof that would lead a person of reasonable caution to believe a crime has been committed or that premises contain evidence of a crime. Creamer goes on to note that according to Justice Rutledge (*Brinegar v. United States* [1948]): "The substance of all definitions of 'probable cause' is a reasonable ground for belief in guilt."

Further, in *Smith v. United States* (1949), probable cause is defined as: "The sum total of layers of information and the synthesis of what the police have heard, what they know, and what they observe as trained officers. We [the courts] weigh not individual layers but the laminated total."

Creamer also points out that the concept of probable cause is one of the oldest and most important in criminal law, having been in existence for more than two thousand years and occurring in both Roman law and the common law of England. According to Creamer (1980, p. 8): "This concept of probable cause has acquired its legal potency in the United States because it has constitutional dimensions and because it is interpreted in the final analysis by impartial judges rather than by the police. The severe penalty that the courts impose on police who fail to abide by the spirit of the Fourth Amendment is to declare the evidence they gathered inadmissible."

Sources of Probable Cause

You recall that probable cause is "a state of facts that lead a man of ordinary care and prudence to believe and conscientiously entertain an honest and strong suspicion that the person is guilty of a crime." That strong suspicion may be founded on several sources: observation by officers, expertise of officers, circumstantial factors, or information communicated to officers.

More often than not, observational probable cause will be supplemented by expertise, circumstantial or informational probable cause. In general, the officer has reason to believe a person is involved in a specific crime. For example, the officer sees a car weaving down the highway at 55 mph, the posted speed limit. Although the driver is not speeding, a car weaving from lane to lane would lead any reasonable person to entertain a strong suspicion that the driver was under the influence of alcohol or drugs. The officer not only has a right but also an obligation to stop the driver because he jeopardizes his own life as well as the lives of other people on the highway.

When he stops the weaving driver, he discovers that the driver is suffering from a sneezing attack caused by a gust of wind blowing a cloud of dust into the car. Obviously an arrest would not be justified even though the probable cause strongly suggested the driver was drunk. On the other hand, if the driver had shown signs of having been drinking, such as the odor of alcohol on his breath, red eyes, slurred speech, or incoodination, the officer would need additional corroboration by administering a sobriety test at the scene and further evidence such as a breath or urine test at the time of booking.

Probable cause may be based on:
- *Observation by officers.*
- *Expertise of officers.*
- *Circumstantial factors*
- *Information communicated to officers.*

Police officers first have to justify an arrest by proving to themselves that a crime has been committed and that sufficient evidence exists to convince a jury ''beyond a reasonable doubt'' that the suspect was involved in the crime. Probable cause to stop a person in reference to a specific crime does not always mean that an arrest will occur.

Observational Probable Cause

Observational probable cause is what the officer sees, hears, or smells, that is, evidence which is presented directly to the officer's senses. This is similar to eyewitness testimony, and it is the strongest form of probable cause. The courts have generally recognized certain types of events as being significant in determining probable cause.

Suspicious activities are generally regarded as contributing to probable cause. For example, a car being driven slowly can be suspicious when (1) the car has circled a block several times, (2) the people in the car are carefully observing a building, (3) the building is closed, and (4) the building is located in a high-crime area. All four factors contribute to probable cause.

Familiar criminal patterns are also generally recognized as contributing to probable cause. The conduct of a person can be indicative of a familiar pattern associated with the sale of stolen property or narcotics or of someone who is casing a building.

Officers assemble factors that contribute to probable cause for arrest. Any one factor by itself may not be sufficient to establish probable cause, but collectively they provide justification—probable cause.

Expertise and Circumstantial Probable Cause

Expertise and circumstantial probable cause are often tied to observational probable cause. Police officers' knowledge of criminal traits and their ability to "put the pieces together" may also contribute to probable cause. For example, two police officers questioned two men seen driving from an alley at two A.M. The officers noted the license number of the car, the occupants' names, and questioned the driver and passenger. The two men were allowed to continue, but a short time later, when the officers learned there had been a burglary in a nearby town, they forwarded the description of the car and its occupants to the local law enforcement officers. The suspects were apprehended, and a search of the vehicle revealed burglary tools as well as the property taken in two burglaries.

In the original confrontation with the suspects, the two officers were not satisfied with the suspects' explanation of why they were there at such an early hour, and even though they did not have sufficient evidence for an arrest, or could not establish probable cause for an arrest, their investigation of the suspicious circumstances eventually led to the arrest and conviction of the suspects, who later pleaded guilty to seven prior offenses, all felonies.

Arrest and conviction in this case were based on the officers' decision as to when there was sufficient reason to act on probable cause. To arrest without a warrant when a felony has been committed, the officers must have reasonable cause to believe that the person(s) arrested committed the crime.

Informational Probable Cause

Informational probable cause covers a wide range of sources. In the case previously described, the information about the two suspects forwarded by the police officers to the police in the nearby town constituted informational probable cause. In addition to official sources, victims of crime and citizen informants can be reliable sources of informational probable cause.

> The major categories of reliable informational probable cause are (1) official sources, (2) victims of crimes, and (3) citizen informants.

Official sources include police bulletins, police broadcasts, and roll call information. This information can be relied upon because it is received through official police channels. Information coming from official sources is, in itself, generally sufficient to justify arrest. Although the police officer may arrest on the basis of information received through official channels, this does not relieve the prosecution from establishing that the original source of information was reliable; that is, the original source of information was sufficient to establish probable cause to arrest.

It is the source of information, not the manner of transmission, that will be considered at a trial. Police officers may testify that the information on which they acted was sent over the police radio, but the defendant has the right to demand to know where the information originated and who passed it on to the dispatcher. In other words, as in any other case, the original source of the information must be reliable. For instances, if police officers make an arrest based on information obtained directly from other police officers, the original officers may be required to testify at the trial as to their sources of information, and it is that source which must establish probable cause to arrest. The source may be a victim of a crime, a witness to a crime, or an informant.

Victims of crimes are also usually reliable sources of informational probable cause. Officers can be and are entitled to rely on the information supplied by victims of crimes committed against their person or property and to use this information in making the decision to arrest suspects. Their statements to police officers can be the source of the officers' belief that they have probable cause to look for a person or persons involved in the commission of a crime.

An example of this comes from the case of *Chambers v. Maroney* (1970) which involved the armed robbery of a Pennsylvania service station and which later went to the Supreme Court on the question of admissibility of evidence. From the attendant at the service station (the victim), police received a description of the two men who had robbed the station. The attendant said one man wore a green sweater and the other a trench coat. The attendant's statement was sufficient for the officers to establish probable cause that the two men described had committed the crime.

Apprehension of the robbers came within an hour because two teenagers had become suspicious of a blue station wagon that had circled the service station block several times. They told the officers that four men were in the vehicle and they had seen it speed out of the parking lot shortly after the robbery. The boys described the man in the green sweater as being one of the four occupants of the station wagon. The information from the boys pin-pointed the robbers' method of escape and established that four men were in the vehicle instead of two. The information from the victim of the crime gave police probable cause to arrest the two men; the information from the boys aided in locating them.

Into which category of informational probable cause does the information supplied by the boys fit? They were not official sources, victims, or informants. They had only witnessed suspicious actions, which are not an adequate basis for arrest. The information does not constitute informational probable cause; it was helpful, but far from sufficient to establish probable cause for an arrest. As a matter of fact, what the boys saw was actually just one of those small pieces of a puzzle assembled to create justification for an arrest—what has already been defined as circumstantial factors.

*Citizen **informants*** quite often provide probable cause. Included in this category are citizens who actually witness a crime and openly aid in the apprehension of the suspect. Eyewitnesses are persons who have observed a crime, who expect no favors from the police, and who do not exchange information for protection or act out of motives for revenge. Complete and otherwise credible information from a citizen informant, based on his personal knowledge that a felony has been committed, is generally sufficient probable cause to justify a felony arrest or to obtain an arrest or search warrant.

Even though information from citizen informants, witnesses to the commission of a crime, is evidence to establish informational probable cause, it is not necessarily absolute evidence. With time permitting, police officers must evaluate as thoroughly as they can that they are, in fact, dealing with an actual witness to a crime. There would be little doubt if a customer was in a store when it was robbed, the owner was shot and killed, and the customer gave police a description of the assailant. The customer would still be at the scene of the crime when the police arrived.

But compare the authenticity of the above witness to the following. A man walked into a police station and identified himself as a serviceman on leave. He gave his address and telephone number and then informed the officers that he had just seen marijuana in the possession of and smoked by a number of people at a given address. The information proved to be accurate; the police went to the address, found people in possession of marijuana, arrested them, and charged them with possession. The judge ruled that the arrest was not justified because the officers had not established probable cause to arrest prior to going into the dwelling and finding the marijuana.

Why? Because they had not established the witness as a reliable informant, nor had they any reason to believe his information was reliable. The serviceman was unknown to them; in fact, the officers did not check his identity further than what he had provided. There were no other circumstances, no additional evidence that would corroborate his information and thus make it reliable.

In the case of the grocery store robbery, in contrast, the officers already had independent evidence that a crime had been committed—a man was killed, and the customer was still at the scene of the crime when they questioned him. The customer was an eyewitness and could be accepted as such. The serviceman had to be considered an untested informant unless additional evidence proved he was a reliable source of information.

The Exclusionary Rule

Without procedures for enforcing the provisions of the Fourth Amendment, the impressive constitutional language would be meaningless. Consequently, the procedures and the power for their enforcement were vested in the courts. They must refuse to consider evidence obtained by unreasonable search and seizure methods, regardless of how relevant the evidence is to the case.

This rule, known as the **Exclusionary Rule,** is the direct result of the Supreme Court decision in the case of *Weeks v. United States* (1914). The Exclusionary Rule, defined in the *Weeks* case as a matter of judicial implications, was made applicable to the federal courts in 1914. In 1961 the Exclusionary Rule reached maturity when the Supreme Court, in the case of *Mapp v. Ohio*, extended the rule to every court and law enforcement officer in the nation.

> *Courts uphold the Fourth Amendment by use of the Exclusionary Rule which demands that no evidence may be admitted in a trial unless it is obtained within the constitutional standards set forth in the Fourth Amendment. Weeks v. United States made the Exclusionary Rule applicable in federal courts. Mapp v. Ohio made it applicable to every court in the country.*

On May 23, 1957, three Cleveland police officers arrived at Dolree Mapp's residence pursuant to information that a person wanted for questioning in connection with a recent bombing was hiding in Miss Mapp's home and that there was also a large amount of gambling paraphernalia hidden there. After telephoning her attorney, Dolree Mapp refused to admit the officers without a search warrant. Three hours later the officers returned with reinforcements and again sought entrance. When she did not come to the door, the police officers gained entry by forcibly opening one of the doors. Miss Mapp demanded to see the search warrant. When a paper, claimed to be the warrant, was held up by one of the officers, she grabbed it and placed it in her bra. A struggle ensued in which the officers recovered the piece of paper and handcuffed Miss Mapp. A thorough search was conducted of the entire apartment, including the basement of the building. Obscene materials, for the possession of which the defendent was ultimately convicted, were discovered as a result of that widespread search.

The state contended that even if the search were made without authority, it was not prevented from using the evidence at the trial because *Wolf v. Colorado* (1949) had authorized the admission of such evidence in a state court; furthermore, Ohio did not follow the Exclusionary Rule. After a discussion of other applicable cases, the Supreme Court decreed that henceforth evidence obtained by procedures which violated Fourth Amendment standards would no longer be admissible in state courts.

Since 1961 the Exclusionary Rule has applied to both the federal and state courts, and evidence secured illegally by federal, state, or local officers has been inadmissible in any court.

The Exclusionary Rule has important implications for the procedures followed by police officers, since neither the most skillful prosecutor nor the most experienced police officer can convince a jury of a defendant's guilt without adequate and lawfully obtained evidence. Police officers must obtain evidence which establishes that a crime has been committed, and they must obtain evidence which connects the defendant to the specific crime—usually long before the case comes to the prosecutor. Further, they must obtain such evidence without violating the rights of the defendant. Only if police officers obtain evidence that will be acceptable in court is there a probability of conviction. But many questions must be answered in determining acceptability of evidence. Consider the following situation.

Two officers stop a motorist driving down a street during the early morning hours. Even without knowing the reasons for stopping the motorist or whether the officers actually suspected he was guilty of a crime, we can assume that since a search was executed, it was a thorough one. In their search the officers find two packets of heroin on the driver. Will the evidence be accepted in court? That depends. What was the justification for stopping the motorist and was the search reasonable? If this individual is brought to trial, the officers will have to provide the judge with justifiable reasons for suspecting the man was carrying drugs.

The Inevitable Discovery Doctrine

On June 11, 1984, the United States Supreme Court ruled that illegally obtained evidence may be admitted at trial if the prosecution can prove that the evidence would "inevitably" have been discovered by lawful means *(Nix v. Williams)*. From this case the Supreme Court adopted what is now known as "the inevitable discovery exception to the Exclusionary Rule."

Chief Justice Warren E. Burger wrote in the majority opinion: "Exclusion of physical evidence that would inevitably have been discovered adds nothing to either the integrity or fairness of a criminal trial." The point of the inevitable discovery doctrine, he said, was to put the police in the same, not a worse, position than they would have been in if no police error or misconduct occurred.

Lawful Searches

Creamer (1980, p. 58) defines a **search** as: "The looking into or prying into hidden places. The term search in the context of the Fourth Amendment involves a governmental invasion of privacy. Searches are intrusions into the privacy for the purpose of obtaining incriminating evidence. . . . However, a search may never be justified by the incriminating evidence it turns up."

Guilty persons are convicted based on the facts which the court finds admissible. Police officers' reports must contain all the reasons for a search or seizure as proof of the reasonableness of their conduct. The questions most frequently asked by the prosecutor and the courts before admitting evidence are: Was the search reasonable? Was the arrest, if there was one, legal? There are rules to guide police officers in answering these questions on a day-to-day basis. The rules often seem contrary to what many people consider to be reasonable; however, these rules, contrary or not, *must* be considered when deciding whether a search or seizure is reasonable. The courts abide by these rules and base their decisions on them.

Since the word *unreasonable* is ambiguous, the courts have adopted guidelines to measure reasonableness and to assure law enforcement personnel that *if* certain rules are adhered to, their search or seizure will be acceptable—reasonable. The three principal justifications established by the court for the right to search are: (1) if the search is incidental to a lawful arrest; (2) if consent is given; (3) if a search warrant has been issued. These circumstances are the preconditions for a reasonable, legal search. A search which occurs under any one of these conditions is considered justified or reasonable.

> *The three principal justifications established by the court for the right to search are:*
>
> 1. *If the search is incidental to a lawful arrest.*
> 2. *If consent is given.*
> 3. *If a search warrant has been issued.*

Limitations on Searches

A reasonable search involves more than justification by an arrest, consent, or a search warrant. **Limitations** on the search itself are set. After establishing the right to search, police officers must determine the limitations on that right—limitations imposed by law and interpreted by the courts. General searches are unconstitutional.

> *The most important limitation imposed upon any search is that the scope must be narrowed. General searches are unconstitutional.*

Limitations on a Search Incidental to a Lawful Arrest

In a search incidental to a lawful arrest (lawful arrest will be discussed later in this chapter) the search must be made simultaneously with the arrest and must be confined to the immediate vicinity of the arrest.

Chimel v. California (1969), involving a search incidental to an arrest, provides a definition of search of a person and a dwelling as well as the limitations of the search. Officers went to the Chimel home with a warrant to arrest Ted Chimel on a charge of burglarizing a coin shop. Mrs. Chimel admitted the officers, who then waited ten to fifteen minutes for her husband to come home. When the arrest warrant was handed to Chimel, he was told that the officers wanted to "look around." He objected, but was informed that the officers had a right to search because it was a lawful arrest.

The officers opened kitchen cabinets, searched through hall and bedroom closets, looked behind furniture in every room, and even searched the garage. (Prior to this case, the courts had accepted fairly extensive searches incidental to an arrest.) On several occasions the officers had the wife open drawers and move the contents so they could look for items removed in the burglary. The search took nearly an hour and resulted in the officers finding numerous coins.

Chimel was convicted in a California court, but he appealed his conviction on burglary charges on the grounds that the evidence—the coins—had been unconstitutionally seized. The United States Supreme Court studied the principle of searches incidental to an arrest and determined:

> When an arrest is made, it is reasonable for the arresting officer to search the person arrested in order to remove any weapons that the latter might seek to use in order to resist arrest or effect his escape.
>
> It is entirely reasonable for the arresting officer to search for and seize any evidence on the arrestee's person in order to prevent its concealment or destruction and the area from within which the arrestee might gain possession of a weapon or destructible evidence.

The officers' justification for extending the search was based on the phrase that "It is entirely reasonable . . . to search . . . the area from within which the arrestee might gain possession of . . . destructible evidence."

In the *Chimel* case, the Supreme Court specified that the area of search could include only the arrestee's person and the area within his immediate control. The court defined **immediate control** as being that area within the person's reach.

> Limitations upon a search made incidental to an arrest are found in the Chimel Rule which states that the area of the search must be within the immediate control of the suspect—that is, it must be within his reach.

The *Chimel* case resulted in a clear definition as to what, beyond the suspect himself, could be searched when officers are using the authority of a search incidental to an arrest. The court pointed out that if an arrest is used as an excuse to conduct a thorough search, such as the search conducted in the *Chimel* case, the police would have power to conduct "general searches" which were declared unconstitutional by the Fourth Amendment over 180 years ago.

One can sympathize with the officers who had alerted Chimel's wife that they were looking for stolen coins and then felt they had to find them or face the possibility she would remove them. But the law allows only a limited search in this situation. Undoubtedly a magistrate would have issued a search warrant for the stolen coins if the officers had realized the limitations on their search and had requested the warrant.

Ironically, prior to the burglary, Chimel had wandered about the coin store, asked the owner where he kept his most valuable coins, inquired into the alarm system, and bragged that he was planning a robbery. Later he took exception to the owner's testimony that it was a "sloppy job," excitedly claiming that the burglary had been "real professional." But the Supreme Court reversed the California decision because the conviction had been based on evidence obtained in a search which was beyond reasonable limits.

An interesting sideline in the *Chimel* case is that three days after the initial search, officers again entered Chimel's house looking for evidence to support a separate charge of robbery. No evidence was seized on the second search, but Chimel was convicted and sentenced on the robbery charge.

Limitations on a Search with Consent

In a search where **consent** is given, the United States Supreme Court provides that the consent must be free and voluntary; therefore, it cannot be given in response to a claim of lawful authority by the officer to conduct the search at the moment. As with searches incidental to lawful arrest, a search with consent must be conducted only in the actual area for which the consent is given.

> Consent must be free and voluntary, and the search must be limited to the area for which the consent is given.

As noted by the Maine Supreme Court *(State v. Barlow, Jr.* [1974]): "It is a well established rule in the federal courts that a consent search is unreasonable under the Fourth Amendment if the consent was induced by deceit, trickery or misrepresentation of the officials making the search.'' A recognized exception to this general rule is when undercover operations are involved.

When a court is asked to determine if consent to search was ''free and voluntary,'' it considers such things as the subject's age, background, mental condition, and education. The number of officers involved should not be a factor if no aggressiveness is displayed. As stated in *People v. Reed* (1975): ''Where aggravating factors are not evident, the number of officers alone will not have an adverse effect on the consent. The presence of a large number of officers in an apartment does not present a situation which is per se coercive.''

The time of day might also be a consideration. Officers should generally avoid seeking voluntary consent to search at night. In *Monroe v. Pape* (1961) Justice Frankfurter said: ''Modern totalitarianisms have been a stark reminder, but did not newly teach, that the kicked-in door is the symbol of a rule of fear and violence fatal to institutions founded on respect for the integrity of man. . . . Searches of the dwelling house were the special object of this universal condemnation of official intrusion. Nighttime search was the evil in its most obnoxious form.''

Perhaps most important is the way in which the request to search is made. It must, indeed, be a request, not a command.

Limitations on a Search Conducted with a Search Warrant

Recall the provision of the Fourth Amendment that the warrant must particularly describe ''the place to be searched and the persons or things to be seized.''

> A search conducted with a warrant must be limited to the specific area and specific items delineated in the warrant.

Search Warrants

We are all protected against unreasonable searches and seizures by the United States Constitution, which guarantees that probable cause, supported by **oath** or **affirmation,** shall be the basis for issuing a search warrant. Our courts have interpreted this guarantee to mean that any search or seizure other than one conducted with a warrant is technically unreasonable. The courts do, however, recognize that emergency situations will arise in which a police officer will not have the opportunity to secure a warrant.

A **search warrant** is an order issued by any court of record or by a justice of the peace in a county having no municipal court other than a probate court. The court must have jurisdiction in the area where the search is to be made.

The warrant must contain the reasons for requesting the search warrant; the names of the persons presenting affidavits, for example, the officer who applied for the warrant, his colleagues, or others who have information to contribute; what specifically is being sought; and the signature of the judge issuing it.

> *A search warrant is a judicial order directing a police officer to search for specific property, seize it, and return it to the court. Probable cause is required for issuance of all warrants. Technically, all searches are to be made under the authority of a search warrant issued by a magistrate.*

The procedures for obtaining and executing search warrants vary from locality to locality, but the following example illustrates what is generally involved. Generally a search warrant may be issued for the following reasons:

- The property or material was stolen or embezzled.
- The possession of the property or material constitutes a crime, e.g., stolen property or drugs.
- The property or material is in the possession of a person with intent to use them to commit a crime, e.g., possession of burglary tools with intent to use them.
- The property or material was used in committing a crime, e.g., a gun, knife, or burglary tools.
- The items or evidence tend to show that a crime has been committed or that a particular person has committed a crime, e.g., letters, clothing.

When police officers present an **affidavit** to a magistrate, their facts must be sufficiently detailed to enable the magistrate to determine that probable cause to search exists. The affidavit need not be as polished as an entry in an essay contest, but it should not skimp on the facts.

The Constitution does not require all necessary information to appear on the face of the complaint, as long as a sworn affidavit made at the time the warrant was issued contains those facts.

> *A police officer must present adequate evidence for a magistrate to determine probable cause. If sufficient facts are contained in the application and supporting affidavit or supplementary facts are presented during questioning of an officer who applies for a warrant, a magistrate will issue the search warrant.*

The use of search warrants has increased since the *Chimel* decision which restricted the area that could be searched incidental to a lawful arrest. Prior to the *Chimel* case, some courts allowed extensive searches incidental to a lawful arrest. The *Chimel* ruling, however, makes it necessary for police officers to obtain a search warrant as well as an arrest warrant if they want to search a suspect's house incidental to the execution of the arrest warrant.

What May Be Seized

A search warrant must clearly specify or describe the things to be seized. The prosecution or the state must accept the burden of proof when items are seized that are not specifically stated in the warrant. This does not mean such items cannot be seized. They can, if a reasonable relationship exists between the search and the seizure of materials not described or if officers discover **contraband**—anything which is illegal for a person to own or have in his possession such as heroin or a machine gun.

> Police may seize items not specified in the search warrant if they are similar in nature to those items described, if they are related to the particular crime described, or if they are contraband.

Consider this example. On two separate occasions, officers arrived at a private dwelling with search warrants authorizing them to seize items taken from burglaries. On both occasions their knock was unanswered, so they entered through a living room window. They seized many items on the search warrants as well as other similar items not specifically mentioned in the warrants. When the case came to court, the defense challenged those items introduced as evidence of the burglaries which were not specifically mentioned in the warrants. The lower court allowed the evidence to be used, and the state supreme court upheld the decision. The high court said the items seized in addition to those mentioned in the warrants were similar to items which the stores had on hand when the burglaries occurred.

In addition, contraband discovered during a search authorized by a warrant may also be seized. It is not necessary that the contraband be connected to the particular crime described in the search warrant.

Gaining Entrance

Police officers are usually required to announce their authority and purpose before entering a home. This protects the citizen's rights and avoids needless destruction of property where the owner or occupant is willing to voluntarily admit a police officer. Sometimes, however, the suspect will not allow entrance, or there may be no one home.

Police officers who arrive to execute a search warrant and find the house unoccupied may forcibly enter the house to search it. If the dwelling is an apartment, they could probably get a passkey from a caretaker, but this would still be considered a **forced entry.** So is opening a closed but unlocked door or window. Officers who are denied entrance to execute a search warrant may break an inner or outer door or window to gain entry.

> Generally police officers must announce themselves. They may enter a house by force to execute a search warrant if they are denied entrance or if there is no one home.

Nighttime and No-Knock Search Warrants

A search warrant will normally be issued to be served during daylight hours, that is, from sunrise to sunset. **Nighttime warrants** may be justified and requested of the court by police officers. They must state the reasons, based on facts, for fearing that unless the search is conducted in the night the objects of the search might be lost, destroyed, or removed.

Similarly, unannounced entries for the purpose of executing search warrants must also receive prior judicial authorization. The **no-knock search warrant** is reserved for situations where the judge recognizes that the normal cooperation of the citizen cannot be expected and that an announced entry may result in loss, destruction, or removal of the objects of the search; for example, surprise entries are often used in searches for narcotics and gambling equipment. In either of these instances, the court will usually acknowledge that evidence can easily be destroyed during the time required to give notice, demand admittance, and accept the citizen's denial of entry.

> *Two special types of search warrants, nighttime and no-knock, must be authorized by a magistrate as a special provision of a search warrant.*

Warrantless Searches

When police officers follow the letter of the law and secure a search warrant, they receive an advance court decision that probable cause does exist. It was originally believed that the magistrate should be the sole judge of probable cause, but when **emergency situations** or **extenuating circumstances** became apparent, the courts decided there were times when reasonable searches and seizures could be based on the decisions of police officers. In all instances where a magistrate has not made the decision of probable cause, the police officer or the prosecution must assume the task of proving that the search was reasonable.

Emergency Situations/Extenuating Circumstances

In situations where police officers sincerely believe they have established probable cause and there is no time to secure a warrant, they can act on their own decision. But it is here that the opportunity for a defense lawyer to challenge the legality of the search can be used. While a number of challenges can be raised, two occur most frequently. The defense may contend that a magistrate would not have issued a warrant had the officers presented the facts before the court (probable cause was not established), or that the officers had ample opportunity to secure a warrant and therefore had no justification to act without one.

If the defense raises one of these challenges in a case involving evidence seized as a result of a warrantless search, the burden of proof is on the officer and the prosecution. It must be proven that the officer was reasonable and prudent and had gathered sufficient facts to make the important decision that probable cause to search existed and that the search must be conducted immediately.

When police officers conduct a search without a warrant, they may be challenged on the basis that:

■ *Probable cause was not established.*

■ *The officers had opportunity to secure a warrant and had no justification to act without one.*

The Fourth Amendment says a great deal in only fifty-four words. It guarantees that United States citizens will not be unjustly searched or arrested and that their property will not be unlawfully seized. With added historical court decisions, most of the language of our present laws governing search and seizure is represented.

The Fourth Amendment was intended to interpose a magistrate between the police and the citizen—requiring a magistrate to study the evidence presented by the police and decide whether a warrant should be issued. The Constitition is a product of a period when authority had been badly misused, and it was presumed magistrates would be more objective than officers.

A strict interpretation of the Constitution requires that a magistrate decide whether probable cause exists. When the officer presents the facts to a magistrate and is granted a warrant, the defense lawyer cannot attack the decision of the individual officer. When the search warrant is issued, it becomes an order from the court, as the Constitution intended it to be. It is no longer the prosecution which has to defend its actions, but the lawyer for the accused who has to prove that a magistrate erred in issuing the warrant.

While the laws are still intended to provide protection, they are also designed to meet emergency situations not considered in the original amendment. There are rules to be observed in such situations; each must fall within the guarantees in the Fourth Amendment. The key is to protect all citizens against unreasonable searches and seizures.

The men who drafted the Constitution understood that other reasonable measures would have to be accepted to uphold the laws of the nation. The Supreme Court, therefore, surveys cases brought before it to determine whether the action taken in a particular situation was reasonable according to the Fourth Amendment. What may be reasonable in one situation may not be reasonable in another. For instance, you could justify a warrantless search of a vehicle by stating the reasons you believed it would be gone if you waited to obtain a search warrant. This same logic, however, cannot be applied to a search of a house or any other fixed object.

We have already looked at three types of warrantless searches:

■ Searches connected with stop and frisk (limited to a search for weapons).

■ Searches incidental to an arrest.

■ Searches when consent has been given.

Although Supreme Court approval of warrantless searches incidental to an arrest was established in cases prior to 1920, it was the *Chimel* opinion in 1969 that confined the search to an area within the immediate control of the person arrested. This opinion did not apply to automobiles, however.

As noted, searches may be conducted without a warrant even though the search is not associated with stop and frisk, incidental to an arrest, or with consent; but when it is conducted under these circumstances, police officers must prove that an emergency existed which did not allow them to secure a search warrant. Very frequently this involves automobiles and other conveyances having **mobility.**

Warrantless Searches of Automobiles and Other Conveyances

When a vehicle is involved, the rules of reasonableness, although within the boundaries of the Constitution, are quite different. The courts have long recognized the need for separate exemptions from the requirement of obtaining a search warrant where mobility is involved.

The precedent for a warrantless search of an automobile resulted from *Carroll v. United States* (1925) which established two basic principles justifying warrantless searches of automobiles: (1) there is probable cause, and (2) the automobile or other conveyance would be gone before a search warrant could be obtained.

> Carroll v. United States *set the precedent for warrantless searches of automobiles provided there is probable cause for the search, and the vehicle would be gone before a search warrant could be obtained.*

The *Carroll* case did not involve a search incidental to an arrest. The concern was with probable cause for a search, not for an arrest.

During Prohibition in the 1920s, some 1,500 agents pursued bootleggers, many of whom brought liquor down from Canada. In addition to the imports, there was so much local production that the 9,500 stills raided in the first six months of prohibition were known to be only a small fraction of the total.

Visualize a scene in a Michigan "honky-tonk" during the 1920s. Four men were sitting at a table holding a meeting; two were supposed buyers, and two were bootleggers. The "buyers" were actually federal prohibition agents. Although the meeting seemed to go well, the two bootleggers, George Carroll and John Kiro, were somewhat suspicious. They indicated that the liquor had to come from the east end of Grand Rapids, Michigan. They would get it and return in about an hour. Later that day, Carroll called and said delivery could not be made until the next day. But the two did not return the next day.

The agents returned to their normal duty of watching a section of road between Grand Rapids and Detroit known to be used by bootleggers. Within a week after their unsuccessful attempt to make the "buy," the agents recognized Carroll and Kiro driving by. They gave chase but lost the car near East Lansing.

Two months later they again recognized Carroll's car coming from the direction of Detroit. They pursued the car and this time were successful in overtaking it. The agents were familiar with Carroll's car, they recognized Carroll and Kiro in the automobile, and they had reason to believe the automobile would contain bootleg liquor. A search of the car revealed sixty-eight bottles of whiskey and gin, most of it behind the upholstery of the seats where the padding had been removed. The contraband was seized, and the two men were arrested.

George Carroll and John Kiro were charged with transporting intoxicating liquor and were convicted in federal court. Carroll's appeal, taken to the United States Supreme Court, resulted in a landmark decision defining the rights and limitations for warrantless searches of vehicles.

The knowledge of the two men and their operation as well as the fact that their car was believed to be used in the transportation of liquor, produced the probable cause necessary to justify a search. So the first principle establishing this as an exception to the rule requiring a search warrant was met.

> The Carroll *decision established that the right to search an automobile is not* dependent on the right to arrest the driver or an occupant, but rather it is dependent upon the probable cause the seizing officer has for believing that the contents of the automobile violate the law.

Regarding the mobility of such a conveyance, the court amplified its opinion to include some of the key reasons why an automobile can be exempted while a house or fixed object cannot:

- A vehicle or conveyance can be quickly moved out of the jurisdiction or locality in which the warrant must be sought.
- The occupants of a vehicle are immediately alerted.
- The vehicle's contents may never be found again if a police officer has to wait to obtain a search warrant before searching the car.

The Supreme Court saw each of these possibilities in the case against George Carroll and, consequently, provided a basis for making a similar judgment in a situation where these circumstances might occur.

The requirement of mobility is also present in the case of *Chambers v. Maroney* (1970). This case involved the armed robbery of a service station. As you may recall from the earlier account of the case, the station attendant described the two men who held guns on him, and two boys provided officers with a description of a vehicle they had seen the men in circling the block prior to the robbery and again speeding out of the area. Within an hour officers spotted the vehicle and identified the occupants as being those whom the three witnesses had described. They stopped the car and arrested the men. The evidence seized and later used to convict Chambers and the other man included two revolvers and a glove filled with change they had taken from the service station.

Chambers based an appeal on the fact that the officers took the car to the police station before searching it. The defense contended that the search was illegal because it was made incidental to rather than simultaneous with the arrest. The defense was right. As a search incidental to an arrest, it would have been illegal. But the Court observed the same set of circumstances in relation to the warrantless search of a vehicle; the seizing officers did have probable cause to believe that the contents of the automobile violated the law. Therefore, it was the right to search, not the right to arrest, that provided the officers with the authority for their actions.

The Supreme Court added another opinion to the *Chambers* case when it said that it was not unreasonable under these circumstances to take the vehicle to the police station to be searched. In other words, the probable cause to search at the scene continued to exist at the police station. Based on the facts, the Supreme Court said there was probable cause to search, and since it was a fleeing target, the Chambers vehicle could have been searched on the spot where it stopped. The Court reasoned that probable cause still existed at the police station, and so did the mobility of the car. The Court quickly pointed out that such actions must be confined to vehicles and other conveyances having mobility.

> *The Chambers case established that a car may retain its mobility even though it is impounded.*

Yet another interpretation of mobility was provided in the case of *Coolidge v. New Hampshire* (1971). The *Coolidge* case, a homicide, tested the requirements of mobility. A fourteen-year-old girl disappeared in Manchester, New Hampshire, and her body was found eight days later. She had been shot. A number of errors were made in the case, including the fact that arrest and search warrants were drawn up and signed by the man who became the chief prosecutor.

A neighbor's tip led police to E.H. Coolidge, whom officers admitted was fully cooperative, even to the point of agreeing to a polygraph examination. The examination was conducted several days after Coolidge was first questioned. During the next two and a half weeks, evidence against Coolidge began to accumulate. The evidence included what the prosecution said was the murder weapon, which officers had obtained from Mrs. Coolidge. The arrest and search warrants were drawn up based on this evidence. The search warrant specifically designated Coolidge's car, which was in the driveway in plain view of the house at the time of the arrest. Mrs. Coolidge was told she was not allowed to use the car, and it was impounded prior to other officers dropping Mrs. Coolidge at a relative's home. During the next fourteen months the car was searched three times, and vacuum sweepings from the car were introduced as evidence.

Coolidge was convicted of the girl's murder. His appeal challenged the legality of the evidence seized from the car. Discounting the fact the warrants were invalid and the prosecution could not prove the search was incidental to an arrest, the prosecution contended the seizure of the car should be allowable based on the standards established by the *Carroll* and *Chambers* cases.

The Court considered the principles of the *Coolidge* case and weighed them against those of the precedent cases. Because testimony from witnesses and from Coolidge indicated that his car was at the scene of the murder, the Court accepted the fact that probable cause to search had been established. But was there sufficient cause to fear the automobile might be moved?

The Court said there was not. Coolidge could not have gained access to the automobile when the officers came to arrest him, and he had, in fact, received sufficient prior warning that he was a prime suspect to have already fled. The only other adult occupant, Mrs. Coolidge, was driven to a relative's home by other officers who were with her after the vehicle was actually taken to the station.

> *Coolidge v. New Hampshire established that the rule of mobility cannot be applied unless there is actually a risk that the vehicle would be moved.*

Table 14–1.   *Searching Cars.*

Method of Search	Leading Case Authority	Justification for Search	Permissible Scope of Search	Time of Search	Purpose of Search
Stop-frisk	*Terry v. Ohio,* 392 U.S. 1 (1968)	Officer's reasonable fear for his own safety	Person and area in his immediate control	At time of stop	Self-protection of officer
Arrest-search	*Preston v. United States,* 376 U.S. 364 1964; *Chimel v. California,* 395 U.S. 752 (1969)	Probable cause to arrest someone in car	Person and area of car in his control	At time of arrest	Self-protection of officer and preservation of evidence
Search warrant	*Spinelli v. United States,* 393 U.S. 410 (1969)	Probable cause presented to judge	Entire car	Any time after warrant issued	Find and preserve evidence
Consent search	*Amos v. United States,* 225 U.S. 313 (1921)	Waiver of 4th Amendment rights by owner or driver	Entire car	Any time after consent	Find and preserve evidence
Custodial search of impounded car	*Cooper v. California,* 386 U.S. 58 (1967)	Police regulations to protect property in their custody	Entire car	Any time	Preserve car and contents
Probable cause search	*Chambers v. Maroney,* 399 U.S. 42 (1970)	Probable cause that car contains contraband, etc.	Entire car	Any time	Find and preserve evidence

Source: The Law of Arrest, Search, and Seizure by J. Shane Creamer. Copyright © 1980 by Holt, Rinehart and Winston. Reprinted by permission of CBS College Publishing.

Neither the *Carroll* nor the *Chambers* opinions could apply here because of the following differences:

- There appeared to be no criminal intent to flee.
- This was not a case of a fleeting opportunity to search on an open highway after a hazardous chase.
- There was no evidence of contraband, stolen goods, or weapons.
- There was no evidence of any friends of Coolidge's waiting to move the car and the evidence therein.
- The automobile in question was secured from intrusion when it was found.

Since the Coolidge premises were guarded throughout the night, and since Mrs. Coolidge was with officers until after the car had been towed in, it had been secured at all times.

The Court could not accept the prosecution's contention that the Coolidge vehicle was included in the category of mobility. The prosecution then contended that the evidence was admissible because it was in plain view. The Court also rejected this contention.

The following rule applies to vehicles or other conveyances when they are used in the commission of serious crimes such as felonies. Such **instruments of a crime** may be seized and searched if the vehicle is an integral part of the defendant's apparatus for the commission of the crime. This generally includes get away vehicles as well as automobiles, trailers, or similar conveyances used to secrete or transport stolen items.

United States v. Ross (1982) held that the police may search a car, including containers, without a warrant as long as they have probable cause to believe contraband is somewhere in the car.

> *Vehicles or other conveyances used in a crime may be seized and searched if the vehicle is an integral part of the defendant's apparatus for the commission of the crime.*

See Table 14–1 for the limitations on searching vehicles.

Plain View

Plain view refers to evidence which is not concealed and which is inadvertently seen by an officer engaged in a lawful activity. Several factors determine what constitutes plain view. First, the police officer must be engaged in lawful activity prior to the discovery of plain view evidence. Such circumstances might occur while the officer is executing a warrant to search for another object, while in pursuit of a suspect, during a search incidental to a lawful arrest, during stop and frisk, or any other legitimate reasons justifying an officer's lawful presence.

Second, the seized items must not be concealed. As the name implies, they must be in "plain view." Third, the discovery of the evidence in plain view must be inadvertent, by accident. Police officers cannot obtain a warrant to search an automobile and fail to mention a particular object they are looking for and then justify its seizure pursuant to the plain view doctrine. If they were looking for it initially, it must be mentioned in the warrant. Fourth, plain view alone is not sufficient to justify the warrantless seizure evidence.

> *Plain view refers to evidence which is not concealed and which is inadvertently seen by an officer engaged in a lawful activity.*

In the *Coolidge* case the Court could not accept the seizure of the car as being within plain view limitations because the officers intended to seize the car when they came onto Coolidge's property. So the rule applied to Coolidge and to all plain view cases following is that the discovery of evidence in plain view must be inadvertent—by accident. The plain view doctrine applies even though the objects seized are not under immediate control of the suspect.

In contrast is a case in which local officers received information that one or two motels in their jurisdiction were to be burglarized during a particular weekend. Patrols in those areas were alerted. When one squad noticed a vehicle slowly driving around one of the motels, the activity was not enough to presume the existence of probable cause to arrest. But since the situation called for investigation, the car was stopped.

While talking to the driver and his passenger, the officers heard conflicting statements as to why the men were in the area. One officer could see a partially concealed television set in the back seat and could identify at least part of the word motel on the set. When questioned, the driver and his passenger presented differing stories as to how they happened to have the television in the car. The men were arrested, and the television set proved to be a valuable piece of evidence in their conviction.

In reviewing the case, the Supreme Court recognized that the stolen item had been seized within the limitations of the plain view rule. The officers had probable cause to stop the vehicle for investigation, and, thus, they had the right to be in a position to see the television set. The discovery of the television set was not the only fact that led to the arrest. The officers were alerted that there might be a motel burglary, and they considered the movement of this particular car to be suspicious. In addition, the men's responses to their questions were contradictory.

Reasonable Seizures—Lawful Arrests

Creamer (1980, p. 56) contends that an **arrest** is: ''The beginning of imprisonment, when a man is first taken by government and restrained of his liberty.'' *Black's Law Dictionary* defines arrest as: ''The apprehension or detaining of the person in order to be forthcoming to answer an alleged or suspected crime.'' Laws of arrest are generally uniform in all fifty states and in federal criminal proceedings.

> *Statutes throughout the United States generally define arrest as the taking of a person into custody by the actual restraint of the person or by his submission to the custody of the officer that he may be held to answer for a public offense before a judge.*

Brandstatter and Hyman (1971, p. 132) warn that: ''The legal definition of arrest has to do with control and detention; not with punishment. This is frequently overlooked or misunderstood. An arrest made for the purpose of punishing an individual is an invalid arrest. Not only will it not hold up in court, but the arresting officer may also face legal charges or departmental disciplinary action for misconduct.''

Elements of Criminal Arrest

According to Creamer (1980, p. 56), the four elements of a criminal arrest are:

1. An *intent* by the peace officer to make an arrest.
2. Real or pretended *authority* to arrest.

3. A *seizure* or *restraint,* actual or constructive.

4. An *understanding* by the person being seized that he is being arrested.

Arrest Warrants

All states have a statute authorizing law enforcement officers to make arrests, but the Constitution stipulates that lawful arrests require an arrest warrant. Klotter and Kanovitz (1985, pp.103-111) note that: ''Aside from constitutional considerations, there is a very practical reason why police officers should, wherever time permits, obtain a warrant before making an arrest. If the warrant is proper on its face and the officer does not abuse his authority in executing the arrest, he will be protected against civil liability for false imprisonment, even though it is later determined that the arrest was unjustified.'' Klotter and Kanovitz list eight requirements for a valid arrest warrant:

1. The warrant must be supported by probable cause. It will be up to the magistrate to determine if probable cause exists.

2. The affidavit for the warrant must be supported by oath or affirmation; that is, some individual must swear to the truth of the facts described in the affidavit.

3. The person to be seized (arrested) must be named.

4. The warrant must state the nature of the offense with sufficient clarity to advise the subject of the accusation.

5. The warrant must designate the officer or class of officers who are directed to carry out the court's order.

6. The warrant must be issued in the name of a state or the United States.

7. The warrant must be issued and signed by a neutral, detached judicial officer, including his/her title.

8. Additional state requirements may also be present.

Arrest Without a Warrant

Lawful arrests require an arrest warrant. If, however, an emergency situation exists and the officers have probable cause to believe a person has committed a crime, they may make an arrest. The courts will determine its legality.

In *Draper v. United States* (1959) the United States Supreme Court stated: ''Probable cause exists where the facts and circumstances within their (the arresting officers') knowledge and of which they had reasonable trustworthy information are sufficient in themselves to warrant a man of reasonable caution in the belief that an offense has been or is being committed.''

Creamer (1980, p. 57) notes that: ''The exact moment when a warrantless arrest occurred is frequently the most important preliminary determination for a court. The legality of a warrantless arrest hinges, in large measure, on the probable cause or guilt-laden facts confronting the police officer up to and including, but never after, the actual moment of arrest. At the moment of arrest, probable cause

An officer frisks a suspect.

ceases to build. Any after-the-arrest, guilt-laden facts that develop will not be considered by the courts as part of the probable cause necessary to justify the arrest.''

> If there is probable cause and an emergency situation exists, an officer may make an arrest without a warrant. The courts will determine whether the arrest was lawful.

Police officers may make lawful arrests without a warrant for felonies or misdemeanors committed in their presence or for felonies not committed in their presence if they have probable cause.

There are four authorities for arrest without a warrant. The first authority allows for an arrest for a public offense committed or attempted in the presence of an officer. Public offense includes both felonies and misdemeanors. To determine whether a public offense has been committed, ask this question: ''Would you be justified in seeking a complaint upon which an arrest warrant would be issued, and could you testify to all the elements of the crime?''

''Committed or attempted in the presence of an officer'' means the crime was apparent to the officer's senses, including sight, hearing, or smelling. A conversation over the telephone is within the officer's presence; therefore, a conversation lawfully overheard that might be indicative of criminal conduct is in the officer's presence. The odor of marijuana is evidence that a crime is being committed in the officer's presence and may constitute probable cause to effect an arrest. In most cases, however, the officer will actually see the crime committed, and this is where the first authority generally applies. A suspect can be arrested without a warrant for a misdemeanor only if the offense is committed in the officer's presence.

The remaining authorities allow an officer to arrest a suspect for a felony which was not committed in his presence. Any lawful arrest, with or without an arrest warrant, requires probable cause. Without an arrest warrant, police officers can arrest a suspect for a felony only if they have probable cause based on their own observations or on information provided to them. They cannot make this same type of arrest for a misdemeanor.

> *The four authorities for arrest without a warrant are:*
>
> 1. *When a public offense is committed or attempted in an officer's presence.*
> 2. *When a person arrested has committed a felony, although not in an officer's presence, for example, an all-points bulletin on a bank robber before a warrant is issued.*
> 3. *When a felony has in fact been committed, and the officer has reasonable cause to believe that the person has committed it; for example, an officer answers a shooting call and the suspect is still at the scene.*
> 4. *On a charge made upon probable cause of the commission of a felony; for example, a person observed running down the street as a burglar alarm sounds is a likely suspect for the crime.*

Stop and Frisk

The courts have stated that suspicious circumstances impose upon police officers the duty to investigate, that is, to stop and question suspects. The procedure of stopping and questioning suspects is directly regulated by the justifications and limitations associated with lawful searches and seizures.

Although we associate a thoroughness to the terms *search* and *seizure* that does not seem to apply to the terms *stop* and *frisk,* the United States Supreme Court (*Terry v. Ohio* [1968]) says there is a **seizure** whenever a police officer restrains an individual's freedom to walk away; and there is a search when an officer makes an exploration of an individual's clothing even though it may be called a ''pat down'' or a ''frisk.''

> *A stop is a seizure if physical force or a show of authority is used. A frisk is a search.*

Although stopping and frisking fall short of being a technical arrest and a full-blown search, they are definitely forms of search and seizure. Police officers stop citizens of their communities as part of their duties. This is daily practice, but most encounters cannot be considered ''seizure of the person'' because the officer does not restrain the individual's liberty. So an officer can stop a citizen without the action being considered a seizure of the person. Defining the term **frisk**, however, leaves no other alternative than to consider it a search.

The United States Supreme Court (*Terry*) had definite opinions about the type of search called a frisk: "It is simply fantastic," the court stated, "to urge that such a procedure, performed in public by a police officer, while the citizen stands helpless, perhaps facing a wall with his hands raised, is a 'petty indignity'. . . . It is a serious intrusion upon the sanctity of the person, which may inflict great indignity and arouse strong resentment, and it is not to be undertaken lightly." The Supreme Court gave its own definition of "**stop and frisk**" by calling it a "protective search for weapons." As always, where there is a justification for taking specific action, there are also limitations. According to the Supreme Court, a protective seizure and search for weapons carries these limitations.

> *Stop and frisk is a protective search for weapons in which the intrusion must be limited to a scope reasonably designed to discover guns, knives, clubs, and other hidden instruments, which may be used for an assault of a police officer or others.*

Since some states do not have stop and frisk laws, when this type of protective search and seizure for weapons is referred to, it is on the basis of the opinion of the United States Supreme Court.

The Supreme Court's opinion on stop and frisk and the rights and limitations for this type of action are illustrated in the case of *Henry v. United States* (1959) which involved an arrest made by officers who had observed Henry and another man stop twice in an alley and load cartons into a car. When the officers saw the two men driving off, they waved Henry's car to stop, searched it, took the cartons, and later made the formal arrest. The men were convicted in Illinois courts of unlawful possession of stolen radios. The Supreme Court overruled the Illinois verdict, saying that an actual arrest had taken place when the officers stopped the suspect's car. The problem in this case was that the officers observed the transaction from a distance of some three hundred feet and could not determine the size, number, or contents of the cartons. The suspects were formally placed under arrest some two hours after they were taken into custody.

The issue in this case was whether there was probable cause for the arrest leading to the search that produced the evidence on which the conviction rested. Since probable cause to arrest had not been established at that time, the Court said the stolen merchandise could not be accepted as evidence. Future cases in many states were decided on this 1959 case, and the accepted opinion was that stopping a vehicle or an individual constituted an actual arrest.

The specific principles which arose from *Terry v. Ohio* (1968) can be applied to most stop and frisk situations.

1. Police officers have the right and duty to approach and interrogate persons in order to investigate crimes.

2. Police officers may stop and make a *limited* search of a suspect if they observe unusual conduct which leads them to reasonably conclude, in light of their experience, that criminal activity may be afoot and that the individual whose suspicious behavior the officers are investigating at close range is armed and probably dangerous.

3. The test of the officers' action is whether a "reasonably prudent man in the same circumstances would be warranted in the belief that his safety or that of others was in danger."

4. Officers may proceed to stop and frisk if nothing occurs to change the officers' theory that criminal activity may occur or that the suspect is armed.

5. The type of search in stop and frisk must be limited. It is a "protective seizure and search for weapons and must be confined to an intrusion which is reasonably designed to discover guns, knives, clubs, or other hidden instruments of assault."

6. If these conditions (principles 1–5) are met, the stop and frisk does *not* constitute an arrest.

7. Since stop and frisk actually involves a search and seizure, it must be governed by the intent of the Fourth Amendment of the Constitution which forbids indiscriminate searches and seizures.

Seven principles applicable to stop and frisk came from the Terry case. It established that the authority to stop and frisk is independent of the power to arrest. A stop is not an arrest, but it is a seizure within the meaning of the Fourth Amendment and therefore requires reasonableness.

While it is true that both the stop and the arrest are seizures and both must be justified by a showing of reasonableness, there are some important differences between a stop and an arrest.

On January 8, 1985, the United States Supreme Court ruled unanimously that the police may act without a warrant to stop and briefly detain a person they know is wanted for investigation by police in another city. In *United States v. Hensley* the Court extended the warrantless stop and frisk rules that the Court established in the 1960s for police who suspect that a crime is about to be committed or is imminent. Police may now sometimes stop, question, and even search people when there is less than probable cause to believe they were involved in a past crime.

Table 14–2.   **Stop and Arrest.**

	STOP	ARREST
JUSTIFICATION	Reasonable suspicion	Probable cause
INTENT OF OFFICER	To resolve an ambiguous situation	To make a formal charge
SEARCH	Possibly a "pat-down" or frisk	Complete body search
RECORD	Minimal	Fingerprints, photographs, and booking

A Caution

Creamer (1980, p. 64) emphasizes that: "Police arrest powers are indeed awe-some, and even while they protect society, they can destroy a citizen. The Fourth Amendment was designed to limit the chances of a citizen being harmed by an unjust arrest. The courts have the responsibility to make sure the Fourth Amendment works to protect the citizen and, at the same time, assure the security of society."

Summary

The constitutional standards for searches and seizures, including arrests, are contained in the Fourth Amendment which requires that searches and seizures be reasonable and be based on probable cause. As the word implies, *reasonable* means sensible, justifiable, logical, based on reason. Probable cause requires more than mere suspicion. It requires facts or proof that would lead a person of reasonable caution to believe a crime has been committed by a specific individual or premises contain evidence of a crime.

Probable cause may be founded on (1) observation, (2) expertise, (3) circumstantial factors, and (4) information conveyed to the officers, including official sources, victims of crimes, and citizen informants.

The Fourth Amendment is reasonable in protecting the rights of the people while allowing law enforcement the right to investigate crime. It is strong enough to protect citizens, but also flexible enough to enable police officers to uphold the Constitution.

The standards established by the Fourth Amendment are enforced by use of the Exclusionary Rule which states that no evidence can be admitted in a trial unless it is obtained within the standards established in the Fourth Amendment. The federal precedent for this rule is found in the case of *Weeks v. United States*. The state precedent is found in the case of *Mapp v. Ohio*.

Reasonable searches and seizures must meet the standards set forth in the Fourth Amendment. The three principal justifications for a search are (1) it is incidental to a lawful arrest, (2) consent is given, or (3) a search warrant is obtained.

Even when one of these conditions is met, certain limitations are placed on the search. The most important limitation imposed upon any search is that the scope must be narrowed. General searches are unconstitutional. The limitations placed on searches incidental to lawful arrest come from the case of *Chimel v. California* which states that the scope of the search must be narrowed to the area within the suspect's immediate control. The limitations to a search made with consent are that the consent must be free and voluntary, not in response to an implied right to search, and the scope must be limited to the area for which consent has been given. The limitations to a search made with a warrant are stated within the warrant itself.

Most searches require a warrant. A search warrant is a judicial order directing a police officer to search for specific property, seize it, and return it to the court. Probable cause is required for issuance of all warrants. Technically, all searches are to be made under the authority of a search warrant issued by a magistrate. If a search is conducted with a warrant, the burden of proof as to admissibility of evidence seized is on the defense; if it is conducted without a warrant, the burden of proof is on the searching officer and the prosecution.

Police may seize items not specified in the search warrant if they are similar in nature to those items described, if they are related to the particular crime described, or if they are contraband.

When police officers execute a search warrant, they generally announce themselves. They may enter a home by force if they are denied entrance or if no one is home. Two special types of search warrants, nighttime and no-knock, may be requested if the officers fear the objects of the search might be lost, destroyed, or removed.

Warrantless searches, based on probable cause, have been justified in stop and frisk, incidental to a lawful arrest, with consent, in an emergency situation, and when mobility is involved.

The two most frequent challenges to such warrantless searches which may be raised by the defense are that (1) there was insufficient evidence to establish probable cause, so a search warrant would not have been issued by a magistrate, and (2) there was sufficient time to obtain a search warrant.

Special provisions have been made for warrantless searches of cars and other conveyances due to their mobility. Precedents for the warrantless search of an automobile were established by the *Carroll* case which demonstrated that probable cause must exist along with mobility—the belief that the car or evidence would be gone by the time a search warrant was obtained. It also demonstrated that the right to search was not dependent on the right to arrest, but rather on probable cause. The *Chambers* case demonstrated that a car may retain its mobility even though it is impounded. The *Coolidge* case demonstrated that the rule of mobility cannot be applied unless there is actually a risk the vehicle will be moved. A car may also be searched without a warrant if it is an instrumentality of a crime.

A special instance of legal seizure of evidence without a warrant exists in the plain view situation; that is, evidence which is not concealed is inadvertently seen by an officer engaged in lawful activity and is supported by other facts or evidence.

Citizens of the United States are also protected against unreasonable arrest (seizure) by the Fourth Amendment. An arrest is usually defined as the taking of a person into custody by the actual restraint of the person or by his submission to the custody of the officer so that he may be held to answer for a public offense before a judge. Such arrests must be reasonable, and they must be predicated on probable cause.

The Fourth Amendment requires that arrests be made by having a magistrate issue an arrest warrant, but police officers may make an arrest without an arrest warrant in an emergency; for example, for a felony or misdemeanor committed in their presence or for a felony not committed in their presence if they have probable cause. A person can be arrested for a misdemeanor only if (1) there is an arrest warrant or (2) the crime was committed in the officer's presence. A person can be arrested for a felony if (1) there is an arrest warrant, (2) the crime is committed in the presence of an officer, or (3) there is probable cause that the person committed a felony.

Stop and frisk is a form of search and seizure and, as such, is governed by the intent of the Fourth Amendment which demands that all searches and seizures be based on reason. A stop is not an arrest; the authority to stop and frisk is independent of the power to search or arrest. A frisk, however, is a search. The type of search allowed under stop and frisk is limited to a protective seizure and search for weapons, and is not a search for evidence of a crime.

Application

A. The background of the case of *Sibron v. New York* (1968) began when an officer watched Sibron for eight hours in one day. The officer had seen him talking to many known narcotic addicts, became suspicious, followed him, and finally asked him to step out of a restaurant where he could be searched. The officer found a packet of heroin on Sibron and charged him with unlawful possession of narcotics. The New York courts, which *do* have a stop and frisk law, convicted Sibron, who then appealed his case to the Supreme Court.
   1. Do you think the Supreme Court upheld the New York decision? Why or why not?

B. A recent district court conviction for aggravated robbery went before the state supreme court when the defendant charged that the arresting officer did not have sufficient knowledge or information to establish probable cause and, therefore, the arrest was illegal. The state admitted that the arresting officer had no personal knowledge of the facts justifying the arrest, except that there was a pickup order for the defendant. The arresting officer had obtained a photograph of the defendant at rollcall. The following circumstances surrounded the case: A woman was knocked down by two men just outside a bank. They took her purse, which contained more than $12,000. One witness told the police that as he was coming toward the bank, he passed a parked car which the two fleeing robbers entered, and he got a good look at the driver—the third man and the defendant in this appeal. He described the man to the police, including the fact that the man was unshaven and wore a dark jacket. Another witness to the robbery wrote down the license number of the car and gave it to the police.

In court, two employees of a parking lot testified that the defendant drove into the lot about thirty minutes after the time of the robbery, parked his car, tossed a jacket through an open window and left. The men originally identified the defendant from photographs shown to them by police. Although residents of the apartment building where the defendant was thought to be living did not know him by the name the police gave them, they were able to identify him from pictures shown to them by a detective. Several weeks had passed since the robbery when this identification was made, and residents of the apartment building told the police that the defendant was getting ready to move. The police entered the building and arrested the suspect.

1. Was there sufficient evidence to establish probable cause?
2. Was a warrantless arrest proper? Why or why not?

Answers

A. 1. No. The Supreme Court reversed the decision because the officer had conducted a search, not a frisk for weapons, without having probable cause to make an arrest. This case demonstrated that the courts will not tolerate the use of ''stop and frisk'' for full-scale searches.

B. 1. There was sufficient evidence to establish probable cause. The state supreme court ruled that the police were in full possession of facts which showed that a felony had been committed and that the defendant was the driver of the getaway vehicle. Probable cause was established by the totality of the information prossessed by the police as a unit.

  2. A warrantless arrest was proper. Although warrantless arrests are not favored, arrest without a warrant for a felony, on probable cause, is proper when circumstances lead the arresting officer to reasonably believe that an immediate arrest is essential to prevent escape.

Discussion Questions

1. Compare the two quotations at the beginning of this chapter. Which seems to support the Exclusionary Rule?

2. Why aren't the police given total freedom to help stop crime? Why aren't they allowed to use evidence which clearly establishes a person's guilt, no matter how they obtained this evidence?

3. In a state where stop and frisk is legal, can a police officer be sued for stopping and frisking someone?

4. According to Sir Arthur Conan Doyle, author of the Sherlock Holmes mystery stories: ''When you have eliminated the impossible, whatever remains, however improbable, must be the truth.'' Discuss this quotation in light of what you know about lawful arrest.

5. What are the most important factors in determining if and when an arrest occurred?

6. Must all elements of probable cause exist prior to a lawful arrest?

7. Why isn't the presence of ten officers considered intimidation when a request to search is made?

8. Have you ever been involved in a search and seizure situation? How was it handled?

9. From what you have learned about search and seizure, do you feel that the restrictions placed upon police officers are reasonable?

10. Why did the Court state that the search in *Coolidge v. New Hampshire* was not valid?

References

Brandstatter, A.F., and Hyman, A.A. *Fundamentals of law enforcement.* Beverly Hills, Cal.: Glencoe Press, 1971.

Creamer, J.S. *The law of arrest, search, and seizure.* 3rd ed. New York: Holt, Rinehart, and Winston, 1980.

Cushman, R.E., and Cushman, R.F. *Cases in constitutional law.* 3rd ed. New York: Appleton-Century-Crofts Educational Division, 1968.

Dowling, J. *Criminal procedure.* St. Paul, Minn.: West Publishing Company, 1976.

Felknes, G.T. *Constitutional law for criminal justice.* Englewood Cliffs, N.J.: Prentice-Hall, 1978.

Ferdico, J. *Criminal procedure for the law enforcement officer.* St. Paul, Minn.: West Publishing Company, 1976.

Friedelbaum, S.H. *Contemporary constitutional law.* Boston: Houghton, Mifflin, 1972.

Greenberg, M.S., and Ruback, R.B. *Social psychology of the criminal justice system.* Belmont, Cal.: Wadsworth, 1982.

Inbau, F.E.; Thompson, J.R.; and Zagel, J.B. *Criminal law and its administration.* Mineola. N.Y.: The Foundation Press, 1974.

Kelly, A.H., and Harbison, W. *The American Constitution.* 4th ed. New York: W.W. Norton, 1970.

Klotter, J.C., and Kanovitz, J.R. *Constitutional law.* 5th ed. Cincinnati: Anderson Publishing Company, 1985.

Lewis, P.W., and Peoples, K.D. *The Supreme Court and the criminal process.* Philadelphia: W.B. Saunders, 1978.

Lockhart, W.B.; Kamisar, Y.; and Choper, J.H. *Constitutional rights and liberties.* 4th ed. St. Paul, Minn.: West Publishing Company, 1975.

Maddex, J.L., Jr. *Constitutional law.* St. Paul, Minn.: West Publishing Company, 1974.

Mendelson, W. *The Constitution and the Supreme Court.* 2d ed. New York: Dodd, Mead and Company, 1968.

Pritchett, C.H. *The American Constitution.* New York: McGraw-Hill, 1977.

The Supreme Court and individual rights. Washington, D.C.: Congressional Quarterly, Inc., December 1979.

The Supreme Court, justice, and law. 3rd ed. Washington, D.C.: Congressional Quarterly, Inc., 1983.

Tresolini, R.J., and Shapiro, M. *American constitutional law.* 3rd ed. New York: Macmillan, 1970.

United States Department of Justice, *Handbook of search and seizure.* Washington, D.C.: U.S. Government Printing Office, 1971.

The Criminal Justice System in Operation

Recall Waldron's description of our criminal justice system as having three inter-related components: the law enforcement community, the judicial community, and the corrections community, each contributing to the criminal justice process, which, according to Waldron: "Is a well-defined legal continuum through which each offender may pass from detection and investigation of the criminal act; to arrest and accusation; to trial, conviction, sentencing, and possible incarceration; to eventual release."*

Section Four looked at the law enforcement community in the criminal justice system. In this section you will be introduced to the role of the courts (Chapter 15), the role of corrections (Chapter 16), and how the juvenile justice system differs from the adult criminal justice system (Chapter 17).

---

*Ronald J. Waldron. *The Criminal Justice System, an Introduction.* 3rd ed. Boston: Houghton Mifflin Company, 1984, p. 57.

One of the ways police officers aid the crimnal justice
system is by testifying in court.

Law Enforcement, the Courts, and the Judicial Process

Do You Know . . .

- What role police officers play in the criminal justice system?
- What the adversary system is?
- What reasonable doubt is?
- What rights the accused has?
- What constitutes due process?
- What landmark decision resulted from *Gideon v. Wainwright?*
- What the critical stages in the criminal justice process are?
- What functions are served by a preliminary hearing? A grand jury? A coroner's jury?
- What the discovery process is?
- What types of pleas may be entered at the time of arraignment?
- What some alternatives to trial are?
- What screening is and when it is appropriate?
- What diversion is?
- What plea bargaining is and what purpose(s) it serves?
- What the typical hierarchy is within the state court system? The federal court system?

■ How jurors are selected and what safeguards are taken to insure against bias?

■ How the defense attorney may attempt to discredit the testimony of a police officer?

■ What common sentencing schemes are?

The truth, the whole truth, and nothing but the truth.
　　　　　　　　　　　　　　　　—Legal Oath

Justice is truth in action.

　　　　　　　　　　　　　　　　　　—Disraeli

Introduction

Numerous aspects of the criminal justice process have been referred to in preceding chapters. The criminal justice system in America is a complex topic constituting a study in itself. This chapter presents only a basic overview of the major components of this system and how police officers function within it.

Police officers are an integral part of the criminal justice process. The criminal codes which guide police officers in enforcing laws are not a set of specific instructions, but rather are rough maps of the territory in which police officers work and assist the criminal justice process. The officer's role in the criminal justice process includes making legal arrests; legally obtaining accurate, relevant information and evidence; writing complete and accurate reports; identifying suspects and witnesses; and providing effective, truthful testimony in court. Regardless of how sketchy or complete the officers' education or experience, in reality they are interpreters of the law and may function as judge and jury at the start of every case. If the case reaches court, the court must subsequently approve or disapprove of the police officers' actions by finding the person guilty or not guilty.

For example, police officers who stop a person for speeding make a judicial decision when they give out a ticket. They might simply warn the next offender. By shooting and killing a fleeing felon who is likely to kill someone while attempting to escape, the police officer delivers a capital penalty for a crime which may otherwise have netted probabion or a prison term. When the officer brings the youngster next door home in the squad car but holds another juvenile in jail for the same offense, the police officer, in a sense, is acting as a judge, for without holding a hearing beyond listening to or ignoring the youth's protests, the officer has "sentenced" the youngster to one or more nights in detention.

Because the police officers' decisions touch so many lives, they are often considered more important than the judge in the criminal justice process. However, officers often know very little about the complex system of justice in which they play such a critical role. Countless police officers have never seen the criminal justice process in action; often they come into court with no experience and with limited time to prepare their testimony. Police officers must be trained to fulfill their role in the criminal justice process: to assist the prosecutor, the judge, and the jury in arriving at just decisions.

> *Police officers aid the criminal justice process by (1) making arrests, (2) obtaining information and evidence, (3) writing reports; (4) identifying suspects and witnesses, and (5) providing testimony in court.*

Errors in any of these roles may seriously damage a case or even prevent a **conviction.**

Equally important to fulfilling their own role is the police officers' understanding of the total system and the other key figures within this system: the prosecutor, the suspect, the defense attorney, the judge, and the jury members. As noted in Standard 1.1. of the American Bar Association Standards Relating to the Urban Police Function:

> Police effectiveness in dealing with crime is often largely dependent upon the effectiveness of other agencies both within and outside of the criminal justice system. Those in the system must work together through liaison, cooperation, and constructive joint effort. This effort is vital to the effective operation of the police and the entire criminal justice system.

In today's society it is imperative that police officers become more familiar with each step of the criminal justice process so they can intelligently bring about desired results.

Before looking at these critical steps in the criminal justice process, however, it is appropriate to consider the underlying assumption of the process—that it is an adversary system—and to consider who the adversaries are.

The Adversary System

Our criminal justice system is based on an adversary system—the accuser versus the accused. The accuser must prove that the one accused is guilty.

> *The adversary criminal justice system requires that the accuser prove beyond a reasonable doubt to a judge or jury that the accused is guilty of a specified crime.*

The assumption is that the one accused is innocent until proof to the contrary is clearly established. Included on the side of the accuser is the citizen (or victim), the prosecutor, and the police officer. On the side of the accused is the defendent and the defense attorney. An impartial judge or jury hears both sides of the controversy and then reaches a decision as to whether the accuser has proven the accused guilty beyond a **reasonable doubt.**

As noted by Inbau, Thompson, and Zagel (1974, p. 229):

It [reasonable doubt] is a term often used, probably pretty well understood, but not easily defined. It is not mere possible doubt because everything relating to human affairs and depending on moral evidence is open to some possible or imaginary doubt. It is that state of the case which, after the entire comparisons and consideration of all evidence, leaves the minds of the jurors in that condition and they cannot say they feel an abiding conviction, to a moral certainty, of the truth of the charge. The burden of proof is upon the prosecutor. All the presumptions of law independent of evidence are in favor of innocence; and every person is presumed to be innocent until he is proved guilty. If upon such proof there is reasonable doubt remaining, the accused is entitled to the benefit of it by an acquittal. For it is not sufficient to establish a probability, though a strong one arising from the doctrine of chances, that the fact charged is more likely to be true than the contrary; but the evidence must establish the truth of the fact to a reasonable and moral certainty; a certainty that convinces and directs the understanding, and satisfies the reason and judgment of those who are bound to act conscientiously upon it. This we take to be proof beyond reasonable doubt; because if the law, which mostly depends upon considerations of a moral nature, should go further than this and require absolute certainty, it would exclude circumstantial evidence altogether.

> *Reasonable doubt means the juror is not morally certain of the truth of the charges.*

The Suspect or Defendant

Until formally accused of a crime and brought to trial, a person accused is called a *suspect*. After formal accusation and court appearance, the person is called a **defendant.**

Everyone, including a person suspected of committing crimes, has certain rights which must be protected at all stages of the criminal justice process. Suspects have all the rights set forth in the Bill of Rights. They may waive these rights, but if they do, the waiver should be in writing because proof of the waiver is up to the police officer or the prosecution. The police officer must be able to show that all rights have been respected and that all required procedures have been complied with.

> *The Fourth Amendment forbids unreasonable search and seizure and requires probable cause. The Fifth Amendment guarantees due process: notice of a hearing, full information regarding the charges made, the opportunity to present evidence before an impartial judge or jury, and the right to refrain from self-incrimination. The Sixth Amendment establishes the requirements for criminal trials including the right to speedy public trial by an impartial jury and the right to have a lawyer. The Eighth Amendment forbids excessive bail and implies the right to such bail in most instances.*

Since our system uses an adversary process to seek out basic truths, the right to counsel is fundamental. However, in *Faretta v. California* (1975) the United States Supreme Court held that the Sixth Amendment guarantees self-represenation in a criminal case, but before the court can allow such self-representation, defendants must intelligently and knowingly waive their right to the assistance of counsel when they formulate and conduct their own defense. A record is usually made stating that counsel is available to the defendant to prevent subesquent claims of improper waiver of counsel or lack of counsel. It has often been said, however, that "one who defends himself has a fool for a client."

The purpose of the right to counsel is to protect the accused from a conviction which may result from ignorance of legal and constitutional rights. Although defendants in all criminal cases have basic constitutional rights, often they do not know how to protect them. The right to counsel is indispensable to their understanding of their other rights under the Constitution.

Although the criminal justice system is sometimes criticized when a defendant is found not guilty because of a technicality, such criticism is unfounded. Even though a person confesses to a hideous crime, if he was not first told of his rights and allowed to have a lawyer present during questioning, his confession should not be considered legal. As noted by the United States Supreme Court in *Escobedo v. Illinois* (1964):

> No system of criminal justice can or should survive if it comes to depend for its continued effectiveness on the citizens' abdication through unawareness of their constitutional rights. No system worth preserving should have to fear that if an accused is premitted to consult with a lawyer, he will became aware of and exercise these rights. If the exercise of constitutional rights will thwart the effectiveness of a system of law enforcement, then there is something very wrong with that system.

During the past several decades many landmark decisions of the Supreme Court have extended the rights of individuals accused of a crime to have counsel at government expense if they cannot afford to hire their own lawyer.

In *Powell v. Alabama* (1932) the Supreme Court ruled that in a capital case, where the defendants are indigent and are incapable of presenting their own defense, the court must assign them counsel as part of the due process of the law.

Between 1932 and 1963 the United States Supreme Court heard a variety of "right to counsel" cases. The Supreme Court ruled in *Johnson v. Zerbst* (1938) that indigent defendants charged with a federal crime had the right to be furnished with counsel. However, this case said nothing about indigents who appeared in state courts.

In *Betts v. Brady* (1942) the Supreme Court ruled that an indigent charged in a state court had *no* right to appointed counsel unless charged with a capital crime. Nineteen years later Clarence Gideon, a habitual criminal, was arrested in Florida for breaking and entering a pool room. Gideon claimed to be an indigent and asked for appointed counsel. The court refused on the grounds that Florida statutes provide for appointment of counsel only in capital cases. Gideon made his request based on the *Betts* case, but he was turned down and subsequently sentenced to the state prison.

Gideon, in a handwritten petition, took his case to the Supreme Court. In the famous *Gideon v. Wainwright* case (1963) the United States Supreme Court overruled *Betts v. Brady* and unanimously held that state courts must appoint counsel for indigent defendants in noncapital as well as capital cases.

> Gideon v. Wainwright *established the court's responsibility for providing counsel for any indigent person charged with a felony.*

Expanding on the "fairness" doctrine in 1972 in the *Argersinger v. Hamlin* case (1972), the United States Supreme Court ruled that all defendants in court who face the possibility of a jail sentence are entitled to legal counsel, and that if the accused cannot afford counsel, the state must provide one.

The Defense Attorney

Lawyers who undertake to represent an accused have the same duties and obligations whether they are privately retained, serving as a legal aid in the system, or appointed by the court. They interview clients about their offenses, whether they are aware of any witnesses who might assist them, and whether they have given a confession. Lawyers investigate the circumstances of the cases and explore facts relevant to the guilt or innocence of their clients. They try to uncover evidence for their clients' defenses and organize the cases to present in court. The **defense attorney** represents the accused in court.

Defense attorneys bring their clients professional objectivity as experts in criminal procedure. Their first goal is to establish a relationship of confidence and trust with their clients. They emphasize the confidential client-lawyer relationship and explain to the accused precisely what the complaint contains, what it means, and what the consequences are. They provide technical and professional skills in analyzing the facts of the case and explaining to their clients how a judge or a jury might view the case. They determine how the law affects their clients and what steps they must take to protect their clients' legal rights.

Defense attorneys also explain to their clients the decisions they as suspects must make; for example, whether to plea bargain the case, what plea to enter, whether to waive a preliminary hearing or a jury trial, and whether to testify in their own behalf. Such decisions of the accused should be fully discussed with the lawyer.

Defense attorneys, too, have to make several decisions: what jurors to accept, what trial motions to make, and whether or how to conduct cross-examinations. All strategies and tactical decisions are the exclusive responsibilities of the defense lawyers, but only after consultation with their clients.

Although the role of the defense attorney has been glamorized by television series, in actuality over 99 percent of all criminal cases involve different kinds of lawyers and defense styles (Glick, 1983, p. 155). Glick notes that criminal law is not emphasized in law school, which instead concentrates on business, property, and tax law, and that criminal law carries little prestige. Part of the reason for this is that the clients are usually poor. In addition, the public generally has little sympathy for criminals and even less for a lawyer who "gets the criminal off."

The majority of criminal cases are assigned to public defenders or to a few private lawyers who handle such cases. Public defenders are full- or part-time lawyers hired by the state or county government to represent people who cannot afford to hire a lawyer. Like prosecutors, most public defenders see the position as a stepping-stone to private practice.

Not all cities have public defenders. In smaller cities, courts may appoint lawyers to represent poor people charged with crimes. In other cities the duty may be rotated among all lawyers practicing in the area as part of their professional obligation to society.

Most cities also have a small group of criminal lawyers who represent people who do not qualify financially for public defense. Known as "regulars," these lawyers usually do not intend to take their case to court since few of the clients have much money. Instead they assist in plea bargaining with the prosecutors.

The Prosecutor

Prosecutors are officials elected to exercise leadership in the criminal justice system. They may be city attorneys, county attorneys, state attorneys, commonwealth attorneys, district attorneys, or solicitors.

Prosecutors are usually elected to a two- or four-year term at the state level. At the federal level they are appointed by the president. Eisenstein (1978, p. 40) notes that: "U.S. attorneys also serve as lawyers for the federal government in civil cases, such as motor vehicle accidents involving postal vehicles. About 40 percent of their work involves noncriminal matters."

According to Jacob (1980, pp. 76–78): "Large cities may have dozens or even a hundred or more assistant prosecutors, a few of whom are interested in developing a political career, but most of whom want to gain experience before starting their own law practice."

Prosecutors are the legal representatives of the people and the police officers. They are responsible to the people who elected them, not to any other state or local official. They determine law enforcement priorities and are the key in determining how much, how little, and what types of crimes the public will tolerate. They serve the public interest and consider the public's need to feel secure, its sense of how justice should be carried out, and the community's attitude toward certain crimes. Sometimes a case becomes so well publicized that the prosecutor is forced to "do something about it" or face defeat in the next election.

Prosecutors not only have great responsibility, but also have a varied amount of discretion. Their own experiences and biases may cause them to be selective in the cases they seek to prosecute. They may, for example, be reluctant to bring to trial cases such as minor bad checks, domestic quarrels involving assaults, or shoplifting by first offenders because they know that juries are usually reluctant to convict these defendants, especially if the offender is a housewife or mother.

In addition, prosecutors must be sensitive to the court's wishes and try to reduce the number of cases brought before it either by referring the complaint to an agency in the community for assistance or by recommending that the case be brought into a civil court or a lower criminal court.

Since prosecutors are lawyers for the public, citizens often go directly to them rather than to the police with their grievances. These cases usually involve business fraud, unfulfilled civil contracts such as default on a financial obligation, and the like. Prosecutors may have a small staff of investigators for such cases to determine if a crime has been committed or if the complainant should pursue a civil course of action.

Prosecutors are also the legal advisors for police officers; they are elected to decide what cases should be prosecuted and how. They rely heavily on the police officers' input in determining if a case should be brought to court or rejected. Often, however, misunderstanding and even ill will may result when a prosecutor refuses a police officer's request for a complaint because of insufficient evidence or some violation of a criminal procedure such as an illegal arrest. Plea bargaining may also cause ill will between a prosecutor and a police officer.

Since both police officers and prosecutors are striving for the same end—justice—they should be familiar with each other's problems. Police officers, for example, should understand what the prosecutor can and cannot do, which types of cases are worth prosecuting, and the need for and advantages of plea bargaining in certain situations. Prosecutors, on the other hand, should be sensitive to the police officers' objections to numerous legal technicalities and excessive paperwork and should include police officers in plea bargaining when possible, or, at the least, inform them when such bargaining has occurred.

Prosecutors perform one other critical function in the criminal justice process; they are responsible for protecting the rights of all involved, including the suspect. In essence they have a dual responsibility: on the one hand they are the leaders in the law enforcement community, the elected representatives of the public, and the legal advisors to the police officer; on the other hand, they are expected to protect the rights of persons accused of crimes. In *Berger* v. *United States* (1935) Justice Sutherland defined the prosecutor's responsibility as being: ". . . the representative not of an ordinary party to a controversy, but of a sovereignty whose obligation to govern impartially is as compelling as its obligation to govern at all; and whose interest, therefore, in a criminal prosecution is not that it shall win a case, but that justice shall be done.

Having looked at the nature of the adversary system and the key "contestants," now consider the critical steps normally involved in the criminal justice process.

Critical Stages in the Criminal Justice System

The criminal justice system consists of several critical stages: the complaint or charge, the arrest, booking, preliminary hearing, grand jury hearing, the arraignment, the trial, and sentencing.

Figure 15–1.   *Diagram of the Criminal Justice System from Complaint to Disposition.*

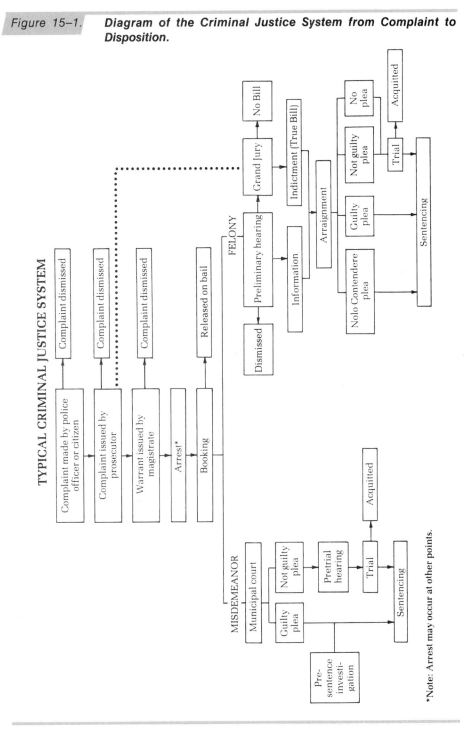

Figure 15–1 illustrates the complexity of the criminal justice system.

The Complaint or Charge

Usually the criminal justice process begins when a police officer or a citizen approaches the prosecutor to obtain a complaint. A **complaint** is a legal document drawn up by a prosecutor which specifies the alleged crime and the supporting facts providing probable cause.

Before making a decision the prosecutor will need answers to numerous questions such as: What is the offense? Who is the suspect? What is the suspect's age? Sex? Does the suspect have a criminal record? Have a series of offenses been committed? What is the evidence? Are the elements of the crime present? Was the evidence obtained legally? Are there witnesses? Will they be cooperative? Has the suspect been arrested? Have the suspect's rights been protected?

If the facts convince the prosecutor that a crime has been committed and adequate probable cause exists that the suspect accused of the offense is guilty, the prosecutor will draw up a legal form specifying the facts in the case.

If, on the other hand, the prosecutor feels insufficient evidence is presented by a police officer or a citizen, he will refuse to issue a formal accusation (complaint) against the suspect. If the suspect is in custody, he will order his release.

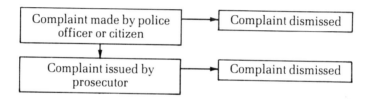

The formal complaint, which is also called the *charge,* contains all necessary evidence and facts to enable a magistrate to make an independent determination that probable cause exists for believing the offense has been committed by the accused.

The Warrant

The police officer or citizen then presents the complaint to a magistrate and, in his presence, swears to the accuracy of the content of the complaint and signs a statement to that effect. If the magistrate, after reading the complaint drawn up by the prosecuting attorney, concurs with the charge, he orders an arrest **warrant** (based on the probable cause established in the complaint) containing the substance of the complaint to be issued. If he does not concur, he dismisses the complaint.

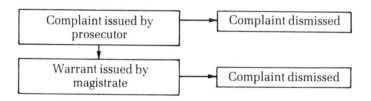

An arrest warrant directs an officer to bring the suspect before the magistrate. The warrant is usually directed to the sheriff or constables of a county or to all police officers of the municipality within the court's jurisdiction. The officer specified then locates the suspect and arrests him if he is not already in custody. The officer may execute the warrant in any part of the county where it is issued or in any part of the state.

The Arrest

Requirements for a legal arrest have been discussed. When making the arrest, officers must inform the suspect that they are acting upon the authority of the warrant. The suspect is entitled to see it. If the officers do not have the warrant in their possession, they must show it to the suspect as soon as possible.

The arrest may occur at other points within the criminal justice process. In a misdemeanor case, it may have occurred without a complaint or warrant, provided the crime was committed in the presence of the arresting officer. Or, as will be discussed later, the prosecutor may choose to present the case to a grand jury for indictment prior to arresting a suspect.

The Booking

After a suspect is taken into custody, he is booked at the police station. The suspect is formally put into the police records system by the booking officer who records on the booking sheet the suspect's name, date, time of arrest, charge, physical description, and physical characteristics. The suspect is photographed and fingerprinted. The prints are placed on file with the FBI in Washington, D.C., and the suspect has what is known as a Police Arrest Record.

Bail and Writ of Habeas Corpus

The Eighth Amendment forbids excessive bail and implies the right to bail in most instances.

One of the accused's rights is usually the right to be released from custody. Not only is this essential to his immediate freedom, but it is in keeping with the premise that a person is innocent until proven guilty. After the formal booking process is completed, the suspect is usually entitled to be released on bail or his own personal recognizance (**R.P.R.d**) if the crime is a misdemeanor, or released on a writ of habeas corpus or bond if the crime is a felony.

The amount of bail for each misdemeanor is determined by the judges of the municipal courts. They decide how much bail (money) is reasonable as a deposit to bring the defendant into court if he is released. However, some statutes allow a judge to set a schedule for the amount of bail required for specific offenses such as violating municipal ordinances on shoplifting, driving under the influence of alcohol, and other violations.

In most cases the judge will set bail when the prisoner comes before the court. The elapsed time between incarceration (jailing) of a suspect and his being brought to court to answer to the charge(s) is determined either by court policy or dictated by statutory law. Therefore, a great variance often exists between jurisdictions. The Sixth Amendment guarantees a suspect a speedy trial; therefore, following an arrest, the officer must take the suspect before a magistrate without unreasonable delay. However, because some court systems do not provide round-the-clock magistrates, courts have ruled that as soon as practicable is sufficient to satisfy the law. Unreasonable delays could jeopardize a case and free a person who might otherwise be found guilty of committing a crime.

Some prisoners are discharged or released on their own recognizance (R.O.R.d), meaning they are responsible for their own behavior and for appearing at their trial. This usually occurs only when the viloation is minor and the suspect is in good standing in the community (for example has a family or steady employment) and is very likely to appear before the court.

Suspects may also post cash or some type of security to guarantee their appearance in court. If they do not have the money, they may have a bail bondsmen post bond for them for a fee.

Periodically a person in jail may be released on a **writ of habeas corpus**—a legal court order literally meaning ''bring forth the body you have''—which commands a person holding a prisoner to being him forth immediately.

This means of determining whether the jailing of the suspect is legal is used primarily when the justice process moves slowly and a prisoner is detained for an unreasonable length of time before the court appearance. Habeas corpus often occurs when a person is arrested without a formal arrest warrant and the follow-up police investigation is taking an unreasonable length of time. Most states have adopted rules or guidelines as to how long a person may be jailed before being charged, released, or making an appearance in court. These rules are somewhat flexible and range from thirty-six to seventy-two hours, taking into consideration Sundays and holidays.

Up to this point in the criminal justice process, it makes little difference as to what type of crime—misdemeanor or felony—has been committed. The process is basically the same.

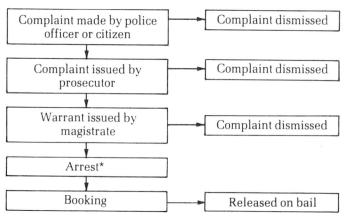

Misdmeanors

Recall that misdemeanors are minor offenses carrying a penalty of a fine or a short imprisonment for less than one year in a local jail. Misdemeanors are usually disposed of by ticket, tab charge, or R.P.R.d, in which case the suspect is ordered to court. The person may plead guilty, not guilty, or have a trial, and the case is disposed of. Failure to appear results in an arrest warrant for contempt of court.

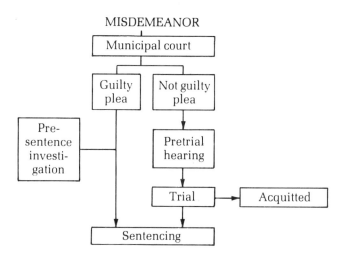

Felonies

Recall that felonies are major crimes carrying a penalty of imprisonment in a state or federal penitentiary for over a year. A fine may also be incurred.

Felony cases are more complex than misdemeanors. The complaint must be filed with the clerk of the district or the superior court. In a felony case the prosecutor may seek an information from a preliminary hearing or an indictment from a grand jury.

A formal written accusation, what we have thus far called the criminal complaint or charge, is also known as an **information.** It contains the substance of the charge against the defendant and usually is associated with a preliminary hearing. However, the United States Constitution requires an indictment by a grand jury for most crimes against federal law.

The Preliminary Hearing

The **preliminary hearing** is the probable cause hearing. The magistrate first determines whether an offense has been committed and if sufficient evidence is presented to believe that the accused committed it.

If the accused is being held, it is important to both the defendant and the prosecutor to hold the hearing within a reasonable time. Most statutes and rules of criminal procedure require a preliminary hearing to be held within a "reasonable time.'' Some jurisdictions require a preliminary hearing to be held immediately after arrest, some within forty-eight to seventy-two hours, other within ten to thirty days.

> *The preliminary hearing seeks to establish probable cause to prevent persons from being indiscriminately brought to trial.*

In a preliminary hearing, the defendant is present, with or without his counsel, and has a right to challenge what is stated against him in court. The defendant can waive counsel, but waiver of this right must be in writing. The defendant also can waive the preliminary hearing. If he does so, the case is sent to a higher court for disposition.

Preliminary hearings are generally held in a lower court or a court which has general jurisdiction such as a municipal court, In fact, 90 percent of all defendants appear in one of the thousands of lower courts in our country.

The magistrate in a preliminary hearing is not bound by the rules of evidence which ordinarily control a trial. Although no one rule is applicable in all parts of the country, a far broader range of evidence is usually admissible. At times the mere presentation of a signed confession is sufficient to move the case to a higher court. The evidence need only show probable cause and reasonably and fairly tends to show the crime is as charged and the accused committed it.

The prosecutor only has to present his evidence; he need not prove the crime was committed beyond a reasonable doubt as long as probable cause is shown. Occasionally the defense attorney or the defendant will demand a preliminary hearing if either is convinced a miscarriage of justice has occurred. Sometimes the defense will test the prosecutor's case by probing the state's potential weak areas. However, as noted, the prosecutor need release only enough evidence to establish probable cause.

The defense attorney can present evidence, cross-examine the prosecutor's witnesses, call defense witnesses, and present any type of defense.

In reality the preliminary hearing is often a minitrial where the defense obtains as much information as possible to strengthen its case should it be bound over to a higher court. Both prosecution and defense often use this stage of the criminal justice process for tactical purposes. In some instances overwhelming evidence may lead to a guilty plea or to a request for plea bargaining.

The preliminary hearing is often a discovery tool for the defendant as he hears the evidence presented against him. If the case went to the grand jury, he would not be aware of the evidence against him. Some states have eliminated this element of surprise by including the **discovery process** in their rules of criminal procedure. The discovery process requires that all pertinent facts on both sides be made available prior to the time of the trial.

Used properly, the discovery process reduces questions of probable cause and other questions normally brought out in a preliminary hearing and encourages more final dispositions before trial, thereby saving court time. Available to both the prosecution and defense attorneys, it eliminates surprise as a legitimate trial tactic.

> *The discovery process requires that all pertinent facts on both sides be made available prior to the time of the trial.*

The preliminary hearing does not determine who is going to win or lose. It merely determines whether further action should be taken. At this point the magistrate usually does not rule on complicated issues of evidence.

Theoretically, at the preliminary hearing, the magistrate determines the guilt or innocence of the accused and dismisses cases he feels the prosecutor should no longer pursue because of lack of sufficient evidence that the person committed the crime (probable cause).

The main intent of the preliminary hearing is to add to the checks and balances of the criminal justice system by preventing the prosecutor from indiscriminately bringing someone to trial. The preliminary hearing, one of the critical stages of due process, is a very formal proceeding insuring that all accused persons are adequately informed and that all their constitutional rights are protected.

The outcome of a preliminary hearing may be to (1) dismiss the charges, (2) present an information and bind the defendant over to a higher court, or (3) send the case to a grand jury.

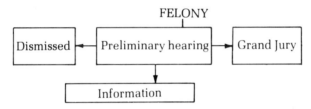

The Grand Jury

The United States Constitution requires an indictment by a federal grand jury before trial for most crimes against federal law. Grand juries frequently hear cases involving misconduct of public officials, violations of election laws, bankruptcy fraud, criminal conduct, and the like.

The consideration of a felony charge by a grand jury is in no sense of the word a trial. Only the prosecution's evidence is usually presented and considered. Contrary to the popular portrayal of grand juries on television and in movies, suspected offenders are usually not heard nor are their lawyers present to offer evidence in their behalf.

A **grand jury** is usually composed of twenty-three voting citizens of the county, selected by either the district or superior judges, jury commissioners, court officials, or some designated county supervisor. These juries may be called to duty any time the court is in session. Sixteen jurors constitute a quorum, and the votes of twelve members are usually necessary to return an indictment.

Grand juries meet in secret sessions and hear from witnesses and victims of crime. Because it meets in secret session, it is an accusatory body and determines only whether enough evidence exists to accuse a person or persons of a crime.

Federal, state, and county grand juries decide whether enough evidence exists to indict (bring to trial) persons in criminal cases whether they are in custody or not.

The prosecutor usually has considerable foundation for believing an offense has been committed before taking a case to the grand jury. The prosecutor is authorized to subpoena witnesses before the jury. Usually only one witness appears at a time before the jury and is questioned under oath by the prosecutor.

In some states, by statute, a grand jury can hear evidence from suspects. However, in order to testify, the persons being considered for indictment must sign a waiver of immunity and agree to answer all questions posed in the grand jury session even though their testimony might be incriminating and lead to an indictment. Their testimony also may be used against them in a criminal trial. Their lawyers are not allowed to be present in the grand jury room if they are testifying.

After the grand jury receives all testimony and evidence, it begins its deliberations. No one else is allowed in the room during these deliberations. Before an indictment can be reached, the jurors must agree that all the evidence presented leads them to believe probable cause exists that the person is guilty of a crime. If the majority of the grand jurors (or a specified number) agree, they instruct the prosecutor to prepare an **indictment** which specifies all the facts of the case and the names of those who appeared before the jury.

The indictment is signed by the grand jury foreman and presented to the district or superior court judge who then orders the issuance of a bench warrant for the arrest of the defendant if not already in custody. If the defendant is indicted, until he is arrested or brought before the court, the fact that an indictment has been found must be kept secret; it is not public information.

Procedures are then implemented for the defendant's appearance in court where a trial jury may be convened to hear the case.

Grand juries may also issue what is called a no bill. If, after hearing all the evidence presented and the witnesses, the jurors believe there is no criminal violation, the grand jury issues a no bill, which means they find no basis for an indictment and will no longer consider the matter unless further evidence is presented which may warrant an indictment.

Grand juries can also take action and conduct investigations on their own initiative. This is known as a presentment and in some jurisdictions is sufficient to support a prosecution. Some states, however, regard a presentment as mere instructions to the prosecutor to draw up a bill of indictment. If, when the grand jury reviews this bill of indictment, they agree it is a true bill, it becomes the basis for prosecution.

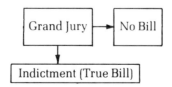

In felony cases, prosecutors sometimes avoid the preliminary hearing by going directly to the grand jury for an indictment. This presents a tactical advantage for the prosecution because grand jury hearings are not public. If the prosecution can convince a grand jury to bring about an indictment based on probable cause, the prosecution does not need a preliminary hearing. An indictment eliminates the need for such a hearing because the defendant goes straight to trial.

The defense attorney or the defendant can demand a preliminary hearing if either feels a miscarriage of justice is occurring.

The Coroner's Jury

Coroners investigate violent deaths where suspicion of foul play exists. By law, coroners may conduct autopsies as to the cause of death, and they may conduct inquests. The **coroner's jury** usually consists of six members. In some states the coroner's jury system has been abandoned and its functions performed by a professional medical examiner, usually a pathologist or a forensic expert.

The coroner's jury is involved in cases where the cause of death is in doubt.

The Arraignment

When defendants are charged with a felony, they must personally appear at an **arraignment.** As in the preliminary hearing, the defendants are entitled to counsel. The procedures of the arraignment vary in some states, but generally defendants appear before the court, are read the complaint, information, or indictment, and, if they have not received a copy, they are given one. They then enter a **plea.**

Defendants have several alternatives when they appear for the formal arraignment. *Standing mute*, that is refusing to answer, is entered by the judge as a not guilty plea.

Nolo contendere means "no contest." By entering a plea of nolo contendere, the defendant, in effect, is throwing himself on the mercy of the court. This plea is often used when a person knows of some forthcoming civil action against him and does not want his plea to jeopardize his defense in the civil trial. (A guilty plea to any criminal offense could become a part of the civil trial.)

Guilty means the accused admits the actual charge or a lesser charge agreed to in a plea bargaining session. A guilty plea has many consequences: possible imprisonment, being labeled a criminal, a waiver of constitutional rights and of all defenses. Still, 90 percent of all criminal defendants plead guilty in the United States, but most plead guilty to offenses reduced from the original charges.

Not guilty means the accused denies the charge. He may have a valid defense for the charge such as intoxication, insanity, self-defense, or mistaken identity. Some states require defendants to automatically plead not guilty to capital crimes such as first-degree murder.

At the arraignment the defendant may stand mute, or enter a plea of nolo contendere, guilty, or not guilty.

If the defendant pleads guilty or nolo contendere, a sentencing time is set. Usually a pre-sentence investigation is ordered to determine if probation is warranted. If the defendant makes no plea or pleads not guilty, he has the choice of a trial by a judge or by a jury who will weigh the facts of the case and make the decision of guilt or innocence. If he wishes a jury trial, the case will be assigned to the court docket and a date set.

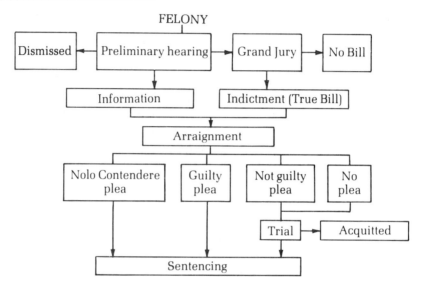

Before looking at the trial itself, the court system within which it occurs, and the sentence that may result, consider first some alternatives to a trial.

Alternatives to a Trial

Alternatives to a trial include screening, diversion, and plea bargaining.

Screening

The National Advisory Commission on Criminal Justice Standards and Goals (*Courts*, 1975, p. 17), notes that: "Screening in a broad sense, means removal of a person from the criminal justice system. Thus, the police officer who makes an investigatory stop and decides not to arrest the subject screens. . . . But here the term will be used in a more restricted sense. Screening is the discretionary decision to stop, prior to trial or plea, all formal proceedings against a person who has become involved in the criminal justice system.'' It is different from diversion, which provides a defendant an alternative to a trial.

> *Screening is the decision to stop all formal proceedings, with nothing further required of the suspect.*

The commission goes on to suggest that screening has two objectives. One objective is to stop proceedings in a case with insufficient evidence to convict; the case appears fruitless, so resources should not be expended on it. It states (p.17): ''Effective allocation of resources dictates that screening for evidence insufficiency be done as early and as accurately as possible. Fairness to the individual also requires that as soon as it is ascertained that he could not be convicted, he be freed from any nonvoluntary involvement with the criminal justice system.''

The second objective is to avoid a conviction that would not serve the dual objectives of the criminal justice system, that is, reducing crime while extending fairness to defendants. Sometimes, even when it is likely that a conviction may be obtained, the sentence may be less effective than having the defendant participate in a rehabilitation program—the purpose of diversion.

> *Screening is appropriate only when neither diversion nor conviction is desirable.*

Diversion

Before the client and his attorney go to court, the defense attorney may explore the possibility of diverting the case from the criminal justice system by using a community agency if the circumstances warrant it; for example, in cases of mental incompetence the attorney may seek to divert the case to a mental institution. **Diversion** gives a defendant an alternative to a trial, e.g., to obtain help from a community agency or to make restitution to the victim of the crime.

The National Advisory Commission on Criminal Justice Standards and Goals (*Courts,* 1975, p. 27) defines diversion as ''halting or suspending, before conviction, formal criminal proceedings against a person on a condition or assumption that he will do something in return.'' This definition is an expansion of an earlier commission statement (*Corrections,* 1973, p. 94):

> Diversion provides society with the opportunity to begin the reordering of the justice system, by redistributing resources to achieve justice and correctional goals . . . to develop truly effective prevention, justice, control, and social restoration programs. . . . Perhaps the biggest contribution that diversion can make during the next decade is to make society more conscious and sensitive to the deficiencies in the justice system, and hence, to force radical changes within the system so that appropriate offenders are successfully diverted from the system while others are provided with programs within the system that offer social restoration instead of criminal condemnation.

The commission notes that diversion uses the threat of possible conviction on criminal charges to "encourage" an accused to agree to take some action such as participate in a rehabilitation program or make restitution to the victim of the offense.

> Diversion gives a defendant an alternative to a trial, e.g., to obtain help from a community agency or to make restitution to the victim of the crime.

The commission also notes that diversion is a discretionary decision that can occur at many points as the case progresses through the criminal justice system. For example, a police officer who assumes custody of an intoxicated person and releases that person to the custody of family or a detoxification center diverts. Likewise, a prosecutor who delays prosecution while a defendant participates in psychiatric treatment diverts. In both instances, a discretionary decision is made that there is a more appropraite way to deal with the defendant than to prosecute.

As might be expected, diversion has its opponents. Some individuals feel this is "letting criminals off easy." However, major benefits can result. According to the commission (1973, p. 27):

> Many individuals come within the language of existing criminal statutes, but their conviction and punishment would not be consistent with the intent of the legislature. . . . By taking the offender out of the criminal justice process before conviction, diversion imposes no stigma of conviction, and unlike screening, prevents the offender from committing future harmful acts or requires him to make restitution. Only diversion provides a means of accommodating this compromise solution. If diversion programs were made available as sentencing alternatives, the objective of avoiding the stigma of a criminal conviction would be nullified.

Another obvious benefit of diversion is economy, eliminating the necessity for what could be a costly court trial.

Plea Bargaining

The client and defense lawyer may also attempt to plea bargain their case. **Plea bargaining** is legal negotiation between the prosecutor and the defense lawyer or the client to reach an agreement that avoids a court trail. The prosecutor is seeking a conviction without going through the formality of a court trial. The defense is looking for some concessions by the prosecutor to reduce the punishment for the defendant.

> Plea bargaining is a compromise between defense and prosecution which pre-arranges the plea and the sentence, conserving manpower and expense.

Basically, plea bargaining involves promises and compromises. From the prosecutor it may mean that if a series of charges are filed, the defendant would only be charged with one; the other charges would be dismissed. Or it might mean that the prosecutor would reduce a charge if only one charge was filed; for example, a charge of burglary might be reduced to breaking and entering which carries a lesser penalty.

For the defendant and the defense attorney, it may mean a guilty plea for the preceding concessions. Or it may mean the defendant pleads guilty to the charges as stated, provided he be placed on probation rather than being sent to a correctional institution.

Prosecutors are always in the stronger bargaining position because they have filed the charge(s) and have all the evidence. The only thing the defendants have with which to bargain is that their guilty plea can save the court both time and money. According to some, however, this explanation is often not the true reason underlying plea bargaining. For example, Rosett and Cressey (1976, pp. 110-111) state:

> Attributing negotiated pleas to overwork is a political explanation of court practice. Voicing this explanation neutralizes important and powerful interest groups who say they want adversary procedures that would maximize the amount of punishment meted out to criminals. If the explanation is accepted, prosecutors can go about their plea-arranging ways of doing justice without encountering too much damning criticism from community leaders who want them to be tough on criminals. They avoid losing elections or being fired.
>
> The successful prosecutor blurs the competing conceptions of what his mission should be. One way to do this is to reduce adversariness in the interests of justice while at the same time arguing—loudly, clearly and publicly—that he engages in informal plea bargaining practices because his officer is overworked, despite careful management.

Although plea bargaining has been in existence for many years, only recently have the courts openly accepted it, often on the basis that without plea bargaining the number of full trials would increase tremendously, requiring enormous amounts of money and manpower. Recently the Supreme Court has expanded the plea bargaining powers of prosecutors. In *Bordenkircher v. Hayes* (1978) the Court told prosecutors that they may threaten criminal defendants with more serious charges in attempts to obtain guilty pleas.

Plea bargaining may seem inconsistent with our legal system, but bargains are made a part of the written record, including the terms of the agreement, the disposition, and an explanation of why a negotiated disposition was appropriate in each case.

A hazard of the plea bargaining system is that it may cause police officers to feel isolated. Throughout the criminal procedures system police officers are valued; the prosecutor, the complainants, the witnesses, and society depend upon them. But when it comes to plea bargaining sessions, they are left out. Often officers will inquire about the disposition of a case of vital interest to them only to find that it has been disposed of in plea bargaining. If officers are to be part of the total system, they should have some input into the disposition of the cases or, at the least, be informed of the disposition. As criminals are placed back into society, the police officers' problems in dealing with crime grow. If police officers are to deal with these problems, they should be consulted.

The Court System

At the beginning of this chapter you were introduced to the adversary nature of our criminal justice system and to the key individuals in conflict with each other. For an adversary system to be truly fair and impartial, certain safeguards must be in place. To this end, a highly structured court system has been established. And the key individuals within this system are the judges and, in some cases, members of a jury.

Judges

Although most people think of trial judges when they hear the word *judge,* many different kinds of judges exist. In fact, if a person comes to trial he will already have encountered certain levels of the court system and judges acting within that system.

Glick (1983, p. 163) suggests that judges have many important functions throughout the entire judicial process: "One of their most important jobs is to decide in preliminary hearings whether a prosecutor has sufficient evidence to justify prosecution. . . . Another important early decision for judges is whether to grant bail, if money bail is required and how much, or if the defendant can remain free without money bail before trial. Judges also make decisions to grant delays to give one side or the other additional time to prepare their case, to attend other legal business, or to give a defense lawyer time to persuade a client to plead guilty or even to pay part of the lawyer's fee."

In many instances the judge has the key role in imposing the sentence to be served if a defendant is found guilty. And, as noted by Glick (1983, p. 177): "Judges have special status and receive great respect from everyone in court . . . their lofty position gives them an opportunity to lead others. If judges choose to exert themselves, they have practically unchallenged opportunities to influence the outcome of cases."

The various types of judges and the functions they serve depend on the court to which they are appointed. At this point a brief review of the justice system, from a somewhat different vantage point, may help to clarify the hierarchy within our court system. The progression depicted in Figure 15–2 can be repeated from a lower court to a higher court, one or more times.

Organizational Structure of the Courts

The courts in the United States operate within a highly structured framework that may vary greatly from state to state. Numerous dualities exist within this framework, the most obvious of which is the dual system of state and federal courts. These two systems will be discussed momentarily, but first some other dualities should be understood. Among the most important are those having to do with a court's jurisdiction—its authority to try a case or to hear an appeal. Technically it does not refer to a geographic area.

Figure 15–2.   ***Typical Progression of Criminal Felony Litigation.***

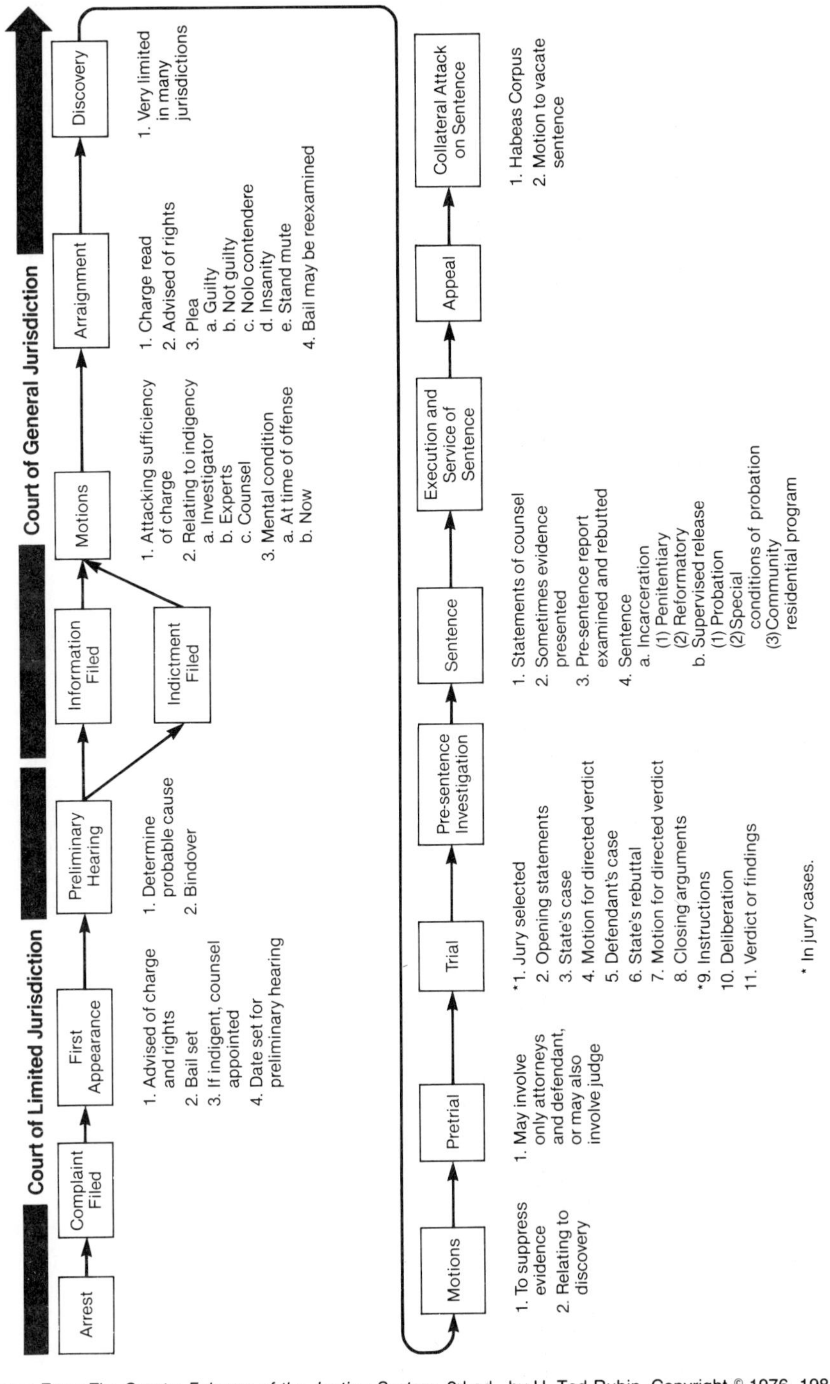

Court of Limited Jurisdiction

Arrest → Complaint Filed → First Appearance → Preliminary Hearing → Information Filed / Indictment Filed

First Appearance
1. Advised of charge and rights
2. Bail set
3. If indigent, counsel appointed
4. Date set for preliminary hearing

Preliminary Hearing
1. Determine probable cause
2. Bindover

Court of General Jurisdiction

Motions → Arraignment → Discovery

Motions
1. Attacking sufficiency of charge
2. Relating to indigency
   a. Investigator
   b. Experts
   c. Counsel
3. Mental condition
   a. At time of offense
   b. Now

Arraignment
1. Charge read
2. Advised of rights
3. Plea
   a. Guilty
   b. Not guilty
   c. Nolo contendere
   d. Insanity
   e. Stand mute
4. Bail may be reexamined

Discovery
1. Very limited in many jurisdictions

Motions → Pretrial → Trial → Pre-sentence Investigation → Sentence → Execution and Service of Sentence → Appeal → Collateral Attack on Sentence

Motions
1. To suppress evidence
2. Relating to discovery

Pretrial
1. May involve only attorneys and defendant, or may also involve judge

Trial
*1. Jury selected
2. Opening statements
3. State's case
4. Motion for directed verdict
5. Defendant's case
6. State's rebuttal
7. Motion for directed verdict
8. Closing arguments
*9. Instructions
10. Deliberation
11. Verdict or findings

* In jury cases.

Sentence
1. Statements of counsel
2. Sometimes evidence presented
3. Pre-sentence report examined and rebutted
4. Sentence
   a. Incarceration
      (1) Penitentiary
      (2) Reformatory
   b. Supervised release
      (1) Probation
      (2) Special conditions of probation
      (3) Community residential program

Collateral Attack on Sentence
1. Habeas Corpus
2. Motion to vacate sentence

Source: From *The Courts: Fulcrum of the Justice System,* 2d ed., by H. Ted Rubin. Copyright © 1976, 1984 by Newberg Award Records, Inc., a subsidiary of Random House, Inc. Reprinted by permission of the publisher.

Figure 15–3.   State Judicial System.

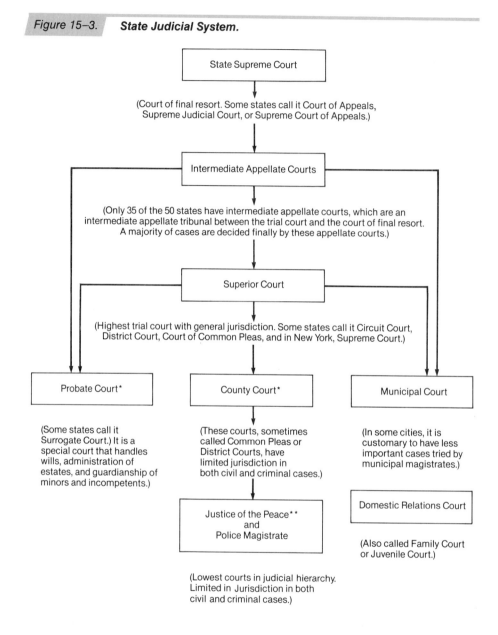

State Supreme Court

(Court of final resort. Some states call it Court of Appeals, Supreme Judicial Court, or Supreme Court of Appeals.)

Intermediate Appellate Courts

(Only 35 of the 50 states have intermediate appellate courts, which are an intermediate appellate tribunal between the trial court and the court of final resort. A majority of cases are decided finally by these appellate courts.)

Superior Court

(Highest trial court with general jurisdiction. Some states call it Circuit Court, District Court, Court of Common Pleas, and in New York, Supreme Court.)

Probate Court*

(Some states call it Surrogate Court.) It is a special court that handles wills, administration of estates, and guardianship of minors and incompetents.)

County Court*

(These courts, sometimes called Common Pleas or District Courts, have limited jurisdiction in both civil and criminal cases.)

Municipal Court

(In some cities, it is customary to have less important cases tried by municipal magistrates.)

Justice of the Peace**
and
Police Magistrate

Domestic Relations Court

(Also called Family Court or Juvenile Court.)

(Lowest courts in judicial hierarchy. Limited in Jurisdiction in both civil and criminal cases.)

---

*Courts of special jurisdiction, such as probate, family, or juvenile courts, and the so-called inferior courts, such as common pleas or municipal courts, may be separate courts or part of the trial court of general jurisdiction.
**Justices of the peace do not exist in all states. Where they do exist, their jurisdictions vary greatly from state to state.
Source: American Bar Association, *Law and the Courts* (Chicago: American Bar Association, 1974), p. 20. Updated information provided by West Publishing Company.

Source: Introduction to Criminal Justice by Joseph J. Senna and Larry J. Siegel. 3rd ed. West Publishing Co. St. Paul, Minn., 1984.

As noted by Waldron (1984, p. 283): "Jurisdiction should not be mistaken for the concept of *venue*, the requirement that the trial for an offense be held in the same area in which the offense occurred. The point to remember is that jurisdiction refers to a court's authority to take notice of and decide a case."

Courts may have *limited* jurisdiction (sometimes called special jurisdiction) and are then referred to as lower or inferior courts. The limits frequently deal with the types of offenses that may be tried or the dollar amounts that may be involved. In contrast are the courts with *general* jurisdiction which are often called higher or superior courts. These courts traditionally have more prestige and the power to overturn the ruling of a lower court.

Another duality within the organizational structure of the courts and their jurisdiction is that of *original* versus *appellate* jurisdiction. A court with original jurisdiction has the authority to try cases, whereas a court with appellate jurisdiction has the authority to hear an **appeal** to set aside a conviction. In some cases a court has both types of jurisdiction, for example, the United States Supreme Court.

A court with the authority to try a case is often called a *trial* court, and since such courts are frequently the first to record the proceedings, they are also referred to as a *court of record*. A court that uses the record from a previous trial in considering an appeal, without calling a new trial, automatically identifies the court below as a court of record.

A *court of last resort* refers to the highest court to which a case may be appealed.

The State Court System. Each state's constitution and statutory law establish the structure of its courts. Consequently, great variety exists in the types of courts established, the names by which they are known, and the number of levels in the heirarchy. For example, until recently, Pennsylvania had eleven different types of courts, each having jurisdiction over a specific kind of case.

> The hierarchy at the state level often goes from courts of special or limited jurisdiction called Justice of the Peace (J.P.) courts, to trial courts or original and general jurisdiction courts, to intermediate appellate courts, to the state supreme court.

The Federal Court System. Within the federal court system a further duality exists: constitutional courts and legislative courts. The constitutional courts include the United States Supreme Court as well as "such inferior Courts as the Congress may from time to time ordain and establish" (Article III, Section 1). These inferior courts include the courts of appeals, the district courts, and numerous specialized courts. Legislative courts are lower in the hierarchy and include trial courts in the United States territories, specialized courts, and the Military Court of Appeals.

> The federal court system is three tiered: district courts, appellate courts, and the United States Supreme Court.

Figure 15–4.   **Federal Judicial System.**

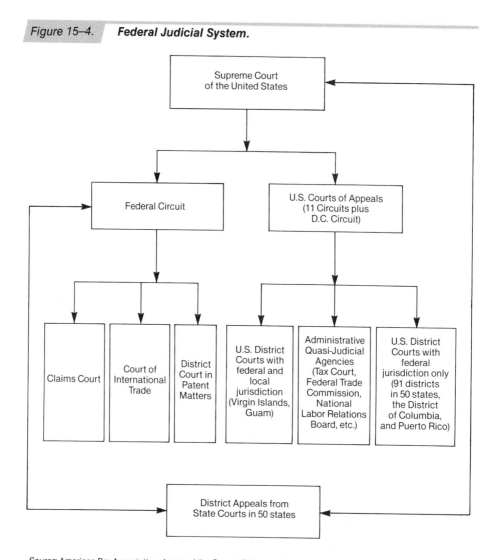

Source: American Bar Association, *Law and the Courts* (Chicago: American Bar Association, 1974), p. 21. Updated information provided by the Federal Courts Improvement Act of 1982 and West Publishing Company.

Source: Introduction to Criminal Justice, by Jospeh J. Senna and Larry J. Siegel. 3d ed. West Publishing Co. St. Paul, Minn, 1984.

The United States Supreme Court.   According to Waldron (1984, p. 198): "The jurisdiction of the Supreme Court is limited, as is the jurisdiction of every other court. Fighting all the way to the Supreme Court may be impossible because of the restrictions imposed by the Constitution and the Congress. Congress has conferred appellate jurisdiction upon the Supreme Court but has no authority to change its original jurisdiction as defined in the Constitution. Actually, cases of original jurisdiction account for less than 1 percent of the cases the Court hears in a term."

The Court is required by law to begin its terms annually on the first Monday in October and to continue until it has heard all the cases scheduled to be heard. This is usually well into the following summer. Each term the Court hears over 3,000 cases.

The United States **Supreme Court** is presided over by nine justices of judges appointed by the president of the United States, subject to Senate confirmation. The president also appoints a chief justice who assigns the cases to the other justices. Most have been lawyers and are from the upper class, white, male, protestant, and graduates of prestigious universities. Over half were judges prior to their appointments as United States Supreme Court justices.

As noted by Glick (1983, p. 105): "Becoming a federal judge requires political visibility, involvement in political activity, party loyalty, and, depending on the court, sharing the political values or ideology of the administration making the appointments. . . . The occasional appointment of Jewish, Catholic, or black justices is a recent and rare event. President Reagan's appointment of Sandra D. O'Connor is the most recent change to occur in recruitment to the Supreme Court."

The Constitution established tenure for "life or good behavior"; therefore the only way to remove a justice is through impeachment unless voluntary retirement can be obtained.

The Trial

When police officers enter the courtroom they realize that the trial is the climax in the criminal justice procedure. All previously made decisions now merge in one finality. The test of how well the police officers have investigated the case, compiled evidence and reported it, and dealt with the victim and witnesses will be weighed in the courtroom.

The key figures in the trial are the judge, members of the jury, the defendant and defense attorney(s), the prosecuting attorney(s), police officer(s), and witnesses.

The judge has charge of the trial and decides all matters with respect to the law. He or she also assures that all the rules of trial procedure are followed. The jury decides all matters of fact. The advocates are the prosecuting attorney(s) and the defense attorney(s). The trial begins with the jury selection.

Jury Selection. Safeguards built into the jury selection process not only protect the rights of the defendant but also assure the public that justice is done. Trial or *petit* jurors are selected at random by district or superior court judges or the commissioners of the county board. The judges or the commissioners randomly select a large group of prospective jurors and, when the trial is about to begin, call these people to the court and inform them of their duties in the particular case for which they may serve.

It is then up to the attorneys trying the case to decide which six or twelve of these individuals will be the jurors in the case. The clerk of courts draws the names of six or twelve jurors from the jury list, and these individuals take their seats in the regular jury box in the order in which their names were drawn. The defense attorney and then the prosecuting attorney question each individual as to his or her qualifications to be a juror in this case. The judge may also question the prospective jurors.

The random selection of potential jurors and the careful questioning of each helps insure selection of six or twelve fair and impartial jurors.

In homicide cases or in other cases involving a great deal of publicity, the system may be altered. All the jurors except the one being questioned by the attorney are excluded from the courtroom (sequestered) to insure that neither the questions asked nor the answers provided will prejudice other jurors.

Challenges may be made to the entire panel of jurors or to individual jurors. *Challenges to the entire panel* may be made if potential jurors were not separated during questioning and one potential juror made a moving speech about the guilt or innocence of the defendant. A challenge to the entire panel might also be made on the basis that the entire group was improperly selected. For example, if the names were not randomly selected, the entire panel could be excluded and a new selection of jurors made.

Challenges to individual jurors are the most frequent type of challenges. Two basic types of individual challenges can be made: challenge for cause (a reason is presented for the challenge) and peremptory challenge (no reason is presented).

Challenge for cause may take several forms. It may be based on the person's background; for example, a prospective juror with a felony record would be disqualified from sitting on any criminal case; or a prospective juror might be related to the defendant, the prosecutor, the judge, or someone involved in the case itself. Challenge for cause may also be based on the answers given during questioning. If, for example, during questioning a prospective juror blurted out, ''I know the man is innocent,'' or ''I know the man is guilty,'' this would clearly indicate bias and constitute grounds for dismissal of that juror. When a prospective juror is challenged for cause, the lawyer presents a factual basis for excluding a particular person, and the judge makes the decision. Sometimes the judge appoints three citizens to listen to the questioning and to decide if a particular person should be excluded. This rather cumbersome method, called the *three triers,* is not normally used except in first-degree murder cases.

Peremptory challenges are based on an attorney's ''gut reaction'' or intuition that a person would be a poor juror. No specific reason is given for excluding the person; the lawyer simply does not want the person on the jury. Both the prosecution and the defense lawyer may exclude persons from the jury without a factual basis by using a limited number of peremptory challenges. Normally the defense is allowed a larger number than the prosecution. For example, in an ordinary criminal case in Minnesota, the defense has five peremptory challenges and the prosecution has three. In a first-degree murder case the defense has twenty peremptory challenges, the prosecution ten.

The National Advisory Commission on Criminal Justice Standards and Goals (*The Courts,* 1973, p. 101) suggests that the twelve-person jury requirement for criminal trials that exists in most jurisdictions is an "accident of history," and that "juries of less than 12 can provide a reliable and competent fact-finding body." In *Williams v. Florida* (1970) the Court stated that the touchstone should be whether the group is "large enough to promote group deliberation, free from outside attempts at intimidation, and to provide a fair possibility for obtaining a representative cross-section of the community." In this same case the Supreme Court held that Florida's use of a six-person jury did not violate the defendant's Eighth and Fourteenth Amendment rights to trial by jury.

The commission goes on to suggest that since scholars maintain that a jury of six or more can reach a reliable verdict, there is no justification for invalidating a trial if one or more jurors becomes incapacitated, as long as six or more members remain. It also contends there is no justification for excluding eighteen-year-olds from jury duty.

Opening Statements. After the jury is selected and instructed by the judge, opening statements are presented. The prosecutor informs the jury of the state's case and how he intends to prove the charges against the defendant. The defense lawyer makes an opening statement in support of his client, or he may waive this opening statement.

Evidence and Testimony. The prosecutor then presents evidence and the testimony of the witnesses, attempting to prove that a crime had been committed and that the defendant did it. He does so by using direct and indirect evidence, a confession, the testimony of witnesses, or the testimony of the police officers whose initial investigation brought the case to trial.

After each bit of evidence is presented, the defense attorney can challenge its validity, and the judge will rule on his objections. In most cases, after each witness testifies, he is subjected to cross-examination by the defense counsel, who tries to discredit the testimony.

After the prosecutor rests his case, the defense presents evidence and witnesses. One tactic frequently used by the defense attorney is to keep his client from taking the witness stand. The well-known privilege against self-incrimination is part of the Fifth Amendment. However, if the defendant takes the witness stand in his own behalf, he gives up this right against self-incrimination—the prosecutor is free to cross-examine him.

Through cross-examination, the defense attorney tries to discredit prosecution witnesses, the evidence, and the testimony of the police officers.

The Police Officer in Court. Almost every officer has his day in court. Because of overloaded court dockets, cases usually come up well after the officers' investigation; therefore, officers must refer to their reports and their original notes to refresh their memories. The notes may remind them that it was a cloudy day, a light rain had fallen and the streets were still wet, that it was midafternoon, and that clearly visible bloodstains trailed out the back door.

Police officers know the defense lawyer will probably try to convince the jury that since the sky was overcast, the officers had trouble seeing the stains clearly—but their notes say differently.

A court appearance is an important part of any police officer's duty. All elements of the investigation are brought together at this point: the report, the statements of the witnesses, the evidence collected, and possibly even a confession from the defendant.

Although the defendant may have given the officers a bad time when he was interrogated, when he enters the courtroom, his lawyer will have him neatly dressed, and he will be polite—the picture of an innocent victim.

The jury will be studying not only the defendant, but also the police officers. They should be neatly dressed and should have left any firearms outside of the courtroom. As police officers walk to the witness stand and take the oath, the jury will judge them, and that judgment affects their readiness to accept the officers' testimony.

Prosecutors also judge officers, for it is upon them that they rely for evidence with which to prosecute the case. Actually the preparation for the courtroom testimony began when the investigation began. The investigators should make accurate, complete notes and from these notes make complete reports. It is extremely difficult to take on a sharp defense lawyer six months and several investigations later unless careful notes and reports have been prepared. The police officers' functions do not end with the invesitgation and the solving of a criminal case; they must be prepared to testify in court regarding the case.

Before going into court, police officers should go over their notes and reports. They may revisit the crime scene to observe any changes. A review of the physical evidence collected is mandatory. They should also review any measurements made.

Even after a thorough review, when police officers enter the courtroom they may not be able to recall certain facts. In such cases they can refer to their notes or reports. Although the defense attorney may offer a challenge upon cross-examination, if officers ask to refresh their memory from their notes or reports, the challenge is unfounded because police officers have that right—provided they are *their* notes or report. If two officers on an investigation agree that one will take notes and make the report, only the officer who took the notes and wrote the report is allowed to testify from them. The other officer cannot use them to recall details.

The prosecution needs to establish the corpus delicti of the crime, which means it has to establish the elements of the crime by testimony of witnesses, physical evidence, documents, recordings, or other admissible evidence. This information usually comes from police officers, their recollections, their notes, and their reports. The prosecutor works with the police officers in presenting the arguments for the prosecution. On the opposing side is the defense attorney.

Defense attorneys use several different techniques for which police officers should be prepared. One frequently used technique is *rapid-fire questioning* with the intent of confusing the officer or obtaining inconsistent answers. To counter this tactic, officers should be deliberate and take their time in answering questions.

They may ask the defense attorney to repeat the question to slow him down and thus thwart his efforts at rapid-fire questioning.

The trial of a criminal case is a contest, a very serious contest. Someone wins and someone loses. The prosecution wins if it establishes the guilt of the defendant. It must prove the defendant is guilty beyond a reasonable doubt. The defendant wins if the prosecution fails in its obligation of proof.

Proof consists of two basic elements: the evidence itself and, equally important, presentation of this evidence. No matter how much evidence exists, if improperly presented, the prosecution will fail. Presenting evidence involves credibility, believability.

In a criminal case, the defense rarely expects to gain helpful information from police officers. The main intent is usually to discredit the officers or their testimony. One common approach is to establish a motive for the officer's testimony, to show that the officer has a personal interest in the case, to question his candor: Is he being open or is he holding back? Is his testimony consistent? Does it contain errors? Is the officer confident and relaxed or nervous, upset, and seemingly afraid? What is his general appearance? Does he give the appearance of a professional doing an important, serious job, or does he give the impression that he takes the trial lightly?

Defense attorneys also attack a police officer's credibility by focusing on the assumptions or inferences of the officer. Assumptions and inferences are natural. We spend our whole lives making assumptions, usually reasonable ones. The law recognizes the validity of assumptions and inferences. As a matter of fact, the court will instruct the jury to make reasonable inferences. From time to time, however, a defense attorney will try to discredit police officers' testimony by asking them if they are making assumptions. If officers have, in fact, drawn inferences or made assumptions, they should not attempt to deny it.

Another cross-examination tactic used by defense counsel from time to time is to present to the jury police officers' reluctance to relinquish their notes. The police officers' notes and their reports, as a general rule, are available to the defense counsel in making cross-examination. When police officers use their notes to testify, they are also available to the defense counsel.

> The defense attorney may try to confuse or discredit a police officer by (1) rapid-fire questioning, (2) establishing that the officer wants to see the defendant found guilty, (3) accusing the officer of making assumptions, or (4) implying that the officer does not want anyone else to know what is in his notes.

Another tactic defense attorneys often use is to inquire as to whether the officer gave the constitutional warning required by the *Miranda* decision. The warning itself, if properly given, is seldom the subject of an attack by the defense counsel. The defense usually focuses on whether the defendant really understood the rights. In some cases on record the defendant has been given a Miranda card to read, waived his rights, and when the case came to trial it was found that the defendant could not read.

These are only a few of the many tactics used by defense attorneys. But no matter how skilled the defense, if police officers are well prepared, well groomed, poised, and present the evidence fairly, openly, and candidly, they will be serving the interests of justice. Perhaps the most important considerations for officers testifying in court are to be composed, truthful, and impartial at all times.

Closing Statements.   After the advocates have concluded their presentations, the jury hears the closing statements—a contest in persuasion first by the prosecution stating the jury should render a guilty verdict, then by the defense attorney concluding his client is surely innocent or at least not proven guilty beyond a reasonable doubt.

Jury Deliberation and Decision.   With the closing of the case, the judge reads the instructions to the jury. He explains the crime, what elements constitute the crime, alternate charges, and the concepts of presumption of innocence and reasonable doubt. The jury then retires behind closed doors to deliberate their findings. They can return one of three findings: guilty, not guilty, or no verdict. No verdict simply means that no agreement can be reached; this is also sometimes referred to as a "hung jury."

After the jury has come to a decision, the judge is notified and the jury returns to the courtroom. With everyone present, the jury foreman announces the verdict. Each juror is then polled as to how he voted and is asked if the verdict which the foreman has read is the verdict of the juror. If the finding is guilty, the defendant may either be sentenced immediately, or he may be given a sentencing date. If he is found not guilty, he is set free. If a hung jury results, the defendant may be retried at the discretion of the prosecutor.

Sentencing

Sentences for individuals convicted of crimes vary considerably from lenient to extremely severe penalties. For one convicted of a crime this may mean the difference between probation and several years in prison.

The National Advisory Commission on Criminal Justice Standards and Goals *(The Courts,* 1973, p. 109) notes that: "The extent to which a defendant regards his sentence as fair may influence his willingness to participate in correctional programs. . . . Sentencing is related to community security insofar as it affects the ability of correctional agencies to change the behavior of convicted offenders. It also may help curtail crimes by persons other than the offender being sentenced. This may occur through deterrence—the creation of conscious fear of swift and certain punishment—or through more complex means, such as reinforcing social norms by the imposition of severe penalties."

The commission also notes that uneven sentencing practices from court to court may endanger a convicted offender's right to "equal treatment under the law." It also notes that every serious study in the last half-century has condemned the practice of having juries impose the sentence, with such jury sentencing being viewed as nonprofessional and more likely than judge sentencing to be arbitrary and emotional.

In many jurisdictions the court has the authority to set, within limits established by state statute, both maximum and minimum sentences. Common characteristics of these schemes are summarized in Table 15–1.

Table 15–1.	*Common Sentencing Schemes.*
Indeterminate	Minimun and maximum terms prescribed by legislature; place and length of sentence controlled by corrections and parole; judge has little discretion over time served; goal is rehabilitation; sentence to fit offender; uncertainty and disparity in sentencing are major problems.
Indefinite	Similar to indeterminate sentence in some states; minimum and maximum terms, or only maximum term prescribed by legislature; sentence to match offender's needs; judge has some sentencing discretion; wide disparity in sentences imposed; parole used for early release.
Definite	Fixed period prescribed by legislature and imposed by judge; goal to punish and deter offender from further crime; allows for same sentence to apply to all convicted of particular offenses; eliminates disparity; judge has no discretion over length of sentence, only over choice of sentence; offender required to serve entire sentence; no parole, inflexibility, and rigidity are major problems.
Determinate	Similar to definite sentence; has one fixed term of years set by judge; offender required to serve entire sentence where no parole exists.
Mandatory	Fixed term set by legislature for particular crimes; sentence must be imposed by judge; judge has no discretion in choice of sentence; goal is punishment and deterrence; contrary to individualized sentence; no sentencing disparity; no parole.
Presumptive	Legislatively prescribed range of sentences for given crimes; minimum and maximum terms with judge setting determinate sentence within these bounds; judge maintains some discretion; guidelines and use of mitigating and aggravating circumstances established by legislature; goal is justice, deterrence, and individualization in sentencing; "just deserts."

Source: Reprinted by permission from *Introduction to Criminal Justice* by Joseph J. Senna and Larry J. Siegel. Copyright © 1984 by West Publishing Co. All rights reserved.

Common sentencing schemes include indeterminate, indefinite, definite, determinate, mandatory, and presumptive.

Case Review and Appeal

To assure that justice is served, the court system provides for a review of cases and for a person convicted to appeal the conviction in most instances. The National Advisory Commission on Criminal Justice Standards and Goals (*The Courts,* 1973, pp. 122–25) states that: "Determining guilt and fixing punishment should not be left to a single trial court. The interests of both society and the defendant are served by providing another tribunal to review the trial court proceedings to insure that no prejudicial error was committed and that justice was done." The commission goes on to note that: "Review also provides a means for the ongoing development of legal doctrine in the common law fashion, as well as a means of insuring evenhanded administration of justice throughout the jurisdiction. Functionally, review is the last stage in the judicial process of determining guilt and fixing sentence. Like the trial proceeding, it should be fair and expeditious.''

You have already been introduced to the appellate courts at both the state and federal level. These courts were established to ease the burden on the state and United States supreme courts. According to the National Advisory Commission on Criminal Justice Standards and Goals a decade ago: ''The review stage is in trouble . . . the process is cumbersome and fragmented. . . . Both state and federal courts are threatened with inundation.'' The commission sees two interrelated defects in the review process. First, appellate review is hampered by rules that limit the court's consideration to matters in the trial record; it cannot review the total case. Second, the defendant not only can obtain collateral review (both federal and state review at the same time), but also can seek and sometimes obtain, multiple reviews.

The result of these defects has been a great increase in the workload of lawyers and judges, protracted periods of litigation following the lower court's decision, and frequently, the ''erosion of finality in convictions. The result of these limitations and fragmentations is a drawn out, sometimes never-ending review cycle. This in turn brings the criminal process into public disrepute and leaves convicted defendants with feelings of injustice mixed with illusory hopes that another round of review will overturn the conviction'' (*The Courts,* 1973, p. 112).

Interestingly, even with the numerous types of review available to persons convicted of crimes, the sentence received, often the most important aspect of the trial, usually cannot be reviewed.

Summary

Police officers aid the criminal justice process by (1) making legal arrests, (2) legally obtaining accurate, relevant information and evidence, (3) writing complete, accurate reports, (4) identifying suspects and witnesses, and (5) providing effective, truthful testimony in court.

Our criminal justice system is based on the adversary system which requires that the accuser prove beyond a reasonable doubt to a judge or jury that the accused is guilty of a specified crime.

The criminal justice system has several safeguards to assure that all citizens are guaranteed their civil rights and civil liberties. The Fourth Amendment forbids unreasonable searches and seizures and requires probable cause. The Fifth Amendment guarantees due process, that is, notice of a hearing, full information regarding the charges made, the opportunity to present evidence before an impartial judge or jury, and the right to refrain from self-incrimination. The Sixth Amendment establishes the requirements for criminal trials including the right to a speedy public trial by an impartial jury and the right to have a lawyer. The Eighth Amendment forbids excessive bail and implies the right to such bail in most instances.

Gideon v. Wainwright established the court's responsibility for providing counsel for any indigent person charged with a felony.

The adult criminal justice system has several critical stages including the complaint or charge, the arrest, the booking, the preliminary hearing, the grand jury hearing, the arraignment, and the trial.

The preliminary hearing is the probable cause hearing. It seeks to prevent persons from being indiscriminately brought to trial. The discovery process requires that all pertinent facts on both sides be made available prior to the time of the hearing. The grand jury may decide whether enough evidence exists to indict (bring to trial) persons in criminal cases whether they are in custody or not. The coroner's jury is involved in cases where the cause of death is in doubt.

Following the preliminary hearing or the grand jury hearing, defendants appear at an arraignment where they enter their plea: they may stand mute, or plead nolo contendere, guilty, or not guilty.

Not all cases go to court. Alternatives to a trial include screening, diversion, or plea bargaining. Screening is the decision to stop all formal proceedings with nothing further required of the suspect. It is appropriate only when neither diversion nor conviction is desirable. Diversion provides the defendant with an alternative to a trial, e.g., obtain help from a community organization or make restitution to the victim. Plea bargaining is a compromise between defense and prosecution which prearranges the plea and the sentence, conserving manpower and expense. The case may or may not go to trial, depending on the circumstances.

If a case does go to trial defendants may often select trial by judge or by jury. If they select jury, the jury will be randomly selected from citizens of the community, and each will be carefully questioned to insure selection of six or twelve fair and impartial jurors. Police officers' testimony at the trial is of great importance. They should be aware of tactics frequently used by defense attorneys to confuse or discredit a police officer who is testifying: (1) rapid-fire questioning, (2) establishing that the officer wants to see the defendant found guilty, (3) accusing the officer of making assumptions, or (4) implying that the officer does not want anyone else to know what is in his notes.

Although the police officer and the prosecutor represent the accuser, in effect, their ultimate responsibility is to see that justice is done—not to see that a conviction is obtained.

Application

Review the following examples of courtroom testimony and decide whether each is effective testimony or not. If it is not effective, what is wrong?

1. *Defense Attorney:* Officer Cooley, isn't it fair to say your job is to arrest people who commit a crime?

   Officer Cooley: That is only partly true. My job is to serve the public and to arrest only those whom I have a warrant for or have probable cause to arrest.

Defense Attorney: Is it fair to say you wouldn't go around arresting innocent people?

Officer Cooley: Yes. I must have probable cause to arrest a person I feel may have disobeyed the law.

Defense Attorney: Isn't it a fair assumption that when you arrest someone, you feel very strongly that she or he committed the offense?

Officer Cooley: Again, it would depend upon the probable cause that the person may have committed the offense.

Defense Attorney: Isn't part of your job to come to court and make sure the defendant is convicted?

Officer Cooley: My appearance in court is to present testimony and evidence which I've gathered related to the commission of a crime.

Defense Attorney: Isn't it true, Officer, that you may have a tendency to shade your testimony a bit to convict this defendant?

Officer Cooley: No, sir; the testimony relates only to the evidence gathered and my knowledge of the crime.

Defense Attorney: Is your principal objective in this case to see that the defendant is convicted?

Officer Cooley: No, my position in this case is to present my testimony and to serve justice to the best of my ability.

2. *Defense Attorney:* Is it fair to say your job is to arrest people who have committed a crime?

Officer Dodd: Yup, that's right.

Defense Attorney: You don't go around arresting innocent people, do you?

Officer Dodd: Never.

Defense Attorney: Do you arrest only guilty people?

Officer Dodd: Yup.

Defense Attorney: Isn't it fair to say, then, that when you arrest someone, you believe he or she is guilty?

Officer Dodd: Sure.

Defense Attorney: Do you believe guilty people should be punished?

Officer Dodd: Sure.

Defense Attorney: Do you believe it is your job to see that they are punished?

Officer Dodd: Sure do.

Defense Attorney: Do you believe you should do everything you can to see that they are punished?

Officer Dodd: Yup.

Defense Attorney: Isn't part of your job to come to the courtroom and offer testimony?

Officer Dodd: Sure is.

Defense Attorney: When you came into this courtroom today, did you believe that Mr. Johnson, the defendant, was guilty?

Officer Dodd: Definitely.

Defense Attorney: You want Mr. Johnson convicted?

Officer Dodd: Definitely.

Defense Attorney: And you want him punished?

Officer Dodd: Definitely.

Defense Attorney: And you'll do everything you can to see that happen?

Officer Dodd: Right.

3. *Defense Attorney:* Officer Thomas, on direct examination you referred to some notes from time to time. May I see those notes, please?

(Officer Thomas glances at the prosecuting attorney and is quite hesitant to turn over the notes.)

Defense Attorney: Officer Thomas, is there something in those notes you don't want me to see?

Officer Thomas: Not particularly.

4. *Defense Attorney:* Officer, you testified on direct examination that when you left the store, walked out the door, and found the sack, you followed a trail of bloodstains. Do you recall that specifically?

Officer Troy: Yes, sir.

Defense Attorney: Did you make a test to determine the nature of these stains?

Officer Troy: No, not me.

Defense Attorney: You made no chemical analysis?

Officer Troy: No.

Defense Attorney: Do you know if anyone else made a chemical analysis?

Officer Troy: No.

Defense Attorney: Did anyone report to you that they made a chemical analysis?

Officer Troy: No.

Defense Attorney: Then, as a matter of fact, you do *not* know now, nor did you know then, that those stains were actually blood.

Officer Troy: Well, I know what blood looks like.

Defense Attorney: What does blood look like?

Officer Troy: When it's dried, it's kind of rusty looking.

Defense Attorney: Are there other things that are rusty looking when they are dried?

Officer Troy: I suppose there are.

Defense Attorney: How about candle wax from a rust-colored candle?

Officer Troy: Could be.

Defense Attorney: We've all seen movies where the prop used is ketchup or something which resembles blood. Many substances are rusty looking when dried, aren't they?

Officer Troy: Not this; this was blood.

Defense Attorney: On what scientific basis do you draw that conclusion? I'll withdraw the question. Officer, it is fair to say that you make assumptions from time to time, isn't it?

Officer Troy: Yes.

Defense Attorney: And that in this particular case you saw a stain that looked sort of rusty and was dried, and you assumed it was blood?

Officer Troy: No. It *was* blood.

5. *Defense Attorney:* Officer Troy, what type of test did you conduct to determine whether or not the defendant understood you when you advised her of her various rights?

Officer Troy: I asked her if she understood the rights as I read them from the card to her.

Defense Attorney: And what was her response?

Officer Troy: She said she did.

Defense Attorney: Well, what tests did you make to determine whether or not she actually understood these rights?

Officer Troy: I asked if she understood what I read to her.

Defense Attorney: Do you know the defendant's I.Q.?

Officer Troy: No, but from my personal observation and conversation with her, she seemed to be reasonably intelligent.

Defense Atorney: Do you know whether or not she can read?

Officer Troy: She said she could.

Defense Attorney: Do you know whether or not she can write?

Officer Troy: She said she could.

Answers

1. This officer has done a good job, has handled himself well in answering some extremely difficult questions.

2. This officer's approach indicates a personal interest in seeing the defendant convicted and punished. He says his job is to arrest people he feels are guilty and wants punished. This is not an ignoble feeling, but the defense counsel can suggest to the jury in his final arguments that Officer Dodd might have stepped beyond the bounds of fairness and honesty in his testimony since he stated under oath he would do everything he could to see Mr. Johnson convicted. Officer Dodd made it quite clear that he has a personal objective—the conviction and punishment of the defendant.

3. The example illustrates the dangers inherent when an officer hesitates to share notes or reports with the defense attorney.

4. This officer has fallen into the trap of not admitting he has made an assumption. He may feel that assumptions are negative or wrong. However, in this case his assumption is legitimate and valid. The court would probably make instructions to the jury as to its legitimacy. However, the officer does not admit he has made an assumption. Therefore, the defense attorney may argue to the jury that the officer refuses to admit making an assumption, when everyone knows he did. Consequently, how reliable and believable is his testimony?

5. This officer has done a good job in response to this line of questioning. Police officers are not expected to conduct tests to determine a suspect's I.Q. They must rely upon their own common sense.

Alternative Application

Diagram as completely as you can the steps in the criminal justice system from complaint to disposition. Then compare your diagram with that in Figure 15–1.

Discussion Questions

1. Is the jury system really fair?

2. What alternatives to the jury system are there?

3. What is the best kind of notebook for police officers to use for testifying in court?

4. Can the defense attorney examine the officer's entire notebook even if it contains notes on other cases?

5. Should the victim of a crime be consulted when plea bargaining is used?

6. How can police officers be sure a person they have just arrested understands the Miranda warning?

7. Is our system truly an adversary system when the prosecutor also has to protect the accused's rights?

References

American Bar Association. *Grand jury policy and model act*. Chicago, 1982.

Eisenstein, J. *Counsel for the United States*. Baltimore: Johns Hopkins University Press, 1978.

Ericson, R.V., and Baranek, P.M. *The ordering of justice: A study of accused persons as defendants in the criminal process*. Toronto: University of Toronto Press, 1982.

Flemming, R.B. *Allocating freedom and punishment*. New York: Longman, 1982.

Glick, H.R. *Who are federal judges*. New York: McGraw-Hill, 1983.

Hermann, R.; Single, E.; and Boston, J. *Counsel for the poor: Criminal defense in urban America.* Lexington, Mass: Heath, Lexington Books, 1977.

Human, G., and von Hirsch, A., eds. *Sentencing.* New York: Oxford University Press, 1981.

Inbau, F.E., and Aspen, M. *Criminal law for the police.* Randor, Penn.: Chilton Book Company, 1969.

Inbau, F.E.; Thompson, J.R.; and Fagel, J.B. *Criminal law and its administration.* Mineola, N.Y.: The Foundation Press, 1974.

Jacob, H. *Crime and justice in urban America.* Englewood Cliffs, N.J.: Prentice-Hall, Inc., 1980.

Jacoby, J.A. *The American prosecutor: A search for identity.* Lexington, Mass.: D.C. Heath and Company, 1980.

Lefstein, N. *Criminal defense services for the poor.* American Bar Association Standing Committee on Legal Aid and Indigent Defendants. Chicago: American Bar Association, 1982.

Lewis, P.W., and Peoples, K.D. *The Supreme Court and the criminal process.* Philadelphia: W.B. Saunders, 1978.

McBarnet, D.J. *Conviction: Law, the state, and the construction of justice.* London: Macmillan, 1981.

Markle, A. *Criminal investigation and presentation of evidence.* St. Paul, Minn.: West Publishing Company, 1976.

National Advisory Commission on Criminal Justice Standards and Goals. *Corrections.* Washington, D.C.: U.S. Government Printing Office, 1973.

National Advisory Commission on Criminal Justice Standards and Goals. *The courts.* Washington, D.C.: U.S. Government Printing Office, 1975.

National Center for State Courts and the Conference of State Court Administrators. *State court organization.* Washington, D.C.: U.S. Government Printing Office, 1982.

Rosett, A., and Cressey, D.R. *Justice by consent.* Philadelphia: J.B. Lippincott, 1976.

Rubin, H.T. *The courts: Fulcrum of the justice system.* 2d ed. New York: Random House, 1984.

Senna, J.J., and Siegel, L.J. *Introduction to criminal justice.* St. Paul, Minn.: West Publishing Company, 1984.

U.S. Department of Justice. National Institute of Justice. *Mandatory sentencing: The experience of two states.* Washington, D.C.: U.S. Government Printing Office, 1982.

Vera Institute of Justice. *Felony arrests: Their prosecution and disposition in New York City's courts.* rev. ed. New York: Longman, 1981.

Waldron, R.J. *The criminal justice system, an introduction.* 3d ed. Boston: Houghton Mifflin Company, 1984.

Williams, V.L; Formby, W.A.; and Watkins, J.C. *Introduction to criminal justice.* Albany, N.Y.: Delmar Publishers, Inc., 1982.

A row of cell blocks at a correctional facility.

Corrections

*The Final Stage in the
Criminal Justice System*

Do You Know . . .

- ■ What corrections is?
- ■ What the primary purpose of any correctional program is? What secondary purposes are served?
- ■ What probation is?
- ■ What the primary goal of a correctional institution is? What secondary goals may be established?
- ■ How jail differs from prison?
- ■ What negative characteristics are associated with our jails?
- ■ What two basic philosophies are evident in our prisons?
- ■ What differences are created by these two philosophies?
- ■ What factors account for the increase in the number of individuals serving prison terms?
- ■ How parole differs from probation? How it is similar to probation?
- ■ What reintegration methods have been used to facilitate the transition from prison to the community?
- ■ How a restitution center differs from a halfway house?
- ■ How corrections relates to the courts? The community? The police?

An eye for an eye, a tooth for a tooth.
—Deuteronomy

Introduction

As noted in the first chapter of this book, since prehistoric times society has found ways to force compliance to its laws. In primitive times burning, branding, maiming, hanging, and other means of punishment were common. And if a member of one tribe committed a crime against a member of another tribe, the result was frequently war between the two tribes. To reduce the amount of fighting between tribes, the notion of restitution was conceived; that is, the offender would pay for whatever damages were caused to the victim, thereby avoiding war.

The concept of restitution is also seen in the laws of Moses which many feel are not a call for revenge, but are rather an appeal that the punishment should fit the crime—an appeal for moderation in delivering justice.

As noted by Williams, Formby, and Watkins (1982, p. 464), when nation-states were formed, crime no longer was dealt with privately. It became the state's responsibility to punish offenders, and if the punishment included any kind of fine, the state kept the money.

Greenberg and Ruback (1983, p. 212) point out that: "Before the 19th century, imprisonment for crimes was virtually unknown. The two most common penalties for violations of the law were the fine and the whip. . . . A punishment for minor crimes often used as an alternative to the fine was the stocks . . . a particularly painful psychological punishment in closely knit communities." They go on to note that frequently offenders were branded or made to wear a letter on their clothes indicating their crime, such as Hester Prynne in Hawthorne's *The Scarlet Letter,* a novel in which Hester wore a scarlet "A" branding her as an adultress. Offenders who did not live in the community were often whipped and then cast out of the community, an inexpensive way to punish vagrants. In addition, according to Greenberg and Ruback (1982, p. 212): "If fines, whippings and public ridicule did not deter an offender from committing more crimes, capital punishment was the usual solution. The criminal codes of the colonies included a large number of crimes that were punishable by hanging. . . ."

It was not until the nineteenth century that imprisonment became a common form of punishment, and not until late in the twentieth century that some states began to allow restitution as an alternative for offenders.

In the present-day criminal justice system the problem of punishment or corrections for offenses against society is seen in most states as a shared responsibility of three levels of government: the county, the state, and the federal.

Corrections Defined

The final stage in the administration of the criminal justice system in the United States is corrections. Corrections is that portion of the criminal justice system that carries out the court's orders. It consists of our probation and parole systems as well as our jails, prisons, and community-based programs to rehabilitate offenders.

According to Eldefonso (1974, p. 4): "Corrections is America's prisons, jails, juvenile training schools, probation and parole machinery, and, as such, is the part of the criminal justice system that the public sees the least of and knows the least about. It seldom gets into the news, unless there is a prison riot, jail break, or a sensational scandal involving corruption or brutality in an institution or by an official." He goes on to suggest that approximately one-third of the individuals being "served" by the corrections program are in institutions, and that these institutions are often in remote rural areas, or in the lower levels of police stations or courthouses. The other two-thirds of the corrections population are on probation or parole and, consequently, are distributed throughout the country and are not readily visible to the general public.

> Corrections is that portion of the criminal justice system that carries out the court's orders. It consists of our probation and parole systems as well as our jails, prisons, and community-based programs to rehabilitate offenders.

Eldefonso also suggests that the underlying philosophy of corrections is to serve and protect society by rehabilitating offenders (1974, p. 5): "The purpose of any correctional program is to make services available, within a client-restrictive status designed to protect society, which will enable the offender to become a useful, productive citizen." The National Advisory Commission on Criminal Justice Standards and Goals (*Corrections*, 1973, p. 222) points out, however, that: "Public protection is not always the sole objective of correctional programming. Some kinds of offenders, especially the most notorious, often could perfectly well be released without jeopardizing public safety. But their release will not be countenanced because public demands for retribution have not been satisfied."

> The primary purpose of a correctional program is to make services available—within a restricted environment—which enable an offender to become a useful, productive citizen.

This notion is also held by Greenberg and Ruback (1982, p. 214) who suggest several purposes for a sentence imposed on an offender: "A sentence imposed on an offender may be for the purpose of individual deterrence, general deterrence, incapacitation, retribution, expression of moral outrage, or rehabilitation." Often a sentence is directly proportional to how the general public views the act.

> Secondary purposes of a correctional program are individual deterrence, general deterrence, incapacitation, retribution, or expression of moral outrage.

Probation

A person who is found guilty of a crime may be placed on probation. Eldefonso (1974, p. 5) defines probation as: "the process of supervision, operating within a frame-work of judicial authority and employing its own disciplines and methods in harmony with basic social casework concepts to effect satisfactory adjustment between the individual's needs and the demands of society." He also notes that probation is the most frequent alternative to a jail or prison sentence.

> *Probation is the conditional suspension of a sentence of a person convicted of a crime but not yet imprisoned for that crime. The defendant is placed under the supervision of a probation officer for a set period of time and must meet specific conditions.*

Probation is most frequently used with first offenders and with crimes that are not considered heinous by society, such as many of the white-collar crimes. A first-time embezzler of high standing in the community might be given probation, avoiding the stigma of a prison record. Probation operates on a "second-chance" philosophy. Consequently, if a person is convicted a second time for a crime, that person is very unlikely to receive probation.

Every county has a probation department that works closely with the courts to carry out its dictates. It is the responsibility of this department to establish rehabilitation programs for those persons placed on probation. A federal probation system also exists to supervise persons convicted of federal offenses and sometimes military personal who have committed crimes against the military.

Correctional Institutions

The first truly correctional institution in the United States opened in Philadelphia in 1790 and was called the Walnut Street Jail. This jail, unlike existing workhouses, prisons, and jails, was used exclusively for the "correction" of convicted felons.

As noted noted earlier, not until the nineteenth century was the use of correctional institutions common in the United States. Eldefonso (1974, p. 6) notes that: "In present-day Western society police power is used in the final attempt to control the offender." He suggests that programs instituted in correctional facilities often serve several purposes, including punishment, treatment, and rehabilitation, usually accomplished with a high degree of regimentation. And he feels that: "The primary goal of correctional institutions, as well as of all corrections should be protection of society."

> *The primary goal of correctional institutions is to protect society. Secondary goals may be to deter, rehabilitate, and reintegrate offenders into society.*

Although corrections attempts to rehabilitate offenders, conditions cannot be such that the prison is a pleasant place to be. Inmates should dread a return. Unfortunately, however, too often our correctional institutions do not rehabilitate but actually contribute to and reward criminal behavior. Greenberg and Ruback

(1982, p. 221) suggest that: "The institutional model for corrections has not been successful in curbing potential crime. But at least it exists, with its physical plant and identified processes of reception, classification, assignment, custody, work, academic and vocational training, religion, and recreation.

The type of correctional institution an offender is sentenced to usually depends on the type of crime committed and the offender's past record. Alternatives include local and county jails and state and federal prisons.

The Jail

The jail is an important part of the criminal justice system in the United States. Jail differs from prison in that its inmates are there for shorter terms and usually for less serious crimes. According to Pursley (1980, p. 417): "A stay in jail is the most widely experienced form of incarceration." People who are in jail may be awaiting trial or serving a sentence. Pursley (1980, p. 416) notes that: "It [jail] is important as an indicator of the interest and concern with justice, punishment, and rehabilitation expressed by society and the local community. The person who is awaiting trial or serving a sentence experiences first-hand and with varying degrees of intensity what it is like to be exposed to the values as they relate to crime and punishment.

Jail differs from prison in that its inmates are there for shorter terms, usually for less serious crimes.

Community values regarding such crimes as prostitution, drunkenness, and vagrancy will directly affect the jail's population. In addition, the court's attitude toward such crimes will also affect the jail's population. It is frequently up to the court's discretion to sentence an offender to jail, to a work program, or to probation. Therefore, the court's decisions directly affect the number and type of persons being sentenced to jail. The court's decisions also dictate how much involvement the jail personnel must have with rehabilitative programs. If, for example, the court specifies that an offender must participate in a work program, the jail must provide such a program.

As part of the corrections segment of the criminal justice system, the jail has an advantage over prison because it is frequently located in the community and can coordinate its services with that of the community. In addition, its offenders are usually more likely to be rehabilitated than prison inmates, many of whom are habitual offenders.

The importance of the jail in the corrections program is stressed by the President's Commission on Law Enforcement and Administration of Justice (1967, pp. 162–63):

On the correction continuum, jails are the beginning of the penal or institutional segment. They are, in fact, the reception units for a greater variety and number of offenders than will be found in any other segment of the correctional process, and it is at this point that the greatest opportunity is offered to make sound decisions on the offender's next step in the correctional process. Indeed, the availability of qualified services at this point could result in promptly removing many from the correctional process who have been swept in unnoticed and undetected and who are more in need of protective, medical and dental care from welfare and health agencies than they are in need of custodial care in penal and correctional institutions. In a broad sense the jails and local institutions are reception centers for the major institutions.

Usually the chief administrator of a jail is a law enforcement officer, often a sheriff. Jail personnel may be sheriff's deputies or other law enforcement officers. Their treatment of people being held in jail will directly affect the offenders' views of the fairness of the corrections program.

Because jails are such an important part of the corrections program and the total criminal justice system, it is imperative that they be of high quality. Unfortunately, however, as noted by Pursley (1980, p. 416): "The jail has traditionally operated below standard." Pursley (1980, p. 420) contends that: "The harsh reality is that most jails remain a serious problem in the system of American justice. For years, criminologists, study commissions, interested citizen groups and some governmental officials have deplored the conditions of our nation's jails. The ill and the healthy, the old and the young, petty offenders and hardened criminals, the mentally defective, the psychotic and sociopathic, the vagrant and the alcoholic, the habitual offender who is serving a life sentence in short installments—all continue to populate our jails in an indiscriminate mass of human neglect." Pursley cites six negative characteristics frequently associated with jails in the United States:

(1) The wide variety of backgrounds of the offenders

(2) The problems of local control and politics

(3) Inadequate personnel

(4) Demeaning physical conditions

(5) Inept administration

(6) Failure to adopt alternative programs and dispositions

Clearly, one of the greatest problems is the variety of offenders either awaiting trial or serving sentences in our jails. Each needs different types of programs and requires different kinds of security. In most instances, the physical facility and lack of personnel make such individualization next to impossible.

> *Negative characteristics of jails in the United States include the following: the wide variety of backgrounds of the offenders in our jails; the problems of local control and politics; inadequate personnel; demeaning physical facilities; inept administration; failure to adopt alternative programs and dispositions.*

The Prison

The word *prison* usually brings to mind an image of rows of cagelike cells, several levels high, crowded mess halls, a "yard" where prisoners engage in physical activities, organized and not so organized, all of which are patrolled by tight-lipped, heavily armed guards. As noted by Greenberg and Ruback (1982, p. 211): ''Prison systems differ among the states, and, even within the same prison system, prisons are of different types and have different programs. Nevertheless, all prisons have certain factors in common: an expensive physical facility, a population of convicted persons who desire to leave, and a much smaller number of guards who must try to maintain order and prevent escape.''

The physical facility itself reflects the philosophy regarding the purpose of imprisonment. Two basic physical designs developed in the United States. The first design consisted of fortresslike structures containing solitary cells, each with a tiny walled-in courtyard. Prisoners were, in effect, in solitary confinement for the duration of their sentences. The second design consisted of cells built back to back and facing a corridor. Meals were eaten in large rooms, and prisoners were expected to work at hard labor. This design, often referred to as the Auburn design because it was first used in the Auburn Penitentiary constructed in 1818 in Auburn, New York, is most frequently used in the United States today.

Both of the early philosophies influencing prison design were basically punitive. Throughout the decades, however, efforts at prison reform have lead to a change in emphasis, seeking to rehabilitate prisoners rather than to punish them.

As Greenberg and Rubeck (1982, p. 214) note: ''All prisons are custodial (and therefore punitive, as custody implies the loss of rights and the denial of certain comforts), but some are more oriented toward treating and rehabilitating offenders than others.'' They go on to cite several important differences between these two orientation.

Table 16–1. **Philosophies of Imprisonment.**

PUNITIVE ORIENTED	TREATMENT ORIENTED
Authority pattern based only on rank. For example, guards obey warden.	Authority pattern based on technical knowledge.
Very specific, measurable rules, with strict emphasis on obedience.	More general goals, more flexibility, more individualized.
Guards have limited decision-making authority, limited discretion.	Guards are encouraged to make their own decisions, use their own discretion.
Communication with inmates is very formal, usually restricted to orders.	Communication is less formal and is encouraged.
Incentives used are usually negative, for example, force and coercion, removal of privileges, solitary confinement, and the like.	Incentives used are usually positive, for example, granting of special privileges, better living quarters, furloughs, and the like.

Greenberg and Rubeck (1982 p. 215) conclude that: ''Although both punitive/custodial prisons and treatment-oriented prisons exist in the United States and although most prisons have elements of both types, most lack the physical and human resources necessary for an effective treatment orientation and, therefore, are primarily of the punitive/custodial type.''

> *Prisons may be punitive or treatment oriented. Punitive oriented prisons are more formal and rigid, with an emphasis on obedience. Obedience is sought through negative incentives. Treatment oriented prisons are more informal and flexible, with positive incentives for good behavior.*

Prisoners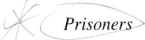

According to the Bureau of Justice Statistics (1983, p. 1): ''At the end of 1982 there were 412,303 inmates in the U.S. State and Federal prisons. The annual increase of almost 43,000 inmates was the highest in any year since data became available in 1925.'' See Figure 16–1.

The Bureau of Justice Statistics (1983, p. 5) notes that: ''Three fourths of the increase [in short-term and unsentenced prisoners] occurred in the seven jurisdictions that operate combined jail-prison systems in North Carolina, where adult misdemeanants with a minimum sentence of 180 days or more are confined in State facilities.'' The incarceration rates by state are summarized in Table 16–2.

Figure 16–1.   *Number of Sentenced State and Federal Prisoners, Yearend 1925–82.*

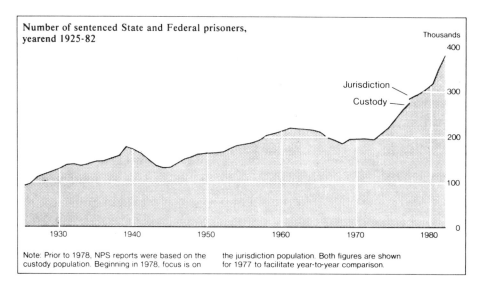

Number of sentenced State and Federal prisoners, yearend 1925-82

Note: Prior to 1978, NPS reports were based on the custody population. Beginning in 1978, focus is on the jurisdiction population. Both figures are shown for 1977 to facilitate year-to-year comparison.

Source: U.S. Department of Justice. *Bureau of Justice Statistics Bulletin.* Washington, D.C.: U.S. Government Printing Office, 1983.

| Table 16–2. | | **The Prison Profile at Yearend 1982.** | | | | | |

States with 10,000 or more prisoners		States with increases of 20% or more since 1981		States with increases of 1,000 or more since 1981		States with in- carceration rates of 200 or more per 100,000 U.S. population	
Texas	36,282	North Dakota	28.2	California	5,257	Nevada	301
California	34,459	Alaska	27.7	Texas	4,780	South Carolina	270
New York	27,910	Nevada	25.4	Florida	4,241	Florida	261
Florida	27,830	New Mexico	23.0	Ohio	2,349	North Carolina	255
Ohio	17,317	Oklahoma	21.0	New York	2,311	Louisiana	251
North Carolina	16,578	Delaware	20.6	Georgia	1,876	Delaware	250
Michigan	14,737			Maryland	1,677	Georgia	247
Georgia	14,320			Louisiana	1,520	Maryland	244
Illinois	13,875			Pennsylvania	1,157	Texas	237
Maryland	11,012			New Jersey	1,115	Alabama	215
Louisiana	10,935			Oklahoma	1,109	Mississippi	210
Pennsylvania	10,522			Alabama	1,030	Arizona	209
Virginia	10,079					Oklahoma	201

NOTE: The District of Columbia, as a wholly urban area, is excluded from the list of States with high incarceration rates.

Source: Bureau of Justice Statistics Bulletin. Washington, D.C.: U.S. Government Printing Office, 1983.

Nearly sixty percent (58.0) of the state prisoner increase occurred in eight states that added more than 1,500 inmates each. The largest gains were in the five largest prison systems—California, Texas, Florida, Ohio, and New York.

Obviously, this large influx of inmates has resulted in adverse living conditions in many of our state and federal prisons. As noted by the Bureau of Justice Statistics (1983, p. 3): ''At year end 31 states were operating under court orders to remedy prison overcrowding, and another 9 were involved in litigation.''

The Bureau of Justice Statistics details several of the causes for the increase in incarceration (1983, p. 3):

Contributing to the increase of prison populations in recent years were strict new laws on the disposition of convicted felons. During the past several years, 37 States passed mandatory sentencing laws and several others enacted determinate sentencing statutes. Both mandatory and determinate sentencing normally require that the convicted person be confined for a fixed period that the parole board may not reduce . . . .

Other new State legislation permits additional time to be added to the sentence of a person who used a firearm in the commission of a crime, who had a prior felony conviction, who committed a property offense involving damages over a certain amount, or who inflicted great bodily harm. Many of these laws also are mandatory in nature, reducing both sentencing and parole discretion.

Along with changes in sentencing laws, many States have adopted new parole policies that raise the requirements of parole, thereby lengthening time served. Fewer releases are being granted because of a more cautious attitude among board members, public pressure to keep criminals in prison longer, and implementation of new criteria for release. Among such criteria are the lengthening of the minimum time served and the availability of a job upon release.

In many states the power of the parole board has lessened, and in 10 states paroling authority has been eliminated.

Other reasons variously cited by States as factors in the 1982 population increase were poor economic conditions, large numbers of young people in the general population, increases in prison capacity, and stricter laws against driving while intoxicated.

> *Reasons for the increase in incarceration rates include stricter new laws and mandatory sentencing practices, longer sentences, new guidelines on sentencing repeat offenders, a "get tough" attitude, a law-and-order mood resulting in stricter law enforcement, a decline in parole releases, and economic conditions resulting in increased crime.*

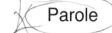

Parole

Parole is the most frequent type of release from a correctional institution. Parole differs from probation in that a person who is paroled has spent some time serving a prison sentence. It is similar to probation in that both require supervision of the offender and set up certain conditions that must be met by the offender.

According to Eldefonso (1974, p. 6): "Parole is administrative and quasi-judicial in nature. It is the process of supervision following an early release from an institution. Using casework principles, it attempts to bridge the gap between the institution and the community."

Factors influencing whether a person serving a sentence is eligible for or, indeed, is granted a parole include the type of offense committed, the offender's prior record, and state statutes. In some jurisdictions, parole is prohibited by statute for certain crimes. In other jurisdictions, however, people sentenced to prison are immediately eligible for parole.

> *Parole differs from probation in that a person who is paroled has spent some time serving a prison sentence. It is similar to probation in that both require supervision of the offender and set up certain conditions that must be met by the offender.*

Community-Based Institutional Programs

In some instances, jail or prison is not the best alternative for an offender.

> *Community-based institutional programs aimed at reintegration of the offender into society include halfway houses and restitution centers.*

Halfway Houses

As the name implies, halfway houses are community-based institutions for individuals who are half way into prison, that is, on probation, or half way out of prison, that is, on or nearing parole. As noted by Williams, Formby, and Watkins (1982, p. 460): "They [halfway houses] are residences for offenders who need fewer restrictions than a prison provides. They are an alternative to prisons."

Halfway houses have been in existence for centuries, with one of the earliest being in sixth-century France, founded by St. Leonard who secured the release of convicts and let them live in his monastery. Williams, Formby, and Watkins (1982, p. 460) note that the first modern halfway house in the United States was founded in 1954 by the Reverend James G. Jones, Jr., chaplain of the Cook County Jail in Chicago. Since that time many halfway houses have been opened in the United States.

Halfway houses typically provide offenders with a place to live, sleep, and eat. Counselors are provided to help with reintegration into society, including help with finding a suitable job and sometimes with transportation to a job.

As noted, halfway houses may serve those who are half way into prison, such as the misdemeanant—a person convicted of a crime requiring no more than a one-year sentence. Or they may serve persons who are half way out of prison—those who are nearing parole or who have actually been paroled but who still need support services. Halfway houses serving those nearing parole or actually discharged from prison are sometimes called "prerelease centers."

Restitution Centers

A new variation of the halfway house is the restitution center. A restitution center differs from a halfway house in that in the restitution center offenders work to partially repay their victims. Like the halfway house, restitution centers offer an alternative to prison, either for those who are half way into prison or those who are half way out of prison.

> *A restitution center differs from a halfway house in that in the restitution center offenders work to partially repay their victims.*

For restitution to be a viable alternative, the amount of money to be repaid must be within reason and the offender must not pose an escape risk. Since persons convicted of crimes typically cannot obtain high-paying jobs, frequently some type of compromise is reached between the victim and the offender, with the agreement being put into a signed contract.

Many sociologists suggest that restitution centers offer advantages to both the victim and the offender. For the victim they provide not only partial repayment, but also a sense that the criminal justice system is indeed fair, and that it is as concerned with the victims of crime as it is with the perpetrators of crime. On the other hand, restitution centers may also benefit the offenders, not only as an alternative to jail or prison, but also as a means of coming to know the victim as an individual who has suffered from the crime committed. Often offenders do not think about their victims as people with the same feelings as themselves. If they can see the harm they have caused, it may assist in their reform.

Other Reintegration Methods

Several methods of reintegration into society have been used, with varying degrees of success. The most common are furloughs, work release, and study release. In all instances the possiblity of escape from the directives of the criminal justice system must be considered.

> *Three common reintegration methods are the use of furloughs, work release, and study release.*

Furloughs

Furloughs are short, temporary leaves from a prison or jail. They may be supervised or unsupervised, although generally they are the latter. Furloughs are often used as positive motivators for good behavior. They may be granted for family emergencies, for a weekend with a spouse, or for job interviewing. Many experts feel that the use of conjugal furloughs for good behavior not only is a positive motivator, but it may also reduce homosexual activity within the correctional facility.

Work and Study Release

Another positive motivator for good behavior that also serves as a means to reintegrate offenders into society is release for either a job or a course of study. Often such programs are conducted through halfway houses. They may also be conducted through local jails. One problem associated with such programs is that those who are released may smuggle contraband back into the correctional facility.

The rules in work release and study release programs are usually very explicit and rigid. For example, a strict curfew may be established; going into a bar may be prohibited; and association with known criminals may be forbidden.

Individuals on work programs usually have their pay closely controlled. They may be required to pay a portion of their room and board, and, if married, to send part of their earnings to their dependents.

Corrections in Context*

As noted previously, corrections does not operate in isolation; it is an integral part of the criminal justice system and is affected by the courts, the community, and the police.

---

*Adapted from National Advisory Commission on Criminal Justice Standards and Goals. *Corrections.* Washington, D.C.: U.S. Government Printing Officer, 1973.

The Courts

The court has a dual role in the criminal justice system; it is (1) a participant in the criminal justice process, determining guilt or innocence and imposing sanctions, and (2) the supervisor of its practices, administering the probation system.

> *The court is a participant in and a supervisor of the criminal justice system. It defines crimes, sets penalties, and imposes sentences.*

If practices of the criminal justice system conflict with other societal values, the courts must also determine which takes precedence over the other. Since the 1970s the courts have increasingly ruled that values reflected in the Constitution take precedence over efficient administration of the correctional programs.

Although correctional officers and sentencing judges do not always agree, most recognize the other's viewpoints. For example, both recognize that sentencing decisions by the courts affect the discretion of correctional administrators in applying correctional programs. The concept of indeterminate sentencing grants correctional administrators broad discretion in individualizing programs.

In addition, recognition is growing that disparity in sentencing limits corrections' ability to develop sound attitudes in offenders. Traditionally sentencing judges felt their responsibility ended with imposing a sentence, and they never fully recognized what would occur if others received a lesser sentence or what might occur after sentence was imposed. If a person is sentenced to ten years for the same offense for which a fellow prisoner is serving three years, the person serving ten years is not likely to accept the justice of the system or the correctional programs it offers. In addition, primarily because of the growing number of lawsuits by prisoners, courts are becoming more aware of the conditions of prison confinement. If alternatives seem warranted, they are more frequently considered. "Use of probation and other community-based programs will continue to grow. The essential ingredient in the integration of courts and corrections into a compatible system of criminal justice is the free flow of information regarding sentencing and its effect on individual offenders." Likewise, "Correctional personnel must recognize that they are to some extent officers of the court. They are carrying out a court order and, like other court officers, are subject to the court's continuing supervision. Corrections has little to lose by this development and may gain a powerful new force for correctional reform (*Corrections,* p. 8)."

The Community

Traditionally correctional institutions were isolated from other human service agencies, and were required merely to hold prisoners and to provide some form of nominal supervision for individuals on probation and parole. More recently, however, as already noted, it is expected that corrections take a more positive approach, seeking rehabilitation whenever possible. These revised expectations make it necessary to link corrections to the community in every phase of operation.

Community-based corrections require a complicated interplay among judicial and correctional personnel from related public and private agencies, citizen volunteers, and civic groups. It also requires leadership.

Community-based corrections includes any activities in the community aimed at helping offenders become law-abiding citizens. The oldest community-based correctional program is supervision under probation, a foundation on which to build a wide range of community-based services. The use of control and surveillance is basic to a sound community corrections system.

> *Community-based corrections includes all correctional activities that occur in the community as an alternative to confinement of an offender at any point in the correctional process.*

A community-based approach to corrections has three significant advantages: humanitarian, restorative, and managerial. The humanitarian aspect is obvious because no one should be subjected to custodial control unnecessarily. To help a person avoid the unfavorable consequences of prison, even though the result of the offender's own criminal actions, is humanitarian. Second, restorative measures should help an offender achieve a position in the community in which he does not violate the law. The accomplishment of this objective can be measured by recidivism.

Finally, the managerial goal of cost-effectiveness can often be obtained from a community-based program. Any shift from custodial control saves money. However, the primary criterion is *not* fiscal. The public must be protected. If offenders can be shifted from custodial control to community-based programs without loss of public protection, a managerial objective can be accomplished.

The Police

The police and corrections are two elements of the criminal justice system that are farthest apart, not only in their sequence of operations, but also frequently in their attitudes toward crime and criminal offenders. The police often view community safety as their responsibility, and removing offenders from the community shifts this responsibility to corrections. The police also often spend more time with the victims of crime and may be more receptive to concepts of retribution and incapacitation than rehabilitation and reintegration.

In contrast, corrections tries to take the long-range view that rehabilitation is the ultimate goal and that this is accomplished by releasing offenders into the community—even though this may pose some risks. Unfortunately, the released offenders whom police encounter are often those who have been bad risks. Consequently, the police acquire an inaccurate view of the risks taken by correctional officers. Nonetheless, these correctional failures, whether parole or probation violators or individuals who fail to return from furloughs, add a burden to already overtaxed police resources and create misunderstandings between police and corrections.

Despite these differences, effective operation of the criminal justice system requires cooperation between police and correctional personnel (*Corrections,* pp. 6–7):

The impact of police practices on corrections, while not so dramatic and tangible as the effects of correctional risk-taking on the police, nonetheless is important and often critical to the correctional system's ability to perform its functions properly. The police officer is the first point of contact with the law for most offenders. He is the initiator of the relationship between the offender and the criminal justice system. He is likewise the ambassador and representative of the society that system serves. To the extent that the offender's attitude toward society and its institutions will affect his willingness to respect society's laws, the police in their initial and continued contact with an offender may have substantial influence on this future behavior.

The police are usually an offender's first contact with the criminal justice system. Police may tend to take the side of the victim and seek confinement rather than integration. Their broad arrest powers directly affect how offenders view the system as well as what type of people are in our jails and prisons.

Police do have broad discretion in the decision to arrest. "In fact, police arrest decisions may have a greater impact on the nature of the correctional clientele than do the legislative decisions delineating what kinds of conduct are criminal. . . . A large number of arrests for offenses that do not involve a significant danger to the community may result in misallocation and improper distribution of scarce correctional resources" (*Corrections,* p. 7).

In addition, any real or imagined discrimination against racial minorities, youth, or other groups such as motorcyclists, can breed hostility and resentment against the police which, inevitably, will influence their behavior within the correctional system.

Further, community-based correctional programs cannot succeed without the understanding and cooperation of the police because individuals within these programs *will* come in contact with the police, and the nature of that contact will directly affect the offender's adjustment.

The police can and must make affirmative contributions to community-based corrections programs. They know the resources available as well as the pitfalls to be avoided.

In essence, the police are an integral part of any successful corrections program, from using good judgment in making arrests to assisting those on parole or probation to reenter the community.

Summary

Corrections is that portion of the criminal justice system that carries out the court's orders. It consists of our probation and parole system as well as our jails, prisons, and community-based programs to rehabilitate offenders. The purpose of any correctional program is to make services available in a restricted environment designed to protect society, which will enable the offender to become a useful, productive citizen. Secondary purposes of a sentence imposed on an offender may be individual deterrence, general deterrence, incapacitation, retribution, or an expression of moral outrage.

The most frequent alternative to a jail or prison sentence is probation—the conditional suspension of a sentence of a person convicted of a crime but not yet imprisoned for that crime. The defendant is placed under the supervision of a probation officer for a set time period and must meet specific conditions.

Many offenders, especially repeat offenders, are sentenced to correctional institutions. The primary goal of correctional institutions is to protect society. Secondary goals may be to deter or rehabilitate and reintegrate offenders into society. Jail differs from prison in that its inmates are there for shorter terms, usually for less serious crimes. Negative characteristics of jails in the United States include: (1) the variety of the offenders, (2) the problems of local control and politics, (3) inadequate personnel, (4) demeaning physical facilities, (5) inept administration, and (6) failure to adopt alternative programs and dispositions.

Prisons may be punitive oriented or treatment oriented. Punitive oriented systems have authority patterns based only on rank; rules are very specific and are emphasized; guards have limited decision-making; communication with inmates is very formal and restricted to orders; and incentives are usually negative. In contrast, treatment oriented systems stress an authority pattern based on technical knowledge; goals are more general, flexible, and individualized; guards are encourged to make thier own decisions and to communicate with the inmates; and incentives are usually positive.

The number of people sentenced to jail and prison has increased greatly in the 1980s. Among the reasons for the increase in incarceration are stricter new laws and mandatory sentencing practices, longer sentences, new guidelines on sentencing repeat offenders, a ''get tough'' attitude, a law-and-order mood resulting in stricter law enforcement, a decline in parole releases, and economic conditions resulting in increased crime.

The vast majority of people sentenced to jail or prison become eligible for parole. Parole differs from probation in that a person who is paroled has spent some time serving a prison sentence. It is similar to probation in that both require supervision of the offender and set up certain conditions that the offender must meet. Parole and probation often involve community-based institutional programs aimed at reintegrating offenders into society, including halfway houses, restitution centers, furloughs, work release, and study release programs. A restitution center differs from a halfway house in that in the restitution center offenders work to partially repay their victims.

The corrections portion of the criminal justice system is directly affected by the courts, the community, and the police. The court is a participant in and a supervisor of the criminal justice system. It defines crimes, sets penalties, and imposes sentences on those found guilty, often including probation. The community is involved because correctional institutions and activities may provide an alternative to confinement of an offender at any point in the correctional process. Equally important are the police, usually an offender's first contact with the criminal justice system. Police may tend to take the side of the victim and to seek confinement of the offender rather than integration. Their broad arrest powers directly affect how offenders view the system as well as what type of people are in our jails and prisons. In addition, the police can and must make affirmative contributions to community-based corrections programs. They know the community resources available as well as the pitfalls which offenders must avoid.

Application

The public's attitude toward community-based corrections is sometimes distorted, biased, and prejudiced. Interview five persons and pose the following question: "Would you be receptive to locating a halfway house for criminals in your neighborhood?"

Assign a numerical value to the responses you feel are the most important and tally up the objections and the agreements as they are stated by those interviewed. Then discuss the results with the class. Both positive and negative attitudes should be noted in the individual's reasons for stating their positions.

Discussion Questions

1. Do you feel the public accepts community-based corrections programs?
2. What are some justifications to support monetary restitution in corrections?
3. What are some obstacles in establishing prison or jail reforms?
4. Are the systems of probation and parole effective tools in dealing with law violators?
5. In our modern society, with its constant changes in corrections philosophy, do you feel that parole boards serve a useful function?

References

Abbot, J.H. *In the belly of the beast: Letters from prison.* New York: Random House, 1981.

Allen, H.E., and Simonsen, C.E. *Corrections in America: An introduction.* 3rd ed. New York: Macmillan Publishing Company, 1981.

American Correctional Association. *The American prison: From the beginning* . . . The American Correctional Association, Publishers, 1983.

American Law Institute. *Modern penal code: Proposed official draft.* Philadelphia: American Law Institute, 1964.

Bartollas, C. *Correctional treatment: Theory and practice.* Englewood Cliffs, N.J.: Prentice-Hall, 1984.

Cullen, F.T., and Gilbert, K. *Reaffirming rehabilitation.* Cincinnati: Anderson Publishing Company, 1982.

Eldefonso, E. *Issues in corrections: A book of readings.* Beverly Hills, Cal.: Glencoe Press, 1974.

Greenberg, M.S., and Ruback, R.B. *Social psychology of the criminal justice system.* Monterey, Cal.: Brooks/Cole Publishing Company, 1982.

Henningsen, R.M. *Probation and parole.* New York: Harcourt Brace Jovanovich, 1981.

Irwin, J. *Prisons in turmoil.* Boston: Little, Brown and Company, 1980.

Keve, P.W. *Corrections.* New York: John Wiley and Sons, Inc., 1981.

Krotcoski, P.C., and Walker, D.B. *Criminal justice in America: Process and issues.* Glenview, Ill.: Scott Foresman and Company, 1978.

National Advisory Commission on Criminal Justice Standards and Goals. *Corrections.* Washington, D.C.: U.S. Government Printing Office, 1973.

National Institute of Justice. *American prisons and jails.* Washington, D.C.: U.S. Government Printing Office, 1980.

President's Commission on Law Enforcement and Administration of Justice. *The challenge of crime in a free society.* Washington, D.C.: U.S. Government Printing Office, 1967.

Pursley, R.D. *Introduction to criminal justice.* 3rd ed. New York: Macmillan Publishing Company, 1980.

Roberg, R.R., and Webb, V.J. *Critical issues in corrections.* St. Paul, Minn.: West Publishing Company, 1981.

Smykla, J.O. *Community-based corrections: Principles and practices.* New York: Macmillan Publishing Company, 1984.

Smykla, J.O. *Probation and parole: Crime control in the community.* New York: Macmillan Publishing Company, 1984.

Snarr, R.W., and Wolford, B.I. *Introduction to corrections.* Dubuque, Iowa: W.C. Brown Publishers, 1984.

Travis, L.F., III; Schwartz, M.D.; and Clear, T.R. *Corrections: An issues approach.* 2d ed. Cincinnati: Anderson Publishing Company, 1983.

U.S. Department of Justice. *1978 Survey of inmates of local jails.* Washington, D.C.: U.S. Government Printing Office, 1980.

U.S. Department of Justice. *Sourcebook of criminal justice statistics—1980.* Washington, D.C.: U.S. Government Printing Office, 1981.

U.S. Department of Justice. Bureau of Justice Statistics. *Prisoners in 1982.* Washington, D.C.: U.S. Government Printing Office, 1983.

U.S. Department of Justice. Bureau of Justice Statistics. *Probation and parole, 1981.* Washington, D.C.: U.S. Government Printing Office, 1982.

U.S. Department of Justice. Bureau of Justice Statistics. *State and local probation and parole systems.* Washington, D.C.: U.S. Government Printing Office, 1982.

Williams, V.L.; Formby, W.A.; and Watkins, J.C. *Introduction to criminal justice.* Albany, N.Y.: Delmar Publishers, Inc., 1982.

The swift apprehension of a suspect aids crime prevention. The initial contact with the law is one of the most important aspects of the juvenile justice system.

The Juvenile Justice System

Police, Courts, Corrections, and the Juvenile Offender

Do You Know . . .

- What four phases of development the juvenile justice system has gone through?

- What is meant by the principle of *parens patriae*?

- What was established by the *Kent* decision? The *Gault* decision? The *Winship* decision? The *McKiever* decision?

- What balance is sought in the juvenile justice system?

- What role the police play in the juvenile justice system?

- How juvenile court differs from adult court?

- What types of correctional facilities have been provided for juvenile delinquents?

> *There is evidence, in fact, that there may be grounds for concern that the child receives the worst of both worlds: that he gets neither the protections accorded to adults nor the solicitious care and regenerative treatment postulated for children.*
> —*Supreme Court Justice Abe Fortas*

Introduction

Gerald Gault was fifteen years old and on probation when he was taken into custody for allegedly making obscene phone calls to a neighbor. At 10:00 A.M., when Gerald was picked up at home, his mother and father were working. No notice was left at the home that Gerald was being taken into custody, nor were any steps taken to notify his parents. Mrs. Gault arrived home about 6:00 P.M. to find Gerald missing. An older brother accidentally discovered that Gerald had been taken into custody.

Mrs. Gault went to the detention home, and the probation officer told her why Gerald was there and that a hearing would be held the next day, June 9. On June 9 the officer filed a petition with the juvenile court making only general allegations of "delinquency." No particular facts of Gerald's behavior were stated.

The hearing was held in the judge's chambers. The complaining witness was not present, no one was sworn in, no attorney was present, and no transcript of the proceedings was made. At the hearing Gerald admitted to making a less obnoxious part of the phone call in question. At the conclusion of the hearing, the judge said he would take the matter under advisement.

Gerald was returned to the detention home for another two days and then released. After the release Mrs. Gault was informed by note from the probation officer that on June 15 further hearings would be held on Gerald's delinquency. The June 15 hearing was also without benefit of complaining witnesses, sworn testimony, transcript, or counsel. The probation officer made a referral report which listed the charge as lewd phone calls and filed it with the court, but it was not made available to Gerald or his parents. At the conclusion of the hearing the judge committed Gerald as a juvenile delinquent to the State Industrial School until age twenty-one. Gerald, only fifteen years old at the time, received a six-year sentence for an action for which an adult would receive a fine or a two-month imprisonment.

 ## Historical Overview

Our juvenile justice system has had its own unique development from the time of the colonists to the 1980s. According to McCreedy (1975), our juvenile justice system has its roots as far back as the feudal period in England when the crown assumed the protection of the property of minors. When the feudal period ended, supervision of the duties previously assumed by the overlord were transferred to the king's court of chancery. This chancery court operated on a principle known as *parens patriae*. Under this doctrine, the king, through his chancellor, was responsible for the general protection of all people in the realm who could not protect their own interests. This included the children of the realm. Consequently, the king, by means of the chancery court and chancellor, assumed supreme guardianship over the persons and property of minors. McCreedy (1975, p. 1) notes that: "In effect, the chancellor acted as a substitute father for those children who were abandoned, neglected, or destitute."

The doctrine of equity was used when dealing with children; that is, decisions were made based on the spirit of the law and on an attempt at fundamental fairness rather than on strict interpretation of the law. This gave much more flexibility in deciding a case.

Another principle in English common law that influenced our juvenile justice system was the belief that children younger than seven years old were considered incapable of criminal intent. Between the ages of seven and fourteen they were presumed to still be incapable of criminal intent unless it could be shown differently. After age fourteen, children, like adults, were held responsible for their acts and treated according to a strict interpretation of the law. In effect, age had a direct bearing on how someone who broke the law was treated.

> *The four major phases of the juvenile justice system have been (1) a Puritan emphasis, (2) an emphasis on providing a refuge for youth, (3) development of the separate juvenile court, and (4) emphasis on juvenile rights.*

The Puritan Emphasis

The concepts of *parens patriae* and the notion that there was an age below which there can be no criminal intent were brought by the colonists to America. However, from the time the colonists first arrived in the United States until the nineteenth century, emphasis was on Puritan values which held that the child was basically evil. Parents were considered responsible for controlling their children who were, in effect, their property. The law dealt very severely with children who broke the law. McCreedy (1975) points out as an example that in 1828 in New Jersey, a boy of thirteen was hanged for an offense committed when he was twelve. This Puritan emphasis lasted until the 1820s.

Providing a Refuge

By the 1820s several states had passed laws to protect children from the punishments associated with criminal laws. According to McCreedy (1975, p. 2): "The first changes came in the area of institutional custody. Central to the reform effort in this area was a recognition of the brutality of confining children in the same institutions with adults convicted of crime. This awareness resulted in attempts to separate children from adult criminal offenders.''

The first American institution that isolated children convicted of crimes from adult criminals was New York City's House of Refuge, established in 1825. This was, in effect, the first juvenile reformatory in the United States.

In 1869 Massachusetts became the first state to pass a law requiring an agent from the State Board of Charity to investigate all cases involving children coming to court, to attend their trials, and to make recommendations to the judge. In 1870 Massachusetts passed legislation that established separate trials for children in Suffolk County, and by 1872 this means of handling juvenile cases extended throughout the state.

Another major development in the mid-1800s was probation, instituted in 1841 by John Augustus, the first probation officer, who was authorized by judges in Boston, Massachusetts, to take into his custody adults and children convicted of crimes.

In 1884 New York passed legislation allowing a trial judge to place a child under the age of sixteen convicted of a crime under the supervision of any suitable person or institution willing to accept him or her.

Table 17–1.	*Antecedents of the Juvenile Court.*
1825	New York House of Refuge was opened, followed by houses in Boston (1826), Philadelphia (1828), and New Orleans (1845).
1831	Illinois passed a law that allowed penalties for certain offenses committed by minors to differ from the penalties imposed on adults.
1841	John Augustus inaugurated probation and became the nation's first probation officer.
1854	State industrial school for girls opened in Lancaster, Massachusetts (first cottage-type institution).
1858	State industrial school for boys in Lancaster, Ohio, adopted a cottage-type system.
1863	Children's Aid Society founded in Boston. Members of the organization attended police and superior court hearings, supervised youngsters selected for probation, and did the investigation on which probation selection was based.
1869	Law enacted in Massachusetts to direct State Board of Charities to send agents to court hearings that involved children. The agents made recommendations to the court that frequently involved probation and the placement of youngsters with suitable families.
1870	Separate hearings for juveniles were required in Suffolk County, Massachusetts. New York followed by requiring separate trials, dockets, and records for children; Rhode Island made similar provisions in 1891.
1899	In April, Illinois adopted legislation creating the first juvenile court in Cook County (Chicago). In May, Colorado established a juvenile court.

Source: Reprinted by permission from *Crime and Justice in America: A Human Perspective,* by Harold J. Vetter and Leonard Territo. Copyright© 1984 by West Publishing Company. All rights reserved.

During this period of development of the juvenile justice system, the state took over the parents' roll of responsibility for their children, but not to the degree that it would do so in the next phase of the system's development.

The Juvenile Court

According to Vetter and Territo (1984, p. 497): "The establishment (by statute) of the first juvenile court in [Chicago] Illinois in 1899 marked the beginning of an era of 'social jurisprudence.' Although the juvenile court was a bona fide court, its procedures were dramatically different from adult court proceedings. Prior to the establishment of juvenile court, children, like adults, were required to furnish bail or be placed in jail; they were indicted by grand juries; they were tried according to adult criminal procedure; and they were sentenced to prison or required to pay fines." In contrast, according to Vetter and Territo (1984, p. 497): "The court's major objective was to help the wayward child become a productive member of the community. The determination of guilt or innocence, using standard rules of evidence, was not of primary importance. Instead, ... court procedures were to be more diagnostic than legal in nature, giving major consideration to the information obtained on the youngster's environment, heredity, as well as his physical and mental condition."

During this period of the development of the juvenile justice system, the philosophy of *parens patriae* was in full effect. The Chicago legislation grew out of the efforts of civic-minded citizens who saw the inhumane treatment of children who were confined in police stations and jails. The legislation, entitled "An Act to Regulate the Treatment and Control of Dependent, Neglected and Delinquent Children," included many of the characteristics of our modern-day juvenile courts, such as a separate court for juveniles, separate and confidential records, informal proceedings, and the possibility of probation.

The Chicago legislation also required that children be given the same care, custody, and discipline that parents should give them. The major goal was to save the child. This was also the first basic principle of the juvenile court—that of *parens patriae*. The state not only acts as a substitute parent to abandoned, neglected, and dependent children; but it also acts as a "superparent" for delinquent children. As noted by McCreedy (1975, p. 7): "In this role, the state can take legal control of a child away from the child's natural parents or guardians. For example, the state acts as a superparent whenever it commits a child to an industrial school or other correctional facility. The juvenile system symbolizes the state's parenthood."

The parens patriae *doctrine made the state legally responsible for the children within that state, providing a legal foundation for state intervention in the family.*

McCreedy goes on to note (p. 7):

The state, as the child's substitute parent, was not supposed to punish the child for his misconduct, but to help him. To reach this noble goal, many of the procedures used in adult criminal proceedings were abandoned or re-

placed with procedures commonly used in non-criminal (civil) court proceedings. A whole new legal vocabulary and new methods of operation were
developed to reflect the new philosophy and procedures used in the juvenile
justice system.

Instead of a complaint being filed against the child, a *petition* was filed.
No longer was the child to be arrested in the strict sense of the term. Instead,
the child was given a *summons*. A *preliminary inquiry* or *initial hearing*
replaced an arraignment on the charge. The child was not required to plead
either guilty or not guilty to the alleged misconduct. Instead of being found

Table 17–2.	*The Language of Juvenile and Adult Courts.*
Juvenile court term	**Adult court term**
Adjudication: decision by the judge that a child has committed delinquent acts.	Conviction of guilt
Adjudicatory hearing: a hearing to determine whether the allegations of a petition are supported by the evidence beyond a reasonable doubt.	Trial
Adjustment: the settling of a matter so that parties agree without official intervention by the court.	Plea bargaining
Aftercare: the supervision given to a child for a limited period of time after he or she is released from training school but while he or she is still under the control of the juvenile court.	Parole
Commitment: a decision by the judge to send a child to training school.	Sentence to imprisonment
Delinquent act: an act that if committed by an adult would be called a crime. The term does not include such ambiguities and noncrimes as "being ungovernable," "truancy," "incorrigibility," and "disobedience."	Crime
Delinquent child: a child who is found to have committed an act that would be considered a crime if committed by an adult.	Criminal
Detention: temporary care of an allegedly delinquent child who requires secure custody in physically restricting facilities pending court disposition or execution of a court order.	Holding in jail
Dispositional hearing: a hearing held subsequent to the adjudicatory hearing to determine what order of disposition should be made for a child adjudicated as delinquent.	Sentencing hearing
Hearing: the presentation of evidence to the juvenile court judge, his or her consideration of it, and his or her decision on dispositon of the case.	Trial

guilty of a crime, the child was found *delinquent*. Moreover, adjudication of delinquency was not to be considered a conviction. None of the liabilities attached to a criminal conviction were to apply to a child found delinquent: for example, disqualification from future civil service appointments, the inability to be licensed by the state or the right to vote.

The second major principle underlying the juvenile justice system, in addition to *parens patriae*, is the individualization of justice. According to McCreedy (1975, p. 8): "This principle stems from the belief that children, like adults differ from one another. Each person has a different family background,

Juvenile court term	Adult court term
Juvenile court: the court that has jurisdiction over children who are alleged to be or found to be delinquent. Juvenile delinquency procedures should not be used for neglected children or for those who need supervision.	Court of record
Petition: an application for a court order or some other judicial action. Hence, a "delinquency petition" is an application for the court to act in a matter involving a juvenile apprehended for a delinquent act.	Accusation or indictment
Probation: the supervision of a delinquent child after the court hearing but without commitment to training school.	Probation (with the same meaning as the juvenile court term)
Residential child care facility: a dwelling (other than a detention or shelter care facility) that is licensed to provide living accommodations, care, treatment, and maintenance for children and youth. Such facilities include foster homes, group homes, and halfway houses.	Halfway house
Shelter: temporary care of a child in physically unrestricting facilities pending court dispostion or execution of a court order for placement. Shelter care is used for dependent and neglected children and minors in need of supervision. Separate shelter care facilities are also used for children apprehended for delinquency who need temporary shelter but not secure detention.	Jail
Take into custody: the act of the police in securing the physical custody of a child engaged in delinquency. The term is used to avoid the stigma of the word "arrest."	Arrest

mentality, physical capability, and personality. . . . As the purpose of the court is to save the child and not to punish him, it is necessary for those individuals involved in the juvenile justice system to consider the background of the child in order to treat him.''

Although the establishment of juvenile courts was a tremendous advancement in our juvenile justice system, it did present some major problems as well. Because children were no longer considered ''criminals,'' they lost many of the constitutional protections of due process in criminal proceedings. In many instances, for example, delinquents were not given notice of the charge, were not provided with a lawyer, and were not given the chance to cross-examine witnesses.

Justification for the informal procedures used in the juvenile justice system prior to 1960 was set forth half a century ago in *Commonwealth v. Fisher* (1905):

> To save a child from becoming a criminal or from continuing in a career in crimes . . . the Legislature may surely provide for the salvation of such a child . . . by bringing it into one of the courts of the state without any process at all, for the purpose of subjecting it to the state's guardianship and protection. The natural parent needs no process to temporarily deprive his child of its liberty by confining it in his own home, to save it from the consequences of persistence in a career of waywardness: nor is the state, when compelled as parens patriae, to take the place of the father for the same purpose, required to adopt any process as a means of placing its hands upon the child to lead it to one of its courts.

By the 1960s, however, the United States Supreme Court began to seriously question the use of *parens patriae* as the sole reason for denying the child many constitutional rights extended to adults charged with a crime, leading into the fourth phase in the development of the juvenile justice system—juvenile rights.

Juvenile Rights

In 1956 a landmark federal case was the first of a series of cases that resulted in drastic changes in the juvenile justice system. In *Shioutakon v. District of Columbia* (1956) the courts established the role of legal counsel in juvenile court. In essence, if a juvenile was to have his or her liberty taken away, that juvenile had the right to be represented by a lawyer in court. If the parents could not afford a lawyer, the court was to appoint counsel.

A second case establishing juvenile rights was *Kent v. United States* (1966). This case involved Morris Kent, a juvenile with a police record, who was arrested at age sixteen in Washington and charged with housebreaking, robbery, and rape. Kent confessed to the charges and was held at a juvenile detention facility for nearly a week. The judge then decided to transfer jurisdiction of his case to an adult criminal court. Kent received no hearing of any kind; the transfer was completely at the judge's discretion and was based on several reports written by probation staff.

In reviewing the *Kent* case, the Supreme Court decreed that: "As a condition to a valid waiver order, petitioner (Kent) was entitled to a hearing, including access by his counsel to the social records and probation or similar reports which are presumably considered by the court, and to a statement of the reasons for Juvenile Court's decision."

> *Kent v. United States established that if a juvenile court transfers a case to adult criminal court, juveniles are entitled to a hearing, their counsel must be given access to probation records used by the court in reaching its decision, and the court must state its reasons for waiving jurisdiction over the case.*

According to Arnold and Brungardt (1983, p. 24): "The impact of the Kent case went far beyond the relatively narrow legal issue—conditions of waiver to criminal court—that it addressed. It served as a warning to the juvenile justice system that the juvenile court's traditional laxity toward procedural and evidentiary standards would no longer be tolerated by the highest court in the land."

An appendix to the *Kent* decision contained the following criteria established by the United States Supreme Court for states to use in deciding on transfer of juveniles to adult criminal courts for trial:

1. The seriousness of the alleged offense and whether the protection of the community requires waiver;
2. Whether the alleged offense was committted in an aggressive, violent, premeditated, or willful manner;
3. Whether the alleged offense was against persons or against property, greater weight being given to offenses against persons, especially if personal injury resulted;
4. The prospective merit of the complaint;
5. The desirability of trial and disposition of the offense in one court when the juvenile's associates in the alleged offense are adults who will be charged with crimes in the adult court;
6. The sophistication and maturity of the juvenile as determined by consideration of his home, environmental situation, emotional attitude, and pattern of living; and
7. The record and previous history of the juvenile.

The following year, another landmark Supreme Court ruling in the *Gault* case resulted in additional major changes in our juvenile justice system. The background of this case served as the introduction to this chapter. Recall that fifteen-year-old Gerald Gault received a six-year sentence for making lewd phone calls, an action for which an adult found guilty would receive a fine or a two-month sentence. The United States Supreme Court overruled Gerald's conviction on the grounds that:

- Neither Gerald nor his parents had notice of the specific charges against him.
- No counsel was offered or provided to Gerald.

- No witnesses were present, thus denying Gerald the right of cross-examination and confrontation.

- No warning of Gerald's privilege against self-incrimination was given to him, thus no waiver of that right took place.

The Gault decision requires that the due process clause of the Fourteenth Amendment apply to proceedings in state juvenile courts, including the right of notice, the right to counsel, the right against self-incrimination, and the right to confront witnesses.

Justice Fortas delivered the opinion of the Court:

Where a person, infant or adult, can be seized by the State, charged and convicted for violating a state criminal law, and then ordered by the State to be confined for six years, I think the Constitution requires that he be tried in accordance with the guarantees of all provisions of the Bill of Rights made applicable to the States by the Fourteenth Amendment. Undoubtedly this would be true of an adult defendant, and it would be a plain denial of equal protection of the laws—an invidious discrimination—to hold that others subject to heavier punishments could, because they are children, be denied these same constitutional safeguards. I consequently agree with the Court that the Arizona law as applied here denied to the parents and their son the right of notice, right to counsel, right against self-incrimination, and right to confront the witnesses against young Gault. Appellants are entitled to these rights, not because ''fairness, impartiality and orderliness—in short, the essentials of due process''—require them and not because they are ''the procedural rules which have been fashioned from the generality of due process,'' but because they are specifically and unequivocally granted by provisions of the Fifth and Sixth Amendments which the Fourteenth Amendment makes applicable to the States.

It is clear that juveniles are to be afforded all of the same rights and privileges as adults in the criminal process. The logical implications of the *Gault* decision require safeguards in the prehearing stage as well as use of the Miranda warning for juveniles, whether at the station house, in the squad car, or on a street corner.

The Supreme Court refused to rule on two questions raised on Gault's behalf: the right to an appeal and the right to a record of court proceedings. *In Re Gault* is a milestone in the history of the juvenile court.

In 1970 another Supreme Court decision expanded juvenile rights. In *In Re Winship* (1970) the United States Supreme Court examined the standard of proof in a 1967 New York case against a twelve-year-old boy who allegedly had stolen $112 from a woman's purse. The New York judge acknowledged that he had operated on the civil court principle of ''preponderance of evidence,'' a standard of proof much weaker than the ''proof beyond a reasonable doubt'' required in a criminal court. In the review of the *Winship* case, the Supreme Court ruled that if adjudication might result in deprivation of liberty for the juvenile, the juvenile court must use the same standards of proof as are required in adult criminal trials.

Table 17–3.	**Juvenile Justice Developments: 1646 to Present.**				
System (Period)	**Major developments**	**Influences**	**Child-State relationship**	**Parent-State relationship**	**Parent-Child relationship**
Puritan (1646-1824)	Massachusetts Stubborn Child Law (1646).	Christian view of child as evil; economically marginal agrarian society.	Law provides symbolic standard of maturity; support for family as economic unit.	Parents considered responsible for and capable of controlling child.	Child considered both property and spiritual responsibility of parents.
Refuge (1824-1899)	Institutionalization of deviants, New York House of Refuge established (1824) for delinquent and dependent children.	Enlightenment; immigration and industrialization.	Child seen as helpless, in need of state intervention.	Parents supplanted as state assumes responsibility for correcting deviant socialization.	Family considered to be a major cause of juvenile deviancy.
Juvenile court (1899-1960)	Establishment of separate legal system for juvenile —Illinois Juvenile Court Act (1899).	Reformism and rehabilitative ideology; increased immigration, urbanaization, large-scale industrialization.	Juvenile court institutionalizes legal irresponsibility of child.	Parens Patriae doctrine gives legal foundation for state intervention of family.	Further abrogation of parents' rights and responsibilities.
Juvenile rights (1960-present)	Increased "legalization" of juvenile law— Gault decison (1966). Juvenile Justice and Delinquency Prevention Act (1974) calls for deinstitutionalization of status offender.	Criticism of juvenile justice system on humane grounds, civil rights movements by disadvantaged groups.	Movement to define and protect rights as well as provide services to children.	Reassertion of responsibility of parents and community for welfare and behavior of children.	Attention given to children's claims against parents. Earlier emancipation of children.

Adapted from U.S. Department of Justice, Reports of the National Juvenile Assessment Centers, A Preliminary National Assessment of the Status Offender and the Juvenile Justice System (Washington, D.C.: U.S. Government Printing Officer, 1980) p. 29, by permission of the U.S. Department of Justice.

The *Winship decision established a juvenile defendant must be found guilty beyond a reasonable doubt.*

One right of adults charged with crimes that is not afforded to juveniles charged with crimes is the right to a trial by jury.

McKiever v. Pennsylvania established that a jury trial is not a constitutional right of juveniles.

McKiever v. Pennsylvania (1971) involved a Pennsylvania youth charged with robbery, larceny, and receiving stolen goods. According to Arnold and Brungardt (1983, p. 24), in this case: "The Supreme Court slowed its march toward reshaping the juvenile court to impose stronger due-process standards and formal procedures. In McKiever, the Court, fearing that jury trials would bring delay and increased formality to the juvenile court, supported noncriminal juvenile hearings and ruled that a jury trial is not a constitutional right of juveniles . . . . The court felt strongly that if the formalities of the criminal adjucative process are to be superimposed upon the juvenile court system, there is little need for its separate existence."

Arnold and Brungardt (p. 24) go on to note:

These Supreme Court decisions, taken as a whole, clearly indicate the Court's support of stronger due-process and evidentiary standards for juvenile court proceedings. However, by declining to rule on the questions of the right to a jury trial and the right to records of the proceedings in Gault, and in issuing the McKiever decision, the Court has pointed to a fundamental dilemma it faces in its juvenile court decisions. On the one hand, the Supreme Court is alarmed by the denial of constitutional rights in juvenile courts; on the other hand, it wants to maintain something of the informality and protectiveness long characteristic of the juvenile court. It appears the movement to bring justice to the juvenile court system has been successful, although the degree to which the orientation of actual court practice has changed is highly visible.

The juvenile justice system seeks to balance the informal and protective emphasis of the parens patriae doctrine with the constitutional rights of juveniles charged with crimes.

See Table 17–3 for the evolution of our juvenile justice system.

The Juvenile Justice System in the 1980s

Just as within the adult criminal justice system, the juvenile justice system has three separate but integrally related components: the police, the court, and corrections—referred to as "Youth Authority." The normal progression of a youth within the juvenile justice system is diagrammed in Figure 17–1.

The Police and the Juvenile Justice System

The police usually are the youth's initial contact with the juvenile justice system. They have broad discretion and may release juveniles to their parents, refer them to other agencies, place them in detention, or refer them to a juvenile court. The

Figure 17–1.   ***From Arrest to Disposition.***

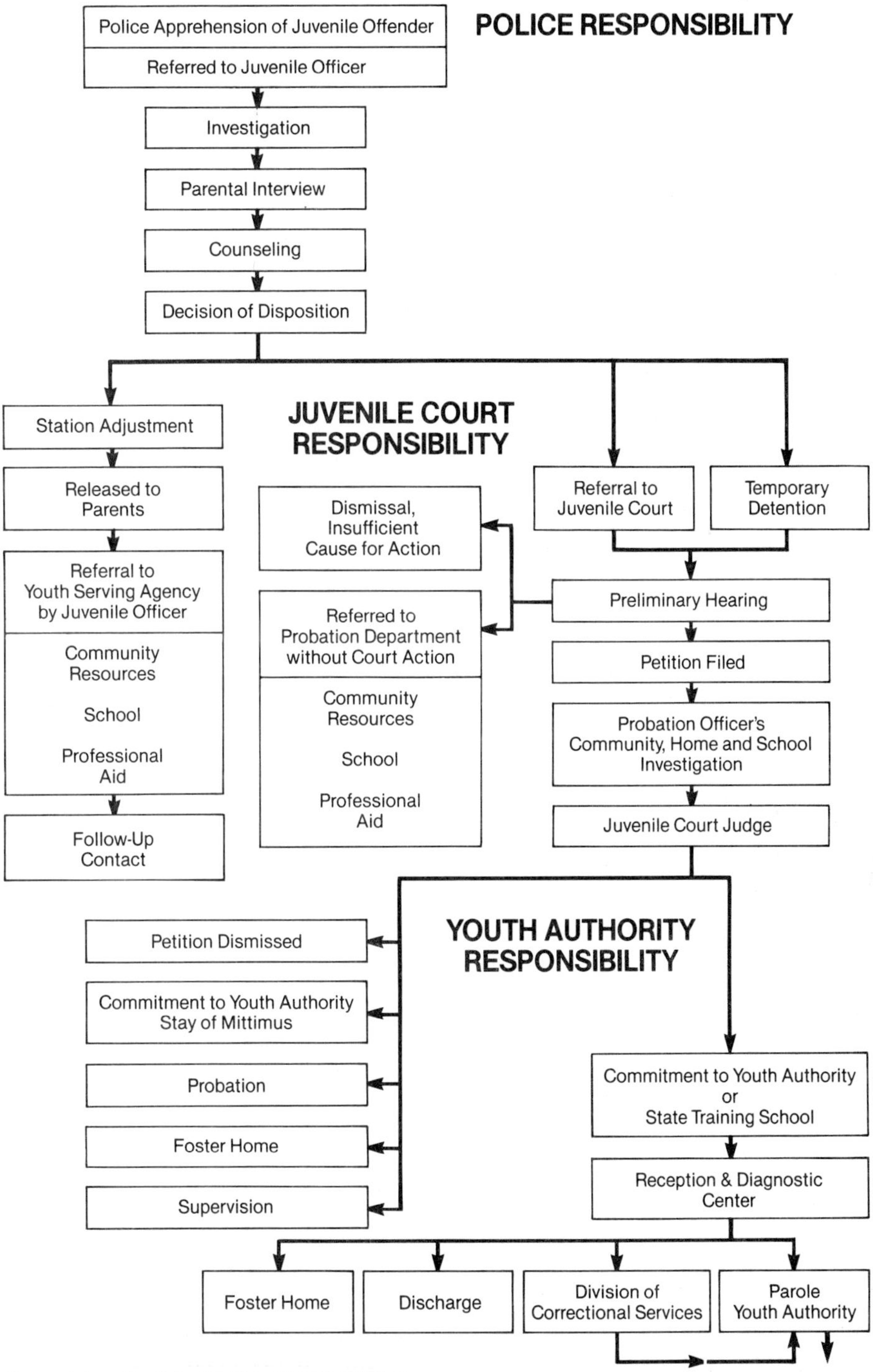

POLICE RESPONSIBILITY

- Police Apprehension of Juvenile Offender
- Referred to Juvenile Officer
- Investigation
- Parental Interview
- Counseling
- Decision of Disposition

JUVENILE COURT RESPONSIBILITY

Station Adjustment

Released to Parents

Referral to Youth Serving Agency by Juvenile Officer

Community Resources

School

Professional Aid

Follow-Up Contact

Dismissal, Insufficient Cause for Action

Referred to Probation Department without Court Action

Community Resources

School

Professional Aid

Referral to Juvenile Court

Temporary Detention

Preliminary Hearing

Petition Filed

Probation Officer's Community, Home and School Investigation

Juvenile Court Judge

YOUTH AUTHORITY RESPONSIBILITY

Petition Dismissed

Commitment to Youth Authority Stay of Mittimus

Probation

Foster Home

Supervision

Commitment to Youth Authority or State Training School

Reception & Diagnostic Center

Foster Home

Discharge

Division of Correctional Services

Parole Youth Authority

Source: International Association of Chiefs of Police.

police may also temporarily detain juveniles, either for their own protection or to assure that they do appear in court.

Trojanowicz (1978, pp. 175–176) feels that:

The intake and screening process is an important aspect of the juvenile justice system. When used properly, it can effectively curtail or interrupt much delinquent behavior before it becomes serious. The intake process can also stimulate community agencies to help parents to better understand their children's behavior and the measures needed to prevent further delinquent acts.

If the child is released at intake and no further processing take place, there should still be a follow-up after any referral to a community agency by either the police or the intake unit. Follow-up facilitates not only the rendering of services to the child, but also promotes closer cooperation between the agencies involved.

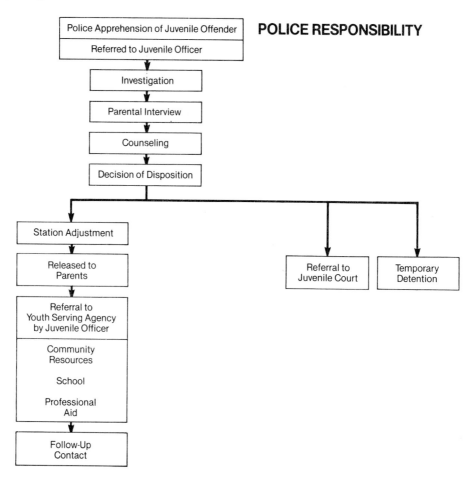

As noted by Eldefonso (1974, p. 3): ''Generally juveniles are referred to local authorities after arrest. . . . In juvenile matters, probation departments provide most of the services for the court from initial screening and filing of a petition in behalf of the juvenile through termination of wardship (i.e., supervision and control).''

> *The police usually are the youth's initial contact with the juvenile justice system. They have broad discretion and may release juveniles to their parents, refer them to other agencies, place them in detention, or refer them to a juvenile court.*

The probation department may or may not be part of a juvenile division. Carey, et al. (1967, p. 26) have diagrammed the decision points in police handling of juveniles (see Figure 17–2):

Figure 17–2. **Decision Points in Probation Handling of Juveniles.**

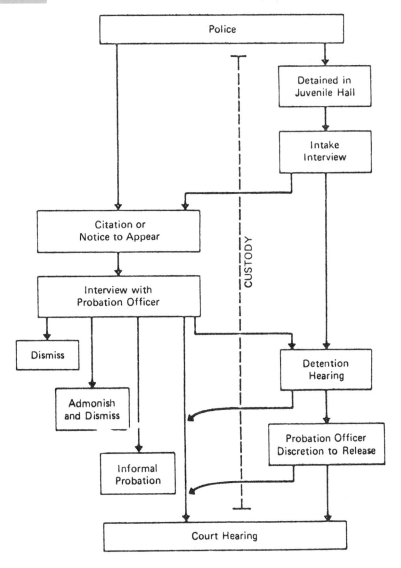

The Courts and the Juvenile Justice System

Laws relating to juvenile courts attempt to secure care and guidance for each minor under the jurisdiction of the court, preferably in the minor's own home. The laws seek to protect the spiritual, emotional, mental, and physical welfare of the minor as well as the best interests of the state. Laws related to juveniles attempt to preserve and strengthen family ties whenever possible, removing minors from parental custody only when the minor's welfare or safety or protection of the public cannot be adequately safeguarded without such removal. When minors are removed from their own families, the courts seek to provide them with custody, care, and discipline as nearly equivalent as possible to that usually given by competent parents.

Juvenile court also has jurisdiction over neglected and dependent children who may suffer from abuse, malnutrition, unsanitary conditions in the home, or who may have been abandoned by their parents. The court also has jurisdiction over those persons who encourage, cause, or contribute to a child's delinquency. Because of the court's scope and clientele, laws relating to juveniles are frequently liberally construed.

Juveniles are subjected to a conglomerate of laws and restraints which do not apply to adults. For example, juveniles are frequently arrested for liquor law violations, curfew violations, absenting from home, truancy, smoking, suspicion, and incorrigibility (these are called status offenses). The courts in which such offenses are judged differ greatly from adult courts.

Juvenile courts are more concerned with rehabilitation of the juvenile than with punishment. These courts are informal, private, and often do not follow formal judiciary procedures. Although adult courts are based on the adversary system, juvenile courts, in contrast, are nonadversary systems, even though they do have the authority of confinement.

> *Juvenile courts are informal, private, nonadversary systems which stress rehabilitation rather than punishment of youth.*

The court may counsel children, their parents, or guardians, or place them in their own homes under the supervision of a probation officer or other suitable person under conditions prescribed by the court. These conditions might include rules for their conduct or that of their parents or guardian designed for the physical, mental, and moral well-being of the children.

When it is in the child's best interests, the court can transfer legal custody of the child. It may order the child placed in a foster home or a child-placing agency, committed to a youth conservation commission, transferred to a county welfare agency, or placed in a special facility if the child requires special treatment and care for physical or mental health. As noted by Trojanowicz (1978), diversion, a popular method of solving juvenile problems in recent times, shows great promise of success.

Juvenile courts vary from state to state, but most begin with some sort of intake, which usually begins as a petition against the child. Frequently the petition

JUVENILE COURT RESPONSIBILITY

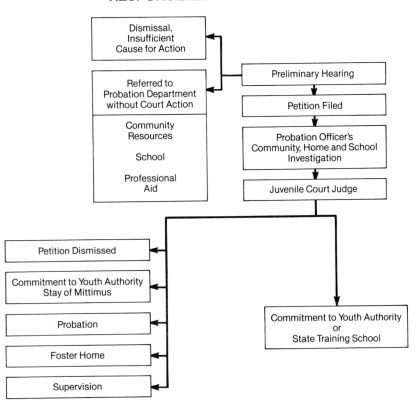

originates with a law enforcement agency, but it can come from another source such as a school, which can refer truancy or vandalism cases, or parents who may feel they cannot control their children. The intake or initial screening is usually controlled and supervised by the juvenile court. As noted by the historic President's Commission on Law Enforcement (1967, p. 14):

> Intake is essentially a screening process to determine whether the court should take action and, if so, what action or whether the matter should be referred elsewhere. Intake is set apart from the screening process used in adult criminal courts by the pervasive attempt to individualize each case and the nature of the personnel administering the discretionary process. In adult proceedings at the post-arrest stage, decisions to screen out are entrusted to the grand jury, the judge, or usually to the prosecutor. The objective is screening as an end in itself: attempts to deliver service to those screened out are rare. . . . At intake in the juvenile courts, screening is an important objective, but referral is an additional goal. Thus, the expressed function of intake is likely to be more ambitious than that of its criminal law counterpart and the function is performed chiefly by persons who are neither legally trained or significantly restricted in the exercise requirements comparable to those of the criminal law.

In addition, the National Advisory Commission on Criminal Justice Standards and Goals (1973, p. 296) recommends that intake units should:

1. Make the initial decision whether to place a juvenile referred to the court in detention or shelter care;
2. Make the decision whether to offer a juvenile referred to the court the opportunity to participate in diversion programs; and
3. Make, in consultation with the prosecutor, the decision whether to make a formal petition in the court alleging that the juvenile is delinquent and ask that the family court assume jurisdiction over him.

At the adjudication hearing, considered to be part of the preliminary hearing, the youth is questioned about the alleged offense. The National Advisory Commission on Criminal Justice Standards and Goals (1973, pp. 302, 474) recommends the following procedures for adjudicatory hearings:

At the adjudicatory hearing, the juvenile alleged to be delinquent should be afforded all of the rights given a defendant in adult criminal prosecution, except that trial by jury should not be available in delinquency cases.

In all delinquency cases a legal officer representing the State should be present in court to present evidence supporting the allegation of delinquency.

The defense counsel should use all methods permissible in a criminal prosecution to prevent determination that the juvenile is delinquent. He should function as the advocate for the juvenile, and his performance should be unaffected by any belief he might have that a finding of delinquency might be in the best interests of the juvenile. As advocate for the juvenile alleged to be delinquent, counsel's actions should not be affected by the wishes of the juvenile's parents or guardian if those differ from the wishes of the juvenile.

At the adjudication hearing, the petition may be dismissed, or, if there is enough evidence that the child is delinquent, a court date is set for the *disposition hearing*.

Ideally, enough time should be allowed between the adjudication and disposition hearings for the probation officer to make a thorough investigation of the case, including an evaluation of the child's home and school environment, the child's attitude and behavior at home, in his neighborhood, his school, and his community, and the amount of supervision provided at home. Often, however, the disposition hearing is the second half of the adjudication hearing.

At the disposition hearing the judge has several alternatives. Based on the findings of the investigation, he may put the youth on probation, place the youth in a foster home, release the child to his parents, commit the child to an institution, or make the child a ward of the court so he can receive the required supervision. The National Advisory Commission on Criminal Justice Standards and Goals recommends that the procedures followed at the disposition hearing be identical to those followed in sentencing adult offenders.

More serious juvenile offenders have been committed to mental institutions, reformatories, prisons, and county and state schools for delinquents. Some cities, such as New York and Chicago, have set up youth courts which are adult courts using the philosophy of juvenile courts. These youth courts usually confine their hearings to misdemeanors. When a juvenile has committed a series of serious crimes, juvenile courts have the legal power to adjudicate anyone under their jurisdiction as an adult. The juvenile is then charged and required to appear in an adult court.

According to the Bureau of Justice Statistics (1984, p. 61): "All states allow juveniles to be tried as adults in criminal courts." This may occur in one of three ways:

Judicial waiver—the juvenile court waives its jurisdiction and transfers the case to criminal court (the procedure is also known as "binding over," "transferring," or "certifying" juvenile cases to criminal courts).

Concurrent jurisdiction—the prosecutor has the discretion of filing charges for certain offenses in either juvenile or criminal courts.

Excluded offenses—the legislature excludes from juvenile court jurisdiction certain offenses, usually either very minor, such as traffic or fishing violations, or very serious, such as murder or rape.

Corrections and the Juvenile Justice System

The philosophy of juvenile court is that ideally children should be kept in their homes pending a hearing. If detention is required for their own welfare or the public safety, it must not be in jails or police stations but in temporary quarters such as boarding homes, protective agency homes, or specially constructed detention homes. The realization of these ideals of the juvenile court system, even in some of the largest United States cities, is far from complete. In many small towns and rural districts no such facilities exist. Although juvenile court acts as the protector of the child, children are still subjected to adverse publicity, criminal procedure, jail detention, and ineffective treatment because of the lack of proper facilities.

According to Pursley (1980, p. 417): "A number of federal courts are now ruling that the confinement of a juvenile in a county jail for adults is in violation of the provision against 'cruel and unusual punishment' of the Eighth Amendment."

**YOUTH AUTHORITY
RESPONSIBILITY**

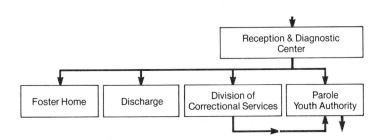

The disposition of juveniles and the problem of the juvenile can be partially gauged by the number of facilities existing in the United States to care for wayward youth.

Reception and diagnostic centers screen juvenile court commitments and assign them to appropriate treatment facilities.

Detention centers provide temporary care in a physically restrictive environment for juveniles in custody pending court disposition and often for juveniles who have been adjudicated delinquent or are awaiting return to another jurisdiction.

Training schools provide strict confinement and instruction in vocational skills. They serve delinquent juveniles committed to them by juvenile courts or placed in them by an agency with such authority.

Shelters provide temporary care similar to that of detention centers but in a physically unrestrictive environment.

Ranches, forestry camps, and farms are residential treatment facilities for juveniles who do not require strict confinement such as in training schools. These ranches, camps, and farms allow juveniles greater contact with members of the community.

Group homes are residences which allow juveniles extensive contact with the community through jobs and schools. Seldom are juveniles placed in group homes on probation or parole.

Halfway houses provide nonrestrictive residential group living where fifty percent or more of the juveniles are on probation or parole. The juveniles are allowed extensive community contact through jobs and schools.

> *Facilities other than punitive correctional institutions for juveniles include reception and diagnostic centers; detention centers; training schools; shelters; ranches, forestry camps, and farms; group homes; and halfway houses.*

In addition to providing facilities for juveniles who have already become delinquent, many communities are attempting to meet the problem of juvenile delinquency by programs which stress prevention rather than rehabilitation, for example, police-school liaison programs as discussed earlier.

Summary

The juvenile justice system has developed through four phases in the United States: (1) a Puritan emphasis with severe penalties for juvenile crime (1776-1823), (2) an emphasis on providing a refuge for youth (1824-1899), (3) development of a separate juvenile court (1899-1960), and (4) emphasis on juvenile rights (1960 to present). Important in the evolution of the juvenile justice system has been the *parens patriae* doctrine which makes the state legally responsible for the children within that state, providing a legal foundation for state intervention in family control.

The most recent phase, that emphasizing juvenile rights, has included several landmark Supreme Court decisions. *Kent v. United States* established that as a valid waiver order to adult criminal court, juveniles are entitled to a hearing, their counsel must be given access to probation records used by the court in reaching its decision, and the court must state its reasons for waiving jurisdiction over the case.

The *Gault* decision required that the due process clause of the Fourteenth Amendment be applied to proceedings in state juvenile courts, including the right of notice, the right to counsel, the right against self-incrimination, and the right to confront witnesses.

The *Winship* decision established that a juvenile defendant must be found guilty beyond a reasonable doubt. And *McKiever v. Pennsylvania* established that a jury trial is not a constitutional right of juveniles.

In the 1980s the juvenile system is continually seeking to balance the informality and protective emphasis of the *parens patriae* doctrine with the constitutional rights of juveniles charged with crimes.

The police usually are the youth's initial contact with the juvenile justice system. They have broad discretion and may release juveniles to their parents, refer them to other agencies, place them in detention, or refer them to juvenile court. Juvenile courts are informal, private, nonadversary systems which stress rehabilitation rather than punishment of youth. Facilities other than punitive correctional institutions for juveniles include reception and diagnostic centers; detention centers; training schools; shelters; ranches, forestry camps, and farms; group homes; and halfway houses. In addition to providing facilities for juveniles who have already become delinquent, many communities are attempting to meet the problem of juvenile delinquency by programs which stress prevention, for example, police-school liaison programs.

Application

Obtain the yearly juvenile report from your local police department and evaluate that report from the standpoint of how many juvenile contacts there were, how many arrests, and how many referrals to juvenile court or other agencies in relation to how many warnings and releases for violations. Determine the percentages in each category.

Discussion Questions

1. Do juvenile courts too often stress rehabilitation and keeping youngsters in the home?
2. Are parents required to testify against their children in court?
3. What correctional facilities are available for juvenile delinquents in our area? Our state?
4. Do you feel the process of justice should be the same for juveniles as it is for adults?
5. Do you feel juveniles should have the right to a jury trial?
6. In what noncriminal matters does the juvenile court become involved?

References

Arnold, W.R., and Brungardt, T. *Juvenile misconduct and delinquency.* Boston: Houghton Mifflin Company, 1983.

Bartollas, C., and Miller, S.J. *The juvenile offender.* Boston: Allyn and Bacon, 1978.

Bureau of Justice Statistics. *Report to the nation on crime and justice.* Washington, D.C.: U.S. Government Printing Office, 1984.

Caldwell, R.G. ''The juvenile court: Its development and some major problems.'' *The journal of criminal law, criminology and police science* 51 (1961): 499.

Carey, J.T.; Goldfarb, J.; Rowe, M.H.; and Lohman, J.D. *The handling of juveniles from offense to disposition.* U.S. Department of Health, Education, and Welfare. Washington, D.C.: U.S. Government Printing Office, 1967.

''Constitutional law—Attorney and client—Right to counsel.'' *Western reserve law review* 19 (June 1968): 1107.

Davis, S.M. *Rights of juveniles: The juvenile justice system.* New York: Clark Boardman Company, Ltd., 1983.

Eldefonso, E., and Hartinger, W. *Control, treatment, and rehabilitation of juvenile offenders.* Beverly Hills, Cal.: Glencoe, Press, 1976.

Finchenauer, J.O. *Juvenile delinquency and corrections: The gap between theory and practice.* Orlando, Fla.: Academic Press, Inc., 1984.

Haskell, M.R., and Yablonsky, L. *Crime and delinquency.* Chicago: Rand McNally and Company, 1970.

Klempner, J., and Parker, R.D. *Juvenile delinquency and juvenile justice.* New York: Franklin Watts, 1981.

Kratcoski, P.C., and Kratcoski, L.C. *Juvenile delinquency.* Englewood Cliffs, N.J.: Prentice-Hall, 1979.

McCreedy, K.R. *Juvenile justice—System and procedures.* Albany, N.Y.: Delmar Publishers, 1975.

National Advisory Commission on Criminal Justice Standards and Goals. *Corrections.* Washington, D.C.: U.S. Government Printing Office, 1973.

President's Commission on Law Enforcement and Administration of Justice. *Task force report: Juvenile delinquency and youth crime.* Washington, D.C.: U.S. Government Printing Office, 1967.

Pursley, R.D. *Introduction to criminal justice.* 3rd ed. New York: Macmillan Publishing Company, 1980.

Sayler, R.H.; Boyer, B.B.; and Gooding, R.E., Jr. *The Warren court.* New York: Chelsea House, 1969.

Sussman, F.D., and Baum, F.S. *Law of juvenile delinquency.* Dobbs Ferry, N.Y.: Oceana Publication, Inc., 1968.

Thornton, W.D.; James, J.A.; and Doerner, W.G. *Delinquency and justice.* Glenview, Ill.: Scott Foresman and Company, 1982.

Trojanowicz, R.C. *Juvenile delinquency, concepts and control.* 2d ed. Englewood CLiffs, N.J.: Prentice-Hall, 1978.

U.S. Department of Justice. Law Enforcement Assistance Administration. *Children in custody. Advance report on the juvenile detention and correctional facility census of 1972–73.* National Criminal Justice Information and Statistics Service, May 1975.

Vetter, H.J., and Territo, L. *Crime and justice in America: A human perspective.* St. Paul, Minn.: West Publishing Company, 1984.

Williams, V.L.; Formby, W.A.; and Watkins, J.C. *Introduction to criminal justice.* Albany, N.Y. Delmar Publishers, Inc., 1982.

A Career in Law Enforcement

A Challenging, Rewarding, Vital Profession

The preceding chapters demonstrate the complex and vital functions performed by law enforcement officers in the United States. The challenges and rewards of this profession should attract well-qualified, dedicated individuals to the field.

This section describes the process involved in becoming a police officer as well as what to expect upon acceptance into the field (Chapter 18). The importance of the police image and factors that affect this image are presented in Chapter 19. The book concludes with a brief look at what might lie ahead for those in law enforcement, including current trend and issues (Chapter 20).

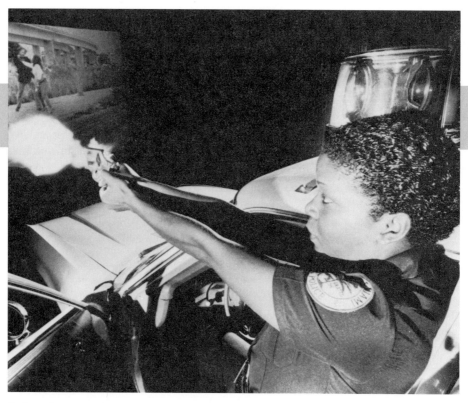
Police officers require a variety of skills. This officer is undergoing stress training in a shooting simulator.

CHAPTER 18

The Police Career

A Challenging Profession

Do You Know . . .

- What qualities are considered essential for an effective police officer?

- What steps are usually involved in the police officer selection process?

- What qualifications are generally required for individuals who wish to become police officers?

- What impact the *Griggs v. Duke Power Company* decision had on the use of tests for employment purposes?

- What most physical fitness tests are like and what they test for?

- What type of information is sought during the oral interview?

- What is of prime importance in the medical examination?

- What occurs during the background investigation?

- What the usual length and purpose of the probationary period in law enforcement are?

- What factors are important in physical fitness and which one factor is of most importance?

- What restrictions are sometimes placed on police officers' off-duty employment?

- What legal considerations in hiring practices are mandated by the Omnibus Civil Rights Law and the Equal Employment Opportunity Act?

■ What benefits are derived from having a police department whose racial makeup reflects that of the community?

■ What preferential hiring is? What reverse discrimination is?

■ How women's performance on patrol has compared to that of men?

> *No one is compelled to choose the profession of a police officer, but having chosen it, everyone is obliged to perform its duties and live up to the high standards of its requirements.*
>
> *—Calvin Coolidge*

Introduction

For years society has sought more effective law enforcement and a criminal justice system to meet its needs. Concurrently, criminologists, psychologists, sociologists, police practitioners, and scientists have worked to solve the crime problem in America. Despite some disillusionment and cynicism, progress has been made, and the future offers encouragement.

The most visible signs of progress in the vast criminal justice system have been in the field of law enforcement, and the most notable advancement within this field has been in the professionalization of the police officer.

This is, in part, because 86-90 percent of most police agencies' budgets are allocated for personnel, and, therefore, they are demanding higher quality performance from them. However, this goal is sometimes difficult to achieve because most police departments are understaffed. The attrition rate throughout the country—approximately 100,000 officers per year—compounds this problem and creates a constant demand for training.

An equally important force behind the professionalization of the police officer is the realization that to a large degree the future of law enforcement, its success or failure, is contingent on the quality and effectiveness of its police officers, their status in the community, and their ability to serve its residents. Members of minority groups and women are now perceived by most departments as necessary and valuable individuals in the department. Although members of minority groups and women have had a long, difficult battle in achieving equal employment rights, not only in the field of law enforcement, but also in most other fields as well, great advancements have been made in the past decade. Today law enforcement offers excellent opportunities for all who are interested in a law enforcement career.

Desired Qualities of
Law Enforcement Officers

If the citizens of a community were asked what traits they felt were desirable in police officers, a compilation of their responses might read something like the following: police officers should be able to work under pressure, to accept direction, to express themselves orally and in writing; they should have self-respect and the ability to command respect from others; they should use good judgment; and they should be considerate, compassionate, dependable, enthusiastic, fair, flexible, honest, humble, industrious, intelligent, logical, motivated, neat, observant, physically fit, prompt, resourceful, self-assured, stable, tactful, warm, and willing to listen and to accept change.

Unfortunately, no one possesses all these traits, but the more of the preceding traits police officers have, the more likely they are to be effective in dealing with not only the citizens of the community, but also lawbreakers as well.

An LEAA funded study conducted at Indiana University ("Indiana University Develops Police Selection Procedure," 1977, p. 1) identified twelve characteristics which separated good police officers from poor ones:

- Reliability
- Leadership
- Judgment
- Persuasiveness
- Communication skills
- Accuracy
- Initiative
- Integrity
- Honesty
- Ego control
- Intelligence
- Sensitivity.

Finding individuals qualified to become police officers is no easy task. The process of recruiting and screening candidates is a continuous and critical function of all police agencies in the country. By examining personnel selection developments over the past years, police administrators can evaluate the effectiveness of their personnel selection procedures. They can assess the recommendations made by the personnel branch and whether they are implemented, and they can assess whether their procedures conform with federal guidelines and regulations.

Qualities of a good police officer include: reliability, leadership, judgment, persuasiveness, communication skills, accuracy, initiative, integrity, honesty, ego control, intelligence, and sensitivity.

Examination Announcements

The most common law enforcement recruitment practice is to place want ads in local newspapers, including minority newspapers to attract more minority candidates. Notices are also sent to colleges and universities inviting students to make application. The actual in-person recruiting on campuses is not as prevalent today as it was in the 1960s when the demand for police officers was at an all-time high.

Police are a good source of recruitment as they frequently have friends who admire them and want to become police officers too. Community bulletin boards have been used effectively by some police agencies. In addition, police professional magazines may be used when many positions are open within a single agency.

Larger cities place spot announcements on television and radio and place notices with state employment agencies. Special posters are often used in advertising on buses, in libraries, and in business establishments. Notices are usually brief, stating something like the following:

· **PROTECT AND SERVE** ·
BE PROUD TO BE A POLICE OFFICER
NOW HIRING

Applications may be made at Mytown Police Department
1001 Main Street, Mytown, USA

When applicants come to the designated place, they are given a fact sheet containing a brief job description, the salary range, fringe benefits, and an application to be filled out and submitted. They are also given a time and place to report for the written examination. Candidates who cannot personally appear may call or write to have the information sent to them.

Most police agencies and civil service commissions accept applications even though no openings are presently listed. The application is placed on file, and when an examination is to be conducted, the applicant is notified by mail or phone.

The Selection Process

Whether a formal merit system or a civil service system is used, good job selection requires sound, equitable procedures. This means that a selection system which measures the predictable success of the officer on the job must be devised if it is not already in existence.

Although procedures differ greatly from agency to agency, several procedures are common to most selection processes, such as a formal application, a preliminary screening, written examination, psychological examination, a physical agility test, an oral interview, medical examination, and a background investigation. Failure at any point in the selection process may disqualify a candidate.

Police officer selection usually includes:

- A formal application.

- A preliminary screening.
    Written examination.
    Psychological examination.

- A physical agility test.

- An oral interview.

- A medical examination.

- A background investigation.

The Formal Application—Basic Requirements to Become a Police Officer

Usually anyone who wishes to become a police officer completes a formal application.

A careful examination of this formal application shows several factors which are evaluated in a candidate: driving record, any criminal record, visual acuity, physical, emotional, and mental condition, and education.

The requirements for becoming a police officer are usually clearly specified by law, as, for example, in the minimum standards for peace officers prescribed in the rules of the Attorney General in Minnesota (Mn. Rules Atty. Gen. 201–218).

Rules and Regulations
AttyGen 207 New Peace Officers
    (a) All appointing agencies, when requested, shall furnish the name, address, date of appointment, and other pertinent information concerning a newly appointed peace officer to the Executive Director.
    (b) No appointing agency shall appoint any new peace officer who does not comply with the minimum selection standard hereinafter enumerated; provided, that these standards shall not be construed to restrict an appointing agency from promulgating more rigid standards in the areas enumerated.
    (1) The applicant must be a citizen of the United States.
    (2) The applicant must possess or be eligible for a valid State of Minnesota driver's license.
    (3) The applicant must successfully pass a written examination demonstrating the possession of all mental skills necessary for the accomplishment of the duties and functions of a peace officer.
    (4) The applicant shall be required to complete and submit to the appointing agency a preliminary application form before testing and a comprehensive application form after testing and just prior to hiring. The prospective employee shall be fingerprinted, and a thorough background search shall be made through the resources of local, state and Federal agencies in order to disclose the existence of any criminal record or the existence of unacceptable standards of conduct which would adversely affect the performance by the individual of his duties as a peace officer.

(5) The applicant shall not have been convicted of a felony in this state or in any other state or in any Federal jurisdiction, or of any offense in any other state or in any Federal jurisdiction, which would have been a felony if committed in this state.

(6) A licensed physician or surgeon shall make a thorough medical examination of the applicant to determine that he or she is free from any physical condition which might adversely affect the performance by the individual of his duties as a peace officer.

(7) An evaluation shall be made by a licensed psychologist to determine that the applicant is free from any emotional or mental condition which might adversely affect the performance by the individual of his or her duties as a peace officer.

(8) The applicant must successfully pass a job-related examination of his or her physical strength and agility demonstrating the possession of physical skills necessary to the accomplishment of the duties and functions of a peace officer.

(9) The applicant must successfully complete an oral examination conducted by or for the appointing agency to demonstrate the possession of communication skills necessary to the accomplishment of the duties and functions of a peace officer.

Although several of the regulations pertain to procedures the applicant must complete, some general qualifications are also cited.

Most agencies require that a police officer:

- *Be a citizen of the United States.*
- *Have or be eligible for a driver's license in the state.*
- *Not have been convicted of a felony.*

Requirements related to education and residency are also frequently stated.

Education.   Opinions differ as to how much education a candidate for police officer should have. Most police agencies require a minimum of a high school education or equivalency certificate. On the other hand, some jurisdictions require at least two years of college and some a four-year degree.

Most police agencies requires a minimum of a high school education.

Some administrators use set educational standards to attain professionalism and upgrade the service. However, police chiefs are at odds as to whether education contributes significantly to the fight against crime. Unquestionably, a college-educated police officer contributes significantly to the quality of police service. On the other hand, some police chiefs feel that too much education makes social service officers of personnel who ought to be fighting crime in the streets. Some surveys indicate that the more education police officers have, the less likely they are to become involved in physical confrontations. Others feel that to require a degreed officer to perform such mundane tasks as issuing traffic tickets and parking tickets, making money runs, and carding juveniles in liquor stores is demeaning, and that such routine tasks soon diminish the highly educated officer's interest in law enforcement. Besides, they argue, most police officers see themselves as crime fighters, not social engineers.

Still, some police agencies (usually in large cities) seek to attract college-educated recruits by offering better career and promotional opportunities, higher salaries, and further educational opportunities. Often such agencies also offer incentive programs for completed education.

Residency Requirements.   Over the years, cities and municipalities have reluctantly waived residency requirements to obtain better candidates. Though generally not required, cities are again beginning to accept only candidates who reside within their boundaries.

> *It is always preferred and sometimes required that police officers live in the community they serve.*

Sometimes compromises have been made whereby candidates are given one year to move into the community they serve. City and municipal politicians feel that by living in the community, a police officer becomes more closely identified with that community, more sensitive to its crime problems, and more readily participates in community activities.

The value of living in the community served cannot be disputed. Police officers are better able to understand the problems and needs of the community. They also develop relationships with the professional groups in the community and can better understand the life-style of the citizens. Additionally, politicians' self-interests dictate that their police officers live in the community so they can contribute their fair share of taxes. However, it may be economically unfeasible for police officers to afford to live in the community they serve.

The issue of preemployment residency raises controversial legal questions. In a Minnesota case, *Carter v. Gallagher* (1971), the legitimacy of the state's Veteran's Preference Law was challenged. The law gave preference for government jobs to those who had lived in Minnesota before entering military service or who had lived in Minnesota for at least five years after completing their military service. The challenge was made that the requirement discriminated against veterans who, although fully qualified, had not lived in Minnesota for the required time. The Minnesota Supreme Court ruled that the state had no interest in the residency requirement and further found that the requirement was inconsistent with the equal protection clause of the Fourteenth Amendment. The court ordered the practice discontintued.

Preliminary Screening Tests

The demands upon police officers are great. Not only are they subjected to emotional and physical stress, but they also are placed in positions of trust and responsibility. Effective screening tests are, therefore, a necessity.

The written examination has assumed a critical importance with the advent of civil rights legislation and the introduction of women into uniformed patrol work. Many unsuccessful applicants have challenged certain written examinations as being arbitrary or discriminatory. Their efforts have led to a reappraisal of the tests.

The use of specific standardized tests and their purpose must be carefully considered and justified, or the agency may run into legal difficulties. For example, in 1971 a class action suit charged the Duke Power Company with discrimination against a group of black employees by using standardized tests to determine promotion. In *Griggs v. Duke Power Company* (1971) the United States Supreme Court ruled that the Civil Rights Act of 1964 was concerned with the *consequences* of testing, not the employer's good intent or lack of intentional discrimination. The Court upheld the Equal Employment Opportunity Commission (EEOC) guidelines of 1966.

> Griggs v. Duke Power Company *established that all tests used for employment purposes must measure a tested person's capability to perform a specific job. Additionally, all requirements and standards established must be business or job related.*

Neither the courts nor the EEOC has drawn a distinction between the requirements for entrance examinations and those for promotional examinations. Consequently, law enforcement agencies have taken a greater interest in the content of written tests, and today's written examinations are generally of a high quality.

Some critics are opposed to any examination of candidates for employment because certain tests have been declared to be arbitrary or discriminatory. However, not all challenges come from members of minority groups. Successful challenges, whatever their origin, have been founded upon evidence that the tests in question were not job related, that is, they were invalid. A valid test measures what it purports to measure: in the case of law enforcement, potential success in law enforcement. The importance of validated tests is twofold. First, a validated test helps an agency discover the best candidates available. Second, it helps avoid time-consuming and costly legal challenges.

Test validation is a difficult procedure beyond the resources of many agencies; therefore, most law enforcement agencies find it more economical to use standardized tests. Seldom, however, does an agency rely upon these tests alone. They also consider physical agility tests, oral interview results, medical examinations, and background check information.

Some police departments have supplemented their preliminary screening procedures with examinations that determine police adaptability, memory retention, reading comprehension, spelling, and potential of the candidate to fit into the present organization.

> *Most candidates are required to complete a preliminary screening consisting of a written examination and a psychological examination. Standardized tests may be used.*

Those candidates who do well on the original preliminary testing or screening procedures of the police agency go on to other testing procedures including physical agility tests, oral interviews, medical examinations, and a thorough background check.

Physical Agility Tests

Physical fitness tests are usually administered to determine a candidate's coordination and muscular strength and to ascertain whether the candidate is in good or poor physical condition. The type of test varies with police agencies throughout the country.

A candidate may be required to run a designated number of yards and while doing so hurdle a three-foot barrier, crawl under a twenty-four inch bar, climb over a four- or six-foot wall with both hands on top of the wall, and sprint the remaining distance—all within a designated time period monitored by a police officer with a stopwatch.

Candidates may also be required to climb ropes or fire ladders, do chin-ups (grasp a bar and pull up a required number of times), or push-ups (from a front leaning rest position, hands flat on the floor with the chest barely touching the floor, push up a required number of times).

Other variations of the physical agility test may be required, but usually only a minimum of strenuous activity is obligatory.

Physical agility tests are necessary because they simulate what an officer may have to do on the street—jumping over a fence, climbing a wall, or chasing someone through back yards or streets. Candidates who are considerably overweight rarely pass the physical agility test.

Usually a candidate unable to pass the test the first time is given a second chance. A second failure results in disqualification.

> *Physical agility tests evaluate a candidate's coordination, speed of movement, and strength. The most common physical agility tests are similar to a military obstacle course which must be completed in a designated time.*

A candidate can prepare for the physical agility test through a regular system of workouts. Running is an excellent general conditioner because it develops endurance and strengthens the legs. Sit-ups, leg-lift exercises, push-ups, and lifting light weights are also helpful in preparing for the physical agility test. Like knowledge, physical fitness does not develop overnight; it develops gradually over an extended period.

The Oral Interview

Oral boards usually consist of three to five skilled interviewers knowledgeable in their fields. They may be staff officers from the agency doing the hiring or from other agencies, psychologists, sociologists, or representatives of a community service organization. The entire interviewing board may consist of members of a police or civil service commission. In smaller jurisdictions, oral boards are sometimes replaced by an interview with the mayor, a councilman, or the chief of police.

The interviews, whether structured or unstructured, are designed to elicit answers revealing the candidates' personalities and suitability for police work, *not* to determine their technical knowledge in the police field.

The candidate should be prepared to answer questions such as the following:

- Why do you want to be a police officer?
- What have you done to prepare for a career in law enforcement?
- What do you feel are the causes of crime?
- What are your favorite hobbies?
- Have you talked with your wife/husband about this position of police officer?
- What does she/he think about it?
- What is the last book you have read?
- What was your favorite subject in school?
- When did you last get drunk?

> *The oral interview seeks information about the candidate's personality and suitability for police work.*

The oral interview will also test the candidate's ability to use good judgment in specific situations such as the following:

- A person is standing on the corner making a speech regarding the overthrow of the government. He is drawing a crowd, and a certain amount of animosity is being shown toward the speaker, indicating future trouble. How would you handle this situation?
- You are working radar and you clock the mayor going 39 mph in a 30 mph zone. How would you handle this situation?
- You are walking a beat and a juvenile thrusts a stick between your legs causing you to fall to the pavement and tear your pants. What would you do?

The interview usually lasts about thirty minutes. The same questions are asked each candidate to allow comparison of answers. After the interview, the qualifications of each candidate are evaluated. Each candidate is given an overall rating which is combined with the scores of the other examinations to yield a composite (total) score.

Candidates should prepare themselves both physically and mentally for the oral interview. They should be well groomed and present a professional appearance. They should have considered in advance responses to questions which are likely to be asked. It is critical to be well prepared since the oral interview generally disqualifies more candidates than it qualifies.

The oral interview usually evaluates appearance, ability to present ideas, social adaptability, alertness, judgment, emotional stability, interest in the job, and communication ability.

The Medical Examination

Medical requirements vary from jurisdiction to jurisdiction, but the purpose is the same. With the modern emphasis on health care, more and more importance is being placed on the medical examination. Citizens, concerned about the possibility of early retirements due to poor health, are demanding physically fit officer candidates.

The medical standards usually include a variety of factors with some—vision, hearing, and the cardiovascular-respiratory system—being more important than others.

Good eyesight is of great importance. Candidates who wear glasses that correct their vision to meet the agency's requirements can qualify in some departments. Likewise, candidates who wear hearing aids that correct their hearing to meet the agency's requirements can qualify.

Because of the stress of the job and the hypertension that frequently accompanies it, the cardiovascular system is thoroughly checked. The respiratory and cardiovascular system play a critical role in fitness. To a great degree, endurance, the ability to continue exertion over a prolonged time, is directly related to the capacity of the cardiovascular-respiratory system to deliver oxygen to the muscles.

A physician who feels a candidate has functional or organic disorder may recommend disqualification of that candidate.

Vision, hearing, and the cardiovascular-respiratory system are of prime importance in the medical examination.

The Background Investigation

The applicant's background is one of the most critical; factors considered in recruitment. In most police agencies an applicant must submit a personal history. The background investigation serves two purposes: (1) it examines the past work and educational record of the candidate, and (2) it determines if anything in the candidate's background might make him unsuitable for police work. The extensiveness of the background investigation is limited only by the number of candidates being investigated and time available.

Normally all information given by the applicant on the history sheet must be verified. Birth and age records are verified through vital statistics, and driving record through the drivers' license bureau. Adverse driving records containing drunken driving, driving after suspension or revocation of license, or a consistent pattern of moving violations may cause disqualification.

Candidates are fingerprinted, and the prints are sent to the Federal Bureau of Investigation in Washington to determine if the candidate has a criminal record. The candidate's criminal record is also checked on the local and state levels, usually through fingerprints, name, and date of birth. Juvenile records are normally discounted unless a person has committed a heinous crime.

Ironically, because of the transient nature of our population, persons wanted on warrants in one part of the country have applied for a police officer's position in another part of the country. The criminal record check has sometimes resulted in the apprehension of such individuals.

Military records are usually checked to verify service and eligibility under the veteran's preference acts of some states. The check also determines if the candidate was involved in any court martials or disciplinary actions.

All personal and professional references and individuals with personal knowledge of the candidate listed on the history sheet are interviewed. Interviewing of references is sometimes criticized because candidates obviously will list only those who see them favorably. However, these references may lead to others who know the candidates and have a different view of them. When candidates list out-of-town references, letters or questionnaires are usually mailed.

Neighbors of the candidate, past or present, are an excellent source of information about a candidate's character and reputation. No department wants police officers who have had prior association with the criminal element, who have been addicted to narcotics or drugs, or who abuse alcohol. Their reputation in the community should be high.

Previous employers are contacted to determine the applicant's work record. Inability to hold continuous employment may indicate trouble getting along with supervisors. A high absentee rate may indicate lack of interest, initiative, or health problems.

The financial status of the candidate is also determined, usually through a credit records check. Individuals whose expenditures exceed their total incomes may be candidates for bankruptcy or bribery. Good credit indicates the person can live within his means and possesses self-control. The candidate may be required to submit a financial statement.

Educational records from high school, college, and any other schools attended are usually checked through personal contact. The education record may indicate interests, achievements, accomplishments, and social life-style while attending school. The scholastic record reflects not only intelligence but also study habits. Any degrees, certificates of achievement, or awards are usually noted.

The use of the polygraph examination as a follow-up to the background investigation is a widely increasing means of verifying the background of a candidate. Although some states have banned its use for preemployment purposes, where it is used to screen police candidates it is necessary to determine why it is being given. Some departments use the polygraph extensively, especially if they have many transient applicants from other parts of the country. Some agencies use it to determine if the candidate has ever engaged in criminal activity and was never apprehended. Some want to know about the candidate's sexual behavior; is he a sex deviant? Others use it to verify the written information the candidate has given them on the application and history sheet.

> The background investigation includes:
> - Verification of all information on the application and history sheet.
> - Check on driving record.
> - Fingerprinting and a check on any criminal record.
> - Check on military records.
> - Interviews with personal references, acquaintances, past employers, neighbors, and teachers.
> - Check on financial status.
> - Check on past performances at school and previous jobs.

It is imperative that the polygraph examiner be ethical and professionally competent. Any questions asked the applicant beyond those pertaining directly to the suitability of the candidate for police service could be construed as discriminatory and negate any information obtained through the use of the polygraph.

The Final Result

After all required tests are completed, they are analyzed and a composite score is given for each candidate. A list is made of eligible candidates, and they are called as openings occur in the police department. Some larger police departments keep their eligibility lists one to two years, depending on civil service requirements or other requirements mandated by states or municipalities.

Probation and Training

When candidates are sworn in as police officers to uphold the laws of the state and the country and they swear to the code of ethics, they are on the way to their life ambition.

Some states have mandated that recruits must be given from 240 to 400 hours of police training within one year of employment. Coincidentally, this is also usually the length of time the officers are placed on probation.

> The probationary period is a trial period, usually one year, during which the officer is observed while obtaining training and applying this training on the streets.

Police officers may obtain their training in a state police academy, a city academy, or a specialized rookie school. The basic training of police officers varies with each jurisdiction and its needs, but most officers will be trained in constitutional law, laws of arrest, search and seizure, and in the various requests for service such as accident investigation, crisis intervention, and giving first aid.

While in training they may be required to come back to the department and spend a specified number of hours on street patrol. Some jurisdictions alternate their training periods every two weeks, allowing an officer to apply on the street what was learned in basic recruit school.

While on the street the recruits ride with a trainer, usually a sergeant, who monitors their movements and helps them apply principles learned in rookie school. While in school, the officers are evaluated and tested by their instructors who periodically send progress reports to the chief of police. After completing training, they continue to ride with one or more training officers who continue to evaluate their street performance.

Following successful completion of the probationary period, they are full-fledged police officers. After probation some states license the person to be a police officer. Legislatures in Texas, Michigan, California, Oregon, Minnesota, and other states have adopted standards for police officers which must be met to satisfy the state's training requirements for licensing.

States have also mandated a certain amount of in-service training to keep the license current. Many of these in-service training requirements revolve around the behavioral sciences so police officers have a better understanding of the entire criminal justice system. Guest speakers from the corrections system, the court system, and on many occasions from minority groups appear to present their philosophy and objectives to police officers.

Physical Fitness Training Programs

Because recruits and experienced officers often face situations involving physical restraint and self-defense, police departments have set up both mandatory and voluntary physical fitness programs for officers. Job-related stress has sometimes affected officers to the extent that many retire early because of physical disability.

Controversy over physical fitness programs exists; some police administrators feel the police are being singled out from other employees. Nevertheless, it is obvious that law enforcement officers should maintain a high level of physical fitness. It is not only desirable from the standpoint of being able to enjoy life to the fullest, but for police officers it is also a necessity because they are frequently faced with situations that place great demands on their physical capacity. Physical fitness may make the difference between success and failure on the job—sometimes even the difference between life and death.

In general terms, physical fitness is a state of well-being which permits one to enjoy life to the fullest; it is the general capacity to adapt and respond favorably to physical effort. Many people evaluate fitness on the basis of appearance alone. Although personal appearance does have some bearing on physical fitness, what is going on inside is more important. The traditional image of fitness—the Charles Atlas physique—has given way to an image which stresses endurance and stamina as the true indicators of fitness.

Although many factors contribute to a well-conditioned body, the prime factor is the condition of the circulatory (cardiovascular) system upon which endurance or stamina is dependent. Other factors important in physical fitness are balance, flexibility, agility, strength, and power.

> *The prime factor in physical fitness is endurance (dependent upon the circulatory system). Other important factors are balance, flexibility, agility, strength, and power.*

Endurance or stamina is the capacity for continued exertion over prolonged periods as well as the ability to withstand pain, distress, and fatigue for extended periods. Physical endurance is required in long distance running, swimming, cycling, and wrestling.

Balance is neuromuscular control—the muscles and nerves working together to perform various movements. Poor balance results in poor body control and may cause the individual to be "accident prone."

Flexibility is mobility of the joints, the ability to "bend without breaking." A flexible person has a wide range of movement; a stiff person has a very restricted range of movement. Loss of flexibility is frequently one of the first signs of physical deterioration.

Agility is the ability to react quickly and easily. Agility is needed to run an obstacle course, to jump or vault fences or barriers, to climb a ladder quickly, or to lie down and spring back up. Agility enables an officer to successfully cope with emergencies and minimizes the chance of personal injury.

Strength and power imply toughness, durability, and vigor, as well as the ability to exert force with the hands, arms, legs, and trunk. *Strength* is needed to

Police academy cadets on a morning run. Physical fitness may make the difference between success and failure on the job.

perform routine or daily tasks. For example, hand and arm strength is needed to lift or pull heavy objects. Leg strength is needed to walk, run, and jump. Trunk strength is needed to support all movements of the arms and legs. *Power* is the explosive force which moves the body suddenly or which propels some object independent of the body. It requires power to run the sprints, to hurdle, or to high-jump.

Salary and Benefits

Salaries among police departments in the country have little uniformity. A variety of factors influence a police officer's salary. Of utmost consideration are the community's ability to pay, the cost of living in the area, and the prevailing wages of similar police departments in the surrounding area.

Normally position-classification plans are implemented under a personnel ordinance or department rule book. Steps on the salary scale are established in each position-classification. New recruits start at the bottom of the salary scale and receive increment raises after six months and each succeeding year until they reach their maximum salary, usually after three to five years. They obtain more salary only if granted a cost-of-living raise. However, a promotion to the next rank would bring them into a different salary bracket. Sergeants, lieutenants, captains, and chiefs, all have minimum and maximum starting levels with the top salary usually reached after three years in the position.

To compensate individuals who do not attain a rank during their police careers, many police departments have adopted longevity plans whereby non-ranking officers receive a certain percentage more of their salary after the tenth year, the fifteenth year, and so on. This seniority system has been attacked, however, on the grounds that is discourages initiative and further education.

When salary schedules are formulated, fringe benefits such as hospitalization and dental plans, insurance, vacation, sick leave, and holidays are all considered. Police officers' indirect benefits from their employers are estimated to be approximately 33 percent, comparable to what business and industry currently allow their employees.

In addition to fringe benefits, most police departments give police officers a yearly clothing allowance to maintain their uniform wardrobe.

Policies vary regarding overtime pay for officers on the job, going to court while on duty, being required to attend training while off duty, and being called back to duty in an emergency. Some departments pay; others give compensatory time off.

Police departments may belong to unions which bargain for them. Usually all conditions of employment are clearly spelled out in their contracts.

Off-Duty Work Limitations

Moonlighting, working at a part-time job while fulfilling the obligations of a full-time position, has been a source of controversy in the police field for many years. Some administrators allow their officers latitude in the off-duty work performed and the number of hours worked. Other administrators are becoming more conservative as a result of poor work performance by some moonlighting officers and lawsuits against the officer and the city or municipality due to some incident while the officer was working off duty.

Some cities allow their police officers to work off duty in only police-related areas; others allow them to work in only nonpolice-related areas. While there are advantages and disadvantages in allowing police officers to work off duty, most cities and municipalities have some limits on the officer's off-duty time.

> *Most police departments restrict the type of work which can be done and the number of hours an officer can work while off duty.*

Federal Guidelines and Regulations

In 1964 Congress enacted the Omnibus Civil Rights Law. Title VII of this law concerns employment opportunities and prohibits discrimination because of sex, race, color, religion, or national origin. The law also established the Equal Employment Opportunity Commission (EEOC) to administer the law and gave this commission authority to establish guidelines. This law affected only private business, not state and local governments; therefore, it had little impact on police agency practices.

> *The 1964 Omnibus Civil Rights Law prohibits discrimination in employment opportunities in private business.*

However, in 1972 Congress passed the Equal Opportunity Act, which modified Title VII to include state and local units of government. This law was passed because six years after the EEOC published guidelines for employment and promotion testing, few state or local central personnel selection agencies had taken positive steps to meet the guidelines. Although not legally required to do so, they should have been forward-looking enough to realize that if such guidelines were not voluntarily followed, steps would be taken to assure compliance.

> *The 1972 Equal Employment Opportunity Act prohibits discrimination due to sex, race, color, religion, or national origin in employment of any kind, public or private, local, state, or federal.*

Minority Group Members in Law Enforcement

According to the Task Force on the Police of the President's Commission on Law Enforcement and the Administration of Justice (1967), police administrators in most large cities are genuinely interested in attracting more officers from minority groups—Puerto Ricans, Mexican-Americans, Orientals, and blacks. However, in many communities, both north and south, discrimination in the selection and promotion of minority officers has occurred in the past and may still exist.

To gain the community's general confidence and acceptance, police department personnel should be representative of the community as a whole. An integrated department helps reduce stereotyping and prejudice. Further, minority officers provide a department with an understanding of minority groups, their languages, and their subcultures, all with practical benefits to successful law enforcement. For example, a police officer with a knowledge of Spanish can help to prevent conflicts between the police and Spanish-speaking residents of the community.

A racially balanced and integrated police department both fosters community relations and increases police effectiveness.

A task force of the President's Commission on Law Enforcement and the Administration of Justice (*The Police,* 1967, p. 167), noted that black officers in black neighborhoods have special competence, as demonstrated in a study in Philadelphia in which three-fourths of the patrol officers thought that black police officers were more effective in black neighborhoods than white police officers: "Personal knowledge of minority groups and slum neighborhoods can lead to information not otherwise available, to earlier anticipation of trouble, and to increased solution of crime."

Reasons for the increased effectiveness of the black officers include: (1) they get along better with, and receive more respect from the black residents, (2) they receive less trouble from the black residents, (3) they can get more information, and (4) they understand black citizens better.

A need for minority police officers has been stated repeatedly. Accomplishing this, however, frequently poses difficult problems for police departments.

Recruitment and Selection of Minority Member Police Officers

Precinct police officers from minority groups are one of the best source of advertising for minority recruits. However, police officers cannot honestly "sell" police work if discrimination exists in their departments. Police departments sincerely wishing to attract minority recruits must abolish internal segregation and discrimination. They must give minority officers full opportunity for promotion and assignment to prestigious units. Minority officers must not be segregated in patrols or in a particular part of the city, but must be welcomed warmly everywhere.

Minority community leaders and civic organizations may disseminate recruitment materials and provide opportunities for recruiters to address groups of potential applicants. Community leaders convinced of the sincerity of the police recruiting minorities may refer applicants to them.

Certain selection standards may unintentionally bar large numbers of minority applicants who could actually perform police work very competently. For example, minimum height restrictions frequently disqualify many Puerto Ricans, Mexican-Americans, and Orientals from police work.

The Task Force on the Police cites national statistics which indicate the underrepresentation of minorities in law enforcement is partly due to the greater percentage of minority applicants who fail to meet police selection standards. This is hardly surprising as minorities are frequently disadvantaged both culturally and educationally.

To hire minority police officers, agencies might apply compensating factors to increase the number of eligible minority members. Compensating factors allow an applicant who fails to meet one qualification but excels in another to be employed; the area of qualification outweighs the deficiency. For example deficiencies in height, weight, or vision may be compensated for by an unusual language skill, leadership experience, or a high level of education. However, certain minimum qualifications such as moral character, mental ability, and psychological health must be met directly rather than by compensation.

An interesting finding of the Rand Study (*The Police,* p. 331) was that salary and job security were *not* primary interests of minority applicants; minority applicants were motivated first by an opportunity to maintain law and order, second by the feeling that comes from helping people, and third by fringe benefits and job security. This study also found that most attrition after initial testing was caused by lack of motivation to follow through on the lengthy processing. At the time of the study, the New York Police Department took up to seventeen months to process an applicant. The Rand Study recommended accelerating the selection process and instituting personal contacts between police department personnel officers and minority applicants to sustain the applicant's interest during the selection process.

As noted by the Task Force Report (1967, p. 169): "Any program to increase the proportion of minority group police officers must begin by persuading qualified candidates to apply. However, the hostility of blacks to police forces is so strong that black officers are frequently disliked by their fellow blacks." The minority officer faces a unique problem in that often members of his own group consider him a traitor. Some young, lawless males resent police in general and hate anyone of their own group who goes into law enforcement.

Promotion

Increasing the number of ranking minority officers is as important as, and closely related to, recruiting new minority officers; successful recruitment and promotional opportunities are closely interdependent.

The limited number of minority officers promoted in comparison to the number recruited and selected is partly due to the recency of recruitment of many minority officers. It usually takes several years to work up through the ranks to supervisory and command positions. Additionally, the more limited educational background of some minority group officers may cause them to do poorly on promotion examinations. Still, to be responsive to the needs of minority neighborhoods, a police department needs several qualified higher-ranking minority group officers. Minority groups should not feel they are policed by an entirely white police force; they should see that minority officers participate in policy-making and other important decisions.

Discrimination

The number of minority applicants will not increase if discrimination in the assignment and promotion of minority officers exists. The total police image will influence minority interest in police careers. The Task Force Report (*The Police*, 1967) identified several policies which limit minority officers' authority to make arrests and restrict them to working only in minority neighborhoods and with other minority officers.

Minority officers should be selected by the same standards as other officers and should compete on an equal basis for every assignment. They should be assigned to minority neighborhoods, but not exclusively; and they should be allowed to advance within the field to positions in supervision, management, or administration.

Preferential Hiring and Promotions and Court Actions

Police agencies must recruit minorities and assure that the selection process is free of unwarranted cultural bias. The federal courts have forbidden cultural bias in the selection process. Some have gone further than that and have demanded preferential minority employment to rectify the effects of past discrimination.

Carter v. Gallagher (1971) dealt with discrimination in the hiring procedures of the Minneapolis Fire Department. The court found that certain selection requirements were not job related and were, in fact, discriminatory. The court ordered the city to correct the situation by hiring one minority group member for every three whites employed until twenty minority members were hired.

A similar decision requiring preferential hiring was made in Philadelphia. In *Allen v. Mobile* (1971) Mobile, Alabama, was charged with discrimination in the assignment and promotion of black officers. The court ordered Mobile to consult with black leaders to develop a recruitment program and to directly advertise that Mobile was an equal opportunity employer.

The Detroit experience with recruitment, hiring, and promotion of minority group members received national attention. In 1971 the Detroit Police Department found it had 13 percent minority personnel compared with 44 percent minority in the community. If the department continued its annual hiring ratio of 20 percent minorities, it would never approach an ethnic makeup reflecting the community. Over half the police officers hired would have to be from minority groups to achieve an ethnic balance by 1980. Therefore, recruitment efforts to attract minority applicants were emphasized in preference to general recruitment techniques.

In July 1974 the Detroit Board of Police Commissioners adopted an affirmative action policy designed to promote equal numbers of blacks and whites, even if it required passing over highly qualified white candidates. At the time Detroit was 50 percent black, but the police force had only 15 percent black personnel. High-ranking black officers were almost nonexistent: only 2 percent black lieutenants and 15 percent black sergeants. Detroit maintained separate lists of black and white candidates for promotion, placed in order of test scores and other criteria. When openings occurred, equal numbers of blacks and whites were drawn from the two lists. Consequently, blacks with lower total scores were promoted over whites with higher scores. This did not, however, mean that blacks were not qualified to fill the position.

> *Preferential hiring and promotion seeks to approximate the minority composition of the community within the employee ranks.*

Reverse Discrimination

In March 1978, as a result of a lawsuit filed by two hundred white officers on the Detroit Police Department, Senior Federal Judge Fred W. Kaess issued a permanent injunction barring the City of Detroit from promoting less-qualified black officers to the rank of sergeant ahead of whites. The injunction barred using racial quotas in promoting police officers to the rank of sergeant only; it did not bar all affirmative action promotions. However, the blow to Detroit's affirmative action program had repercussions throughout the country.

The Fourteenth Amendment guarantees *every* American citizen equal protection under the law, and a long series of civil rights laws assert that a person must not be discriminated against because of color. Judge Kaess noted: "While the purpose of the quota system is generally compassionate, its effect is intolerable because it denigrates individuals by reducing them to a single immutable birth characteristic—skin pigmentation." Kaess also rejected the commonly used term "reverse discrimination" as a misnomer: "Racial discrimination is as indefensible when practiced against whites as it is when practiced against blacks and does not become 'reverse' merely because it is practiced against whites."

> *Reverse discrimination exists when a more qualified person (usually a white male) is denied a position or promotion because it is reserved to fill a quota established by affirmative action plans.*

A Promising Future for Minority Police Officers

Police administrators should aggressively seek out, employ, and promote qualified members of minority groups (or the courts may well dictate that they do so). Several recruitment techniques and programs are effective in attracting minorities. When it is necessary to overcome a distrust of the police, minority recruiters may establish rapport with minority groups. Minority recruiters have been successful across the country, especially in Phoenix, Washington, Kansas City, New York, and Detroit.

Although employment of persons from all ethnic groups within the community should be a recruitment goal, primary consideration should be given to employing the best-qualified candidate available, regardless of ethnic background. The ethnic makeup of the community should be a guide for recruitment policies, not a basis for quota hiring.

One way to assure well-qualified candidates from minority groups is to promote educational programs for minority group members. For example, in 1977 a little-publicized program to increase minority participation at master's and doctoral degree levels in criminal justice education was begun in eight traditionally black colleges. Participating colleges include Mississippi Valley State University; Itta Bena, Mississippi; Grambling State University, Louisiana; Talladega College, Alabama; Texas Southern University; Fayetteville State University and Shaw University, North Carolina; Bishop College of Dallas; and Shaw College of Detroit.

The program, known as Positive Features, Inc. (PFI) was conducted under an LEAA grant and sought to improve the image of the criminal justice system in the black community by using black criminal justice students, graduates, and interns to conduct community relations meetings, workshops, and other related projects.

Such innovations and others in the development stages should help to assure that minority group members have the opportunity for a successful future in law enforcement.

Women in Law Enforcement

Deborah Lancaster (1983, p. 43) notes that: ''In 1970, women constituted only 1 percent of sworn law enforcement officers. Today that figure is 4 percent and it continues to slowly rise each year. The men who are entering police work today are, for the most part, a new generation. They have been raised in an era of equal opportunity with the idea that women are equal and capable of performing just about any job. As these men rise through the ranks of police departments across the nation, I believe women will continue to enter and rise in the profession as well.''

Initially women were restricted to processing female prisoners and to positions as police matrons. Many misconceptions about the female's ability to perform certain ''masculine'' tasks have been dispelled as a result of changing social attitudes; yet room for improvement remains.

Just before the turn of the century, a movement to employ women as regular police officers gained support. The first woman police officer in the United States was Marie Owen, appointed in 1893 by the Detroit Bureau of Police. In 1910 the first regular policewoman under civil service was appointed in Los Angeles. Shortly thereafter, in 1912, in New York, the first woman chief of police was appointed by the mayor of Milford, Ohio. By the end of World War I, over 220 cities employed policewomen.

A major reason for this relatively rapid acceptance of female peace officers was a change in the public's view of the police function. The acceptance of women paralleled the newly accepted emphasis on citizen protection and crime prevention rather than exclusive concentration on the enforcement of laws and detection of crimes.

Despite early rapid progress in breaking into the police field, women have met with several barriers in becoming equal to their male counterparts. Many agencies have excluded women altogether by quota systems, discriminatory hiring, and promotional policies. Some women officers are not eligible to take the exam for promotion available to men. Only within the last ten years have many agencies allowed women to take supervisory exams. Some agencies required women to have more education than male applicants. For example, before 1969 the Washington, D.C. Metropolitan Police Department required women applicants to possess a college degree; men needed only a high school diploma.

Practitioners at every level within the police service have resisted the expansion of the woman's role in law enforcement. Some believe police work requires more strength and physical agility than most women possess; few women have the strength to perform many of the difficult tasks required of patrol officers. Some argue that if they allow shorter, lighter women to become patrol officers, they must also allow shorter, lighter men. They contend that physical standards should not be altered to bring women into the service. However, if standards are not altered, only 3.5 percent of the women in the country would be eligible for work in the police field because 96 percent of American women are shorter than 5'8'' and 98 percent weight less than 140 pounds (National Advisory Commission on Criminal Justice Standards and Goals, 1973, p. 345).

Another concern of police administrators is women's ability to supervise male officers. Some administrators believe all female supervisors should be assigned to the juvenile aid division and supervise only policewomen. Some administrators feel women supervisors are too lenient with the men, do not have the respect of the patrolmen, and fail to get voluntary compliance from subordinates. Other police officials claim deployment of women limits their command flexibility and that social, domestic, and disciplinary problems occur when ''coeducational cop cars'' are used.

In addition, many agencies neglect training of female personnel. Some conduct separate training classes for women, geared toward investigative rather than line functions of police work. Women are also excused from the qualifying examination in physical fitness and are passed automatically. However, such exemptions perpetuate the image of ''weakness'' of women officers and promote an overprotective attitude in male officers. More importantly, the exemptions are a form of discrimination against male officers.

Further, in many agencies substantial numbers of policewomen are assigned to clerical duties, and many are not paid on the same basis as the men who perform similar functions. For example, five Detroit policewomen filed a complaint with the Michigan Civil Rights Commission alleging that their salaries were not equal to their male counterparts.

Often promotions are based on experience, knowledge, and ability as determined by an examination. Women, because of discrimination, have been unable or unwilling to compete successfully in this process. Their duties do not lead to attainment of comprehensive knowledge or experience in police work, especially in basic line functions. Since they cannot qualify for positions requiring such background, some agencies systematically exclude them from the promotional process.

Across the country, many police departments have tried to keep physical agility tests, height standards, and other requirements to restrict the number of women on police forces. However, the Equal Employment Act of 1972 forbids such practices, demanding that *all* jobs must be open to both men and women unless it can be proved that sex "is a bonafide occupational qualification necessary to the normal operation of that particular business or enterprise."

Suits have charged that women have been discriminated against regarding promotions, job assignments, seniority practices, maternity policies, and physical requirements. Yet no one has proved that a taller, heavier person can perform the functions required of a police officer better than a smaller, lighter person. However, because most police work does require physical strength and agility, agencies must not establish criteria which will result in the hiring of police officers unable to perform police duties. Agency standards should not be changed to employ women at the cost of reduced physical effectiveness of individual police officers (although discriminatory height and weight restrictions may be changed).

Police agencies cannot maintain different hiring qualifications for men and women. They must establish criteria to facilitate the employment of both without restricting their capability to carry out their functions. The federal government has taken steps in this direction. In 1971 the Secret Service administered the oath of office to five women, the first in the history of the agency. In 1972 the nation's first female FBI agents were sworn in. Dallas, Miami, and New York City police departments have opened their promotional examinations to women. And the Washington, D.C., Metropolitan Police Department has gone a step further in an innovative promotional policy that maintains only one promotional list including both male and female officers. When a vacancy occurs, the next eligible person is elevated, regardless of sex.

Effectiveness of Women on Patrol

In 1971 Miami promoted the first women to sergeant to command a patrol sector of six to ten men from a mixture of ethnic backgrounds. The woman sergeant not only did a highly competent job, she helped change the department uniform regulations so female officers could wear slacks on duty.

According to Miami Chief of Police Bernard L. Garmire (1974, pp. 11–13), female officers proved to be effective in all phases of police work in Miami. Women officers were well accepted by male officers and by the public. In fact, the classification of policewomen was eliminated with all personnel classified as police officers. As noted by Garmire: "Crime makes no distinction between sexes, and neither should law enforcement in its effort to combat it (p. 13)."

> *Studies have shown that women perform as well as men in police patrol work.*

The LEAA financed a seven-month study in New York City ("Women on Patrol," 1978, p. 43) which found that women generally perform as well as men in police patrol work, although some small differences exist. The study, based on direct observation of 3,625 patrols and 2,400 police-civilian encounters, examined an equal number of men and women. It analyzed the actions required of the officers, their style of patrol, their methods of gaining control, their initiative, physical strength, and the reactions of the public.

The study found that the performance of policewomen is more like that of policemen than it is different, although the women made a better impression on the public. Citizens said women officers were more competent, pleasant, and respectful than the men. The women's performance created a better civilian regard for the New York Police Department.

The study also found that women were less likely to join male partners in taking control of a situation or jointly making decision. However, in the few incidents judged to be dangerous, men and women were equally likely to attempt to gain control. Women were neither more nor less likely than men to use force, display a weapon, or rely on a direct order. In addition, the behavior of women who patrolled with women was more active, assertive, and self-sufficient.

Other findings of the study were that women were slightly less physically agile in such activities as climbing ladders or steep stairs. Women took more sick leave than men—consistent with earlier research showing that, in general, women are absent from work more frequently than men, perhaps because they are more likely to stay home when family members are ill.

The report attributed the small but consistent differences to socially conditioned attitudes such as protectiveness, disdain, or skepticism by men and passivity by women. The study concluded that: "The results offer little support either to those who hold that women are unsuited to patrol or to those who argue that women do the job better than men. By and large, patrol performance of the women was more like that of the men than it was different."

According to James M.H. Gregg, former LEAA administrator: "This report is another important step toward creating equal opportunities for women in law enforcement. . . . Today's police patrolwomen are pioneering in what has always been a man's world, and there are obstacles to overcome. This report makes it clear that they are being overcome."

A later survey of women on patrol (Bouza, 1975, pp. 2–7) revealed that women were confident of their ability to perform all aspects of the patrol function: they could drive automobiles as well as males, they would rather work on the street than in the station house, they acknowledged their physical limitations but were confident of their ability to cope—either through persuasion or through the display of superior force—and the initial male resistance was subsiding and acceptance was growing; they felt accepted and respected by the public as well.

The situation does seem to be improving for women. "Women on Patrol" (1977, pp. 45–53) described some gains made. From 1971 to 1975 the number of women police officers doubled from 3,157 to 6,139, yet this number represented less than 2 percent of all police officers. In 1978 Atlanta had 71 of 126 women police officers on the streets; Dallas had more than 50, San Francisco 46, Miami 35. Houston had only five women out of 2,700 officers riding in patrol cars in 1978. St. Louis had fewer than twenty women on patrol and New York had only 112.

Washington, D.C., was the first city to assign large numbers of women to patrol. In 1977 more than 200 of their 299 policewomen were on patrol—walking beats and riding in patrol cars. They constituted almost 10 percent of the total police force (Kiernan and Cusick, 1977, pp. 45–53). Women were assigned to each of the twenty-three divisions and bureaus, from traffic to homicide. Most were young, still in their twenties. Two-thirds were black. Only six achieved the rank of sergeant, only one that of lieutenant. These female uniformed police officers have drawn great interest and undergone more professional scrutiny over the last ten years than any other category of police officers in the country. The question inevitably asked is, "Can women perform patrol work as well as men?" And, almost without exception, the answer, from the women, their male partners, and the professionals who have studied them is: "Yes."

Barbara Lewis (1983, p. 33) quotes Police Chief Robert Norman of Forest City, California: "Some officers have a resistance to change. In fact, I was very skeptical when I worked as a patrol officer and women were introduced on the force. But, my first female partner was exceptional and that turned around my skepticism." Lewis also notes that most police chiefs feel female officers are interchangeable with male officers as far as job responsibilities are concerned. Some police chiefs, however, disagree, feeling that female officers excel in certain areas within the department, for example, rape cases, child abuse cases, domestic disputes, undercover work, violent confrontations, and traffic details.

Whichever view is held, it seems clear that most police chiefs surveyed are very positive about the female officers on their force. Lewis (1983, p. 34) quotes Sergeant George Scharm of the Evanston, Illinois, police department as saying: "A woman is as versatile as any man and they can handle any job. Without a doubt, we are happy with our women officers. In fact, I wish that we could get more."

Although the use of policewomen has been a success in many departments, problems do occur. The questions most frequently asked about putting women on patrol include:

- Can women handle situations involving force and violence?
- What changes in training and equipment must be made?
- Do women resent the loss of the "specialist" role they have usually had in police work?
- Should women compete with men for promotions?
- Does the law require police departments to hire women and put them on patrol?

As these questions are satisfactorily answered, less resistance to putting women on patrol should be encountered. It must be remembered, however, that women differ from one another as much as men do. Among the differences in the women on the Washington police force were the following:

- They range in height from 5 feet to more than 6 feet and in age from 20 to 44.

■ All finished high school, but many had additional schooling; some had completed college.

■ They joined for a variety of reasons; money, adventure, or to help people.

■ Their views of their male colleagues ranged from complaints of continual teasing and harassment to flowing praise that the male officers "were like brothers."

The men on the force also differed in their opinions of the policewomen. Some women were described as "nice guys, people who want to help people." However, one women was so aggressive she was nicknamed "Mad Dog."

Susan Ek (1983) conducted a survey of female police officers in Minnesota, receiving a return rate of approximately 50 percent. According to this survey, the average female officer in Minnesota was twenty-nine years old, five feet six inches tall, married, and had a college degree. Eighty-two percent indicated that their families supported their law enforcement career choices and 92 percent indicated that their families still supported the choice. Over half (52 percent) were patrol officers and almost half (44 percent) worked a rotating shift.

Ek's survey also revealed that 56 percent of the female officers had been in a "knock-down, drag'em out fight on-duty," primarily with drunks, and 36 percent had been injured on duty, with 22 percent of the injuries occurring while making an arrest. Well over half (59 percent) indicated that their jobs did hurt their off-duty lives, with 38 percent indicating that the odd hours limited social and family life. And 86 percent indicated that they had been bothered by job stress at least once in a while.

In 1972 the Police Foundation funded a comparison study of male and female recruits in Washington, D.C. Completed in 1974, the study concluded that from a performance viewpoint it was appropriate to hire women for patrol on the same basis as men. Among its specific findings were the following (Kiernan and Cusik, 1977):

■ Both men and women officers obtained similar results in handling angry or violent citizens. No incidents cast serious doubt on a female officer's ability to patrol satisfactorily.

■ Women made fewer arrests and gave fewer traffic citations. However, they also had fewer opportunities to do so, as they were not given patrol assignments as often as men. Arrests made by women and men were equally likely to result in convictions.

■ Men were more likely to engage in serious misconduct than women, for example, to be arrested for drunk and disorderly conduct while off duty. Women, on the other hand, were more likely to be late for work.

■ A majority of Washington residents approved of the use of women in patrol work, although they were "moderately skeptical" of women's abilities to handle violent suspects.

■ There were no differences between men and women in the number of sick days used, number of injuries sustained, or number of days absent from work because of injuries.

- Male and female partners shared driving equally, took charge with about the same frequency, and were about equal in giving each other instructions.

- Resignation rates were also similar: 14 percent for women and 12 percent for men.

Perhaps the most graphic illustration of the equal role played by men and women on police patrol is that of Gail A. Cobb who joined the Washington, D.C. Police Department in 1973 and had been assigned to patrol duty for only five months when she responded to her last police call.

Around noon one Friday in September, Officer Cobb was patrolling downtown Washington when she was called to help search for two suspected bank robbers who had exchanged shots with police and then fled. Officer Cobb saw a man dash down a ramp into an underground parking garage and followed him. Then, moments after entering the garage, she was shot in the chest. Only twenty-four years old, Officer Gail Cobb became the first United States policewoman to be killed in the line of duty. As noted by Police Chaplain Reverend R. Joseph Dooley, her death "established the fact that the criminal makes no distinction between the sexes. It is the badge and the blue uniform that makes the difference."

Concurring with this view is Susan Ek (1983, p. 4) who notes that:

Today's women compete for and achieve the same duties, responsibilities, and accomplishments as their male counterparts. . . . Success, however is not automatically guaranteed to every woman (or man) entering law enforcement. Success is an *individual* achievement based largely on good common sense, self-confidence, and a sense of fair play. . . . Preparation is a key factor in any field, but especially critical in law enforcement where "unpredictable" is the norm. It is not easy to deal with the constant physical and emotional job stress, the erratic working hours, and the inevitable pressure on family and friends, but for those individuals who have given law enforcement careful consideration and come prepared, it is the most rewarding career opportunity of a lifetime.

Employment Opportunities in Law Enforcement

Although this chapter has focused on the local police department, numerous other employment opportunities exist for individuals interested in a career in law enforcement. A review of Chapter 6 will provide several opportunities on the state and federal level.

More information about specific requirements for positions at the federal level can be obtained through the nearest Federal Job Information Center which is usually listed in the white pages of local telephone directories under "U.S. Government." If there is no listing, call the toll-free information number (800-555-1212) and ask for the nearest Federal Job Information Center.

Information about opportunities in law enforcement at the state level can be obtained by contacting the state department of personnel or any local state employment office.

Summary

The future success (or failure) of our law enforcement system depends in large part on the effectiveness of our police officers. Therefore, valid recruitment, screening, testing, and selection procedures must be used to assure that only well-qualified candidates are hired. Qualities identified in good police officers include: reliability, leadership, judgment, persuasiveness, communication skills, accuracy, initiative, integrity, honesty, ego control, intelligence, and sensitivity. Individuals possessing such skills are sought through a careful selection procedure.

Police officer selection usually includes (1) a formal application, (2) a preliminary screening including a written examination and a psychological examination, (3) a physical agility test, (4) an oral interview, (5) a medical examination, and (6) a thorough background investigation. Most agencies require that a police officer candidate be a citizen of the United States, have or be eligible for a driver's license in the state, and not have been convicted of a felony. Additional requirements may specify educational level and residency in the community served.

Tests used in the selection process must be valid, as established in *Griggs v. Duke Power Company*. All tests used for employment purposes must measure a tested person's capability to perform a specific job, and all requirements and standards established must be business or job related.

Once candidates have passed all tests in the selection process, they usually enter a one-year probationary period during which they are observed while obtaining training and while applying this training on the streets. This probationary period allows for evaluation of the selected candidates. After the probation, the officers should continue to receive periodic in-service training to maintain already acquired skills and to achieve proficiency in new ones.

Physical fitness is of critical importance to police officers. The prime factor in physical fitness is endurance. Other important factors are balance, flexibility, agility, strength, and power.

In addition to local and state requirements for recruitment and selection of police officers, certain federal guidelines and regulations must be met. Most important are the 1964 Omnibus Civil Rights Law, which prohibits discrimination in employment opportunities in private business, and the Equal Employment Opportunity Act of 1972, which prohibits discrimination due to sex, race, color, religion, or national origin in employment of any kind, public or private, local, state, or federal. All individuals meeting the specific requirements of the department should be given the opportunity to apply for and successfully compete with other candidates.

Members of minority groups are highly beneficial in a police department. A racially balanced and integrated police department fosters community relations and increases police effectiveness. However, discrimination has been found in the recruitment, selection, and promotional practices of some police departments as well as in some policies which limit minority officers' authority to make arrests and restrict them to working in certain areas on certain types of assignments and only with other members of their minority group. Progress is being made in eliminating such discrimination. In some instances preferential hiring and promotion have been implemented to attract minority group members to police departments. However, preferential hiring and affirmative action programs have resulted in claims of reverse discrimination from white male police officers who feel their civil rights are being violated when quotas for minority members are established.

Just as members of minority groups have a promising future in law enforcement, so do women. The acceptance of women into law enforcement paralleled the newly accepted emphasis on citizen protection and crime prevention rather than exclusive concentration on the enforcement of laws and detection of crimes. Women have not always been welcomed onto the force, however. Those opposed to women in police work feel they are not strong enough to perform many of the required tasks, are given an unfair advantage over men because of lower height and weight standards, and they are not able to supervise male officers. In spite of such contentions, surveys have shown that women perform as well as men on police patrol.

All police officers, be they white, black, brown, male or female, are subjected to the hazards of police work, and all are expected to fulfill the responsibilities of the job. Each must be given an equal chance to become a police officer, to be adequately trained, and to be promoted. Each offers the profession an added dimension and one more means of fulfilling its mission.

Application

Students who graduate from law enforcement programs frequently are uncertain about what agency they would like to work for. With 20,000 law enforcement agencies in the United States, 155 on the federal level, most students have no idea where their talents should go. So that most students in the class have an idea of the differences in agencies, have students complete a research project that summarizes the following information:

Federal Agencies

- What are the educational requirements?
- What are the benefits?
- What are the responsibilities?
- What is the pay scale?
- What are the promotion possibilities?
- What is the probability of a transfer to another city?

State Agencies

- Are there any state investigative agencies I would be interested in?
- What about the highway patrol? Would I like to patrol the highways eight hours a day?

■ Are there supervisory positions available through promotion?

■ What is the pay scale?

■ What are the fringe benefits?

■ Am I qualified to get a job with the Department of Natural Resources?

Municipal Agencies

■ What would it be like to work in a medium size city?

■ What would it be like to work in a small police department?

■ What is the pay scale?

■ What are the fringe benefits?

■ What are the promotion possibilities?

■ Would I ever become a detective or a juvenile officer?

■ What hours would I be working?

Private Security

■ With over one million private security officers in the United States, would I be interested in a supervisory and eventually a managerial position with one of the fifteen hundred corporations in the United States that have security departments?

In some instances, students may find that they may want to consider furthering their education and focusing on a specific goal within a specific agency.

Discussion Questions

1. What is the most common restriction for off-duty work for a police officer?
2. Where are the U.S. Civil Service Commission offices in our area?
3. Is a newspaper advertisement placed by a police department requesting that only women apply for a job opening fair?
4. What is the most common reason for rejection during the selection process?
5. What employment opportunities in law enforcement are available locally? In our county? Our state?
6. What is the percentage of minorities and women on our police force? Is this ''balanced''? How did this situation come to be?

References

Bopp, W.J. *Police personnel administration.* Boston: Holbrook Press, 1974.

Bopp, W.J., and Whisenand, P.M. *Police personnel administration.* 2d ed. Boston: Allyn and Bacon, 1980.

Bouza, A.V. "Women in policing." *FBI law enforcement bulletin* 44, no. 9 (September 1975): 2–7.

Ek, S. "The female officer." Editorial. *Police* 7, no. 9 (September 1983): 4.

Ek, S.G. "Female officer survey." *Police* 7, no. 9 (September 1983): 38–41.

Garmire, B.L. "Female officers in the department. *FBI law enforcement bulletin* (June 1974): 11–13.

"Indiana University develops police selection procedure." *Target* 6 no. 8 (September 1977): 1.

Kiernan, M., and Cusick, J. "Women on patrol: The nation's capitol gives them high marks." *Police magazine* (1977): 45–53.

Lancaster, D.A. "One woman's struggle." *Police* 7, no. 9 (September 1983): 42–43.

Lewis, B. "Women behind the badge." *Police* 7, no. 9 (September 1983): 33–35.

National Advisory Commission on Criminal Justice Standards and Goals. *Police.* Washington, D.C.: U.S. Government Printing Office, 1973.

President's Commission on Law Enforcement and Administration of Justice. Task Force Report. *The police.* Washington, D.C.: U.S. Government Printing Office, 1967.

Sturner, L.J. "Personnel selection and promotion processes: Some consideration. *FBI law enforcement bulletin* 46, no. 6 (June 1977): 6–12.

Swaton, J., and Morgan, L. *Administration of justice.* New York: D. Van Nostrand Company, 1975.

Territo, L.; Swanson, C.R., Jr.; and Chamelin, N.C. *The police personnel selection process.* Indianapolis: Bobbs-Merrill, 1977.

"Women on patrol." *Minnesota police journal* 50, no. 1. (February 1978): 43.

Good community relations and a positive police image formed by daily contacts with citizens are necessary if officers are to fulfill their assigned responsibilities.

CHAPTER 19

The Police Image

A Critical Factor

Do You Know . . .

- How the police image originates?
- What factors influence this image?
- What negative character traits are sometimes part of the police image?
- What emotional dangers are involved in police work?
- Why police image is important?

> No one means all he says, and yet very few say all
> they mean for words are slippery and thought is
> vicious.
>
> —Henry Brooks Adams

Introduction

Before beginning the discussion of police image, we must first recognize that each police officer is an individual. Police officers are fathers, mothers, sons, daughters, uncles, aunts, coaches of Little League teams, church members, and neighbors. As people, they like to be liked, but often their profession requires that they take negative actions against those who break the law. As a result, they are often criticized and berated for simply doing their job.

Although police officers are individuals just like those in the community they have sworn to "serve and protect," their behavior is very public. As noted by More (1976, p. 126): "Policemen may simply be very ordinary people who happen to be extraordinarily visible."

Still, the public's image of the police varies greatly. Some see police officers as saviors; others see them as militaristic harassers. The sight of a police officer arouses feelings of respect, confidence, and security in some citizens; fear, hostility, and hatred in others; and indifferences in yet others.

The image of the police officer frequently portrayed on television has not been very helpful. The "Starsky and Hutch" tactics, with much violence and disregard for civil rights, is often presented as *the* way a police officer should behave.

The effects of television on both the police image and the fight against crime cannot be accurately measured. Certainly, it must be having its impact. In one evening a person can learn how to steal a car, rape a woman, rob a bank, mug a senior citizen, and commit murder in a variety of bizarre ways. This continuous diet of murder and violence is an insult to our citizens' integrity and a threat to our youth. Youngsters spend more time watching TV than they do in school classrooms. Each successful television crime serves as an advertisement to entice and encourage some youths to commit crimes.

In addition, hardly an hour passes without an illegal search, a coerced confession, police brutality, and general violence dealt out by the police officers. Many modern-day police "heroes" are shown blatantly indulging in illegal and unconstitutional behavior, which in effect instills in the public the opinion that police misconduct is acceptable and, in fact, sometimes the only way to apprehend criminals. The same criticisms may be applied to our movies. It would be unfortunate if citizens came to accept (or expect) such behavior from their police officers in real life.

In spite of what is written in books or portrayed on television and in movies, the abstraction we call the ''police image'' is primarily the result of day-to-day contacts between police and citizens. It is the behavior of police officers at the patrol level rather than at the command level that is of greatest importance in establishing the police image. In turn, the individual behavior of the police officer who creates the police image is the result of several factors including length of service, the community served (ghetto or exclusive suburb), training, and experience.

> *The police image results from everyday contacts between individual police officers and citizens.*

Factors Influencing Police Behavior and Image

In addition to easily identifiable and predictable factors such as experience, training, and locality served, numerous subtle factors influence police behavior and image, including the nature of police work itself, a confusion of identity, the police officer's unique relation to the criminal justice system, the democratic nature of our society, and the individual officer's personality.

> *Police behavior and image are influenced by the nature of police work.*

Numerous demands are placed upon the police officer. Police officers are under constant pressure and faced with rapidly changing conditions, sometimes life-threatening situations, with few guidelines and little supervision; they frequently must ''play it by ear.'' Skolnick (1967) describes two principal variables of the policeman on the beat—danger and authority. He cautions that these variables must be interpreted in the light of constant pressure to appear efficient.

The stressfulness of the situation in which police officers are placed is described by More (1976, p. 33):

> It is obviously difficult and often impossible for police officers to respond in an appropriate manner to the numerous incidents called to their attention. They are under constant pressure, especially in highly congested areas, to handle a volume of cases that is beyond their capacity—forcing them to develop short-cut responses to run-of-the-mill situations. They lack adequate training with respect to some of the more complex social problems. And there has been little effort to provide individual officers with the guidelines which they require if they are expected to make more effective and judicious decisions in disposing of the incidents which come to their attention. In the absence of adequate resources, training, and guidance, the tendency is for individual police officers to attempt to meet largely by improvisation the varied demands made upon them.

Police officers cannot be expected to perform expertly in every situation; it is not humanly possible. Such expectations are as unrealistic as those expressed by a man who had just hired a new secretary and told her: "What do you mean you can't type; you have ten fingers don't you?" Simply because a person is a police officer does *not* mean that he can handle every situation which arises. The observation of Lord Wavell, a British Army field marshal, might apply equally to an American police officer (Tanner, 1960, p. 4):

> Stupidity in (army) generals shouldn't excite or surprise one since they were selected from an extremely small class of human beings who were tough enough to be generals at all. The essential quality was not that they should be extremely clever or sensitive, but that they should continue to function even if not particularly well, in situations in which a more sensitive and less stable organism would have stopped functioning altogether.

In addition to having to improvise in many situations, police officers must deal with people from all walks of life who are involved in criminal and non-criminal activities and must use broad discretion in a wide variety of situations with little supervision. They deal with crimes already committed, with people who are hurt, confused, angry, and upset; yet they must remain neutral, calm, objective. They may appear indifferent or unsympathetic, but, much like physicians, they cannot become personally involved and still do a professional job. They must remain detached and objective.

Police work also requires constant decision-making by the law officer. In fact, law enforcement has been described as a sequence of discretionary decisions. This discretion may lead to wide variations and inconsistencies in how the law is enforced, which citizens rightly criticize. Just as children need consistent discipline, adults in a community need and expect consistent enforcement of the laws—fairness and impartiality.

Police officers must also decide whether to give priority to a situation or not. They may encounter a cat in a tree, a downed power line, people locked out of cars or houses, noisy teenagers, and family disputes. If the officer does respond to such situations, there is often little to do other than give support, advice, or assistance.

Frequently police officers are called to make someone who is not breaking the law stop doing something which someone else views as "bad," for example, noisy kids playing ball in a vacant lot next door to a woman who is trying to sleep. Formerly the family, the church, or the school usually kept people "in line," but more and more often people see the police as their only chance to force someone who is misbehaving to "straighten up." However, in such situations, police officers cannot do much. In fact, they may add to the problem. Trying to make someone "be good" when they do not want to is a thankless task which is usually doomed to failure. When citizens see such failure, they have a reduced opinion of the effectiveness of law enforcement, without realizing that in such instances the law has no authority.

The image resulting from the nature of police work might easily be compared to the image of a football referee. It is readily accepted that referees are necessary to the game. Without them chaos would reign, and the team with the strongest, "dirtiest" players would always win. Despite their criticality, however, their image is frequently negative. No matter what call they make, a great many people are unhappy with them. They are usually perceived as being on the opponent's side. Defeats are frequently blamed on referees; however, seldom is a referee given credit for a team's victory. It is often a thankless, sometimes dangerous job. Fans have thrown pop bottles at and attempted to physically assault referees. Likewise, abusive names are frequently hurled at the referee. It often makes one wonder what type of individual could continue to work under such pressures.

Police officers are sworn to "serve and protect" the people in their community and at the same time to enforce the laws. We talked earlier about the controversy regarding how much service police departments should provide to the community. In reality, most police officers spend as much as 80 percent of their time being helpful rather than making arrests. Frequently, however, the public does not see them as helpful. Help that is not asked for is very often interpreted as interference; "When I want help, I'll ask for it" is a common and natural response to an unsolicited offer of assistance.

A case in point is the domestic call. Neighbors may call the police to report a wife, husband, or child beating. (Surprisingly, a recent survey reports that over two million husbands per year are severely beaten up by their wives.) The police response to such calls is frequently fraught with danger to the officer; 22 percent of all police fatalities occur during response to domestics. These are unglamorous, potentially highly dangerous calls.

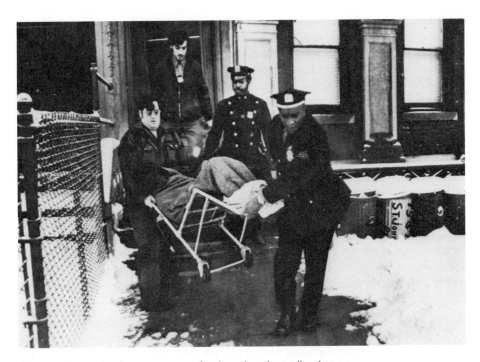

Community service is one means of enhancing the police image.

The role conflict faced by many police officers has a direct influence on the image projected (More, 1976, p. 180):

> He wants to function as a crime fighter, but does not. He is not trained or rewarded for being a peace keeper or community service agent. His quasi-judicial role is poorly differentiated. He works on the one hand in an autonomous situation on the street, but on the other hand is supposed to be highly responsive to a chain of command. All these issues engender role conflict in the police officer.

Police behavior and image are influenced by a confusion of identity.

Most police officers feel they are law enforcement officers, not social workers. They didn't create nor can they control the social problems which exist and which prompt numerous service calls. When they do respond to such calls, their help is often perceived as interference; they may be berated or even assaulted.

Another factor influencing the police image is the officers' relationship to the law. Although police officers frequently initiate the criminal justice system by investigating and apprehending criminals, they often feel like outsiders in the judicial system. They may feel their investigation and apprehension of criminals is hampered by legal restrictions and that the suspect has more rights than the victim of the crime.

Although police officers are frequently blamed for rising crime rates, their participation in the legal system is often minimized. They may be made to feel as if they were on trial during the court proceedings as the defense attorney cross-examines them. They are seldom included in any plea bargaining. And frequently defendants are found not guilty because of loopholes or legal technicalities. When a confessed robber is acquitted on a technicality or a known rapist is not brought to trial by the prosecutor, police officers may take this as a personal affront, as a criticism of their investigative expertise. In addition, citizens of the community may also blame the police officers for the unsuccessful prosecution of the suspect. Further, legal technicalities may even result in the police officer being sued for false arrest.

Police behavior and image are influenced by their unique relation to the criminal justice system.

Although police represent the law, they are *not* the law. However, some police officers, consciously or subconsciously, feel they have a very special relationship to the law. And, indeed, they do. Obviously, police officers cannot and do not arrest all the offenders they encounter. Because of their discretionary powers, the individual police officer, in effect, makes law enforcement policy on a daily basis.

It is extremely difficult to be a law officer in a diverse, democratic society. Civil rights and civil liberties are stressed so heavily that often police officers feel they cannot function effectively; they perceive that the criminals have all the breaks on their side. However, herein lies the special challenge which, faced squarely, can make police work the highly challenging and rewarding profession that it is to many police officers. At an annual meeting of the International Association of Chiefs of Police, Quinn Tamm stressed that (Germann, Day, and Gallati, 1966, pp. 112–113):

> The theme that must run beneath every police training program is that the rule of law is the very heart and soul of American police action. It must be the golden thread which ties together all the varied subjects that constitute the curricula of our schools. . . . No matter how carefully we teach our young officers and no matter how skilled they become at such techniques as interviewing, patrol, sketching, plaster casting, photography, and the like, they will not be real officers until the conviction has become part of their very being that everything they do must be done in a reasonable and constitutional manner. This is the true mark of a professional officer. In the final analysis we are not so much interested in developing good photographers and good interviewers as we are in sending into the community officers truly knowledgeable of their role in a free country who are incidentally good photographers and good interviewers.

Police behavior and image are influenced by the democratic nature of our society.

The Police Personality

Popular and scientific literature related to the police image often identifies several personality traits of the "typical" police officer.

Police officers are frequently described as being suspicious, cynical, bigoted, indifferent, authoritarian, and brutal.

Suspicious.   Police work requires a police officer to be wary of situations which are out of the ordinary, for example, a person with an umbrella on a sunny day or a person wearing sunglasses at midnight. Not only is keen observation critical to effective investigation and crime prevention, it is critical to self-defense. Danger is always possible in any situation. Skolnick (1967, pp. 45–46) believes that the police officer "develops a perceptual shorthand to identify certain kinds of people as symbolic assailants, that is, as persons who use gesture, language, and attire that the policeman has come to recognize as a prelude to violence. This does not mean that violence by the symbolic assailant is necessarily predictable. On the contrary, the policeman responds to the vague indication of danger suggested by appearance."

Cynical.   Because police officers deal with criminals, they are constantly on guard against human faults. Police officers see people at their worst. They know that people lie, cheat, steal, torture, kill. They deal with people who do not like police, who even hate them, and they feel the hatred. Additionally, they may see persons they firmly believe to be guilty of a heinous crime freed by a legal technicality. Neiderhoffer (1967) asserts that ''the kind of cynicism that is directed against life, the world, and people in general . . . is endemic to policemen of all ranks and persuasions.'' This cynicism may also lead to paranoia.

Bigoted.   Police are frequently victims of problems they have nothing to do with and over which they have no control. They are not to blame for the injustices suffered by members of minority groups: housing, educational, and employment discrimination. Yet often members of minority groups perceive the police officers as a symbol of the society which has denied them its privileges and benefits. Tension between minority group members and any representatives of ''authority'' has become almost a way of life in many parts of large cities. The minority group members vent their anger and frustration on the police, and some police, understandably, come to feel anger and dislike for them.

Indifferent.   When police officers are called to the scene of a homicide, they are expected to conduct a thorough, impartial investigation. Their objectivity may be perceived by grieving relatives of the victim as indifference or coldness. However, police officers must remain detached; one of the grieving relatives might well be the murderer. Further, a certain amount of distancing is required to work with difficult situations. Ellison and Genz (1978, p. 4) state that officers who must deal with assignments involving mutilation and death develop coping mechanisms: ''These defenses, which permit one to do an important job well, often prevent him from doing the work which involves interacting with others.''

Authoritarian.   Effective law enforcement requires authority; authoritarianism comes with the job. Without authority and respect, the police officer could not effectively compel citizens of the community to obey the law. As noted by the French philosopher Pascal: ''Justice without force is powerless; force without justice is tyrannical.'' The physical appearance of the police officer adds to this authoritarian image. The uniform, gun, club, and handcuffs project an image to which most people respond with uneasiness or even fear. Yet this image projects the right of the police to exercise the lawful force of the state in serving and protecting as well as in enforcing laws. The difficulty arises when the power that comes with the position is transferred to ''personal power.'' Perhaps Henry Brooks Adams was correct in 1907 when he said, ''The effect of power and publicity on all men is the aggravation of self, a sort of tumor that ends by killing the victim's sympathies.''

Brutal.   Sometimes force is required to subdue suspects. Unfortunately, the crime-related aspects of a police officer's job are what frequently draw public attention. When police officers have to physically subdue a suspect, people notice. When they help someone get into his locked car, few notice. Sometimes, however, more force is used than is required. This, too, is easier to understand if one thinks of the other personality traits which often become part of the police ''personality,'' particularly cynicism and authoritarianism. Police officers may use excessive force with a rapist if they believe that the probability is great that the rapist will never be brought to trial because of the prosecutor's policies on rape cases. They may also erroneously believe that violence is necessary to obtain respect from individuals who seem to respect nothing but force and power.

Table 19–1.	**Police Actions Seen Negatively and Positively.**	

Action by Officer	Negative Person	Positive Person
Steps in to stop a fight in a bar.	Interference.	Preserving the peace.
Questions a rape victim.	Indifferent, cold.	Objective.
Uses a baton to break up a violent mob.	Brutal.	Commanding respect.
Steadily watches three youths on a corner.	Suspicious.	Observant.

Significance of the Negative Personality Traits

The purpose of the preceding discussion was not to excuse the negative traits frequently found in some police officers. It was intended to provide some insight into the possible causes for such negative traits in the hope that police officers new to the field will be aware of and avoid these common pitfalls in logic. Even though understandable, such negative traits are not excusable. Sometimes, however, the fault is not in the behavior but in the *perception* of the behavior.

The eyes of the beholder determine how a police officer's actions will be interpreted or described. A person who dislikes police officers will probably perceive a specific behavior negatively, while the same behavior might be perceived positively by an individual who has a high regard for police officers. Consider, for example, the following actions and the way each is described by an individual who feels negatively about the police and one who feels positively about the police.

Given the fact that the police have numerous encounters with people who do not like them, that they must frequently take action against lawbreakers which elicits highly negative reactions, and that they are often presented on television and in the movies and newspapers in mob-control situations where public dislike of the police is most strongly displayed, it is small wonder that most police officers believe the public is against them. According to W. Westley (1970), 73 percent of policemen interviewed believed the average citizen disliked police officers. Evidence from field surveys, however, suggests the opposite—that attitudes are predominantly positive and supportive of police (*Law and Society Review*, 1973, pp. 135–152).

The Police Culture

Police officers work nights and weekends; they deal with highly confidential material which cannot be shared with friends; they must enforce the law impartially, whether it is a friend or a stranger who violates a law; and they frequently face public hostility, abuse, name-calling, and biased reporting in the media. A combination of the preceding factors largely accounts for the existence of a "police culture."

Individuals who become police officers frequently find that they lose their nonpolice friends within a few years. They work different hours—nights and weekends—and they may make some of their friends uneasy, especially their friends who drink and drive or who habitually speed. Police officers' friends often do not understand some of the actions police are forced to take in fulfilling their responsibilities.

Police officers not only frequently lose their nonpolice friends, they may come to realize that they are now a part of a group which is isolated from the rest of society. Although they are highly visible, they are set apart. They may be feared, disliked, hated, or even assaulted by citizens, making them close ranks for protection and security. The closer they become, the greater the suspicion and fear on the part of the citizens, leading to even tighter ranks, and so the cycle goes. Police officers are expected to take the place of mother, father, church, and school—to be ''family''—to those who will not accept them.

The police become the ''in group'' and everyone else is the ''out group.'' As noted by Skolnick (1967, p. 52), social isolation produces a we-they view of the world. To a police officer the world consists of cops and civilians, or perhaps better phrased as cops versus civilians.

This ''them versus us'' attitude leads to defensiveness exhibited in such ways as reluctance to give up traditional police responsibilities (for example, traffic control on state highways), or reluctance to explain their actions to citizens. Official police silence is sometimes necessary to protect the rights of others or to safeguard an investigation, but sometimes it is, in reality, a defensive response.

> *The dominant characteristic of the police culture is isolationism. It may result in a ''them versus us'' situation.*

Police officers who isolate themselves from the community and from their nonpolice friends frequently develop a ''one-track'' life with the central focus being law enforcement. They may have few outside interests, devoting their attention to reading articles and watching programs related to law enforcement and socializing only with other individuals in the law enforcement field.

The result of such isolation from the rest of society is frequently a paranoia similar to that typically seen in some members of minority groups. But there is an important difference between the isolation of a minority group member and that of police officers. Police officers have physical powers—guns and clubs—and the authority to use them to preserve law and order for the very individuals who they feel have rejected them. This can pose a highly inflammatory situation and may partially account for the extensive riots of the 1960s.

Whether it did or not, the riots of the sixties highlighted the dire need for better relations between the police and the citizens they serve. Often, however, efforts are directed only at changing the public's attitude, not at changing police behavior as well. It must always be remembered that the public responds to what is presented to them.

Image Building—Public and Community Relations

The relationship between police officers and citizens is not always good. Some citizens do not want to get involved or are apathetic. Other citizens are suspicious of the police and of the entire criminal justice system. Still others have no regard for laws or police officers.

The Importance of Police-Community Relations

The criticality of good police-community relations is well illustrated by looking at what happens when relations are poor. As noted by the President's Commission on Law Enforcement and the Administration of Justice in their Task Force Report (*The Police*, 1967, p. 144):

> Hostility, or even a lack of confidence of a significant portion of the public has extremely serious implications for the police. These attitudes interfere with recruiting, since able young men generally seek occupations which are not inordinately dangerous and which have the respect and support of their relatives and friends.
>
> Public hostility affects morale and makes police officers less enthusiastic about doing their job well. It may lead some officers to leave the force, to accept more prestigious or less demanding employment.

In addition, poor police-community relations have a direct effect on law enforcement. You learned earlier how important citizen cooperation is in preventing crime and detecting those responsible for crimes committed.

Good police-community relations are important not only to recruit and retain high-caliber individuals as police officers, but also to effectively fulfill the responsibilities assigned to police officers.

Stress and Burnout

No discussion of the real life of a police officer would be complete without again recognizing the highly stressful nature of this profession. Police officers deal with crisis on a daily basis, usually that of someone else. Sometimes, however, the demands of the roles and how they are expected to be performed create enough stress to put police officers themselves into a crisis situation.

A police officer's job is highly stressful and may result in a personal crisis for the officer.

Several writers and researchers have stated that police work is, indeed, stressful:

- "Police work is a high stress occupation. It affects, shapes, and, at times, scars the individuals and families involved" (Dash and Reiser, 1978, p. 18).

■ "Police work has been identified as the most psychologically dangerous job in the world" (Axelberd and Valle, 1978, p. 13).

■ "Police officers have the highest rate of divorce of all professions and, according to recent research, most of it is due to a combination of the traditional demands imposed on an officer by himself, society, and the organization as well as the social change affecting today's marriages" (Somodevilla, et al., 1978, p. 10).

■ "The law enforcement profession is notorious for the incidence of heart problems and in fact runs close to the top of professions in cardiovascular insufficiency and/or impairment" (Somodevilla, et al., 1978, p. 18).

Terry (1981, pp. 61–65) discusses four sets of stressors functioning in police work:

External stressors include frustrations with the criminal justice system, particularly in terms of the apparent leniency of court decisions and the scheduling of court appearances, discontent with unfavorable media coverage, resentment of certain opinions arising out of minority communities, and dislike of the decisions and interests of government and administrative bodies affecting the performance of police work.

Internal stressors cover a large number of problem areas, many of which are organizational, including training that is felt to be inadequate, equipment that is thought to be substandard or in a state of disrepair, poor pay, and ambiguously defined reward structures, as well as inadequate career development guidelines, offensive departmental policies, excessive paperwork, and intradepartmental political favoritism.

Task-related stressors include role conflicts, the rigors of shift work, boredom, fear, danger, being exposed to the miseries and brutalities of life, and work overload.

Finally *individual* stressors include fears about job competence, individual success, and safety. Discussions of individual stressors also include consideration of stressors arising out of performing police work, particularly health problems, alcoholism, marital problems, divorce, and suicide.

Bennett-Sandler and Ubell (1977, pp. 47–51) state that some modern departments have hired psychologists or counselors to help their members deal with the symptoms of job-related stress: alcoholism, suicide attempts, and the like. When faced with severe or prolonged stress, many police officers become what has been called "burned-out samaritans" (Maslach, 1976, pp. 16–22).

According to Ellison and Genz (1978, p. 3): "A situation is more likely to be stressful and result in crisis reactions if it is unpredictable and if the individual has, or feels he has, little or no control over it." When stress results in "burnout," the individual tends to place himself at a great distance from the situation in which he is involved: he tends to go by the book rather than by the specific situation; a major symptom of burnout is "the transformation of a person with original thought and creativity on the job into a mechanical bureaucrat" (Maslach, 1976, p. 18).

Maslach (1976, p. 18) also describes symptoms which indicate when a person is burning out: "He becomes cynical and develops negative feelings about his clients. He may begin to talk of them as other than human, and to withdraw from contact with them.''

According to Ellison and Genz (1978, p. 3): ''The reactions described by Maslach are seen all too frequently in police officers.'' Niederhoffer (1967), too, describes the increasing alienation and cynicism in urban police officers which are similar to Maslach's example of burnout. In fact, he asserts that the kind of cynicism that is directed against life, the world, and people in general is endemic to police officers of all ranks and persuasion.

Ellison and Genz examine some of the specific factors which might account for burnout. They first identify two specific types of particularly stressful situations: the first is the wounding or death of a fellow officer, especially one's partner; the second is the maiming or sexual assault of a child. They note that as long as only one kind of basic skill is required in a job, problems are minimal, but that when assignments require different, contradictory skills, problems do arise: ''When the necessity for interaction and sensitivity to human feelings and behavior is combined in an assignment with the necessity for dealing with situations which demand distancing because they (police officers) deal with basic human fears of mutilation, trauma, and death, the officer must attempt to perform the almost impossible balancing act of working appropriately with 'clients' who are undergoing ego-threatening crisis and protecting his own ego'' (1978, pp. 4–5).

Ellison and Benz feel that burnout is more of a problem when officers are required to handle large numbers of serious calls or when they are not equipped or trained to handle them. Further, they believe that ''job-related stress is exacerbated, and indeed, may be caused by certain traditional police practices. One of the most devastating of these is the indiscriminate use of a military model. This model sees police skills as technological ones. It assumes that every assignment involves skills that do not vary greatly from individual to individual or with the setting. It views discretion as unimportant and inappropriate for all but top brass'' (1978, pp. 4–5). Unfortunately, this model simply does not work in many situations.

Summary

The police and the citizens of a community are dependent on each other. How each views the other and how effectively they can communicate together will have a vital influence on the effectiveness of police officers in fulfilling their responsibilities.

The police image results largely from everyday contacts between individual citizens and individual police officers. The police officer's behavior and the resulting image conveyed are influenced by the nature of police work, by the frequent confusion of identity and role conflict, by the police officer's unique relation to the criminal justice system, by the democratic nature of our society with its emphasis on civil rights and civil liberties, and by the police officer's personality.

Police officers are frequently described as being suspicious, cynical, bigoted, indifferent, authoritarian, and brutal. Although these negative personality traits may be explained by the factors previously enumerated, they may not be excused. Sometimes, however, the fault is not in the behavior of the police officer, but in the way it is perceived by the citizen.

The dominant characteristic of the "police culture" is isolationism which may result in a "them versus us" orientation which does little to further good community relations.

A positive image and good community relations are important not only to recruit and retain high-caliber individuals as police officers, but also to effectively fulfill the responsibilities assigned to police officers.

Application

Watch three different drama shows and write a brief character sketch of the main character in each. Comment on what is being portrayed.

Discussion Questions

1. How do police officers deal with their own lives when they spend so much time with the worst of people?
2. How can police get away from the superhuman image?
3. What are some societal factors interfering with police work?
4. Why is the police officer on the street responsible for the success of police-community relations programs and the police image?
5. What is the dominant characteristic of the police culture?
6. What are some ways the police can get the public on their side?
7. Whose problem is it when the police and the community don't get along?
8. Has the police image changed in the past ten years? The past hundred years?
9. What do you feel is the police image?
10. What do you think is the general image of the police in our community?

References

Axelbred, M., and Valle, J. "South Florida's approach to police stress management." *Police stress* 1, no. 2, (1978): 13–14.

Bennett-Sandler, G., and Ubell, E. "Time bombs in blue." *New York magazine* (March 21, 1977): 47–51.

Bent, A.E., and Rossum, R.A. *Police, criminal justice, and the community.* New York: Harper and Row, 1976.

Cohn, A.W., and Viano, E.C. *Police community relations: Images, roles, realities.* Philadelphia: J.B. Lippincott Company, 1976.

Dash, J., and Reiser, M. "Suicide among police in urban law enforcement agencies." *Journal of police science and administration,* (1978): 18–21.

Ellison, W.K., and Genz, J.L. "The police officer as burned-out samaritan. *FBI law enforcement bulletin* (March 1978): 2–7.

Garmire, B.L. "The police role in an urban society." In *The police and the community,* edited by R.F. Steadman. Baltimore: Johns Hopkins University Press, 1972.

Genz, J.L., and Lester, D. "Authoritarianism in policemen as a function of experience." *Journal of police science and administration* 4, no. 1 (1976): 9–13.

Germann, A.; Day, F.; and Gallati, R. *Introduction to law enforcement and criminal justice.* Springfield, Ill.: Charles C. Thomas Publishers, 1966.

Law and society review 8, no. 1 (Fall 1973): 135–152.

Maslach, C. "Burned-out." *Human behavior* (September 1976): 16–22.

More, H.W., Jr. *The American police.* Text and readings. Criminal Justice Series. St. Paul, Minn.: West Publishing Company, 1976.

McNamara, R. "Uncertainties in police work: The revelance of police recruits' backgrounds and training." In *The police: Six sociological essays,* edited by D. Bordua. New York: John Wiley & Sons, 1967.

Munro, J.L. *Administrative behavior and police organization.* Cincinnati: W.H. Anderson Company, 1974.

Niederhoffer, A. *Behind the shield.* New York: Anchor, 1967.

Police and community relationships . . . is a two-way street! New York: National Conference of Christians and Jews, 1969.

The President's Commission on Law Enforcement and Administration of Justice. *The police.* Task Force Report. Washington, D.C.: U.S. Government Printing Office, 1967.

Skolnick, J.H. *Justice without trial: Law enforcement in a democratic society.* New York: John Wiley and Sons, 1967.

Somodevilla, S.A.; Baker, C.J.; Hill, W.R.; and the Dallas Police Department. Departmental memorandum prepared by the psychological services unit of the Dallas Police Department, (January 1978).

Stang, D.P. *The police and their problems: Law and order reconsidered.* Washington, D.C.: U.S. Government Printing Office, 1969.

Tanner, J.M. *Stress and psychiatric disorder.* Oxford: Blackwell Scientific Publications, 1960.

Terry, W.C. III, "Police stress: The empirical evidence." *Journal of police science and administration* 9, no. 1 (1981): 61–65.

Westley, W.A. *Violence and the police: A sociological study of law, custom, and morality.* Cambridge: MIT Press, 1970.

Officer teaching handgun safety. One of the issues facing police officers today is the legal and moral aspects of using deadly force.

Critical Issues in Law Enforcement and Criminal Justice

No Easy Answers

Do You Think . . .

- Law enforcement is a profession?
- Police departments should be accredited?
- Police departments should be unionized?
- Certain police activities are corrupt?
- Police officers are justified in using deadly force?
- Police effectiveness can be determined?
- Civilian review is of value to police departments?
- Police officers should be held civilly liable?
- Some provisions of the Bill of Rights are controversial?
- Some crimes might be decriminalized?
- Plea bargaining is in the best interests of society?
- Our correctional system is effective?

> *He who will not reason, is a bigot; he who cannot is a fool; and he who dares not is a slave.*
> —*William Drummond*

Introduction

The criminal justice system has several vital issues facing it in the last part of the twentieth century. The issues encompass law enforcement, the courts, and corrections. Several issues affect all three. Although this chapter concentrates on those issues that directly affect law enforcement, issues related to the courts and corrections that may also affect law enforcement are also discussed briefly.

Police Professionalism

Throughout this book the field of law enforcement has been referred to as a profession; however, whether law enforcement technically qualifies as a profession is extremely controversial. Several years ago, Wilson (1973, p. 283) called the police ''subprofessionals'' and ''members of the craft.'' But changes have occurred since then.

Part of the problem is that definitions of professionalism vary. To some, a professional means simply an important job. Sociologists, however, have identified certain elements that qualify an occupation as a profession. Moore (1970, pp. 3-22) summarized the key elements of a profession as professional knowledge, professional autonomy, and the service ideal.

> *The three key elements of professionalism are (1) professional knowledge, (2) professional autonomy, and (3) the service ideal.*

Professional knowledge is generally considered to consist of a complex subject requiring extensive training over a period of years. The most obvious example is a medical doctor who completes four years of undergraduate education, four years of medical school, and one year of internship at minimum. Most also complete three to five additional years of externship or residencies, specializing in one aspect of medicine. In contrast, law enforcement officers receive relatively limited training—approximately 400 hours is the standard commonly used. According to Walker (1983, p. 244): ''The most important parts of the body of knowledge (the relevant local criminal law, criminal procedure, departmental procedures) could be mastered by a reasonably intelligent person in a relatively short period of time.''

The second key element, *professional autonomy,* refers to the ability to control entrance into the profession, to define the content of the knowledge to be obtained, and to be responsible for self-monitoring and disciplining. In addition, the autonomy of a profession is usually authorized by the power of the state; for example physicians, dentists, lawyers, and teachers are licensed by the state. These professions are, in effect, legalized monopolies. In contrast, the police do not control entry into the profession, the content of knowledge to be obtained, nor their own self-monitoring.

The third element of a profession, the *service ideal,* requires that members of the profession follow a formal code of ethics and be committed to serving the community. In this area, police officers do qualify as professionals provided the department stresses the public servant aspects of police work.

Walker (1983, p. 244) notes that:

> Despite the fact that the police lack many of the key elements of a true profession, they continue to insist that they are professionals. For most reform-oriented police officials, progress is defined in terms of professionalization. To understand the nature of the professional self-concept of the police it is necessary to analyze the nature and direction of police professionalization.
>
> Police professionalization emerged at the beginning of the twentieth century. The reform agenda included eliminating political interference, attracting qualified police officials, upgrading personnel standards, and developing improved techniques of management control.

Walker cites two reasons for the police insistence on calling themselves professionals. First is the considerable progress that has been made in policing, and second is the improvement of self-image. According to Manning (1977, pp. 127–128), viewing oneself as a professional builds self-esteem and cohesiveness. By calling themselves professionals, the police set themselves up as experts on crime and law enforcement and, in essense, obtain a measure of autonomy.

Another distinctive characteristic frequently attributed to professionals is that they belong to professional organizations such as the American Bar Association or the American Medical Association; they shun unions.

Law Enforcement Accreditation

Closely related to the issue of professionalism is the issue of accreditation for law enforcement agencies. Should they or should they not seek accreditation? The Commission on Accreditation for Law Enforcement Agencies was formed in 1979 to develop a set of law enforcement standards and to establish and administer an accreditation process to which law enforcement agencies could voluntarily apply to demonstrate that they met professional criteria.

The commission is the combined effort of the International Association of Chiefs of Police (IACP), the National Organization of Black Law Enforcement Executives (NOBLE), the National Sheriffs' Association (NSA), and the Police Executive Research Forum (PERF). Members of these four organizations direct approximately 80 percent of the law enforcement community in the United States.

The standards address six major areas:

- The law enforcement role and responsibilities, and relationships with other agencies
- Organization, management, and administration
- Personnel administration
- Law enforcement operations, operational support, and traffic law enforcement
- Prisoner and court-related services
- Auxiliary and technical services

The standards were developed to help law enforcement agencies: (1) increase agency capabilities to prevent and control crime, (2) enhance agency effectiveness and efficiency in the delivery of law enforcement services, (3) improve cooperation and coordination with other law enforcement agencies and with other components of the criminal justice system, and (4) increase citizen and employee confidence in the goals, objectives, policies, and practices of the agency.

> *The Commission on Accreditation for Law Enforcement Agencies was formed to develop a set of professional standards and to establish and administer a voluntary accreditation process.*

Any "legally constituted governmental entities having mandated responsibilities to enforce laws and having personnel with general or special law enforcement powers" are eligible to apply. If accepted, the accreditation fee is contingent upon the size of the agency, based on the number of full-time employees. In 1983 the rates ranged from $3,800 for an agency with fewer than ten full-time employees to $14,700 for agencies with more than 3,000 full-time employees. Whether this cost is justifiable is strongly debated in many departments.

Further information regarding accreditation can be obtained by writing to The Commission on Accreditation for Law Enforcement Agencies, Inc., 4242B Chain Bridge Road, Fairfax, Virginia 22030.

Unionism

According to Cole (1983, p. 214): "For much of this century, police employee organizations were mainly fraternal associations that existed to provide opportunities for fellowship, to serve the welfare needs (death benefits, insurance) of police families, and to promote charitable activities." He notes that the 1950s saw a dramatic rise in membership in police unions, partly due to job dissatisfaction, particularly regarding pay and working conditions; the perception that other public employees were improving their positions through collective bargaining; the feeling that the public was hostile to police needs; and an influx of younger officers with less traditional views on police-employee relations. In addition, during this time organized labor was making strong recruitment efforts.

Most police officers are members of local employee organizations. Cole (1983, p. 216) feels the police unions are locally based because the key decisions related to law enforcement are made at this level. And, although most police officers have joined local organizations rather than become affiliates of the AFL-CIO or other national unions, the strength of police unions has increased in many cities.

Most police officers are currently members of local employee organizations and are not directly enrolled in a national labor union.

One common objection to unionism is the tactics commonly employed, including slowdowns, "sickouts," and strikes. Although it is usually illegal for most public employees to strike, strikes by law enforcement officers have occurred in San Francisco, California; Tucson, Arizona; Oklahoma City, Oklahoma; Las Cruces, New Mexico; and Youngstown, Ohio (Gentel and Handman, 1980, p. 5). Some of the strikes lasted only a few days, but others lasted weeks. In some instances strikers lost their jobs, but in other instances they obtained raises.

Other objections raised against unionism include the fear of law enforcement administrators and public officials that unionized police employees could abuse their collective bargaining power, and that specific aspects of administration such as transfers and promotions could become bound up in arbitration and grievance procedures. Cole (1983, p. 214) states that: "Many administrators view the union as interfering with their law enforcement leadership and with the officers in the ranks." In addition, police unions have resisted changes in law enforcement organizations and techniques that affect their membership. According to Juris and Feuille (1974, p. 206), the unions opposed attempts to shift from two-person to one-person patrol cars in at least two of the twenty-two cities studied. Unions have also objected to efforts to hire civilians in clerical positions, and they have resisted affirmative action efforts, seeking to maintain the status quo rather than to increase recruitment of women and minorities into law enforcement.

In discussing the future of police unions, Cole (1983, p. 217) suggests that: "Clearly, collective bargaining is a concept whose time has come, and police officials are going to have to recognize this new influence on law enforcement administration. At the same time, note that in a public sector of diminished resources, state and local governments may not have the funds to increase salaries to meet inflation. Already New York City and Boston have reduced the size of their police force as one way of reducing budget deficits. But in other cities, particularly those in expanding regions of the country and in the more affluent suburbs, police unions are making greater headway and can be expected to retain their influence. There are still, however, crucial questions about the rule that unions should play in determining police department policies and the methods that they can use to influence bargaining agreements."

Police Corruption

According to Walker (1980, p. 19): "Corruption is the oldest and most persistent problem in American policing. The history of law enforcement agencies is the story of repeated scandals over corrupt practices." Numerous definitions have been set forth for police corruption. One very plausible definition has been stated by Goldstein (1975, p. 3): "Police corruption consists of acts involving the misuse of authority by a police officer in a manner designed to produce personal gain for himself or for others."

The two key elements in the definition are: (1) the misuse of authority and (2) personal gain. Both elements must be present. The officer must be acting as a police officer, for example, using the authority of the badge to gain entrance to a building and then committing a theft. The act must also result in personal gain. Illegal acts of police officers such as excessive use of force or an illegal search do not constitute police corruption because they do not result in personal gain.

Walker (1983, p. 174) notes that: "Police corruption is a problem of enormous magnitude." He contends that to deal with the problem effectively, it is necessary to understand the types of corruption that exist, why it exists, and how it might be controlled.

> *Police corruption is the misuse of authority by an officer for personal gain. It includes accepting gratuities and bribes as well as committing theft or burglary. The most common and extensive type of corruption is accepting small gratuities or tips.*

Walker notes that a great difference exists between the officer who accepts a free meal and one who accepts, perhaps even encourages, a cash payment. In fact, many cities do not consider gratuities as corruption. A restaurant owner may sincerely want to do something extra for those who "serve and protect" him, and may also feel that having police cars parked in the lot may deter crime in the area.

Although discounts and free service are usually not regarded as important, cash payments to police officers are quite another matter. The Knapp Commission (1973, p. 4) distinguished between "grass eaters" and "meat eaters," with the grass eaters being officers who passively accepted gratuities offered to them, in contrast to meat eaters who aggressively solicited payments.

Even more serious are outright bribes to avoid arrest or a fine. The most common instance of this occurs in traffic violations, particularly speeding. All too often a person who has been stopped for speeding may include a ten or twenty dollar bill along with the requested driver's license and end up with a warning rather than a ticket. In some instances, officers may actually suggest that a bribe be made, perhaps in the form of buying tickets to a police benefit.

Another form of extremely serious police corruption is appropriating material or money that comes into their possession in the line of duty. For example, according to Daley (1978), New York detectives regularly divided their "scores" of narcotics and cash, sometimes amounting to thousands of dollars. Or property may be taken from the property room and then mysteriously "disappear."

The seriousness of the problem cannot be ignored. According to Walker (1983, p. 187): "Corruption undermines the basic law enforcement function of the police. Whether the corrupt act involves a small bribe to ignore a traffic violation or a sizable and regular payoff to protect a gambling operation, illegal activity is being tolerated." And this communicates the message that criminal activity is acceptable behavior, undermining the basic mission of the police and damaging the reputation of the entire police department. As noted frequently throughout this book, the police depend on citizen cooperation to do an effective job. If the police are perceived to be corrupt, it is unlikely that citizens will be cooperative. They may, in fact, become hostile toward the police.

There is univeral agreement that police corruption is a major problem. What is controversial is what can be done about it. Is it inevitable? Or can it be reduced or eliminated completely?

Use of Deadly Force

Pursley (1984, p. 244) notes that: "An issue that has grown in importance in recent years has been the use of deadly force by the police. This issue is usually tied inextricably to the broader issues of police-minority relations and the supporting issues of police violence and/or police brutality." Pursley also cites an extensive analysis of police use of deadly force conducted by the Police Foundation, the research findings of which are summarized as follows (Milton, et al, 1977, pp. 10–11):

1. Police departments differ widely in their policies and review procedures relating to the use of deadly force. There is no universally accepted standard dictating when an officer should use a firearm.

2. There is a clear national trend in police departments toward the enactment of written policies governing the use of firearms. Often, however, these policies are not set forth in any single document, but are scattered among several department orders or bulletins. Many of these policy statements are poorly organized and confusing.

3. Many departments appear to shy away from adopting firearms policies that are much more restrictive than state law, for fear of increasing their vulnerability to civil suits. In addition, police administrators have to cope with increasing police union opposition to the adoption of more restrictive standards.

4. The rates of shootings by police officers vary widely among jurisdictions, and it is impossible (within the limits of the study) to say what specific factors are responsible for these differences.

5. Many departments are beginning to develop record-keeping procedures designed to identify and monitor officer conduct involving the use of excessive and repeated involvement in shooting incidents.

6. It is difficult, after the fact, to categorize certain shootings as "justified" or "unjustified." Some shootings are clearly and unequivocally acts of self-defense. Some manifestly fail to meet the requirements of law and local policy, or appear to have served no compelling purpose, in that no lives were saved and no dangerous felons apprehended. Many incidents, however, fall into a middle ground where the officer's word may be pitted against that of a friend or friends of the victim, or where one or two facts appear to be inconsistent with the officer's version of events.

7. Most shootings are called ''justified'' by departments, and very few are referred to criminal charges. When an officer is formally charged in connection with an incident occurring in the line of duty, juries generally do not convict, perhaps because most witnesses are themselves participants and not impartial observers. Department discipline in such cases rarely goes beyond a verbal or written reprimand to the officer involved.

8. The formal review of shooting incidents by a civilian or part-time civilian body does not in itself guarantee a fairer or more systematic resolution.

9. The number of blacks and other minorities shot by police is substantially greater than their proportion in the general population, but is not inconsistent with the number of blacks arrested for serious (Part I) crimes. Shootings of minority juveniles, in particular, have been responsible for increased tensions and occasionally violent disturbances in ghetto neighborhoods.

10. The review of shooting incidents in the cities surveyed for this study indicates that a sizable percentage involved out-of-uniform officers (both on duty in plainclothes and off duty), perhaps because out-of-uniform officers are less conspicuous and thus more able to intervene in situations in which criminal or suspicious activity is still going on.

When considering the justifiable use of deadly force, two interrelated rights are important: the legal right to use such force and the moral right compelling the officer to do so.

State legislators have generally given the police very broad discretion in this area, with most politicians fearful of being labeled as ''soft on criminals'' if they did otherwise. Many state statutes authorize use of deadly force to prevent the commission of a felony or to prevent a fleeing felon from escaping. In fact, in one state, it is a felony to run from the police, thus making it legal for police to shoot the person. Although this is legally right, is it morally right?

To balance the legal and moral rights involved, several states have adopted penal codes that do not rely solely on a crime being classified as a felony. They focus instead on the danger posed by the suspect to the officer and society.

> *Justification for use of deadly force must take into consideration not only the legal right, but also the need to apprehend the suspect compared to the safety of the arresting officer and compared to the value of human life.*

Pursley (1984, p. 245) concludes that: ''Like so many other concerns surrounding crime and criminals, discussion of such issues tends to be more emotional rather than logical. To minorities it is simply a means to further oppress and show disregard for Blacks or Chicanos; for many white Americans it is simply giving the robbers, the rapists, the murderers what they deserve—after all, they say, it's not our problem that a disproportionate number of them are Black or Chicanos. For the police themselves, it's an issue of perceived safety, and they naturally feel at 'greater risk' when confronting the more perceived prevalence of violence among minorities.''

A recent Supreme Court ruling, *Tennessee v. Garner* (1985), is of extreme importance in the issue of use of deadly force. This ruling bars police from shooting to kill fleeing felons unless there is an imminent danger to life. This ruling invalidates laws in almost half the states that allow police officers to use deadly force to prevent the escape of a suspected felon. According to Nislow (*Law Enforcement News,* April 22, 1985, p. 1): "The current ruling sprang from a 1974 incident in which a Memphis police officer fatally shot an unarmed 15-year-old, fleeing from police after having stolen $10 in money and jewelry from an unoccupied house. . . . The police officer who fired the fatal shot testified that he had fired because he believed the suspect would otherwise escape and because he had been trained that Tennessee state law permitted him, in such situations, to shoot a suspected fleeing felon." This ruling has the backing of the several national law enforcement agencies.

Accountability of the Police

The last decade has emphasized accountability—for the schools, for the medical profession, and for law enforcement. But it is extremely difficult to measure the effectiveness of the police. If they are doing an effective job of detecting crime, the crime rate statistics will increase, even though the rate of actual crime may not have changed at all. Likewise, a police department may have relatively few arrests or reported crimes, but this low crime rate does not mean the department is effective. Nonetheless, official crime statistics are the usual means of assessing the effectiveness of a police department.

Pursley (1984, p. 235) suggests that "The effective measurement of police services . . . will not occur overnight. Like other public service agencies, police departments perform functions that almost defy quantitative measurement. The problem is compounded by the fact that where public safety is an issue, tolerances for misjudgments are very limited and the case for an insurance margin most compelling." Pursley notes that some measures that might be applied to police productivity are available. These factors are summarized in Table 20–1.

Measures of police productivity might include police patrol operations, provision of noncrime services, human resource management, and crime statistics.

Civilian Review

Another major law enforcement controversy centers on use of civilian review boards to deal with alleged police officer misconduct. Civilian review boards were created as independent bodies to review instances of alleged police misconduct. Such boards are extremely popular with critics of the police, but are extremely unpopular with the police themselves. Recall that one key element of a profession is autonomy—the ability to self-monitor. And this is a responsibility police departments guard ardently. Nonetheless, critics argue that the "police culture"

Table 20–1. *Some Recommended Measures of Police Productivity.*

Police Function Being Measured	Measure Employed
Police patrol operations	1. Number of patrol officers assigned to street patrol in terms of total patrol officers
	2. Work-hours of patrol time spent on activities contributing to patrol objectives in terms of total patrol work-hours
	3. Number of calls of a given type and response time for answering these calls
	4. Arrests resulting from patrol that survive the first judicial screening
	5. Felony arrests from patrol surviving the first judicial screening
	6. Arrests (felonies and misdemeanors) that result in convictions
Provision of noncrime services	1. Number of noncrime calls for service that are satisfactorily responded to in terms of work-hours devoted to noncrime service calls
	2. Medical emergency calls that emergency room personnel evaluate as having received appropriate first aid
Human resource management	1. Number of disciplinary charges filed and number substantiated in terms of total departmental personnel
	2. Number of work-hours lost during the year due to illness, injury, or disciplinary action
Miscellaneous considerations	1. Population served per police employee and per dollar
	2. Crime rates and changes in crime rates for reported crimes (relative to dollars or employees per capita)
	3. Clearance rates of reported crimes (relative to dollars or employees per capita)
	4. Arrests per police department employee and per dollar
	5. Crime rates, including estimates of unreported crimes based on victimization studies
	6. Clearance rates, including estimates of unreported crimes based on victimization studies
	7. Percentage of crimes solved in less than x days
	8. Percentage of population indicating a lack of feeling of security
	9. Percentage of population expressing dissatisfaction with police services

Sources: The National Commission on Productivity, *Opportunities for Improving Productivity in Police Services* (Washington, D.C.: National Commission on Productivity, 1973), pp. 14-28, 49-52: and The Urban Institute, *The Challenge of Productivity Diversity: Improving Local Government Productivity Measurement and Evaluation, Part III, Measuring Police-Crime Control Productivity* (Washington, D.C.: The Urban Institute, June 1972). p. 11.

provides a type of solidarity that protects officers who do not act responsibly or honorably.

According to Walker (1983, p. 237): "The most famous civilian review board was the New York City Civilian Complaint Review Board (CCRB)." This board illustrates the many problems associated with civilian review. The board was established in the 1950s and originally was not actually a citizen review board at all. Complaints about police misconduct were sent to the deputy commissioner who reviewed them and made recommendations. During its first two years the CCRB reviewed approximately eighty cases a year and recommended charges in approximately 20 percent of the cases.

During the next decade Mayor Robert Wagner gradually expanded the powers of the CCRB, and the number of complaints filed increased. Then, in the 1960s Mayor John Lindsay transformed the board, expanding it to seven members—four civilians appointed by the mayor and three police officials appointed by the commissioner—creating a truly civilian review board. This board reviewed 146 cases in its four-month existence and recommended charges in only four of the cases—less than 3 percent. The civilian majority on the review board so angered police officers that they took it to their fraternal group and then to their union and were able to have the question of the CCRB put on the ballot for the November general election. New York voters voted to abolish the CCRB by a two-to-one margin.

According to Walker (1983, pp. 240–241), there are both advantages and disadvantages of civilian review. On the positive side, such boards would help dispel the belief that police departments "whitewash" the acts of misconduct of fellow officers. They would ensure justice being carried out and improve public trust in the police. In addition, they would lessen the isolation of the police from the community.

On the negative side, however, is the fact that civilian review would be singling out law enforcement from among all other social agencies to be reviewed by a civilian board. In addition, the cases often receive much publicity and the officer involved may be subjected to "trial by publicity." Finally, since the review boards themselves are controversial, they become ineffective.

As noted in the study by the Police Foundation (Milton, *et al.,* 1977, pp. 10–11): "The formal review of shooting incidents by a civilian or part-time civilian body does not in itself guarantee a fairer or more systematic resolution."

> *Civilian review boards were created as independent bodies to review instances of alleged police misconduct. Most such boards have had very limited authority and, consequently, have been ineffective.*

Interpreting the Constitution and the Bill of Rights

The law is a living reality which encourages the opening of new avenues of human conduct. As Oliver Wendell Holmes put it: "The life of the law has not been logic; it has been experience." People who view the Constitution as an outdated document fail to see that it is the best structure so far in history for a growing society with changing institutions.

Issues related to the Constitution and the Bill of Rights include:

- The Second Amendment—gun control.
- The Fourth and Fifth Amendment—the Exclusionary Rule and the *Miranda* decision.
- The Eighth Amendment—capital punishment.

As noted in Chapter 13, the Second Amendment to the Constitution is one continuing source of controversy. Those who oppose gun control state that outlawing handguns would arm criminals and disarm law-abiding citizens. They say the criminals will get guns anyway. The question revolves around whether the government should regulate handguns—the number one weapon of killers. Some 18,000 murders occur every year in the United States, often committed by "law-abiding" people shooting other "law-abiding" people. In addition, an average of more than ninety police officers are slain by handguns every year.

Some polls consistently show that the majority of United States citizens support sensible handgun legislation. However, when Massachusetts held a referendum proposing to ban handguns, it was defeated by a 70 percent majority. Possibly they realized what New York's tough gun law has shown: if only one state outlaws guns, a person can easily get one in another state. Nevertheless, it seems clear that the federal government should establish some uniform regulation of handguns before they cause more tragedy and terror.

Controversy also exists over the Exclusionary Rule and the *Miranda* decision. You will recall that the Exclusionary Rule disallows the introduction of illegally seized evidence from a trial, and the *Miranda* decision forbids confessions as evidence if the suspects have not been informed of their constitutional rights. The Exclusionary Rule has been regularly challenged in our courts. Opponents of the rule say that it penalizes society and rewards the defendant for any mistakes made by the police. When the *Miranda* decision was handed down in 1966, many people felt the criminals were decidedly given the upper hand; consequently the U.S. Supreme Court came under blistering attack from some police, prosecutors, and citizens. Since 1966 twenty-two states have sought to overturn the *Miranda* decision through the U.S. Supreme Court, but to no avail. Today's police officers are functioning and performing their jobs better than before *Miranda;* they are not hindered by it. Police officers, above all others, ought to obey the laws. Further, withdrawal of the rights provided by the Fourth and Fifth Amendments could lead to a police state.

Another controversial amendment is the Eighth Amendment, which forbids "cruel and unusual punishment." The question of capital punishment has been in the courts for the past quarter-century. In 1976 the U.S. Supreme Court ruled that states which used certain guidelines could pass laws allowing them to execute convicted murderers, but the Court reserved any decision on whether the death penalty is constitutional for any other crime. Still unresolved are such questions as how far prosecutors can go in making emotional charges in their closing arguments to a jury in a capital punishment case and whether rape can be punished by death.

The Police Officer's Civil Liability

Section 1983 of the Civil Rights Act of 1964, often referred to as "1983 Action," was intended to protect citizens against excesses and misuses of official power, including police power. 1983 Action has served as a basis for federal jurisdiction in cases alleging police misconduct in the following areas: (1) use of unnecessary force, (2) assault and battery, (3) coercion to obtain a confession, (4) malicious prosecution, (5) false arrest and imprisonment, and (6) illegal searches and seizures.

Traditionally, false arrest and imprisonment suits have accounted for the great majority of civil suits against police officers. As noted at several points throughout this book, one way to avoid such suits is to act under the authority of a search of arrest warrant.

In 1967, in *Pierson v. Ray,* the Supreme Court extended to police officers the defenses of good faith and probable cause. These defenses are generally viewed as having two elements. First, the officer must allege in any defense that he or she acted without malice or other improper intentions. Second,the officer must allege that the action taken was reasonable.

In *Tennessee v. Garner* (1985), the Supreme Court decision that cut down the fleeing felon rule, no charges were brought against the officer because of his good faith reliance on Tennessee law and the rules of the Memphis Police Department.

> *1983 Action has served as a basis for federal jurisdiction in cases alleging police misconduct, including use of unnecessary force, assault, battery, coercion, malicious prosecution, false arrest and imprisonment, and illegal search and seizure.*

Decriminalization

The basic issues involved in decriminalization are: If a crime is victimless, is there really a crime? Can you legislate morality?

According to Williams, *et al.* (1982, p. 336): "The overreach of modern American criminal law is notorious. We have for years operated under a 'pass a law' syndrome regarding the criminalization of behavior deemed distasteful or dangerous by the lawmaking branch of government. Such a state of affairs has placed an enormous strain on all segments of the criminal justice establishment."

Obviously, the criminal justice system has limited resources. Should it not concentrate those resources on the Part I offenses such as murder, robbery, and rape?

Unfortunately, the crime-related portion of most police officers' responsibilities is devoted to lesser offenses such as prostitution or gambling. Decriminalization of certain offenses would allow concentration of resources on serious crime and might also legalize certain actions such as gambling and prostitution that are major revenue sources for organized crime. However, the acts now considered criminal may be engaged in more frequently by law-abiding citizens if they were decriminalized, thus lowering our country's moral standards.

Williams, *et al.* (1982, p. 337) say if "the offense so repealed is one that has heretofore created and sustained a major underground or blackmarket operation, a repeal may mean that such endeavors will ultimately cease operation because of the now legal nature of the enterprise."

Law-Abiding Citizens Select the Laws They Obey

Many good citizens disobey the law every day and justify it as "not hurting anyone else." For example, countless citizens break speed laws, drive after drinking, and pilfer from their employers. Even more serious, many citizens, although abhorring organized crime in general, foster, promote, and support it daily by gambling and using its many other "services." Perhaps the deeply entrenched force of organized crime has gone beyond the comprehension of the general public. Many notorious criminals of the present era wear the mantle of respectability because they have bought into legitimate business with their illegal money or have simply strong-armed their way in. These criminals have gained social prominence and often community acceptance.

Decriminalization would likely focus on those crimes that are now selectively enforced and would return emphasis to the more serious crimes. Offenses that would be candidates for decriminalization include prostitution, sexual activities between consenting adults, gambling, public drunkenness, certain types of juvenile delinquency (status offenses), narcotics and drug offenses, vagrancy, and disorderly conduct. This would conserve resources that have come to be over-extended in many communities.

Over a decade ago, the National Advisory Commission on Criminal Justice Standards and Goals (*Corrections,* 1973) recommended that the states: "Re-evaluate laws on gambling, marijuana use and possession for use, pornography, prostitution, and sexual acts between consenting adults in private. Such re-evaluation should determine if current laws best serve the purpose of the state and the needs of the public."

This recommendation is reiterated by Williams, *et al.* (1982, p. 339): "Criminal justice policymakers in the 1980s and beyond must come to grips with the criminal laws' overreach. Until such is done, we will continue to have a system of criminal law enforcement in the United States that is administratively cumbersome, selectively unjust,and economically wasteful."

> *Offenses that would be candidates for decriminalization include prostitution, sexual activities between consenting adults, gambling, public drunkenness, certain types of juvenile delinquency (status offenses), narcotics and drug offenses, vagrancy, and disorderly conduct.*

The Plea Bargaining Controversy

As previously discussed, plea bargaining is a system whereby a defendant pleads guilty to a crime in exchange for a reduced punishment. According to Levine, *et al.* (1980, p. 214): ''In many courts, more than 90 percent of criminal convictions are not obtained by the verdict of a jury or the decision of a judge. Rather, they are based upon the defendant's own plea of guilty.'' The prevalence of plea bargaining is also noted by Glick (1983, p. 164) who says: ''In 1971, the U.S. Supreme Court also acknowledged plea bargaining as a fact and a necessity of judicial life (Santobello v. New York, 104 U.S. 257). But, many people oppose plea bargaining and argue that it provides few benefits for courts, criminal defendants, or the public. Since nearly all cases are settled short of a trial, plea bargaining is a central feature of the judicial process and we need to evaluate carefully its place in American justice.''

Glick (1983, pp. 164–165) also notes:

Once a prosecutor decides to pursue a case and a judge refuses to grant motions to dismiss, *the chances of conviction are overwhelming.* Usually the crimes involved are serious or the evidence against defendants is so clear that the chances of being acquitted of a crime are extremely remote. Some readily plead guilty because they recognize the odds are against them and want to put an end to the stress and disruption. They simply want to get out of the system. Others plead guilty because they expect leniency or have negotiated specific bargains with prosecutors and judges.

The mechanics and details of bargained guilty pleas vary considerably. Arrangements may involve reducing criminal charges to less serious crimes, dropping certain charges altogether, promising light sentences for guilty pleas to original charges, and possible combinations. Whatever the arrangements, the key element to any bargain is that in return for pleading guilty and avoiding a trial, cooperative defendants expect to receive lighter sentences. Through plea bargaining, almost all cases end with convictions, but not with trials.

Plea bargaining not only involves avoiding a trial, but it also involves the defendant surrendering such constitutional rights as the right to take the witness stand, the right to confront witnesses against him, the right to trial by jury, and the right to be assumed innocent until proven guilty by proof beyond a reasonable doubt. Levine, *et al.* (1980, p. 42) warn that: ''A system that encourages the waiver of such fundamental rights is defensible only if it deals justly with the person waiving those rights. On the other hand, plea bargaining also affects the police, who have accumulated evidence of guilt; the victim, who has suffered at the hands of the offender; and the public at large, who demand protection against future offenses. These interests also must be dealt with justly in the plea negotiation process, or the process is as indefensible as if it violated the rights of the offender.''

A high percentage of cases are settled through plea bargaining. While plea bargaining is acknowledged to be a central part of the judicial process, some critics warn that it might not be in the best interests of society at large.

The case *Bordenkircher v. Hayes* (1978) expanded the power of plea bargaining from the prosecution's side, upholding the prosecutor's right to threaten

Table 20–2.	*Arguments For and Against Plea Bargaining.*

PRO: Allows courts to move cases quickly and efficiently.

Lightens the burden on judges, prosecutors, lawyers, and other court employees.

Spares victims the stress and possible humiliation of public trial.

Cooperative defendants are screened from the system and receive reduced penalties for not requiring everyone to prepare for a trial.

Allows the punishment to fit the crime and the individual criminal.

Few professional, hardened criminals are allowed to go free.

CON: Cheapens the image of justice by using hurried, secret negotiations to obtain convictions.

The prosecutor comes out ahead by the guilty plea and the defendant gets the best deal he can on the sentence.

Places pressure on defendants to plead guilty.

Forces defendants to give up constitutional protections and safeguards.

Legal errors made by police, prosecutors, or trial judges can rarely be reviewed by an appellate court.

Amounts to a coerced confession which violates the Fifth Amendment.

Produces sentences that are too lenient.

criminal defendants with more serious charges if they refuse to plead guilty to the charges offered. In this case Hayes was indicted by a grand jury for forging an $88.30 check. In pre-trial meetings the prosecutor told Hayes and his lawyer that if Hayes pleaded guilty, making a trial unnecessary, the prosecution would recommend a five-year sentence. (The sentence under Kentucky law, where the case was being tried, would have carried a sentences of two to ten years.) The prosecutor also said that since Hayes had two previous felony convictions, if he refused to plead guilty, prosecution would seek a new indictment—a habitual offender charge, which would bring a life sentence. Hayes refused to plea bargain, was convicted, and was sentenced to life. His appeal to the U.S. Circuit Court of Appeals was that the prosecutor's "reverse plea-bargaining" violated Hayes's due process rights. This appeal was granted, but then overturned by the United States Supreme Court which said prosecutors must have broad discretionary powers in plea bargaining.

Glick (1983, pp. 165–167) sets forth numerous arguments for and against plea bargaining, as summarized in Table 20–2. The basic issues involved are important to understand and investigate.

Correctional Institutions

The message from the National Advisory Commission on Criminal Justice Standards and Goals (*Corrections*, 1973) still has relevance ten years later.

The pressures for change in the American correctional system today are building so fast that even the most complacent are finding them impossible to ignore. The pressures come not only from prisoners, but also from the press, the courts, the rest of the criminal justice system, and even practicing correctional personnel.

During the past decade, conditions in several prison systems have been found by the courts to constitute cruel and unusual punishment in violation of the Constitution. Over the last decade, the U.S. Supreme Court has decided numerous cases directly affecting offenders, and in a majority of them, the offender's contention prevailed.

The riots and other disturbances that continue to occur in the Nation's prisons and jails confirm the feeling of thoughtful citizens that such institutions contribute little to the national effort to reduce crime. Some maintain that time spent in prison is, in fact, counterproductive.

It is clear that a dramatic realignment of correctional methods is called for. It is essential to abate use of institutions. Meanwhile much can be done to eliminate the worst effects of the institution—its crippling idleness, anonymous brutality, and destructive impact. Insofar as the institution has to be relied on, it must be small enough, so located, and so operated that it can relate to the problems offenders pose for themselves and the community.

The Commission suggests that: "The failure of major institutions to reduce crime is incontestable. . . . Correctional history has demonstrated clearly that tinkering with the system by changing specific program areas without attention to the larger problems can achieve only incidental and haphazard improvement. . . . Corrections must seek ways to become more attuned to its role of reducing criminal behavior. Changing corrections' role from one of merely housing society's rejects to one of sharing responsibility for their reintegration requires a major commitment on the part of correctional personnel and the rest of the criminal justice system."

Correctional institutions have failed to reduce crime or recidivism; they succeed in punishing but not in deterring. They protect the community only temporarily, and they often cause negative changes in committed offenders.

According to the commission, corrections must use "greater selectivity and sophistication in the use of crime control and correctional methods. These great powers should be reserved for controlling persons who seriously threaten others. They should not be applied to the nuisances, the troublesome, and the rejected who now clutter our prisons and reformatories and fill our jails and youth detention facilities. The criminal justice system should become the agency of last resort for social problems. The institution should be the last resort for correctional problems."

One major handicap to correctional reform, according to Allen and Simonsen (1981, p. 487) is: "Lack of conclusive evidence as to which techniques work and which do not."

Summary

Numerous issues are important in law enforcement. One such issue is whether law enforcement qualifies as a profession. According to sociologists, the three key elements of professionalism are (1) professional knowledge, (2) professional autonomy, and (3) the service ideal. The Commission on Accreditation for Law Enforcement Agencies was formed in 1979 to develop a set of law enforcement standards and to establish and administer an accreditation process to which law enforcement agencies could voluntarily apply to demonstrate that they met professional criteria. Whether the cost is justifiable is a strongly contested issue in many departments. Most police officers are currently members of local employee organizations and are not directly enrolled in a national labor union.

Another issue is police corruption and what can be done about it. Police corruption consists of acts involving the misuse of authority by a police officer in a manner designed to produce personal gain for himself or for others. It is a problem of enormous magnitude and takes several forms, including accepting gratuities and bribes as well as committing theft or burglary. The most common and extensive type of corruption is accepting small gratuities or tips.

A fourth important question is when police are justified in using deadly force. Any such use must take into consideration not only the legal right, but also the moral right to use deadly force—the need to apprehend the suspect compared to the safety of the arresting officer and compared to the value of human life.

A fifth issue is how police might be made more accountable. Measures of police productivity might include police patrol operations, provision of noncrime services, human resource management, and crime statistics.

A closely related issue is the use of civilian review boards. Such boards have been created as independent bodies to review instances of alleged police misconduct. Most such boards have had very limited authority and, consequently, have been relatively ineffective.

Other issues in law enforcement involve interpretation of the Constitution and the Bill of Rights, including the Second Amendment and gun control controversies; the Fifth and Sixth Amendments and the associated Exclusionary Rule and *Miranda* decision; and the Eighth Amendment and the use of capital punishment as cruel and unusual.

Closely related to issues regarding interpretation of the Constitution and the Bill of Rights is the controversy of when police officers are to be held civilly liable for their actions. The "1983 Action" has made police open to civil suits for use of unnecessary force, assault and battery, coercion to obtain a confession, malicious prosecution, false arrest and imprisonment, and illegal searches and seizures.

Controversy also exists as to whether certain offenses should be decriminalized. Such decriminalization would allow concentration of resources on serious crime and might also legalize certain actions such as gambling and prostitution which are major revenue sources for organized crime. On the other hand, acts now considered criminal may be engaged in more frequently by law-abiding citizens if they were decriminalized, thus lowering our country's moral standards.

Offenses that would be candidates for decriminalization include prostitution, sexual activities between consenting adults, gambling, public drunkenness, certain types of juvenile delinquency, narcotics and drug offenses, vagrancy, and disorderly conduct.

Heated controversy surrounds the practice of plea bargaining. In many courts more than 90 percent of criminal convictions are not obtained by the verdict of a jury or the decision of a judge. Rather, they are based upon the defendant's own plea of guilty. Convincing arguments exist both for and against plea bargaining. However, there is general agreement that it is practiced extensively.

One final area of controversy involves our correctional system. Our correctional institutions have failed to reduce crime or recidivism; they succeed in punishing, but not in deterring. They protect the community only temporarily, and they often cause negative changes in committed offenders.

An understanding of these basic problems is vital for individuals in law enforcement if they are to make informed contributions to discussion of the issues.

Application

Decriminalization is a controversial issue. On a 3 × 5 card, put your answer as to whether "yes," you favor decriminalization or "no," you do not favor it. A tally of the total of the class will give an indication of what may happen in the future.

___ Prostitution	___ Absenting from home
___ Public drunkenness	___ Truancy from school
___ Marijuana smoking	___ Smoking under legal age
___ Gambling	___ Drinking under legal age
___ Pornography	___ Breaking curfew
___ Heroin or cocaine use	

Discussion Questions

1. Will police departments be totally professionalized?
2. Unions have played a vital role in the economic development of this country. Do they have a place in police work?
3. How serious is police corruption?
4. When will the curtailments on the use of deadly force be lifted so that an officer will be free to act as he or she sees fit without constraints?
5. How can police accountability be measured?
6. What are civilian review boards? Do we have one in our community?
7. Are the police doing an effective job in apprehending criminals?
8. What role should police officers play in the plea bargaining process, if any?
9. How effective is our correctional system? How might it be improved?

References

Allen, H.E., and Simonsen, C.E. *Corrections in America: An introduction.* 3rd ed. New York: Macmillan Publishing Company, 1981.

Cole, G.F. *The American system of criminal justice.* 3rd ed. Monterey, Cal.. Brooks/Cole Publishing Company, 1983.

Daley, R. *Prince of the city: The true story of a cop who knew too much.* Boston: Houghton-Mifflin, 1978.

Fyfe, J.J. *Readings on police use of deadly force.* Washington, D.C.: Police Foundation, 1982.

Gentel, W.D., and Handman, M.L. *Police strikes: Causes and prevention.* U.S. Department of Justice. Washington, D.C.: U.S. Government Printing Office, 1980.

Glick, H.R. *Courts, politics, and justice.* New York: McGraw-Hill, 1983.

Goldstein, H. *Police corruption: A perspective on its nature and control.* Washington, D.C.: Police Foundation, 1975.

Juris, H.A., and Feuille, P. "Employee organizations." In *Police personnel administration,* edited by O.G. Stahl and R.A. Staufenberger. Monterey, Cal.: Duxbury Press, 1974.

Knapp Commission. *Report on police corruption.* New York: George Braziller, 1973.

Levine, J.P.; Husheno, M.C.; and Palumbo, D.J. *Criminal justice, a public policy approach.* New York: Harcourt Brace Jovanovich, 1980.

Lundman, R.J. *Police and policing.* New York: Holt, Rinehart and Winston, 1980.

Manning, P.K. *Police work.* Cambridge: MIT Press, 1977.

Milton, C.H.; Halleck, J.W.; Lardner, J.; and Abrecht, G.L. *Police use of deadly force.* Washington, D.C.: Police Foundation, 1977.

Moore, W.E. *The professionals: Rules and roles.* New York: Russell Sage, 1970.

National Advisory Commission on Criminal Justice Standards and Goals. *Corrections.* Washington, D.C.: U.S. Government Printing Office, 1973.

National Advisory Commission on Criminal Justice Standards and Goals. *Courts.* Washington, D.C.: U.S. Government Printing Office, 1973.

Nislow, "Fleeing-felon rule cut down." *Law enforcement news* XI, no. 8 (April 22, 1985): 1.

Pursley, R.D. *Introduction to criminal justice.* 3rd ed. New York: Macmillan Publishing Company, 1984.

Seherman, L.W. *Scandal and reform: Controlling police corruption.* Berkeley: University of California Press, 1978.

Walker, S. *The police in America: An introduction.* New York: McGraw-Hill, 1983.

Walker, S. *Popular justice.* New York: Oxford University Press, 1980.

Williams, V.L.; Formby, W.A.; and Watkins, J.C. *Introduction to criminal justice*. Albany, N.Y.: Delmar Publishers, 1982.

Wilson, J.Q. *Varieties of police behavior*. New York: Atheneum, 1973.

Epilogue
Why Become a Police Officer Today?

With violence a constant threat in communities and to individuals in the form of hijackings, murders, assaults, rapes, and kidnappings, the future police officer must be a true professional dedicated to the American creed of justice and liberty.

It is evident that the general public has become somewhat suspicious of the rhetoric of politicians, and many citizens want simple solutions to the crime problem where none exist. Police agencies themselves have become more militant and political; some ambitious administrators have even used a police agency to launch themselves into high political office. Many police have problems with poor image, low status, and limited training, while at the same time they are asked to perform the most skilled, important, and dangerous police work.

What leads us to believe that the next ten years will be much better? Not much, on the surface. Only 1.5 percent of the convicted criminals are ever imprisoned. The odds are ninety-nine to one that you could commit a crime and never go to jail for it. Besides, if we were to imprison every convicted criminal, we would have to build thousands more jails, and the public simply would not stand the cost.

The question today is whether our citizens can succeed in controlling crime by resurrecting the determined pioneering spirit exhibited by our ''heroes'' in history. Seldom have city dwellers been as apprehensive about their safety as they are today, even though statistics show there is more fear of crime than actual crime itself.

Our forefathers fought to gain liberty for us; today we struggle to maintain and perpetuate that liberty. The police must enforce the law, but citizens must help. They must express their outrage at crime by reporting it. They must cooperate fully in its investigation and prosecution. They must give full support to law enforcement and criminal justice programs. As citizens see for themselves the correction of inequities in their communities, crime will start to be contained.

We need to rekindle the spirit of self-esteem in America, and police officers can provide the leadership. It will take intelligence, courage, and determination.

So why does anyone want to be a police officer today? Because, despite all that is terribly wrong with our country, the majority of citizens do not commit crimes, and they need protection. Law violators are a minority. Most people in our country are honest and good, and among them are many men and women who, although realizing that no one ever said being a police officer is easy, nonetheless want the challenge of service to their community, which is implicit in being a law enforcement officer.

Glossary

Administrative services—those services such as recruitment, training, planning and research, records and communications, crime laboratories and facilities including the police headquarters and jail.

Affidavit—a statement reduced to writing, sworn to before an officer or notary having authority to administer an oath.

Affirmation—usually related to an oath.

American creed—the national conscience.

Amphetamine—a stimulant taken orally as a tablet or capsule or intravenously to reduce appetite and/or to relieve mental depression.

Appeal—the removal of a decision from a lower to a higher court.

Arraignment—a court procedure whereby the accused is read the charges against him and is then asked how he pleads.

Arrest—to deprive a person of his liberty by legal authority. Usually applied to the seizure of a person to answer before a judge for a suspected or alleged crime.

Arson—intentionally damaging or destroying or attempting to damage or destroy by means of fire or explosion the property of another without the consent of the owner or one's own property, with or without the intent to defraud.

Assault—an unlawful attack by one person upon another for the purpose of inflicting bodily harm.

Ballistics—a science dealing with the motion and impact of projectiles such as bullets and bombs.

Barbiturate—a depressant usually taken orally as a small tablet or capsule to induce sleep and/or to relieve tension.

Bill of Rights—the first ten amendments to the Constitution.

Bow Street Runners—the first detective unit; established in London by Henry Fielding in 1750.

Burglary—an unlawful entry into a building to commit a theft or felony.

Case law—a collection of summaries of how statutes have been applied by judges in various situations; the precedents that have been established by the courts.

Chief of police—the chief law enforcement officer at the local level.

Civil law—all restrictions placed upon individuals which are noncriminal in nature; seeks restitution rather than punishment.

Civil liberties—an individual's immunity from governmental oppression.

Civil rights—claims which the citizen has to the affirmative assistance of government.

Commission—the highest ruling body of the Mafia.

Common law—in England, the customary law set by the judges as disputes arose; the law in force before and independent of legislation.

Complainant—a person who makes a charge against another person.

Complaint—a legal document drawn up by a prosecutor which specifies the alleged crime and the supporting facts providing probable cause.

Consent—to agree; to give permission; voluntary oral or written permission to search a person's premises or property.

Constitution—the basic instrument of government and the supreme law of the United States; the written instrument defining the power, limitations, and functions of the United States government and that of each state.

Contraband—any article forbidden by law to be imported or exported; any article of which possession is prohibited by law and constitutes a crime.

Coroner's jury—an inquest, usually before a jury of six members, to establish cause of death occurring under unusual circumstances.

Crime—an action which is harmful to another person and/or to society, and which is made punishable by law.

Criminal intent—a resolve, design, or mutual determination to commit a crime, with full knowledge of the consequences and exercise of free will.

Criminalistics—the scientific study of evidence in a criminal case and of individuals involved in such cases.

Criminal law—the body of law which defines crimes and fixes punishments for them.

Dangerous drugs—addicting, mind-altering drugs such as depressants, stimulants, and hallucinogens.

Data privacy act—the regulation of confidential and private information gathered by governmental agencies on individuals in the records, files, and processes of a state and its political subdivisions.

Defendant—the person accused in a criminal proceeding.

Defense attorney—the representative of the accused in court.

Deliriant—a volatile chemical which can be sniffed or inhaled to produce a ''high'' similar to that produced by alcohol.

Deposition—a written statement made by a witness under oath to be used in court.

Discovery process—a system that requires all pertinent facts be available to the prosecutor and the defense attorney prior to the time of trial.

Diversion—bypassing the criminal justice system by assigning an individual to a social agency or other institution rather than bringing to trial.

Emergency situation—circumstances where a police officer must act without a magistrate's approval (without a warrant).

Equity—a concept that requires that the ''spirit of the law'' take precedence over the ''letter of the law.''

Evidence—all the means by which any alleged matter or act is either established or disproved.

Exclusionary Rule—a United States Supreme Court ruling that any evidence seized in violation of the Fourth Amendment will not be admissible in a federal or state trial.

Extenuating circumstances—requiring immediate action; an emergency situation.

Felony—a major crime, for example murder, rape, arson; the penalty is usually death or imprisonment for more than one year in a state prison or penitentiary.

Field services—the operations or line divisions of a law enforcement agency such as patrol, traffic control, investigation, and community services.

Forced entry—an announced or unannounced entry into a dwelling or a building by force for the purpose of executing a search or arrest warrant to avoid the needless destruction of property, to prevent violent and deadly force against the officer, and to prevent the escape of a suspect.

Frisk—a patting down or minimal search of a person to determine the presence of a dangerous weapon.

Goal—a broad, general, or desired result for a law enforcement agency.

Grand jury—a group of citizens, usually twenty-three, convened to hear testimony in secret and to issue formal criminal accusations (indictments) based upon probable cause if justified.

Habeas corpus—a judicial order to bring a person being held in custody to court.

Hallucinogen—a drug whose physical characteristics allow it to be disguised as a tablet, capsule, liquid, or powder; hallucinogens produce distortion, intensify sensory perception, and lessen the ability to discriminate between fact and fantasy.

Homicide—the willful killing of a human being by another human being; also *Murder.*

Immediate control—within a person's reach.

Indictment—a written accusation based on probable cause, returned by a grand jury charging an individual with a specific crime.

Informant—a person who furnishes information concerning accusations against another person or persons.

Information—a formal written accusation of a crime resulting from a preliminary hearing; a charging document.

Informational probable cause—statements which are made to officers that can be relied upon and are generally sufficient in themselves to justify an arrest.

Instruments of a crime—the means by which a crime is committed or the suspects and/or victims transported; for example: gun, knife, burglary tools, car, truck.

Intent—see *Criminal Intent.*

Interrogation—the questioning of a suspect.

Interview—the questioning of a witness.

Justification—a sufficiently lawful reason why a person did or did not do the thing charged.

Juvenile delinquency—behavior by a person not of legal age (usually under age eighteen, but in a few states under age twenty-one) that violates a law or an ordinance.

Larceny/theft—the unlawful taking and removing of the property of another with the intent of permanently depriving the legal holder of the property.

Law—a body of rules for human conduct which are enforced by imposing penalties for their violation.

Lawful arrest—lawfully taking a person into custody (with or without a warrant) for the purpose of holding that person to answer for a public offense; all legal standards must be satisfied, particularly probable cause.

Legal—authorized by law.

Leges Henrici—a document that made law enforcement a public matter and separated offenses into felonies and misdemeanors.

Limitation—a legal restriction of time or authority relating to an offense.

Loan-sharking—lending money at higher than legally prescribed rates.

Mafia—an Italian word referring to the lawless, violent bands of criminals who engaged in kidnapping and extortion in Sicily in the nineteenth and twentieth century; used today to refer to organized crime.

Magna Carta—a decisive document in the development of constitutional government in England that checked royal power and placed the king under the law (1215).

Misdemeanor—a minor offense, for example, breaking a municipal ordinance, speeding; the penalty is usually a fine or a short imprisonment, usually less than one year, in a local jail or workhouse.

Mobility—movable; not firm, stationary, or fixed; for example, an automobile that is capable of being moved quickly with relative ease.

Murder—see *Homicide.*

Narcotic—a drug that produces sleep and lethargy or relieves pain; usually an opiate.

NCIC (National Crime Information Center)—the computerized files of the Federal Bureau of Investigation containing records of stolen property and wanted persons.

Nighttime warrant—a search or arrest warrant issued by a magistrate that authorizes a police officer to execute the warrant during the night.

No-knock warrant—authorization by a magistrate upon the issuance of a search warrant to enter a premise by force without notification to avoid the chance that evidence may be destroyed if the officer's presence were announced.

Oath—a legal attestation or promise to perform an act or make a statement in good faith and under a responsibility to God.

Objective—a specific, measureable means of achieving a goal.

Offense—an act prohibited by law, either by commission or omission.

Offense report—a preliminary report filled out by the responding officer for all crimes, attempts, investigations, and incidents to be made a matter of record.

Omerta—a rigid ethical code which binds Mafia members together and requires any member who suffers an injustice to take personal vengeance without contacting the law.

Ordinary care—such degree of care, skills, and diligence as a person of ordinary prudence would employ under similar circumstances.

Organized crime—conspiratorial crime involving a hierarchy of persons who coordinate, plan, and execute illegal acts using enforcement and corruptive tactics.

Parish constable system—an early system of law enforcement used primarily in rural areas of the United States.

Pennsylvania Constabulary—organized in 1905 and considered the first modern state police agency.

Plain view—evidence which is not concealed and which is inadvertently seen by an officer engaged in a lawful activity; what is observed in plain view is not construed within the meaning of the Fourth Amendment as a search.

Plea—the accused's answer to formal charges in court.

Plea bargaining—a compromise between the defense and prosecuting attorneys which prearranges the plea and the sentence, conserving manpower and court expense.

Police authority—the right to direct and command.

Police power—the power of the federal, state, or municipal governments to pass laws regulating private interests, to protect the health and safety of the people, to prevent fraud and oppression, and to promote public convenience, prosperity, and welfare.

Preliminary hearing—a court process to establish probable cause to continue the prosecution of the defendant.

Probable cause—reasonable grounds for presuming guilt; facts which lead a person of ordinary care and prudence to believe and conscientiously entertain an honest and strong suspicion that a person is guilty of a crime.

Prosecutor—an elected or appointed official who serves as the public's lawyer.

Rape—carnal knowledge of a woman or man through the use of force or the threat of force.

Reasonable—sensible; just; well-balanced; good, sound judgment; that which would be attributed to a prudent person.

Reasonable doubt—when a juror is not morally certain of the truth of the charges.

Reasonable force—force not greater than that needed to achieve the desired end.

Reasonable search—a search conducted in a manner consistent with the Fourth Amendment.

Reasonable seizure—the seizure of evidence or persons according to constitutional standards set forth in the Fourth Amendment.

Relevant—having a direct relationship to the issue in question.

Restraint—to restrain; to prohibit; to bar further movement; to limit freedom.

Robbery—the stealing of anything of value from the care, custody, or control of a person in his presence, by force or by the threat of force.

Roll call—the briefing of officers prior to their tour of duty to update them on criminal activity and calls for service.

R.O.R.d—released on own recognizance.

Scandinavian-type law—prohibits driving with blood alcohol concentrations exceeding specific levels and establishes severe penalties for disobedience.

Search—examination of a person or property for the purpose of discovering evidence to prove guilt in relation to a crime.

Search warrant—a judicial order directing a peace officer to search for specific property, seize it, and return it to the court; it may be a written order or an order given over the telephone.

Seizure—a forcible detention or taking of a person or property in an arrest.

Sheriff—the principal law enforcement officer of a county.

Sir Robert Peel—often referred to as the ''Father of Police Administration,'' his efforts organized the Metropolitan Police of London (1829).

Spoils system—a political system whereby ''friends'' of politicians were rewarded with key positions in the police department.

Status offense—a crime restricted to persons under the legal age, e.g., smoking, drinking, breaking curfew, absenting from home, truancy, incorrigibility.

Statutory law—law passed by a legislature.

Stop and frisk—a protective search for weapons which could be used to assault police officers and others, for example, knives, guns, and clubs.

Submission—placing of one's person or property under the control of another; yielding to authority.

Subpoena—a written legal document ordering the person named in the document to appear in court to give testimony.

Supreme Court—the highest court in the United States and the only court established by the Constitution.

Task—a specified activity which contributes to reaching an objective.

Texas Rangers—established in 1835 as the first agency similar to our present-day state police.

Tithing system—in Anglo-Saxon England, a unit of civil administration consisting of ten families; established the principle of collective responsibility for maintaining law and order.

Tort—a civil wrong for which the court seeks a remedy in the form of damages to be paid.

U.S. Attorney General—the head of the Department of Justice and the chief law officer of the federal government.

Warrant—a written order issued by an officer of the court, usually a judge, directing a person in authority to arrest the person named, charged with the named offense, and to bring that person before the issuing person or court of jurisdiction.

Watch and Ward—a system of law enforcement which was used to protect citizens twenty-four hours a day; the day shift was called the ''ward'' and the night shift the ''watch.''

White-collar crime—occupational or business-related crime.

Witness—a complainant, an accuser, a victim, an observer of an incident, a source of information, or a scientific examiner of physical evidence.

Writ of habeas corpus—see *Habeas corpus.*

Table of Cases

Index